Helen Z. Papanikolas

The Editor

Helen Z. Papanikolas was born in
the little town of Cameron, Carbon
County, of Greek immigrant parents.
Later, her family moved to Salt
Lake City where she completed her
education, receiving a bachelor's
degree from the University of Utah.
She has written and lectured
extensively on Utah history and
folklore. Her publications include
the well-known *Toil and Rage in a
New Land: The Greek Immigrants
in Utah* and a variety of articles on
Utah's immigrant and mining
communities. She is a member of
the Board of State History, a
Fellow of the Utah State Historical
Society, and coordinator of the
Greek Archives, Western
Americana, Marriott Library,
University of Utah. With her
pioneering research, writing, and
collecting of materials on
immigrant culture, Mrs.
Papanikolas has encouraged many
young scholars to explore this
important aspect of social history.

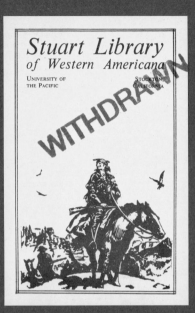

The Peoples of Utah

The Peoples of Utah

Edited by
Helen Z. Papanikolas

UTAH STATE
HISTORICAL SOCIETY
Salt Lake City

FIRST EDITION

Library of Congress Catalog Card Number 76–12311
SBN 0-913738-26-3
Printed in the United States of America

ACKNOWLEDGMENTS

The editor and publisher wish to acknowledge the grant received from the Utah American Revolution Bicentennial Commission toward the publication of this book and the support and encouragement given by the publications committee headed by Professor Brigham D. Madsen.

The editor is grateful for the cooperation of the authors of the various chapters and those who donated photographs and for the dedication and resourcefulness of the staff of the Utah State Historical Society, especially Miriam B. Murphy and Stanford J. Layton of the publications office, Margaret D. Lester, curator of photographs, and Martha R. Stewart, reference librarian.

CONTENTS

INTRODUCTION   1

1   THE FIRST PEOPLES OF UTAH
    My Native Land   FRED CONETAH   11
    The Navajos   CLYDE J. BENALLY   13
    *The Utes, Southern Paiutes,
    and Gosiutes*   FLOYD A. O'NEIL   27

2   IMPERIAL ZION: THE BRITISH
    OCCUPATION OF UTAH   FREDERICK S. BUCHANAN   61

3   BLACKS IN UTAH HISTORY:
    AN UNKNOWN LEGACY   RONALD G. COLEMAN   115

4   SCANDINAVIAN SAGA   WILLIAM MULDER   141

5   JEWS IN ZION   JACK GOODMAN   187

6   THE CONTINENTAL INHERITANCE   DAVIS BITTON
                                             GORDON IRVING   221

7   THE PIONEER CHINESE OF UTAH   DON C. CONLEY   251

8   THE OFT-CROSSED BORDER:
    CANADIANS IN UTAH   MAUREEN URSENBACH
                                          RICHARD L. JENSEN   279

9   ITALIANITA IN UTAH:
    THE IMMIGRANT EXPERIENCE   PHILIP F. NOTARIANNI   303

10 JAPANESE LIFE IN UTAH   HELEN Z. PAPANIKOLAS
                                             ALICE KASAI   333

11 FALCONS IN FLIGHT:
    THE YUGOSLAVS   JOSEPH STIPANOVICH   363

12 FROM BABYLON TO BABYLON:
    IMMIGRATION FROM THE MIDDLE EAST   ROBERT F. ZEIDNER   385

13 THE EXILED GREEKS   HELEN Z. PAPANIKOLAS   409

14 AFTER ESCALANTE: THE SPANISH-
    SPEAKING PEOPLE OF UTAH   VICENTE V. MAYER   437

    THE AUTHORS   469

    INDEX   473

    PICTURE CREDITS   498

THE NEW COLOSSUS

Not like the brazen giant of Greek fame,
With conquering limbs astride from land to land;
Here at our sea-washed, sunset gates shall stand
A mighty woman with a torch, whose flame
Is the imprisoned lightning, and her name
Mother of Exiles. From her beacon-hand
Glows world-wide welcome; her mild eyes command
The air-bridged harbor that twin cities frame.
"Keep ancient lands your storied pomp!" cries she
With silent lips. "Give me your tired, your poor,
Your huddled masses yearning to breathe free,
The wretched refuse of your teeming shore.
Send these, the homeless, tempest-tost to me,
I lift my lamp beside the golden door!"

—EMMA LAZARUS
*Tablet on pedestal
of Statue of Liberty*

INTRODUCTION

Utah has long ceased being an agrarian society of a "peculiar people." Although still predominately Mormon, many cultures have contributed to its unique essence in this lost domain of the Indians. Only a few Spanish priests in 1776 and, later, explorers and trappers had briefly entered that varied, spectacular realm. Within their ancestral boundaries, the Gosiutes, Utes, Paiutes, and Navajos had sovereignty over plains of acrid sagebrush and alkaline wasteland, the Great Salt Lake and its surrounding desert, fresh lakes and rivers, the Wasatch and Uinta mountains, and the red-earth country with its awesome monoliths. Their great chiefs, Washakie, Wakara, and Kanosh were known far beyond these borders; and Indian life flowed in orderly, rigid observance to the laws of nature, to blood ties and mores, and with proper esteem or terror for near and distant tribes.

Then, in 1847, Mormons in wagon trains weighted with the rudiments of existence, a few Negro slaves among them, animals trailing, moved resolutely forward to settle once and for all this little-known territory. They belonged, John A. Widtsoe said, "to the civilization that Anglo-Saxon peoples had won for themselves through centuries of struggle."

With the first sowing of seed, the Mormons formed in their Zion an enclave within the United States. Having been persecuted by "Gentiles," they wanted none in their gathering. Peace and isolation was their goal. The Indians, the Lamanites of the Book of Mormon, were to be fed, not fought: they were to be converted to fulfill prophecy; their women would become plural wives; they would be taught to drop their primitive ways and become civilized. As westward expansion had done to all tribes, the Utah Indians began to lose their traditional freedoms and their ancient lands.

For twenty years the Mormons were squatters, unable to secure a federal land office for the territory. Their numbers continued to increase rapidly through a high birthrate, dramatically accelerated by plural marriages, and through immigration of converts. Missionary work intensified in the first natural field, the British Isles, the land of their forebears, from where the new dispensation continued to be spread worldwide to all parts of the empire, especially Australia. Canadians, among the first white men in Utah, had been drawn to Mormonism from its early beginnings and steadily added converts to Zion.

Social and religious upheavals in Sweden, Denmark, and Norway attracted Scandinavians to Mormon missionaries, bringing the second largest group of converts to Zion. Icelandic Mormons were sparse in numbers, yet culturally significant. Although fewer missionaries preached the faith in Germany, France, Switzerland, and Italy, converts were made, the Swiss responding readily. Expanding missionary activity included the Netherlands, and another ethnic strain set sail for the New World. Thousands of these new believers pushed handcarts across the plains toward distant mountain tops spoken of by Isaiah.

As Mormon communal villages became secure from Indian attacks, the great expanses of sagebrush were broken at long intervals by a lone adobe house and root cellar surrounded by patches of plowed earth and the green of winter wheat. An irrigation stream flowed by, lined with a row of Mormon poplars for windbreaks. With desperate innovation, or they would have starved, the settlers became America's irrigation pioneers and set the laws and rules for all people living "under the ditch." They experimented with varieties of wheat and grasses, brought in livestock to improve their meager animals, spread their gospel, and attempted idealistic societies, the United Orders.

Hardly had the Mormons arrived when their leaders began calling them on more epic journeys to colonize the territory. For the kingdom of God they left newly made fields in alluvial earth where sagebrush grew as high as a man's waist, land such as John Holladay's that he sowed with a drill and reaped sixty bushels to the acre. On hostile land of stunted sagebrush and extreme isolation, they made oases.

In an act of genius Brigham Young counseled his people to keep journals. The past is there for us on fragile brown pages, in terse sentences—often of great beauty from writers with little education. A long-awaited letter arrives from Scotland; a steer is rescued from a flood; the "feds" are hoodwinked; a midwife saves a threatened mother and child; a father makes his way home through snowstorms, near death from starvation, his horse and provisions stolen by Indians; a young mother dies in a dugout.

Heroic endurance, a common occurrence among men — there was nothing else to do — was a phenomenon among Mormon women. For as Erik Erikson has said, the hard work of pioneering fell to women; men could escape from time to time. Mormon women carried added burdens: polygamy and their men's long absences on missions left them to colonize and to raise families alone. Many of them did not have the solace of living among their own people. As plural wives they were forced to Canada and Mexico to begin new lives.

A heritage of strength and of rich folklore grew out of the life of this "peculiar people." Miraculous healings in times of deepest despair fired their faith; divine promptings averted tragedies; and seagulls swept down to devour grasshoppers gorging on priceless wheat. During the crucial early years, the Three Nephites of the Book of Mormon, Christ's apostles in the New World, appeared often when need was greatest.

A theocracy based on an agrarian culture was the vision of church leaders. Beyond religious matters their attitudes reflected the nativism of the nation. The goal of gathering to Zion and the supremacy of the church in all matters submerged national origins and hastened the Americanization of Mormon immigrants. Native languages and customs became the subjects of anecdotes and passed into folklore.

From the beginning, though, intrepid Jewish merchants, better educated than the mass of immigrants, and Gentiles of various occupations came to Zion. Some, like the federal officials who were imposed on the Mormons for their resistance to the antipolygamy laws, were more unwanted than others. Besides the long struggle for statehood, other disruptions eroded the grand vision of Mormon theocracy. The transcontinental railroad, joined at the same time as Major Powell's historic journeys on the Green and Colorado rivers, made it economically possible to unearth the state's abundant coal, gold, silver, copper, and other minerals. Industrialists rushed in; for laborers they could choose non-Mormon immigrants from the British Isles, Scandinavia, and northern Europe. Many of the Chinese who had worked on the Central Pacific Railroad remained as section-gang workers, miners, and shop owners.

With the beginning of the new century the character of the state began to change drastically. The opening of numerous mines in arid, juniper-covered mountains and the branching of rail lines to transport valuable minerals required many thousands of laborers.

Mormon leaders warned their people against forsaking the agrarian life for the licentiousness of mining towns. Mass apostasies were feared.

English-speaking people began leaving pick-and-shovel labor and moving upward. Immigrants from the Mediterranean, the Balkans, and a lesser number from Asia Minor and the Middle East took their places. Absentee landlords used alien labor agents to bring in gangs of these unskilled laborers who were willing to work for less than Americans would. Often they were used as strike-breakers. In this way Italians, Finns, South Slavs, Greeks, and Mexicans came in large numbers to Utah.

The "Yellow Peril" coincided with the arrival of the first of the new immigrants. Chinese were replaced by "whites and Italians." Japanese, "less objectionable" than the Chinese who wore their hair in braids and dressed in old-country clothing, remained longer on section crews and in the mines until the growing numbers of Balkan and Mediterranean immigrants were deemed "less objection-able" than they and used to replace them. The frugality of the Japanese enabled those who remained in the state to become farmers, open produce markets, and buy property.

The Mormon pioneers had taken months to cross the plains and to cut roads through forested mountains. The new immigrants traveled by boxcar and at times by railroad coach. They left the safety of big city ghettos, where their people crowded into tenements and worked in factories, and began precarious odysseys through prairies, mountains, and deserts. By the time they reached Utah, they had been hounded by officials, who assessed a head tax on them or jailed them for vagrancy while they looked for work, and been repulsed by Americans of all classes for their "foreign looks" and language. Fearful that the aliens would take their jobs, American workmen stalked them.

For these later immigrants, Utah was a stop on a tedious journey out of poverty. They expected to remain in America long enough to make sufficient money to return to their own countries to buy property, become shopkeepers, moneylenders, or merchants. They unnerved Americans and immigrants from the British Isles and northern Europe with their intense nationalism. They had been impelled into Mormon country not by the grand vision of the pioneers but by coincidence: by meeting a labor agent who was recruiting gangs for Utah mines, section gangs, mills, and smelters; by receiving a letter from a brother or cousin in a Carbon County or

Bingham Canyon mining camp; by merely jumping off a freight train and finding themselves in a place called Utah.

Utah and all the West teemed with the movement of these young, single men of "foreign looks." They moved constantly, in and out of the state and back again. They laid rails for branch lines and replaced narrow-gauge tracks with standard gauge. They spent months isolated on plains and in mountains, building roads and bridges. They went from mine to mine, from mill to smelter, living in tents, railroad cars, and in shacks they built themselves out of gunpowder boxes. Company boardinghouses were few. No one, least of all the companies, gave thought to the immigrants' housing and sanitation needs.

They kept on moving, beyond the census takers. Their mail was sent in care of coffeehouses, labor agents, and interpreters. It was not until the early 1920s that most of them had remained in one place long enough to complete the five-year residency required for citizenship.

The clang of sledges on steel was heard on homesteaded farmland that increasingly pushed back the sagebrush. Hamlets and towns were now surrounded by fields in patterns of yellow and green. Frame and brick houses had replaced adobe and log cabins, and rows of Mormon poplars were familiar landmarks. The old inhabitants saw the large labor gangs and were alarmed: after a half-century they had succeeded in "making the desert blossom as the rose," and suddenly foreigners who had neither fought nor suffered for Zion were invading it.

The new "unassimilable" immigrants were castigated and reviled in Utah as in the entire nation. The Mormons had contained the Indians, but they could not control the kind of labor brought in by eastern management. They would prefer to hire Mormons, the mine and mill bosses said, but not enough of them came forward. The nationwide view that the Balkan and Mediterranean immigrants were of inferior heredity was deepened in Utah by the Mormon notion that the invaders had "tainted blood."

Besides having to contend with prejudice and suspicion from Mormons, these later aliens brought old-country dissensions with them. Mine, mill, and smelter rolls record them: North Italians, South Italians; Greeks, Bulgarians, Albanians, Cretans; Spanish, Mexican; and the various contentious peoples who were to make up the nation of Yugoslavia in 1928—Slovenes, Croatians, Serbs, Bosnians, Herzegovinians, Dalmatians, and Montenegrins, all usually

5

listed as Austrians. Only in labor troubles and attempted lynchings did they unite against the Americans.

For mutual help and for the comfort of familiarity, each national group formed "colonies," more often called Wop Towns, Greek Towns, Bohunk Towns, and Jap Towns. In these enclaves within the larger enclave of Mormondom, they carried on as if they were in their fatherlands. They had churches, midwives, folkhealers, lodges, newspapers, coffeehouses, other meeting places, and belligerent factions upholding political parties in their homelands. Although they were remaining longer in the new country than they had anticipated and were bringing over picture brides, almost all of them were still thinking of returning to their native countries. America's and Utah's life, and politics especially, were of superficial interest to them.

A few of them found work in small towns, beyond the reaches of their enclaves. Like the Wild Bunch outlaws who left the fringes of Mormon society and soon lost their identity with it, these immigrants, cut off from their compatriots, married into pioneer families, and although never fully absorbed by Mormonism, their native culture became increasingly remote to them.

Unlike the Mormons who kept journals, these new immigrants came from people who spoke and sang their history. The few who had more than several years' schooling formed circles and wrote poems and stories for their foreign-language publications. The women had a high illiteracy rate and lived circumscribed lives of inordinately hard work caring for large families and young countrymen as boarders. Restrictive custom and folklore of their native countries determined their existence. The life of these various nationalities can be glimpsed through their few extant newspapers, reports, often virulent, in Utah publications, and the reminiscences of the aged.

Among the thrifty Mormons, then, the thrifty new immigrants came. Except on Sundays they dressed poorly. Their houses were barren, yet they bought real estate and regularly sent money back to their families. Their religions were ancient, a natural infusion into life. To insure themselves the proper ceremonies of life and death, they built churches. They were not called upon to make great emotional and financial sacrifices to spread a new religion throughout the world. The church was there. It was not the primary preoccupation of life; the family was.

The immigrants continued coming, drawn not only by the traditional poverty of their countries but by political events in them, by the Mexican Revolution, and by the Balkan Wars. The First World War disrupted immigration patterns and set off vicious campaigns against aliens and other minorities 'n America. Lynchings of Negroes had averaged a yearly seventy since 1900, but race riots increased. Between forty and a hundred people were killed in the 1917 riot in East Saint Louis; in the Red Summer of 1919, 38 were killed and 537 were injured in Chicago. The immigration laws of 1921 and 1924 and the Ku Klux Klan attacks of 1924 to 1925 were attempts to control these "un-American" aliens and native-born who "would take over" if they were not stringently watched.

The peak years for the alien population in Utah were reached before the First World War when mine employment, railroad building and maintenance were at their height. The most numerous, the Greeks and Italians, accounted for 11.1 percent of Utah's foreign-born population in 1910 and 1920. When quotas were set, immigrants "without papers" entered the state illegally and were hidden on sheep ranches or moved constantly from one mining town to another.

Of these thousands of men who did the industrial work for the state, many left with a small sum of money to start modest businesses elsewhere in the country. Few of some groups remain. Albanians disappeared. The Lebanese who were numerous enough at one time to require two labor agents can be tallied quickly. Montenegrins, too, were once a sizeable portion of mine and mill payrolls. Serbs and Croats remember several Bosnians who lived among them. Bulgarians found the climate among their coreligionists, but traditional enemies, the Greek Orthodox, so hostile that church records show they did not avail themselves of the sacraments.

The 361 Turks (Turkish nationals included) counted in the 1910 Census, greatly outnumbered by 4,039 Greeks and a smaller number of Serbs, the animosities of over four centuries of Ottoman rule alive in them, did not remain to be counted in the 1920 Census. Of the nearly six hundred Russians reported in the same census, only a few communicants remain in the Salt Lake City Greek churches. They have generally disappeared from the Intermountain West as have their wooden churches with onion-shaped domes, once incongruously set in western mining towns. The hundreds of Finn miners who annoyed mining camps with their Temperance associations that also espoused socialism dwindled to 1.4 percent of Utah's foreign-born population by 1920.

There were a few Armenian families who escaped Turkish persecution and came to Utah as Mormon converts. Syrians sold rugs, tablecloths, and bedspreads in mining camps, transplanted nomads. Gypsies made the rounds of industrial towns to tell fortunes and to sell flowerpot stands, made of rough wood and willows, and garish shawls. As late as the 1940s, twenty-six nationalities were counted in Helper, Carbon County, many of them listed in the census as "all others." One small group that continues to be distinguishable is the Basques, one hundred of them in Salt Lake City, a fewer number in Ogden, and several more throughout the state. Enabling legislation to supply the state with sheepherders has kept their numbers from diminishing further.

The depression years of the thirties began the ultimate acceptance of America by these later immigrants as their primary country: if America was in trouble, they feared what life would be in their perpetually impoverished fatherlands. Loyalty to their homelands became increasingly tempered by concern for American life. The Second World War completed the metamorphosis. Children of immigrants were in America's armed services and these sons and daughters knew America as their country. Children of Japanese immigrants were also serving this, their country, yet thousands of first, second, and third generation people of Japanese ancestry were interned in the Topaz relocation center in Millard County. Hundreds stayed on to relive the immigrant experience of frugality leading to financial independence.

After the war the relaxation of immigration quotas again brought increased numbers of diverse peoples into Utah. The missionary program of the Latter-day Saints church still adds that vitality that is immigration's primary contribution to America.

Although Chicanos and Blacks live in specific neighborhoods, there are no longer "colonies" and "towns." Native languages are lost beyond the second generation, except for the Greeks, Jews, and Japanese who continue their schools and traditions. Italians gather annually to acknowledge a cultural commonality. Basques meet in a westside hotel and restaurant. Swiss days are celebrated and a German hour is heard on radio. Spanish-speaking performers entertain with ethnic dances and songs on television. On the first day of May, a small band of Finnish ancestry drive to the Scofield cemetery where sixty-three Finns, victims of the 1900 Winter Quarters explosion, are buried.

An increasing number of Koreans have been coming to Utah since the Korean War, mostly as students. Filipinos have never been in the state in large numbers, fewer than four hundred were counted in the 1970 Census. Hawaiians are remembered for their courageous efforts to establish an LDS colony in Skull Valley. They stayed for twenty-eight years, during which they created a small town and planted fruit and shade trees and yellow roses. They were unable, however, to adjust to the extremes of heat and cold of the desert, and leprosy added to the graves in the sagebrush. The younger Hawaiians left for Salt Lake City and mining camps to look for work. When a Mormon Temple was built in Laie, Oahu, Hawaii, the small band of converts returned to their island and Iosepa became a desert once more.

Following the Second World War when ethnic and racial prejudices began to decline, a new awareness for people's origins grew. The Latter-day Saints church stresses now the relearning and preserving of cultural heritage. Universities are documenting the immigrant experience in Utah.

Today there are only scatterings and patches of sagebrush around the cities and towns of Utah. Where sagebrush covered mountain slopes, wheat and orchards now grow. There are plains of it still, but far into isolated places. Industries and factories increase. Utah is no longer an agrarian society of a "peculiar people."

This book is a commemoration of the early peoples of Utah, of the pioneer Mormons who sought religious freedom, and of the later immigrants who came for economic security. More than a dozen of Utah's distinctive cultural groups are represented between these covers. Each is surveyed by a historian especially qualified by blood ties and training to comment on the particular role served by that group in shaping our state's complex and fascinating history. They join with me in dedicating this effort to the memory of our ancestors, who left us a unique and rich legacy, and to the present Bicentennial generation which carries it forth.

HZP

1 THE FIRST PEOPLES OF UTAH

My Native Land

BY FRED CONETAH

I am standing on a high hill overlooking a vast amount of country and wondering if one of my forefathers stood here and saw the same country as I see now. If so, he saw a completely different kind of country. He saw the wonders of nature and how they were created for him. Nothing was overlooked, for if he missed certain things, part of his life was gone. He saw the mountains and knew that from those mountains came part of his livelihood. He knew in those mountains were the deer, elk, bear, mountain sheep, and the different kinds of birds, and in the streams, many kinds of fish; likewise, he looked at the prairie and saw the buffalo, antelope, and other creatures meant to live in the lower area. He saw the many kinds of trees, brush, and plants that would become a part of him. This was his native land.

In order to make use of the things and creatures created for him, he had to come up with his own idea of producing crude weapons and the apparatus needed to harvest his own needs and those of his fellow tribesmen. He developed many kinds of weapons and tools to make his life easier. He made tools for the women to use at home and around the encampment, and he had to have the knowledge to get the right kind of materials to make them work for his purposes. He had to find the right kind of wood, bone, and clay to make his cooking and eating utensils; the right kind of stone to make into grinding stone, ax, hammer, or battle ax. The flint stone he knew would be good for knives, scrapers, spears, and arrowheads because of its keen edge and hardness. He had to know what part of the country would contain certain woods, flints, paints, and other useful items. He knew that wood, stones, and flints were located within the territory of his enemies, and therefore certain wood and stones were considered sacred by him. This was good for him because this was his native land.

I wonder, as I stand here, if he knew that he would be labeled as a renegade, savage, a blocker of another civilization, a hindrance to progress, and, someday be thought of as not even a human being by people of other races.

I wonder if he saw the dark clouds coming over the horizon, an atmosphere that would soon change or try to change his way of living or his beliefs. I believe the natives had the philosophy to accept anything that was true. Their faith evolved from the understanding that the Father was the creator of everything that was on this earth.

I know there was a conflict of beliefs when Christianity was brought by the strangers and the invaders. This was merely part of the movement to destroy the natives' attitudes, beliefs, customs, and culture. The natives could not say God is Red, White, Black, or any other color. They only thought the Great Spirit was the color of the universe, which no people can claim. The native people could see this because his creation was tangible.

My people saw the explorer who was employed by an alien government to make geographical discoveries. They saw the white trappers and fur traders who first came into our country for economic reasons, then the woodsmen who followed and lived in log cabins with hunting, fishing, and small-scale farming as their means of subsistence. Then the farmers came to stay and built their schools, churches, town halls, and established an urban community.

The native land changed with the coming of these white people but more completely when the Office of Indian Affairs was established within the War Department in 1824. In 1832 Congress authorized the appointment of a commissioner of Indian affairs who reported to the secretary of war on Indian matters. In 1849 the office of the commissioner of Indian affairs was transferred from the War Department to the new Department of the Interior, where it has remained.

The policy was first to do away with the natives, confiscate their crude weapons, destroy their beliefs, tradition, and culture, and encourage them to adopt the white man's ways; but the natives found it hard to accept beliefs and customs of any alien culture. They faced starvation. Their main source of subsistence had been the buffalo. After it was exterminated by the great white buffalo hunters, the natives were quickly reduced to poverty, making them dependent on government annuity goods and rations for their daily bread.

As I stand here, I can see it has been a long, hard road back toward the natives' economic independence. We have moved from our tepees to better living and housing conditions. We are caretakers of the natives' once-beloved, ever-dwindling land. The question now comes, as a descendant of that person who might have stood on this same hill a long time ago, whether or not I have forgotten his beliefs, traditions, customs, and culture. To truly understand our native land, we have to learn about our own people and the many great leaders and chiefs who were charged with taking care of the Great Spirit's creation. We have to find ways to cope with the policies and restrictions that do not allow us to be free in exercising our lifestyle.

I stand here and know this is my native land.

The Navajos

BY CLYDE J. BENALLY

In beauty (happily) I walk.
With beauty before me I walk.
With beauty behind me I walk.
With beauty below me I walk.
With beauty above me I walk.
It is finished (again) in beauty.
It is finished in beauty.

— Night Chant

It is generally agreed that the Navajos, the largest Indian tribe in the United States, came into the Southwest sometime after A.D. 1300, even though the Dine' ("the People") themselves do not attest to this. The Dine' mention their strong relationship to their Anasazi, the Ancient Ones, in their mythology and ceremonies. This relationship justifies to them permanent ties and absolute use-rights to the native land that is bounded by four sacred mountains: the Blanca Peaks in New Mexico on the east, Mount Taylor in New Mexico on the south, the San Francisco Peaks in Arizona on the west, and the

Hesperus Peaks in Colorado on the north. The Navajos live "in severely eroded plateau country . . . colorful, beautiful to look at, but hard to make a living from." [1]

In this red earth country of monoliths, buttes, and bridges of rock made by erosion of time, the Dine' had no concept of real ownership of land but instead one of communal property. Use-rights were established by anyone who used and needed the land. The Dine' philosophy embodied Father Sky and Mother Earth as the parents of all and gave no individual absolute title to a piece of the sky or the earth. Also, they asked, who in his right mind would hold absolute ownership when his existence on this earth is but brief?

Father Sky is sacred as are his offerings: air, wind, thunder, lightning, and rain. Mother Earth is also sacred and all that she offers the Navajos is therefore sacred: mountains, vegetation, animals, and water. Many prayers for blessings are addressed to Mother Earth, Father Sky, the Four Winds, and White Dawn, to name a few.

Food and shelter are more than utilitarian objects for the Navajos who are always conscious that they are Mother Earth's gifts. Their food is simple and easily prepared. Mutton is commonly eaten; other meats are small game like rabbits and prairie dogs and large game such as deer and antelope. Infrequently a horse is butchered and all of the animal is used: the meat and entrails are eaten fresh or dried for later needs and the hide is made into footwear, belts, and articles of clothing. Corn is used not only for food but for offerings to the gods and for the mundane yet useful repair of leaky baskets. A large portion of Navajo myth is centered around corn, telling how Changing Woman (Nature), who created the ancestors of the Dine', gave instructions on how it should be raised. The dependability of corn for food is emphasized; cornmeal mush, cakes, and bread are some of the corn foods.

When wheat flour was stocked by trading posts, the Navajos conceived their well known fried bread, made from flour, baking powder, salt, and water (sugar and milk may be added), formed into flat rounds, and fried in lard or animal fat. Every cook has her own special recipe. For baking loaf bread, an outdoor earth oven is used.

[1] Leland C. Wyman, ed., *Beautyway: A Navaho Ceremonial* (New York, 1957), p. 5.

The hogan, like corn, has deep religious importance. A similar structure, the Navajos believe, was used by the gods when they first laid down the ceremonies for the people. Every ceremony ends with a sacred hogan chant and everyone inside the hogan must be awake when it is sung.

There are two types of hogan, both built according to religious dictates that require four main support posts: one each in the east, west, south, and north for the different gods in these directions. The hogan always faces east and the space inside is organized around the centrally placed fireplace.

The conical type of hogan is the original kind and is made by leaning cedar logs together to form a smoke hole and doorway. The domed-roof, or round hogan, is larger and has support posts arranged in a circle with logs laid horizontally from post to post. The logs are intersticed one upon the other until a small smoke hole is left at the top of the dome. The support poles are usually in multiples of four. A typical domed hogan usually has eight supports, but there could be as many as twelve. The logs are covered with brush, bark, and dirt.

Chants for the purification and blessing of the hogan belong to a multitude of rituals that are the fabric of the complex Navajo religion. Religious rites and the conduct of daily life are centered in the Navajo ideal: to live in sacred harmony, in beauty, and in blessedness. A vast knowledge of Navajo myths, history, and folk tales is needed to understand the repetitive, seemingly meaningless chants—often called "sings" or "dances."

Some rites are short, like the diagnostic ritual in which the hand trembler (diviner) observes a sick person to determine the nature of his illness and the appropriate healing ceremony. A significant short rite is the morning prayer to White Dawn to welcome a new day. Pollen from corn tassels is used and is richly symbolic of purity as well as of peace, happiness, and prosperity. Pollen-sprinkling along with specific chants consecrate and sanctify hogans, patients, prayer sticks, dry (sand) paintings, and cornmeal mush that is eaten ceremonially. Navajos call the haze in the air, pollen of morning sky and pollen of evening sky.[2]

The complex and lengthy rituals include, among many, the various three-day sings, five-day sings, and the nine-day sings. Some

---

[2] Gladys A. Reichard, *Navajo Religion: A Study of Symbolism* (New York, 1963), 2d ed. in one vol., pp. 251–52.

of these are often referred to as the Squaw Dance (Enemyway or Enemy chant), the *Yei bi chai* (Night chantway), and the Fire Dance (Mountain chantway).[3]

The roster of mythical figures in these sings appears to be endless; each has an important role in the history of the Dine', and their names instantly relate the Navajos to certain periods of time in their past. A few of these names are Rock Crystal Talking God, Happiness Boy, White Shell Woman, White Corn Boy, Yellow Corn Girl, First Man, Big Snake, Pollen Boy, and Cornbeetle Girl. While the lengthy sings go on, the medicine man performs an extremely complicated ritual with his bundle of herbs, prayer sticks, pollen, emetics (at times), and sand and sandstone for the dry paintings. The following, taken from a Beautyway ceremony, sung to the medicine man's ministrations, has only perplexity for the uninitiated:

> Dusty Body [Rattler], youth chief, I have made
> you an offering . . . Dusty Body maiden
> chief an offering . . .
> Pollen Body [Bull Snake], youth chief . . .
> Pollen Body maiden chief . . . Arrowsnake,
> youth chief . . .
> Arrowsnake, maiden chief. . . .[4]

For the Navajos, however, every line of a sing is important.

Under the two categories of ceremonies, Blessingway and Evilway, there are far too many ceremonies for any one medicine man (singer) to know all of them. Most medicine men specialize in one to six or seven ceremonies, and rarely will a medicine man specialize in more than eight. Everything has to be learned by memory. It takes years to learn the songs or chants, the myths and origins of each song, each ceremonial ritual, and the design and interpretation of sand paintings—if they are used. Learning is accomplished through apprenticeship to noted medicine men. After their education, medicine men have to be ceremonially ordained for each ceremony they perform.

During his training, each medicine man must acquire his own medicine bundle. This can be done by the ritualistic gathering of a bundle from an aging medicine man or by making up a new bundle. The type of ceremony that the medicine man knows will determine

[3] See Wyman, *Beautyway*, and Leland C. Wyman, *Blessingway* (Tucson, 1970). A discussion of Enemyway is found in the latter.

[4] Wyman, *Beautyway*, p. 105.

the kind and size of the medicine bundle. Collection of a new medicine bundle is time-consuming and includes herbs, pollens, feathers, sacred mountain dirt, stones, scrub oak branches, juniper bark, cattail flags, wild rice grass, rock sage, bear grass, plants with pods, and many other grasses and tree branches.

The medicine man, further, must be able to identify exactly every herb, plant, and other necessary object required in particular ceremonies. Like a medical doctor, he is on call at all times but goes to the patient's hogan to perform the necessary ceremony. The Navajo people usually know which medicine man in their area specializes in each ceremony. The chants are followed by serving food to the spectators, and, with the medicine man's fee, the expense can be large.

Navajo society is close-knit; families are organized around the mother, grandmother, and, sometimes, older sisters. A man usually lives with his wife in her mother's community. (Marriages are exogamous, outside the parents' clans.) The children inherit the mother's clan, and the cousins of the clan are referred to as brothers and sisters. Because of these strong ties, a Navajo has deep obligations in helping and in participating in functions involving his kin. If a ceremony is to be performed, the patient's kin are expected to assist in it. Males are obligated to their maternal clans and it is not unusual for a husband to leave his family to help his mother's kin.

Present Navajo society has had a long evolution. The first contact with foreigners occurred in the sixteenth century. From the Spanish the Dine' adopted practices that changed them from food hunters to sheep raisers. Besides acquiring sheep and horses from the Spanish, they discarded their buckskin clothing for the wool of the white men and learned silversmithing and the use of money (beso) as a medium of exchange. Intermarriage with the Spaniards produced the Nakai-di-nee clan.

From the time of this Spanish intrusion, the Dine' had to adapt to an ever-changing environment. The Navajos believe that almost all cultural practices originated within the tribe, but that weaving, farming, livestock raising, and some legends were learned from the Spanish and other southwestern Indian tribes. The Navajos are known as the most innovative of tribes, taking from other cultures what could be useful, discarding what could not, and being self-supporting under the poorest economy. Their flocks of sheep that must graze on vegetation so sparse that hogans are miles from each

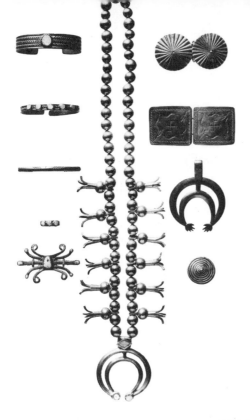

Above: *Goulding's trading post, Monument Valley, near the Utah-Arizona border, 1947. The Navajos learned silversmithing from the Spanish and became consummate artists.*

Above: *Squaw dance in Monument Valley.* Left: *The Navajos learned weaving from neighboring tribes and then surpassed them in skill. Monument Valley, 1941.*

Exhibit 1st Navajo Fair. Sept 21st 1899. Bluff. Utah.

From the top: *Exhibit in the first Navajo fair, September 1899, in Bluff. After a sing, a medicine man gathers up his fee, coins tossed onto a blanket by the patient's family and spectators. Potato race held during a celebration in Monument Valley. Horse racing is a favorite diversion for the Navajos.*

Opposite, from the top: *During the* Kin-nahl-dah *celebration marking a girl's reaching puberty, women pour batter into a pit to bake ceremonial bread. Navajo women butchering a beef to serve guests at a Squaw Dance. A Monument Valley hogan.* Above: *A Navajo medicine man.* Right: *Sweat house used at sings during which a medicine man conducts ancient healing rituals.* Below: *The high altar at Saint Christopher's, Bluff, San Juan County, an Episcopal mission established by Father H. Baxter Liebler in 1943.*

21

other attest to the great adaptability of the Navajos. In 1871 Willy Arny, a trader, persuaded a few Navajos to sell their wool at Fort Defiance, Arizona. The animals were spindly and

> gave no more than a pound or two of wool, hacked off with a homemade knife shaped from a tin can. But when the Navajos saw an economic advantage they took it. By 1886, they had a million pounds of wool to trade, and by 1890, two million.[5]

By crossing their Merino ewes with Rambouillet rams, the Navajos produced a hardy sheep with thick wool. Today sheep, the wealth of the Navajos, move through all of Navajoland, watched over by excellent male and female herders of all ages.

In both silversmithing—using bold, simple designs often with embedded turquoise—and in weaving, the Navajos became superb craftsmen.[6] Weaving with cotton was learned from the agricultural Pueblo Indians. Later when the Spanish drove sheep north into Arizona and New Mexico in 1540, wool was used. Mastering wool dyeing by using native roots, berries, and bark, the Navajos are credited with creating the first native tapestries in the United States. The predilection for red of traders, like Don Lorenzo Hubbell, and tourists coming into the land of the Dine' on Fred Harvey buses, together with new analine dyes in bright colors, threatened the craft for a while. Navajo weavers were given pictures to reproduce and in their experimentation with the analine dyes and their hurry to sell more of their work, a period of poor-quality rugs came off the looms. The market for Navajo rugs never waned, and weavers gave all their time to this source of income, always steady while drought and floods regularly ruined their crops. Blankets for their own use were no longer made; instead the softer wool blankets from Pendleton, Oregon, were bought at trading posts.

The Southwest Museum in Los Angeles displays many rugs in traditional designs that were original to the Navajos. The principal Utah Navajo weaving district is part of Monument Valley in the Four Corners area and is called Teec Nos Pos. The designs from this area are the most complex, "the least Indian and the most like

---

[5] Ruth M. Underhill, *The Navajos* (Norman, Okla., 1956), p. 181.

[6] See Elizabeth Compton Hegemann, "Pioneer Silversmiths," *The Masterkey* 36–37 (1962): 44–59, 102–113; David L. Neumann, "Navajo Silversmithing," *El Palacio* 77, no. 2 (1971): 13–32; and *Arizona Highways,* July 1974.

oriental. . . ." [7] Outstanding weavers from this area are Alice Nelson, Hilda Begay, Emma Yabeney, Mrs. Saltwater, and Esther Williams.[8]

After the Spanish, who changed Navajo life with horses, sheep, and silver works, the next contacts with white men were the English-speaking *Bilagáana* ("white man"). This major event in the lives of the Navajos began when Mexico gave the responsibilities for the Dine' to the United States under the Treaty of Guadalupe Hidalgo in 1848. The preceding eight decades and the following two were the bloodiest in Navajo history, with wars against the Apaches, Utes, Spanish, Pueblos, and Comanches over slave raiding. Until the treaty, the Navajos governed themselves in clan units with the eldest or medicine man acting as head or chief. There was no head chief over all the Navajos, and trouble arose when a few chiefs signed treaties with white men who thought the clan leaders were representing the whole tribe. The treaty, for example, of November 22, 1846, signed by Narbona and other leaders was not accepted by Manuelito and other younger Navajos. Raiding continued, despite the treaty, until 1864 when large forces under Kit Carson conquered the Navajos. About eighty-five hundred Navajos were forced to take the "Long Walk" to Bosque Redondo in New Mexico. For four terrible years they were confined in a concentration camp, their self-sufficiency and independence destroyed. The captive Dine' began their homeward journey after the Treaty of 1868, and those who endured and survived regarded themselves with high esteem.

Navajos, living in the western part of the Navajo country, who had escaped from the United States militia into the rugged steep canyons of the San Juan and Colorado rivers of Arizona and Utah and were able to survive untouched, also thought of themselves as heroes because of their cunning and ability to elude capture.

The Treaty of 1868 ended the intense suffering of the Navajos and made them amenable to trading with whites. By 1877 six trading posts were established on the Navajo Reservation; by 1943, the peak in trading, ninety-five traders were licensed. The reservation trader was far different from the early itinerant trader who brought guns, liquor, and trinkets to Indian camps in return for furs. The reservation trader lived among confined Indians in his trading post

[7] See Carl Schaefer Dentzel, "Native American Tapestries of the Navajo," *Arizona Highways,* July 1974.
[8] *Ibid.,* p. 6.

with a reliable water supply nearby.[9] Because the Navajos lived far off in inaccessible terrain, the trader was often the only white man they ever saw. This isolation insured the Navajos' keeping their culture free from the white man's influence; it also, until the 1930s, gave traders great authority that was often misused, resulting in exploitation of the Dine' when selling their wool, rugs, and silver jewelry. Although 25 percent profit was the federally set limit, the isolation of the trading post gave dishonest traders the opportunity to buy and sell at their prices.

The trading post was the central meeting point for the widely scattered Navajos. For trading information, advice from the trader in business, personal, and government matters, medical help, the fearful burial of the dead, Indians rode hundreds of miles, first on horseback and later in pickup trucks. The trader continued in this role until the federal relief programs, begun in 1933, brought an increase in white personnel and diminished somewhat his status. A poignant novel of this period is Oliver La Farge's *Laughing Boy,* the story of a young Indian who was demoralized by his first contact with whites.

Navajo women wearing full orange, purple, and green sateen skirts and velveteen tops, their wealth in necklaces of silver, coral, and turquoise around their necks and silver bracelets on their arms, haggled with the trader over their rugs. Silver bracelets, bridles, squash necklaces, and buttons—often made of United States dimes and quarters—were pawned for supplies. The pawn could remain hanging in the trading post for years. Wool and rugs were sold to cut down the price on the pawn ticket. A sample pawn ticket on a silver bracelet:

Woman - Who - Doesn't Smoke [10]		
flour and coffee	$1.45	2/19/30
sateen	1.80	3/15/30
	3.25	
rug pd.	2.00	4/ 3/30
	1.25	

[9] See Elizabeth Compton Hegemann, *Navaho Trading Days* (Albuquerque, 1963) and Frank McNitt, *The Indian Traders* (Norman, Okla., 1962).

[10] Hegemann, *Navaho Trading Days,* p. 341.

velveteen	2.50	5/20/30
	3.25 [sic]	
coffee, sugar	1.10	6/ 5/30
	4.35	
wool	4.35	6/10/30
plus $2 to trade out	$0.00	

Navajos near the Utah border traded at Oljato, Gouldings, Gap (for many years run by Joe Lee, son of John D. Lee who was held responsible for the Mountain Meadows Massacre), Hatch's, Aneth, and trading posts in Bluff and Blanding.

It has been a long and slow progress from the trader representing the Indians to the present tribal government begun by United States agents. The policy of the government in education and in tribal affairs was to transform Navajos into white men.

The United States directed social and cultural change at every level of tribal society. Although Navajos were given livestock and farm implements, they also were forced, in many cases, to cut their *conjos* (long hair tied in a bun) before receiving wagons, and children, frightened by separation from their families and far from their hogans, had their hair cut as soon as they arrived at school. The proud tradition of wearing *conjos* was destroyed with severe loss of self-esteem.

At the beginning the tribal government was merely administrative in nature and carried out the programs of the Bureau of Indian Affairs. Since then the Navajos have learned the intricacies of laws and bureaucracy and are now on the verge of total self-government. The various branches of the Navajo tribal government plan, control, and administer their own programs. The overriding theme is self-determination in conducting their own affairs. To accomplish these goals, there is a big push by the tribe toward education while keeping its Navajoness.

No longer working only with the Bureau of Indian Affairs, Navajos today run for local school boards, county commissions, and state legislatures. The tribe communicates and works directly with the state and national governments. All in all, the Navajo, a great learner, has mastered the white man's politics.

Since the Treaty of 1868, Navajoland has been expanded many times. Westward expansion was initiated by unilateral executive order of May 17, 1884, and took in northeastern Arizona and southeastern Utah below the San Juan River. The order of March 10, 1905, added the Aneth area north of the San Juan. The Paiute Strip had been classified in various ways until it was added to the reservation along the Aneth Extension by act of March 1, 1933. The Land Exchange Act of September 2, 1958, added McCracken Mesa and other lands north of the Aneth Extension area. This exchange was for land that is presently covered by the water of Lake Powell.

The United States Indian policy is slowly changing, giving Indians a voice in the policies and programs that affect them. This makes education more meaningful and develops expertise in the handling of tribal affairs.

While the future looks bright, a tremendous amount of effort is needed to improve Navajo education and to introduce industrial development to create jobs on the reservation, even though more Navajos are moving into the cities for work.

In Navajoland today adults in both Indian and "American" dress and little girls wearing cotton dresses, boys in jeans still travel the dusty road to trading posts where cases of the ubiquitous soda pop bottles are stacked. Some of the Navajos attend Father Baxter Liebler's Saint Christopher Episcopal Mission church or Catholic and Mormon services. For medical services they have, besides their medicine men, the Seventh Day Adventist Hospital near Goulding's Trading Post. Their children ride hours on yellow school buses for their education and when of high school age attend boarding schools as far away as the Indian school in Brigham City, Utah, where they meet students from other tribes. Many never return to live on the reservation where mothers still admonish children not to kill spiders because they are friends. It was Mrs. Spider, they say, who taught Navajo women how to spin fine threads from leaf fibers, cotton, and wool into useful articles.[11]

Great-grandfathers still explain the beginning of time through folk tales and how the First People were led out of the pitch in the center of the earth to the outside by Coyote and Badger. Coyote (usually the epitome of irresponsibility) told them, "Our tunnel is straight and will lead you to the dry land of the new world, but if

[11] Franc Johnson Newcomb, *Navajo Folk Tales* (Santa Fe, 1967), p. xiii.

you follow the crooked tunnels of the blind mole you will always live in the earth."[12]

The First People followed Coyote and Badger and emerged into Navajoland where on its red earth they lived close to nature and where they survive to this day in their hogans, looms nearby, and flocks of sheep spread out, grazing on the sparse life-nurturing plants.

[12] *Ibid.,* p. 53.

The Utes, Southern Paiutes, and Gosiutes

BY FLOYD A. O'NEIL

THE UTES

". . . teach 'em to speak Ute. And don't let them ever forget how we're supposed to live, who we are, where we came from." —Connor Chapoose

Confined on reservations, no longer free to range over the mountains and deserts of their lands in the incessant quest for food, the hard-pressed Utes never completely forgot how they were supposed to live, who they were, and where they came from. The elders handed this knowledge down to them in family tepees, during tribal ceremonies, and in the everyday practice of religion and acknowledgment of their myths. They knew that once their lands had stretched as far east to what is now the city of Denver, as far west to the Great Salt Lake Desert, and from northern Colorado and northern Utah south to the New Mexico pueblos. In these lands of mountains and deserts, the Utes were assured of ample food. The White River band of Indians hunted and fished in the Colorado Rockies and the Uintas during the summers while their women gathered seeds and berries. Buffalo meat was sliced thinly and dried; bones and marrow were boiled and ground into a gelatinous food; seeds were crushed into flour; and berries were dried, with part of the harvest pounded into dried meat (pemmican) and stored to be eaten in wintertime. The desert Indians ingeniously gathered myriad kinds of seeds and cacti to augment the large and small animals that were their main source of food. Not all of the Ute bands, however, were so fortunate as the Utes of the Utah Lake area who had an abundance of trout available as well as berries, seeds, roots, venison, and fowl; but as with most Indian tribes, they well understood the uses of the earth.

The shelters for the largest portion of the tribe were tepees, but brush and willow houses that were easily heated by an open fire were used as well. These structures were also cool in summer. One family might build several, depending on where they chose to live during that portion of the year: one at a fishing camp in winter, another near the place where seeds were gathered in July, another for the gathering of wild berries and fruits in August and September, and yet another in the pine forests where the women could gather the nuts and men could hunt in late summer and fall.

Their myths, together with their traditions, told the Utes how they were "supposed to live." It was far from the stereotype of Indians as an aimlessly roaming people ruled by primitive whims, ruthless to their women, children, and enemies. The Utes used their territory with systematic efficiency for the gathering of food and for the comfort of the season. Economics determined that they live in small bands of probably fewer than two hundred people, except for the large encampment at Utah Lake. This allowed them to maintain their food supply without endangering the size of herds, the grasses, or plants on which they subsisted.

Long before white contact, the Ute people believed in the immortality of the soul. They believed in a Creator God, Senawahv, and other lesser gods—a God of Blood, healer of the sick; a God of Weather, controller of thunder and lightning; a God of War; and a God of Peace. The Ute people believed in the pervasive power of Senawahv who fought and won over evil forces, and therefore their view of life and afterlife was essentially optimistic. None of the religions of the people from the European continent has ever been successful in altering this view among the Ute people.

The religion of the Ute people has always been highly individualistic in its application. Group rituals were not common, although two celebrations, the Bear Dance and the Sun Dance, have remained important to the present day. The religion was dominated by shamans (medicine men), people possessing special powers. Persons sought through the shaman the power of the supernatural to help them gain good health, courage, ability in the hunt, and defense of the groups. The practices of the shamans were not alike, nor were they formalized systems. Each shaman acted, sang, and used items which were different for each occasion and each manifestation of power. Some items used regularly by the shamans were eagle feathers, eagle bones, fetish bags, and certain medicinal plants. In performing their acts, especially in healing, the shamans often used songs and prayer to assist them. The practice of using shamans' services has increased in some of the Ute communities in the recent past.

The family was the center of Indian life and loyalty to it was the fabric of existence. The family included not only the immediate members as in European cultures, but extended to uncles, cousins, and maternal and paternal grandparents. Grandparents were extremely important for their judgment and for their intimate involvement in the rearing of children.

The honors extended to the aged were many—first to be served, seated in honored spots, and accorded special respect by the children. Work was expected of all, with the exception of small children. Prowess in hunting and defending the people was admired in men. In women, integrity, the ability to gather foods, prepare them, and the tanning and sewing of leather for clothing were admired traits. The woman who could feed, clothe, and shelter her family well was extended prestige. Babies were welcomed; their *khans* ("cradle boards") were decorated with beaded flowers and rosettes in blue for girls and often butterflies and rosettes in red for boys. The aromatic smooth inner bark of cedar was shredded for use as diapers.

The songs and stories of the people were the entertainment and the learning systems of the Utes. An infinite number of stories were told, some for moral instruction, some of bravery, some illustrative of the foolish acts of men, while others were of lyrical beauty describing nature as the handiwork of God. The stories and songs provided a milieu for nearly every act: birth, reaching manhood or womanhood, going to war, marriage, or death. Each storyteller and singer of songs had his own style and variation of which he was proud.

Surrounded by a large family, a plentiful earth ruled over by a beneficent God, the Ute child grew to maturity in a world where he felt himself an integral and welcome part.

Beyond the family, leadership was shared by many people rather than a "leader" in the commonly held sense of the word. Leaders were chosen from time to time to perform duties such as to lead a war party in defense of the Ute domain, or to lead the hunt for food. The most common form of leadership was simply respect for the wisdom of the elders of the tribe who assembled and came to decisions concerning matters. Following European contact, persons who were chosen to perform certain duties for the tribe were assumed by outsiders to be chiefs or rulers. They were not. They were respected members of the tribe performing certain functions.

Women, too, were given leadership roles. Chipeta, the wife of Ouray of the Uncompahgre band, is one of the celebrated women in the history of Colorado and Utah. John Wesley Powell was impressed with chief Tsau'-wi-ats's wife and wrote in his journal:

> His wife, "The Bishop," as she is called, is a very garrulous old woman; she exerts a great influence, and is much revered. She is the only Indian woman I have known to occupy a place in the council ring.[1]

This ordered life began to change, imperceptibly, with the coming of the first Europeans into their territory. The Utes received many goods of great value from the Spanish: metal points for arrows, metal cooking pots, mirrors, guns, and most important, the horse. They enjoyed an additional advantage: since the northward thrust of the Spanish empire stopped at the edge of Ute territory, they, unlike the Pueblo people, did not endure Spanish and Mexican administration.[2] The advantages of trade were also broadened. Even though the Utes had traded at Taos and other pueblos for generations prior to the arrival of the Spanish, their wealth now grew with the Europeans' increased demand for meat and hides that were bartered at Taos.

Although the Spanish drive to the north stopped at Abiquiu in the Chama Valley, its influence was felt much farther. Some trips were made into Ute country: in 1765 the Rivera expedition to

---

[1] John Wesley Powell, *Report of J. W. Powell, Exploration of the Colorado River of the West and its Tributaries* (Washington, D. C., 1875), p. 42.

[2] Lyman Tyler, "The Spaniard and the Ute," *Utah Historical Quarterly* 22 (1954): 344–45.

the Uncompahgre River in Colorado; the Dominguez-Escalante journey mostly through Ute country in 1776; the Arze-Garcia expedition of 1813; and many journeys to Ute country by one Maestas who was interpreter and legal officer on the northern frontier for Spain and later Mexico. These and other incursions were but momentary, however, and the integrity of Ute territory was maintained.

In the 1820s, when the Santa Fe Trail from Missouri to New Mexico was opened, some of the people who came to New Mexico were men interested in fur trapping. From Santa Fe and Taos the trappers moved northward into Ute country to gather the furs from the mountains the Utes called home.[3] Also coming from Missouri were trappers who moved directly into Ute country from the east and north. Those who came from Missouri up the Platte River route into Ute country became legendary figures in the early history of the West: William Henry Ashley, Jedediah Smith, Jim Bridger, Thomas Fitzpatrick, and Thomas L. (Pegleg) Smith, to name a few.

The trappers who came from Taos and Santa Fe also left their mark on the land: Antoine Robidoux, Etienne Provost, Denis Julien, and the elusive Duchaine. Elderly Utes of today recall hearing about them: ". . . my mother [said] Chambeau Reed . . . had his first trading post at Whiterocks. . . . He traded calico, beads, knives, and stuff like that to the Indians, and buckskin and furs."[4]

During the time of the fur trappers, a commercial route of lasting import was opened through Ute country in the early 1830s: more than half of the Old Spanish Trail from Santa Fe to Los Angeles led through Ute lands, with an additional portion through Paiute lands in Utah.[5] During the 1820s to the 1840s, the Utes began experiencing an increasing number of intruders who sought their resources. In the 1830s the Missouri French fur traders working from Taos opened two trading posts in Ute country, one in the Uinta Basin and one on the Uncompahgre River in Colorado.

Then, in the 1840s, two events changed Ute life forever. The first was the rapid defeat of the Spanish-speaking people to the south. The Mexican War altered the powerful force with whom

---

[3] The best treatment of this subject is to be found in David J. Weber, *The Taos Trappers* (Norman, Okla., 1970).

[4] The complete interview with Henry Harris, Jr., of the Uintah-Ouray Reservation, is in the collection of the Duke Indian Oral History Project at the University of Utah.

[5] Leroy R. Hafen and Ann W. Hafen, *The Old Spanish Trail from Santa Fe to Los Angeles* (Glendale, Calif., 1954).

Ouray, seated center, and other Ute leaders: Warets, Shavano, Ankatosh, and Guero on a peace mission to Washington, D. C.

A Ute warrior and his dog on the eastern slope of the Wasatch Mountains.

An encampment in the Uinta Valley, ca. 1873.

*Above: A Ute warrior and his bride in the Uinta Valley, ca. 1873.
Below: Ute mother with child in a beaded cradle board.
Government allotment day on the Uintah-Ouray Reservation.*

Poke, Jess Posey, Chief Posey, and Tse-ne-gat were arrested in San Juan County during the Posey War, 1915, a dispute involving land rights.

The Ouray school, Uintah-Ouray Reservation, Randlett. Ute Bear Dance.

From the top: *Uncompahgre Indians who joined four hundred others in marching to South Dakota in 1906, hoping to convince Indians there to fight the government. Red Cap, seated, was one of the Ute leaders on the long march to South Dakota. The long trek began at Whiterocks.*

the Utes had traded and made treaties. Secondly, the Mormons arrived in Ute borderlands and began a rapid dispersion of their people into the most fertile areas of the western fringe of Ute lands. Game, wild berries, and roots that Utes depended on for food became depleted. The pioneers hunted the game for themselves and they uprooted the roots and fruit-bearing bushes to cultivate fields.

The Americans moved rapidly. In the first decade following the Mexican War, they defeated the Ute bands who opposed them, founded Fort Massachusetts in southern Colorado, placed a military force on the northern border with two forts in Wyoming, and started the occupation of the lands in Colorado.

In all of this, the Utes remained remarkably peaceful. Only the Walker War in Utah and some raiding on the northern New Mexico-southern Colorado border by the Utes were exceptions. These breaches were experienced only after great provocation.

For the Utes, the occupation of the lands was troublesome on the eastern front, troublesome in the south, but fraught with disaster in Utah. By the winter of 1856 starvation had begun.[6] Brigham Young said, soon after the Mormons settled in the Salt Lake Valley:

> When we came here, they could catch fish in great abundance in the lake in the season thereof, and live upon them pretty much through the summer. But now their game has gone and they are left to starve. It is our duty to feed . . . these poor ignorant Indians; we are living on their possessions and in their homeland.[7]

Although some charity was given, the settlers ignored the basis for Indian raids: that ". . . Indians . . . rapidly reduced to a point of starvation . . . followed nature's law which predicates that a hungry man always goes in search of food and will follow the course which promises the most speedy relief." [8] Instead, most settlers looked on the Indians as mere thieves. A *Deseret News* article was typical of this attitude:

> The Indians in and about Cache Valley are represented as being considerably inclined of late to be saucy and belligerent in their deportment, and have committed some depreda-

[6] Floyd A. O'Neil, "A History of the Ute Indians of Utah until 1890" (Ph.D. diss., University of Utah, 1973), p. 50.

[7] Jesse D. Jennings, Elmer R. Smith, and Charles E. Dibble, *Indians of Utah: Past and Present* (Salt Lake City, 1959), p. 100.

[8] *Ibid.,* p. 106.

tions and threaten to do more. They are reported to be unusually fond of beef, which if they cannot get in one way, they will take in another.[9]

Inadequate federal response to the Indian agent's appeals for food and funds coupled with the dramatic rise in Utah's population spelled trouble. The Indian farms in central Utah, which had been started in the 1850s, were closed by agent Benjamin Davies and all furnishings sold to feed the starving Utes. The agent at the time described them as being in a "state of nakedness and starvation, destitute and dying of want." [10] Even the conservative historian Bancroft observed, "The natives had no alternative but to steal or starve; the white man was in possession of their pastures; game was rapidly disappearing, in the depth of winter they were starving and almost unclad. . . ." [11] The Utes increased their raids on cattle and other livestock of the Mormon settlers. The answer in Utah to this situation was expected: the populace demanded the removal of the Indians.

The location was anticipated to be the Uinta River Valley. Before the designation was made, however, the Mormons explored it to see if they wanted it for themselves. They rejected the areas as too poor for white settlement.[12] It took only six weeks after the Mormon rejection of the area for Indian Affairs officials to persuade President Abraham Lincoln to set it aside as a home for the starving Utes, October 3, 1861. But Congress was slow to ratify Lincoln's designation; not until May 5, 1864, did the confirmation come, and by then many Utes had died of starvation. Federal responsibility was not fulfilled for several reasons: Congress was penurious, cabinet officials did not grasp the problems, and the energies of the federal government were directed toward survival in the Civil War. The problem was so great that the occasional charity given by settlers and institutional efforts were unequal to a solution.

The Mormon settlers pressed to have the Indians removed. Naturally, the Indians resisted leaving the areas of Provo, Spanish Fork, and Sanpete for the bitter cold of winter and the small food supply of the Uinta Basin. Indian resistance gathered behind a

[9] Quoted in *ibid.*, p. 107.

[10] Benjamin Davies to Commissioner Dole, June 30, 1861, in *Report of the Commissioner of Indian Affairs* (Washington, D. C., 1861), p. 129.

[11] Hubert Howe Bancroft, *History of Utah* (San Francisco, 1890), p. 629.

[12] *Deseret News,* September 25, 1861.

new leader named Black Hawk, a man recently raised from obscurity. By 1865, when the Civil War had ended and the United States government could direct its officers to settle the Indian question in Utah, the Black Hawk War had reached serious proportions. It was to be the largest and costliest war in Utah history. The Mormon settlers were forced to abandon entire counties, build forts, and raise and maintain a levee of troops in the Nauvoo Legion. Because the conflict was mainly over raids on livestock herds, the guerrilla nature of the fighting was a war of attrition on both sides.

In the long run, the technical ability, the supplies, and the superior numbers of the whites made the outcome an inevitable Indian defeat. In 1865 a hope for peace came when O. H. Irish offered a relatively good treaty to the Utes to induce them to move. Brigham Young was at the treaty negotiations and urged the Utes to leave. But Congress never ratified the treaty, and the native people felt betrayed. This failure by Congress added fuel to the resistance which was already afire across the territory of Utah.

After another series of raids the Utes were defeated, and Black Hawk was replaced by a man who recommended peace—Tabby-to Kwana ("Child of the Sun"). He led the reluctant and defeated Utes to the Uinta Basin; there they found almost no preparations had been made for their coming. As the raids renewed, Brigham Young gathered up about seventy-five head of cattle and had them driven to the new reservation. The act helped to stop the raiding.

Within the boundaries of their new, inhospitable domain, the quality of Ute life changed. Symbolic of the whole was the replacement of wild game, berries, and roots with a weekly government ration issued for each family.

A typical allotment was as follows:

Bean coffee	2 lbs.	Bulk soap	½ lb.
Bulk lard	2 lbs.	Sugar	2 lbs.
Salt bacon	2 lbs.	Salt	½ lbs.
Flour	10 lbs.	Fresh beef	10 lbs.[13]
Navy beans	2 lbs.		

As Frank Beckwith said in his small treasure, *Indian Joe,* the Utes traded their ancestral lands for "beef, sugar, and a blanket." [14]

[13] Jennings, Smith, and Dibble, *Indians of Utah,* p. 662.

[14] Frank Beckwith, *Indian Joe, in Person and in Background* [Delta, Utah, 1939], p. 53c. Only seven copies of this unusual monograph were printed privately by Beckwith to send to friends as "my Christmas Greeting Card for 1939." The Utah State Historical Society's copy is the gift of J. Cecil Alter.

The first Indian agents were disappointed with their situation and refused to stay. In 1871 John J. Critchlow came to the Uintah Reservation and for the next decade moved with relentless energy to make the reservation a home for the Utes and to induce them to farm. He founded a sawmill, invited traders to come from Kentucky to open trading posts, increased the size of the cattle herds, established a day school, broke new lands for agricultural pursuits, and distributed supplies carefully until the agency could be nearer to self-supporting. The Utes came to trust him and were in far better condition when he left than when he took up his labors there.

Most of the Utes from central Utah became firmly planted in their new home, although a few small groups remained on the fringes of Mormon towns.[15] But barely a decade of troubled peace was allowed to the Utah Utes when events again radically altered their situation. The Utes in Colorado had been given a treaty in 1868 in which they held about one-third of western Colorado. Then gold was discovered in southwestern Colorado, and the government renegotiated for a quadrangle of land in the San Juan Mountains for the gold and other minerals there. The Utes were reluctant, but the pressures on the United States government were so great that their giving up of this land was inevitable. The "Bruno Cession" occurred in 1873.[16]

The increased population and power of Colorado Territory were recognized by the federal officials, and statehood was granted in 1876. The citizens of this new state were unwilling to accept the idea that nearly one-third of their territory was still Indian reservation. A demand that "the Utes must go" soon developed into a statewide movement.[17]

That opportunity came in 1879. The Utes of the White River band had been dissatisfied with the effort of their agent to get them to farm. The agent, Nathan C. Meeker, was a figure of national reputation who had been a writer, journalist, and Socialist experimenter. He was a friend of Horace Greeley and had named a Socialist community in Colorado after him. When the Greeley colony failed, Meeker decided to reform and remake the Utes into farmers after his design. He ordered them to sell their beloved ponies and began

[15] O'Neil, "A History of the Ute Indians of Utah until 1890."

[16] Gregory Coyne Thompson, *Southern Ute Lands, 1848–1899: The Creation of a Reservation,* Occasional Papers of the Center of Southwest Studies, no. 1 (Durango, Colo., 1975), p. 6.

[17] Dee Brown, *Bury My Heart at Wounded Knee* (New York, 1972), p. 367.

to plow up their pasture to plant crops. The Utes fired on the plowman. Instead of negotiating with his wards, Meeker sent for troops. The Utes warned that if the soldiers came on the reservation, war would ensue; the White Rivers were known to be more warlike than other Ute bands.

The detachment from Fort Steele, Wyoming, under the command of Maj. Thomas Thornburg moved close to the White River Agency. The Utes attacked under their powerful leaders: Captain Jack, Douglas, Chief Johnson, Atchee, and Sow-a-wick. In the battle, Major Thornburg was killed and his troops surrounded. The Utes moved back to the agency where they killed twelve people, including Nathan Meeker. A second force was then sent to relieve Thornburg's trapped men. At that time a leader of the neighboring band of Utes, Ouray, intervened and persuaded the White River Utes that the whites had too many soldiers to resist. Peace was restored, captives returned, and officials descended upon the scene for the inevitable readjustment.[18]

"The Utes must go!" the crowd demanded. The White Rivers were forced to leave Colorado and take up residence on the Uintah Reservation in Utah. Ouray, who had long befriended the whites and who had mediated to stop the battle with Thornburg's troops, was similarly punished. Ouray ("Arrow") spoke four languages: Ute, Apache, Spanish, and some English. As a result of his linguistic ability, he had been chosen as a *negotiator* in dealing with the white men, who immediately began referring to him as "chief." (Later he assumed a more important role in tribal affairs internally because many of the tribal interests at that time involved dealing with outsiders. Ouray has been given far more importance in histories written by whites than the Ute people assign to him.) He and his Uncompahgre band were forced from their homes to the Utah lands. Ouray died before the exodus began and Sapavanaro and Guero replaced him. Around these new leaders was a group of strong men, capable of leading: Billy, Wass, Peak, Curecante, McCook, Cohoe, Chavanaux, Red Moon, Unca Sam, Alhandra, Wyasket, and Ar-reep.

Sapavanaro and Guero rode with military personnel out of the home they had always known, out of Colorado toward the Uintah Agency to search for a place to put more than one thousand Utes.[19] The military men selected the Uncompahgre Reserve by simply rid-

---

[18] Marshall Sprague, "The Bloody End of Meeker's Utopia," *American Heritage* 8 (1957): 94.

[19] *Report of the Ute Commission*, 1881, pp. 331–32.

ing down the White River to the Green River. The river valleys into which the Uncompahgres were to be sent were but narrow ribbons of green through an expanse of poor desert land almost bare of vegetation. The choice was made hastily and without any real knowledge of the country.

Rather than move there, the Utes attempted to negotiate with the army—to no avail. Capt. James Parker of the Fourth Cavalry reported:

> After a debate lasting several hours they sent for Mackenzie. They proposed a compromise. They said they had concluded they must go, but first they had wished to go back to their camp and talk with their old men. "No," said Mackenzie. "If you have not moved by nine o'clock tomorrow morning, I will be at your camp and make you move."
>
> The next morning, shortly after sunrise, we saw a thrilling and pitiful sight. The whole Ute nation on horseback and on foot was streaming by. As they passed our camps their gait broke into a run. Sheep were abandoned, blankets and personal possessions strewn along the road, women and children were loudly wailing.
>
> . . . It was inevitable that they should move, and better then, than after a fruitless and bloody struggle. They should think, too, that the land was lost beyond recovery.
>
> . . . As we pushed the Indians onward, we permitted the whites to follow, and in three days the rich lands of the Uncompahgre were all occupied, towns were being laid out and lots being sold at high prices.[20]

The Uncompahgres were moved from the high San Juan Mountains of Colorado, the "Switzerland of America," to their desert. The shock embittered them. Little had been done to found an agency at Ouray, and so it was decided that extra efforts—a new military post—would be needed to keep the Utes on their new reservation. To guard the Indians, Fort Thornburg was founded across the river while the new agency was being constructed. The Utes had received what was to be their permanent home. The location of the fort was seen to be a threat to the peace of the area, and it was moved to a site near the mouth of Ashley Creek Canyon. There it existed for three short years and was abandoned in 1884.

[20] Quoted in Robert Emmitt, *The Last War Trail* (Norman, Okla., 1954), pp. 292–95.

Almost from the day of the founding of the Uncompahgre Reserve the agents there complained bitterly of the location. One agent described the land as

> . . . extremely rugged and fearfully riven, being pinnacled with mountains, crags, and cliffs and torn with cañons, arroyos, and ravines . . . . a wild and ragged desolation, valuable for nothing unless it shall be found to contain mineral deposits.[21]

As poverty and starvation deepened, the Utes began to return to Colorado to hunt, causing a great outcry. In addition, they would not send their children to school or adapt to what Secretary of War L.Q.C. Lamar called "civilized pursuits." [22] Using this as a pretext, Lamar ordered Fort Duchesne to be founded in September 1886. The Utes were angered at the arrival of troops but decided that resistance was useless.

In 1886, with the new fort in existence, the Uintah Agency and the Ouray Agency were combined and the agent moved to Fort Duchesne. From that day to this it has been known as the Uintah-Ouray Agency. Yet, only one year after the founding of Fort Duchesne and the consolidation of the agencies, Congress passed the Dawes Act designed to break up the reservations and to make Indians into individuals farmers. The Uintah-Ouray Reservation had hardly been founded when the dismantling began. Additionally, a hydrocarbon mineral called gilsonite was discovered in the northeastern corner of the reservation, and powerful new voices were added to demands that the Indian people be removed from that spot. In the early 1890s a large portion of the Uncompahgre band was allowed to take up farmlands along the Uinta and Duchesne rivers in the old Uinta Valley reservation.

Some of the new lands given the Uncompahgres were lost to white settlers by 1898, and seven years later, despite loud protests and threats by the Utes, the bulk of the reservation was opened by Congress to white settlement in 1905. Under Red Cap's leadership, with the assistance of two other White River Utes, Mosisco and Appah, nearly four hundred Utes traveled from Utah to South Dakota hoping to make an alliance with the Sioux to war on the United States. But the harsh memories of Wounded Knee and the

[21] U.S., Congress, House, House Report No. 3305, 51st Cong., 2d sess., February 2, 1890, Serial 2885, p. 4.

[22] *Report of the Secretary of the Interior,* 1886, pp. 16–17.

total poverty of the Sioux made the entire venture hopeless. Two years later, even more ragged, they returned home, escorted by the United States Army, to face their fate as reservation Indians surrounded by whites.[23]

The white settlers were never satisfied with the Indian land given them. They wanted more of it, for they could get the water shares necessary for cultivation while the Indians could not. The Pahvants at Kanosh, for example, were entitled to 120 shares of water for their 3,200 acres but for all their efforts were never able to get more than 20.

> When the Ibapah Indians met in the Capitol Building of Utah this spring with the assistant Attorney General, seeking their rights, complaining about encroachments by whites on their farms, their water rights, their hunting, they referred to a specific treaty, "Indians remember it—but white men forgot it. . . ."
>
> A white woman storekeeper at Kanosh was drawing gas for my car; I inquired: "Are the Indians making their farms pay" "No, and never will. Why don't they give that land to us who want it, and go to the reservation and let the Government take care of 'em? Why they've even got 3,200 acres! We could do something with that!"
>
> (Yes, 20 shares of water, and 3,000 acres of mountain tops. . . .)[24]

The Indians continued to be the dispossessed in all areas of life: property, education, and employment. The old saying "the only good Indian is a dead one" dogged Indians throughout their poverty-blighted lives. During the Great Depression they were refused WPA work. Their children were neglected in schools, their culture arrogantly dismissed. Struggling to keep their pride in being Indian, they have tenaciously held on to their culture and their religion.

However, since the arrival of the Europeans, Christian churches of the Episcopal, Catholic, and Latter-day Saints faiths have won converts. A further influence, the Native American church, was brought to the Uintah-Ouray Reservation in the early years of the twentieth century. This "peyote" church has had a strong effect on

---

[23] Floyd A. O'Neil, "An Anguished Odyssey: The Flight of the Utes, 1906–1908," *Utah Historical Quarterly* 36 (1968): 315–27.

[24] Beckwith, *Indian Joe,* p. 61a.

the Utes and is renewing its strength after some decline during the quarter century after 1940.

The ancient rituals continue to be held; the oldest is the Bear Dance in spring, at about the time bears leave hibernation. The dance takes place within a large circle made from willows and brush. All ages join in. The music comes from native instruments or modified ones using modern materials. The men and women form separate lines, face each other, and move back and forth in unison to the rhythm of the drums and the singing. The singers are usually women. But the Bear Dance is more than just a dance. It is a festival, a time of great socializing; card playing, hand games, and courting are carried on. Feasting and visiting last into the night.

The ritual having the greatest influence on the present-day Utes is the Sun Dance. This important celebration was introduced by tribes from farther north about 1890. The dance is an elaborate ceremony associated with gaining power or regeneration. It lasts for four days and nights, and the dancers neither drink nor eat during this time. The ceremony is a combination of ancient Indian and Christian symbolism. A permanent site for the Sun Dance has been established near Whiterocks, Utah. A twenty-acre plot holds the ceremonial edifice as well as providing room for the scores of tribal members who camp at the site. The dates of these summer dances vary, but July is more often the time for the event than June or August.

Since the Indian Reorganization Act of 1934, the tribe has held periodic elections. Two members of each of the three bands are elected to govern the tribe. The elected committee then chooses a chairman who serves as the executive officer of the Utes. Women have also served on the Tribal Business Committee which has governed the tribe since 1936.

The present condition of the Utes of Utah is by and large far better than the condition of most other American Indian tribes, especially in economic pursuits. They own a substantial reservation with income derived from oil and natural gas leasing, from an impressive cattle industry, a furniture factory, and a major tourist facility called Bottle Hollow Resort. Great strides have recently been taken by the tribe in providing houses for their members. Several housing complexes have been completed in the past decade, and the standard of living has sustained a sharp upward trend.

In education, many of the Ute students are enrolled in the public schools of the Uintah and Duchesne school districts. However, many families prefer to send their children to all-Indian boarding schools provided by the Bureau of Indian Affairs, such as the Intermountain School at Brigham City, Utah; the Stewart School at Carson City, Nevada; Haskell in Kansas; and the Institute of American Indian Arts at Santa Fe, New Mexico.

Education, economic stability, social and legal justice, and the maintenance of the Ute culture remain as basic challenges to the Tribal Business Committee and the Ute citizenry at large.

The Southern Paiutes

In Spring and Summer the Pahutes lived in the valleys of the red mountains where they planted corn, beans, and grass seeds. In Fall they harvested, held a feast to thank their gods Tabats and Shinob for their bounty, and lived in mountain caves during Winter. The rains and snows diminished. Seeds, corn, beans, and grass plants withered for want of water. The bountiful animals, deer and elk; the smaller ones, squirrels, rabbits, chipmunks; the wild fowl fled. The starving Pahutes called their gods for food. Shinob answered, "You should have as much sense as the animals and birds. The country is large and somewhere there is always food. If you follow the animals and the birds they will lead you to it. . . ."

From that day to this the Pahutes have been a nomadic people. Leaving their homes in the caves, they have followed the game from high land to low and gathered in gratitude the foods which the gods distribute every year over the face of tu-weap, the earth.[25]

The country that the god Shinob told the Shoshonean Paiutes about was large, encompassing extensive parts of southern Utah, northern Arizona, southern Nevada, and southeastern California. Throughout it, the Paiutes hunted, gathered, and farmed small plots. They organized themselves loosely into bands of several families, each of which controlled a definite territory. There was little or no tribal organization, although several bands or band members might temporarily join together for a certain project. The Paiutes were slow to acquire and effectively use horses. (When they did come into possession of one, they usually killed and ate

---

[25] William R. Palmer, *Pahute Indian Legends* (Salt Lake City, 1946), pp. 113–23.
The Southern Paiutes section was written with the help of John R. Alley.

it.) As a result they became victims of the Utes who raided them on horseback and captured their women and children as slaves, either for themselves or to be sold to the New Mexican Spanish settlements.

Some Paiutes who lived southeast of the Colorado River visited the Spanish settlements before 1776, but the central body of Paiutes living on the tributaries of the Virgin River first encountered white men when the Dominguez-Escalante expedition crossed their lands on their return to Santa Fe. Father Escalante wrote of coming upon women who were gathering seeds and were

> so frightened that they could not even speak. . . . we saw other Indians who were running away. . . . We did our best to know what kind of people those were who already planted corn. . . .[26]

In the interim between the Escalante expedition and the beginning of commercial traffic on the Spanish Trail, the Spanish began to take a more active role in the slave trade, penetrating deep into Ute country to buy Paiute slaves. The successful establishment of the Spanish Trail that ran directly through the heart of Paiute country made the slave trade an important part of Spanish-Indian relations. In 1843 Thomas J. Farnham wrote of the slaves:

> These poor creatures are hunted in the spring of the year, when weak and helpless . . . and when taken, are fattened, carried to Santa Fe and sold as slaves.

To elude capture the Indians carried water with them and avoided springs.[27]

Although the Paiutes partially retreated from the areas the whites had invaded, the aggressiveness of American trappers and explorers who began to enter the area in the 1820s forced the relations between Paiutes and whites to a low point. This was the condition when the Mormons arrived in Utah. The Paiutes experienced the usual displacement from their best hunting and gathering lands. Grazing animals, timbering, and cultivation drastically cut their food supply.

One of the first outer settlements established by the Mormons was located at Parowan, well within Paiute territory. By that time,

---

[26] *Father Escalante's Journal*, 1776–77, ed. Herbert S. Auerbach (Salt Lake City, 1943), pp. 82–83, published as vol. 11 of *Utah Historical Quarterly*.

[27] Thomas J. Farnham, *Travels in the Great Western Prairies*, 2 vols. (New York, 1973), 2:11.

the Paiutes had attained the reputation of being hostile, but the Mormons were able to establish peaceful and secure relations with them because they provided a buffer against Ute and Spanish raids, supplied trade that increased material wealth, and introduced productive farming methods.

The Mormons came from a religious culture that emphasized a special role for Indians (the Lamanites of the Book of Mormon), and the Paiutes were an easily controlled group upon which these beliefs could be practiced. One of the earliest, largest, and most successful Indian missionary efforts was called the Southern Indian Mission established at Fort Harmony, south of Cedar City in 1854.

Missionary work, principally by Jacob Hamblin and Howard Egan, kept confrontations from becoming serious. John Wesley Powell records in his journal:

> This man, Hamblin, speaks their language well, and has a great influence over all the Indians in the region round about. He is a silent, reserved man, and when he speaks, it is in a slow, quiet way, that inspires awe. . . . When he finishes a measured sentence, the chief repeats it and they all give a solemn grunt. . . .
>
> Then their chief replies [to Powell]: "Your talk is good, and we believe what you say. We believe in Jacob. . . . When you are hungry, you may have our game. You may gather our sweet fruits. . . . We will show you the springs, and you may drink; the water is good. . . . We are very poor. Look at our women and children; they are naked. We have no horses; we climb the rocks, and our feet are sore. We live among the rocks, and they yield little food and many thorns. When the cold moons come, our children are hungry. We have not much to give; you must not think us mean. . . . We love our country; we know not other lands. We hear other lands are better; we do not know. The pines sing, and we are glad. Our children play in the warm sand; we hear them sing, and are glad. The seeds ripen, and we have to eat, and we are glad. We do not want their good lands; we want our rocks, and the great mountains where our fathers lived. . . .[28]

In addition to converting the Indians to Mormonism, the Mormons also sought to end the New Mexican slave trade. This came about in 1852 through an act of the Utah territorial legislature that substituted indentured servitude for slavery, a system

[28] Powell, *Exploration of the Colorado,* pp. 128–29, 130.

that was in practice limited to Mormons. The slave trade decimated the Paiute population; the Mormon version of servitude continued the process. Although generally treated well, the Paiutes who lived in Mormon houses were torn between two cultures. They rarely married, but those who married whites had childen who most often considered themselves whites. Hence, the Paiute population declined further. The diseases which the whites brought with them continued the process of shrinking the Paiute population, and by the 1890s it was difficult to find any survivors at all of a majority of the original Paiute bands.

Although Paiutes continued to have skirmishes with travelers on the Spanish Trail and occasionally even with Mormon settlers, their dwindling population usually came under domination of the white settlement nearest them. The establishment of the first Southern Paiute Agency at Saint Thomas in 1869 and also the Moapa Indian Reservation in 1873 resulted from tensions between the Nevada Paiutes and miners when mineral discoveries were made in Meadow Valley and Pahranagat Valley in the late 1860s and early 1870s.

The problem then arose of removing all the Southern Paiutes to a reservation in accordance with current government policy. In 1865 a few Utah Paiutes had signed a treaty relinquishing southern Utah in return for their removal to the Ute reservation in the Uinta Basin. This treaty had never been ratified, but, nevertheless, it became the basis of government policy. John Wesley Powell and George W. Ingalls were sent to the area to determine Paiute status. In 1873 they recommended that all of the Southern Paiutes be removed to Moapa. This policy was continued for the next decade. Either through lack of interest or forgetfulness, the government neglected the Indians for many years.

With lack of supervision and aid, the Moapa reservation sank into corruption and neglect. Occasional government inspections found the reservation almost totally abandoned by the Paiutes who had become an integral part of the local white economy by providing a cheap labor force. Jacob Hamblin wrote to Major Powell in 1880 of the Paiutes'

> destitute situation. . . . The watering places are all occupied by white man. The grass that product mutch seed is all et out. The sunflowere seed is all destroyed in fact thare is nothing for them to depend upon but beg or starve. . . . I assisted them some this last season to put in some corn and

squash. They got nothing on account of the drouth. They are now living on cactus fruit and no pine nuts this season.[29]

In 1891 the government provided a reservation for the Southern Paiutes in an area cut through by the Santa Clara River. This location had historically supported one of the largest segments of Paiute population. However, this reservation did not provide for the Tonoquint or Paroosit Paiutes who had once farmed its bottomlands. It did provide for the remainder of the Shivwits Paiutes who lived deep in the Arizona Strip on the Shivwits Plateau near the Grand Canyon. There were not enough living members of the other bands to even perpetuate their names.

In the early part of the twentieth century a partial attempt was made by the government to regain control over Indian affairs at Moapa. Land was acquired at Las Vegas for an Indian colony, and the Moapa Agency was temporarily moved there in 1912. Other Paiute reservations were established: the Kaibab Reservation in northern Arizona in 1907, the Koosharem Reservation in central Utah in 1928, and the Indian Peaks Reservation in western Utah in 1915.

A colony of Paiutes had existed at Cedar City since the Mormons first settled there in 1851. The government twice offered to buy land for these Indians, but the local residents replied that they would provide the land.

The twentieth century has not changed the relative economic standing of the Paiutes significantly. The Indians who work are still mainly limited to manual labor; most depend on welfare to some degree for sustenance. Only on the Moapa and Kaibab reservations has there been much success in establishing a healthy economic community. The United States government has also largely continued its traditional role of ignoring the Indians and their problems. This practice had its logical conclusion in 1957 when the Southern Paiutes of Utah had their special trustee relationship with the government terminated. They had become the victims of a government policy advocating immediate Indian integration into the general American culture and economy. Although the Paiutes had been judged unready for such termination by preparatory reports, they were one of the first tribes to go through the process. Of the Utah Paiutes, only the Cedar City band escaped this fate, probably because they did not own any land.

[29] U.S., Department of Interior, Bureau of Ethnology, Letters Received 1880, Bureau of American Ethnology Collection, Smithsonian National Anthropology Archives, Washington D. C.

Paiute seed gatherers. Seeds and small animals were their main foods.

Paiute arrowmaker and children.

Latter-day Saints baptism near Saint George.

Left: *Paiutes playing the game of "kill the bone" on the Kaibab Plateau in the 1870s.*

The Circle Dance on the Kaibab Plateau, 1870s.

everal bands of Paiutes met with federal respresentatives in 1873 on
ie Rio Virgin, a tributary of the Colorado in southern Utah.

From the top: *Paiutes in Koosharem, 1905. Gosiute mother and child. Gosiute rider at Ibapah, 1924. "Go-Shoot Habitation, Pleasant Valley" is the title of an illustration made during Capt. James H. Simpson's expedition in 1859.*

From the top: *A Gosiute house in Deep Creek, 1940s. Canvas was placed over log section for shelter. Brush section was used for cooking and weaving. Mrs. Teddy McCury weaving a* kono, *or cradle board. Genevieve Henroid, Mollie Bonamont, and Lillie Pete with articles made by their craft club at Ibapah.*

Once among the poorest Indian groups in the United States, the Gosiutes won a $7.1 million settlement from the federal government in 1975 in a hundred-year-old land dispute. Tribal authorities plan to use the money to improve housing and set up businesses.

The Southern Paiute land claims decision of 1965, a controversial case that was settled out of court without even the normal determination of date of taking or territorial boundaries, partially repaid the Paiutes for the land they had lost. However, money could never begin to restore the Paiutes' lives, peace, and pride that had been gradually but relentlessly destroyed in the face of white advancement into their territory.

For all their adversity, the Paiutes can still say as did the old chief to Major Powell: "We love our country; we know not other lands." Federal and state training programs have been unsuccessful because they require relocation that threatens close family ties. Still, the native language is heard less today. Fewer religious beliefs are retained, but herbs for medicine and berries and pine nuts for food are still gathered. Summertime is also visiting time, as it has always been, and families travel long distances to attend rodeos and Ute Sun Dances and Bear Dances. But many Paiutes no longer know that when their people were as free as the eagle, their costumes were adorned with its feathers. Now turkey feathers are used. "The young, they go away to school. They forget. They need to spend more time with their elders, learning, listening. They talk about their heritage but they don't want to take the time to really feel it." [30]

THE GOSIUTES

Early travelers through Gosiute country, southwest of the Great Salt Lake, were appalled at the small tribe's miserable existence and amazed that human beings could survive in that desolate country of alkaline earth and sagebrush. Mark Twain wrote:

> . . . we came across the wretchedest type of mankind . . . I refer to the Goshoot Indians . . . [who] have no villages, and no gatherings together into strictly defined tribal communities—a people whose only shelter is a rag cast on a bush to keep off a portion of the snow, and yet who inhabit one of the most rocky, wintry, repulsive wastes that our country or any other can exhibit.[31]

Capt. J. H. Simpson, exploring the Great Basin in 1859, was repelled by the Gosiute food of crickets and ants, rats and other small animals; their scrawny nakedness; and their dogged clinging

---

[30] Clifford Jake, quoted in *Salt Lake Tribune,* July 6, 1975.

[31] Mark Twain, *Roughing It* (Hartford, Conn., 1872), pp. 146–47.

to life. They illustrated, he said, the theory that man's terrain is "intimately connected with [his] development. . . ." [32]

The Gosiutes had no horses; their shelters in the summer heat and winter cold were made of piled-up sagebrush called *wickiups*. They used twine to bind juniper and sage, as well as rabbit skins, to make blankets. Moccasins were a prized rarity. Explorers thought of the Gosiutes as near-animals and were surprised when they showed human emotions.

> These Indians appear worse in condition than the meanest of the animal creation. Their garment is only a rabbit-skin cape . . . and the children go naked. It is refreshing, however, . . . to see the mother studiously careful of her little one, by causing it to nestle under her rabbit-skin mantle.[33]

The same explorer gave bread to

> a very old woman, bent over with infirmities . . . and the most lean, wretched-looking object it has ever been my lot to see. . . . [Although the old woman] was famished, it was very touching to see her deal out her bread, first to the little child at her side, and then only after the others had come up and got their share, to take the small balance for herself.[34]

With hunger a constant, the Gosiute birthrate was low, keeping the tribe at several hundred in number. They survived through the ingenious use of the desert wasteland.[35] Their entire lives were devoted to the search for food, leaving hardly any time for ceremonies. Only the round dance was known, a sideways shuffling to the beat of a drum, an invocation to make grass seeds grow; at infrequent times it was also a social dance. Because they were constantly moving in their food search, their possessions were few: baskets to collect seeds, knives and flint scrapers to skin and dress the small animals, and grinding stones for crushing seeds. Except for communal animal hunts, each family moved alone in its gathering of food, and this made solidarity and tribal development impossible.

---

[32] J. H. Simpson, *Explorations Across the Great Basin of the Territory of Utah* (Washington, D.C., 1876), p. 36.

[33] *Ibid.,* p. 56.

[34] *Ibid.*

[35] See Jennings, Smith, and Dibble, *Indians of Utah,* pp. 16–19 and 69–85.

The Gosiutes exploited the desert to its fullest. They used eighty-one species of wild vegetables: forty-seven gave seeds, twelve berries, eight roots, and twelve greens. The most important food was the pine nut. Large quantities were stored because it was not an annual crop, and when it failed starvation neared. A good crop meant a good winter.

It was in winter when seed gathering could not be done that the Gosiutes huddled in their sagebrush wickiups and told their myths.[36] Summer was not the proper time for telling myths; it was even dangerous to do so. Hawks and coyotes were actors in many of the myths. Coyote was feared and even when starving, the Gosiutes would not eat its flesh. It was a quarrel between hawk and coyote on a large mountain that formed the mountains of Gosiute land. In anger hawk flew high, then swooped down on the mountain and clawed it, breaking off the top and scattering it into smaller mountains. Besides animal myths, there were stories of "Little Man" who gave shamans power and "Water Baby" who cried at night but disappeared by day. In the winter, also, a few simple games were played: hoop and pole game, hand game, and races.

In the harsh life of the Gosiutes, communal hunts were exciting events. The most common game pursued was the black-tailed rabbit. Hunts for antelope were not held yearly because they greatly reduced the herds. Preparation for an antelope drive brought several familes together to erect mile-long, V-shaped traps of stone and sagebrush under the medicine man's direction. Twenty miles away from the mouth of the trap, hunters stationed themselves and slowly converged toward it. Antelope would run from the hunters toward the trap. They would then be enclosed in the small end where a few at a time would be taken out, killed, the meat dried, and the skins tanned.

This barren, simple Gosiute life was destined to change when Capt. Howard Stansbury, surveying for the Corps of Topographic Engineers, built an adobe house in Tooele Valley. Timbering began nearby and a mill was built. By 1853 there were farms surrounding the townsite of Tooele and the cycle began: settlers invading Indian regions and uprooting the land to make farms; their cattle, sheep, and horses eating the grasses that the Indians needed for seeds; and the Indians retaliating by raiding the settler's livestock.[37]

[36] Carling Malouf and Elmer R. Smith, "Some Gosiute Mythological Characters and Concepts," *Utah Humanities Review* 1 (1947): 369–78.

[37] See James B. Allen and Ted J. Warner, "The Gosiute Indians in Pioneer Utah," *Utah Historical Quarterly* 39 (1971): 162–77.

An incident during these first years when whites began crossing Gosiute lands has become legendary. Capt. Absolom Woodward's company of ten men had camped in Ibapah land ("Deep Water" or "Deep Creek") near a cluster of Gosiute wickiups. Four soldiers were later discovered killed, food for scavengers, and the mail they were transporting strewn over their bodies. Rumors that the killings were not senseless acts of the Gosiutes but motivated by revenge continued for decades. An amateur historian, James P. Sharp, attempted for years to learn the truth behind the rumors, but the Indians would tell him nothing. He had his opportunity when an old Indian, Antelope Jake, came to ask him for work. Sharp knew that Antelope Jake was said to be one of the men who had killed the soldiers and hired him as a sheepherder. While gaining his confidence, Sharp found that Antelope Jake was fond of canned tomatoes. Taking four cans with him, he visited Jake's sheep camp and displayed them. He soon had Antelope Jake's story: the soldiers camped near the wickiups had learned that the tribe had gone antelope hunting and had left their girls behind to tend the elderly and the small children. They raped the girls and moved on. When the tribe returned, six of the men on foot, armed with bows and arrows, stalked the company through falling snow, hiding on the mountain slopes, knowing that they were no match for men armed with guns and riding horses. They ambushed five of the men in a mountain draw; one escaped and rode on to spread the story of wanton murder.[38]

Indian raids in search of food became more frequent. To put an end to them, Robert Jarvis, an Indian agent, tried to convince the Gosiutes to learn farming. One of the bands had already plowed the ground by using sticks and had planted forty acres of wheat, but most of the Gosiutes were unwilling to give up their traditional life. To prevent further raids, the government and the mail company provided provisions for the Indians who, however, were not placated. They killed three employees and wounded another during the winter of 1862–63. A treaty that followed gave the president of the United States the right to remove the Indians to reservations, but when the Uinta Basin was chosen for the relocation of Utah tribes and most Indians submitted, the Gosiutes refused to leave their land.

Federal annuities continued for the Gosiutes; their game was gone and their territory reclaimed for farms. Again farming was

[38] *Salt Lake Tribune*, May 22, 1960; Earl Spendlove, "The Goshute Revenge," *Golden West* 5 (1968–69), pp. 24–27, 50–52.

tried, but the wheat crop was destroyed by grasshoppers. Further efforts were made to induce the Gosiutes to move to a reservation but they were afraid, they said, of living among other Indians. Only the Gosiutes in Skull Valley had had success with farming, entirely through their own efforts. The government had given them no help and continued to press for the removal of all Gosiutes to the Uintah Reservation although the tribe repeatedly avowed they would never leave their land. John Wesley Powell and George W. Ingalls were among the government officials recommending relocation and to insure the success of their proposal advised that no annuities be given except at the designated reservations. Negotiations went on for the removal of the Gosiutes to the Uinta Basin, but the years passed and they remained in Skull Valley. They were absent from official correspondence and forgotten by the government.

Two reservations were eventually established for the Gosiutes on their own lands: in 1912 eighty acres were reserved for their use in Skull Valley with an additional 17,920 acres added in 1919, and in 1914 the Deep Creek Reservation in western Tooele County and eastern Nevada was founded with 34,560 acres.

A young doctor who arrived to practice in the area in 1912 said:

> The agent in charge at this time was an old-time bureaucrat who worried more about his reports than about the Indians. In addition to his other duties he was busily trying to make the Gosiutes over into Ohio Presbyterians like the ones he had known back home. . . . His sister-in-law was supposed to be the schoolteacher, but nary an Indian ever darkened the door of her temple of learning in quest of an education. . . . [39]

The doctor came to like the Gosiutes and pondered:

> Were these Gosiute women wiser than I when they . . . let the unfit die? They were good mothers, kind and gentle with their children. Were they also kind in eliminating the weak that the tribe might be perpetuated only by the strong?[40]

From the tenacious Gosiutes Dr. Joseph H. Peck learned about "psychosomatic medicine ten years before anything about it appeared in medicine journals." [41] Dr. Peck discovered little about the Indians'

[39] Joseph H. Peck, *What Next, Doctor Peck?* (Englewood Cliffs, N.J., 1959), p. 157.
[40] *Ibid.*, p. 170.
[41] *Ibid.*, p. 165.

Great Spirit and religion. "Their yearly binges upon marijuana and peote [*sic*] had somewhat the nature of a religious festival. When questioned about it they always said it was too long and complicated to explain to a white man and we would not understand, a conclusion that was probably true." [42]

Dr. Peck practiced medicine in Deep Creek country and Tooele for twenty-seven years before moving away. In 1967, fifty years after first coming to the Gosiute lands, he returned to Deep Creek.

> Where there had been nothing but sagebrush and tin cans, now there were green alfalfa fields with plenty of good stock grazing upon them. The wickiups were gone and each little cabin had a radio aerial sticking up out of the roof. I stopped at the first one and asked for some of my old friends. Most of them had gone to the happy hunting grounds. . . .[43]

Only three of the sixty-one Skull Valley Gosiutes remain on the reservation. The rest have migrated for school and employment opportunities and live mostly in Tooele and Grantsville. They will soon be dispersed like members of the Shoshone communities that were disbanded after World War II and reside now in northern Utah towns. (Washakie in Box Elder County existed with close ties to the Mormon church until that time.)

The Deep Creek Reservation in 1970 numbered eleven families. Nine women began meeting every Tuesday of that year to make necklaces, bolo ties, moccasins, women's purses, belts, headbands, and earrings. They had to learn beadwork from others; the craft was not part of their tribal skills. ". . . they are 'building culture.' Culture is something the tribe never had." [44] It went directly from rabbit-skin robes to store-bought clothing.

The ingeniousness of the old Gosiutes is still with them. Men skin the deer, killed on the reservation; and women tan the hides, making lye from charcoal for removing the hair. The women would make more buckskin articles if they had hides. "We don't have many deer, and our men would have to buy licenses to hunt off the reservation." [45]

Perhaps these Deep Creek Indians will continue the Gosiute tenacity of refusing to give up their ancestral lands and to improve them with time.

[42] *Ibid.*, p. 171.
[43] *Ibid.*, pp. 207–8.
[44] *Salt Lake Tribune,* April 25, 1970.
[45] *Ibid.*

2 IMPERIAL ZION: THE BRITISH OCCUPATION OF UTAH

BY FREDERICK S. BUCHANAN

On board the "International"
All joyful and lighthearted.
Bound Zionward, four hundred Saints,
From Liverpool we started.
We're English, Irish, Scotch, and Welsh
Assembled here together;
Resolved to do the will of God,
Whate'er the wind and weather.

To the tune of "Yankee Doodle" so sang Henry Maiben of Brighton, England, to an audience of British Mormon converts in mid-Atlantic in the spring of 1853. In a variety of regional accents belonging to the English, Irish, Scots, and Welsh, they affirmed in the chorus their reason for undertaking the voyage:

Then sing aloud ye Saints of God,
In one united chorus;
Old Babylon we'll leave behind,
For, Zion is before us.[1]

This synthesis of British Saints, religious conviction, and "Yankee Doodle" was a combination that was repeated frequently between 1850 and 1880 and in time became an important factor in the development of America's Intermountain empire—their Zion of the latter days.

[1] *Diary of a Voyage from Liverpool to New Orleans on Board the Ship International* (Salt Lake City, n.d.). As far as is known the only printed copy of this diary is in the possession of T. Edgar Lyon, Salt Lake City. It is reproduced in its entirety in Frederick S. Buchanan, "The Emigration of Scottish Mormons to Utah, 1847–1900" (M.S. thesis, University of Utah, 1961), Appendix A, pp. 141–59. Note: for convenience, the term "British" will be used in this essay to indicate all persons born in the British Isles including Ireland. During the nineteenth century, Ireland was, politically, a part of the United Kingdom.

They were not, of course, the first Britons to view America as Zion; an earlier group of "Saints" had viewed their settlement in New England as part of a divine plan to civilize the wilderness and set the light of true religion upon a hill. But these Mormon counterparts of Pilgrims and Puritans were no less avid in their belief that their journey was but a precursor to the establishment of the kingdom of God on earth, aided and abetted by one of the most efficiently organized mass emigration schemes to ply the Atlantic routes.[2]

The exodus of British Mormons to the United States had its origins in the crisis-ridden events that almost engulfed the fledging church at Kirtland, Ohio, in 1837. Faced with rebellion and subversion when his Kirtland Safety Society Anti-Banking Company failed, Joseph Smith, the prophet of the "New Dispensation," saw the church shaken to its roots by apostasy and dissension. From the midst of the turmoil, Joseph declared that the Lord had revealed to him "that something new must be done for the salvation of His Church."[3] The something new was the establishment of missionary activity in the British Isles in 1837. Beginning in Preston, Lancashire, the Mormon missionaries within a few years had spread into Wales, Scotland, and Ireland, and the infusion of loyal blood that Joseph Smith had desired eventually began to swell and sustain the church-ordered society at Nauvoo, Illinois.

In his study of Nauvoo's early development, Robert Flanders has observed that "Utah had its roots in Nauvoo; without that seven years' experience in Illinois, the development of the Great Basin, and of the West, would not have been the same."[4] Nauvoo's character and its history were also influenced by the British Mormons who settled there. By 1845 some 25 percent of the city's population were from the British Isles and included among their ranks stonemasons, weavers, bootmakers, potters, and carriage makers and settlers like James Sloan of County Tyrone, Ireland, who became Nauvoo's first city recorder, Welshman Dan Jones who com-

---

[2] A detailed account of the organization of the migration of Mormons to Utah is Philip A. M. Taylor, *Expectations Westward* (Edinburgh and London, 1965), chaps. 3, 6, 9.

[3] R. Kent Fielding, "The Mormon Economy in Kirtland, Ohio," *Utah Historical Quarterly* 27 (1959): 331–56; Brigham H. Roberts, *A Comprehensive History of the Church of Jesus Christ of Latter-day Saints*, 6 vols. (Salt Lake City, 1930), 1:396–97.

[4] Robert B. Flanders, *Kingdom on the Mississippi* (Urbana, Ill., 1965), pp. v, 86.

manded Joseph Smith's riverboat on the Mississippi, and Miles Romney, the English architect who was foreman of construction on the Nauvoo Temple. A Scottish minister who visited the city in 1844 observed that "Nauvoo . . . acts as a kind of receptacle for all the odd and fantastic minds, not only in America but of Great Britain," but he felt that their presence and enthusiasm in Nauvoo "works less dangerously than in crowded cities." [5]

Odd and fantastic these immigrants may have seemed, but they were a significant component of the Mormon migration to the valley of the Great Salt Lake and the vanguard of a future enthusiastic invasion of the Mountain West by Mormons from the British Isles. Given a common language and similar cultural roots, it is not surprising that men and women from the British Isles have since those early years played such a significant role in the affairs of the Mormon church. Because these early Mormons interpreted the establishment of the kingdom of God in a very literal and physical sense, it might also be expected that the Mormons from the British Isles would make significant contributions to Utah's social, economic, and cultural history.

They were not, however, the first British citizens to leave their impress upon the territory that in time became Utah. A Captain Welles, a British army officer and veteran of Waterloo and New Orleans, shared with Miles Goodyear in the establishment of one of the earliest permanent settlements in Utah when they built Fort Buenaventura on the Weber River in 1846, the year before Mormon immigrants entered the Salt Lake Valley.[6] At least twenty years prior to Welles's brief appearance on the Utah stage, a much larger drama was acted out by rival British and American trappers as they sought to gain control of the disputed Oregon country. The Hudson's Bay Company sent its British and Canadian trappers into the region, which now includes Utah, in order to assert the British claim to this wilderness empire, and they did so by making it a veritable "fur desert" through overtrapping it and making it un-

---

[5] Quoted in *ibid.*, p. 86. For details on individual immigrants see entries in Andrew Jenson, *Latter-day Saints Biographical Encyclopedia,* 4 vols. (Salt Lake City, 1901–31). For a contemporary view of British settlers in Nauvoo see Eudacia B. Marsh, "A Reminiscence," ed. Douglas L. Wilson and Rodney O. Davis, in *Journal of the Illinois State Historical Society* 64 (1971): 31–32.

[6] Dale L. Morgan, "Miles Goodyear and the Founding of Ogden," *Utah Historical Quarterly* 21 (1953): 213–15.

attractive and unprofitable to the American trappers and traders.[7] The western explorations of trappers like Alexander Ross opened up the Rocky Mountain region to permanent settlement, and one of their number, Charles McKay, a native of Sutherlandshire explored northern Utah and in 1825 sighted the Great Salt Lake.[8] In blazing the trail as trappers and traders these Britons prepared the way for the colonization of the Great Basin by later immigrants, including the Mormon pioneers.

While the objective of securing the Oregon country as a British domain was never achieved in a literal sense, it was in a way realized through the occupation of Utah's valleys by thousands of British settlers who came in response to a prophet's promise rather than the promise of profit. From the first pioneer company to enter the Salt Lake Valley in July 1847 through the arduous journey of the hand-cart pioneers and the much later "Pullman pioneers," there was a marked British presence in Utah. In 1848 Franklin D. Richards led a company of some one hundred thirty British Saints to Utah and so reestablished large-scale Mormon migration, the practice having been temporarily discontinued during the exodus from Nauvoo.[9]

The British-born population between 1860 and 1880 averaged some 22 percent of the total population of Utah and over 67 percent of the foreign-born population. During that period, almost two out of every ten persons in Utah had been born in Britain, while two out of every three foreigners in Utah were of British origin. The reduction in the percentage of British-born residents in the last two decades of the nineteenth century can be accounted for in part by the large influx of Scandinavian and German immigrants and by a tapering off of British immigrants. This trend continued into the twentieth century, so that by 1930 the British-born population in Utah was a mere 2.7 percent of the total population. In 1970, one hundred years after the British population had made up almost one-quarter of Utah's population and two-thirds of her foreign-born

---

[7] LeRoy R. Hafen, ed., *The Mountain Men and the Fur Trade of the Far West,* 10 vols. (Glendale, Calif., 1965–72), 1:165, 3:217, 227.

[8] *Ibid.,* 6:387, 9:255. Another western trapper and trader, Kenneth McKenzie, was so successful that he was called "Emperor of the West" by his contemporaries. *Ibid.,* 2:222.

[9] Franklin L. West, *Life of Franklin D. Richards* (Salt Lake City, 1924), p. 83.

population, it had shrunk to 22.7 percent of the foreign-born and 2.8 percent of the total population.[10]

The period of heaviest immigration to Utah (1850–70) bears a strong relationship to Mormon missionary activity and conversions in Britain and the numbers of British-born residents who appear on United States Census returns in Utah. Of course, some defected before reaching the promised land and others had resided in Canada and the United States before joining the trek to Utah. As the conversion rate declined, so also did the numbers of potential and actual immigrants.[11] During the 1870s and 1880s the opening up of Utah mineral resources coupled with the decline in Mormon missionary activity (or at least conversions) in Britain led to a larger proportion of non-Mormons entering the territory, especially those involved in mining operations.

Generally urban dwellers in the old country, Britons continued to be urban in the United States; in the 1870–80 period 40 percent of all British-born residents in the United States lived in the fifty largest cities.[12] Even in Utah, which was essentially a rural territory, the British clustered in the most populous counties (with the exception of Sanpete where they were vastly outnumbered by the Scandinavians).

At the peak period, 71 percent of all British-born Utahns resided in the six Wasatch Front counties of Utah, Salt Lake, Davis, Weber, Box Elder, and Cache, an area that contained almost two-thirds of Utah's total population. Those counties with sparsest populations (0.6 per cent of the total) also had the fewest number of British-born residents, Rio Virgin (Washington) County representing only 0.28 percent, Piute County, 0.07 percent, and Sevier a miniscule 0.04 percent of the British population.[13]

But the census returns are not the only indication of the British "occupation." They left their marks on the landscape in the form of place names. The family names of British immigrants dot the Utah map as villages, towns, and areas. Adamsville, Penrose, Bennion, Nibley, Stoddard, Talmage, Teasdale, Eccles Creek, and Bryce Canyon recall men and women who made settlement a reality. They brought with them a sense of loyalty to their origins when they

[10] 1850, 1860, 1870, 1880, 1890, 1900, and 1970 Censuses.

[11] Taylor, *Expectations Westward*, pp. 151–55.

[12] R. T. Berthoff, *British Immigrants in Industrial America* (Cambridge, Mass., 1953), p. 125.

[13] 1870, 1880 Censuses.

named their new homes Avon, Glendale, Leeds, Croydon, Cornish, Lynne, Chester, Elgin, and Wales. The latter town, in Sanpete County, was perhaps the only settlement inhabited by an entirely British-born population, although it was not the first distinctively Welsh settlement in Utah. As early as 1849 Dan Jones and Reese Williams had located a group of Welsh immigrants in a settlement near the "English Canal" on the west side of the Jordan River near present-day Granger. The farming venture failed, however, and by 1854 it was referred to as the "old Welsh settlement." [14] Almost two-thirds of the Welsh in Utah in 1890 resided in Salt Lake and neighboring counties, a pattern similar to that of the English and Scots. By virtue of its almost exclusive settlement by Welsh miners, the main street of Wales, Sanpete County, was lined with the homes of Price Williams, John Llewellyn, John Jones, Henry Rees, Thomas Davis, John Rees, John Price, William Richards, Nathaniel Edmunds, Thomas Rees, David Nicholas, Richard Davis, Benjamin Davis, and Evan Thomas, all traditional Welsh names, which made it a veritable Cymric village in the heart of Utah. [15]

While no Utah towns were officially named "England" or "Scotland," in the 1850s the area lying southwest of present-day Salt Lake City near Granger was referred to as "English Fort" and "British Fort." Layton and Kaysville, both named for English Mormon bishops, were predominantly English towns in the 1850s, with two-thirds of Kaysville's twenty-nine families of English origin. [16]

In the vicinity of Layton, an area inhabited by Scots was known locally as "Scotland"; and Wellsville in Cache Valley became the "Scotch Town" of Utah's north country with its Nibleys, Jardines, Murrays, Kerrs, Leishmans, and Stoddards among some twenty Scottish families who settled the area. [17] Also in northern Utah, the existence of a large group of Scottish immigrants gave rise to the Argyle Ward in Rich County, a name that pleased the settlers when

[14] "Historical Sites and Landmarks," vol. 2, p. 17, typescript. Archives Division, Historical Department, Church of Jesus Christ of Latter-day Saints, Salt Lake City; "Journal History," September 2, 1854, LDS Archives.

[15] Names recorded on a sketch map in "Manuscript History of Wales Ward," LDS Archives.

[16] Joseph Harker Journal, November 12, 1856, July 1858, LDS Archives; Daughters of Utah Pioneers, *East of Antelope Island: History of the First Fifty Years of Davis County,* 4th ed. rev. ([Bountiful?] 1971), p. 123.

[17] DUP, *East of Antelope Island,* pp. 104–5; Preston Nibley, *et al.,* eds., *Charles W. Nibley Reminiscences* (Salt Lake City, 1934), pp. 23–24, 35; interview with Preston Nibley, 1960; "Record of Members, Wellsville Ward, 1869–90," LDS Archives.

announced at a Mormon conference.[18] In Sevier County, William Morrison named his settlement Inverury (Gaelic for "between two waters"), and Mary Wilson recalled the romance of the Highlands when, during a pang of loneliness for her native land, she named a Utah mountain Ben Lomond.[19]

A plan to establish an Irish agricultural colony in Bear River Valley near the Gentile town of Corinne "died a-borning for lack of interest among the Irish it was intended to serve," and it appears that in general the Irish in Utah were much less likely to be identified with permanent community building than the English, Welsh, or Scottish settlers.[20] As soldiers, miners, and railroad workers, they were basically transient and left little imprint by way of distinctive communities. In 1890 two-thirds of the Irish lived in Salt Lake County and vicinity. Summit County with its mining community of Park City accounted for some 14 percent of the total Irish population in 1880 and 1890; Juab County had 11 percent.[21]

Another factor contributing to the Irish settlement pattern was their non-Mormon orientation (according to Robert J. Dwyer, most Irish were Catholics), so clearly demonstrated in the make-up of the populations of two adjacent towns in southern Utah, Saint George and Silver Reef. Saint George with its emphasis on agriculture, stability, and "humble domestic virtues" had but one Irishborn resident, a male, in 1880. In contrast, Silver Reef, a "worldly" mining community, the very antithesis of Mormon Saint George, had an Irish-born population of eighty-six males and twenty-five females, 26 percent of the total foreign-born population.[22]

In time, of course, the meanings attached to particular names disappeared: Inverury became Central (perhaps because the former was too difficult to pronounce, or perhaps the water in Sevier disappeared), and Argyle Ward is no longer; but, like the Prince of

[18] "Manuscript History of Woodruff Stake," December 22, 1895, LDS Archives.

[19] "Manuscript History of Inverury Ward," February 7, 1877, LDS Archives; Milton R. Hunter, ed., *Beneath Ben Lomond's Peak: A History of Weber County, 1824–1900* (Salt Lake City, 1941), p. 3. Sources for origins of place names are scattered, but useful data may be found in State of Utah, Department of Public Instruction, *Origins of Utah Places Names* (Salt Lake City, 1960) and Andrew Jenson, *Encyclopedic History of the Church of Jesus Christ of Latter-day Saints* (Salt Lake City, 1941).

[20] Robert J. Dwyer, "The Irish in the Building of the Intermountain West," *Utah Historical Quarterly* 25 (1957): 232–33.

[21] 1880, 1890 Censuses.

[22] Nels Anderson, *Desert Saints* (Chicago, 1966), pp. 428–30.

Wales mine and the Highland Boy mine, they served their purpose in reinforcing the British identity of these immigrants who made Utah their work place and home just as surely as Henry Maiben's words to "Yankee Doodle" gave American identity to the movement that brought most of them from Britain's maritime islands to Utah's arid valleys.

LABOUR AND DILIGENCE

It is apparent then that British-born residents in Utah made a significantly large numerical contribution to the territory during the nineteenth century. If they had done no more, their physical presence at a time when Utah was lacking in population could be considered important. As it was, they were more than just place fillers—they were colonizers and imperialists in a sense, but they claimed the land not for the kingdom of Great Britain as their kin had done in India, Australia, Africa, and New Zealand, but for the kingdom of God.

While the Mormon perception of the kingdom was interlaced with otherworldly overtones, yet, in the final analysis, it was a very physical conception, as a report to the *Millennial Star* made clear in admonishing the converts to banish

> the peculiarly imaginative ideas that have long lingered in the minds of the Saints that the Kingdom of God would be built like some castle in the air, or by the touch of some magician's wand . . . . these notions are fast being replaced by the stern realities that the kingdom of our God has to be built by the labour and diligence of his Saints. . . .[23]

In the "land of treasures—the home of the righteous" [24] these British pioneers hoped to fulfill God's will here on earth. Their desire, too, was to "have a part of the soil we can call our own and work it for ourselves and own no master but our God." [25]

With the development of Deseret viewed as a cooperative rather than a competitive effort, the Mormon leaders adopted the policy of attracting the kinds of workers most needed to secure Zion for the "chosen people." And just as Joseph Smith had turned to the British Isles to save the church in 1837, so Brigham Young

[23] *Millennial Star* 20 (1858) : 523.

[24] *Millennial Star* 11 (1849) : 91.

[25] William Gibson Journal, p. 113, LDS Archives.

advised the British Mormons to organize immigration companies according to their trades and to come to Zion prepared with machinery, tools, and materials for the establishment of new settlements.[26] Specifically, the church leadership asked for iron workers, potters, cutlers, woolen workers, comb makers, millers, and coal miners. The Sixth Epistle requested that

> if some of the brethren who are tanners, would come home and attend to their calling here, they would receive the blessings of many souls. Some attempts are now making at this business, but more help is wanted.[27]

The president of the British Mission was instructed to have the presiding elders search out "blowers, moulders and all kinds of furnace operators to immediately immigrate to the valley without delay." [28]

These early British settlers came to Utah with the specific intent of contributing their technical expertise to the new economy and to meet the needs of Utah's burgeoning population. John Taylor expressed the ideal when he claimed that the people in Utah would not need to send to Sheffield for tools, ". . . we will set the Welsh boys to get the ore in the mountains, and then set the Sheffield boys to work in fixing it up into tools, and into forks and knives. . . ." [29]

In reality, however, many of these early attempts to industrialize Utah failed. The Deseret Pottery, established by using pottery workers from Staffordshire, was abandoned in 1853; the sugar mill with machinery and operators imported from Britain was also aborted after the first attempts. One relatively successful industry and one of crucial importance in supplying the immediate needs of Utah's inhabitants was the manufacturing of woolen goods. Initially given impetus by a call to Ayrshire shepherd John Murdoch (and his collie) to herd sheep for Brigham Young, the woolen mills were operated by men and women trained in the English and Scottish mill towns.[30] In responding to his call, John Murdoch revealed how

[26] *Millennial Star* 11 (1849) : 246.

[27] *Millennial Star* 14 (1852) : 21.

[28] *Millennial Star* 11 (1849) : 248–49.

[29] *Millennial Star* 12 (1850) : 359.

[30] Leonard J. Arrington discusses Utah enterprises related to the occupations of British immigrants in chap. 4 of his *Great Basin Kingdom, An Economic History of the Latter-day Saints, 1830–1900* (Cambridge, Mass., 1958); Franklin D. Richards to Brigham Young, February 24, 1852, in "Journal History." Richards said he was sending Scottish shepherds and sheep dogs to Utah.

close a connection exists in Mormon thought between the spiritual
and the material aspects of the kingdom of God. At a farewell party
John sang:

> Farewell then my kindred, my home and my all
> When duty requires it we bow to the call.
> We brave every danger and conquer each foe
> To the words of the Prophet, Oh, then let me bow.[31]

It is difficult to make a precise assessment of the financial contribution these skilled craftsmen made to Utah's development. But, trained
in another land as they were, they brought with them indirectly the
"wealth" Britain had invested in their training. Whether it was in
herding sheep, making rope, tanning leather, mining coal, or manufacturing bicarbonate of soda, these immigrants made positive
material contributions to the development of their new home with
a minimum investment from their adopted homeland.

In addition to skills, they brought with them their social
philosophy concerning trade unions and working men's associations,
evidenced by the appearance of tradesmen marching in units in an
1861 Fourth of July parade in Salt Lake City. Henry McEwan, a
Scottish immigrant who later became first president of the Deseret
Typographical Association, Local 115, in 1868 led the "Printers
of Deseret" in this parade, followed by the blacksmiths led by
Jonathan Pugmire of Carlisle, England. The carpenters and joiners
marched under a banner of "Union is Strength" led by English
architect and builder Miles Romney. The painters followed another
British artisan, Edward Martin, as did the Boot and Shoe Makers
under Edward Snelgrove and the stonecutters led by Charles Lambert who had been an active member of a trade union in his native
land.[32]

In a biographical account of 535 prominent persons in the
vicinity of Salt Lake City (published in 1902), 134, or 25 percent,
of the entries were born in the British Isles. If one includes those
residents who were born of British parents in Canada or the United

---

[31] R. Philip Rasmussen, comp., "A History of the James Murdoch and
Mary Murray Murdoch Family and Their Children Who Came to America,"
(Salt Lake City, 1959).

[32] *Deseret News*, July 5, 1861. I am indebted to Professor Kenneth
Davies of Brigham Young University for this reference. See his essay "The
Secularization of the Utah Labor Market," presented at the Fall 1974 meeting,
Utah Academy of Arts, Sciences, and Letters, Logan, Utah.

States (including Utah), the British contribution in terms of percentage makes up 36 percent of the total entries. Imprecise as these indicators may be, yet they afford the reader an opportunity of seeing the British impact on Utah's economics, particularly in Salt Lake City. Three percent of these British-born residents came to Utah as infants, 15 percent as children, 24 percent were in their teens, 52 percent were adults, and 5 percent were between forty and fifty years of age. Only 1 percent were in their sixties.[33]

From the admittedly unrefined data emerges a picture of an immigrant group that came as settlers in their prime in terms of productive industrial capacity and also in the child-bearing years, of crucial importance to the colonization and holding of a virgin land. The median age of these colonists was twenty-two; and they came not primarily as individual adventurers but as members of stable families. Of this particular group, approximately fifty were involved in agriculture (despite an urban origin); the others were related to professions, building trades, and other commercial pursuits. Only 8 of the 134 British-born were not Mormons, and only 12 of the entries mentioned were engaged in mining.[34]

In the 1870s and 1880s, however, the contributions of non-Mormon British-born were of immense importance, especially in the development of Utah's mineral resources. Mormon policy had chosen to emphasize home manufacturing and agricultural pursuits with an occasional bow in the direction of light industry, and British Mormons were generally faithful in their adherence to the church policy of avoiding the development of the region's mineral resources, leaving it to Gentile expertise and capital.[35] However, one Mormon who openly opposed Brigham Young's policy of discouraging industry that might attract a non-Mormon population was Londoner William S. Godbe. Despite his estrangement from the church he actively

[33] *Biographical Record of Salt Lake City and Vicinity* . . . (Chicago, 1902).

[34] *Ibid.*, Of the Gentiles, four were involved in mining: R. Forrester, J. Farrell, M. Cullen and J. W. Donnellan; W. Nelson was a federal marshal and publisher; Peter Lochree was a lawyer and judge; Boyd Park was a jeweler and Lawrence Scanlan, a clergyman. See entries under their respective names.

[35] W. Turrentine Jackson, "British Impact on the Utah Mining Industry," *Utah Historical Quarterly* 31 (1963): 347–75; Clark C. Spence, *British Investments and the American Mining Frontier 1850–1901* (Ithaca, N.Y., 1958). See especially chap. 8 for a discussion of British involvement in the financially disastrous Utah Emma Mining Company in Little Cottonwood Canyon.

pursued British capital that contributed substantially to the development of Utah's mining industry.[36]

The title of father of Utah's mining industry, of course, rightly belongs to Patrick Edward Connor, Brigham Young's nemesis and commander of federal troops at Camp Douglas. Described by Archbishop Dwyer as the "Kerryman out of Stockton, California," Connor's contribution led to an influx of non-Mormon Irish and Cornish miners and in the 1880s and 1890s to greatly increased Gentile political and economic power.[37] Other sons of Erin who contributed leadership brain (if not brawn) to the mines of Utah included Col. John W. Donnellan and Matthew Cullen of whom it was said, "The career which he has made entitled him to a front rank among pioneers of the state." [38]

British entrepreneurs and business leaders in Utah also included John Sharp and William Jennings. Sharp, often referred to as the "Mormon railroad bishop" for his part in the development of Utah's railroads, was also known among both Gentiles and Mormons as "the smartest man in the church." From a coal miner in Scotland he rose to be superintendent of Utah's Central Railway in 1871 and a director of the Union Pacific.[39] William Jennings of Birmingham was involved in a variety of enterprises, including the first Utah tannery, cloth manufacturing, mining, and cooperative merchandising. Both he and his wife, Priscilla Paul of Cornwall, participated actively in the commercial affairs of Salt Lake City. In 1867 they purchased Salt Lake City's first mansion and named it "Devereaux House" after an estate near his home town of Birmingham.[40]

Among the earliest merchants in Utah were the Walker brothers from Yorkshire, England: Samuel, Joseph, David, and Matthew. They established one of the first mercantile centers in Salt Lake City and later founded the Walker Bank, an institution that has played an important part in stimulating and maintaining Utah's economic growth during and since the pioneer era. Although Latter-day Saints, the Walker brothers broke with the church in the 1860s. Refusing to pay tithes to the church, they offered to set aside money

[36] Hubert H. Bancroft, *History of Utah* (San Francisco, 1889), pp. 650–51. Godbe claimed that through his business efforts hundreds of people were gainfully employed and thousands of dollars pumped into Utah's economy.

[37] Dwyer, "Irish in the West," 221–35.

[38] *Biographical Record,* pp. 99, 137, 609.

[39] Walter G. Marshall, *Through America or Nine Months in the United States* (London, 1881), p. 233.

[40] *Biographical Record,* pp. 105–6.

for charitable purposes. For their defiance, coming as it did during a period when Mormon leadership was attempting to resist Gentile challenges to its hegemony in Utah, the Walker brothers were excommunicated and ostracized, but they nevertheless succeeded.[41]

Other Britons' skills also became part of Utah's economy: Boyd Park in jewelry, Charles Nibley in sugar and lumber, William Silver in mechanical engineering and iron manufacturing, David Eccles in banking, Henry Dinwoodey in furniture manufacturing; the roster of distinguished Britons is virtually endless.[42] This should not be surprising considering the large number of immigrants from Great Britain who settled in the Salt Lake area.

Numerous children were also an important "product" of Utah's society, and British midwives, among them Janet Hardie who had studied under Sir James Simpson in Edinburgh, lent their skill in replenishing Utah's population.[43] Utah's health and social welfare laws were also influenced by Welsh-born Martha Hughes Cannon, one of Utah's early women physicians and, in 1896, the first woman to become a state senator in the United States, defeating her own husband, a Manxman, Angus M. Cannon, in the process.[44]

In singling out a few individuals, one may be prone to forget that for every "distinguished" immigrant there were perhaps thousands whose everyday deeds were a necessary part of the warp and woof of Utah's economic and social fabric. The reader who follows the life of a man like Henry Hamilton of Fifeshire, who came to Utah in 1856, finds recorded not acts of leadership or feats of daring, but the day-in, day-out fight against ever-present poverty and hunger, grubbing his land by hand, trading his blanket for wheat seed, hiring out to do chores for others, being dismissed from one job because of being slowed down by a sunburned leg and yet, withal, raising his hand to sustain the brethren and having a "right good time of it" at religious meetings.[45]

[41] Edward W. Tullidge, *History of Salt Lake City* (Salt Lake City, 1886), p. 380; Edward Larkin Journal, April 9, 1864, LDS Archives.

[42] See Jenson, *LDS Biographical Encyclopedia* and *Sketches of the Intermountain States . . .* (Salt Lake City, 1909) for numerous references to British entrepreneurs in Utah.

[43] Claire Noall, "Mormon Midwives," *Utah Historical Quarterly* 10 (1942): 114–25.

[44] Jean Bickmore White, "Gentle Persuaders: Utah's First Women Legislators," *Utah Historical Quarterly* 38 (1970): 31–33, 42–48.

[45] Henry Hamilton Journal, LDS Archives.

In a similar vein, one can read of Welshman Christopher Arthur's complaint of a lack of "breadstuffs" in 1856 and then adding, "It had been kisses without the bread and cheese, but we had happiness and contentment." [46] These men then, the laborers and artisans from Britain's industrial centers, with their wives and families, though not remembered in marble and bronze or even in "Who's Who" publications, left their imprint nonetheless. In describing the contribution of these ordinary folk, Edward W. Tullidge told how they brought not only their skills and technical knowledge but also the tools of their trade and the best of their personal possessions to the promised land:

> . . . excepting furniture and cumbersome articles, it may be said that from the opening of the general emigration to Utah in 1849–50, a thousand English, Scotch and Welsh *homes* were yearly transposed to Utah from the mother country.[47]

Their lives and their homes brought the promise of the land to fruition. Some, of course, like silk-printer Charles Parkinson of Lancaster or marine engineer John Rider of County Mongham, Ireland, found little call for their expertise in Utah and had to turn their hand to other pursuits, in Rider's case to assisting William Howard build a distillery in Salt Lake City. Samuel Francis of Wiltshire had been involved in the manufacture of woolen goods in Britain and attempted to do the same in Utah without success. Shetland Islander John Sutherland had spent most of his life on the sea and had plied the United States coast in trading ships. His move to Utah left him unemployed, shipwrecked as it were, and he and Francis turned to agriculture.[48]

Speaking of these British artisans, mechanics, and manufacturers turned farmers "which the Mormon Church every season poured into the Territory," Tullidge said:

> they soon lost their original character in consequence of the necessities of the country and the strict method through which the Mormons have built up their cities and settlements. . . . Devoting their lives and industries toward general results as a community, the emigrants were directed by the bishops over the whole extent of country mapped out by the

[46] Christopher J. Arthur Journal, vol. 2, p. 16, typescript, Utah State Historical Society.

[47] Tullidge, *History of Salt Lake City*, p. 667.

[48] *Biographical Record*, pp. 464, 355, 303, 196.

authorities to be subdued by Mormon industry and enterprise. Thus, a people originally artisans and manufacturers, became agricultural in their pursuits of life; and it was not until the last decade, under the new era and development of the railroads and mines, that they resumed their original activities.[49]

As agrarians then, rather than as miners or manufacturers, the British Mormon settlers contributed their brain and brawn to the building of Zion's chief defense against Gentile incursions, solid Mormon communities.

The development of Utah's resources and the growth of her economy were closely allied with spiritual motives, but the immigrant men and women who helped make Zion an earthly reality were involved in more than otherworldly pursuits. Whether Mormon, Gentile, or dissident, they labored with diligence to produce if not quite the kingdom of God then a relatively successful secular economy in the Great Basin.

CULTURAL TONIC

Important as business leadership and daily toil are in the establishing of a successful, civilized society, yet the sum is much more than statements of profit and loss. Despite the seriousness with which Mormon settlers took the task of building the kingdom, they found time for recreation. Notwithstanding his New England puritanism, Brigham Young had taken part in stage plays in Nauvoo; and as the Saints moved westward, music and dance continued to be very much a part of social life. Englishman William Pitt's Nauvoo Brass Band left Nauvoo on the same day as Brigham Young and was the nucleus from which grew Utah's first musical and theatrical associations. According to Tullidge, three men, Hiram B. Clawson, John T. Caine, and David O. Calder (the latter two being British immigrants) were instrumental in convincing Brigham Young that early Utah society "needed toning up" in a professional sense. Calder, who in his native Scotland had organized the Falkirk Musical Association under the patronage of the earl of Zetland, prevailed upon Utah's nobleman to give his patronage and church financial support to the organization of philharmonic societies

---

[49] Tullidge, *History of Salt Lake City*, p. 670.

throughout the territory in the form of the Deseret Musical Association.[50]

Another musician who did much to support Brigham Young's belief in music and drama as a necessary part of civilized society was Charles J. Thomas who had had wide experience in metropolitan orchestras in London and who, according to Tullidge, transformed the Mormon Tabernacle Choir from an ordinary country church choir into a "fairly metropolitan" group that performed good anthem music "to the delight of the congregation, the majority of whom had come from the musical cities of Great Britain." The presence of such a large number of British immigrants has also been viewed as a primary stimulus to the development of theatre in Salt Lake City:

> . . . the community were socially starving for public amusements and recreation to enliven the isolation of a "thousand miles from everywhere," as their locality was then described. The majority of the citizens in 1851 and 1852 were fresh from a land of theatres. . . . where the common people for generations have been accustomed to go to the theatre and to the philharmonic concerts, to see the best of acting and hear the divinest singing, at a few pence, to the galleries. Such a community could not possibly have got along without their theatre, nor been content with their isolation without something to awaken pleasurable reminiscences of the intellectual culture and dramatic art of their native land. Their sagacious head sensed all this, and he at once gave to the newly formed "Musical and Dramatic Company" the "Old Bowery," where the congregation of Saints met Sabbath days, and it was there—in the only temple or tabernacle Zion had in those days—that home theatricals took their rise.[51]

Tullidge may be guilty of filopietism in his assessment—after all, not only was he from Britain, but his father John, Sr., and his brother John, Jr., made important contributions to music and painting in Utah. But even at that, when one examines the accounts of cultural activities in early Utah, the British presence is dominant. James Ferguson, Phil Margetts, Robert Campbell, William Clayton, David McKenzie, John Lindsay, James Hardie, to name a few, Britons all, were active participants in the Salt Lake Theatre and its earlier

[50] *Ibid.*, pp. 771–72.
[51] *Ibid.*, p. 737.

counterpart, the Musical and Dramatic Company. Only two days after his arrival in Salt Lake City, David McKenzie became involved with the Deseret Dramatic Association. Within a week he was on the stage of Social Hall; and in time John McCullough, the American critic, described him as the best Polonius he had ever seen, no mean accomplishment for the immigrant apprentice engraver.[52]

British immigrants not only contributed to the secular scene in music and drama, but the sacred songs of the Mormon people bear their imprint. Welsh-born Evan Stephens, Utah's most prolific composer, was for many years conductor of the Tabernacle Choir, leading it to its Second Place award at the Chicago World Fair in 1893. William Clayton, Joseph Daynes, John Jaques, Ellen Knowles Melling, James Baird, Ebenezer Beesley, Henry Naisbitt, George Careless, John M. MacFarlane are among the immigrant composers, musicians, and song writers whose names and words are still on the lips of thousands of Utahns today. Their songs and singers even played a minor role in Utah's dramatic history as in 1858 when federal peace commissioners were negotiating with Brigham Young regarding the positioning of the federal army in Utah. During the meeting, word was received that Johnston's army was on the move. Brigham Young, no doubt intending to impress the commissioners with the Mormon resolve to resist, called on David Dunbar, a Scottish immigrant, to sing "Zion," the words of which say in part:

> In thy mountain retreat
> God will strengthen thy feet;
> On the necks of thy foes
> Thou shalt tread. . . .
> Thy deliverance is nigh
> Thy oppressors shall die
> And the wicked shall bow 'neath thy rod.

The commissioners were suitably impressed; and after several stormy sessions, a peaceful settlement of the movement of the troops was concluded. As an expression of Mormon solidarity, "Zion" was

---

[52] George D. Pyper, *Romance of an Old Playhouse,* rev. ed. (Salt Lake City, 1937), p. 58; Tullidge, *History of Salt Lake City,* p. 759. David McKenzie, an engraver, acted out another role in an off-stage drama. While living in the Beehive House he was engaged to engrave plates for the Deseret currency, but in 1859 he was arrested on charges of counterfeiting U.S. drafts and sentenced to a two-year prison term. In 1868 he became private secretary to Brigham Young. See Juanita Brooks, ed., *On the Mormon Frontier: The Diary of Hosea Stout,* 2 vols. (Salt Lake City, 1964), 2:698 n. 58.

written in England in 1856 by Charles W. Penrose who had never been to Utah, and it was originally sung to a Scottish tune, "O Minnie, O Minnie, Come o'er the Lea." [53]

At the heart of any community's intellectual life lie the books and journals, outside of local publications, that are necessary for the sustenance and renewal of the life of the mind. In 1860 Utah was fortunate to have an enterprising and congenial Irish bookman from Tipperary who played the role of community intellectual through his vending of books and magazines and his liberality in allowing his back rooms to be used for educational meetings and community dialogue. James Dwyer's Salt Lake City bookstore was in reality an educational center—the "gathering place for the educated society of Utah" and according to one writer "many of Utah's advancements started as conversations in the back room of Dwyer's." [54] The availability of books and of stimulating conversation was a necessary adjunct to Utah's cultural and intellectual development and an added stimulus for Dwyer's fellow immigrants to continue their literary pursuits in isolated Utah.

One such writer was John Lyon, the Mormon poet from Kilmarnock, Ayrshire, who, prior to his conversion, had written an 1832 report on unemployment in Scotland for the British House of Commons. As a Mormon he put his pen at the service of another social cause, the Perpetual Emigrating Fund, and helped many a poor British family go "home to Zion" with proceeds from the sale of *The Harp of Zion* published at Liverpool in 1852. Once in Zion, John Lyon contributed poems and articles to Utah's developing literary periodicals, served as drama critic for the *Daily Telegraph* and as assistant territorial librarian under another British settler, William C. Staines, the territorial librarian. [55]

[53] J. Spencer Cornwall, *Stories of Our Mormon Hymns* (Salt Lake City, 1963), pp. 159–60.

[54] Chris Rigby, "Ada Dwyer: Bright Lights and Lilacs," *Utah Historical Quarterly* 43 (1975): 42.

[55] *Deseret News*, September 7, 1901; See John Lyon's contribution in *Tullidge's Quarterly Magazine;* Maude Adams, Utah's most distinguished actress, claimed that John Lyon introduced her to the art of elocution and Sarah Elizabeth Carmichael, the Utah poet, gave "Father Lyon" credit for teaching her the basics of poetry writing. Lyon with other kindred spirits (many of whom were British) made up the membership of Salt Lake City's Twentieth Ward which under the leadership of Bishop John Sharp was considered one of the city's "most intellectual and liberal Wards." Interview with T. Edgar Lyon, March 27, 1975, Salt Lake City. See sketch of John Sharp in Jenson, *LDS Biographical Encyclopedia* 1:677.

Still another British writer, Edward W. Tullidge, promoted the publication of Utah's first literary journals. The son of relatively affluent and Eton-educated John E. Tullidge of Weymouth, England, Edward was converted to Mormonism in 1848. After serving as an editor of the church publication *Millennial Star* and as an active proselytizer for the church, he felt "called" to write a history of Joseph Smith and came to Utah in 1861 to pursue this. He was hired as an assistant in the Church Historian's Office to facilitate his research but soon became disillusioned with the close integration of church and secular affairs in Utah. In 1864 in cooperation with an English friend, Elias L. T. Harrison, he published the *Peep O'Day,* reputed to be the first magazine published west of the Missouri. The magazine soon became identified as "anti-Mormon"; and although its publisher disclaimed any attempt to destroy Mormonism, it was condemned by the church and ceased publication after only five issues.

After a stay in the East where he wrote for the *New York Galaxy,* Tullidge returned to Utah and took over publication of the *Utah Magazine* founded by Harrison and another Briton, William S. Godbe. In time the *Utah Magazine* evolved into a weekly newspaper, the *Mormon Tribune,* the immediate fore-runner of the *Salt Lake Tribune.* Despite his disagreements with church authorities, Tullidge produced a *History of Salt Lake City* in 1886 that received acclaim and financial support not only from businessmen but from civic and church officials and was regarded in its day as containing a balanced view of Utah's early history.[56]

Paralleling the literary accomplishments of Tullidge were those of his contemporaries Thomas B. H. Stenhouse and his wife Fanny. Natives of Dalkeith, Scotland, and Jersey, Channel Islands, respectively, the Stenhouses began as fervent defenders of the faith in the British Isles, on the Continent, and in America, but, according to historian Ronald W. Walker, through such books as his *Rocky Mountain Saints* and her *Tell It All* they eventually "helped to fashion throughout the United States and Great Britain the negative image of nineteenth century Mormonism."[57] However, in the interim between their arrival in Utah in 1859 and their subsequent disaffection with Mormonism some ten years later, they were among

[56] William F. Lye, "Edward Wheelock Tullidge, The Mormon's Rebel Historian," *Utah Historical Quarterly* 28 (1960) : 57–75.
[57] Ronald W. Walker, "The Stenhouses and the Making of a Mormon Image," *Journal of Mormon History* 1 (1974) : 51–52.

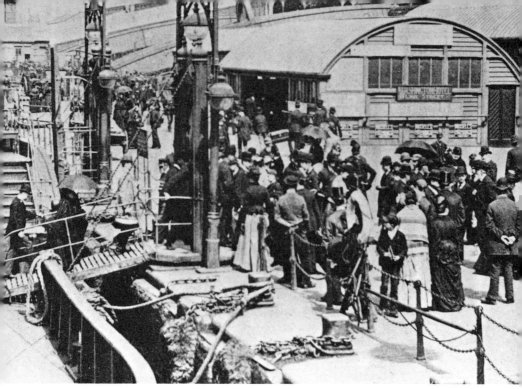

Above: *Thousands of immigrants bound for America embarked from Liverpool, England.*

Left: *James and Mary Jane Ewer Palmer from England represent dedicated builders whom history often ignores.*

Right: *Ebenezer Beesley of Oxfordshire, England, came to Utah with a hand cart company. He directed the Tabernacle Choir and founded a music company.*

From the top: *William Spry of Berkshire,
England, served as governor of Utah,
1909–17. He directed the building of the
State Capitol and was embroiled in the
controversial Joe Hill case. Hannah Tapfield
King, born near Cambridge, England, brought
a taste for culture and poetry to the Utah
frontier. Charles R. Savage, left, and George
M. Ottinger, right, on a photographic and
sketching trip in the Wasatch Mountains. A
native of Southampton, England, Savage was
famous as a photographer.*

Left: *The Tullidges were an exceptionally talented English family: John, Sr., noted musician; Edward, editor, publisher, and historian; John, Jr., whose shop is pictured, an artist.*

Right: *Born in Llandudno, Wales, Martha Hughes Cannon was a physician, suffragist, and ardent Democrat. The fourth wife of Angus M. Cannon, she defeated her Republican husband to become the first woman state senator. Below: Welsh gatherings always included singing and other musical contests popular with the public.*

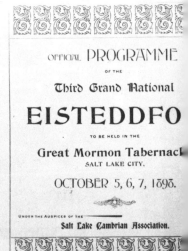

From the top: *Welsh stonemason Shadrach Jones built many homes in Willard, Box Elder County, that remain as precious examples of folk architecture. Thomas Davis Giles of Wales, blinded in an accident, was known in Utah for his harp playing. Music and words to the Welsh national anthem sung at eisteddfods.*

GEMS IN GLASSWARE, QUEENSWARE, ETC., AT Z. C. M. I.

HEN WLAD FY NHADAU.
(THE LAND OF MY FATHERS).

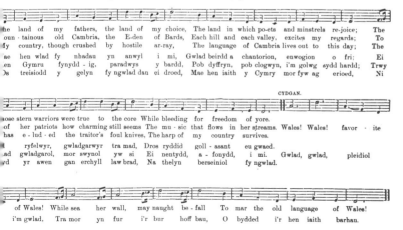

Above: *Irish-born Martha Spence Heywood made hats, taught
school, settled Nephi, yearned for culture, and kept one of the most vivid
diaries of the 1850s. Patrick Edward Connor, a Kerryman by birth,
led the California Volunteers to Salt Lake City in 1862, founded Fort
Douglas, and generated interest in mining.* Below: *Hundreds of Irish
tracklayers under John S. Casement, in foreground, lived in boxcars
during the building of the Union Pacific.*

Left: *The bookstore owned by James Dwyer of Tipperary, Ireland, was a meetingplace for intellectuals.* Above: *Educated at All Hallows, Dublin, Irishman Lawrence Scanlan brought schools, health care, and the spiritual life to his widespread flock.*

Patrick J. Moran, second from left, began a successful contracting firm in Utah that installed steam heating and, later, paved roads.

Above: *Elizabeth Bonnemort from Glasgow, Scotland, became Utah's "sheep queen" with large holdings at Deep Creek, Tooele County. Another Scot, Richard Ballantyne, founded the LDS Sunday School system, farmed, and held civic posts in Ogden.* Below: *John Taffe McDonald began a family candy business that has continued to prosper.*

Left: *David O. McKay at Loch Lomond. The LDS president was proud of his Scottish heritage.*

ove: *Traditional dances and events like tossing the caber are* pular *among Utahns of Scottish ancestry today.* Below: *Kilted* pers *and drummers at Temple Square. Several bands keep the sounds* Scotland *alive in Utah.*

Zion's leading exponents and were at the center of Utah's intellectual and artistic life. As Utah's "most cultured missionaries," they contributed through their personal contacts to the favorable image of Mormonism as expressed by Sir Richard Burton and other observers. T.B.H. Stenhouse in particular played a prominent role as a publisher, patron of the arts, and as a university regent. As founder and publisher of Salt Lake City's *Telegraph,* this articulate immigrant put his pen at the disposal of the Mormon cause in its conflict with Colonel Connor and the *Union Vedette* of Camp Douglas. His literary skills and sophisticated perceptions were also recognized by the non-Mormon press in the East and in California. In Walker's view, "his journalistic voice was undoubtedly the most powerful in the territory." [58]

Although Fanny Stenhouse apparently shared the limelight with her husband as "among Deseret's most cultured missionaries," in male-dominated Utah, as in the nation at large, the social roles played by women were rigidly prescribed by custom and tradition. The education of women was still viewed as an unnecessary frill, and those women in Utah who wished to enlarge their cultural or intellectual horizons had to rely almost entirely on informal educational institutions. The Elocution Society and the Polysophical Society, for example, drew much of their support (both in attendance and creative contributions) from such pioneer women as "cultured, educated and creative" Hannah Tapfield King, an immigrant from Cambridgeshire, England. Hannah found intellectual gatherings "a spur to cultivate our thinking faculties more," and she persisted in the view that her "sisters" should cultivate their minds. However, after one social meeting with some American "sisters" who apparently were trying too hard to match her own intellectual acumen, she exclaimed: "Silly women! They only exposed their ignorance and ill manners, and what do *they* know of the English, or English society." [59] On the Utah frontier in the 1850s survival was paramount, and perhaps Hannah was expecting too much from her sisters; she personally refused to be cowed by the environment and instead was eager to shape its cultural perspectives.

Another immigrant who broke the traditional stereotype of the pioneer woman with no interests but husband, kitchen, and

<hr>

[58] *Ibid.,* pp. 54–56. Scottish Mormon William Gibson recalls that he knew Stenhouse in Britain "and was not at all surprised at the course he took. . . ." in Utah. William Gibson Journal, p. 147, LDS Archives.

[59] Maureen Ursenbach, "Three Women and the Life of the Mind," *Utah Historical Quarterly* 43 (1975): 33, 27.

children was Martha Spence Heywood, a native of Dublin, Ireland, who in the 1850s was involved in founding an Elocution Society in Salt Lake City, and who when called to settle isolated Salt Creek (Nephi, Utah) with her husband in 1851, set about organizing the Mount Nebo Literary Association. On returning to Salt Lake City she and Hannah Tapfield King participated in the affairs of the Polysophical Society until that organization fell a victim to the reforming zeal of brethren who viewed its intellectual pursuits with some alarm.[60] Given the circumstances of pioneer Utah, with its necessary emphasis upon physical and economic survival, it is noteworthy that these pioneer women were not oblivious to the life of the mind and made the desert places not entirely devoid of cultural refinement and intellectual interests.

In assuming their roles as journalists, actors, composers, poets, and historians, these literate immigrants from the United Kingdom contributed to a broadening of Utah's social and cultural base, promoting thereby the development of a frontier society that was not only atypical in its theocratic emphasis but also in its cultural pursuits.

PROTESTORS OF MORMONISM

In the history of the United States a vigorous free press has often challenged the claims of authority put forward by the official establishment. It should not, therefore, come as a surprise to find that articulate persons with access to a printing press would become a focal point of resistance to the Mormon establishment. Writers with the ability of a Tullidge or the Stenhouses were able to direct their criticisms against the source of their once fervent faith, and their expertise contributed substantially to a movement that challenged the authority of Mormon leaders in the 1860s.

Discussing the impact that early Utah society had on British immigrants, Philip Taylor contended that the change from Britain to Utah "gave them both security and restriction." [61] For men like Edward W. Tullidge, Thomas B. H. Stenhouse, Elias L. T. Harrison, and William S. Godbe, the sense of restriction was perhaps more intense than their sense of security. They were articulate, cultured, and critical; and eventually they challenged Brigham Young's authority in secular affairs through the *Utah Magazine*. Consequently,

[60] *Ibid.*, 29–32.
[61] Taylor, *Expectations Westward*, p. 246.

they left the church either through excommunication or voluntary withdrawal. Along with another Briton, William Shearman, Canadian Henry Lawrence, and Eli B. Kelsey who had spent many years in the British Mission, these men formed the nucleus of what became known as the Godbeite conspiracy. Godbe, much admired by Brigham Young for his economic talents, wanted to reform the church and to reduce the priesthood's domination of secular affairs. Mormonism was one thing in Britain, where it could not possibly wield such far-reaching power over secular life, and quite another in isolated Utah where these Britons apparently felt stifled by church domination over every aspect of life, spiritual and temporal. Through the Church of Zion, organized as a result of spiritualist manifestations to Harrison and Godbe, the reformers hoped to reestablish a freer Mormonism on a more spiritual basis. However, the movement failed to generate widespread support among faithful Mormons and eventually lost its religious character, becoming instead an element of the emerging Liberal party of the 1870s.[62]

The defection of Godbe and Harrison and their British Mission associates had an intellectual basis, even if mixed with spiritualism. A different challenge to Brigham Young's authority of a charismatic nature occurred shortly after Tullidge's arrival in Utah. This short-lived movement was also headed by a Briton, Joseph Morris, who had come from Wales in the 1850s. Described by Dwyer as a "fanatical visionary," Morris claimed to have received direct revelations regarding his role as leader of the church in 1860. When Brigham Young refused to accept Morris as the Lord's anointed, he led some five hundred followers to Weber Canyon where they awaited the Second Coming of Christ and where Morris was crowned king, the crown used having been fashioned by another immigrant, tinsmith Alexander Dow. Morris's chief counselor was Englishman John Banks who had at one time served as assistant presiding bishop of the church under Brigham Young. The "kingdom" in Weber County came to an end in June 1862 when the Nauvoo Legion under Col. R. T. Burton arrived and attempted to arrest Morris and Banks on charges of murder and plundering neighboring farms. Morris, Banks, and two women died as a result of the ensuing con-

[62] Ronald W. Walker, "The Commencement of the Godbeite Protest: Another View," *Utah Historical Quarterly* 42 (1974): 217–44; G. II. Palmer, "The Godbeite Movement: A Dissent Against Temporal Control" (M.A. thesis, Brigham Young University, 1968).

flict, and eventually some of the group were resettled near Soda Springs, Idaho.[63] Brigham Young still led the faithful.

Individual disillusionment and apostasy were, of course, not uncommon among the Utah settlers, and a visitor to Utah in the early 1850s reported meeting one embittered Scot who in attempting to get his surplus money out of the "common exchequer" so that he could try his luck in California, was refused and rebuked for his lust for gain. The Scot complained that he "dinna se whar' this wad lead to, or how it wad end." [64]

For some, estrangement from church policy and practice led to removing themselves from Utah; for others it led to a disrupting of friendships and family relationships in the heart of Zion. One veteran who became disaffected after years of distinguished service was George P. Watt, the first person baptized into the Mormon church in Great Britain, private secretary to Brigham Young, publisher of the *Journal of Discourses* and a leading proponent of the Deseret alphabet. Watts opted to stay in Utah and although associating himself with Godbeites for a short period, he seemed to have lost faith in Mormonism or its leaders prior to the Godbeites' emergence. Personally disenchanted with Brigham Young, Watts publicly confessed his defection, blaming his waywardness and stubborn disposition on his "mixture of English and Scottish blood," which he said "could not be driven, but would respond to sympathy and kindness." [65]

Another dissident Briton, F. W. Blake of Birmingham, was much more discreet in giving voice to his changed perceptions of Mormonism. After participating in the rites in the Endowment House, he "walked forth in Zion's Street ever afterwards an unbeliever in the pretensions of Brigham Young and an apostate to the doctrines of Mormonism." However, he restrained his public criticism and "sarcastic puffs at authority and discipline" on purely pragmatic grounds; open dissent, he felt, might be dangerous and besides he

[63] Robert J. Dwyer, *The Gentile Comes to Utah: A Study in Religious and Social Conflicts (1862–1890)* (Washington, D. C., 1941), pp. 107–8. Gibson Condie mentions that Alexander Dow made Morris's crown. See his Journal, p. 47, LDS Archives.

[64] William Kelly, "The Mormon Settlement in the Great Salt Lake Valley," cited in J. Cecil Alter, ed., *Utah—The Storied Domain*, 3 vols. (Chicago, 1932), 1:97. Because the Scot had voluntarily deposited his money with the church, Kelly commented that "notwithstanding his strong dialect, I question if he is clean-bred Scotch."

[65] Ronald G. Watt, "George D. Watt: Old Ship Zion or Devil's Harrow," essay in possession of Ronald G. Watt, Salt Lake City.

enjoyed the company of his Mormon friends. His "air of faithfulness was merely assumed," he wrote, and caused him some discomfort; but even at that he was ordained to the office of a seventy in the Mormon priesthood.[66]

The attempt of the British-led Morrisites and Godbeites to challenge Brigham Young's leadership and the individual apostasy of prominent individuals or of rank and file members left the dominant position of Mormon authority in Utah virtually unscathed. But these "Mormon Protestants" of various hues and complexity might well be viewed as evidence that in pioneer Utah the human spirit could transcend social limitations and respond to a variety of religious beliefs, and to freedom of expression.

The Faith of Saints and Gentiles

How many immigrants put on an "air of faithfulness" as F. W. Blake did is unknown, but there can be little doubt that substantial numbers of British immigrants remained faithful in belief and in practice and were entrusted with a significant role in the leadership echelons of the kingdom of God, as Andrew Jenson's *Latter-day Saint Biographical Encyclopedia* readily reveals. When the British traveler Walter Gore Marshall visited Utah in 1879, he reported that thirteen of the twenty-nine bishops in the Salt Lake Stake were British.[67] Over the course of its history the Mormon church has drawn heavily on the administrative and intellectual talents of its British population: between 1850 and 1925 a dozen native sons of the British Isles served as General Authorities of the Mormon church and often, by virtue of their church position, as leaders in Utah's secular affairs, too. John Banks and Alfred Cardon of Lancashire were ordained assisting presiding bishops of the church in 1851 and served in that capacity until 1853. (Banks was excommunicated in 1859 and became a leader in the Morrisite movement which, as noted above, led to his death in 1862.)

The appointment of George Q. Cannon to the Quorum of the Twelve Apostles in 1860 "began a process of appointing foreign-born men that characterized the Mormon Hierarchy for the next seventy years." [68] It appears to have been an unwritten policy to

[66] F. W. Blake Diary, November 24, 1861, LDS Archives.

[67] Marshall, *Through America*, p. 229.

[68] Dennis Michael Quinn, "Organizational Development and Social Origins of the Mormon Hierarchy 1830–1932: A Prosopographical Study" (M.A.

have the dominant national groups in the church represented in the General Authorities; and reflecting the large British sector of the church population, "British" General Authorities are prominent. Indeed, from 1838 to 1932 with the exception of two years, there was always a native-born Briton among the church apostles; included were such notables as Cannon, George Teasdale, John Winder, Charles Penrose, and James E. Talmage. In the First Quorum of Seventy in the years 1888–1933, were Brigham H. Roberts and George Reynolds. Roberts was elected to a seat in the House of Representatives in 1900 but was refused admission on the grounds that he was a polygamist. Sterling M. McMurrin described him as "the most interesting and exciting and stimulating person in [the church's] leadership, its most prolific writer, its chief theologian and historian, and its most capable defender." [69] Roberts was somewhat of a maverick, being disfellowshipped in 1896, reinstated the same year, and then denounced by Joseph F. Smith for showing disrespect to the First Presidency of the church. His *Comprehensive History of the Church of Jesus Christ of Latter-day Saints* is still viewed as one of the most balanced accounts of Mormonism's beginnings, written as it was by a practicing Mormon and a nonprofessional historian.

Controversy seems to have been an endemic element of British participation in Mormon affairs. The name of George Reynolds, an immigrant of 1865, was attached to the Supreme Court decision that marked the beginning of the end of Utah's peculiar institution, polygamy. As a result of *United States* v. *Reynolds,* this Englishman, who had volunteered as a test case, served time in the Nebraska State Penitentiary for his polygamous beliefs and actions and was accorded a hero's welcome on his return to Salt Lake City, much to the chagrin of the Utah Gentiles. [70] He was appointed a member of the Council of Seventy in 1890, six months before the church issued its Manifesto that in effect accepted the Reynolds decision of 1879.

During the seventies and eighties two Englishmen, John Taylor and his nephew George Q. Cannon, served in the First Presidency, the highest council of the Mormon hierarchy. The influence they

thesis, University of Utah, 1973), pp. 95–96. This is the most useful single volume reference for personal data on the Mormon General Authorities.

[69] Sterling M. McMurrin, "Notes on a Mormon Historian," in Brigham H. Roberts, *Joseph Smith—The Prophet Teacher* (Princeton, N. J., 1967), p. vi. See also Robert H. Malan, *B. H. Roberts: A Biography* (Salt Lake City, 1966).

[70] Dwyer, *The Gentile Comes to Utah,* pp. 112–17.

wielded there led anti-Mormons, like the editor of the *Salt Lake Tribune,* to charge that after Brigham Young's death, Mormonism was completely controlled by these two Englishmen. According to C. C. Goodwin, Taylor and Cannon "make the controlling power and give direction to the whole system." [71] They may not have had the absolute power attributed to them, but they assuredly played important roles in the development of Mormonism and of Utah.

John Taylor, a native of the north of England, had been a close associate of Joseph Smith and was wounded at Carthage when Joseph was killed. Upon Brigham Young's death in 1877, he presided over Mormon affairs as president of the Quorum of the Twelve for three years and then in 1880 became Mormonism's third "prophet, seer and revelator." To celebrate the church's jubilee in 1880, the new leader initiated a movement to reduce the indebtedness of poor immigrants to the Perpetual Emigrating Fund by one half, to reduce tithing indebtedness also by one half, and to distribute a thousand head of cattle and five thousand head of sheep to the deserving poor. Despite this auspicious beginning, Taylor's administration was plagued by increased federal pressure on Mormon polygamists, and the aged leader spent much of his time evading federal warrants, dying in virtual exile in 1887.[72]

George Q. Cannon, converted to Mormonism by his uncle, John Taylor, during the latter's mission in England in 1840, was not, strictly speaking, English; he was born in Liverpool of Manx parents. In 1842 he emigrated to Nauvoo and came to Utah in 1847. After a mission to California and the Sandwich Islands, he became a member of the Quorum of the Twelve in 1860, serving as an assistant counselor to Brigham Young from 1873 to 1877. In 1880 he began his service in the First Presidency under John Taylor and continued in this capacity with the next three presidents until his death in 1901.

Few important events in Utah were not in some way shaped or influenced by George Q. Cannon: education, publication, and politics as well as religion felt his impress. He represented Utah as its territorial delegate at a time when every election in Utah was challenged by the Gentile minority who longed for power but could not

---

[71] C. C. Goodwin, "The Mormon Situation," *Harper's New Monthly Magazine* 63 (1881): 759. Goodwin claimed the government of Utah was "monarchial" and "more absolute than ever was the Czar of Russia."

[72] Brigham H. Roberts, *Life of John Taylor* (Salt Lake City, 1963); Tullidge, *History of Salt Lake City,* pp. 23–28.

break the solidarity of the church-dominated People's party. Eventually Cannon was refused his place as a delegate because of his polygamous relationships and was succeeded by another Englishman, John T. Caine, a Mormon who did not practice polygamy. Pursued by the "feds" and finally apprehended, Cannon served with other "prisoners for conscience' sake" in the Utah Territorial Penitentiary and then paradoxically played a major role, through his son, Frank, in the negotiations with federal authorities (including President Grover Cleveland) that resulted in the issuance of the Manifesto and the disavowal of polygamy as a practice of the Mormon people.[73]

Cannon's trail from Liverpool to Nauvoo, to Washington, D. C., and to the penitentiary is in many ways the story of the most tumultuous years in Utah history. As one of its leading lights, he has been variously described as "the sweetest, smoothest, and most plausible sophist on all this round earth" as well as the "Mormon premier" and the "Mormon Richelieu" during his long tenure as Mormonism's political spokesman. Bernard DeVoto recognized Cannon's place in Mormon history when he characterized him as "the last great leader of the Saints." [74]

DeVoto's judgment might be correct, but Cannon was certainly not the last Briton to wield influence in the hierarchy of the church. British influence continued with the selection of John R. Winder to replace Cannon in 1901. Then, in 1907 Charles W. Penrose was elevated to the First Presidency and served until his death in 1924 when he was succeeded by the last person of British birth to be a counselor to the church president, Charles W. Nibley. A native of Scotland, Nibley served until his death in 1931. As presiding bishop he had administered the temporal affairs of the Mormon church since 1907, and in 1918 he chose as one of his counselors John Wells of Nottinghamshire, England. An immigrant of 1860, Nibley had been in partnership with financier David Eccles and had played an important role in developing Utah's sugar industry. Bishop Nibley also spearheaded the drive to construct a

[73] For details on Cannon's role as a territorial delegate during the height of the polygamy controversy see Mark W. Cannon, "The Mormon Issue in Congress 1872–1882: Drawing on the Experience of Territorial Delegate George Q. Cannon" (Ph.D. diss., Harvard University, 1960).

[74] C. C. Goodwin, "The Political Attitude of the Mormons," *The North American Review* (March 1881): 282–83; A. S. Street, "The Mormon Richelieu," *Ainslee's Magazine* 4 (1900): 699–706. DeVoto quote cited in Cannon, "The Mormon Issue," p. 4.

church office building that would meet the needs of the times and was instrumental in having the church pay cash rather than scrip for services performed by its employees.[75]

Given the role that the Mormon church has played in Utah's history, it is understandable that when the term "the church" is used in Utah, it often has reference to the dominant Mormon organization. From the earliest years, however, non-Mormons or Gentiles have had a different view of what "church" means, and some had leaders who saw their mission as one of combating the errors of Mormonism and of weakening Mormon control of Utah society. This was especially true of Congregational and Presbyterian missionaries whose very names reveal their national origins, although none was actually born in the British Isles. During the 1870s the Reverends D. J. McMillan, Robert G. McNiece, and Norman McLeod were the principal antagonists of Mormon control; they hoped by preaching in churches and teaching in schools to break the grip of "Brighamism" on the territory. They contributed substantially to Utah's educational development, but, much to their dismay, the Mormons filled their classrooms during the week but returned to "Brighamism" on Sundays.[76]

Unlike these Protestants, Catholics, who were numerically the largest of the Gentile groups, were more concerned with keeping their own people faithful than changing the Mormons. Priests from Ireland, like Fathers Edward Kelly, Patrick Walsh, and Thomas Galligan, were among the earliest Catholic clergy in Utah. Father Lawrence Scanlan, whose major task in life was to keep Catholicism's flame burning in Utah, was also a son of the Emerald Isle. A graduate of All Hallows College, Dublin, Scanlan came to the United States shortly after his ordination as a priest in 1868 and in 1873 arrived in Salt Lake City just as the influx of Irish miners began. It was to these Irishmen that Scanlan's labors were primarily directed. In the tradition of mining, his parishioners were notori-

[75] Nibley, *Reminiscences;* Jenson, *LDS Biographical Encyclopedia,* 3:768–69. For sketches on Winder, Penrose, and Wells see *ibid.* For examples of lower echelon leadership in the Mormon church such as Britons John Steele and Christopher Layton, see Taylor, *Expectations Westward,* p. 72.

[76] Dwyer, *The Gentile Comes to Utah,* chap. 6, "The Torchbearers," discusses the evangelical Protestant efforts to convert the Mormons. T. Edgar Lyon, "Evangelical Protestant Missionary Activities in Mormon Dominated Areas 1865–1900" (Ph.D. diss., University of Utah, 1962), p. 251. Lyon quotes one Protestant evangelist as saying that the Mormons "take our profferred [*sic*] education, but not our religion, and use it to strengthen their own institution."

ously impermanent; and his missions in Ophir, Silver Reef, and other mining locations were the very antithesis of Mormonism's religiously motivated colonization. That the Irish miners moved away as the veins of ore were drained was no reason for complacency; the faith must be preserved, and Scanlan's energies matched the needs. Not only were spiritual needs met by this Irish priest, but through his efforts the Sisters of the Holy Cross established hospitals in Salt Lake City and Ogden, and academies and parochial schools were promoted that served not only Catholics but were "patronized by children of Mormon parentage." [77] Scanlan's policy was to cultivate amicable relations with Mormons as individuals and, unlike the evangelical groups, he did not practice Mormon-baiting. In May 1879, during a visit to Silver Reef (a mining community with a large Irish population), Scanlan was invited by the Mormon leadership to utilize the nearby Saint George Tabernacle for a Catholic mass. The Tabernacle Choir practiced and sang "Peter's Mass" in Latin under the direction of an Edinburgh native, John MacFarlane. In 1887 Scanlan was appointed vicar apostolic of Utah, and in 1886 titular bishop of Laranda, culminating in his elevation to bishop of Salt Lake in 1891. His success in promoting the growth and stability of the Catholic church in Utah was made possible in large measure by those very Irish miners whose religious needs he had devoted his life to serving. In the 1890s they were among the wealthiest men of the territory and were "characteristically generous toward their church" making the Cathedral of the Madeleine a unique reality for such a numerically small diocese.[78] In so doing these Irish immigrants not only strengthened their own particular religion, they added to the diversity and pluralism of Utah's cultural inheritance.

Illustrative of the role that British immigrants and their children assumed in Utah's religious affairs was the life of Utah-born David O. McKay, the son of David McKay of Scotland and Jennette Evans of Wales. Long an apostle, this educator son of immigrants became Mormonism's chief spokesman in 1951 when he

[77] Dwyer, *The Gentile Comes to Utah*, pp. 157–59; Robert J. Dwyer, "Pioneer Bishop: Lawrence Scanlan 1843–1915," *Utah Historical Quarterly* 20 (1952): 135–58.

[78] Addressing the Mormons in the audience Scanlan said "I think you are wrong, and you think I am wrong, but this should not prevent us from treating each other with due consideration and respect." See "Manuscript History of St. George Stake," May 25, 1879, LDS Archives; M.A. Pendleton, "Memories of Silver Reef," *Utah Historical Quarterly* 3 (1930): 116.

was sustained as president of the church, a position he held until his death in 1970. In striking contrast to the open hostility directed at the John Taylors and George Q. Cannons of an earlier generation, President McKay was widely respected and admired by non-Mormons and symbolized the amicable relationship between Mormons and Gentiles which has characterized Utah's recent history.[79]

NATIVE PRIDE

Because British immigrants in the United States were less likely to establish separate and distinct British settlements than other immigrants, they have been in large measure invisible as a group. But, as Charlotte Erickson has pointed out, it should not be assumed that they were, therefore, automatically assimilated into the mainstream of American life. This assumption overlooks the role that the informal immigrant "communities and their institutions played in the accommodation of the first generation immigrant and in the long-run assimilation of his children." [80] In addition to the psychological and physical support received from the immigrant communities, the settlers' adaptation to life in America was facilitated by their political activity, their close family association, their common use of the English language, and their lack of a "prickly British nationalism, which might have hindered their adjustment." [81]

These factors are plainly evident when one considers the British settlers in Utah. With the British-born making up a significant proportion of the population, there was a large immigrant community capable of lending support to newcomers; the Mormon emphasis on family unity made settlement in Utah a family affair; the full participation of British immigrants in the social and political life of Utah no doubt gave the new settlers a sense of control over their own destiny; and, of course, the peculiarly Mormon interpretation of America as the land of Zion subdued any lingering nationalism. As William Morrison expressed it: "I long for citizenship in Zion, the metropolis of God's kingdom." [82] However, like British settlers in the United States at large, the immigrants in Utah never

[79] See, for instance, the account of a dinner given by community friends honoring David O. McKay on his ninetieth birthday in *Deseret News*, December 11, 1962.

[80] Charlotte Erickson, *Invisible Immigrants: The Adaptation of English and Scottish Immigrants in Nineteenth Century America* (Miami, 1972), p. 407.

[81] *Ibid.*, p. 256.

[82] William Morrison Diary, July 13, 1851, Utah State Historical Society.

completely divested themselves of their cultural heritage. Indeed, that heritage may even have promoted their gradual accommodation and adaptation to the new environment by keeping intact a sense of personal and group integrity. As Horace Kallen has observed, genuine cultural pluralism does not require the debasement or neglect of one's origins; rather pluralism is strengthened by the promotion of individual and group diversity.[83]

There can be no doubt, however, that early Mormonism was less concerned with preserving cultural identity and cultural pluralism than with building a holy commonwealth whose citizens would have allegiance to God (and to his chosen representatives). John Taylor, an immigrant himself and a prominent Mormon leader, proclaimed as his motto, "The Kingdom of God or nothing," and an early editorial of the *Deseret News* took note of the problem of discord arising among Utah's settlers, gathered as they were from so many nations. Not only was language seen as a barrier, but habits, native prejudices, customs, superstition, credulity "imbibed in childhood and riper years, not wholly divested of native pride" were pointed out as weaknesses which had to be overcome. The editorial then asked rhetorically:

> Does it ever occur to you that you are a Swede, or a German, or a Dane, or an Englishman, or a Scotch, or an Irishman, Canadian or Yankee; that your nation understands their business *most* perfectly and that you don't like a man of another nation to be foreman over you?

If such thoughts have ever arisen, then "so far you have fallen short of the Savior's rule; you are not one with your brethren." Decrying the notion that a Welshman understands foundry work because he is Welsh or an Englishman cotton spinning because he is English or a Yankee is more inventive because of birth, the immigrants were cautioned to be "like little children, and learn to do their master's will" so that the society they labored to build would succeed.[84] Nor was the friction between groups simply a matter of English versus a foreign tongue; when Erastus Snow visited the settlers in Iron County, he reported that he found there a Scotch party, a Welsh party, an English party, and an American party. Using a metaphor

[83] Horace Kallen, *Cultural Pluralism and the American Idea* (Philadelphia, 1956), pp. 52–53; Berthoff, *British Immigrants in Industrial America,* chap. 11, "National Cultures and Immigrant Societies," discusses the efforts of British immigrants to maintain their English, Scottish, and Welsh customs and traditions in the United States; see also Erickson, *Invisible Immigrants,* pp. 85–86, 484.

[84] *Deseret News,* February 5, 1853.

that these iron-workers understood, he "undertook to put all these parties through the furnace and run out a party of Saints for the Kingdom of God." [85]

The notion that the church should be a melting pot was, of course, very much a matter of physical survival in those early years. Later, unity would also be stressed as a means of combating the Gentile influence. Added to these practical reasons were the ever present spiritual motivations as Jedediah M. Grant expressed them in a discourse in 1856:

> I like to see the English, the Scotch, Welsh, French, Danes, and men from every nation, kindred, tongue and people come forth and unite under the standard of truth, obey God and be one. [86]

Even those who spoke foreign languages were promised that in time the Lord would restore the "pure" language so that misunderstandings arising out of different tongues would cease. [87] The long-term success of this policy of stressing unity is quite evident in recent studies of the Mormons: sociologist Thomas F. O'Dea defined them as "a people" and D. W. Meinig, a geographer, said:

> as a group they constitute a highly self-conscious subculture whose chief bond is religion and one which has long established its mark upon the life and landscape of a particular area, i.e., Utah and parts of surrounding states. [88]

It is almost axiomatic that they did not achieve the status of a "self-conscious subculture" by promoting the separate cultural identity of the diverse groups from which they drew their strength. Indeed, it seemed as if the Mormon message (mixed with American self-confidence) helped promote the notion that their native lands were not worthy of loyalty. What else would one expect when new converts sang of their homes as the epitomy of evil:

> Oh Babylon, Oh Babylon
> We bid you farewell
> We're going to the mountains
> Of Ephraim to Dwell. [89]

[85] "Journal History," December 12, 1852.

[86] "Journal History," January 27, 1853.

[87] *Deseret News*, February 5, 1853.

[88] Thomas F. O'Dea, *Sociology of Religion* (Englewood Cliffs, N. J., 1966), p. 70; D. W. Meinig, "The Mormon Culture Region: Strategies and Patterns in the Geography of the American West," *Annals of the Association of American Geographers* 55 (1965): 191.

[89] *Latter-day Saints Psalmody* (Salt Lake City, 1896).

Similarly, James Burgess wrote as he sailed for Zion:

> In darkness long we have been o'er whelmed
> Upon proud Brittons land
> But now the Lord has called us forth
> By his divine command.[90]

Charles Penrose, who referred to Utah as his "old mountain home" years before seeing it, gave notice of his break with England not only physically but mentally when he virtually disowned her during his return mission in 1866. Acknowledging that he had become disenchanted with his native land, to the tune of the Irish National song, "Erin go Bragh," he sang: "The spots on the face of thy beauty I see" and ended praising Utah as a land free of political corruption:

> "Where poverty lives not,
>   and bondage is banished."
> . . . .
> Where righteous men govern,
>   where Zion is rising.
> To spread forth her glory to every shore.
> "Tis the rest of the Saints,
>   and my home of adoption,
> Oh, England! I'll call thee my country no more." [91]

In Utah the struggle for economic, political, and social survival during the first forty years preempted the formation of distinctive nationalistic institutions among immigrants; and, as has been suggested, the Mormon concept of the kingdom and stress on unity was not particularly conducive to separatism among the British national groups. The English, of course, because of their dominant position numerically had the least need for formal organizations to perpetuate their cultural identity in Utah. They were, after all, a major influence in shaping the overall Utah scene. As in the nation at large, the Scots, Welsh, and Irish were much more given to nationalistic sentiments, however muted by Utah circumstances.[92]

In contrast to the English as an immigrant group, the Irish were the smallest of those who settled in Utah from the British Isles.

---

[90] Burgess's verse is from his journal, LDS Archives.

[91] *Improvement Era* 25 (1922): 354–56.

[92] Berthoff, *British Immigrants in Industrial America,* chap. 11, *passim.*

They were the least likely of the four groups to come to Utah as Mormon converts, although the first white child born in the Salt Lake Valley was the daughter of Irish Mormon immigrants, John and Catherine Steele.[93] Instead, the increased Irish population of the territory paralleled the extension of the railroad westward and the opening of the Utah mines. For instance, between 1869 and 1880, while the number of Scots in Utah tripled, the Irish increased by almost 500 percent. Most of the Catholics in Utah were of Irish birth or extraction, and the Catholic church played an important role in maintaining their Irish identity. Before mining and railroads, however, Irish soldiers came to Utah as members of Johnston's army in 1858 to help put down the "Mormon rebellion" and were included among the garrison at Camp Douglas in the 1860s. That native Irish were included in occupation forces may have contributed in some way to the hostility that existed between them and the Mormons, and Archbishop Dwyer's suggestion that "the relative peace and quiet of that decade [1847–57] was due in part to the fact that so few Irishmen were around" [94] has, perhaps, some merit. Given the relatively large English population in Utah and the centuries of hostility existing between the two groups, conflict between English settlers and Irish soldiers might be expected. However, although a branch of the ultra-nationalistic Fenian Brotherhood (which "hated England with a consuming hatred") was established among Patrick Connor's Irish soldiers at Camp Douglas in 1864, there is no documentary evidence to suggest that the soldiers (as Irishmen) were involved in any specifically anti-English activities among the English population of the Salt Lake Valley.[95] At a later date the centuries of rivalry between Irish Catholics and Protestants was recalled when a Mrs. Creedon, the Irish landlady of a boarding house in Bingham, displayed a sign on her front porch that read "No Orangemen Allowed." The Battle of the Boyne had reached into Bingham Canyon.[96]

[93] "Extracts from the Journal of John Steele," *Utah Historical Quarterly* 6 (1933): 18.

[94] Dwyer, "The Irish in the West," 226.

[95] The quote on Fenian hatred of England is from Alfred L. Burt, *The Evolution of the British Empire and Commonwealth from the American Revolution* (Boston, 1956), p. 372. Dwyer expressed the view that the Fenian group were not politically active in Utah in a letter to the author, January 10, 1975.

[96] This anecdote was related to the author by Helen Z. Papanikolas, Salt Lake City, September 30, 1974.

Although Scots had been in Utah from the earliest days of settlement, it was not until 1876 that a "Scotch Gathering" was organized. In June of that year some two hundred Scots and their "freens wha dinna come frae the Land O'Cakes" gathered at Fuller's Hall in Salt Lake City to hear bagpipes played by W. C. Dunbar and an old veteran of the 42d Highland Regiment and also to participate in the program of Scottish dances, songs, and poetry. Quoting Burns, the *Deseret News* reported that the pipers "screwed their pipes an' gart them skirl, till roof an' rafters a' did dirl." Orson Pratt reminisced about his early missionary work in Scotland, and the assembly, gathering in small knots and responding to the invitation to "sit ye doon mon, an' ye'r crack. . . . reenacted in the forcible word painting of the strong willed Scot, the scenes and circumstances of Auld Lang Syne." [97] Eight years elapsed before a more formal group came into being. In 1884 some "canny Scots" organized a Caledonia Society, the purposes of which were "mental improvement, social enjoyment, healthful recreation, and mutual benefit." Despite its name, however, membership in this Caledonia Society was not confined to Scots; but there is every indication that it *was* an exclusively Mormon group, "Latter-day Saints of any nationality" being eligible for membership.[98]

Another Scottish group was formed as the Caledonia Club in 1892, and its purposes were decidedly more social although not limited to Scots or to Mormons. The meetings, it was announced, would have "Scottish characteristics, but both our American and English friends can enjoy them." [99] Through such institutions as the Thistle Social Club, the Caledonia Football Club, the Scottish Missionary Reunion, Scottish Club, the annual Burns Supper, the Caledonia Pipe Band, the Utah Pipe Band, and the Salt Lake Scots Pipe Band, Utahns of Scottish birth and extraction perpetuated aspects of their unique heritage.[100]

Of all the British immigrants in the United States, the Welsh have been characterized as those who were "the most clannish and

[97] *Deseret News,* June 21, 1876. Note: "June 22" is regarded as the date of the Battle of Bannockburn when Scotland established its independence from England.

[98] *Deseret News,* February 12, 1884.

[99] *Deseret News,* September 20, 1892.

[100] The author is indebted to Archie McNair, an immigrant of 1922, for information concerning Scottish social groups in Salt Lake City. Mr. McNair was "Chief" of the Salt Lake Scottish Club for a total of 25 years. Interview, January 21, 1975.

worked hardest to uphold their national customs and language." [101]
Nationally, the most separate of the British groups, in Utah as in the
nation at large, the Welsh "burned to re-create their folkways." [102]
That they spoke the ancient Welsh language helped promote their
sense of separateness, especially in religious affairs. The use of English,
the language of materialism and secular affairs, in a religious context
was viewed as highly inappropriate, and every attempt was made to
preserve the traditional faith and the language of their fathers.
Mormon recognition of the importance which the Welsh attach to
Cymric (even though most converts were made in the most in-
dustrialized and Anglicized southern region of Wales) was seen in
the production of *Prophwyd y Jubili,* the first non-English Mormon
publication, and in the translation of the Mormon scriptures into
the ancient Welsh tongue. [103]

While the Welsh celebrated Saint David's Day in Salt Lake
City as early as 1852, [104] the re-creation of Welsh folkways was given
its greatest impetus by a mass meeting of Utah's Welsh citizens in
1885 when they assembled in Salt Lake City for a reunion that
concluded with a proposal by Elias Morris to establish in Utah a
"Welsh eisteddfod, an organization peculiar to the Welsh people,
for the development of literary and musical ability." [105] On Saint
David's Day 1893 such a gathering was held at Spanish Fork "to
maintain the Welsh language and customs of the country and to
foster and cultivate a patriotic spirit among the people." The group
was addressed by the Gentile territorial governor, A. L. Thomas,
who, though born in the United States of Welsh parents, regarded
himself a Welshman. [106] In 1895 a formal organization, the Cam-

[101] Oscar Handlin, *A Pictorial History of Immigration* (New York, 1972),
p. 186; Berthoff, *British Immigrants in Industrial America,* p. 183.

[102] Berthoff, *British Immigrants,* p. 172.

[103] Handlin, *A Pictorial History of Immigration,* pp. 145–46; Jenson,
Encyclopedic History, p. 681.

[104] *Salt Lake Tribune,* February 27, 1937. This article recounts the 1852
meeting attended by two hundred fifty immigrants at the home of Daniel
Daniels.

[105] *Deseret News,* August 21, 1885; *Salt Lake Tribune,* August 21, 1885.
The *Deseret News* reported that some eight hundred to one thousand Welsh
gathered at this meeting. The *Tribune* reported three hundred to four hundred.

[106] *Deseret News,* March 2, 1893. The first formal meeting of the "Cambrian Association of Utah" was apparently held in Salt Lake City on March
2, 1891, at which time E. M. Bynon, the president of the association, gave an
address "The Welsh in America." One of the organizers of this "First Annual
Anniversary," William N. Williams, later became president of the group and on
his death in 1927 was described by his fellow Welshmen as "an ardent devotee
of his native land and one who reverently cherished her finest traditions and

brian Society, came into being, and at Spanish Fork ex-governor Thomas was elected its president. A *Deseret News* description of the Spanish Fork *eisteddfod* gives the impression that it was a community affair not just a Welsh reunion:

> St. David's Day is being celebrated here amid great enthusiasm by the largest delegation of Welshmen ever assembled in this Territory. Representatives are in attendance from nearly every county in Utah, Salt Lake in particular, many coming a great distance to participate in the day's festivities. Business is entirely suspended and the principal buildings are beautifully decorated. The Spanish Fork brass band met the visitors and treated them to some excellent music. Promptly at eleven o'clock the exercises of the day commenced.
>
> At two o'clock the Eisteddfod was held and prizes were given for choruses, solos, essays, poetry and instrumentalist. The music was grand, and especially when the vast assemblage sang in unison the Welsh anthem. The afternoon's exercises concluded with addresses from D. L. Davis and W. W. Williams and the carrying out of Welsh customs.
>
> Tonight a concert will be given with short addresses by prominent Welshmen.[107]

Later in 1895, Salt Lake City was the site of a regional *eisteddfod,* and Welsh Americans from Utah and surrounding states came to perpetuate their cultural heritage which, though Welsh in origin, was credited in 1908 with being instrumental in contributing substantially to the literary and musical culture of Utah. An editorial in the *Deseret News* expressed the hope that the Cambrian Society would long be "a blessing to the community." [108]

Perhaps more important than formal organization as far as helping immigrants feel at home in the earlier years were the countless small, informal reunions where old friends could reminisce about the old country and where the natural loneliness of being in a strange, albeit chosen, land would be softened. Loneliness pervaded

loftiest ideals and did much to extend them in the land of his adoption to which *he was even more patriotically devoted as a broad minded and loyal American. . . ."* (emphasis added). A "Resolution of Respect and Sympathy," January 20, 1928, in possession of a granddaughter, Mrs. Evalyn D. Bennett, Salt Lake City, Utah. No matter how much devotion was shown to their native land, it was invariably superseded by loyalty to the United States. Information derived from Saint David's Day Programme, March 2, 1891.

[107] *Deseret News,* March 1, 1895.

[108] *Deseret News,* October 5, 1908.

William Grant when he wrote of the heartbreak he and his wife experienced when one of their children died shortly after their arrival in Utah: "as we did not have relatives nor many friends we were left alone with our dead. There was none but our Neibor came to help us." Longingly, he remembered the happy times in England where he had been a member of a musical group "who shared a fine appreciation of my talent [as a coronet player]." But he brought himself up short in his revery and self-pity when he added ". . . but I must turn from these old Country scenes to real life in the Valleys of the Mountains, the Zion of the Latter days." [109]

James Steele, an Ulster Scot, reminisced that although the first contacts made in Utah were with American and English families, "as the Scotch are considered clannish," he and his friends would get together in the houses of other Scotch immigrants and with William Park at the fiddle, dance traditional Scottish dances to perpetuate the clannishness.[110]

About three months after his arrival, Elijah Larkin held a party for old friends from England and new ones met since his settlement in Utah. At this party a discussion on why they should have come to Utah ensued. According to Larkin, it was agreed that coming to Utah to build up the kingdom of God was the best course for them to have pursued.[111] Larkin may well have had some doubts about his new environment when later he clashed with drunken Camp Douglas soldiers trying to enter the Salt Lake Theatre where he was a guard. A strict law-and-order constable in Oxford, England, he stood his ground in Utah and was subjected to public criticism for refusing to yield. A few days later he personally complained to Brigham Young that he "could not walk up and down the street without being called the Stiff Englishman." According to Larkin's account, Brigham Young "put his hand, very fatherly on my shoulder" and said "if I do not find fault with you you need not mind what others say." [112] Larkin might have rejoiced thirty years later when the *Contributor* published an article in praise of "The Reserved Englishman" who added a sense of stability amid sweeping change.[113]

[109] William Grant Journal, pp. 23, 24, LDS Archives.

[110] "Extracts from Journal of John Steele," *Utah Historical Quarterly* 6 (1933): 22–23.

[111] Elijah Larkin Diary, October 3 and 8, 1863, photocopy of typescript, LDS Archives.

[112] *Ibid.,* October 29, November 4, 1863.

[113] "A Reserved Englishman," *Contributor* 14 (1893): 88–89.

That these early settlers were not as uncomplaining as folklore sometimes would have us believe is indicated in November 1864, when W. C. Staines, an immigrant himself, preached a sermon on "Letter Writing to the Old Country" in the tabernacle. Elijah Larkin recorded that Staines "advised the Saints when they wrote to write the truth and not represent the dark side of the Picture all the time. . . ." As was his wont on many occasions, Brigham Young took issue with Staines and told the assembly to "write just what they liked and paint things as black as they choose and the honest in heart would come anyway." [114]

And some letter writers did indeed portray the bitter side of life in Utah. A Welsh woman writing in 1862 to a friend in Wales confessed that since coming to Utah she had "seen little besides pain, sorrow, darkness and trouble. We are wearing out a miserable existence, anxiously looking for something we may never attain." The dread of polygamy, she said, made her so miserable that at times "I almost wished myself at the bottom of the sea instead of in Utah." [115]

Joseph Harker recalled that many of their meals were thistles and roots and that when his son heard that thistles were the main course, "he would lay down until we had eaten our thistles and then he would go out and play." [116] William Greenwood summed up the year 1855 by saying it would be a year "long remembered by the Saints in the Mountains for destruction of crops and cattle." [117] Joseph Cooper complained of a lack of clothes and food in Cache Valley in 1858, and describing his home of 1872 he said that "when it rained outside, it also rained inside, only raining two or three days after the rain quit." Not enough rain, however, was the problem when Cooper went to Arizona as a colonist and preserved for the future a veritable litany of pioneer failure:

> We planted our grain, but it failed. We planted some peas, they came up fine but all turned yellow and died. We built a dam across the Little Colorado River . . . the dam washed

[114] Larkin Diary, November 20, 1864.

[115] "Jane ——————— in Utah to A ———————," September 16, 1862, in A. Conway, ed., *The Welsh in America: Letters from the Immigrants* (Minneapolis, 1961), p. 318.

[116] Joseph Harker Journal, p. 43, LDS Archives.

[117] Journal of William Greenwood, pp. 24–25, Western Americana, Marriott Library, University of Utah, Salt Lake City.

out and we rebuilt it, and it washed out again. . . . Our crops were a total failure.[118]

Writing to his brother Thomas in Yorkshire in 1854, Stephen Longstrath conveyed to him the high cost of imported items such as cloth, sugar, and tea, adding that they had "maney inderances and hevey taxes it being a new conterey there is a maney roads and bridges to make," but despite these difficulties "we have a plenty of the necereys of life," a common refrain in letters and journals and so poignantly expressed by Alfred Cardon when he records the celebration of Pioneer Day on July 24, 1868: "There was nothing to mar our peace only the thought that the Locust were destroying our crops . . . they eat our clothing as we sat in the Bowery." The next day he mentioned that the locusts had stripped everything, but "what little there was left we were thankful for." [119]

All this, of course, simply says that British immigrants partook of pioneer life and reacted to it not as Britons, but simply as people. The heat, the dry climate, the food, the altitude, the different social system prompted different responses depending perhaps as much on personality as on anything else. Even the dread of polygamy had another side as expressed by Eliza Knowles's letter to her parents in Gloucester, England, in 1856. Inviting her sister to come to Utah she asked her parents to "tell her if she doos believe in Plurality of wives she may have half of my man. Tell her he is a good man and she had better have half of a good man than have hole of a bad one." [120]

The differences the immigrant had to contend with were not always matters of life or death. For instance, in Pennsylvania, en route to Utah from England, William Atkin described his first encounter with a yellow cake eaten with meals. He thought this the "height of American extravigances in very deed" and determined to eat the cake as dessert. One bite of the cake convinced him it was made of sawdust. He commented that he knew then why cornbread was eaten with, rather than after, the meal; it could not be eaten other-

---

[118] "Autobiography of Joseph Cooper," pp. 3, 10, typescript, Utah State Historical Society.

[119] Stephen Longstrath to Thomas Longstrath, May 1, 1854, copy at Utah State Historical Society; Alfred Cardon Journal, July 24, July 25, 1868, LDS Archives.

[120] Eliza Knowles to Mathew Barrett, Sr., 1856, in Kate B. Carter, ed., *Heart Throbs of the West*, 12 vols. (Salt Lake City, 1938–51) 5:421.

wise. Finding it to be called corndodger he "dodged it for a long while after that." [121]

When Christopher Arthur was introduced to Brigham Young in 1853, the president served watermelon, the first Arthur had ever seen, and he "hardly knew how to go to work upon the piece meted out to him." [122] John Jones Davies wrote home to Wales in praise of the variety of food available in his lodgings unlike the "scanty meals of the Old Country" and what is more "Everyone has complete freedom to help themselves. The cook does not put everyone's share in front of him, such an act would be an unforgivable insult." [123]

Davies mentioned that English is the common language of his English, Scottish, Yankee, Irish, French, Welsh, Swiss, Swedish, Danish neighbors in Sugarhouse, but there is a "great deal of difference between the English spoken in America and that in England." [124] Quite apart from differences in meanings, British accents made for different pronunciations of English, too, and "Come, Come Ye Saints" was more likely to sound like "Coom, Coom Ye Synts" when sung by Lancashire immigrants.[125] In the journals and letters of English immigrants one can find traces of the peculiar language idiosyncracies of the English settlers: adding an "h" to some words and dropping it in others. William Blood, who came to the United States when five years old, recorded in 1863 that "Helder Horson Hyde" (Elder Orson Hyde) preached, and in 1872 he referred to "Hangus" (Angus) M. Cannon. Toward the end of his life he was still adding or dropping an "h": he observed the "national oliday" in 1915 and a year later referred to trouble he had with the pain in his "hear" and noted that his daughter had a "hoperation." George Dunford reported that his father had been "hailing" for some years and used "as" for "has" on occasion. George Barber "itched up the ponies" and Joseph Harker complained that Samuel Bennion had lost his wife's "arnice." One might well think that Elijah Larkin had seen a "magic deer" on the stage of

[121] William Atkin, "Autobiography," pp. 18–19, typescript, Utah State Historical Society.

[122] Journal of Christopher J. Arthur, part 1, p. 6, typescript, Utah State Historical Society.

[123] "John Jones Davies at Sugarhouse Ward, Salt Lake City, to Ed." in Conway, *The Welsh in America*, pp. 319–20.

[124] *Ibid.*

[125] An observation made by James Kimball, Jr., in a conversation with the author, June 1974.

the Salt Lake Theatre when he referred to a "Magic Hart" show, if one is not aware that these unforeign foreigners had difficulty with the aspirant "h".[126]

When the parents of Daniel MacIntosh inquired if he could still speak "the Gaelic," he responded, "Would I forget my mother's tongue?" [127] But in fact he had little occasion to use Gaelic as secretary to Brigham Young, and few there were of Gaelic-speaking Highlanders in Utah with whom he could converse. The Scots in Utah were principally Lowlanders, speaking that combination of standard English and Scottish dialect, Lallans, that no doubt sounded foreign enough to untrained ears. James Henderson complained that he had difficulty making Americans understand his Glasgow tongue,[128] a matter of no small wonder when one considers the rolled "r's," broad "a's," and glottal stops so characteristic of Scottish Lowlands speech. Charles Nibley, who was a child when his parents emigrated, claimed that it was easy for him to "talk Scotch and read Scotch." [129] But the theatre critic for the *Daily Union Vedette* in 1863 was disturbed over David McKenzie's accent as a Scottish fisherman in the melodrama *Warlock of the Glen*:

> We have no doubt that his accent was Scotch all over and was rendered in the most natural way. Yet, if he had given us a little more English idiom and a trifle less of Scotch dialect, we think the audience would have been better able to appreciate and understand the good things, which we have no doubt old Andrew said.[130]

"Good plain Scotch" as James Lindsay referred to his native dialect was a minor but yet personally important mark of distinction for the Scot, and even second generation Scots like Joseph H. McPhie of Salt Lake City and Alexander Calderwood of Tremonton could in later years with David O. McKay, Mormon church president, "lapse into a Scottish accent with ease." [131]

[126] Journal of William Blood, 1863, February 25, 1872, July 15, 1915, November 13, 1916, May 22, 1914; George Dunford Journal, p. 38; George Barber Journal, July 13, 1862; Joseph Harker Journal, p. 71; Elijah Larkin Diary, February 6, 1864; all in LDS Archives.

[127] Daniel MacIntosh to his parents, November 22, 1858, holograph, Utah State Historical Society.

[128] Carter, *Heart Throbs*, 12:419.

[129] Nibley, *Reminiscences of Charles W. Nibley*, p. 41.

[130] *Daily Union Vedette*, December 11, 1863.

[131] James Lindsay, "Autobiography," 1863–64, Utah State Historical Society; interview with Joseph McPhie and Alexander Calderwood, 1960; *Aberdeen*

Because Cymric (the language of Wales) is not a dialect of English, like Scottish Lallans or the Irish brogue, the Welsh in Utah had a natural and more secure base from which to maintain their cultural heritage. Through the Cambrian Association and its sponsorship of the *eisteddfod* festivals and *gymanfa ghani* (the hymn-singing festivals) the Welsh immigrants helped perpetuate the ancient language and culture of the Cymri in Utah. According to one account, this ancient Celtic tongue even played a role in the founding of Wales in Sanpete County. Because of their experience as miners in old Wales, John Rees and John Price were called by Brigham Young to open up a coal mine in Sanpete in 1854. While digging at the site shown them by an Indian guide, they were asked to bless a sick Indian chief and, being more fluent in their native tongue than in English, they gave the chief a blessing in Welsh. The chief, recognizing that they did not speak English when praying, informed his followers that these men were good and that "they had talked with the Great Spirit in a new tongue, and made him well." Later when some of the Indians decided to attack the settlers, the Welshmen called in alarm to each other in Welsh and the Indians, thinking that the strange tongue was indeed a sacred language used only in time of need, retreated from the planned annihilation.[132] The Welshmen would probably have agreed that their language was never more sacred to them than at that time.

Utah's Irish, English, Scottish, and Welsh settlers, in uniting with Americans and other immigrants to build their new home and despite pressures to conform, never quite forgot their origins or their native pride.

The religious and social impulses that stimulated the initial massive flow of immigrants from the British Isles to Utah in the nineteenth century have long ceased to be. Zion is no longer regarded in solely geographic terms. A Mormon temple stands on Britain's "green and pleasant land"; and the Mormon church discourages, on pragmatic if not on theological grounds, any sense of gathering to Utah from the "isles of the sea." In addition, the labor of foreign Gentiles is no longer needed to build railroads and to mine Utah's ores. However, though much reduced, the trickle of immigrants has per-

Evening News, August 12, 1953. As the son of British immigrants, David O. McKay was deeply proud of his heritage. He could quote the poetry of Burns and Scott and pronounce Welsh names with facility. The writer toured the Scottish Trossachs with President McKay in 1952.

[132] "Manuscript History of Wales Ward."

sisted during the twentieth century. Although, by 1970 British-born residents in Utah were a meager 2.8 percent of the total population, they were still the largest immigrant group in the state, comprising 23 percent of the foreign-born population. Through the contributions of such scholars as Dr. Arthur Beeley, the founder of the University of Utah's School of Social Work, artists like Alvin Gittins, skilled tradesmen such as James S. Campbell, or teachers like the Irish Catholic Sisters of Saint Vincent's School in Salt Lake City, immigrants from the British Isles have continued to enhance Utah's social, cultural, and economic fabric.

At this point the historian of immigrant contributions may be tempted to engage in speculation as to the decisive difference that any one group, or for that matter, any one person, made to America's and Utah's development. Did it really make a significant difference to Utah's educational development that for a large part of its first forty years its schools were under the superintendency of a Scot, Robert L. Campbell, who urged free schools and criticized the easygoing attitude which the populace had toward improved education for their children? Or has Utah's educational development been significantly influenced in the long run by two-thirds of the eighteen county superintendents in 1868 being of British birth and education?[133] Was it decisive when immigrant Peter Lochrie, a Gentile, was elected prosecuting attorney in Beaver Couny rather than some other person?[134] Probably not—if Campbell had not been superintendent, others would have undoubtedly urged free schools. Again, Lochrie was not the only Gentile in Beaver and perhaps a Mormon bishop would have served the community as well. When Utah's electorate chose John Cutler and William Spry, both native Englishmen, to be the state's governors between 1905 and 1917, they were undoubtedly influenced more by the candidates' political capability than by their particular nationality.[135] The prominent position occupied by Britons in Utah is more a function of their numerical majority than any intellectual or social superiority.

Ultimately, one is driven to the realization that it is human beings who accomplish what nationalities are credited with. Al-

---

[133] Robert L. Campbell, *Annual Report of the Territorial Superintendent of Common Schools for the year 1868* (Salt Lake City, 1868).

[134] *Biographical Record*, p. 217.

[135] William L. Roper and Leonard J. Arrington, *William Spry: Man of Firmness, Governor of Utah* (Salt Lake City, 1971), pp. 62, 67–102; L. H. Kirkpatrick, ed., *Know Your Utah and Its Governors* (Salt Lake City, n.d.), pp. 34–35.

though native pride may not be sufficient to explain the British contribution to Utah, it is a necessary component in any assessment of Utah's people and institutions. Through maintenance of their cultural heritage these British immigrants were able to relate to their new environment not as a dispossessed and helpless minority but as a relatively powerful, "imperial" minority. Neither completely assimilated nor yet entirely segregated, they shaped the character of Utah's history and development through daily toil, leadership, faith, dissent, and diversity.

In celebrating the exploits of the "great" men and women, there may be a tendency to neglect the daily ploddings of common British people in Utah who, because they were in a particular place at a particular time, became an essential element in Utah's development from a religious colony to a modern state. When Jacob Peart, a British settler of 1847, died in 1914, it was said of him that he "led an honorable, unassuming life and leaves a large family," [136] a tribute that could be extended to the thousands of unsung common contributors who are

> . . . the caldron and reservoir
> Of the human reserves that shape history.[137]

---

[136] *Deseret News,* June 25, 1914.

[137] Carl Sandburg, "The People Speak," *The People, Yes* (New York, 1936).

3 BLACKS IN UTAH HISTORY: AN UNKNOWN LEGACY

BY RONALD G. COLEMAN

This essay is gratefully dedicated to Mary Lucille Perkins Bankhead, a descendant of three Black pioneer families and related through marriage to others. She has contributed greatly to this writer's research and to that of others in quest of the role of Blacks in Utah history.

The history of Blacks in Utah is a microcosm of the history of Blacks in the United States. Black experience in Utah began during the exploration and fur-trapping period. James P. Beckwourth, a mulatto whose mother may have been a slave, is the best known Black of this period. A trapper for the Rocky Mountain Fur Company, guide, Indian fighter, and hunter, Beckwourth is a legendary figure in this early history of the Far West. He was a participant in the Seminole and Mexican War, the California gold rush, and for several years lived with the Crow Indians.

Beckwourth came to Utah between 1824 and 1826. For several years he traveled in and out of Cache Valley and the Salt Lake-Ogden areas trapping, hunting, and exploring. Among his comrades were Jim Bridger, Kit Carson, James Clyman, William Sublette, and Jedediah Smith. Fortunately for historians, Beckwourth left a record of his life and adventures; in addition to providing information about his life, the work gives valuable detail about the history of the Far West. Scholars have disagreed as to the veracity of parts of Beckwourth's autobiography. In keeping with the tradition of mountain men, Beckwourth was known to stretch the truth, especially when glorifying his own accomplishments. The main faults of his autobiography were due to lapses of memory and misuse of statistics.[1]

[1] James P. Beckwourth, *The Life and Adventures of James P. Beckwourth,* ed. Thomas Bonner; new introduction and epilogue by D. R. Oswald (Lincoln, Nebr., 1972), introduction, vii–xiii, pp. 541–43.

As historian Hubert Howe Bancroft wrote:

> Beckwourth was by no means a bad man, though he had his faults, the greatest of which was being born too late. He should have swum the Scamander after Grecian horses, captured Ajax when calling for light, or scalped Achilles in his tent. Then had not been denied him the honor of dying like a Roman on his shield in a lightning of lances, or a storm of Blackfoot braves.[2]

Other Blacks were in Utah at approximately the same time as Beckwourth, long before Mormon settlement. One adventurer, Jacob Dodson, was a member of two of John C. Fremont's expeditions into Utah and other parts of the West between 1843 and 1847. Dodson was about eighteen years old when he volunteered to accompany the Fremont expedition. The financial report of the exploration lists him as a voyager and shows payment of $493 for his services between May 3, 1843, and September 6, 1844. Fremont said Jacob Dodson "performed his duty manfully throughout the voyage."[3]

Blacks, therefore, were in Utah almost a quarter of a century before the arrival of the Mormons in 1847; however, permanent Black settlement began with the pioneers and established the foundation for today's Black community. Approximately one hundred fifty descendants of the early Black pioneers presently live in Utah.[4]

Three Black men entered Utah with the initial Mormon pioneer group. Folk tradition says that Green Flake drove the wagon that brought Brigham Young into the valley. Oscar Crosby and Hark Lay also appear in various historical works on the pioneers. Their names are engraved along with those of other first pioneers on a tablet on the Brigham Young Monument at the intersection of Main and South Temple streets in Salt Lake City.[5]

Except for these three men, the Black pioneers of Utah have remained relatively anonymous in the annals of Utah history. Black pioneers were both slave and free, Mormon and non-Mormon.

---

[2] *Ibid.,* p. 628.

[3] *The Expeditions of John Charles Fremont,* ed. Donald Jackson and Mary Lee Spence, 2 vols. (Chicago, 1970) 1:383, 388, 427–28.

[4] Interview with Mary Lucille Perkins Bankhead, August 1974.

[5] Andrew Jenson, *Latter-day Saints Biographical Encyclopedia,* 4 vols. (Salt Lake City, 1901–36), 4:703. The names are listed separately from other pioneers and appear under the heading "colored servants." The three men were slaves of southern converts to the LDS church.

They shared the experiences of journeying to a new land and participating in its settlement and subsequent development.

The 1850 Census of Utah Territory indicates the presence of fifty Blacks in Utah. Of this number, twenty-four are listed as free and twenty-six as slaves.[6] In most instances census schedules do not include the names of those Blacks in bondage. However, the 1850 Census of Utah Territory lists the names of Blacks in bondage and notes they were enroute to California.[7] Thus, one might be led to believe that with the removal of those twenty-six individuals, Utah's slave population was eliminated. This is inaccurate; the 1860 Census indicates the presence of fifty-nine Blacks in Utah, twenty-nine of whom were slaves.[8] The Utah territorial legislature in 1852 had passed a law that recognized the legality of slavery in the territory.[9] Acceptance of Black bondage in Utah began with the settlement of Mormon pioneers in 1847 and became illegal when the United States Congress abolished slavery in the territories in June 1862.[10] While there is evidence of some masters emancipating their slaves before 1862, it appears that the majority did so only after slavery was abolished by law.

Mormon masters had come from the South and leaving there brought some of their slaves with them.[11] Black slaves also accompanied non-Mormons to Utah.[12] The exact number of Black slaves in Utah is unknown; some pioneer companies did not differentiate between slaves and free Blacks.[13] In addition, the census report of 1850 is incorrect in reporting the number of Blacks, free or slave in the Utah territory.[14]

[6] 1850 Census.

[7] *Ibid.* Microfilm copies of the holograph schedules are available at Marriott Library, University of Utah, and Utah State Historical Society, both in Salt Lake City.

[8] 1860 Census.

[9] "An Act in Relation to Service" in Utah Territory, Legislative Assembly, *Acts Resolutions and Memorials* (Salt Lake City, 1852), pp. 80–82.

[10] Alfred H. Kelley and Winfred A. Harbison, *The American Constitution: Its Origins and Development* (New York, 1970), p. 433.

[11] Kate B. Carter, *The Story of the Negro Pioneer* (Salt Lake City, 1965), pp. 17–26.

[12] *Ibid.,* pp. 47–48.

[13] O. D. Flake, *William J. Flake, Pioneer-Colonizer* (Salt Lake City, 1948), pp. 10–11.

[14] A comparison of the Utah census schedules of 1850 and 1860 indicates that several of the Blacks listed as free in the 1850 Census were slaves and that the slaves living in Bountiful, Utah, were not included in the census.

There is more information about Green Flake, one of the three Blacks accompanying the initial pioneer group into Utah, than there is about either Oscar Crosby or Hark Lay. This is largely because of his residing in Utah longer than they did. Crosby and Lay were members of a group of slaves taken to San Bernardino, California, in 1851 by Mormon masters who went to colonize the area.[15] Because California law prohibited slavery, the Blacks became free.[16]

Green Flake was the slave of James M. Flake, a southerner who had moved from North Carolina to Mississippi. In 1843 James Flake and his family joined the Mormon church, and shortly thereafter he sold or emancipated the majority of his slaves and moved to the Mormon settlement in Nauvoo, Illinois.[17] Flake took Green and Liz, a young Black girl who was Mrs. Agnes Flake's personal maid, to Nauvoo with the family. As the Mormon pioneers made preparations for the journey to Salt Lake in 1847, James Flake sent Green to help Brigham Young's pioneer company on the journey.[18] Green helped the pioneers in planting crops and building homes. Then he returned east with others to aid the Mormon immigrants coming west. Between 1848 and 1850 Green married Martha Crosby and became the father of two children, Lucinda and Abraham. For a while Green Flake worked for Brigham Young, and by 1860 he had acquired property and was living with his family in Union, Utah. Although he moved to Idaho in 1885, he continued to correspond with his friends in Utah and journeyed to Salt Lake to participate in the pioneer celebration of 1897. When Green died, his body was returned to Utah for burial next to Martha in the Union cemetery.[19]

Among the Blacks coming to Utah with Mormon pioneers at least three families were known to be free. The James family arrived in Salt Lake in 1847 and consisted of Isaac and Jane along with their children, Sylvester and Silas. Jane Manning James was the matriarch of Utah's early Black community. She and her

[15] Andrew L. Neff, *History of Utah: 1847–1869*, ed. Leland H. Creer (Salt Lake City, 1940), p. 219; 1850 Census.

[16] Eugene Brewer, *The Frontier Against Slavery; Western Anti-Negro Prejudice and the Slavery Extension Controversy* (Urbana, Ill., 1967), p. 65.

[17] Flake, *William J. Flake*, pp. 3–12.

[18] "Pioneers of 1847—A Collective Narrative," manuscript, Archives Division, Historical Department, Church of Jesus Christ of Latter-day Saints, Salt Lake City. This narrative was compiled from several pioneer journals.

[19] Carter, *Negro Pioneer*, pp. 5–7.

brother, Isaac Manning, had lived and worked in the Nauvoo home of Joseph Smith, the founder of the Mormon church.[20] Although Isaac Manning did not arrive in Salt Lake until 1893, both he and his sister Jane were accorded a special status within the local community.[21]

After the James family settled in Salt Lake, they went into farming. Although they were far from being financially secure, by 1865 the family's real estate and personal property were valued at $1,100.[22] Sylvester James, the oldest of the children, was listed in 1861 as a member of the Nauvoo Legion and was in possession of his ten pounds of ammunition and musket. He later married Mary Perkins and was a successful farmer. Sylvester James is the only Black listed in Frank Esshom's *Pioneers and Prominent Men of Utah.*[23]

The financial success of Isaac and Jane did not prevent them from having personal difficulties, and by 1870 they had separated. Only two of her seven children outlived her, and many of her grandchildren died at an early age. Despite her difficulties, Jane Manning James maintained her poise and self-respect. When she died in 1908, newspapers noted her death and President Joseph Fielding Smith spoke at her funeral.[24]

In 1847 a mulatto named Elijah Abel and his family journeyed to Utah with other Mormons. Abel had been baptized in September of 1832, ordained an elder in the Melchizedek priesthood on March 3, 1836, and made a member of the Nauvoo Seventies Quorum in 1839. His membership certificate was renewed in 1841 in Nauvoo and again in Salt Lake City. The Abels also lived in Ogden for a short time. A carpenter by trade, Abel contributed his work to the building of the Mormon temple in Salt Lake City where he and his wife Mary Ann managed the Farnham Hotel. Almost forty years after arriving in Utah, Abel went on a mission for his church to Canada, proselytizing in the United States on the way. A year later,

[20] Henry J. Wolfinger, "A Test of Faith: Jane Elizabeth James and the Origin of the Utah Black Community," research paper, 1972, pp. 2–7, 19–22, LDS Archives.

[21] Carter, *Negro Pioneers*, pp. 9–13.

[22] Wolfinger, "Jane Elizabeth James," p. 5.

[23] Frank Esshom, *Pioneers and Prominent Men of Utah* (Salt Lake City, 1913), p. 85.

[24] Wolfinger, "Jane Elizabeth James," pp. 6–9, 10; Carter, *Negro Pioneer,* p. 11.

in 1884, he returned and died shortly afterwards "in full faith of the gospel." [25]

Fredrick Sion, a mulatto from England, came to Utah in 1862. Along with his wife, Ellen, and daughter, Eliza, Sion sailed on the ship *William Tapscott* which arrived in New York in June 1862. The family then made the long journey to Utah and settled in Millville where Sion continued to work as a shoemaker. Three more children had been born by 1870.[26]

The treatment of Black slaves in Utah can be seen in "An Act in Relation to Service." Approved in 1852, the law recognized the legality of slavery and clearly explained the responsibilities of both the slave and slave master.

Slave holders coming into the territory were required to file evidence of lawful bondage with the probate court, and any transfer of slaves to another master or removal of them from the territory required court approval and the consent of the slaves themselves. Four sections of the act dealt with the issues of miscegenation; food, clothing, and shelter; punishment; and education:

> Sec. 4. That if any master or mistress shall have sexual or carnal intercourse with his or her servant or servants of the African race, he or she shall forfeit all claim to said servant or servants to the commonwealth; and if any white person shall be guilty of sexual intercourse with any of the African race, they shall be subject, on conviction thereof to a fine of not exceeding one thousand dollars, nor less than five hundred, to the use of the Territory, and imprisonment, not exceeding three years.

> Sec. 5. It shall be the duty of masters or mistresses, to provide for his, her, or their servants comfortable habitations, clothing, bedding, sufficient food, and recreation. And it shall be the duty of the servant in return therefor, to labor faithfully all reasonable hours, and do such service with fidelity as may be required by his, or her master or mistress.

> Sec. 6. It shall be the duty of the master to correct and punish his servant in a reasonable manner when it may be necessary, being guided by prudence and humanity; and if he shall be guilty of cruelty or abuse, or neglect to feed,

[25] Lester E. Bush Jr., "Mormonism's Negro Doctrine: An Historical Overview," *Dialogue: A Journal of Mormon Thought* 8 (1973): 16–17. Jenson, *Biographical Encyclopedia*, 3:577. Notes taken from Elijah Abel File, LDS Archives.

[26] "Pioneer Emigrants From Europe," microfilm, LDS Archives; 1870 Census.

clothe, or shelter his servants in a proper manner, the Probate Court may declare the contract between master and servant or servants void, according to the provisions of the fourth section of this act.

Sec. 9. It shall further be the duty of all masters or mistresses, to send their servant or servants to school, not less than eighteen months between the ages of six years and twenty years.[27]

The seeming benevolence contained in certain parts of the act when compared with similar legislation in regards to Indian slavery demonstrates a higher regard for Indians than for people of African descent. The preamble to "An Act for the Relief of Indian Slaves and Prisoners" says the act ". . . will be most conducive to ameliorate their condition, preserve their lives, and their liberties, and redeem them from a worse than African bondage. . . ."[28] Furthermore, the masters of Indians were obligated to send Indians between the ages of seven and sixteen to school three months of each year if a school was within the area of residence.[29] Finally, the restrictions against sexual relations between all Blacks and whites were not applicable to Indians; some Mormons were induced to take Indian wives in the early period of colonization. That both acts were adopted within a month of each other shows a greater aversion to people of African descent.[30]

Slave owners also had no reservations about selling their slaves, and the local courts recognized the right of a slave owner to secure his property. The legality of such transactions is attested to by numerous examples. Alexander Bankhead was originally brought to Utah by George and John Bankhead and later purchased by Abraham O. Smoot and taken to Provo.[31] Marinda Redd, who later became the wife of Alexander Bankhead, initially journeyed to Spanish Fork with John Hardison Redd, his family, and five other Black slaves.[32] Later she became the property of Dr. Pinney, a resident of

---

[27] "An Act in Relation to Service," pp. 80–82.

[28] "A Preamble and an Act for the Further Relief of Indian Slaves and Prisoners," in *Acts, Resolutions, and Memorials*, pp. 93–95.

[29] *Ibid.*

[30] *Ibid.*, pp. 82, 94.

[31] *Broad Ax*, March 25, 1899. Alexander and Marinda Bankhead, former slaves, were interviewed by Julius Taylor, owner and publisher of the *Broad Ax*, a Black newspaper.

[32] Carter, *The Negro Pioneer*, pp. 25–26.

Salem, Utah.[33] In August 1859 "Dan," a twenty-six-year-old Black man was sold by Thomas S. Williams to William H. Hooper. Williams had purchased Dan a year earlier from Williams Washington Camp for $800.[34] Perhaps the reason for Williams Camp selling Dan arose from a court case in June 1856. Camp was accused of kidnapping Dan, who earlier had run away from him. Upon proving that Dan was his slave, Camp was acquitted of the kidnapping charge.[35]

An 1899 editorial in the Salt Lake City Black newspaper, the *Broad Ax*, records the reminiscences of two Black pioneers, Alex Bankhead who arrived from Alabama in 1848 and his wife who was born in North Carolina and came to Utah in 1850.

> She was the property of a gentleman by the name of Redd. She, in company with a number of other slaves, were on their way to Utah; and while passing through the State of Kansas, during the dark hours of the night, the majority of them made good their escape, which was a great loss to their owner. But Mrs. Bankhead was not so successful in that direction, and she was brought on to Utah. . . . They both have a very distinct recollection of the joyful expressions which were upon the faces of all the slaves when they ascertained that they had acquired their freedom through the fortunes of war. At that time many negroes, according to Mr. Bankhead's statement, "Left Salt Lake City and other sections of the Territory, for California and other states". . . . He informed us that when this city was in its infancy, the slaves always congregated in a large room or hall on State street almost opposite the city and county building. There they would discuss their condition, and gaze in wonderment at the lofty mountains, which reared their snowy peaks heavenward, and completely forbade them from ascertaining how they could make their escape back to the South, or to more congenial climes. For we were assured that their lives in the then new wilderness, was far from being happy, and many of them were subjected to the same treatment that was accorded the plantation negroes of the South. Mr. and Mrs. Bankhead now own a little home, including twenty acres of land. They are both devout and strict Mormons.[36]

[33] *Broad Ax*, March 25, 1899.

[34] Carter, *The Negro Pioneer*, pp. 42–43.

[35] Dennis L. Lythgoe, "Negro Slavery in Utah," *Utah Historical Quarterly* 39(1971): 41–42.

[36] *Broad Ax*, March 25, 1899. The city and county building referred to was the old City Hall located on First South near State Street.

The interest of slaves in the progress of the Civil War and what the outcome might mean for their condition is shown by Sam Bankhead's continuing desire for news from the East. He was heard to comment, "My God, I hope de Souf get licked." [37] For many slaves the wish for freedom did not imply negative feelings toward their masters. Freedom meant that they could be their own masters.

Although many former slaves left the area, others remained in Utah and together with the early free Black residents and new arrivals sought to elevate and improve their condition in Utah. These people intermarried and lived in close proximity to one another in Union, the east Millcreek area, and the Eighth LDS Ward, now called Central City. [38]

The completion of the transcontinental railroad in 1869 and the expansion of railroads from Utah to other states greatly improved the economic opportunities for individual investors and corporate concerns. Not only did the railroads profit but the improved transportation network was valuable to mining and agricultural interests. Black workers, like other Americans east of the Missouri, responded to new employment opportunities with the railroads.

During this post-Reconstruction period, Black involvement in the settlement of the West continued in earnest—the awareness of its extent is but a recent addition to western history. The Black cowboy quickly became myth. There were at least two Blacks who worked the range in the Brown's Hole area on the Utah, Wyoming, and Colorado borders. Albert "Speck" (because of his freckles) Williams operated a ferry on the Green River. [39] Isom Dart, known primarily as a cattle rustler, was an outstanding bronco-buster. "I have seen all the great riders," a westerner said in William Katz's *The Black West,* "but for all around skill as a cowman, Isom Dart was unexcelled. . . . He could outride any of them; but never entered a contest." [40]

[37] Charles W. Nibley, *Reminiscences: 1849–1931* (Salt Lake City, 1934), pp. 35–36.

[38] Wolfinger, "Jane Elizabeth James," pp. 12–15.

[39] Charles Kelly, *The Outlaw Trail: A History of Butch Cassidy and his Wild Bunch,* rev. ed. (New York, 1959), pp. 320–22.

[40] William Loren Katz, *The Black West: A Documentary and Pictorial History,* rev. ed. (Garden City, N.Y., 1973), p. 158.

James P. Beckwourth, the
legendary Black mountain
man explored and trapped in
Utah in the 1820s. He became
a leader among the Crow
Indians and later published a
vivid account of his adventures.

124

Folklore says Green Flake, opposite, drove Brigham Young's wagon into Salt Lake Valley in 1847. Shown are five generations of his descendants. Opposite: Martha J. Perkins Howell, granddaughter; Lucinda Flake Stevens, daughter; Belle Oglesby, granddaughter. Above: Martha J. Perkins Howell, granddaughter; Mary Lucille Perkins Bankhead, great granddaughter; Ruth Jackson, great great granddaughter; Juanita Spillman, great great great granddaughter, now the mother of a sixth generation.

Right: Isom Dart, cowboy in the Brown's Hole area. Amanada Leggroan Chambers and her husband, Samuel D. Chambers, came to Utah in 1870.

Right: *William James, son of Mary Ann and Sylvester James, posed with his uncle, Sylvester Perkins, standing.* Below: *Black pioneer Mary Ann Perkins James was a sister of Sylvester Perkins and the wife of Sylvester James, a member of the Nauvoo Legion and son of Jane Manning James. Fashionable Lottie Campbell was a sister of Sylvester Perkins and Mary Ann James.*

Below: *Don Freeman Bankhead was the first freeborn Black in Utah, his middle name proudly stating his status.*

126

Right: *Detective Paul Cephas Howell served on the police force for more than twenty years.* Above: *Chaplain Allan Allensworth was stationed at Fort Douglas with the Twenty-Fourth Infantry.* Below: *Black veterans of the Spanish-American War return to Utah.*

From the top: *Frederic Remington traveled with
the Black cavalry and in 1889 published his drawings
of them, including this campfire scene, in* Century
Magazine. *Church group posed in 1963 with the
Reverend Thomas J. Townsend of Trinity African
Methodist Episcopal Church. The Reverend David D.
Wilson of Trinity AME Church in 1975.*

From the top: *The Esquire Club, ca. 1946,
at the White City Ballroom, Ogden. Albert Fritz
presented annual Civil Rights Worker Award,
given in his honor, to Alberta Henry at NAACP
banquet in 1971. NAACP leaders James Dooley
of Salt Lake City and Roy Wilkins of the
national office visited in 1971. Robert E. Freed,
posthumously honored by the Salt Lake City
NAACP for his efforts to desegregate entertainment
facilities before civil rights legislation.*

129

Despite his reputation for stealing cattle, Isom Dart appears to have been a man of character. Joe Philbrick, a deputy sheriff from Wyoming, went to Brown's Hole to arrest Dart on suspicion of cattle rustling. While returning to Rock Springs, Philbrick was badly injured in an accident. Rather than escaping, Isom gave Philbrick what help he could and returned him to Rock Springs. After leaving Philbrick in the hospital, he turned himself in to the local authorities. At his trial Philbrick appeared as a character witness, the charges were dropped, and Isom returned to Brown's Hole.[41]

Another Black cowboy, and one of the few to leave an account of his life on the trail, was Nat Love. His autobiography is titled *The Life and Adventures of Nat Love: Better known in the Cattle Country as "Deadwood Dick."* On his retirement from the cowboy trail, Deadwood Dick worked as a porter for the Pullman service. For a period in the 1890s he lived with his family in Salt Lake City.[42]

In the last quarter of the nineteenth century the military brought many Blacks to Utah. In 1869 Congress created two Black infantry regiments and two Black cavalry regiments. All four of these units saw action in the West for over thirty years after the Civil War.[43] Three of the four units, the Ninth Cavalry, the Twenty-fourth Infantry, and the Twenty-fifth Infantry served in Utah.[44] To the Indians, the short wool-like hair of the Black soldiers resembled the shaggy mane of the buffalo. Hence, the Indians called the Black soldiers of the Ninth and Tenth cavalries the "buffalo soldiers." [45]

Because of difficulties with Ute Indians, authorities in Washington decided to establish a military post on the Uintah frontier. The post was named Fort Duchesne, and in 1886 two troops of the Ninth Cavalry arrived with four companies of infantry to man the fort. In addition to building the post, the soldiers were charged with protecting and controlling the Indian populations of eastern Utah, western Colorado, and southwestern Wyoming. The Black soldiers were stationed at Fort Duchesne for approximately twelve

[41] Philip Durham and Everett L. Jones, *The Negro Cowboys* (New York, 1965), pp. 185–86.

[42] *Ibid.,* pp. 203–5; Byrdie Howell Langon, *Utah and the Early Black Settlers* (Los Angeles, 1969), pp. 31–32.

[43] Jack D. Foner, *Blacks and the Military in American History* (New York, 1974), pp. 52–55.

[44] Michael J. Clark, "A History of the Twenty-fourth United States Infantry Regiment 1896–1899" research paper, University of Utah History Department, 1974, p. 12.

[45] Durham and Jones, *Negro Cowboys,* p. 10.

years. With the outbreak of the Spanish-American War in 1898, members of the Ninth Cavalry were sent to Mobile, Alabama, to prepare for the journey to Cuba.[46] Some members of the Ninth Cavalry were sent to Salt Lake City's Fort Douglas in June 1899.

The placement of members of the Ninth Cavalry at Fort Douglas in 1899 was not the first time Black soldiers had been stationed at the fort. In October 1896 the Twenty-fourth Infantry arrived for duty there. For the first time in history, the United States Army had stationed a Black unit in an area with a substantial Black population within a large white population. Before this, Black soldiers had been stationed in isolated areas. With all of the companies intact, the number of men in the Twenty-fourth Infantry was approximately four hundred fifty. The members of the Twenty-fourth regiment were elated when they first learned of the transfer to Fort Douglas. Having spent many years in the Arizona-New Mexico region, the men wanted a more pleasant location. Fort Douglas, at the time, was considered an ideal location by all soldiers, Black and white.

The joy of the Black soldiers was not shared by many of Salt Lake's white residents. The *Salt Lake Tribune* and Sen. Frank J. Cannon did everything possible to persuade officials in Washington not to send Black soldiers to Fort Douglas. An editorial in the *Tribune* questioned the character of Black soldiers and suggested that under the influence of liquor Black soldiers might become aggressive in the presence of white women.[47] The *Tribune* and Cannon failed to change the minds of Washington officials. As members of the Twenty-fourth prepared to come to Fort Douglas, a letter written by Pvt. Thomas A. Ernest, of Company E, Twenty-fourth Infantry, appeared in the *Salt Lake Tribune:*

> The enlisted men of the Twenty-Fourth infantry, as probably the people of Salt Lake City know, are negroes. . . . They have enlisted to uphold the honor and dignity of their country as their fathers enlisted to found and preserve it. . . .
>
> We object to being classed as lawless barbarians. We were men before we were soldiers, we are men now, and will continue to be men after we are through soldiering. We ask the people of Salt Lake to treat us as such." [48]

[46] Thomas G. Alexander and Leonard J. Arrington, "The Utah Military Frontier, 1872–1912, Forts Cameron, Thornburgh and Duchesne," *Utah Historical Quarterly* 32 (1964) : 344–52.

[47] Clark, "The Twenty-fourth Infantry," pp. 14–16, 19, 21.

[48] Foner, *Blacks and the Military,* pp. 70–71.

Within a relatively short time, the members of the Twenty-fourth developed close ties with the Salt Lake City community. Black and white citizens were entertained and impressed by the Twenty-fourth's "outstanding band, . . . crack drilling and the ability of many of its members in athletics, both track and baseball." Chaplain Allan Allensworth, one of two Black chaplains in the United States Army at the time, was impressive. College educated and urbane, he sought to aid the members of the regiment in improving their educational skills and emphasized the importance of the soldiers' maintaining good conduct. In addition, Allensworth was active in local affairs. On December 21, 1896, he met with Mormon church president Wilford Woodruff who welcomed the members of the Twenty-fourth Infantry to Salt Lake City.

During the Spanish-American War members of the Twenty-fourth saw duty in both Cuba and the Philippine Islands. Many Salt Lake and Provo residents, Black and white, turned out to bid them farewell when they left and a joyful welcome upon their return to Salt Lake. Upon completion of their duty in the Philippine Islands, the companies of the Twenty-fourth were dispersed to different parts of the United States.[49] Several of the soldiers liked their experience at Fort Douglas and eventually made Salt Lake City their permanent residence.[50]

Since the turn of the century a majority of Utah Blacks have lived in the cities of Salt Lake and Ogden. Employment opportunities for Blacks have been greater in these cities and their surrounding areas. Despite the tendency of Blacks to settle in urban centers, wherever employment opportunities existed in other parts of the state, Black workers willingly moved there. In the period between 1920 and 1930, Carbon and Emery counties had a number of Blacks working in the coal mines and other related industrial activities.[51] The Black population in these areas declined when employment was reduced.

For many years the majority of Blacks residing in Salt Lake and Weber counties were primarily employed in domestic and personal services for the civilian population. When Ogden became the railroad center for the Union Pacific, Southern Pacific, and other railroads, many Blacks, both local and new arrivals, found work. Rail-

[49] Clark, "The Twenty-fourth Infantry," pp. 22, 25, 33–35.

[50] Carter, *The Negro Pioneer*, pp. 71–73.

[51] George Ramjoue, "The Negro In Utah: A Geographical Study in Population" (M.A. thesis, University of Utah, 1968), pp. 19–21, 71–73.

roads advertised widely for men to fill their various labor needs. Word was sent out through newspapers, by word-of-mouth, by correspondence between relatives and friends, and through cards handed out on streets by railroad agents. "Wanted 1,000 Men" the cards read, with the address of the railroad's hiring office underneath the words. Between 1890 and 1940, the railroad was the most important employer of Blacks. Some of them worked in railroad roundhouses and on construction crews, but Blacks were mainly porters, cooks, and waiters for the railroads' hotel and restaurant services.[52] Fantley Jones, a forty-year resident of Ogden, recalls that he was living in Oklahoma when he received a letter from a cousin telling him that the Union Pacific railroad needed men, and if he could get to Kansas City, a ticket and job would be waiting for him. "I sold a calf and used the money to get to Kansas City," Jones said. In Kansas City, Jones was hired as a cook by the railroad's local agent, a man named Beanland, and put aboard a train to Ogden. Jones began learning his job on the way and remained as a cook for the Union Pacific until he retired in 1969.[53]

The influx of Black railroad workers required hotel and restaurant facilities, because white-owned services were barred to Blacks. In Salt Lake City, near the railyards, several hotels, restaurants, and clubs, such as the Porters and Waiters Club, were operated by Blacks. Blacks in Ogden also provided similar services near the Union Pacific depot. Lonnie Davis and his wife owned the Royal Hotel where Blacks, temporarily in the area, stayed. Billy Weekly managed the Porters and Waiters Club.

Railroads, the military, and military-related activities influenced the further growth of Utah's Black community. World War II with its increased number of military camps and defense plants provided employment for Blacks at Hill Air Force Base in Ogden, the Dugway Proving Grounds in Tooele, and other military installations in Utah.[54]

Blacks in Utah, like Blacks in many states, were excluded from participating in the general social and cultural life and consequently developed their own churches, fraternal organizations, a literary club, a press, and a community center. Blacks have participated on

[52] Interviews with Fantley Jones, February 1974, and William Gregory, August 1974. Mr. Gregory arrived in Salt Lake City in 1913. He worked as a Pullman porter for over forty years.

[53] Jones interview.

[54] *Ibid.*

semi-professional baseball teams, sponsored by state industries since the early 1900s. (The Leggroan brothers are remembered as outstanding players of the 1920s. A teammate of one of the brothers on the Denver and Rio Grande Western team recalls, "He was a fine player and a gentleman. When we went out of town, he didn't come with us." [55] The inference was that he would not cause embarrassment to the team by being refused service in restaurants and hotels.)

In the 1890s Trinity African Methodist Episcopal Church was the first Black church to be established and Calvary Baptist Church was founded shortly afterward. Both of these churches were located in Salt Lake City. Early in the century Wall Street Baptist Church was founded in Ogden. [56]

Black newspapers were first published in Utah during the late 1890s. The *Democratic Headlight,* published by J. Gordon McPherson, appeared briefly in 1899. The *Tri City Oracle* was published for a few years by Rev. James W. Washington, pastor of the Calvary Baptist Church. The two most interesting Black papers were the *Utah Plain Dealer,* published by William W. Taylor, and the *Broad Ax,* published by Julius Taylor. The *Broad Ax* was discontinued in 1899 when Julius Taylor moved to Chicago. The *Plain Dealer* continued to appear until 1909. [57] The two editors were continually arguing through their respective papers over which publication truly represented the best interests of the Black race. William Taylor supported the Republican party and Julius Taylor, surprisingly, supported the Democratic party. [58] Besides waging their private war, both editors sought to inform the community of local and national news.

Every year the Black community celebrated Emancipation Day. The sponsor of this event was the Abraham Lincoln Club, a Black

[55] Interview with Nick Papanikolas, March 12, 1975, who recalled this information from a previous talk with Lee Brown, Denver and Rio Grande Western ballplayer of the 1920s, and Claude Engberg, president of the Pioneer Baseball League for many years.

[56] Wolfinger, "Jane Elizabeth James," p. 15. Interview with Rev. Frances Davis, minister of Calvary Baptist Church, December 1974, Salt Lake City.

[57] J. Cecil Alter, *Early Utah Journalism* (Salt Lake City, 1938), pp. 274, 330, 390.

[58] *Broad Ax,* September 14, 1895. The majority of Blacks in the United States during this period supported the Republican party. The party of Abraham Lincoln had ended slavery and made an issue of Black rights during Reconstruction.

Republican organization.[59] The Democratic counterpart was the Salt Lake Colored Political Club.[60] Several of the old Black Mormon pioneers participated in the annual Old Folks Day celebration. There would be an annual free excursion to some point in the area for them.[61] Many Blacks would turn out to watch and some took part in the celebration of the "Days of Forty-seven." [62]

Blacks formed local lodges of the Odd Fellows and Elks. The Ladies Civic and Study Club of Salt Lake City, the Camelia Arts and Crafts Club, and the Nimble Thimble Club were three Black women's groups. The Nimble Thimble Club was responsible for initiating the idea of building a community center for Blacks. The Nettie Gregory Community Center, named for an outstanding member of the club, was completed in 1964 at Seventh West and South Temple streets in Salt Lake City. Besides joining the various fraternal and social groups, Blacks often went to dance and to listen to the music at some of the local night clubs. Dixie Land, the Jazz Bo, the Porters and Waiters Club, and the Hi Marine were places where Blacks and some whites went for entertainment.[63] The well-known bandleader and arranger Fletcher Henderson and his brother Horace had a club north of Salt Lake City in the 1940s.[64]

Paul C. Howell was Salt Lake City's first Black policeman and today his great-grandson, Jake Green, is a member of the Salt Lake City Police Department.[65] D. H. Oliver was a Black attorney who was active in civic affairs. He is the author of *A Negro on Mormonism.*[66] One of the outstanding Black writers of the 1920s and early 1930s, Wallace Thurman, was born in Salt Lake City. He wrote two novels, *The Blacker the Berry* and *Infants of the Spring,* two plays, and was a ghostwriter for a magazine. Because of his dedication to art and excellence, Thurman was critical of Black writers who did not strive for perfection. He died in 1934 at the age of thirty-two.[67]

[59] *Broad Ax,* September 14, 1895.

[60] *Ibid.,* November 20, 1897.

[61] *Ibid.,* July 25, 1896.

[62] Interview with Mary Lucille Perkins Bankhead.

[63] *Ibid.;* interview with William Gregory.

[64] Edward "Duke" Ellington, *Music Is My Mistress* (Garden City, N.Y., 1973), pp. 49–50.

[65] Interview with Officer Jake Green, Salt Lake City Police Department, February 1974; Langon, *Utah and the Early Black Settlers.*

[66] Gregory interview.

[67] Nathaniel Irvin Huggins, *Harlem Renaissance* (London, 1973), pp. 191–95, 239–43.

It is in discrimination against Utah Blacks that their history here becomes a microcosm of Black history in the United States. The age-old attitude of white superiority and Black inferiority continues to prevail. With immigrants from the Balkans and the Mediterranean initial discrimination was strong but of relatively short duration and never so virulent as that experienced by Blacks. Public opinion kept the new immigrants out of certain areas in towns and cities and frowned on intermarriage, but laws restricted Blacks in housing and public accommodations and through the Anti-Miscegenation Law (1898–1963) prohibited marriage with whites.[68]

One of the paradoxes of Black-white relationships lies in the entertainment field: whites flocked to hear Black artists but would not allow them rooms in their hotels or service in their restaurants. Local Blacks faced the ignominy of having to sit in the balcony sections of theatres and stand outside the ballrooms of Lagoon, Saltair, and the Rainbow Gardens to hear the music of their fellow Blacks.[69]

Before World War II, a French Black singer, Lillian Yvanti, stayed with the Frank Johnsons while in Salt Lake City because she was denied rooms in leading hotels in town. During the 1940s and 1950s similar incidents continued. Marian Anderson, famed concert singer, was allowed to stay at Hotel Utah on condition that she use the freight elevator. Harry Belafonte was also refused rooms at Hotel Utah but was accepted at the Hotel Newhouse which had previously barred Blacks. Ella Fitzgerald and her entourage were placed in a Black hotel on the west side of Salt Lake City because no white hotel would take them. To avoid embarrassment, pianist Lionel Hampton's wife used the ploy of asking local sponsors to find a hotel for them that would take her two small dogs.[70] This discrimination against nationally known entertainers occurred frequently in other parts of the United States as well as in the South.

The breakthrough in Utah was the result of the determined efforts of Robert E. Freed, a prominent leader in civil rights. When the Freed family and their partner, Ranch Kimball, took over

[68] Margaret Judy Maag, "Discrimination Against the Negro and Institutional Efforts to Eliminate It" (M.A. thesis, University of Utah, 1971), pp. 87–88.

[69] Wallace R. Bennett, "The Legal Status of the Negro in Utah," *Symposium on the Negro in Utah,* Utah Academy of Sciences, Arts, and Letters, Weber College, 1954.

[70] Harmond O. Cole "Status of the Negro in Utah," *Symposium on the Negro in Utah,* p. 1. Interview, May 5, 1975, with Peggy Johnson Clark; interview May 5, 1975, with Peter Freed, president of Lagoon.

the lease of Lagoon, the terms forbade Blacks in the swimming pool and the ballroom in accordance with a Farmington town ordinance. By the late 1940s, Robert Freed had succeeded in fully opening Lagoon to Blacks; and when his company acquired the Rainbow Gardens (Terrace), the same policy was adopted. The NAACP Fifty-sixth Annual Membership and Freedom Banquet Program on April 25, 1975, honored Freed posthumously.[71] Providing entertainers with first-class accommodations had to wait until the state and federal legislation of the 1960s.

Overt discrimination against Blacks has ranged from lynchings to rejections in housing, public accommodations, and employment.[72] In 1869 a Black was shot and hanged at Uintah in Weber County. The reason given was "he is a damned Nigger." [73] In 1925 Robert Marshall was taken from his jail cell in Price by a mob and hanged "in slow stages." The rope was pulled until he lost consciousness; he was then revived by burning his bare soles with matches. The pulling and burning continued until Marshall died to the cheers of men, women, and children who smiled for a photographer while the dead Black swung from the hanging tree in the background. Law officers arrived unaccountably late.[74]

Lynching was the extreme form of discrimination and housing difficulties the common form. In 1939 Salt Lake City commissioners received a petition with one thousand signatures asking that Blacks living in Salt Lake be restricted to one residential area. This area would be located away from the City and County Building where visitors to the city would not come in contact with a sizeable number of Blacks. The petition was initiated by Sheldon Brewster, a realtor and bishop of a Mormon ward.[75] Brewster employed a local Black in the attempt to persuade Blacks to sell their houses and agree to be colonized in one location, but he failed to secure their cooperation. Blacks rose up in indignation and marched to the Capitol to protest Brewster's action.[76] When the petition failed to get the approval of the commissioners, a restrictive covenant policy was used

[71] See *Salt Lake Tribune,* July 18, 1974, for Robert E. Freed obituary and *Deseret News,* July 18, 1974, for obituary and July 19, 1974, for editorial.
In earlier years Lagoon had closed to the "public" after Labor Day. Then, on one day following the holiday, Black families were allowed to use the resort facilities before they were shut down for the winter.

[72] Maag, "Discrimination Against the Negro," pp. 29–31.

[73] Robert G. Athearn, *Union Pacific Country* (Chicago, 1971), p. 87.

[74] *News Advocate* (Price), June 18, 1925.

[75] Maag, "Discrimination Against the Negro," pp. 45–47.

[76] Bankhead interview.

to limit Black opportunities in housing. Real estate companies inserted a Form 30 clause in real estate contracts:

> The buyer, his heirs, executors, administrators, successors, or assigns agree that no estate in possession of the said premises shall be sold, transferred, granted, or conveyed to any person not of the Caucasian race.

Although restrictive clauses were ruled unconstitutional in 1948, many deeds continued to include them.

Typical statements from whites on the issue of Blacks and housing are:

> A Negro is all right in his place, but his place is down below you. You can't treat them as an equal or they will take advantage of you every time. You have to keep them down. Yet, the property around here isn't worth as much since they moved on the block, but I guess they have to have some place to live. I understand there is some kind of a city ordinance against selling to them, but it hasn't kept them out of here.
>
> I don't like them around here but there is nothing you can do about it. One thing, they train their dogs and kids right. They are a lot better mannered than the white kids in the neighborhood. Once in a while you see a drunk Nigger, but he is no worse than a drunk white man. But those that are good, you can bet that it is the white blood they got in them.[77]

Even with the protection of recent federal law, Blacks still have problems in renting or purchasing homes.[78]

In the area of public accommodations, more specifically hotels, restaurants, and social organizations, Blacks have suffered the indignity of being refused admittance or service. In instances where a Black was accommodated, he sometimes would have to accept second-class treatment. As in housing, Blacks are often confronted with discrimination in public accommodations despite federal law.[79]

---

[77] Maag, "Discrimination Against the Negro," pp. 47–48.

[78] This writer has personal knowledge of Blacks in Salt Lake City who have been refused housing because of their color. Professor Shelby Steele, a former member of the University of Utah faculty, and Professor Raymond Horton, a former graduate student at the University of Utah, filed suits against individuals who denied them housing because of their race.

[79] Interview with Grady Farley, former graduate student, University of Utah, fall 1973. There are some nightclubs in Salt Lake City that have refused to permit a Black to enter, even though the Black person possessed a membership card.

Employment opportunities, while somewhat improved for Blacks (largely because of federal law), nevertheless continue to be limited, specifically in the area of job-advancement opportunities. While many employers have made meaningful attempts to guarantee equal employment opportunities, others have sought merely to stay within the limits of the law. As a result tokenism is common when it comes to Blacks in visible positions. Even where progress has been more or less a token gesture, it is the result of a long, hard struggle. Mignon Richmond, who was graduated from Utah State Agricultural College (now Utah State University) in 1921, was unable to find work as a teacher and for many years worked as a laboratory technician and school lunch supervisor. Mrs. Richmond has given many years of active service to both the NAACP and the YWCA.[80]

There are two branches of the National Association for the Advancement of Colored People in Utah. The Salt Lake City group was organized in February 1919, ten years after the founding of the national body. The Ogden branch was organized in 1943. Despite limited membership and funds, both branches have been active in the struggle for human rights. In addition to the NAACP, there have been several other organizations such as B'nai Brith, the Japanese-American Civic League, and the Urban League that have worked to bring rights to all people.[81]

In Utah the Mormon church's denial of its priesthood to Black men has hampered their fight for human dignity. Blacks see it as a hindrance to gaining full rights in that they cannot be held in equal esteem with others because denial implies inferiority. The LDS church maintains that it is possible to support civil rights and preserve existing religious opinion. The assertion that denial of priesthood to Blacks is a theological position with no sociopolitical relevance is a specious dichotomy to Blacks.[82]

Nevertheless, Blacks have joined the Mormon church. It has been suggested that their roots in fundamentalism made them amenable to accepting the doctrines of LDS theology and that the self-sufficiency, unity, and independence from outside institutions, advocated by fundamentalist religions and mirrored in the Mormon church, further increase its appeal for Black converts.

[80] Maag, "Discrimination Against the Negro," pp. 40–41.

[81] *Ibid.,* pp. 63–73.

[82] Bush, "Mormonism's Negro Doctrine," 44–45, 67. This article is the most comprehensive study to date on the subject.

Blacks have lived in Utah for more than a century and a quarter and in the United States for more than three and a half centuries. During these years progress has been limited to individuals and not to the race as a whole. In considering the historical experience of Blacks in Utah and the United States, encompassing the struggle from slavery and the continuing quest for human rights, one is reminded of words uttered by a female slave of the nineteenth century: "Oh, Lord Jesus, how long, how long. . . ." [83]

[83] Leslie H. Fishel, Jr., and Benjamin Quarles, eds., *The Black American: A Documentary History,* rev. ed. (Glenview, Ill., 1970), pp. 86–87.

4

SCANDINAVIAN SAGA

BY WILLIAM MULDER

I

In the telephone directories, Utah looks decidedly Anglo-Scandinavian. History and the statistics confirm the impression. Utah's Scandinavians and their descendants, as with most of the state's other immigrants from northern Europe, are largely the fruit of over a century of Mormon proselyting abroad. During the second half of the nineteenth century, when Mormonism preached its doctrine of the "gathering" with vigor and conducted a program of organized migration to Zion, some thirty thousand converts from Norway, Denmark, and Sweden felt persuaded that the valleys of Deseret were Kingdom Come and set out for a frontier far beyond the broader acres their countrymen were homesteading in Minnesota and Wisconsin and well ahead of the Scandinavian invasion of Nebraska and the Dakotas. Backsliders among the Mormon Scandinavians helped people the great West between the Mississippi and the Rockies: disillusioned or quarrelsome, they defected from their church emigrant companies en route and stayed behind to become first settlers in towns and counties in Iowa and Nebraska that by now have forgotten their Mormon origin. Some disaffected among the Scandinavians backtrailed to the Midwest from Zion itself, notably the family of woodcarver James Borglum from Jutland, whereby Utah lost a pair of famous future sculptors in sons Gutzon and Solon Hannibal, who one day would carve Mount Rushmore.

Zion as lodestone, however, proved strong enough to attract fresh arrivals from Scandinavia down the years. The mighty stream of the late 1800s diminished in the 1900s, reflecting changes in Mormon policy and program. The trickle swelled briefly after World War II when Mormon converts, many of whom had waited for years, put Europe and the holocaust gladly behind them. In every

This essay is based on the author's *Homeward to Zion: The Mormon Migration from Scandinavia* (Minneapolis, 1957).

141

census in the hundred years from 1850 to 1950, Utah residents born in Scandinavia as well as those of Scandinavian stock (those having Scandinavian or mixed parentage) appear consistently as the second largest group of foreign-born or foreign stock in the state, second only to British-born and those of British stock.[1] In 1900 Scandinavians formed 34 percent of Utah's foreign-born, and Scandinavian stock that year formed 16 percent of the total population. Two years later Anthon H. Lund, Danish immigrant of 1862, could tell a big reunion of Scandinavians in Brigham City, "We are now 45,000 and are a great power in our state." [2] His own appointment the year before to the high office of counselor in the First Presidency of the Mormon church was a recognition of that power, an official acknowledgement of the role his countrymen were playing in Utah's affairs. But by 1910 more Greeks (657) than Scandinavians (479) were giving Utah as their destination at American ports. In the decades that followed, the Scandinavian percentage of Utah's foreign-born gradually but steadily declined. By 1950, one hundred years after the first Mormon missionaries went from Utah to Scandinavia, Scandinavians comprised 18 percent of the foreign-born in the state. In 1960 they comprised 20 percent, reflecting the influx after the war. In 1970 the figures, whether absolute or in percentages, seem slight: the Scandinavian-born barely 9 percent of the foreign-born; Scandinavian stock only 19 percent of the foreign stock and just a fraction, slightly under 2 percent, of the total population.

But these figures are deceptive, yielding at best a thin profile of late immigration; to stop with them is to look at recent passports only, to the neglect of family portraits in the album of the past. The

[1] In 1960 and 1970 the German-*born* exceeded both the British- and Scandianavian-born (in 1970: 4,890 born in Germany, 4,431 born in Great Britain, 2,751 born in Scandinavia), but British and Scandinavian *stock* still led (in 1970: 9,289 of German stock, 24,100 of British stock, 19,303 of Scandinavian stock). In 1970, to refrain for a moment from lumping all Scandinavians together and give nationalism its due, Scandinavian distribution in the state, by country of birth, showed 724 born in Norway (3,389 of Norwegian stock), 842 born in Sweden (6,635 of Swedish stock), and 1,185 born in Denmark (9,279 of Danish stock), maintaining the same ranking among the three countries that had been true from the beginning. In the state at large, 12,736 reported one of the Scandinavian languages as their mother tongue. In Salt Lake City, metropolitan center for most of the late immigration, 7,714 residents in 1970 still spoke one of the Scandinavian languages as their mother tongue, exceeded only by the 13,704 who claimed German and the 17,972 who claimed Spanish, the latter evidence of the growing presence of the Mexican-Americans and an index of a radically different rate of assimilation: the Nordic immigrant in Utah was inclined to lose his mother tongue quickly.

[2] The U.S. Twelfth Census (1900) shows 24,751 inhabitants of Danish stock, 14,578 of Swedish, and 4,554 of Norwegian in Utah for a total of 43,883 of Scandinavian stock, or very close to Lund's round figure of 45,000.

Scandinavian die was cast early, and the imprint on the state today is unmistakable, even though it is no longer common to call certain towns and neighborhoods in Utah Swede Town [3] or Little Denmark and even though many descendants of the early convert-emigrants no longer think of themselves as Mormons. Utah's Scandinavian saga, moreover, is not exclusively a Mormon story, as flourishing Lutheran congregations bear witness. Scandinavian goldseekers passed through Salt Lake Valley on their way to California as early as 1850, forerunners of the non-Mormon visitors from Scandinavia (journalists, educators, reformers, artists, adventurers, evangelists, tradesmen) who would tarry among the Saints for a season, some to stay. But the branches of the Scandinavian tree, even where secularized and obscured, owe much to the parent trunk. It is a story of a transplanting rather than an uprooting, with Mormon methods in proselyting, emigration, and settlement providing a humane husbandry.

II

The earliest Scandinavian converts to Mormonism were won not in Europe but in the United States among the Norwegian immigrants in the storied settlements at Fox Rixer in Illinois, Sugar Creek in Iowa, and Koshkonong in Wisconsin Territory, within missionary striking distance of Nauvoo, the rising Mormon capital of the 1840s. Joseph Smith, the Mormon prophet, hoped to recruit missionaries for Scandinavia among them who would lead their countrymen to settle in and around Nauvoo to strengthen Zion as converts from the British Isles were already doing. By 1843 the Norwegian Mormon congregation at Fox River numbered fifty-eight, including several of the famous "sloop folk" of 1825; Knud Peterson of Hardangar, immigrant of 1837, better known in Utah history as Canute, who would be one of the early settlers of Lehi; and Aagaata Sondra Ystensdatter, eighteen and also an immigrant of 1837, from Telemarken, who as Ellen Sanders Kimball, wife of Brigham Young's counselor Heber C. Kimball, would be one of the three women in the first company of Mormon pioneers to enter Salt Lake Valley in 1847. Norwegian congregations sprang up in Iowa and Wisconsin as well, and by 1845 one Lutheran minister lamented that nearly a hundred and fifty Norwegians in the western

[3] Yet as late as January 1975 a letter appeared in the *Salt Lake Tribune*'s "Public Forum" captioned "Advice from Swede Town" and beginning, "I live in 'Swede Town,' which is in the very northwest end of the Capitol Hill area at 1550 North."

settlements—some eighty in the Fox River colony alone—had followed the "Mormon delusion."

After the death of Joseph Smith, Brigham Young visited the outlying congregations of the Saints in quick succession trying to hold the pieces together. He called on the Norwegian Branch at Fox River in October of the martyr year and on a hundred acres northeast of nearby Ottawa "laid out a city," called it Norway, and "dedicated it to the Lord." Brigham Young declared that it would be a gathering place for the Scandinavian people and that they would build a temple there. But the Norwegian converts had to abandon that hope as the Mormons had to abandon Nauvoo. A hundred Norwegian Mormon families made ready to go west with Brigham Young, but the dissenter James J. Strang threw them into confusion with his counterclaims to the succession. Most of the Norwegian congregation eventually joined the reorganization under Joseph Smith III, son of the prophet, who in the 1850s united many splinter groups and individuals adrift around Nauvoo following the "Brighamite" exodus.

Brigham Young, meanwhile, did not forget the Fox River converts. In December 1847, back with news of fresh beginnings in the valley of the Great Salt Lake, he sent word from Council Bluffs to the Norwegian settlement urging them to come west. In April 1849 twenty-two Norwegians, Canute Peterson among them, left Fox River in six wagons headed for the valley. At Kanesville, Iowa, they joined Apostle Ezra Taft Benson's camp on the east bank of the Missouri River to become known in Mormon history as the Norwegian Company. Already on the grounds were a group of Welsh emigrants under Capt. Dan Jones. From Kanesville the companies traveled together, a mingling of tongues typical of Mormon migration. At the Weber River they encountered Apostle Erastus Snow and two Scandinavians, John Erik Forsgren and Peter Ole Hansen, eastward bound to carry the gospel to the old countries. After battling waist-deep snows in the mountains, the Norwegian Company reached the valley on October 25, in time to be numbered in Utah's first census, along with one Swede and two Danes. An early Gentile Scandinavian on the scene was Christian Hoier, a Norwegian forty-niner on his way to California, who wrote a letter to Bratsberg's *Amtstidende* about these *Thelebonder* among the Mormons—the first of many letters and travelers' accounts about Utah that would find their way into Scandinavian newspapers.

The Swede in that first census was John Erik Forsgren and the Danes were Peter Ole Hansen and his brother Hans Christian. John Erik and Hans Christian, both sailors, had embraced Mormonism in Boston in the early 1840s and had gone to Nauvoo. Hans Christian had written the news of his conversion to his younger brother Peter Ole in Copenhagen, who hastened to Nauvoo, where Brigham Young set him to work on a Danish translation of the Book of Mormon while Hans Christian entertained the Saints with his fiddle. After the fall of Nauvoo, Forsgren marched to California with the Mormon Battalion in 1846 and Hans Christian Hansen came west in 1847 with the pioneer vanguard, Peter Ole following soon after. It is a smiling coincidence of history that in these early representatives Norway, Denmark, and Sweden were all three "present at the creation," significant tokens of the important role the three kingdoms (and Iceland as well before the decade was out)[4] were to play in the peopling of Utah, harbingers of the harvest to come from "the land of the north."

III

Most Mormon converts were won in the compact villages of Denmark and southern-most Sweden. In far-stretching Norway and northern Sweden the needle of emigration to America was already oriented, and Utah seemed a meager offering alongside the riches of Minnesota's "New Scandinavia." But the leaven of religious dissent and social unrest was at work in all three countries. The times were ripe for the "Gospel of America." The Mormons found many poor and not a few notable exceptions among the affluent who were persuaded the ancient gospel had been restored and were eager to dedicate their worldly possessions to the upbuilding of God's kingdom in the West. The first American missionaries recruited

---

[4] Some Mormon proselytes were made in Iceland as early as 1851 when two natives, Thorarinn Halflidason, a cabinetmaker, and Gudmundur Gudmundson, a jeweler, learning their trades in Copenhagen, were baptized there and on returning to Iceland won several followers. Numbering fewer than four hundred during the half century to 1900, Icelandic Mormons emigrated a handful at a time, usually via Liverpool. A group of sixteen settled in Spanish Fork in 1855–56 forming the nucleus of what is claimed to be the first Icelandic colony in America in modern times. Possessed of literary and musical gifts, and skilled in a variety of crafts, the small but influential settlement deserves separate study. Kate Bjarnason Carter, perennial president of the Daughters of Utah Pioneers, is a descendant of the first settlers. Halldor Laxness, internationally known Icelandic novelist, has written a fanciful novel about them: *Paradisarheimt*, translated by Magnus Magnusson as *Paradise Reclaimed* (1960).

preachers among the converts themselves, laymen from all walks of
life—farm laborers, shoemakers, tailors, carpenters, stonemasons—
who went two by two through most of the provinces of Denmark
and ventured into Sweden and Norway to spread the Mormon
contagion as fortune favored them and the letter of the law allowed.
These native elders became so well known they were celebrated
in the street ballads of the time. In 1856 the itinerant artist Christen
Dalsgaard encountered them in a carpenter's cottage and recorded
the scene in *Mormon-praedikanter* ("Mormon Preachers"), a colorful genre painting notable for its sympathetic realism, which hangs
in the Statens Museum for Kunst ("the State Museum for Art") in
Copenhagen today.

Through the labors of these tenacious laymen, preaching a
Zion they had never seen (*"O Du Zion i Vest"* was the Danish equivalent of "O Ye Mountains High"), Mormonism gained its own
momentum in Scandinavia. They were its mustard seed. The first
ten years of the mission were largely their story, some of them serving
six and seven years before emigrating. During that first decade,
Utah itself sent only thirteen missionaries to Scandinavia, and six
of these were Scandinavians who had joined the church in America.
The elders from Zion arrived in greater numbers with each passing
year. Altogether 1,361 missionaries were sent out from Utah during
the half century 1850–1900. "The Kingdom is beleaguered by this
missionary army from Utah," complained a Swedish official. The
strength was more than numerical. To a surprising degree the manpower from America was Scandinavian—converts and the sons of
converts who had emigrated and had answered a call to devote two
or three years in the homeland as elders from Zion.[5]

[5] Of the 1,361 missionaries sent from Utah by 1900, only 24, or less than
2 percent, were not Scandinavian; 516, or 41 percent, were first-generation
Danes; 417, or 30 percent, were first-generation Swedes (the Swedes nearly
equaling the Danes after 1886); and 130, or about 10 percent, first-generation
Norwegians. Ten were Icelanders. The American-born missionaries of Scandinavian parents, the first of whom arrived in 1882, numbered 247, or about 19
percent. The proportion of these second-generation missionaries rose sharply
after 1896, for the five years 1895–1900 surpassing the first generation. By June
4, 1905, when the Scandinavian Mission was divided into separate Swedish and
Danish-Norwegian administrations, another 388 missionaries had spent the
usual two and a half years in the field, totaling 1,749 for the life of the
undivided mission since Erastus Snow and his companions had founded it in
1850. Some 67 of these returned to Scandinavia on second and third missions,
among them many of the old-timers who had formed the earliest native ministry.
Anthon Skanchy, Norwegian ropemaker who became a building contractor in
America, served five terms. It is still a matter of pride in many families that a
son, a grandson or great-grandson should return to the old country "on a mission." The Utah-Scandinavia axis has been well traveled.

The return of the native on such a grand scale advertised Utah more effectively than the literature and efforts of the Boards of Immigration and railroad land agents serving other states. *Skandinaviens Stjerne* ("Scandinavian Star"), the mission periodical founded in October 1851, became a rich repository of news from Utah: territorial and national news, church communiques and doctrine, editorials from the *Deseret News* and the *Millennial Star* (*Stjerne's* British counterpart), and, above all, letters from convert-emigrants. Their postmarks provided a romantic roll call of Zion's habitations, names of far places yet familiar, endeared by the knowledge of friends and kinfolk writing from their own firesides. From Sanpete Valley, itself an Indian name, and the "Little Denmark" of the settlements, came numerous letters bearing lovely names: Springtown, Mount Pleasant, Fountain Green, and Fairview; a biblical name like Ephraim—at first Fort Ephraim and then Ephraim City, the change speaking a whole history; a Book of Mormon name like Moroni; a historical name like Gunnison. And of course a great many letters came from *Store Saltsostad,* "Great Salt Lake City" itself. Letters from emigrants en route were an education in United States geography: "Fort Laramie," so explained *Stjerne's* editor in introducing a letter from that outpost in 1861, "lies about midway on the prairies and about 500 English miles from Florence." Later, business houses with immigrant names advertised in the state's foreign-language papers which were sent abroad—but even these papers were church-sponsored. In 1895 a Lucerne Land and Water Company issued an "Invitation to Danish Farmers and Dairymen," Utah's closest approach to the immigration literature of other states.

Utah's early invitation to prospective settlers clearly required a special motivation and indoctrination, a mingling of spiritual and practical inducements. For anyone to be content in Zion, conversion —at least conditioning—had to precede emigration. Mormon missionaries were "heralds of salvation" first and only incidentally immigration agents. After arrival in Utah, should the faith falter, the glow subside, the disaffected became the object of the counterefforts of Lutheran evangelicals, whose tracts against the Mormons also found their way to Scandinavia, where a flood of anti-Mormon literature (and hence hurtful to Utah) had flourished from the beginning. Denominational societies in America as well as in Scandinavia were zealous distributors. As late as 1907 the Lutheran Mission in Utah was distributing *Luk Doren for Mormonerne!*

Advarsel! (*"Lock Your Door against the Mormons! Warning!"*)
Balladeers in Scandinavia hawked "the latest new verse about the
Copenhagen apprentice masons" who sold their wives to the Mormons for two thousand kroner and riotously drowned their sorrows
in the taverns. In the doctrine of polygamy, of course, the opposition in Scandinavia saw in Mormon proselyting a bid for concubines
for Zion.

The popular image of the Mormon proselytes—their poverty,
their ignorance, their fanaticism—made them Europe's ugly duck-
lings, objects of scorn and ridicule, though the novelist Ole Rolvaag
called emigrants from the same class "giants in the earth." It was
precisely the poor and humble the Mormons were after. Poverty
and ignorance were ills for which America itself was the remedy,
an assurance that was one of Mormonism's enthusiasms. The hidden
resources of the humble could be magnificent. There was no way to
measure the intangibles that were to be their greatest assets once
settled in Utah. How could fellow Lollanders ever see in Elsie
Rasmussen and Jens Nielsen more than simple, hard-working hands
hiring out from one farm to another, now and then walking arm and
arm to dance away the night and return in time to do the chores?
How could anyone predict their heroic history? Underway to Zion,
Jens's courage would fail him crossing Wyoming's snowbound
plateau, and Elsie would load him, his feet frozen, into her handcart and pull him till his courage returned, saving him, though
permanently crippled, to pioneer five settlements and build as many
homes to make good his dedication to the Lord for his deliverance.
As colonizer, Indian peacemaker, merchant, stockman, bishop, and
patriarch he would make his broken-tongued maxim *sticket to trude*
—"stick to the truth"—a badge of honor, while in sandswept Bluff,
Elsie would plant mulberry trees to raise silkworms, tend beehives to
provide the settlement its only sweets, spend long hours at the loom,
giving her days to manual labor, her evenings to the Bible and other
good books, and devote herself as foster mother to the children of
her husband's plural wives.

It was just such recruits Zion needed. Conversion called thousands like Jens and Elsie Nielsen out of obscurity. But conversion
cost dearly. Nearly a third of the proselytes could not pay the price
but disavowed the faith in Scandinavia itself, with others following
suit after emigration. The winnowing was part of a general reformation in which conversion, itself such a profound education, was only
the beginning. Mormonism took its converts where it found them and

prepared them for the American experience in an indoctrination unique among European emigrants. To this end the mission considered itself "Eden's nursery," where the gospel was sown and the seedlings readied for transplanting to Zion, the garden itself. Mormonism's practicality gave its vision substance, intended to purify motives and to improve habits.

Directly related to preparation for America was the sustained effort on the part of young and old to learn English. Classes, held often on Sunday morning, a prelude to church service, were in a real sense religious exercises; a phrase in Peter Nielsen's journal unconsciously reflects the natural affinity of the worldly and the spiritual in their lives: H.T.W. Eriksen, he says, who held an evening school in Nyby for the children, "taught them English, religion, and writing." [6] The private journals themselves, many of them fortunately preserved by the descendants or in Utah archives today, moved from Norwegian, Swedish, or Danish to English, the language mixed at first, then more confidently in the new tongue, though spelling remained woefully uncertain. Zion's meetinghouses would hear an odd admixture of sin and syntax in the "testimony meetings" in congregations dominated by Scandinavian immigrants. The desire to learn English, revered as the language of the Book of Mormon and of latter-day prophets, was another evidence of how completely Mormonism produced a break with the convert's past, separating him from mother church, fatherland, and native tongue, the transition begun even before he left. It was a striking contrast to the congregations Lutheranism transplanted to New Scandinavia that kept the old tongue alive as the one vital link with the homeland.

Not only English was important to salvation; so was soap. "It is not enough for a person to believe, be converted, and be baptized for forgiveness of sins. The gospel promotes a reformation in every respect where many customs and habits inherited from the fathers are not in harmony with the gospel." So went the official admonitions. Cleanliness was paramount. The Holy Spirit did not dwell in unclean tabernacles. "The first step in this so important reformation is to wash the whole body at least once a week and

---

[6] Peter Nielsen Diary, April 23, 1859, original holograph in possession of Frederik J. Nielsen, Blue Water, New Mexico, typescript translation in Archives Division, Historical Department, Church of Jesus Christ of Latter-day Saints, Salt Lake City.

change linen as often. Thus may health be preserved, peace and good cheer, and sickness and death kept at bay." [7]

In Scandinavia the training in this inclusive morality was intense and diligent. The converts were to legalize their common-law marriages, cease card-playing, abstain from tobacco and strong drink, and pay their debts. Converts emigrating without settling old obligations damaged the cause. False promises, gossip, and backbiting were sources of grievance and unbecoming to a people who should be united. The ideal of social and religious harmony was arduously pursued. They even attempted to erase national prejudices; their identity as Danes or Swedes or Norwegians was supposed to be lost in their association as Latter-day Saints—a fraternal feeling not always preserved in Utah. The number who fell by the wayside, often over trivial matters, only indicates how serious a commitment membership was and how far the converts had to go. Though in Utah itself Anglo-American elements might patronize them and look on the converts from Scandinavia as "dumb Swede" and "ignorant Danishman," in all respects they were expected to be an example to an already critical world. The country crudities of some converts would furnish Utah with the comic figure of the "Sanpete farmer" and his household, earthy and unsanitary as a scene from Breughel, and they offended fastidious converts whose idealism had not anticipated such a lowly brotherhood and who did not stay long in such company. But those with tougher sensibilities remained to lift up their fellows and provide an effective native leadership. The convert-emigrants who returned from Utah on missions also served as living models of what the new life could do. They attracted their kind and strengthened the work of reformation.

Products of a conversion that shook most of them to the roots, objects of a thoroughgoing reformation in their manner of living, welded by doctrine and tried by experience, the proselytes found themselves impatient to "go up to Zion," for in Mormon thinking, conversion was practically synonymous with emigration. Raising means to go to America became the great preoccupation of the faithful. "Everywhere among the Saints," one of them remembered, "the next year's emigration is almost their every thought. This circumscribes their prayers, their anxieties, and their exertions." [8]

[7] "Et Vink til Emigranterne," *Skandinaviens Stjerne*, 11:200–201 (April 1, 1862).

[8] Christian A. Madsen to John Van Cott, July 24, 1861, in Scandinavian Mission General History, LDS Archives.

IV

Contrary to the folklore about the Mormons as abductors of women to supply Utah's supposed harems, the movement in Scandinavia was a family phenomenon. The majority of the emigrants were in their vigorous thirties and forties. A great many eligible young women in the emigrant companies married young men, their own countrymen, before journey's end.

Although the collector of customs at New Orleans, on March 17, 1853, indiscriminately labeled the first chartered company of converts "Labourers and Shoemakers"—and had them coming from "Ireland"—they were in reality Danish farmers and artisans representing the same variety of skills that marked the whole emigration: the original roll of the *Forest Monarch* company has not survived, but it included several weavers and blacksmiths, a tailor, wagonmaker, seaman, miller, wheelwright, carpenter, cabinetmaker, cooper, a government clerk, a former Baptist lay preacher, a village choirmaster, a school trustee, and a good many farmers. Farmers and their families (including an occasional shepherd and a few called gardeners or agriculturalists) made up fully half the emigration in the 1850s, 57 percent in one company. In the 1860s they made up about a third, their numbers steadily declining with each decade as the proportion of laborers rose. Arrived in Utah, the later immigration would not know what to do on a farm. Carl Madsen, a carriagemaker, on his arrival in 1881 went home with Bishop Barton to Kaysville: "The next morning I was handed a bucket and directed to go to the barn. I caught the idea I was to milk the cows, a thing I had never done before." [9]

The "farmers" of the shipping lists were small farmers, Europe's familiar peasants—freeholders, tenants, or simply journeyman hands. Their peasant ancestry would figure years later in directives from the Genealogical Society of Utah outlining "how we must go to work if we want to construct a genealogical table of a farmer family." They included a few like the well-to-do Peter Thomsen of Bregninge on Falster Island, so prominent his conversion rocked the village, and the landed Anders Eliason of Ennerkulen, Sweden, who provided a hundred of his fellow converts with passage to America. At the other extreme were young hands like Christian Lund, who remembered herding cattle one winter for his board

---

[9] Carl Madsen, "My Conversion to Mormonism," typescript in possession of Brigham D. Madsen.

and a pair of wooden shoes, and Hans Christensen, whose sole possession was the sheep his father gave him as his share of the family property. In between were freeholders like Jens Nielsen, who at thirty years of age could buy five acres of land and build a cottage enabling him to be "looked upon as a respectable neighbor and many times invited to the higher class of society." [10]

The great majority in the 1850s and 1860s, decades of Mormonism's largest rural following in Scandinavia, were independent enough to pay their passage to Zion, at least as far as the frontier, where wagons from Utah Territory awaited them, and to assist those without enough saleable goods to scrape their passage together. They were, besides, a vanguard which, once established in Utah, sent help to the old country and made possible the greater emigration, proportionately, of the 1870s and 1880s. The well-to-do farmers were few enough to be especially noticed, though of course wealth was relative: James Jensen remembered that owning a cow gave his parents "some recognition socially" in the village of Haugerup. Certainly the farmers of those early years were far from the indigent serfs they were commonly imagined to be. They were seed corn for Zion, supplying it with a skill most sorely needed. Better fitted for an agrarian experience than the urban British migration, they were destined to make the valleys where they settled known as the granaries and creampots of Utah.

Like the farmers, the artisans, who outnumbered the unskilled laborers, included the prosperous and the poor. Among them were masters, journeymen, and apprentices—at one extreme, established proprietors like Hans Jensen, whose blacksmith works in Aalborg was valued at $4,000, and tailor Jens Weibye of Vendsyssel, who kept fourteen employees busy in his shop; at the other extreme, a journeyman carriagemaker like Jens Christopher Kempe, who had nothing but the tools of his trade. Others, like weaver Hans Zobell, owned their cottage worksteads, which they could sell when they emigrated. Ola Nilsson Liljenquist, a tailor, whose wife could afford silks and a servant, was one of the few early converts enjoying the privileges of burghership.

[10] *Scandinavian Jubilee Album* (Salt Lake City, 1900), p. 228; "Across the Plains in 1863," in Kate B. Carter, comp., *Heart Throbs of the West,* 12 vols. (Salt Lake City, 1939–51), 4:351; C.N. Lund, "Autobiography"; Hans Christensen, "Memoirs"; Jens Nielsen, letter to son Urian, in Albert R. Lyman, "Sketch of Bishop Jens Nielsen"; Hans Jensen Hals, "Autobiography" in WPA Writers' Project Collection, Utah State Historical Society, Salt Lake City.

Among the artisans, carpenters and related craftsmen like cabinetmakers, coopers, wheelwrights, joiners, turners, and carriage-makers made up a considerable group. The next largest group of artisans were the tailors, seamstresses, dyers, and weavers. Smiths— blacksmiths, ironfounders, coppersmiths, tinsmiths, and an occasional machinist—followed these, with shoemakers, tanners, saddle- and harness-makers almost as large a group, not far outnumbering stonecutters, masons, and bricklayers.

There were about the same number of butchers, brewers, bakers, and millers as there were fishermen and seamen. The sailors were few. Landlocked in Utah, they might on some glorious Fourth of July climb the community flagpole like a mast, or like bargeman Hans "Pram Stikker" Larsen, work the block and tackle to hoist the stone for meetinghouses and temples. Four ropemakers, two house painters, a miner, a matmaker, a hairdresser, a hunter, a bookbinder, a printer, a thatcher, a sailmaker, a shipbuilder, five watch- or instrument-makers, four clerks, four potters, and a furrier complete the inventory of occupations. Three musicians—all members of the *Monarch of the Sea* company in 1861—alone saved the day for the professions, though the *B.S. Kimball* emigrants included a homeopath. For a budding artist like young Carl Christian Anton Christensen, whose expert silhouettes won him a scholarship to Copenhagen's Royal Academy until he joined the Mormons, Zion had at first no call. He had to content himself with farming when he emigrated in 1857, though he kept his interest alive as an amateur, painting scenery for the Salt Lake Theatre and creating a traveling panorama of church history that won him at last a kind of fame. The panorama was rediscovered in the 1960s and went on tour again, a twentieth-century resurrection.

The basic skills were all there; others would be developed in the settlements. "I would never have believed," wrote Christensen in 1872, after visiting the Utah Territorial Fair, "so much talent could be found among us as a people who are nearly all gathered from among the poor and most downtrodden classes of mankind." Someone from his hometown, the Danish settlement of Ephraim, had won the silver medal for a landscape painting showing several children gleaning corn in the field just outside "our town"; a Swedish sister had received the premium for *haararbeide,* or "hair artistry"; "our friend W." (without doubt the Norwegian painter Dan Weggeland) had received the silver medal for his portraits; a young Norwegian brother had taken the prize for wood-carving; a Swede for an artistic watch; "and many others won premiums. . . . It's only a small part of what can be accomplished." [11] Twenty years later Christensen observed that he met Scandinavians "nearly everywhere" in his travels and found his countrymen in many places holding "the most responsible positions both in church and civic affairs," which he found "a greatly satisfying witness to our national character by the world's most practical nation—the Americans." He would have taken pride in their descendants in the twentieth century: scientists, university presidents, school superintendents, poets and novelists, musicians, legislators.

V

The emigrants were rich in human resources, but they came, most of them, on a shoestring. In 1852 the Mormon mission established a *Vedvarende Emigrationsfond,* or revolving fund, designed as a branch of the churchwide Perpetual Emigrating Fund, the PEF. Translating the doctrine of the gathering into Danish rigsdaler and Swedish kroner spelled formidable difficulties. Eager brethren in Copenhagen in 1852 circulated a subscription to buy their own ship, for which they advertised in Norwegian papers, but abandoned the plan in favor of the British example of using chartered vessels. Scandinavia could profit from a dozen years of Mormon experience in transporting Mormons from England, and from a longer apprenticeship on the frontier during movements of the church from New York to Ohio, Missouri, Illinois, and finally to Utah. The Mormons were old hands at chartering ships, organizing emigrants into self-governing, self-helping communities on board, securing train or steamboat connections in the States, and, before the transcontinental railroad, assembling wagons, oxen, mules, flour, and tents at river and railroad terminals.

Mormon operations were a kind of consumer cooperative, a pooling of the emigrants' meager resources into the hands of church agents which, together with support from those already in Utah, gave them bargaining power. It meant cheaper travel for those who paid their own way, and it created a carrier for those who could not—the "Lord's poor" for whom Brigham Young pleaded ceaselessly but who, given labor and opportunity in Zion, could soon repay their passage. An air of dedication marked this activity. Mor-

[11] C.C.A. Christensen to Edward H. Anderson, December 29, 1891, *Nordstjarnan,* 16:47 (February 1, 1892).

mon representatives at ports of departure and arrival and at out-fitting stations on the frontier considered their work "missions." Even teamsters were "called" from season to season to haul im-migrants to the valley. Christian Michelsen in 1866 was shocked by the rawness of the Mormon teamsters: dressed in wide-brimmed hats, short jackets, and leather breeches, with a revolver or bowie knife in the bootleg, a long bull whip around their necks, some with a quid of tobacco in their mouths, and cursing, they did not look like "Saints." But the three hundred Scandinavian converts arriving at New Orleans on the *Jesse Munn* in 1854 were grateful to James Brown who met them: going aboard he "laid hands on their sick and felt to rejoice that I was where I could do good to the people of God." They raised "their hands to heaven" and in their broken language exclaimed, "Our brother has come from the land of Zion to help us." [12]

Church assistance was businesslike, but in the interest of the emigrant himself: all future help depended on keeping the PEF alive as a revolving fund; outgoing aid was not a gift but a loan, not unlike the federal student loan program today. Whether for the entire passage or for emergency aid along the way, he signed a promissory note. At Florence, Nebraska Territory, in 1860, for ex-ample, Johan Storstrom and Christian Christensen "having received the benefit of three hand cart shares" promised to pay "on demand" the sum of $39.60. Anders Jensen, evidently in return for some service, received a voucher issued by the "Emigration Office" at Florence in 1863 drawing on the "Warehouse" for "four dollars in rations." [13]

Of 10,843 Scandinavian converts setting out for Utah by 1869, before the completion of the transcontinental railroad, at least 6,810 were transported from the frontier to the Salt Lake Valley in church wagons, signing IOUs for thirty-six dollars for a share of a wagon as one of eight passengers—though they more often walked. This was wholly in the 1860s. In the 1850s 1,032 went through by handcarts, which they could either purchase outright or sign for at eighteen dollars a share, four shares to the handcart. The rest, or about three thousand, went all the way as "independents," having been able to buy their own equipment and provisions. To the enemies

[12] James Brown to his family, February 22, 1854, typescript in Utah Humanities Research Foundation Archives, Marriott Library, University of Utah.

[13] Photostatic copies of these notes and the voucher are preserved in the Utah Humanities Research Foundation Archives.

of the Mormons, the pledge exacted from the converts that "We will hold ourselves, our time, and our labour, subject to the appropriation of the Perpetual Emigrating Fund Company, until the full cost of our emigration debt is paid, with interest if required," seemed a form of indenture and they accused the church of grinding the faces of the immigrant poor. The bark was worse than the bite. Threats, complaints, and pleadings rang down the years as the church tried to collect, but the PEF agreement remained a merciful instrument. At Brigham Young's death the fund's accounts receivable ran to over a million dollars, without interest.

Contributions from church members both at home and abroad, advance deposits from intending emigrants, and prepayment of passage money by those sending for friends and relatives made up the working capital of the PEF, augmented by occasional investments (PEF herds and farms in Utah), but it was not known from one year to the next how much assistance could be made available. In Scandinavia the converts helped themselves and they helped each other. For those few who possessed property and saleable goods, the proceeds were often enough to carry them through. Anna Widtsoe, widow of a schoolmaster in Trondhjem, Norway, whose son John A. would become a noted soil and water scientist, president of the University of Utah, and an apostle, auctioned the family library in 1883; Hans Zobell, weaver, sold his Danish cottage for 400 kroner ($100) in 1869; and Andrew M. Israelsen, as a boy of seven, remembered the heavy red box of silver coins his parents received when they sold their little farm in Norway. The five hundred farmers, shoemakers, smiths, masons, tailors, and weavers and their families who made ready to leave on the sailship *James Nesmith* in January 1855 footed their own bill, some 3,813 English pounds, of which 1,638 pounds was sent to the frontiers in advance as "cattle and waggon money." In 1862 Soren Larsen Berstrup, a fifty-two-year-old farmer from northern Jutland, deposited 1,815 rigsdaler at Mormon mission headquarters in Copenhagen as one of over fifteen hundred converts, all financially independent, preparing for spring departure from Hamburg in a special caravan of four ships. Few could equal the treasure of farmer A.P. Kjersgaard Olsen, thirty-five, of Rakkeby, who in 1867 deposited 7,000 rigsdalers, which, after disbursements for passage, plains equipment, and advances to various persons, left him a comfortable $1,050 in exchange.[14]

By far the greater number, to judge from the ledger entries, had little or nothing to spare after paying their passage. Those with ampler means assisted their less fortunate fellow believers. A deliverer who like Moses never set his own feet on the promised land was Jens Andersen of Veddern, Aalborg, who had assisted no fewer than sixty of his fellows to emigrate; he met death on the North Sea in 1862, soon after leaving Cuxhaven. Almost as dolorous was the history of another benefactor, Hans Rasmussen of Ammendrup: before he emigrated in 1856 he paid the church a tithe amounting to 700 rigsdaler, contributed 1,400 rigsdaler to the mission's emigration fund, and paid, besides, the emigrant fare for thirty fellow converts. He lost everything except his life and his family in the snowstorms that overtook his company in the mountains, and he arrived in Salt Lake Valley destitute. Settled in Sanpete Valley, he sustained successive losses from Indian wars, droughts, and grasshoppers, to die at seventy-two, a severely tried Saint. The redeemed, once settled, did not always repay with kindness; some shirked their debt, which led to some fallings out among the convert-emigrants. It grieved the editor of *Morgenstjernen,* Danish monthly in Salt Lake City, that year after year many remained indifferent to their obligation: "Have you forgotten how eagerly you seized every means which would make your emigration possible?" he asked, and he upbraided those whose "views of the latter-day work" had changed: they should still honor their debt.[15]

One third of the means for the 567 emigrants leaving Scandinavia in 1869 was sent from Utah. Work on the approaching railroad proved a boon because it was the one type of labor for which cash was paid, cash that could be sent to waiting relatives in the old country. Scandinavians in Utah contributed twenty-five cents a month to a missionary fund, and they organized local emigrant aid societies whose contributions showed up on the emigration ledgers in Copenhagen as the Moroni Fund, the Ephraim Fund, the Provo Fund. The renowned Scandinavian Choir in Salt Lake

---

[14] John A. Widtsoe, *In the Gospel Net: The Story of Anna Karine Widtsoe, 1849–1919* (Salt Lake City, 1941), p. 74; H.J. Zobell, "Autobiography," typescript in possession of Albert Zobell, Jr., Salt Lake City; Andrew M. Israelsen, *Utah Pioneering, An Autobiography* (Salt Lake City, 1938), p. 12; Emigration Records (Copenhagen), *passim.*

[15] "Betal Eders Emigrationsgjaeld," *Morgenstjernen,* 1:168 (1882).

City held benefit concerts. In Ephraim, Sarah Ann Peterson of the Women's Relief Society urged her sisters to donate all Sunday eggs to the fund, and other settlements followed. In 1872, to mark the twenty-fifth anniversary of the arrival of the Mormons in the Great Salt Lake Valley, friends and relatives in Utah sent $10,000 to Scandinavia. In 1883 they sent $30,000 more to Sweden alone, enabling so many to emigrate that the mission could hardly function.

Prepaid tickets were among the forms of assistance from Utah. J.A. Peterson, steamship passenger agent in Salt Lake, advertised regularly in the Scandinavian weeklies that his tickets were good for a year and those who wished could travel "with the Latter-day Saint emigration." Copenhagen headquarters received deposits to individual accounts which led to a regular savings system in a bank called significantly *Bikuben* ("The Beehive"). The *Regenskabs Bog* or "account book" was as important to Mormon migration from Scandinavia as the Book of Mormon itself. It required long years for some to save enough from their pittance to accumulate even the few dollars needed for passage. "The great question among the Saints is 'How shall we get to Zion?' " wrote Niels C. Flygare in 1878. "Many have been in the church for fifteen or twenty-five years and grown old, but they are not tired of assisting in the good cause." Mission leaders advised thrift. By saving ten örer (2.5 cents) daily, the young, unmarried folk, who were unburdened and earning a living, would save 300 kroner ($75) in ten years. It was slow; painful saving, but it brought them one by one, family by family, ever closer to the great day when they could go "home to Zion."

VI

Going to America involved more than stepping aboard a vessel on one side of the Atlantic and disembarking on the other. For the Scandinavian converts it was a whole series of journeys. They first had to make their way to Copenhagen, main assembly point, then to Hamburg and across the North Sea to Grimsby or Hull for the train ride to Liverpool. The North Sea passage was often the roughest part of the whole journey: accounts describe the horrible retching in the holds of the vessels, sometimes little better than cattle boats. Shelter at various stages of the journey certainly had none of the comforts of home; a sensitive Norwegian woman found the "poor Saints" packed into a large hall in Copenhagen, given beds on straw in a loft in Hamburg, with no segregation of men and women, quartered in a "kind of stable" in Grimsby, and sheltered in "a rude shed" in Liverpool.

From Scandinavia to England was but a foretaste of interminable changes, endless distances. After the Atlantic, crossed in sailing vessels until 1869, there stretched a continent to cross. Until 1855 Mormon emigrants traveled the New Orleans route, utilizing the waterways to get as far inland as possible—Keokuk or Quincy on the Mississippi, Atchison or Saint Joseph on the Missouri. To avoid the murderous climate of the lower Mississippi, all emigration after 1855 passed through eastern ports. The route in the states was determined by the best contract Mormon representatives were able to make. Scandinavian companies made up whole wagon trains and, after the full journey could be made by rail, occupied entire coaches. Brigham Young once toured the coaches carrying six hundred Scandinavians arriving in September 1872, going midway to Ogden to greet these "strange brothers and sisters from across the sea."

The tortuous itinerary did not disturb the Saints as they prepared to leave the old country, for there was too much excitement at departure. A Dane remembered the scene in Copenhagen in 1869: with his mother and sister he stayed with four hundred other emigrants, the greater part Mormons and "mostly farm folk," at the Bolles Hotel. The sitting room was in constant motion. Some people went about in the crowd begging to be taken along. "It was a sight to behold"—four hundred people marching from the hotel to the dock, lugging their worldly goods to the clanging of loose tinware and singing "Think not when you gather to Zion your trials and troubles are o'er. . . ." At the dock he remembered vividly how a mother gave her three small girls a last embrace before turning them over to a young woman to be taken to Utah.[16]

The first emigrants to go all the way from Scandinavia to Utah (not counting the Norwegian forerunners converted in Illinois) numbered a small band of twenty-eight, whom Erastus Snow in January 1852 — with his following nearly six hundred and growing daily — ventured to send out like doves from the ark. They made hurried preparations to join a company of British Saints embarking from Liverpool in February on the *Ellen Maria*, but they missed connections, and it was March 11 before they boarded the *Italy*. Snow himself caught up with them four months later in Kanesville, Iowa, from where he escorted them to Salt Lake Valley in Eli

---

[16] Zobell, "Autobiography," p. 52.

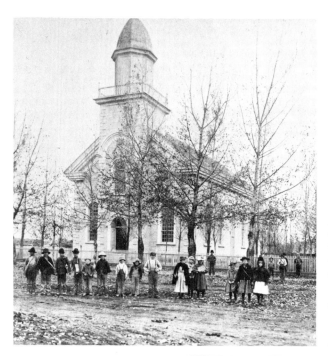

Left: *Scandinavian immigrants began settling in Ephraim, Sanpete County, in 1854. As the town prospered, these Latter-day Saints built a handsome meetinghouse for worship.*

Right: *Scandinavian stonemasons built the beautiful Spring City chapel of Sanpete limestone. Gothic in design, it reflects the finest craftsmanship inside and out.*

From the top: *Children could trade eggs for candy at Jensen, Christiansen and Co. the "Green Store" of Richfield, Sevier County. Many Danes and other Scandinavians settled in central Utah. Rev. Harald Jensen served as pastor of the Danish Evangelical Lutheran Church in Salt Lake City in the early 1900s. Hans Peter Olsen, Danish-born farmer and member of the town board of Fountain Green built his home in 1877. It is now listed on the National Register of Historic Places.*

From the top: *The Elsinore Hotel,
operated by Jens and Inger Jensen, was
popular with salesmen and other
travelers. Augusta Lund of Copenhagen
came to Utah in the early 1900s where
she married Joseph L. Lund, a son of
Danish immigrant parents in Mount
Pleasant, Sanpete County. Employees
of the Jensen Creamery in Salt Lake
City worked for Danish entrepreneur
Wiggo F. Jensen.*

From the top: *Kate B. Carter, long-time president of the Daughters of Utah Pioneers, represents the state's unique Icelandic heritage. Many Finns came to Utah to work in the mining camps. When 200 coal miners lost their lives on May 1, 1900, in the Winter Quarters mine explosion at Scofield, Carbon County more than sixty of the dead were of Finnish extraction.*

Left: *Ellen Sanders Kimball, a native of Norway, was one of three women in the pioneer company of 1847 and one of two Scandinavians (the other: Hans Christian Hansen). Below: Two Norwegians, John A. Widtsoe and Torleif S. Knaphus, brought diverse talents to Utah: Widtsoe as an agricultural scientist and Knaphus as a sculptor.*

Below: *A Scandinavian celebration at the Logan Tabernacle in 1903.*

Left: *Ski jumping meet at Ecker's Hill, 1937. Utahns of Norwegian ancestry led in the development of the state's winter sports.*

Right: *Danquart A. Weggeland of Norway painted the Bennion farm and other Utah scenes.* Below: *Another Scandinavian artist, C.C.A. Christensen of Copenhagen, painted panoramic scenes from Mormon history.*

Ola N. Liljenquist, Swedish-born bishop of Hyrum, established the most successful cooperative in Cache County.

Above: Hyrum Dairy was managed by the United Order of Hyrum under Bishop Liljenquist. Below: Swedish Evangelical Lutheran Church was built in 1885.

Another Swede, John Erik Forsgren, served in the Mormon Battalion and led the famed Forsgren company of Scandinavian immigrants to Utah in 1853.

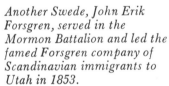

Left: *Hilda Anderson Erickson, a native of Sweden, studied under Dr. Romania B. Pratt in order to serve both Indians and whites at Ibapah, Tooele County, by delivering babies, extracting teeth, and performing minor surgery.* Below: *Costumed members of a glee club,* Det Norske Sangkor, *proudly displayed the Norwegian flag.*

B. Kelsey's ox train. *Stjerne* could tell its anxious readers in Scandinavia that the "little flock of Danish Saints" had arrived on October 16 "alive and well satisfied and they urge their friends to follow them." [17]

A few of the emigrants had already bought places to live and turned the first soil. Niels Jensen and his nephew Frederik Petersen were getting ready to build a pottery in Salt Lake's Second Ward, soon to be known as Little Denmark. Clerk Conrad Svanevelt's wife had a new baby, a girl they called Josephine Brighamine in honor of the two prophets; the Rasmus Petersens were staying temporarily with Erastus Snow, turnabout for the time he had made his home with them in Denmark; tailor Wilhelm Knudsen looked forward to the arrival of his father's family the next year and went north to the settlement at Box Elder to get ready for them; midwife Augusta Dorius married Henry Stevens and went south to Sanpete Valley, where Cecelia Jorgensen followed to become in time the plural wife of Hans Jensens Hals. It was a sad day when *Stjerne* had to report Svanevelt's defection, removal to California, and final return to Denmark, but a happy one when it could announce his reunion with the Saints. So ran the news about the five families, six bachelors, and four spinsters who were the vanguard of the Scandinavian emigration.[18] They were never out of mind, though it was not until death that some of them figured again in the news from Utah: the obituary always remembered they were "one of the first twenty-eight," and that paid them the highest respect.

An even greater watchfulness followed the adventures of the company led by John Erik Forsgren that sailed with 199 adults and 95 children under twelve from Liverpool on January 16, 1853, aboard the *Forest Monarch,* the *Mayflower* of the Mormon migration from Scandinavia. (In 1953, the centennial year of its departure, the *Forest Monarch* figured as a float in Salt Lake City's Pioneer Day parade.) It was a long nine months before the Forsgren company could record in their journals: "September 30, 1853. This day we entered the Valley and camped in the center of the

[17] *Stjerne,* 2:110 (January 1, 1853).

[18] "Efterretninger fra Emigranterne," *Stjerne,* 2:288 (June 15, 1853); "Fra Vesten," *Stjerne,* 3:187 (March 13, 1854); "Niels Jensen," *Stjerne,* 19:314 (July 15, 1860); Andrew Jenson, *Latter-day Saints Biographical Encyclopedia,* 4 vols. (Salt Lake City, 1901–26), 2:67, 3:126; "O.U.C. Monster," *Morgenstjernen,* 3:192 (1884); *Scandinavian Jubilee Album 1850–1900* (Salt Lake City, 1900), p. 220; Salt Lake City Second Ward, Historical Record, LDS Archives.

city." [19] More characteristic of the future emigration in numbers and organization than the first group, the Forsgren pilgrims provided a more genuine test of the ability of the Scandinavian Saints to make their way to Zion and establish themselves as equal citizens of the kingdom.

Some of the immigrants found a temporary home with the first twenty-eight, who had already given their neighborhood a distinctly Danish character. Some followed John Forsgren north to Fort Box Elder, where his wife was living with her father, Bishop William Davis, founder of the settlement. With John went his brother Peter, a weaver, and wife, and his sister Erika, who would become the bishop's plural wife. Most of the company, on Brigham Young's advice, went south within a few days to the high country of Sanpete Valley to strengthen Father Isaac Morley's colony at Manti. They became first settlers of Spring Town (New Denmark) and Fort Ephraim. "The first thing we did," Anders Thomsen remembered, when he arrived in Spring Town in mid-October, "was to go down to the river bottom and cut some frozen grass. We had some ox teams which had to be cared for. When we had done this we had to build a fort wall against the Indians." [20] In Manti, Christian Nielsen built a grist mill "after the Danish fashion." A number of artisans remained in Salt Lake City, their immigrant skills helping to build public works like the Council House, the Old Tabernacle, the Social Hall, the Endowment House, the Bath House, the Tithing Store, the Church Office, and the Beehive House and the Lion House in the 1850s, as those who followed them would work on the Salt Lake Theatre and the new Salt Lake Tabernacle in the 1860s, the Assembly Hall in the 1870s, and the Salt Lake Temple, under construction until 1893. Purely to "keep the English and Danes at work," and to set a good example for the

---

[19] The history of the Forsgren company has to be drawn from several sources: Daughters of Utah Pioneers, *A Pioneer Journal, Forsgren Company,* (Salt Lake City, 1944), pp. 1–40; Willard Snow Journal, excerpted in Scandinavian Mission General History, which also quotes a number of journals by members of the company and provides a partial list of emigrants; Christian Nielsen, Letter, April 27, 1856, original holograph in Royal Library, Copenhagen; "History of Anders Thomsen, Sr., by Himself," typescript in possession of Woodruff Thomsen; letters from the emigrants published in *Stjerne, passim* for 1852–54. The story of the Forsgren company also survives in fleeting references in many memoirs and in the oral tradition of Mormon families who take pride in their descent from the emigrants.

[20] "History of Anders Thomsen, Sr., by Himself."

other settlements, Brigham Young ordered six miles of stone wall erected around Salt Lake City in the winter of 1853–54.

The Forsgren company left a golden track in Utah history. An ounce of their success was worth a pound of propaganda in Scandinavia, and a hundred companies confidently followed in their wake, their adventures continually renewing the twice-told tale of the first voyagers and pioneers. They gave the migration of Scandinavian Mormons a distinctive pattern. Later immigration naturally gravitated to the early centers—Sanpete and Sevier counties in the south, Salt Lake County in the middle, and Box Elder and Cache in the north becoming early, and remaining, the strongholds of Scandinavian population. "The people are like bees," wrote Christian Nielsen from Manti; "when they fill up one place, they swarm out and build up a new one. . . . About three hundred Danish families live in this town, and about seven English miles north of us there are about as many." [21] *Morgenstjernen,* the Danish monthly, in 1884 had eighty-three agents in as many settlements, evidence of the extent of Scandinavian concentration.

Scandinavian Mormons colonized Idaho and Nevada in the 1860s and Wyoming, Arizona, New Mexico, and Colorado in the 1870s; some joined refugee colonies of polygamists in Mexico and Canada in the 1880s; a few followed Mormon entrepreneurs to Oregon in the 1890s to carry on lumbering operations. Scandinavians participated in two of Mormonism's most heartbreaking colonizing expeditions: the Muddy River mission in 1868–71, consistently wiped out by floods, and the San Juan mission in 1880 in the badlands of southeastern Utah, which they had to reach by way of Hole-in-the-Rock, a treacherous cleft in the sheer wall of the Colorado, down which they blasted a trail and a history. Scandinavians were among the seasoned colonizers who led what might be called the second wave of Mormon pioneering that sought to build up "the waste places of Zion" and extend its borders, a vigorous and far-flung program after the death of Brigham Young.

The Scandinavians gave their names to some places: Jensen, for Lars Jensen, who built the ferry on Green River in 1885; Axtell in Sanpete County, after Axel Einersen; Anderson in Washington County, after Peter Anderson's orchard in 1869; Peterson in Morgan County, for Charles Shreeve Peterson, its bishop; Elsinore in Sevier

---

[21] Letter, April 27, 1856, *Bikuben* (Salt Lake City), December 19, 1912. Original holograph in Royal Library, Copenhagen.

County, founded in 1874, after the Danish town where Hamlet once stalked a ghost; Widtsoe in Garfield County, for John A. Widtsoe; Lockerby in San Juan after an early resident; Yost in Box Elder County, after Charles Yost in 1880; Swedish Knoll in Sanpete because Niels Anderson herded sheep there; Christianson Canyon in Tooele County, for an early Swedish settler along Deep Creek; Borgeson Canyon, for Anders Borgeson, who built the first molasses mill in Santaquin. There were, besides, nicknames like Little Copenhagen for Mantua, a hamlet of Danish families in Little Valley; and Little Denmark for a half dozen towns. Rural communities dominantly Scandinavian invariably had a Danish Ditch, a Danish Field, a Danish Bench, and a Danish Woods, indicative that language needs determined how to divide up the commons.

Scandinavian distinctions persisted: in a country where building materials were scarce, the thatched roof and the half-timbered house of the Skane countryside in southern Sweden were welcome importations, and the blue doors and bright-colored trim of the houses and the woven willow fences surrounding the yards also became characteristic of the New World communities. Old-country skills often spelled the difference in a community between want and prosperity. Sanpete Scandinavians might be accused of going to bed with the pigs and the chickens, but nowhere were the animals better housed in winter or the stock better cared for, and the butter improved as a result. A Danish farmer began Utah's first dairy cooperative, rounding up four hundred cows from his fellow townsmen in Brigham City to pasture and tend them on shares. A Yankee might raise flax for linseed oil and not know what to do with the straw, but his Danish neighbor, a flaxman, could construct a simple instrument for shredding and preparing it for the loom. The state's land grant college was from the beginning heavily staffed by Scandinavians and their offspring seeking ways to conserve the land their fathers had dearly bought.

In a number of communities Scandinavians outnumbered all other foreign-born, and their second generation formed the greater part of the native-born. But there were no exclusively Scandinavian colonies, which would have been contrary to the idea of the kingdom, whose fellowship overrode ethnic distinctions. Salt Lake City by 1885 did have a Swede Town, but it was a suburban development promoted by businessmen eager to profit from the great influx of Swedes into the capital in the 1880s. The Scandinavian Building Society in Salt Lake in 1889 was simply an urban expression,

171

through united cash, of what once could be done through united labor in the settlements.

The Little Denmark of Salt Lake City's Second Ward, steadily augmented since the arrival of the first twenty-eight in 1852, was not exclusive: though twenty-nine of its fifty-eight households in 1860 were Scandinavian, they lived side by side with their Yankee, English, and Scotch neighbors in a community as mixed as the country settlements. (The ward, only nine blocks from the center of the city, was still decidedly rural, devoted to dairying; other occupations among the Scandinavians there included potter, shoemaker, cabinetmaker, blacksmith, wheelwright, laborer, carpenter.) Relations were not always amicable: Charles L. Walker, later of Dixie fame, noted in his journal on Sunday, October 23, 1859, that he had "calculated to go to the Tabernacle but a Danish Brother came for me to settle a difficulty between him and a scotch man both parties were near to fighting point." After "laboring with them for about 2 hours" Walker got them to shake hands and feel "pretty well toward each other." [22] After 1860 the Second Ward became less the Scandinavian center, the immigrants scattering freely throughout the city, where their friends and relatives following after were naturally attracted to them and soon gave other neighborhoods a Scandinavian complexion. Scandinavian domestics, moreover, served in numerous non-Scandinavian households.

Polygamy led to international households: the Dane John T. Dorcheus married Danish, English, and Scotch wives to beget seventeen children. Twelve percent of the wives of 147 Scandinavian polygamists listed in Esshom's *Pioneers and Prominent Men of Utah* were non-Scandinavian; and 101 Scandinavian women were married as plural wives to men of other nationalities. Some of these women were married to civic leaders and leading churchmen. Mayor A.O. Smoot married Anna Mauritzen of Norway as his fifth wife, who became the mother of Reed Smoot, long-term apostle and United States senator from Utah. Apostle Lorenzo Snow, enterprising leader of Brigham City cooperatives, and one day to become president of the Mormon church, took to wife Minnie Jensen, daughter of iron founder Hans Peter Jensen, early stalwart from Aalborg, and his wife Sarah Josephine, who had translated the revelation on plural marriage when it reached Denmark in 1853.

---

[22] Charles L. Walker Journal, entries for October 20, 23, 1859, typescript, Utah State Historical Society.

Scandinavians, as Mormons and farmers, shunned Gentile establishments like Corinne, a railroad boom town, and Silver Reef, a briefly prosperous mining community, but they did not hesitate to sell their produce to the unbelievers at a profit; the cash from soldiers, miners, and railroad workers was often the only money they saw in their early barter economy. The full-scale development of the copper mine in Bingham after 1890, and its accompanying smelters and refineries, appealed particularly to the populous Swedes of Salt Lake and Grantsville who found employment there. By 1970 the census showed few first- or second-generation immigrants on the farm: 90 out of 3,389 of Norwegian stock, 195 out of 6,635 of Swedish stock, 241 out of 9,279 of Danish stock.

Some Scandinavians in the early immigration were inevitably tempted by California or were overcome by longing for the old home, or for causes either profound or trivial, backtrailed to Nebraska and Iowa to join those who had fallen by the way. Departures of the disillusioned from Zion were common enough for *Bikuben,* Danish-language newspaper in Salt Lake City, to run a facetious advertisement in 1877: "In case someone in Utah becomes tired of living among the Mormons, here is an opportunity which you will seldom find," and it went on to describe the offer of some-one in Nebraska ready to "sell or trade" an eighty-acre farm for property in Utah. The ill-at-ease at first preferred to leave, but in time they asserted their claim to a stake in the new country on other than church terms and remained, often affiliating themselves with Protestant denominations that carried on educational and evangelical missions as part of the national effort after 1869 to "Christianize" Utah.[23] Rev. M.T. Lamb, looking for a bright spot in "all the dark canvas" of Mormonism, found immigration itself a blessing in disguise. "Through the strange providence of God there have been thrust upon the Christian workers of our country 50,000 young people in Utah, who, if they can be brought under the influences of the truth . . . are worth ten times as much . . . as they could have been had their parents remained in the stagnant, uneventful life of the old country."[24]

[23] By 1880 the Protestants had twenty-two ministers serving twenty-five mission day schools with 54 teachers and 2,250 pupils; by 1890, the high-water mark of their activity, they had sixty-two ministers serving sixty-three churches and sixty-four schools with 323 teachers and 7,007 pupils. T.C. Iliff estimated that by 1895 the Methodist Episcopal church had spent $500,000, the Presbyterians $880,000 on Utah.

[24] M.T. Lamb, "Lessons from Mormonism," in *The Situation in Utah: Proceedings of the Christian Convention 1888* (Salt Lake City, 1889), p. 88.

With Scandinavian immigrants so numerous, the denominations sensed a special opportunity and were soon making urgent appeals to the home mission societies and boards for ministers and teachers who could speak the language. "If a Norwegian or Danish Lutheran priest should go to Sanpete County," wrote Andreas Mortensen in 1887, "he would have half the Mormons follow him." [25] He scolded the establishment in Scandinavia, whose missions had neglected Utah. Oddly enough, it was not the Lutherans but the Presbyterians, closely followed by the Methodist Episcopal church and the Baptists, who first made inroads among the immigrants. The Reverend Duncan J. McMillan, whom Brigham Young called "a mischievous stranger," appeared in Mount Pleasant in 1875, the first denominational missionary to work in an exclusively Mormon community. Feeling himself "100 miles by stage from any Christian brother or Gentile friend," he converted Liberal Hall, being built by disaffected Mormons, into a Presbyterian chapel and opened a school. The town, as would prove true with denominational effort everywhere else in Utah, was more interested in the school than in the church, but by 1880, five years after McMillan's courageous beginnings, the Presbyterian church was organized with eleven members, the elected elders and deacons bearing names that once honored Mormon rolls in Scandinavia. Services were carried on in English, Danish, and Swedish, with hymnals ordered printed in all three languages. By 1893 the church had seventy-three members, with a Sunday school of forty-five and a home for boarding girls where they could be under "Christian influence and receive practical instruction in housekeeping." [26] The home was part of the Wasatch Academy, a major development out of McMillan's mission school. Still operating today under the auspices of the Women's Executive Committee of Home Missions, it was the forerunner of successful Presbyterian academies in other towns in Utah, most notably among them the still flourishing Westminster College of Salt Lake City.

McMillan extended his work to nearby Ephraim and Manti, the county seat, about equally English and Scandinavian, where his brother J.S. McMillan and wife opened a mission school in September 1877. The Reverend R. G. McNiece came down from Salt Lake

---

[25] Andreas Mortensen, *Fra mit Besog blandt Mormonerne* (Christiania, 1887), p. 283.

[26] "The History of Presbyterian Work in Utah," in *World's Fair Ecclesiastical History of Utah* (Salt Lake City, 1893), p. 238.

City the next spring to preach in Fox's Hall and organize the church with ten members. One of the ruling elders was Andrew Nelson, Presbyterianism's most spectacular conversion: as Anders Nielsen he had come to Utah in 1853 with the famous Forsgren company to settle in Spring Town; he had filled a Mormon mission to Scandinavia twelve years later, had married four wives, and, as a prosperous farmer, stockholder, and justice of the peace, was looked upon as a pillar of the community. Differences with his Mormon bishop over nothing more serious than card-playing ripened him in disaffection, to be plucked by the Presbyterians and become their mainstay when they came to Manti. He lived with his third wife, but to travelers he seemed that curiosity, a Presbyterian polygamist. Nelson sent his eighteen children to Manti's mission school, where attendance had ranged from 60 to 125 since its beginning in 1877, and which in 1881 was housed in a handsome building of native oölite—the same beautiful stone as the Mormon temple, the Presbyterians always added. Its pupils became public school teachers, one of them a county superintendent and another a city principal. One of Nelson's sons was Lowry Nelson, who became a well-known sociologist and, fittingly, wrote a study called *The Mormon Village*.

After McMillan's fruitful undertaking in Sanpete Valley, where the Swedish evangels of the Free Christian Church followed in his wake, the Presbyterians were emboldened to proselyte in other Scandinavian centers: Brigham City, or Box Elder, as it was known, and the settlements in Cache Valley. Hyrum, Wellsville, and Millville kept the minister busy preaching twelve trilingual sermons a month. In 1884 the day schools in the three towns were enrolling 107, the Sunday schools 130. By 1892 Hyrum flourished with 101 in the day school. In Mendon, across the valley from Hyrum, the Scandinavian keeper of the Mendon Ward Historical Record compared the Presbyterians to the Pharisees of old, but by 1895 they could claim for Mendon "a strong and rapidly growing sentiment in favor of higher Christian education." [27]

The Congregationalists, despite their admirable New West Education Commission, which began an academy in Salt Lake in 1878 and by 1895 had schools in many towns with two hundred teachers and seven thousand students, paid no special attention to the Scandinavians. The Methodists did, writing a whole chapter of

[27] "Scandinavian Work in Utah," *Church Review,* 4:55 (December 29, 1895).

Scandinavian Methodist activity into their Utah history. They maintained a Sanpete Valley circuit, and established a First Norwegian Church in Salt Lake, with an attendant Norwegian school. The Scandinavian Methodists had small congregations in at least a dozen communities besides Salt Lake, in the main where Presbyterians had already made a beginning. "The work is hard, but looking up," was a familiar phrase in their reports. Often the Scandinavians shared the same facilities with the English Methodists, as in Brigham City. By 1897 the work in Mount Pleasant among the English and the Scandinavians was consolidated under a single pastor, a common pattern by that time. All the day and Sunday schools were conducted in English, though the congregational singing employed Norwegian and Danish Methodist hymnals as well as the Epworth Hymnal and Gospel Hymns. *Vidnesbyrdet,* the Norwegian and Danish weekly Methodist church paper, was "largely circulated in the Territory." [28]

The Baptists had Swedish missionaries in Salt Lake by the end of 1884, and the following year the American Baptist Home Mission Society sent five workers to Utah, two of them Scandinavians. Anna B. Nilsson, a missionary, found the work in Utah "the hardest she had ever done." Her greatest success came in the Industrial School in Ogden, in women's meetings, and in the homes, but she regretted there was no preacher to speak to them in a language they could understand. She pleaded for Scandinavian preachers. At length, in 1891, some Scandinavian brethren in Salt Lake City withdrew from the First Baptist Church to form the Swedish Baptist Church. Four years later, however, it had only a dozen members.[29]

The Lutherans came late and their activity was largely urban. The earlier immigrants had little love for the Establishment and failed to kindle to it no matter what their eventual quarrel with Mormonism. The Augustana Synod had the Mormon proselytes in mind for ten years before actually sending two missionaries among them in 1882, but they found the discouragements great and the soil stony. In twenty-seven years, which saw long vacancies, the only fruits were seven congregations, with 294 communicants and six churches.

[28] "Scandinavian Methodist Episcopal Missions in Utah," in *World's Fair Ecclesiastical History of Utah,* p. 273.
[29] "The Baptist Church," in *World's Fair Ecclesiastical History of Utah,* p. 284.

The yield for other Lutheran synods was equally barren. Danish Lutherans were tardiest of all, strange in view of the overwhelming proportion of Danes among Utah's Scandinavians, but it reflected the general indifference of Danish immigrants elsewhere in the United States to the home church. It was not until 1906 that the *Utah-Missionens Udvalg,* conceived in Denmark, sent Pastor Harald Jensen to Salt Lake City to found a Danish Evangelical Lutheran congregation. Denmark paid for all but $2,700 of the $17,000 to build the church Tabor, constructed in 1908.[30]

The denominational effort in Utah was an aspect of the extraordinary national attention directed to the state's immigration, seen by extremists as a means of strengthening Mormonism and its resistance to the federal government's attempts to prosecute it for polygamy. Reported the Omaha *Herald* in 1885: "The arrival in the United States of a few hundred Danes who have been brought here by the Mormon church is the signal for an outcry in the eastern press against their admission into the country, and calling on the government to stop this kind of immigration." But the *Herald* defended a program that might be "a plain matter of business" in increasing the wealth of the territory and the church, but which "combines with it positive Christian charity." [31] That seemed to be the opinion with Utah itself, where even an Englishman, usually condescending toward "dumb Swede" and "simple Dane," spoke well of his Scandinavian neighbors and described how the newcomers struck root:

> I have seen many Scandinavian families come into Manti in pioneer days with no means of support. Most of them had small trunks that contained all their earthly wealth, a few clothes and some bedding. Some walked from Salt Lake City to Sanpete County. Former countrymen would take them into their homes for a few weeks. Then the new immigrant would acquire a lot, build himself a small adobe home, surround it with a willow woven fence. Soon a few acres of ground were added to his accumulations, every foot of which was utilized. Mother and father and every child in the Scandinavian home worked. None of the wheat they raised was wasted and after it was threshed with the flail, the Scandinavians cleaned their wheat with hand-turned

[30] *Danske i Salt Lake City* (Salt Lake City, 1910), p. 18.

[31] Quoted without date in "De skandinaviske Emigranter," *Skandinaviens Stjerne,* 35:93 (December 15, 1885).

mills. They chopped their animal feed with a hand chopper so that it would go farther, and provide better animal food. There was no waste. I am an Englishman, but I have always said that the Scandinavian was thrifty, honest and God fearing, and set us a worthy example.[32]

VII

Unremitting as the demands of getting started seemed to be, the immigrants from Scandinavia were not forever pitched in a sober key. There were times when, as Christian Larsen urged, they gave up "the cares of the harvest and hay field." In their own tongue they enjoyed a considerable life of the spirit, as indispensable to their well-being as their lands and increase and the water they had learned to bring down from the hills.

The Mormon church tolerated the old tongue only as an expedient mediator, a means of teaching the gospel and informing the immigrant of the affairs of the kingdom in a language he could understand until he learned English; and in Brigham Young's time it even produced a phonetic system, the Deseret alphabet, that was expected to "prove highly beneficial in acquiring the English language to foreigners as well as the youth of our country." [33] But the ugly new alphabet was short-lived. The mother tongue itself proved a better instrument of adjustment than the artificial spelling reform. At least it was alive. The immigrants did not form autonomous congregations for worship in their own tongue, but for their instruction and welfare the church did foster a Scandinavian meeting in every community large enough to support one, with presiding officers drawn from the three countries. The Scandinavian meeting, or organization as it was sometimes called, in turn sponsored choirs, amateur theatricals, and outings and reunions on Old World holidays and mission anniversaries. Such lay activities growing up around the church kept it the center of the immigrants' intellectual life and went a long way toward preserving church loyalties when they were threatened in the 1870s by the denominational missions that tried to make an appeal through services in Scandinavian.

Whatever the Mormon church promoted was always inclusively Scandinavian, making no distinctions among Danes,

[32] Daughters of Utah Pioneers, *Scandinavia's Contribution to Utah* (Salt Lake City, 1939), pp. 25–26.

[33] "Eleventh General Epistle of the Presidency of the Church of Jesus Christ of Latter-day Saints," in *Deseret News,* April 13, 1854.

Swedes, and Norwegians—an ideal inherent in their new fellowship as Saints' and a union paralleling the organization of the mission in Scandinavia itself, which until 1905 was administered as a single unit. In the face of history, which had seen the three countries often at odds, the church urged harmony. Scandinavian unity seemed so complete in 1890 that "the young people of Zion do not know there are three nations in Scandinavia." [34] The turn of the century, however, saw the idyll rudely disturbed in Salt Lake City when a Swedish editor attacked the *Skandinavisme* that was making mere "Swedish Scandinavians" out of his people, or worse, changing them into "Danish Scandinavians." Otto Rydman, talented and somewhat histrionic editor of *Utah Korrespondenten,* had little use for Scandinavian union which he felt made for a bastard culture at best and at worst a Danish imposition on the less numerous Swedes and Norwegians. In his paper, founded in 1890 at first to serve the church, only later to antagonize it, he stumped for unadulterated Swedish culture and called for separate Swedish meetings. It was one thing to promote Swedish cultural autonomy in nonreligious activities but quite another to advocate Swedish separatism within the church. Besides, Rydman's invective angered church authorities and they rebuked him. When in 1901 he tried to observe *Julottan* in a ward meetinghouse on Christmas morning —a service in Mormon eyes too reminiscent of Lutheranism—he found the doors closed against him. He retaliated by vilifying the leaders of the Scandinavian meeting and the editors of the rival and conservative *Utah Posten,* who had him tried before a church court and excommunicated. But Rydman, an accomplished performer with Thalia, a Swedish dramatic society, and an engaging satirist in his column signed "Tomte," or Robin Goodfellow, was personally popular, and eighteen hundred petitioners from all over the state protested his dismissal, appealed to the First Presidency for a hearing, and endorsed his plea for a Swedish auxiliary within the church separate from the Scandinavian. When their petition was denied, they staged a mass meeting, a dramatic episode in what the American papers called "The Swedish Uprising."

After a silence of some months, during which it studied conditions in every place where Scandinavian meetings were held and determined the status of every petitioner, the church answered the

[34] Edward H. Anderson, "Scandinavia," *The Contributor* (Salt Lake City), 12:108 (December 1890).

malcontents in an epistle from the First Presidency: "To the Swedish Saints: Instructions in Regard to the Holding of Meetings, Amusements, Social Gatherings, etc." The epistle reaffirmed an established policy: "The counsel of the Church to all Saints of foreign birth who come here is that they should learn to speak English as soon as possible, adopt the manners and customs of the American people, fit themselves to become good and loyal citizens of this country, and by their good works show that they are true and faithful Latter-day Saints." The declaration advanced some telling arguments: the Scandinavian meeting in Salt Lake City was actually presided over by a Swede, with a Dane and Norwegian for counselors. Out of 521 names on the Salt Lake City portion of the petition, but 311 were members of the church, and most of these withdrew their names. The Scandinavian meetings regularly heard Swedish speakers and Swedish singing. Swedish gatherings were actually being held in the Fourteenth Ward twice a month. The joint social gatherings were always agreeable. A great many of the Scandinavians were intermarried; it would be absurd to separate husband and wife in meetings, social gatherings, excursions, and conferences. There was no objection to separate meetings where the numbers in each nationality justified them. "The inconvenience of the difference in the languages is smaller than the inconveniences of that division which has been advocated by a few extremists." Eighty percent of the signers of the petition, the epistle noted, could speak and understand English: let these attend the regular meetings in their own wards and leave the foreign-language meetings primarily for the aged and the recently arrived. "We deprecate the attempt to build walls of separation between Saints from different countries, and fanning into flame the dying embers of former national hatreds." [35]

The accent was on assimilation, as it had been from the beginning. The *Deseret News*, writing on "The Scandinavian Element" in 1886, had complimented the Scandinavians on "the facility with which they—the younger portion especially—acquire the language and customs of the country," and it defended those with "an accent that betrays their nationality" against "undeserved ridicule" and the charge of dullness because they could not understand the lan-

---

[35] *Deseret Evening News*, April 5, 1903. "The Swedish Uprising" was striking enough for the Swedish observer A.O. Assar to make note of it in his *Mormonernas Zion* (Stockholm, 1911), pp. 45–49. See *Utah Posten* and *Utah Korrespondenten* for August 1902 for the charges and countercharges and *Utah Korrespondenten*, January 9, 1903, for Rydman's account of the petitioners.

guage. The *News,* like the church itself, was sympathetic, but the ideal, plainly enough, as in the United States at large at the time, was the melting pot. Cultural pluralism was still in the future.

The Scandinavian meeting faded in time as immigration declined, to revive briefly after World War II to accommodate the new immigration; and the great annual reunions that used to bring Scandinavians together in one town or another from all over the state dwindled. Brigham City hosted four thousand Scandinavians at a reunion in 1902. Provo drew only fifty in the mid-1950s. The celebration in 1950 of the hundredth anniversary of the opening of the Scandinavian Mission saw the last large united gatherings: an outing at Liberty Park, a pageant in the University of Utah stadium, a meeting in the Salt Lake Tabernacle.

For several generations, however, the annual infusion of fresh arrivals from Scandinavia kept activities in the mother tongue (or tongues) alive, and the denominational missions, as already noted, were especially alert to language as their opportunity, providing services in the mother tongue and schools to learn English and other arts that would broaden horizons too narrowly confined by the Mormon outlook. A happy memory in Mount Pleasant was its first public celebration of Christmas, when many saw their first Christmas tree laden with presents from eastern missionary barrels and their first oranges, which children mistook for yellow apples. Despite the fearsome image of the denominational workers as Gentiles, their students, beneficiaries of their kindly and cultured influence, remembered them with gratitude. The granddaughter of a Danish immigrant who was one of the founders of Ephraim remembered that Rev. and Mrs. G. W. Martin were "wonderful examples of people who stuck with their post" and "made friends if not converts." They were interesting, different: they would hitch up the surrey and visit the southern canyons and bring home Indian relics and wonders of nature "that the local people did not value." Their home was the town's library and their Temperance Union sponsored a reading room, "warm, well lighted and furnished with tables and comfortable chairs, with plenty of good books, current magazines, and daily papers." [36] Utah history owes Martin a debt: he kept the only complete file of the Manti *Messenger.*

[36] Kate C. Snow on Manti, Sanpete County, in "Non-Mormon Religious Denominations in Utah," Daughters of Utah Pioneers, *Heart Throbs of the West,* 7:262–64.

Altogether, whether inside the church or out, there was considerably more life of the spirit in the mother tongue than outsiders, imagining the immigrant ignorant and deprived, were aware. Ephraim by 1876 had built a little theatre where a small company of Scandinavians produced the Norwegian comedy *Til Saeters*. Most of the settlements had their local dramatic group or at least a good choir; several even had a brass band, the instruments in one instance brought in an emigrant company from the homeland. Nearly every settlement could match Ephraim's zeal. Provo and Salt Lake had Scandinavian choirs. In 1891 Salt Lake's Scandinavian Dramatic Club, which sometimes performed in the Salt Lake Theatre, as did the Swedish acting society Thalia, gave fifteen performances in southern Utah, typical of its road-show activity for the benefit of countrymen in the settlements. *Danske Klub,* another amateur group of actors, had done the same in the 1880s.

The 1890s saw a Scandinavian Mercantile Association and a Scandinavian Democratic Club. In the same decade the Swedes formed Norden Society, *Svenska Gleeklubben, Harmonien,* and *Svea,* and after the turn of the century those most estranged from the Mormon church joined less indigenous associations like *Vasa Orden,* just as the Danes formed lodges of the *Danske Broderskap.* English classes, insurance brotherhoods, emigration fund societies, and sport clubs multiplied. In their patriotic eagerness to celebrate Old World holidays, the national orders often ran competition with the church-sponsored organizations. Both *Vasa Orden* and the Swedish Mormons celebrated Midsommarfest at the same resort on the same afternoon, sharpening the rivalry. But seven hundred Scandinavians joined hands in Salt Lake City on New Year's Eve in 1901–2 in a ball, concert, and supper at Christensen's Hall where Gov. Heber Wells addressed them.[37]

A natural association, antecedent to the formal organizations and never losing its vitality, was the informal evening over the coffee cups in each other's homes when in the early days the guests, as Emma Anderson of Hyrum remembered, brought their own lump sugar in their pockets. The church frowned on infractions of the Word of Wisdom, the brethren bearing down on the use of tea, coffee, tobacco, and strong drink; but the Scandinavians believed they had a special dispensation to drink coffee and their homemade beer. "Not all the goot tings," as one of them put it, "should be

[37] *Stjerne,* 11:59–60 (February 15, 1902).

left to the yentiles." With at least one Dane it was a particular mark of devotion to go without coffee on Sunday. God-fearing and obedient, the Scandinavians were, if anything, more indulgent in their entertainments, their eating and drinking, than the converts from Old or New England. The past, too recently left behind, broke through the discipline of the new faith especially on festive occasions. It was then the old stories were remembered and new ones told, born of unique situations in the Mormon community. Ephraim in time came to be known as "the town that laughs at itself."

It was twenty years before Utah Scandinavians issued an organ in their own tongues, but meanwhile they contributed letters and amateur verses to *Skandinaviens Stjerne,* the mission periodical they had come to know so well as converts and which many continued to read in the settlements. *Stjerne* made isolated inlanders surprisingly well read in international affairs, but it could not satisfy their provincial and immediate needs. At last, on December 20, 1873, pricked on by the threat of denominational proselyting among the immigrants, the Danish-Norwegian *Utah Posten* made its appearance, the first foreign-language publication in Utah and the first of three weeklies to bear the name through several metamorphoses during the next fifty years. Other publications followed in its wake, often with mixed political, cultural, and religious objectives: in 1874 the trilingual *Utah Skandinav,* which proved to be too liberal for Mormon readers and lasted only three years; *Bikuben* ("The Beehive") in 1876, destined for a long life of fifty-nine years. In 1895 it became church property, in time joined by the German *Beobachter,* the Swedish *Utah Posten,* and the Dutch *Utah Nederlander* to form the Associated Newspapers that the church subsidized until 1935. One of *Bikuben's* editors was Andrew Jenson, who became assistant church historian and founded *Morgenstjernen,* a historical journal that flourished in Danish from 1882 to 1886 and proved so valuable it became the *Historical Record* in English and ran to nine volumes. Jenson's labors were prodigious: he collected the archival records and biographical reminiscences from church missions around the world that have put all historians in his debt. The Swedes established an organ of their own in *Svenska Härolden* in 1885, which lasted until 1892, undermined, they felt, by Otto Rydman's *Korrespondenten* in 1890. In 1900 they founded a *Utah Posten* in Swedish, though Rydman took delight in pointing out that the officers of the Scandinavian Publishing Company, backers of the new venture, were anything but Swedish: three of its officers were Norwegian, two were Danish, and its two Swedes were really "Swedish Scandinavians."

Almost a footnote to the history of Swedish publication in Utah was *Utah Bladet,* founded in 1924 by Frank Malmstedt, former Swedish vice-consul in Salt Lake. A monthly, without any religious or political axe to grind but devoted to biographies of leading Swedish citizens and articles on business, national, and international affairs, it lived less than a year. *The Northern Light,* half in English, half in Danish, lasted for a few months in Logan in 1879; the *Utah Danske Amerikaner,* a monthly "family magazine," appeared for about a year in Huntsville. Its editor, Carl C. Ericksen, who called himself The Danish Publishing Company, went broke: "What did you suppose," his townsmen asked, "would become of a man who would start a newspaper in Huntsville?" [38] A cultured but equally luckless effort among the Norwegians was *Varden* ("The Beacon"), founded in 1910 at the peak of Norwegian population in Utah (2,304), intended to foster "affection for Norwegian language, music, and literature." It was the outgrowth of the activity of the *Norske Literaire Forening,* with Josef Straaberg, local literary and dramatic light, and Christian Johannessen, who would become known as the father of concert pianist Grant Johannessen, as co-editors. It lived only two years, but in that short time it promoted, among other things, a Norwegian exhibit of art and handicraft at the state fair, and published lives of prominent Norwegians in the state: John A. Widtsoe, scientist; Nephi Anderson, novelist; Ramm Hansen, architect; C.M. Nielsen, judge; Martin Christophersen, landscapist and gardener; Willard Weihe, violinist; Hans A. Pedersen, businessman—a talented array Norwegians were proud of.

More than an aspect of culture in the mother tongue, the Scandinavian papers were also an instrument promoting all its other forms—its musical and literary and dramatic societies, the social evenings, the reunions. The papers advertised them, previewed them, described and reviewed them, stirring up friendly rivalry between communities, establishing standards of performance, effecting communication where before had been only association. An unfailing delight were the contributions from immigrant writers who through the papers reached their widest audience. There was not a professional among them. Even the editors had to supplement their income

[38] J. Cecil Alter, *Early Utah Journalism* (Salt Lake City, 1938), p. 89. For a full account of publishing ventures among the Scandinavians in Utah, see my master's thesis, "Utah's Nordic-Language Press: Aspect and Instrument of Immigrant Culture" (University of Utah, 1947).

at other tasks. Their reward was small except in the affection and esteem of those for whom they wrote—and in the appreciation of a later generation slow to discover them but grateful for their legacy.

VIII

The Scandinavian presence in Utah persists, a strong and vital strain. The -sons and the -sens still predominate in many a small town, and even in the capital, more metropolitan and ethnically mixed by now, daily life in Utah continues to be full of reminders that one can be served by Scandinavian talent and tradition in a variety of ways, some more visible than others as they appeal to nostalgia and trade on Scandinavian associations. Shall we eat out at Finn's or Scandia Kaffe House? Shall we buy our imports from the Scandinavian Shop, our plants and flowers from Engh's? Shall we read a novel by Virginia Eggertsen Sorensen, listen to the Scandia Male Chorus or to Grant Johannessen play the piano, attend Willam Christensen's Nutcracker Ballet, admire Scandinavian architecture, see the handcart sculpture on Temple Square by Torleif Knaphus? Shall we watch the Vikings play soccer, ski on Ecker Hill, dance with the Swedes at Midsommarfest, celebrate Norwegian Constitution Day in May, laugh with Kris Kringle or be served by Lucia and her crown of lighted candles at Christmas? Shall we have Ryberg build our house and Christiansen or Madsen furnish it? Shall we go to church at Mount Tabor or Zion or Saint John's Lutheran? Shall we call Dr. Lund or Lagerquist or Larsen, get our prescription filled at Erickson Pharmacy, attend a viewing at Lindquist Mortuary?

From the cradle to the grave, Scandinavian energies, bone and sinew, mind and imagination, continue to contribute to the life of Utah's communities. We may not be aware of it. The musical lilt of Scandinavian English is seldom heard any more. Old-country customs, to be sure, are revived on festival occasions, when food and music and the old lore are brought expectantly out of their ancestral wrappings to create a special atmosphere. For the most part, daily life among the Scandinavians themselves is American, in a Utah setting, seasoned by pioneer and immigrant memories. The hyphen is less and less in evidence in Scandinavian-American. Though sometimes we point out the elements that built Utah in the way we recite "The House That Jack Built," the house is there for all to see, and who can say where the Scandinavian, or any other, contribution began and where it ends?

5

JEWS IN ZION

BY JACK GOODMAN

Except for the pitifully few American Indians occupying remnants of their once pristine homeland, we are a nation peopled solely by the descendants of immigrants. "Americans all, immigrants all," Franklin Roosevelt once said. Rather than a melting pot, the United States as a whole, and each segment of the federal union, is the sum of a hundred cultures, cultures washing across the North American continent in successive waves. From the time of Columbus until today, those waves have crossed the Alleghenies, the wide Missouri, and the Rockies, with eddies and crosscurrents washing west to east, north to south, and vice-versa after the continent-spanning nation "filled up."

Our viewpoints, mores, and folkways—the foundations of those diverse cultures—are themselves accretions having their beginnings in lands lapped by the Baltic, the Aegean, the Mediterranean, the waters of the Bristol Channel, the Irish Sea, even the Java Sea, or Mozambique Gulf. In any of the globe's lands, on the shores of scores of seas, oceans, gulfs, and bays, men and women came from upland moors or backcountry villages to peer across the restless waters towards a new world.

Americans all—immigrants all, with some, to be sure, emigrating and immigrating earlier than others. Some came penned in the holds of slave ships, others freely ventured aboard the *Mayflower*. Some came in steerage, some few traveled first cabin. Some journeyed in sleek clippers, others were crowded into the lower decks of four-funneled Nordeutscher Lloyd liners. Most would never again venture upon the sea to visit lost homelands on another continent. Instead, on dry land at long last and after fervent prayer, they began treading a continent extending far beyond their earliest imagined childhood horizons. Some settled in coastal cities, some migrated across the new land earlier and farther than their peers, thereby gaining pride of place among their descendants.

The Spanish explorers, the mountain men, the straggling, struggling Donner party, the Mormon settlers and government mapmakers, the forty-niners, the railroad builders, irrigators, merchants, miners, dam-builders, military men—all were caught up in a westering wave that washed across the boundaries of what came to be called Utah. And with them all, or almost all, came the wandering Jew, an emigrant and immigrant before, during, and even more so since biblical times. To Utah—to Zion—as elsewhere in the West, there came a trickle, a thin stream, of Jewish settlers. By reason of limitations set by geography and economics, the number of Jews crossing the Wasatch was never large in any year— perhaps never greater than one thousand per annum, although most such figures are at best conjectural. Indeed, the number of Jewish immigrants in the nation as a whole was not great at first. Then upheavals (ca. 1848) in the Austrian and German states caused a major outpouring of Jews from Central Europe. Later, when the pressures of pogroms or of czarist military programs caused the largest out-migration of Jews Europe had ever known, most Jews were content to settle wearily in the cities of the East Coast, in New York, Philadelphia, Providence, New Haven, where earlier immigrants, often relatives, could help them find shelter, food, and work. If there were attractions in the "outback," they were more likely to be found in Saint Louis, Cincinnati, New Orleans, and golden California than in the isolated, semi-arid Zion of a foreign faith.

At this juncture it is necessary to try to explain—for most readers in this dot on the globe where Jews are Gentiles—what a Jew is, and what a Jew is not. Definitions are imprecise, but one can begin by pointing out that Jews are Hebrews, the Semites whose sages and scholars gave the world three major monotheistic religions —Judaism, Christianity, and Islam.

But Jews are no longer members of a single race. Since the Diaspora, the dispersion of the People of the Book, nearly two thousand years ago, Jews have made their homes in many lands in the Mediterranean littoral, in eastern and western Europe, in Asia and Africa. Living in such lands so long, they have acquired some physical characteristics of the natives who people those lands. Does anyone look more "Spanish" than a Spanish Jew? Meeting one of the handful residing in Toledo, one may learn of an ancestor who crossed with Columbus on the great navigator's second voyage, while *his* ancestors had lived in Spain throughout the Moorish era.

Why should he not look "Spanish?" However, Americans—Jews as well as Gentiles—insist there is a characteristic "Jewish look" recognizable in some of their neighbors. This "look" may make such neighbors more, less, or just as acceptable as the red-headed "Irish look" or the pink-cheeked "Scottish look" or the sleek-haired, dark "Italian look." But there are "black Irishmen" and blonde Italians—blonde Jews, too. In truth, in the case of most American Jews, their "racial" appearance is of eastern or middle European origin. While early Utah Jews were of German origin, the majority of Utah's few thousand present-day Jews had parents, grand-parents, or prior ancestors who arrived in the great wave of immi-gration that brought two and one-half million Russian, Polish, and Rumanian-Hungarian Jews to American shores between 1881 (immediately after the assassination of Czar Alexander II and the resultant pogroms) and 1924 (when the Johnson-Lodge immigra-tion bill effectively shut off the flow).

While American Jews, and therefore Utah's Jews, are not members of a single ethnic stock, they are not a cohesive religious unit either. While some would debate the point, virtually all Jewish scholars hold that to be born Jewish is to be Jewish forever. One may choose not to practice the Hebrew religion; one may have taken leave of synagogue, temple, or congregation formally or informally. In the main, justly or not, fellow Jews will continue to consider such a person Jewish. One can depart most faiths at will, or at least after excommunication. But as many Jews learned to their sorrow in Nazi Germany and elsewhere during the holocaust, most neighbors, including former coreligionists, will continue to consider a Jew Jewish, even if he or she had parents or grandparents who departed the faith a half-century earlier.

This brings us to the Jews of Utah, a scant twenty-five hundred men, women, and children residing in Utah in the 1970s and some of those who came before.

It is easy, to be sure, to count as Jews those who have been members of Utah's Orthodox, Conservative, and Reform Hebrew congregations. Presently, for example, Salt Lake's Kol Ami, which combines Reform and Conservative congregants, lists 310 family memberships, with perhaps seven hundred people affiliated and fairly active. But how many Jews have resided in Utah, in Utah Territory, in Deseret, down through the years? Although no one is certain, the number is doubtless small, perhaps no more than twenty-five thousand in the century-plus history of Jews in the area. That number includes the few hundred from outside Salt Lake City whose friends and family saw fit to give them proper burial in the sanctified earth of Salt Lake's Jewish cemetery established in 1864. However, one can only estimate the number of Jews who scattered across Zion in Utah's early years as merchants, farmers, ranchers, and miners outside of what was first called Great Salt Lake City. Certainly there were only a score or so in the territory's initial two decades.

Long before forming the territory's initial congregation, a few obviously heeded the scriptural "Hear, O Israel, the Lord our God is One; and thou shall love the Lord thy God with all thy heart, and with all thy soul, and with all thy might." Jews, unlike Latterday Saints, were not given to keeping "journals" of the everyday affairs. How many fastened a *mezuzah* [1] upon their tentposts or cabin lintels in isolated new settlements? And for every Utah Jew who placed a tiny, rolled sampling of the Lord's Word upon his door as commanded in Deuteronomy, how many others quietly bound their *Tefillin* [2] upon their forearms, or continued to set "frontlets between thine eyes" as they had done in Prussia, Austria, Holland, or England? We shall never know precisely.

There are no Jewish names among the "First Company" members of 1847 listed on the Brigham Young Monument at South Temple and Main in the Utah capital city. Just a few years later, however, Jews in some number crossed the territory in the whitetopped wagons heading for California and Oregon. According to journal-keeping Lorenzo Brown, on March 1, 1851, he "called to see some Hungarian Jews living in the ward. . . . emigrants bound for the [California] mines . . . forced to leave their native land because of the revolution." [3]

Aside from this anonymous vanguard of the larger number of Jews who would soon be fleeing Europe's wars, revolutions, and pogroms, the first Jewish arrivals to "settle in" were Julius Gerson Brooks and his wife Isabell, usually identified by her nickname, Fanny. The Brooks, or Brucks, family were natives of Silesia. Born in 1821, Julius left Germany at twenty-one, took passage to New York, lived with a sister, and, according to Leon Watters, "peddled

[1] A small scroll containing scriptural passages affixed to a doorpost.

[2] Phylactery, a small leather box containing scriptural passages bound to the forehead during prayer.

[3] Quoted in Juanita Brooks, *The History of the Jews in Utah and Idaho* (Salt Lake City, 1973), p. 13.

in New England." Like many immigrants of the period, he earned a modest sum, returned to Silesia, and took a bride of sixteen summers back to the New World.[4]

The young couple's story is almost a standard tale of the period. They journeyed to Illinois, were fascinated by tales of the Far West told them by a recently returned army man, then headed for Oregon country by way of Utah. They reached the Salt Lake Valley in July 1854 as members of a train of fifteen wagons and decided to stay. Soon afterwards, the *Millennial Star,* listing twenty-two business establishments in Great Salt Lake City, recorded among them "Mrs. Brooks, Millinery Store and Bakery."[5] Julius and Fanny Brooks were to become solid citizens of the business, religious, and social community, their name recalled in the brick and stone Brooks Arcade building at State and Third South streets. However, Julius was a bit restless, operating shops in the California mining towns and junketing to New York, Portland, Boise, and San Francisco. Years later Brooks told his daughter, Mrs. Samuel H. Auerbach, that the army man whose tales had spurred them west from Galena, Illinois, starting place of their wagon, was Ulysses S. Grant—an army lieutenant turned unsuccessful farmer.

Another early arrival was a thirty-nine-year-old artist-photographer of considerable talent, luck, and fame, whose name, Solomon Nunes Carvalho, turns up with some frequency in volumes devoted to the military exploration of the West. A South Carolina native of Portuguese and Sephardic Jewish descent, Carvalho had the good or bad fortune to join John C. Fremont's 1853–54 mapping expedition to the Rocky Mountains, one of a series of ventures that brought Fremont the rank of general, the popular title of the Pathfinder, and even made him a candidate for the presidency (he was soundly trounced).

Carvalho signed on with Fremont as artist and daguerreotypist for the expedition on August 22, 1853.[6] In fulfilling his assignment, he faced familiar hazards of western exploration: dwindling rations, freezing temperatures, and hostile Indians. Added to these difficulties were the particular challenges of wet-plate photography:

[4] A short biography of Julius and Fanny Brooks is found in Leon L. Watters, *The Pioneer Jews of Utah* (New York, 1952), pp. 123–25.

[5] *Millennial Star,* August 29, 1854.

[6] Solomon Nunes Carvalho, *Incidents of Travel and Adventure in the Far West,* ed. Bertram Wallace Korn (Philadelphia, 1954), p. 77. This centennial edition provides an excellent introduction by Korn with many details on Carvalho's life.

While suffering from frozen feet and hands, without food for twenty-four hours, travelling on foot over mountains of snow, I have stopped on the trail, made pictures of the country, repacked my materials, and found myself frequently with my friend Egloffstien [sic], who generally remained with me to make barometrical observations, and a muleteer, some five or six miles behind camp, which was only reached with great expense of bodily as well as mental suffering.[7]

Fighting against bitter cold, but determined to cheer himself and his companions, Carvalho "had reserved with religious care, two boxes containing one pound each, of Alden's preserved eggs and milk . . . . Nobody knew I had them. A paper of arrow root . . . I had also reserved. These three comestibles, boiled in six gallons of water, made as fine a blanc mange as ever was *mangéd* on Mount Blanc." Dreaming perhaps of traditional Rosh Hashanah observances, Carvalho served his dessert on the secular New Year's Day, January 1, 1854, to the "satisfaction and astonishment of the whole party," a fitting climax to a meal of horse soup and horse steaks fried in buffalo tallow.[8]

In February the expedition nearly perished in the mountains outside of Parowan, but settlers rescued the party and took them into their homes. Carvalho stayed at the home of a Mr. Heap for fourteen days, suffering from severe frostbite, diarrhea, and the symptoms of scurvy. The artist, accompanied by "Egloffstien," was taken by wagon to Salt Lake City where the topographer would join the remnants of the Gunnison party and where Carvalho would set up as a portraitist, hoping to earn cash for his trek back to Baltimore. Among the results of this effort were paintings of Brigham Young, Daniel H. Wells, Wilford Woodruff, and other church and civic leaders. Then Carvalho journeyed south with Brigham Young, sketched Chief Walker and other local Indian leaders, and joined Parley P. Pratt and a group headed toward Las Vegas and San Bernardino, sites of new Mormon settlements. He went on to Los Angeles, met a few fellow Jews, then returned east where in 1857 his *Incidents of Travel and Adventure in the Far West* was published. Carvalho's vivid narrative of the expedition remains one of the most readable accounts of travel in the

---

[7] *Ibid.*, p. 81.

[8] *Ibid.*, pp. 148–49.

West and continues to be a prime source of information on the 1853 expedition for which Fremont kept only sketchy notes. During just ten weeks in Salt Lake City and another few months on the trail in the territory, Carvalho filled sketchbooks and notebooks with drawings, paintings, and meticulous observations that are still studied for a record of pioneer times in Utah.

While the Brookses became Utah's first Jewish family, and Carvalho the first Jew of prominence to limn the territory, several Jewish converts to Mormonism had preceded them. Watters and other historians cite Alexander Neibaur who reached Utah in 1848 as having been "educated to be a rabbi." Levi Abrahams came to Utah in 1854 and joined the Mormon church, and there obviously were other converts. But the most important newcomers to Utah in the context of "Jewish pioneering" were the merchants who arrived shortly after Johnston's army.

As most Utah-educated children and adults know, friction akin to war had developed between Mormon leaders and federal officials within the first decade of settlement. Brigham Young had sought to develop a self-sustaining, theologically based Zion in the mountains, in what had been Mexican territory; federal laws, courts, and troops followed close behind his wagons to ensure that Deseret would be a part of the Union. In 1857, following serio-comic stresses and strains between none-too-judicious federal judges and a people who looked inward for guidance, President James Buchanan sent a new territorial governor to Utah—plus the troops deemed necessary to support the laws of the land. One result of the "Utah War" that followed was the departure, for a ten-year period, of Mr. and Mrs. Julius Brooks, who wanted no part of the bloodshed they foresaw. Another and more significant result was the establishment of Camp Floyd, thirty-five miles south and west of the city, on the Pony Express route of the period.

The troops led by Col. Albert Sidney Johnston fired few, if any, shots in anger; and whether or not abandonment of Mormon settlements in California and Nevada, plus Brigham Young's evacuation of his capital city, was indeed necessary has long been debated by Utah historians. But the troops who marched through a deserted Great Salt Lake City in June 1858 to set up camp in Cedar Valley brought with them large supplies of "eastern goods," including harness, hardware, uniforms, and the like. All of their stores became available at a few cents on the dollar when a far

more serious revolt led President Lincoln's War Department to recall its bluecoats from the Jordan to the Potomac.

To improve supply services and communications for military
and civil establishments, both the Pony Express and the Overland
Stage services were soon initiated. Even before the men of Johnston's command marched off to battle in the Civil War, settlers,
wagoners, freighters, and shopkeepers clustered in the Camp Floyd
vicinity where hard cash and government paper money had become available. Previously, barter or church scrip had usually substituted for more familiar forms of legal tender.

While such firms as Walker Brothers were on hand earlier,
Jewish merchants and freighters were doing business with the military at Camp Floyd by 1858. Apparently the first to arrive was
Nicholas Siegfried Ransohoff, whose name appears on bills of lad-
ing in 1858, then as a member of Utah's first Masonic Lodge which
was founded at Camp Floyd in April 1859. Ransohoff apparently
had Orthodox dietary scruples—there is a fairly well authenticated
story that he lent Brigham Young $30,000 to purchase Camp
Floyd's entire supply of pork when the post closed, due to Ransohoff's distaste for the *treyfa* ("unclean, forbidden") meat.[9]

The most important arrival of 1859—or so it was to prove—
was Samuel H. Auerbach, who wheeled in with a wagonload of
goods from California where he had set up in business with his
brothers Frederick and Theodore during the gold rush. Natives of
Prussia, the brothers ran tent and woodshack stores at Rabbit
Creek and Bodie, California, and later at Austin, Nevada, after
first spending a few years on the eastern seaboard. Although they
traded in Camp Floyd in 1859, it was 1864 before Frederick came to
Salt Lake with a wagonload of general merchandise, conferred with
Brigham Young, and was able to set up "The People's Store" in a
Main Street adobe. Samuel, eleven years his junior, became Fred's
partner, while Theodore moved back east to New York City.

F. Auerbach & Bro. flourished, moving to larger and larger
locations and finally settling in at State and Broadway where it
continues under family direction as one of the city's best-known
institutions. However, in the interim, the Auerbach brothers had
simultaneously set up branches at railheads along the line of the
Union Pacific Railroad as it advanced from Bryan, Wyoming, to

[9] Watters, *Pioneer Jews,* pp. 126–27.

Ogden and then Promontory. The Auerbachs prospered, paying such San Francisco creditors as Levi Strauss in gold, "until 1868 when the institution known as Z.C.M.I. was started . . . for a time this seemed to threaten our existence as merchants. . . ." [10]

The brothers Auerbach, with other "Gentile" merchants, found themselves caught up in an ideological-economic war unique to Utah. This short-lived struggle had its roots in the openly expressed belief on the part of church leaders that non-Mormon businessmen were guilty of outrageously overcharging the general populace. By the time the situation came to a head, the city's Jewish merchants included three Siegel brothers, Ichel and Abraham Watters, Charles Popper, Nathan and James Ellis, as well as the Auerbachs. And it must be stressed that the economic warfare that soon centered around the ZCMI and later at the new Gentile city of Corinne was not anti-Semitic in nature. In fact, church leaders looked with rather more favor upon Jewish businessmen such as the Ransohoffs and Auerbachs than they did upon the Walker brothers and other non-Mormon or ex-Mormon merchants and traders.

Indeed, open-minded reading makes it clear that, from its earliest days, the founders and leaders of the Church of Jesus Christ of Latter-day Saints gave those who professed the Hebrew faith special consideration. This appears to be due to Mormon acceptance of the Jews as God's chosen people, their literal belief "in the gathering of Israel and the restoration of the Ten tribes," Mormon acceptance of the Old Testament, and the Mormon belief that Jews will be returned to Jerusalem prior to Christ's Second Coming. Back in Kirtland, Ohio, in 1836, Joseph Smith had persuaded the highly regarded Joshua Seixas to instruct church leaders in Hebrew; at Nauvoo in 1842, when Joseph Smith officiated as chaplain at the installation of a new Masonic Lodge, the grand master who came from Columbus, Ohio, for the installation was Abraham Jonas, a Jew.[11]

In part as the result of a national anathema towards Mormons linked to the practice of polygamy, in part as the residue of the Utah War and ill will bred by the presence of federal troops and

[10] *Ibid.,* pp. 131–33.

[11] While official Mormon doctrine has been generally favorable regarding Jews, anti-Semitism has nevertheless existed within the church fold. For example, a Salt Lake attorney recalls as a boy that a member of his ward's leadership was outspoken in his contempt for Jews. Interview with Justin C. Stewart, July 28, 1975, Salt Lake City.

courts, in part because of the approach of the railroad and an end to isolation in the mountains, and, of course, due to matters economic centering around charges of villainous profiteering, local frictions led to shootings and at least a pair of murders. There was preaching against dealing with non-Mormons—and finally a near panic among the Gentile merchants, who, on December 20, 1866, sent Brigham Young a most remarkable petition, signed with twenty-three names, including many Jews. The petitioners offered to sell out and move on, providing that all outstanding accounts of church members be settled and that all "goods, merchandise, chattels, houses, improvements . . . be taken at cash valuation, and we make a deduction of twenty-five per cent from the total amount." [12]

President Young would have none of the bargain, perhaps realizing that the departure of the Gentile merchants would be followed by the departure of all non-Mormons and the raising of questions in Congress and elsewhere concerning the situation under which the members of a single religious faith could persuade all others to vacate a territory of the United States. Young took a different tack, apparently reasoning that establishment of a church-owned "yardstick" would show Saints and Gentiles alike what prices and profits were deemed fair and reasonable. Reversing former precedent, the church leader developed the idea that the Latter-day Saints should engage in business cooperatively. In establishing Zion's Cooperative Mercantile Institution, the church purchased six Mormon-owned businesses, and one Jewish-owned establishment, that of Nicholas Ransohoff, Young's good friend.

When the ZCMI opened, signboards bearing an "all-seeing eye" with the inscription "holiness to the Lord" appeared over the doorways of its scattered shops. Mormons were exhorted in tabernacle and wardhouse meetings to patronize their own cooperative, and dealings with Gentile merchants were discouraged. Sales at the Auerbach brothers' store fell sharply. While Auerbach figures are not available, business at the large Walker Brothers shop was reported to have fallen from a $60,000 a month figure to $5,000 monthly in the second year of ZCMI operation.[13] Auerbachs, the Kahn, Siegel, and other sizeable Jewish businesses apparently were hit as severely. As a result, many small merchants shuttered their shops and moved out of the territory or to Corinne. This new metropolis of mud streets and wood fronts gave signs of becoming Utah's

[12] Brooks, *Jews of Utah and Idaho,* p. 60.

[13] Watters, *Pioneer Jews,* p. 58.

Gentile city, serving mining towns in Idaho and Montana and east into Wyoming, as well as Utah communities. By 1873 Corinne had nearly four thousand residents and its streets were alive with freight wagons meeting Central and Union Pacific trains. But Utah's business as well as religious center remained in Salt Lake.

In two decades Corinne was a ghost town. The prevailing church had gradually eased its strictures on trade with Gentiles; its parallel effort at cooperative communal ownership, the United Order, had failed in rural Utah, although the ZCMI flourished. Jewish merchants again set up shop in Salt Lake City, Provo, and along the lines of the new railroads. But Corinne—or rather the isolationist efforts by church leaders that brought it into being— had produced something of a new political spirit among Gentiles. Utah's first opposition political party, the Liberal party, took shape in the hamlet on the Bear River. Its initial members included such Jewish citizens as Samuel Kahn, Gumpert Goldberg, Julius Malsh, and a newcomer, Simon Bamberger. A short, quick-spoken, eminently energetic man, Bamberger became a major figure in Utah business, railroading, mining, and its only Jewish governor.[14]

While the territory's score or two of Jews were busily trying to survive economically in this strange new sector of a strange new land, they were almost equally active trying to keep their old religious way of life viable.

Although it is just conjecture, it must be presumed that many of the score or two of Jews who had wandered to and through Utah Territory in the era of the Utah War, Civil War, and Gentile economic war, carried *Siddurs* (prayer books) in their wagons or packs and carried the faith of their fathers in their hearts. In October 1864 the *Salt Lake Telegraph* reported that Jews of the territory's largest city had celebrated the Day of Atonement in the "home of an East Temple Street merchant, since a synagogue is lacking." Illustrative of the way in which news got around, the *Archives Isrealites* in distant Paris reported with some amazement that Salt Lake's Jewry comprised members enough for a *minyan*[15] and closed their places of business on Holy Days—this in 1865. Somehow a *Torah,* or sacred scroll, turned up, for a year later the *Salt Lake Telegraph* reported services at which H. M. Cohen "read ably" from such a hand-lettered scroll at services in the

---

[14] *Ibid.,* pp. 60–64.

[15] Male quorum necessary for services.

197

Masonic Hall presided over by Nathan Ellis. In 1866 services were held in the Seventies Hall, and a committee resolution signed by Ellis, Auerbach, and Siegel formally thanked Brigham Young for his kindness in furnishing this site for High Holy Days worship.[16]

At the midpoint in this same decade, the community's half-hundred Jews joined Gentiles of other persuasions in raising funds for the purchase of land and construction of a building called Independence Hall, which was to be the first non-Mormon church in Utah Territory. Although the deed was entered in the name of "Trustees of the First Church of Jesus Christ Congregation," one trustee, Samuel Kahn, was indubitably Jewish, and the building, at Third South just west of Main, was utilized for Jewish Holy Days as well as Sabbath services. However, on occasion Jewish services were again held in such quarters as the Masonic Hall, the Seventies Hall on Temple Square, and even at Richard's Skating Rink.

Lacking a rabbi, services were variously conducted by Ichel Watters, Moses Caspar Phillips, or other local savants. The community was also lacking a *moel* to perform circumcisions. However, by 1872 the *Salt Lake Tribune* was able to report the temporary availability of a visitor, Rabbi H. Lovenberg, of Elko, Nevada, who circumsized a trio of youngsters. And from that year forward the *Tribune* and *Telegram* took regular note of Passover, New Year, and Atonement services held by the tiny Jewish community.

It is obvious, particularly from the notes left by the Watters and Auerbach families, that the impossibility of maintaining dietary laws centering around kosher meats was recognized early by Utah Jews, but it is equally obvious that holiday ceremonies were observed as fully as possible. The Watters home was apparently a center and haven, with as many as thirty persons, including most of the city's Jewish bachelors, often on hand for Passover meals where *matzohs* ("unleavened bread"), wine, the requisite bitter herbs, and traditional songs were all features.

During thirty or so years following the entry of the first Jews into Zion, there was social fellowship and economic cooperation of the sort to be expected among newcomers of similar antecedents

[16] For a more detailed look at the beginnings of Jewish religious activity in Utah, see Watters, *Pioneer Jews,* chapter 8; Brooks, *Jews of Utah and Idaho,* chapters 6 and 7; and the Jewish Archives, Western Americana, Marriott Library, University of Utah, Salt Lake City. Additional data have been uncovered recently by Norton B. Stern in "The Founding of the Jewish Community in Utah," *Western States Jewish Historical Quarterly* 8 (1975):65–69.

far from their homelands. And there were discussions concerning formal establishment of a religious congregation and construction of a suitable house of worship. However, numbers were considered insufficient until March 1, 1881, when twenty-three solid citizens met to form B'nai Israel of Salt Lake City. Board President Henry Siegel and his aides purchased a $2,600 lot at Third South and First West as a building site. Planning and fund-raising continued until, by September 30, 1883, the city's first Jewish house of worship was dedicated, a brick structure that served as both Hebrew school and synagogue.

Ideological problems paralleling those still surfacing during present days arose almost immediately. Congregation B'nai Israel, formed by the community's few Jewish families, initially followed Orthodox ritual using Hebrew texts, with members wearing hats, or *yarmulkahs* ("skull caps"), and, apparently, with women separated from men at services in traditional fashion. But in 1884 Rabbi Leon Strauss of Belleville, Ohio, was called to the congregation, after consultation with Dr. Isaac M. Wise of Cincinnati, one of the founders of the American "Reform" movement. Heads were uncovered during the ensuing High Holy Days, the *Minhag America,* or Reform, prayers were used, and dissension flared. The combined Hebrew and English services aroused the displeasure of Isadore Morris, Moses Phillips, and others, and factionalism was given as a reason for the resignation of Rabbi Strauss in July 1885. Those who know the present Congregation Kol Ami, itself a merger of Temple B'nai Israel (Reform) and Congregation Montefiore (Conservative), will instantly and sadly realize that ecumenical movements in Utah Judaism are a bit hard to achieve, or will quickly appreciate that problems perplexing today's Salt Lake Jewry have a historical base.

With the schism came a decline in income as well as membership. By 1886 peacemaker Samuel Auerbach was suggesting return to the older ritual for the High Holy Days to appease the former members who held to Orthodox tenets. But B'nai Israel struggled on and made considerable fiscal progress by selling its building for a reputed $20,000 in 1889, after which the present property at Fourth East between Second and Third souths was purchased as a site for "old B'nai Israel." A youthful graduate of the new Hebrew Union College, Rabbi Heiman J. Elkin was employed, and under him the Reform ritual became the established form at B'nai Israel.

199

Shortly afterwards the congregation had a new home, a structure that proved reasonably adequate to its needs for some eighty years—with a few additions, to be sure. The building, costing about $37,500 and still standing, is in effect a small replica of the Great Synagogue in Berlin. Its architect was Philip Meyer, a nephew of Frederick Auerbach. The Salt Lake merchant brought his nephew to Utah at his own expense, and Meyer prepared the architectural designs for the domed, kyune sandstone building gratis. As if to illustrate the subtleties of fate, Berlin's Great Synagogue was to have its glass smashed in the *Kristalnacht* of the Nazis and then to be smashed to rubble by bombing planes. Some may have been piloted by Jewish lads from Utah. As for Philip Meyer—he was to die in one of Hitler's death camps. Not a few of the congregants at B'nai Israel, thousands of miles from the holocaust, found it difficult to believe, in the initial years of National Socialism, that German Jews who had successfully accommodated themselves to the ways of Bismark and the kaisers could really be threatened by an Austrian house-painter named Adolph Hitler.

Congregation Montefiore had its inception in 1889 when a gathering of Orthodox and Conservative Jews took place at the home of Nathan Rosenblatt at Eighth South and State Street. While it would be an oversimplification to state that Utah by that year was seeing a major influx of Russian, Polish, and Central European Jews, it seems likely that the proportion of Jews of Germanic extraction was dropping perceptibly and that immigrants from the Russo-Polish "Pale of Settlement" would soon be numerically in the ascendancy. Certainly census figures reflecting arrivals at Castle Garden and later Ellis Island in New York show increasing thousands were migrating from the *shtettels* ("villages") and ghettos of czarist Russia. By the turn of the century, shortly after Utah Mormons at long last rejected polygamy and achieved statehood, it seems likely that Yiddish-speakers who had spent their childhoods under the kaisers or Emperor Franz Josef were beginning to be outnumbered, in Utah, by Yiddish-speakers who had departed the embrace of the Russian Bear.

Total familial membership at Congregation Montefiore reached thirty by 1904. Morris Levy donated a lot, Isadore Morris led off contributions with $150 in gold dust, and such worthies as Joshua Shapiro, Benjamin Kahn, Nathan Rosenblatt, Moses Nathan, and assorted Levitts, Levys, and Lewises set about building the twin-domed, Moorish-looking structure that stands today. The Mormon church, apparently at the urging of Isadore Morris, contributed $650 to the building fund. This donation came partially in gratitude for the activities of Morris who earlier had gone to Washington to successfully petition for the release from prison of Bishop William R. Smith. Smith had been imprisoned for polygamy under the Edmunds Act, along with a score of other Mormon leaders, and church officials were grateful for the support they had received from Jews—among them Fred Simon, who had insisted discrimination against Mormons be ended in the Salt Lake Chamber of Commerce of which he was president. It was Simon who wrote Governor Caleb West protesting federal and state disfranchisement of Mormons for the crime of polygamy—said "crime" being part and parcel of their sincerely held religious beliefs. Such an argument, Simon wrote of the Cullom Bill, sets precedents so far reaching as to "terminate by gradually disenfranchising the Catholic for believing too much and the Infidel for believing too little." [17]

Setting benchmarks in the history of any group, large or small, can be more of a vice than a virtue, but for convenience one can broadly assert that the pioneering days of Utah's Jewry closed at about the beginning of the new century, just as the pioneering days for the Utah Saints ended with the coming of the transcontinental railroad. Not only were there two congregations in Salt Lake City, plus a B'nai Brith Lodge, plus the much-needed women's auxiliaries, but Jewish stores and businesses were pretty firmly established in a dozen Utah towns by 1900–15. Except in Ogden, there were never enough families in these towns for the *minyan*. But there was a Lessing Hotel in Minersville, and A. B. Cline's Golden Rule Store in Beaver. Arthur Frank had set up in the clothing business at Midvale, and Louis Frank in Nephi. Max and Sol Krotki operated stores first in Richfield, then Kimberly, then Marysvale. Max Cohen's general store in Gunnison thrived to the point he became president of the local bank; in the coal towns Harry Lowenstein and Sam Stein had stores in Price and Helper, while one Morris Glassman branched out from Vernal to Castle Dale and Huntington. There were success stories and failures. Nate Horne, who operated a store in Payson, sold out to his clerk Ben Roe in 1920. Roe and his brother expanded, operated a sizeable store on State Street in Salt Lake, and Ben Roe became one of the city's best regarded community members. But in addition to shopkeepers, there were

[17] Watters, *Pioneer Jews,* p. 171.

Right: *Sarah Cohen Kahn, wife of businessman and civic leader Samuel Kahn, was one of Salt Lake City's prominent hostesses, entertaining dignitaries such as Vice-President Schuyler Colfax at the family home on Main Street.* Below: *The corner of Second South and Main in Salt Lake City in the 1880s showed the influence of pioneer Jews in merchandising.*

From the top: *The Auerbach brothers and others opened branch stores in Corinne in the 1870s. Jews helped found the first opposition political party in Utah, the Liberal party, at Corinne. Entrepreneur Samuel Newhouse built the Boston and Newhouse office buildings on Exchange Place. This view was taken from the Newhouse Hotel. Gov. William Spry spoke at a harvest celebration in the Jewish agricultural colony of Clarion, Piute County, 1912. Despite the efforts of many, the colony had to be abandoned.*

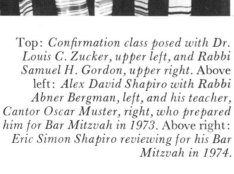

Top: *Confirmation class posed with Dr. Louis C. Zucker, upper left, and Rabbi Samuel H. Gordon, upper right.* Above left: *Alex David Shapiro with Rabbi Abner Bergman, left, and his teacher, Cantor Oscar Muster, right, who prepared him for Bar Mitzvah in 1973.* Above right: *Eric Simon Shapiro reviewing for his Bar Mitzvah in 1974.*

Simon Bamberger, one of the first Jewish governors in the United States, founded the interurban Bamberger Railroad and the well-known Lagoon resort in Davis County.

Right: *Temple B'nai Israel, built in 1891, was modeled by architect Philip Meyer after the famous Berlin temple. Below: Rabbi Mordecai Podet, left, and Cantor Harry Sterling at ground-breaking ceremonies for the Jewish Community Center in 1956.*

Top: *Utah-born scientist,
industrialist, and author
Leon L. Watters with friend
and colleague Albert Einstein.*
Above left: *Congregation
Montefiore.* Above right: *Ben
M. Roe and Dr. Louis C.
Zucker examine Chai Award
given to Mr. Roe by Israel for
his activities in behalf of that
nation.*

Jewish peddlers who worked manfully but never quite made money enough to set up proper stores. There were dealers in furs and hides, dealers in scrap iron or "junk" who prospered mightily; there were others who failed and moved on as the market for their wares rose and fell.

This might be a good time to cite Nathan Rosenblatt, who arrived in the valley a few years prior to the turn of the century, then went peddling to the nearby mining towns of Alta, Park City, and Bingham with wagonloads of goods from the Auerbach brothers' stores. Rather than return to State Street with an empty wagon, young Rosenblatt began buying odds and ends of outworn mining machinery—scrap iron, or junk. By the time his sons Simon and Morris grew to adulthood, peddling was abandoned for an iron foundry and machinery business, which eventually became the multi-million dollar Eimco firm. The surviving son, Joseph, headed it prior to its sale a dozen years ago. Much earlier, during World War I, the father-and-sons firm ventured its capital and all it could borrow to set up Utah's first steel mill at Midvale. The Armistice brought cancellation of wartime contracts, and Nathan Rosenblatt found himself heavily in debt. "It's a great country," he is reputed to have said. "I came here without a dime, and now I owe a million dollars." The debt was paid in full.

A major success story is, of course, that of Simon Bamberger, one of four brothers who came to Utah from Hesse, Germany, by way of New York and Saint Louis. Fourteen years old when he reached New York, Simon took the steam-cars to Cincinnati to board with relatives but failed to change trains and wound up in Indianapolis, an error all too typical of the travels and travails of "greenhorns" fresh off the boat and unable to speak the language of the new land. Luckily there was a Bamberger cousin in Indianapolis who employed the youngster. After a few months he joined an older brother, Herman, at Wilmington, Ohio. There, during the Civil War, "Herman guarded bridges and I guarded his store," Simon recalled.[18]

When the Civil War ended, Bamberger worked his way west in an effort to make collections of some bad debts. Then, keeping pace with the work camps of the Union Pacific as its rails were laid, he began cashing and rediscounting paychecks for construc-

---

[18] *Ibid.*, pp. 163–69. There is a wealth of source material available on the career of Simon Bamberger.

tion workers. Soon the youthful businessman was erecting and renting tents and shacks in the rough, tough camps. Reaching Ogden, he had cash enough to buy a half-interest in the Lester House Hotel, operated by Mr. and Mrs. Briner Cohen. A smallpox epidemic wrote finis to the hotel in 1869 or thereabouts, after which the venturesome Bamberger joined the Cohens as partner in the Delmonico Hotel (renamed the White House) at the southwest corner of Main and Second South in Salt Lake City.

By 1872 Bamberger was "in mining," at the Sailor Jack operation in Tintic. As his brothers Jacob, Herman, and Louis arrived, he set them up in business but made his major strike with W. S. McCornick and W. W. Chisholm in the Centennial Eureka mine in the silver-rich district. Looking into some coal mines in Sanpete County, Bamberger began to realize that a railroad to Nephi was necessary for successful operation. According to an interview with Watters, he promptly set off for England, where he raised a million dollars. He then built the requisite railroad, "but the coal turned out to be of inferior quality and the venture was a failure."

Untroubled by his million-dollar loss—or perhaps spurred on to meet the venture's debts—he obtained a franchise for a new railroad extending north from Salt Lake City to Ogden, in competition with the existing steam lines. The line reached Ogden in 1908, but earlier, after completion to Beck's Hot Springs, Bamberger had built the Lagoon resort, still operating successfully. Electrified in 1910, the railroad ran profitably through the World War II years, when its rails served the complex of military depots south of Ogden. The line shut down in the mid-1950s. Had it remained viable, Simon Bamberger's visionary electric interurban line might today be helping cut traffic and pollution along the Wasatch Front.

Gentiles and Mormons alike recognized Bamberger as a vigorous, honest man—outspoken and dealing fairly with miners, railroaders, and clerical help in a period when relationships between capital and labor were increasingly strained. He was a Board of Education member from 1898 until 1903, a time when bitter battles between Mormons, Masons, and Gentile groups filled the columns of Salt Lake's daily newspapers. He became a state senator and served from 1903 to 1907, gaining considerable respect despite an accent that troubled some fellow solons. In 1916 he was elected Utah's governor on the Democratic ticket, promising the state's half-million citizens a liberal and progressive administration acceptable to followers of both Theodore Roosevelt and Woodrow Wilson. Despite his business ties, he pressed firmly for a state public utilities commission capable of regulating utilities and railroads, fostered efficient budgeting practices, helped gain annual salaries for teachers, planned successfully for establishment of a public health department, worked vigorously for a workmen's compensation measure, and stressed the right of labor to organize. Considerably ahead of his time, Governor Bamberger proposed a corrupt practices act, limits of expeditures by candidates, and nonpartisan election of judges. A feisty, short-statured, volatile redhead, he was a teetotaler, an anti-tobacconist—again a man somewhat ahead of his time.

Utah's first and only Jewish governor was as intrigued by the problems of local and national Jewry as by state and business affairs. One involvement that met ultimate failure was the effort to establish a Jewish agricultural colony called Clarion, near Gunnison. During that era, when Zionist colonies were being painfully established in Israel through the efforts of Theodore Herzel, American Jews were giving thought to similar agricultural efforts, hoping to shift as many Jews as possible from eastern ghettos to the nation's vacant lands.[19]

The Clarion effort began in 1910 with ninety-five pioneers from New York City and fifty-five from the Philadelphia area. Samuel Newhouse, the mining man whose name is memorialized in the Newhouse Hotel and Newhouse Building on Salt Lake's Main Street, was a major backer, along with George Auerbach. Nearly six thousand acres of central Utah land were purchased. Gov. William Spry and state officials agreed to set aside sufficient irrigating water for inital needs. With further funding necessary, a Utah Colonization Fund was established with the Auerbachs, Bambergers, and such distinguished community members as Daniel Alexander, Henry Cohen, Adolf Baer, Adolph Simon, David Spitz, and Rabbi Charles Freund helping underwrite a $150,000 bond issue. Back east, Jacob Schiff and Julius Rosenwald, two of Jewry's most potent leaders, were interested in the venture; the Mormon church contributed some funds; and by 1913 grain, hay, and vegetables were being raised on 1,560 acres, with colonists living in forty-six homes.

However, the settlers had ignored the advice of natives to insulate plank cottages with adobe or plaster, and as a result the

[19] For a more detailed study of Clarion, see Everett L. Cooley, "Clarion, Utah, Jewish Colony in 'Zion'," *Utah Historical Quarterly* 36 (1968): 113–31.

houses were freezing in winter and sweltering in summer. In addition many of the colonists were city dwellers, totally unprepared for the problems of handling farm animals, cultivation, and irrigation. As had happened in poorly sited Mormon colonies from Pariah to Iosepa, buildings were abandoned, ditches crumbled, and the plow that broke the plains was itself broken. However, Clarion was to lead to two successful Utah enterprises and careers. Benjamin Brown, one of the colonists, stayed on in the state to found the Utah Poultry Cooperative Association that slowly built up a market for the state's eggs and fowl. And one youthful settler, Maurice Warshaw, moved on to California, then back to Utah, to peddle produce from a wagon, open a small store, develop it to a sizeable market, then expand into today's Grand Central and Warshaw market chains, familiar to thousands of Utah patrons.

Jewish immigrants to Utah in the initial decade of the twentieth century came by train, rather than in white-topped wagons from the broad Missouri or across mountains and desert lands from California. They crossed the Atlantic in steamships, instead of sailing by clipper to New York, or around the Horn, or to the Isthmus of Panama. The journey was easier but not without pain or pangs of loneliness. Usually half-a-week's time was spent departing Russia or Poland, in a manner not unlike that in *Fiddler on the Roof.* There were passport problems, inspection problems, ticketing problems, baggage problems, first at Hamburg, or Rotterdam, or any of a dozen ports of embarkation—and equally frightening health inspection problems in the Ports of New York, Philadelphia, Baltimore, or Boston.

The very enormity of the influx of newcomers baffled the immigration authorities working at Ellis Island, within sight of the Statue of Liberty and its inscription—written by a Jewish woman— inviting the wretched and stormtossed to these shores. The *New York Post,* reporting on January 7, 1905, that 70 percent of all Russian immigrants were Jewish, noted that one hundred thousand persons came from the czarist empire in the previous year, plus at least twenty thousand from Austria-Hungary and another six thousand from Rumania. The newspaper cited "midnight expulsions from Moscow, the awful suffering at St. Petersburg and Kiev . . . the revival of persecution reaching its most intolerable manifestation at Kishenev" as reasons for the tide of emigrants. There were to be other horrors, other waves of refugees, a quarter century later.

Numerically, the number of Jews reaching Utah was a trickle, but although they now arrived by train, they had often suffered as much in the old country, in steerage quarters in the bowels of pitching steamships, and in a few bewildering days in the New York ghettos as their brethren who came via sail and wagon. Early or late, as Dr. Louis C. Zucker succinctly put it in his "Shalom Paper" of 1972, they were animated by Horatio Alger motives and virtues, plus a resolve to find a permanent, viable home.

The newcomers of the new century were, like those who came before, most likely to find their livelihood as shopkeepers, often serving an informal apprenticeship in the stores of fellow Jews of the earlier generation. A cluster of stores on Main Street, State Street, and "Broadway" in Utah's metropolis remains as a memorial to their diligence, their hours of toil. Unlike the situation in New York or Chicago, where the family "lived in back," in a few drafty rooms behind a clothing, grocery, cigar, furniture, or dry goods shop, Utah's newcomers were usually able to find a side-street rental house or apartment and would walk to work or ride the trolley to their labors. Talk with today's Shapiros, Wolfes, Axelrads, Tannenbaums, Ziniks, Franks, or their peers about parents or grandparents and the story comes through basically the same. First, a weary arrival from the seaboard, perhaps after a halt at Denver. There a larger Jewish colony thrived due partly to a hospital specializing in tuberculosis and other lung diseases to which the people of the ghettos were especially prone. Somehow parents and grandparents put a few dollars together, rented a tiny shop, persuaded wholesalers to take credit risks, and a new luggage, furniture, or dry goods establishment came into being. Cash was the commodity lacking—faith and the ability to work agonizingly long and hard were present in abundance. "Poor relations" kept arriving, and, as in the tales of Sholem Aleichem, there was always room at the table, on a couch, or even on the floor. A job? Someone had knowledge of one—not through the State Employment Service, but down the street at some fellow Jew's store, or at meetings of the temple or synagogue auxiliary, or at Hadassah, or "Council," or "Sisterhood." From 1916 till 1940 there was an Orthodox congregation, Shaarey Tzadek, for those newcomers who chose not to depart old forms and ritual.[20]

---

[20] The story of this fascinating congregation is told by Hynda Rudd in an article prepared for a forthcoming issue of *Western States Jewish Historical Quarterly.*

Now and again the community had a kosher butcher, but not too frequently, which seems to have been one reason ultra-Orthodox faithful departed the city. Somehow, since the community's earliest beginnings, residents found a way to maintain a Hebrew school where some rudimentary training in biblical lore and Jewish history was available. Dollars for the rabbi's salary were hard to come by, but the Lord—and his adherents—provided.

As Sholem Aleichem might have said, "the community didn't exactly prosper, but it survived." A few Jews, as might be expected, prospered more than others. Down through the years many Utah Jews have taken pride in the achievements of their fellows in business, education, science, medicine, and the arts.

The business roster is the longest. Some firms, such as the candy company founded by Leon Sweet have a regional reputation. Eimco, became one of the city's largest employers. Standard Optical, founded by the Schubach brothers, is operated by a second generation of Schubach brothers. New faces with established old names operate such well-regarded firms as Pepper's Allied Metals, Shapiro's Luggage, Tannenbaum's National Store, Axelrad Furniture, Wolfe's, and Makoff's. In quite a few instances the older generation comes around to see how children or grandchildren are doing.

A multitude of visionaries come to mind. Utah's television and radio industry recently honored Sid Fox, who founded KDYL and Channel 4. Louis Marcus was a Salt Lake motion picture pioneer as well as one of the city's more efficient and honest mayors. Sid Cohen pioneered television film-buying and the little theatre presentation of fine foreign films. Joe Dupler was long known as the city's largest furrier and a major mink rancher. Charlie McGillis grew with newspaper distribution, starting with a news wagon and winding up handling virtually the entire run of the city's largest daily. The growth of the insurance business found Herbert Hirschman and son, and then Jack Weinstock and son, in leading local roles. One of the city's major fortunes was earned by James A. White, who came down from Ogden, early saw the potential of coal mine company stock and arbitrage, and later gave his name to Salt Lake's handsome Jewish Community Center.

As with Jews everywhere, members of the earlier generations sought the best in education for their youngsters—in Utah, as elsewhere, Jews remain People of the Book in more ways than one. Prior to the turn of the century, a handful of Utah young people went east or to California to attend universities. In the first three decades of the new century, increasing numbers of parents could speak with pride of children at Stanford and Pennsylvania, Columbia and Yale. In more than a few instances those youngsters, accustomed to the free and easy camaraderie of old Salt Lake High, (or East, South, or West highs after such schools were built) unhappily discovered overt anti-Semitism for the first time. Perhaps more important, Utah's Jewish collegians found they could, by and large, succeed in campus life—scholastically at least—in competition with the easterners they were encountering for the first time.

Those same years were years of great growth for the University of Utah, which earlier lagged behind state institutions in the Midwest. As the university's offerings increased, more and more Jewish graduates of city and county high schools found it a gateway to chosen professions in law, medicine, engineering, mining, or business. The university served a leavening function for the community as well. Dr. Louis Zucker was its single Jewish faculty member in 1928, but there were a dozen during the war years and upwards of fifty today. When a four year College of Medicine was established at the end of World War II, men who wrote the textbooks, including Dr. Max Wintrobe, Dr. Leo Samuels, and Dr. Louis Goodman, took major roles in winning the institution a national reputation. In addition, it attracted part-time faculty members interested in both research and the practice of medical specialties, men such as Dr. Irving Ershler and Dr. David Dolowitz who settled in to stay, side by side with the few native sons, such as Dr. Milton Pepper, practicing medicine in the valley.

Today a parallel situation is evident in legal circles, with Law School faculty members, such as Lionel Frankel and relative newcomers to the community such as Dan Berman and David Geldzahler winning prominent legal or political roles equaling those long since gained by established community members, including A. Wally Sandack, Irving Arnowitz, and Alvin Smith. Just as the university was attracting new professionals to the area, the campus and the businesses it fostered have been bringing local Jewry a leavening of physical and social scientists. This had also happened during and shortly after World War II, when hundreds of Jewish men, stationed at Camp Kearns, Wendover, Hill, the Ogden General Depot, or Clearfield, liked what they found in Utah—perhaps the mountains, perhaps a pert college girl—and decided to settle in Zion at war's end.

214

Unfortunately, to match the influx of new professionals and businessmen, students, artisans, and a handful of retirees, Utah's Jewish community, along with Mormon and other groups, suffered the attrition of mortality and the debilitating out-migration that has long plagued the state. Just as rabbis came and departed, just as collegians and faculty members came and went, so too have bright young Jews of both sexes come of age, taken a long look at available opportunities, and departed. Utah may indeed be Zion to some, but to others it is a small provincial state in the hinterland of a far larger nation. As always, far fields seem greenest to those hoping to make their mark in the world. Again, statistics are impossible to gather, but a great many Utah-born Jews are actively engaged in communications, medicine, law, sciences, arts, and just plain seeking a livelihood, across the Sierras in California, or back east in Washington, D.C., and New York City.

To be sure, there are opportunities in such slightly esoteric fields as the dance, music, and the visual arts that might have caused some headshaking among old-timers in the valley before Maurice Abravanel arrived to conduct the Utah Symphony. His orchestra has a sizeable number of Jewish names in its string and wind sections, as well as on its boards and lists of donors. Salt Lake City now has a ballet, modern dance group, art center and museum, plus a half-dozen small and large theatres able to absorb a proportion of the talent that once of necessity went elsewhere.

It is a matter of curiosity to some that Utah's Jews have as yet produced no painter or sculptor of major reputation. Pianist Gladys Gladstone, the Jewish community's major performing artist, is herself an import—albeit of a quarter-century standing. No author of both stature and Jewish persuasion (or even non-persuasion) has yet loomed on the horizon. Helen Sandack and her Temple Sisterhood Follies have not as yet brought a Utah-born Jewish stage, screen, or television star of national prominence to the public ken. Nor has Utah Jewry produced politicians of note since Governor Bamberger, Mayor Marcus, or Tooele's State Senator Sol Selvin made local headlines. Perhaps the distaff side with prominent women such as Esther Landa or Corrinne Sweet will produce the next Jewish vote-getter.

Analyzing Jewish life in Zion a bit more seriously, it seems apparent—although many will argue the point—that the state's Jews, like many Mormons, remain more than a mite removed from the mainstream of American life, not to mention worldwide Jewry.

215

The world across the sheltering Wasatch does impinge on occasion. In the 1917–18 war that shook the Old World of their parents to its foundations, thirty-seven members of the Jewish community wore khaki leggings or navy blue, a list extending alphabetically from Alexander to Weitz. When Pearl Harbor erupted in 1941 and the nation had a need for a two-ocean navy, a huge army, and an air force capable of reaching the heartland of both Germany and Japan, 180 Utahns left Jewish homes for military duty. Harold Glazier, Morris Romick, Sherman Pomerance, and Edward Cherenik never returned, their young lives taken by a global conflagration from which many of their neighbors had believed Zion isolated. Korea and Vietnam once again saw Jewish men in uniform. In the latter conflict, at least a few Jewish young people deliberately stood aside, making clear their distaste for a war they felt should never have been visited upon the world.

Meanwhile, like it or not, Utah Jews have come to a realization that they cannot escape the woes of their fellows in Israel, in the lands fringing the Mediterranean, or in the regions governed by the Soviets. Things were rather different earlier on, when, in the 1920s, as Dr. Louis Zucker has indicated, a majority of the members of the Utah community wore blinders, and initially felt the woes of Germany's Jews were of little concern to Americans. In his "Recollections and Observations," he makes clear "the Zionist movement languished," while B'nai B'rith lodge meetings were spent in "parliamentary skirmishes about nothing of importance." [21] Rabbis Joseph Krikstein of Montefiore and Sam Gordon of B'nai Israel were "militant ideologues" chiefly concerned with the faithfulness of the folk to Rabbinic Judaism and the routine of confirmation or Bar Mitzvah.

Hitler's regime and its overt anti-Semitism changed the isolation of Utah's Jews. By 1936 the local United Jewish Council and Salt Lake's Jewish Welfare Fund were raising thousands of dollars to bring refugees to a free land. By war's end, after Hitler's holocaust had eradicated millions of Jews, newcomers as diverse as the Edgar Bodenheimers (both law professors) and the Lu Dornbush family (they founded the city's finest Jewish delicatessen; he wears a concentration camp tattoo on one arm) were making new homes in Salt Lake City. Refugee families brought a new language and ancient customs to the city's suburbs, to Ogden, Cedar City, and points

---

[21] Brooks, *Jews of Utah and Idaho,* pp. 205–13.

north and south. Many of the newly arrived prewar and postwar refugees were to move on to major West Coast centers, but Utahns take pride in the role they played in providing an initial emergency haven for the new wave of tempest-tossed.

To coin a phrase, there were always Zionists in Zion, dating back to the movement's inception at Basle in 1897. The local Hadassah, the feminine arm of this activist movement, was formed just six years later, in 1903. Looking back over the past few decades, Simon Shapiro, Ben Roe, and Louis and Ethel Zucker can be seen as the early goads and spurs of a community conscience too long unconscious of overseas needs and goals. When World War II ended, and it was obvious that the pitiful remnants of European Jewry needed a land of their own, the city's earliest Zionists were joined by Simon Rosenblatt and young Joel Shapiro in approaching Mormon leader George Albert Smith, gaining meaningful Latter-day Saints backing in the local Jewish effort to support a reborn Jewish state named Israel.

Since those years, Zion's Jews have donated millions of dollars to help keep that tiny but plucky land viable. Like their brethren from coast to coast, Utah Jews groan when approached to buy tickets for dinners, luncheons, concerts, motion pictures, and plays, to attend lectures and benefits, to pledge dollars, to hear ambassadors and authors. They groan, but, admitting to the grievous need, contribute their tithes, buy bonds, sign checks.

What of the future? Two struggling congregations have joined forces in an effort to weld a single living congregation, Kol Ami. Vigorous, youthful Rabbi Abner Bergman spreads the gospel to the members who regularly attend Sabbath services and to the far greater number of Jews crowding two old houses of worship on the High Holy Days. Arguments concerning the use of Hebrew and English, cantor, choir, and organist sound much like those of a century ago when Orthodox and Reform contended. An article in a January 1975 *Deseret News* concerning the impossibility of finding kosher foodstuffs in Utah parallels one found in a city daily seventy-five years earlier.

However, Utah's Jews have happily been spared many of the abrasive and frustrating problems that, in all too many American communities, have been rooted in anti-Semitism. Utahns have generally accepted Jews as neighbors, as business associates, as fellow citizens, and as the folks next door. Perhaps because of the rather special role Mormon theology accords them, perhaps because of

217

their small numbers, overt anti-Semitism is largely unknown. When the Ku Klux Klan was being resurrected and at the time when Father Coughlin inveighed against "foreigners" from his radio pulpit, crosses occasionally burned in Salt Lake's foothills, but old-timers say the principal targets of such bitter demonstrations were the region's Catholics and outlanders of any persuasion. However, some Utahns joined Silver Shirt groups in support of Nazism in the 1930s. A Salt Lake City attorney, Justin C. Stewart, remembers serving as moderator on a public forum broadcast by KUTA radio in 1938. One program featured Rabbi Samuel H. Gordon and a local Silver Shirt representative:

> The Silver Shirt said, "you can always tell a Jew just by looking at him." Rabbi Gordon challenged him to pick out the Jews in the audience of fifty or sixty people. Well, of course, he missed as many as he got. He was forced to admit that he didn't think even Rabbi Gordon looked especially Jewish.[22]

As Hitler gained strength, a few Mormon missionaries in Germany, along with some LDS converts, were infected with the Nazi's racist ideology, but their views never seriously affected the ethical course chosen by the Latter-day Saints' leadership.

On the national level the Anti-Defamation League of the B'nai B'rith has assessed anti-Semitism in business, industry, education, labor, and the professions, as well as in social matters. By ADL standards, Utah comes off well, especially if numbers are the criteria. The country clubs and downtown clubs where businessmen and their spouses congregate to dine and play bridge have Jewish members, although they may or may not have implicit quotas. There seems to be no problem concerning admission of Jews to the state's public and private schools, colleges, and universities, although Jews here as elsewhere were once excluded from fraternities and sororities that restricted membership to believers in Christ. As in other parts of the nation, Utah's Jews have long taken an active role in seeking to keep church affairs, school affairs, and state affairs strictly separate, and have sought to keep curricula, texts, and teaching clear of taint.[23]

[22] Stewart interview.

[23] Anti-Semitism is largely a covert, unorganized phenomena in present-day Utah. In its overt form it most often comes from a fringe group such as the Keep America Committee. A tract circulated by this group contains a message from a woman with a Salt Lake City post office box number, lumping

Down through the years, national surveys indicate Jews have had few posts of consequence in railroading, utilities, banking, or mining. While Utah Jews have held few such positions in railroading and utilities, they have been conspicuous in mining. Sam Newhouse and Simon Bamberger were followed by Louis Buchman, who rose from the ranks to head Kennecott Copper's western operations, and Wallace Woolf, a University of Utah graduate who directed Bunker Hill's facilities in neighboring Idaho. Although Jews have not risen to leadership posts in local banking, Joseph Rosenblatt is a long-time director of the Federal Reserve Bank of San Francisco, and Jewish names dot the directorships of major Utah corporations.

Enter almost any Jewish home in Salt Lake or Ogden, or find a group of Jewish youngsters at the University of Utah Commons, and the conversations concerning intermarriage, conversion, and just plain "falling away" from the faith of parents and grandparents will likely produce a feeling of *déjà vu* in auditors fortyish or older. Intermarriage, whether the Jewish party be male or female, still causes concern, misgiving, and wrangling in Jewish homes in Utah, as it assuredly does in Catholic, Lutheran, Baptist, Mormon, Greek Orthodox, and even nondenominational settings across the nation.

However, when the High Holy Days come around annually, as they have done for five thousand or so years, male or female members of an interfaith marriage will as likely as not put aside their daily chores, or even call off a round of golf, and set forth for a day of communal devotion. Following in parental footsteps, they keep the youngsters home from school on Rosh Hashanah ("New Year's Day") and Yom Kippur ("Day of Atonement"), dress the children in Sabbath best, and join, family style, in intoning prayers as long-lived as any in the history of mankind.

As in generations past, Utah's Jews will stream to their house of worship, observe the fast day, ask the Lord to inscribe them in the Book of Life. A strong-lunged member of the congregation will sound the *shofar* on a simple ram's horn—echoing the ancient times when shepherds tended flocks in a very different place and time.

Jews, Negroes, aliens, and racketeers as "parasites" threatening the American way of life. See "Bits of Information for Christians, 'Extreme Rightists,' 'Featherheads' " (Los Angeles, [1963?]), in the pamphlet collection of the Utah State Historical Society, Salt Lake City.

On the Passover, a tattered, treasured *Hagodah* [24] will be read to the assembled family by the clan's elder sage, while the youngest answers questions concerning the Exodus that have been put to Jewish children in a multitude of lands and in a multitude of conditions. The household's finest napery will be on the table, a special set of cutlery, tableware, and china will gleam, candles will cast their glow upon a treasured samovar brought from the old country.

Next, the odors of *k'nedlach* and *charoses, matzoh brie* and a roasting fowl mingle with the sharper aroma of *gefulte* fish and *t'simmas*.[25] There is food enough for all comers — indeed, someone will order the door opened for Elijah or any hungry stranger, while a napkin-wrapped matzoh will be hidden, to be sought later by the family's children.

Seated at such a ceremonial dinner, a few oldsters will recall similar Passovers years ago—in Brest Litovsk, or Kiev, in Berlin, perhaps, or Salonika, Warsaw, Riga, or Budapest. Members of a younger generation can realize, with some awe, that the Passover being celebrated near Utah's Jordan and the Great Salt Lake is being marked in precisely the same fashion beside another River Jordan and Dead Sea.

And so, two hundred years after a Declaration of enduring Independence signed near the banks of the Delaware, it can be hazarded that Jewry in distant Utah will survive—perhaps even flourish—not because of, or as the result of, or in spite of, classes in Hebrew at the temple, a library of Judaica at the university, nor even classes in weaving, finger-painting, or skiing at the Jewish Community Center. Perhaps it will live and develop because of nostalgia, a hidden hunger for old songs as well as grandmother's cooking, or because of some inner knowledge that greater Jewish faith is indeed needed, but that faith alone will not suffice in perpetuating an ancient heritage.

Having settled in a Zion very different in space and time from the land of their ethnic and ethical beginnings, Utah's Jews remain, along with their neighbors, Americans all, with their roots as firmly in this place as any People of the Book anywhere.

[24] A book, often richly illustrated, containing the story of Exodus and the Passover service.

[25] These traditional foods, in order, are: matzoh balls (often cooked in chicken soup); chopped apples, cinnamon, nuts, and sugar mixed in wine; matzohs in gravy; chopped fish (usually pike or carp) cooked in balls; simmered prunes, carrots, and matzoh balls.

6 THE CONTINENTAL INHERITANCE

BY DAVIS BITTON AND GORDON IRVING

[We are] all the descendants of immigrants. That is, in fact, the quality and the experience all of us have in common; the differences are of degree only in that for some of us the experience is immediate and personal, for others inherited, and for still others vicarious. Immigration is then the oldest theme in our history and the most nearly universal.

— Henry Steele Commager

Adding to the variety of Utah's population were immigrants from western Europe. Those to be dealt with in the present chapter are the western Europeans exclusive of the British Isles, Scandinavia, and Italy, each of which receives separate treatment, and of Spain, whose immigrants to Utah are few and mainly limited to Basques. In other words, these are the German, French, Belgian, Swiss, and Dutch immigrants in Utah.

To lump these nationalities together is to do something that would annoy most of them, convinced as they are of the importance of their own national backgrounds. But they did have some things in common. They were not Scandinavian, which in practical terms meant that they did not belong to the single largest non-English immigrant group. They were not from the British Isles, which meant that they had to wrestle with a new language; for the first generation this meant a difficult obstacle to amalgamation, as they usually spoke English with some kind of accent. Finally, the religious background of these Europeans (prior to the conversion of many of them to Mormonism) was mainly Protestant, with the handful of Utahns from France an apparent exception.

Compared with the population of Utah as a whole, the immigrants from western Europe were few. From the beginning the majority of Utahns were American-born, and most immigrants came from the British Isles, Canada, and Scandinavia. Yet the western Europeans had their importance. And they made significant contributions to the richness of Utah's cultural heritage.

Patterns of Immigration and Settlement

It will be helpful first to gain an idea of how many people we are talking about, where they came from, where they settled, and how these patterns varied from generation to generation. Considering that so high a percentage of those who did come from the Continent came as converts to the LDS church, nineteenth-century patterns of immigration are explained in large part by emphases in Mormon missionary work. Prior to 1890 most LDS missionaries laboring in Europe were sent to the British Isles or Scandinavia. From 1860, when records began to be kept, until 1889, 160 missionaries were sent from Salt Lake City to German-speaking countries, with only 24 going to the Netherlands and apparently none being assigned to French-speaking areas.[1] As a result, although there were some conversions and subsequent migrations to Utah, the lack of a concentrated effort to make proselytes on the Continent meant that such people were few in number. The most successful early missionary effort took place in Switzerland, with 1,040 Swiss-born Mormons appearing in the 1880 Census, compared with 885 from the German Empire and a handful of settlers born in the other countries being considered in this chapter.[2]

After 1890 the numbers grew in all LDS missions, with a much greater emphasis being given to proselyting on the Continent. For example, between 1890 and 1909 there were 980 missionaries called to German-speaking lands and 282 called to the Netherlands, a tremendous increase over earlier years. Growth in the missionary force, coupled with socio-economic factors, brought a considerable increase in LDS immigration from these areas, some seventy-five hundred Utah residents born in German-speaking countries being listed in the 1910 Census, with nearly fourteen hundred born in the Netherlands.

Although difficult to put in quantitative terms, it would appear that non-Mormon immigration to Utah from continental Europe began in the late 1860s with the coming of the railroad and greater

[1] Discussion regarding numbers of missionaries and their geographical distribution is based on Gordon Irving, "A Preliminary Compilation of Data Relating to Numerical Strength and Geographical Distribution of the LDS Missionary Force, 1830–1973" (unpublished paper, 1974).

[2] Numerical data in this chapter relating to the foreign-born population of Utah are drawn from appropriate sections of the U.S. Census returns for Utah, 1850–1970. Data for 1850–1880 and 1900–1950 are conveniently summarized in Douglas A. Alder, "German-speaking Immigration to Utah, 1850–1950" (M.A. thesis, University of Utah, 1959), pp. 124–34.

activity in mining ventures in the territory. For example, many of the foreign-born listed in the biographical volumes of *Utah Since Statehood* came seeking mineral wealth. Many others came with the idea of going into business, seeing Utah as a likely place to pursue the trades they had learned in Europe.[3] In general the non-Mormon Europeans differed from their Mormon brethren in that they did not come to America with the idea of settling in Utah. Many came west only after living for years in other parts of the country, attracted by opportunities in Utah as the region became increasingly integrated into the national economy.

As the western Europeans came to Utah they initially spread out through most of the inhabited portions of the territory. The nineteenth-century Mormon immigrants were either used to agricultural work in their homelands or felt the need to pursue agricultural careers in the new land. However, there was a tendency for European immigrants to cluster in certain areas. The German-born in particular tended to settle near the major centers of population in the territory, although less typically there were sizeable concentrations of Germans in Box Elder County in the 1870s and in Juab County in the 1880s and 1890s.[4] Many of the Swiss-born settled in or near the larger towns, particularly in Salt Lake and Cache counties. Providence, in the latter county, was long known as a Swiss settlement. Still, there were also Swiss colonies in less densely populated areas, such as the one at Santa Clara in southern Utah and the colony at Midway in Wasatch County, during much of the nineteenth century.

After the turn of the century European patterns of immigration to Utah changed considerably. The efforts of the Mormon church to de-emphasize the doctrine of gathering and encourage foreign members to stay in their homelands slowed immigration in many cases. For instance, although there was some Swiss immigration following 1910, the Swiss-born population of the state has declined in every census year since that time, only 566 being listed in 1970. However, in other countries unsettled political and economic conditions outweighed the ecclesiastical urgings to stay at home. German immigrants, probably encouraged by the problems connected with World War I and the economic chaos of the Weimar Republic

---

[3] Noble Warrum, ed., *Utah Since Statehood,* 4 vols. (Chicago and Salt Lake City, 1919), vols. 2–4, *passim.*

[4] Data relating to patterns of settlement within Utah are drawn from U.S. Census returns, such material being available by county only from 1870 to 1950, with some of the nationalities under consideration in this chapter not being listed during all of those years.

years, came to Utah in fairly large numbers. A fairly typical response
to a questionnaire sent to German-born Utahns illustrates this
point:

Question: Why did you want to leave Germany?
Answer: To better my life.
Q: Why did you choose Utah?
A: I am an LDS member.[5]

Mormon missionaries in Germany, nearly eleven hundred of them
during the 1920s, found many people responsive to their message
and attracted to Zion in the New World, until the depression of the
thirties tarnished the vision of Utah as land of opportunity. Dutch
immigration followed much the same pattern, the Dutch-born population of Utah peaking in 1930, as was also the case with the
German-born.

Economic disorder following World War II occasioned another
influx of German and Dutch immigrants to Utah, although government restrictions on immigration were much tighter than they had
been in the 1920s. Waiting periods, the finding of sponsors, and
other such problems delayed the peak in postwar immigration from
the Continent until the early 1950s. Although available immigration
statistics are very incomplete, the censuses indicate that the German-
born and Dutch-born populations of Utah increased 2,251 and
1,569, respectively, between 1950 and 1960, which represents a considerable postwar immigration, especially considering that such
figures represent not total immigration, but rather net variations, including as they do both the effect of deaths and out-migration.
Great increases, relatively speaking, can also be noted in the French-
and Belgian-born populations of Utah following World War II,
although these groups were not nearly so significant numerically
as the Germans and Dutch. With the economic reconstruction of
Europe and the easing of cold war tensions, immigration from
western Europe dropped off considerably after the 1950s, the number
of Utah residents born in the countries under consideration declining
nearly 25 percent from 1960 to 1970, indicating that death and out-
migration are now far more significant demographic features than
is immigration. The establishment of the LDS church in Europe on

[5] Questionnaire completed in August 1974 by Erich W. Kuehne of Salt
Lake City, a 1929 immigrant from Hamburg. Questionnaires relating to immigration and adjustment experiences in Utah were sent by the authors to
roughly one hundred German-, Dutch, and Swiss-born Utahns during August
1974.

a much more solid foundation since the end of World War II has also played some role in encouraging potential immigrants to stay at home.

Although the number of foreign-born in Utah is on the decline, western Europe now provides a greater share of Utah's foreign-born population than in the past. Representing only about 3 percent of the foreign-born population of the territory in the 1850s and 1860s, new patterns of immigration in the twentieth century saw the proportion climb to some 15 percent between 1900 and 1920, reaching a peak of 35 percent of the total foreign-born group in 1960.

Twentieth-century immigrants have been largely drawn from urban areas of Europe, or at least they have been more inclined to settle in what can be called urban areas in Utah. Of course, opportunities for employment in agriculture have declined in Utah since the turn of the century, the general Utah population itself becoming increasingly more urban. However, the European-born in Utah are much more likely than is the general population to live and work in urban areas. The Dutch in particular have usually settled in or near large population centers. In the period since 1900 over 90 percent of the Dutch-born have lived in Salt Lake, Weber, Utah, and Cache counties. Initially favoring Weber County, and particularly Ogden, the Dutch-born since the twenties have tended to settle in Salt Lake County, where two-thirds of them lived in 1950.

The Germans have long tended to settle in the four counties mentioned above, especially Salt Lake County, where 76 percent of the German-born lived in 1950. Initially spread more widely through the state than the Germans, the Swiss-born, too, have since 1900 become more highly concentrated in what may be considered as urban counties. Although a large number still lived in Cache County in 1950, more than half lived in Salt Lake County. In the case of the Swiss, as with the Germans, when old settlers in less densely populated areas died off, they were not replaced, new immigrants preferring to settle in the cities and large towns of Utah. In many cases the new arrivals were city-bred and sought employment only available in large population centers.

The French-born population, although small, presents a contrast to the Germanic groups. The French have been no more likely than the average Utahn to live in the counties referred to here as urban. To some extent this is because up to 1950 nearly a quarter of the French immigrants lived in Carbon County, where many of them were involved in the sheep industry or in mining activities in that area.

So immigration to Utah from western Europe tended to increase in the late nineteenth century, as the foreign missionary effort of the LDS church increased and as business opportunities in Utah became more attractive. Unsettled conditions following two world wars also encouraged large-scale immigration to Utah, with periods of peace and prosperity deterring European migration. Although the foreign-born population of Utah has declined sharply both absolutely and relative to the general population, western Europe has come to represent an increasing share of Utah's foreign-born population. Finally, the settlement of European immigrants has increasingly tended to be in what can be termed urban areas, particularly in Salt Lake County.

Problems of Adjustment

The difficulty of adjustment to a new environment is one of the constants of the immigrant experience. Along with excitement and challenge, to move from a homeland to an alien shore presented practical problems of finding work, making a home, earning enough to sustain life, and making new friends. The putting down of new roots can never have been easy, even under the best circumstances. For the Europeans coming to Utah, whether in the nineteenth or twentieth century, there were undeniable problems.

First and foremost was the necessity of finding work. Agriculture was the backbone of Utah's economy, and it was natural for the immigrants to do farm work for others or, as quickly as possible, to stake out farm claims for themselves. In the twentieth century, especially after World War I, farming was a shrinking opportunity in Utah, and it was more natural for the newcomers to stay in the towns. For those who had a saleable skill as artisans or craftsmen, the transition was often fairly smooth, but for others coming to the new land meant not an improvement in financial status but a downgrading. When asked if they found work commensurate with their skill and education upon first arriving in Utah, about half of those contacted in 1974 answered in the negative—not that they experienced out-and-out discrimination, although such may have been the case at times. Often the difficulty of satisfying the technical requirements of professional certification (doctors with degrees from

European medical schools faced exclusion at first) or of union membership (nativist proclivities of unions have been notorious) reduced employment opportunities.

There was also the matter of language. Those who spoke English with great difficulty, or not at all, simply could not move smoothly into many kinds of jobs. It is not surprising, perhaps, that a fairly large number of men and women immigrating from the Continent found work as servants or hired hands or custodians. The following statement from presidents of the German-speaking LDS missions in 1958 was intended to discourage immigration, but the disappointments and difficulties of employment it describes were often real enough:

> A man in Germany who held a responsible position became a janitor in America because he did not master the language sufficiently to hold down a more important job. The head of a large firm in Europe had to accept simple bookkeeping work. Here [in Europe] he was in charge of fifty to sixty people, but there [in Utah] he is on the lowest rung of the ladder and he has to live under conditions which seriously curtail his activity.

> A highly qualified beautician achieved very little in America because the styles were completely different from those in Europe. She finally had to accept household work which she very much disliked. A construction foreman who supervised large projects here had to carry bricks in America because the construction methods were strange to him. A successful teacher from here had to accept work as a waitress. We could multiply these examples. . . .[6]

Behind every individual's search for a job and the frequent disappointment and the eventual accepting of a menial task that would enable him to stay alive is a story of human pathos. But there are encouraging stories of resourcefulness and success as well. Money was saved even from the meager income of day laborers and household help, and relatives were sent for. Some upgrading in employment took place eventually, especially for those still young and energetic at the time of their arrival. And the next generation, the children of the immigrant parents, sought to prove themselves

---

[6] "Emigration" by Burtis F. Robbins, president of North German Mission, Jesse R. Curtis, president of Swiss-Austrian Mission, and Theodore M. Burton, president of West German Mission, in *Der Stern* 84 (1958) : 343–46, translation in Alder, "German-speaking Immigration," pp. 114–18.

with a vengeance. Of course, all of this is not different from the general pattern of immigrant adjustment in the New World.

In addition to the all-important influence of language limitations on ability to get jobs, there was the subtle but pervasive sense of inadequacy it symbolized, the frustration of poor and slow communication and the inexcusable, if human, tendency of some established citizens to ridicule and look down upon these "funny-speaking foreigners." Henri Edouard Desaules, from Switzerland, was a skilled carpenter and made furniture at Kingston, Utah, in the 1880s. Although he read widely, his command of English was inadequate. The poor man was often lonely and on July 4, 1884, could not bring himself to join the rest of the community in celebration. "I staid home by my own lone[l]y cussed self," he wrote. "Well, allright, this is my cursed fate. I must grin and bear it." [7] Desaules was not alone in being the butt of ridicule, especially from children. Who has not heard the immigrant speaking in meetings to the accompaniment of snickers from unruly boys? Of such experiences were compounded the pain and suffering, psychological as much as economic, of adjustment to the Utah scene.

Beyond these problems experienced by many of the first-generation immigrants from the Continent, the German-speaking people had an additional difficulty at the time of World War I. Even before the entrance of the United States into the war, the tendency of most Americans and most Utahns was to sympathize with the Allies, reflecting the strong Anglo-Saxon strain of the American population and perhaps the economic self-interest of the country. Even though few of the immigrants from Germany still retained any feeling of political allegiance to that country, a few defended the behavior of their fellow countrymen or at least tried to point out that the responsibility for the conflict should be shared by more than one country. Some Germans, in Utah as elsewhere in the United States, experienced ridicule and discrimination, and their loyalty to their new country was impugned. After the entrance of the United States into the war in 1917, feelings became even more intense. The *Deseret News* of March 30, 1917, deplored the "rumor about suspicion of loyalty of German-Americans." In a public meeting American citizens of German and Austrian birth or extraction reaffirmed their loyalty to America, one of their speakers denouncing

[7] Henri Edouard Desaules Diary, holograph, Archives Division, Historical Department, Church of Jesus Christ of Latter-day Saints, Salt Lake City.

charges "that the German-Americans are unpatriotic." Obviously such statements were reacting to something—to widespread fear and suspicion of the Germans in Utah and elsewhere. In 1918, due to "a growing sentiment against gatherings of German people," meetings of German Mormons in Logan and elsewhere were discontinued. That same year all teaching of the German language was brought to an abrupt end in both church and state schools.[8] Simply bearing a German name, speaking with a German accent, or learning the language was sufficient to label one as disloyal.

With the rise of Hitler in the 1930s a similar situation began to develop. The problem of loyalty to the German government was, of course, acute among Latter-day Saints in Germany, but it was not totally absent among those who had immigrated to Utah. Some expressions of sympathy and support for the new National Socialist regime were voiced by Utah Germans, as by other Germans and Bundists in the United States. One of the authors remembers hearing a speaker in church in the late 1930s, an American whose wife was German, staunchly defend the German dictator. In 1937 J. M. Sjodahl, a Utahn from Sweden who had been involved in the publication of several foreign-language newspapers, wrote an editorial entitled "Some Things in Their Favor," referring to the Germans.[9] As might have been expected, the reaction to these scattered signs of pro-Naziism was ridicule and discrimination from the larger community. With the outbreak of hostilities in 1939 and with the entrance of the United States into the war at the end of 1941, anything German was suspicious. German Mormons, who had held regular meetings in the Assembly Hall in Salt Lake City, ceased their gathering, obviously hoping to maintain a low profile. Like the Japanese-Americans, the German-Americans were overwhelmingly loyal to their new country during the war, but both groups suffered humiliation and mistreatment due to official fears and widespread public prejudice. For the German-speaking immigrants in Utah both wars brought brief periods of discomfort.

For the few French (and the French-speaking Belgians and Swiss), another subtle form of discrimination raised its ugly head. Reflecting general American attitudes, Utah newspapers as early as 1909 were describing the degeneracy and decadence of the

[8] "Journal History," October 2, 1892, April 7, 1918, April 13, 1918, July 19, 1918, December 3, 1921. This is a huge, multi-volume compilation of letters, clippings, and other primary sources located in LDS Church Archives.

[9] "Journal History," August 28, 1937.

French, an impression reinforced by the one-sided experiences of American troops during the two wars. In a religious context, some French Mormons have noticed that for many years almost all sons of General Authorities went on British Missions, and more than one Mormon leader was heard to say that there was no "blood of Israel" in France, which in Mormon terms was condemnation indeed.[10] Since World War II these old prejudices have been almost entirely overcome both by the experience of the Mormon missionaries in France and by the highly respectable record achieved by French-speaking immigrants.

ORGANIZATIONS

To help them face up to these problems—the sense of displacement and malaise, the feeling of being outsiders, the ridicule and prejudice, the employment handicaps—continental Europeans in Utah very early developed agencies of their own to provide mutual support and encouragement. On a simple level this was the natural pulling together of family and friends who spoke the same language. Newly arrived immigrants would be taken into the homes of fellow countrymen until they could get their feet on the ground. The tendency for members of a given national group to gather in neighborhoods of a town or into certain areas of the state—the Swiss in Midway or Santa Clara, for example—is mostly explained by this natural tendency to self-help and mutual encouragement, although during the nineteenth century, the LDS church seems to have encouraged such gathering to some extent.

Going beyond such simple manifestations of group activity, in the case of some nationalities, meetings were held, officers elected, and organizations formed. Although there were Europeans in Utah almost from the beginning, at first only the Swiss were present in sufficient number to organize. Their own communities and wards provided most of their needs. Then by the last decade of the century, the Germans of Salt Lake City were holding meetings. In the early 1870s the Germans organized a choir, which was still in existence fifty years later under the sponsorship of the Ensign Stake. After World War II the Dutch had their Dutch Club AVIO [*Alle Vermark Is Ous*], a chapter of an international organization. And the Swiss had their choir, which functioned much as a club and brought together Swiss Utahns. The French and French-speaking Swiss and Belgians were fewer. "The French are not very good at emigrating. Usually they stay where they are," said Flore G. Chappuis. But even without an official organization (except for language clubs at the universities), they have enjoyed some of the same mutual reinforcement of the larger groups. As Mrs. Chappuis has remarked, "All of us who have been here for years, when somebody comes, we help them." [11]

Going beyond organizations set up merely for fraternal purposes, German immigrants in Salt Lake City during the depression expanded the *Chemnitzer Vereinigung,* basically a social group, into the German-American Federal Credit Union. Finding it difficult to obtain loans from banks, the German-born, by joining together, were able to finance not only the immigration of the friends and relatives of the organization's members but also to provide loans for other ends, such as helping Germans go into business for themselves. Known since World War II as the Utah C. V. [*Chemnitzer Vereinigung*] Federal Credit Union, the group now has fifty-four hundred members, including those of German background as well as those who have married into German families. [12]

Besides clubs and organizations, newspapers also encouraged continuing national identification for these western Europeans. After two premature attempts to found German newspapers, Dr. Joseph Walter Dietrich founded the Salt Lake City *Intelligenz-Blatt* in 1890; lasting only six months, it "promoted things of the Germans, by the Germans, and for the Germans." The successor newspaper *Der Salt Lake City Beobachter* followed the same general editorial policy of catering to the special interests and emotional attachments of the Germans in Utah. There was even a humorous columnist, "Hans Besenstiel," who in the 1890s satirized various features of the surroundings. After 1905 *Der Beobachter* was published by the Beobachter Publishing Company and was subsidized by the Mormon church. [13]

For the Dutch in Utah there was a small periodical entitled *De Huisvriend* as early as 1905, published in Ogden by William

[11] Interview with Flore Chappuis, LDS Church Oral History Program, transcript in LDS Archives.

[12] Conversation with Carl E. Ebert, credit union manager, September 1974.

[13] William Mulder, "Utah's Nordic-Language Press: Aspect and Instrument of Immigrant Culture" (M.A. thesis, University of Utah, 1947), p. 64–67.

Above: *Pioneer Swiss families were
sent to Santa Clara to raise wine grapes
and other fruit to help support the Dixie
mission.* Right: *John Hafen came from his
native Switzerland as a child in the 1860s
and achieved note as a Utah landscape
painter.*

*John Held, in white jacket, conducted
a well known local band and was an
inventor and businessman. Born in
Geneva, Switzerland, he was the father
of John Held, Jr., a famous American
artist.*

Above: *Women from Switzerland, France, and other European countries used their knowledge of sericulture to found Utah's short-lived but fascinating silk industry.* Below: *Elise Furer Musser, a native of Neuchatel, Switzerland, achieved an international reputation during the 1930s as a United States delegate to peace conferences in Latin America. Her photograph was taken with Franklin D. Roosevelt in 1937.*

233

Martin M. Reenders, second from left, was born in the Netherlands and came to Utah as a young man. He began as a grocery clerk, managed the Grabeteria on Main Street in Salt Lake City, and was an owner of Maxfield Lodge.

Gerrit de Jong, Jr., founder of the College of Fine Arts at Brigham Young University, with members of his first graduating class. The de Jong Concert Hall at BYU was named in honor of the accomplished Dutchman.

Left: *Frenchman Henry Dusserre, left, a prominent Carbon County sheepman posed before sacked wool with another sheepman, Harry Mahleras.*

Right: *Jean A. DeBouzek, born in Alsace-Lorraine, France, founded an engraving business and invented several photo-mechanical processes.* Below: *The Hogar Hotel in Salt Lake City serves as a headquarters for the state's small but significant Basque population.*

235

*German-born Richard K. A. Kletting,
shown with his family, was the architect
for many notable Utah buildings, including
the Saltair pavilion, above, and the Utah
State Capitol.*

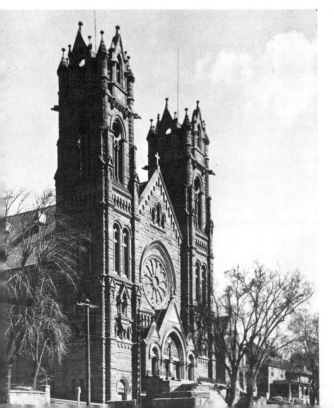

*Carl M. Neuhausen, another
German-born architect,
designed the Cathedral
of the Madeleine, left, the
Utah State Historical
Society (Kearns) Mansion,
and many other structures.*

ESTABLISHED 1864.   W. P. KISER, Mgr.   INCORPORATED 1897.

HENRY WAGENER BREWING CO.,   BOTTLED   BEER and PORTER

... 74 E. 1st South.   'Phone 218.   For Family Trade a Specialty.

Above: Henry Wagener was one of several German immigrants who founded breweries in Utah. Right: Karl G. Maeser, a native of Saxony, Germany, founded Brigham Young Academy in Provo (later Brigham Young University) and supervised the LDS Sunday School system. Below left: Charles M. Stoffel, son of German immigrants, operated a pharmacy in Salt Lake City. Below right: German prisoners of war interned at Camp Ogden during World War II. Propaganda against the German-born was high during wartime.

DeBry, who preferred to be known as a Netherlander. Briefly in 1907 there was *De Hollander* published in Salt Lake City and edited by Frank I. Kooyman, a young bookkeeper. Seven years later, with some Mormon church support but largely dependent on subscriptions, DeBry began *De Utah Nederlander*. His editorials, according to William Mulder, were "clear, vigorous, intelligent, directed at assisting his people to find their way in the new environment without at the same time losing the refining influence of the homeland." [14] Kooyman helped with this paper, too, and published a series of humorous verses.

In 1914 these foreign-language papers were brought under the LDS church's official direction. The need for them in Utah was diminishing—dependent as it was on the ebb and flow of immigration—and even their role overseas, where something like two hundred copies of each newspaper were sent for proselyting purposes in the late 1920s and early 1930s, was less important. Finally in 1935 the foreign papers were brought to an end "for lack of patronage." Not only had their subscriptions declined, but also they had been standardized and brought under central editing and management. Mulder notes that their closing at least spared them "the dotage of further dependency and old age." While they lasted, however, the newspapers were a response to the needs of immigrants from western Europe, helping to smooth the transition from the Old World to the New World.

Much of the institutional involvement of European immigrants in Utah has been in the area of religion. Among the Latter-day Saints, religious meetings for those of European origin have been held for more than a century. For example, an Ogden record states

> The first Dutch meeting was held in Ogden City in the house of Br. P. J. Lammers and R. van Dyke return[ed] missionaries from the Netherlands in the year 1870 which were held once a week. The average attendance was 10 persons, about all the Holland speaking people in the Weber stake or county of Weber. Those meetings were held of[f] and on for a number of jears [sic].[15]

Similarly, meetings were probably held for German-speaking immigrants in Salt Lake City and elsewhere in the early days.

---

[14] *Ibid.*, pp. 77–78.
[15] Dutch Organization, Ogden, Utah, Historical Record, 1911–1929, p. 1, LDS Archives.

Although such meetings were held, full-scale ecclesiastical organizations did not generally develop, due to the desire of LDS church leaders to see immigrant Mormons assimilated into existing English-language units; however, a German branch existed for several years in Logan. During the twentieth century the pattern until recently was to sponsor in Salt Lake City and Ogden German or Dutch "organizations." These held weekly meetings—sometimes on a weeknight, sometimes on Sunday—in which hymns were sung, sometimes by choirs, prayers were offered, and sermons were delivered in the native languages of the congregations. But the Germans and the Dutch still had to attend English-speaking wards to receive the sacrament or to participate in the activities of church auxiliaries and priesthood quorums. The exception to this was that in some cases a foreign-language Sunday School might be organized for those elderly people for whom there existed no possibility of learning the English language.[16]

Although interrupted by the two world wars, some of the LDS foreign-language associations survived into the 1960s, although, in at least the case of the German organization, now meeting only once a month. In 1963 the German and Dutch LDS organizations in Salt Lake Valley were abolished in connection with the formation of foreign-language branches of the church, including the Netherlands Branch and the German Branch. These units were established to insure those having trouble mastering the English language a fuller religious participation, those who could assimilate still being encouraged to participate in the English-speaking wards within which they resided. These foreign-language branches proved popular, the German Branch increasing enough in membership within the first two years to become a ward. For the Germans the meetings attracted not only the elderly, but also the young, who had been encouraged to assimilate. This resulted in the rather anomalous situation in the 1970s that some of the children's classes in the German ward had to be taught in English.[17]

On the whole, LDS European immigrants to Utah have entered into the group life of local English-speaking wards and stakes, serving

[16] Conversations with John A. Dahl, Nicholas J. Teerlink, and Alfred A. Lippold, all of Salt Lake City, September 1974. The church archives has records for Dutch organization meetings in Ogden and Salt Lake City, as well as the German organization in Salt Lake City and the German Branch in Logan.

[17] Conversations with Dahl, Teerlink, and Lippold; also Theodore A. Mebius of Salt Lake City, July 1974.

as teachers and officers in the units within which they resided. Some have achieved prominence in church activity. At the leadership level Carl W. Buehner, a German immigrant, served for some years, as a counselor in the Presiding Bishopric. Frederick Tadje was president of the German-Austrian and Swiss-German Missions during the 1920s, and J. Peter Loscher was called to preside over the Austrian and North German Missions in the 1960s. German converts were also instrumental in extending LDS proselyting to South America. K. B. Reinhold Stoof, an officer in the Imperial Army converted to Mormonism, served during 1926–35 in Argentina as president of the South American Mission; Emil Schindler spent several years under Stoof's direction as head of the missionary effort in Brazil. Both were active members of the Salt Lake German community.

Germans and Dutch have played a prominent role in LDS church administration at the local level as well. Bart Wolthuis, Nicholas J. Teerlink, and Louis Roos, among the Dutch immigrants, have served as stake presidents, and others have served as counselors in stake presidencies. Considering the proportion of the population that is Dutch, a surprisingly large number of Dutch immigrants have been bishops in LDS wards in the Salt Lake City area. Among German-born Mormons, Manfred R. Deus has served as a stake president, with others acting as counselors, several also having been called to be bishops.

Not all of the Utah Europeans have been Latter-day Saints. Although for many years most were Mormon and came as the result of Mormon gathering, from the first there was some falling away. "Of the Hollanders who journeyed with me, six have apostatized, and my mother and I were the only ones who remained faithful," wrote Johanna Carolina Lammers, who had come to Utah in 1867.[18] And increasingly, especially in the twentieth century, there were non-Mormons who came, contributing to university and community life. Between the active Mormons, the apostates, and the Gentiles some tension has always existed, but there are also occasions when their common nationality helps to bridge the gap. An organization like AVIO for the Dutch includes both Mormon and non-Mormon Dutch nationals.

[18] Johanna Carolina Lammers, "A Journey to Utah in the Year 1867," *Utah Nederlander* 1 (July 23, 1914): 17, translation in Mulder, "Nordic-Language Press," pp. 15–57.

Those Europeans who were not Mormons were long so few in number that Protestant foreign-language congregations were not established until quite late in the nineteenth century. By 1890 enough German Lutherans had arrived in the territory to justify the presence of a Lutheran missionary. Then, in 1892, Rev. Otto Kuhr established the German Evangelical Lutheran Saint John's Church in Salt Lake City, with another congregation being organized shortly thereafter in Ogden. Although there was some question as to which national Lutheran body to affiliate with, since 1900 Saint John's has been part of the Missouri Synod's Utah mission. Lutheran organizations in Utah were basically German-language congregations until World War I. The war marked the turning point in accommodation to American culture, as was the case in other areas. After the war, services were partly in German and partly in English for some time but are now in English. Although more than half the members of Saint John's Church, for example, are of Germanic descent, the group does not foster the preservation of the German cultural heritage. Since the establishment of Saint John's, other Lutheran churches have been established in the state; like the mother church in Utah, these have become increasingly less German in their orientation. Besides churches there have been Lutheran missions to Utah mining camps, to German prisoners of war during World War II, and to other German-language groups.[19]

The organization of a Dutch-oriented Protestant congregation did not take place in Utah until after World War II. Prior to that time Dutch-born Utahns in the Salt Lake area attended existing Protestant churches or met together in small groups in homes. The First Christian Reformed Church was established in downtown Salt Lake City shortly after the war, with the Immanuel Christian Reformed Church being set up in the Cottonwood area of Salt Lake County in the early 1960s. Two other branches of the Christian Reformed Church of America exist in Utah—one in Ogden and a small church in Brigham City—giving the denomination a Utah membership of several hundred. Services are not held in Dutch, nor is there a conscious effort made to preserve the Dutch heritage, but many of the members are Dutch and some of the social organiza-

---

[19] Conversation with Rev. Lawrence Meinzen of Saint John's Lutheran Church, Salt Lake City, September 1974. Ronnie L. Stellhorn, a graduate student at Utah State University, supplied much of the information given here with regard to the Lutheran church in Utah. Stellhorn is preparing a master's thesis titled "A History of the Lutheran Church in Utah."

tions sponsored by the church could be considered Dutch in their orientation. In some cases Dutch immigrants came to Utah because the mother church in Grand Rapids, Michigan, asked the Salt Lake unit to sponsor immigrants following World War II.[20]

CONTRIBUTIONS

It is impossible to enumerate the many kinds of activities continental Europeans engaged in after their coming to Utah. As with other people, most of their time and energies were consumed in the business of making a living. But in both vocation and avocation they made contributions to many aspects of Utah life. Without seeking to maintain that this small minority of the state's population was anything like a dominant force, it can safely be argued that many activities and occupations were strengthened and enriched by the Europeans' contribution.

Most European immigrants settled down into the economy of Utah as it was, taking jobs in agriculture, in shops, or in the various industries of the state. It was primarily a question, in other words, of fitting into a new environment, making a living, establishing oneself. In a few areas, however, the previous experience and expertise of the immigrants from the Continent became fairly important. Three areas are deserving of mention.

During the Brigham Young period of Utah history one of the goals consciously promoted by the territory's leaders was that of self-sufficiency. This meant, among other things, producing wine that could be sold to travelers, used for the sacrament in LDS services, and indulged in to a greater or lesser degree by both Mormon and Gentile Utahns. Sent to Utah's Dixie for the special purpose of establishing grape culture were Swiss Mormons under the leadership of Daniel Bonelli, and it was John C. Naegle who became the leader of wine production in Toquerville for many years.[21]

---

[20] Conversations with Rev. Clarence Van Slooten of First Christian Reformed Church of Salt Lake City and Rev. Adriaan Van Heyst of Immanuel Christian Reformed Church in the Cottonwood area of Salt Lake County, September 1974.

[21] On the wine industry in early Utah see Leonard J. Arrington, *Great Basin Kingdom: An Economic History of the Latter-day Saints, 1830–1900* (Cambridge, Mass., 1958), pp. 216–22, 477; Nels Anderson, *Desert Saints: The Mormon Frontier in Utah* (Chicago, 1942), pp. 373–74, 434–37; and the chapter on John Naegle in Thomas G. Romney, *The Gospel in Action* (Salt Lake City, 1949).

Another goal for several years was the establishment of silk production in Utah. For this purpose mulberry seeds and cocoons were brought from France by Octave Ursenbach and others. Paul and Susanna Cardon, French-speaking immigrants from the Piedmont valleys of alpine Italy, taught Utahns how to raise and use silk. And one Frenchman, Louis Bertrand, was a one-man champion of sericulture, devoting several lengthy articles in the *Deseret News* to a discussion of silk production and its possibilities for Utah. Ultimately, the silk industry in Utah fizzled out, unable to compete with cheaper fabrics from outside, but while it lasted those who had had some experience with it on the Continent were listened to.[22]

Finally, there was Swiss cheese. Some of the Swiss families— the Hubers, Abplanalps, Mosers, Abbeglens—who settled in Midway in the 1860s would graze their cattle in the canyons in the summer and in the fall drive the herds back to town, bringing cheese they had made. Later, Fred Buher established a cheese factory in Midway. On an even larger scale was the cheese industry in Cache Valley, said to produce more cheese than all of Switzerland. Although Danish settlers originally established the industry there, Swiss immigrants played a key role in the major expansion and diversification that started in the 1930s.[23]

Some energetic continental Europeans became builders and contractors, as did Charles Schmalz, who in 1871 moved to Ogden. After World War II, Joseph Hasoppe from Belgium came to Utah and established a family construction firm that continued active through the generation after the war. Although he had some experience in building houses in Belgium, Hasoppe found construction methods different in Utah. He worked as a laborer and carpenter for others, but he paid particular attention to learning the new methods. "I was working hard," he said, "but my eyes and my mind were working harder." Soon he started building a house on his own, working early in the mornings and in the evening. After four years, when he could get along fairly well in English, he launched his own construction company.[24] Another builder was Cornelius Kapteyn, from the Netherlands, who did everything from simple carpentry to the building of houses in the 1960s and 1970s. Show-

[22] Arrington, *Great Basin Kingdom,* pp. 227–28, 254, 347.

[23] The great expansion of cheese-making in Cache Valley occurred in the 1930s. One example of a Swiss who was a moving force in the making of cheese there is Edwin Gossner, whose company continues.

[24] Interview with Joseph Hasoppe, LDS Church Oral History Program, transcript in LDS Archives.

ing the brotherly concern and cooperation that was necessary in the new environment, both of these builders frequently used fellow immigrants as painters, plumbers, and other subcontractors.

Coming from a continent where the apprentice system was still strong throughout the nineteenth century, many of the immigrants were skilled artisans and tradesmen. Watchmakers from Switzerland like Octave Ursenbach brought this skill across the Atlantic and plied the trade in Utah. In the mid-twentieth century it was still noticeable that for certain kinds of skilled work—fine antique painting, woodcarving, furniture upholstering, bookbinding, cabinet making, and the like—European immigrants were among the best. A contemporary example of European craftsmanship transplanted to Utah is Peter Paul Prier's Professional Violin Making School of America. Prier, who was trained in Bavaria as a violin maker, came to Utah in 1960 to take charge of the violin department of a Salt Lake music store. A few years later he opened his own shop and then in 1972 initiated his violin-making academy, apparently the only school of its kind in America. Beginning with four students who followed a three- to four-year curriculum, demand for violin makers in America had become so great by 1974 that there were twenty-six students, and Prier had had to expand his original facilities.[25]

Moving to another field of endeavor, in the nineteenth century most schooling in Utah was not influenced by anything beyond American models, although within that context there were important innovations. In the field of education, especially higher education, immigrants from Europe have exerted a pronounced influence. In the 1880s a German, Karl Gottfried Maeser, became president of Brigham Young Academy. Maeser's conception of education and his advice on organizing the curriculum grew out of his experience as head teacher at the Budich Institute in Dresden. In Utah several hundred academy students came under his direct tutelage, and as head of the Latter-day Saint Department of Education Maeser traveled to many communities and sought to raise educational standards. During the same generation, at the end of the nineteenth century, German-born Louis F. Moench became an important leader at Weber Stake Academy.

In the twentieth century it is mainly individual professors who have made valuable contributions to the educational experiences of

[25] Peter Prier Clipping File, Deseret News Library, Salt Lake City.

Utah young people. Gerrit de Jong, who emigrated from the Netherlands in 1906, made important contributions to Brigham Young University as dean of fine arts and established a Portuguese language program second to none in the country. Almost constantly from the 1930s on, Utah universities included in their language faculties native-speaking professors, many of whom settled down as permanent residents. Belgian Andrée Barnett, professor of French at the University of Utah, was graduate advisor and in 1974 was named assistant dean of humanities. Robert E. Helbling, from Lucerne, Switzerland, became an acknowledged authority on the writings of Rudolf Kleist. A master teacher, Helbling became head of the Department of Languages at the University of Utah and for three years was director of the Honors Program.

It was not only in language departments that Europeans made themselves felt. Helmut Callis, born in Leipzig, Germany, became the University of Utah's expert on Asian history. In the Department of English at the Salt Lake school one of the most respected faculty members was William Mulder, from the Netherlands, author of the highly regarded work *Homeward to Zion,* a study of Mormon emigration from Scandinavia. Mulder, who obtained his doctorate at Harvard University, taught American literature and, broad-gauged person that he is, served on two occasions as advisor to India in the establishment of American Studies programs there. One of the most celebrated adopted Utahns in the 1970s was Willem Kolff of the University of Utah Medical School, who was one of the nation's acknowledged leaders in research on artificial organs. Several dozen other names of European professors in Utah's universities could be listed.[26]

For the great majority of immigrants, of course, the American institutions they encountered most directly were less likely to be universities than business and politics. As for Utah politics, if the immigrants in higher education were few, all who obtained citizenship had to come to grips with Utah's political system. Seldom did those of the first generation become directly involved except as voters. Prejudice against foreign-sounding names discouraged entrance into the political arena as candidates, and the challenge of adjustment to the new environment was enough to keep most of them occupied. They did not constitute large enough voting blocs to form powerful

[26] A brief survey of the faculty at the University of Utah in 1974 indicated that at least two or three dozen professors obtained their degrees in Europe and, to judge from the names, must be of European origin.

interest groups, although occasionally their newspapers did venture to give cautious advice to their readers.

With all of these discouragements, however, some immigrants made their mark. The French-born Alex Toponce was elected mayor of Corinne; the Swiss Eugene Santschi, mayor of Hiawatha and county commissioner in Carbon County; the Frenchman Paul Droubay, commissioner in Tooele County; Fred J. Kiesel, mayor of Ogden. Later in the century, Dutch-born Nicholas Teerlink served in the state legislature. Another Netherlander, Bart Wolthuis, was elected mayor of Ogden. A good example of a continental European who refused to be discouraged in her determination to be involved in public service in her adopted country was Elise Furer Musser, who emigrated from Switzerland in 1897. A state senator, Salt Lake County recorder, and trustee of the Utah Unemployment Commission during the 1930s, Mrs. Musser was a representative at international peace conferences, a Democratic national committee-woman, and a crusader for child welfare.[27]

In the world of music in Utah the Europeans were noticeable. The Dutch and Germans had a choir as part of their LDS congregation, and the Swiss organized an independent choral society, the Swiss Chorus Edelweiss, which gave numerous concerts from the 1940s on. Following the disbanding of the German LDS organization, the German choir became the Chorus Harmonie. Other German choruses have also performed in Utah, among them a male chorus and a children's chorus. Alexander Schreiner, an immigrant from Germany, became Tabernacle organist and won renown for his broadcast performances, starting in the 1930s. Gerrit de Jong, already mentioned with regard to his contributions in the field of education, was also an accomplished musician, playing and teaching piano and organ and leading orchestral groups at BYU. Margrit Feh Lohner, from Zurich, Switzerland, joined the Tabernacle Choir and the Swiss Chorus Edelweiss upon her arrival in Utah in 1940. In 1957 she became the director of Edelweiss. The group, dressed colorfully in Swiss costumes, gives many concerts each year and participates in the conventions of the Pacific Coast Swiss Singing societies. Mrs. Lohner also joined the Symphony Singers and was featured as a soloist for some five years.[28] Most notable in the post-

[27] Richard Jensen, "A New Home, A New Life: Contributions of the European Saints in Building the Kingdom," *The Ensign* 3 (August 1973): 62.

[28] Margrit Feh Lohner, LDS Church Oral History Program, transcript in LDS Archives.

World War II period was Maurice Abravanel, who took over the leadership of the Utah Symphony and raised it to a respectable level among American symphony orchestras. Although technically not a native of the countries being discussed here, Abravanel was truly a European with broad background—of Spanish-Portuguese ancestry, born in Greece, reared in Lausanne, Switzerland, and student of music and guest conductor in both Germany and France—and he has made such significant contributions to Utah music since 1947 that he deserves mention as an example of western Europe's cultural impact.

In the visual arts Europeans played a relatively small role. Although a group of Utah artists went to Paris to study at the end of the century and there absorbed important western European influences, only one of these, John Hafen, was himself a European. Born in Scherzingen, Switzerland, in 1856, Hafen came to America at age six and learned painting in Utah at the studios of Ottinger and Weggeland, beyond what he taught himself. After studying in Paris in the 1890s, Hafen traveled extensively throughout the United States and finally settled in Indiana. Returning to Utah, he produced many paintings of recognized merit. Another European who came to Utah as a boy was Herman H. Hagg, painter and instructor of art at the end of the last century.

In Salt Lake City the Deutsches Theater, under the direction of Siegfried Guertler, has fostered the preservation of the German dramatic tradition.

Like other Americans, the immigrants were on the whole less interested in the arts than in more popular activities. Sports presented an interesting challenge of adjustment. Not accustomed to playing traditional American sports such as football and baseball, European immigrants to Utah have done much to popularize soccer in the state. German and Dutch immigrants promoted the formation of athletic clubs both before and after World War II to provide athletic and social activities for their young men. Initially the clubs fielded teams divided along national lines, some of the more prominent being the Germania and Alemania clubs among the Germans and the Salt Lake Athletic Club and the Sports Club Rapids, which were predominantly Dutch teams. These and other teams came to form the Utah Soccer Association, which soon branched out to include teams sponsored by some of Utah's universities. An unusual club was Sports Club Berlin, whose team was mostly comprised of East German refugees. The adult league grew until by the mid-1960s there were fifteen teams in three Utah cities, although the teams now are organized more by ability than nationality. The Germania and Hollandia clubs have visited Europe in recent years on exhibition tours.[29]

Two immigrants from Germany were among the prime movers in interesting the young people of Utah in soccer. Hermann Neumann came to Utah in 1929 and played for the Germania Club for thirty-two years until an injury forced him to retire at age sixty-two. Arthur Zander came in 1952. Together these two organized the Utah High School Soccer Association, with the first teams being fielded at South, West, East, and Highland high schools in Salt Lake City in the mid-1950s. Not recognized by the Utah High School Activities Association until 1974 and therefore not funded by those schools having teams, the soccer program in Wasatch Front high schools long had to operate with volunteer coaches and officials. Zander served as coach of the first high school team. As soccer became increasingly popular in the late 1960s, membership in the association swelled to thirty-two teams in 1972, involving more than five hundred players.

As soccer became of greater interest to older boys, the Alemania and Hollandia clubs in 1967 organized the Junior Soccer Association to encourage play by young men from ages nine to fourteen, with Hermann Neumann as commissioner. The league was soon expanded to include three age groups. Although soccer is still not so popular as it is in many countries outside the United States, it would appear that the efforts of continental immigrants in Utah have guaranteed the sport an ever greater popularity in future years.

Besides participation in a team sport like soccer, there has also been the opportunity for Europeans in Utah to participate in individual sports. German young men participated in a physical fitness program known as *Sport Abzeichen,* in which awards were given according to the physical performance of individual participants. Gaston Chappuis, from French Switzerland, was Utah's handball champion seven different times and also showed his ability in chess, winning the state championships of Nevada, Idaho, and Utah.[30]

[29] Section on soccer in Utah is based on articles in Soccer Clipping File, Deseret News Library.

[30] Conversation with John A. Dahl of Salt Lake City, September 1974. Interview with Flore Chappuis, LDS Church Oral History Program, transcript in LDS Archives.

Conclusion

Certain aspects of the immigrant impact are almost impossible to discern. Because of the arbitrary custom of wives taking the surnames of their husbands, many young women from the Continent drop out of sight in Utah. Foreign-born wives of former servicemen, returned missionaries, or others certainly influence their families as much as any mother, and many of them participate actively in church and community affairs. But because their name is Smith or Johnson rather than Schroeder or Chateaubriand they are not usually noticed as obvious examples of foreign influence.

Even more important is the second generation. Since those born in Utah after the arrival of their families were native Utahns in the strict sense, they have not been considered here. But in the immigrant experience generally in the United States, it is the business of the first generation to get its feet on the ground and establish a secure existence, while it is the second and third generations that go on to dramatic achievements. In a sense it is artificial to divide these generations, counting some and excluding others, for the parents would undoubtedly count their children as the most important single "contribution" to the new environment—children who could draw from the strength of their European inheritance but who, more at home in the new environment than their parents, could go on to excel in their chosen profession. Since this is the way the immigrant families saw their own experience, it is artificial to include only those of the first generation, artificial, but inevitable; for the succeeding generations are American in language, education, experience, self-consciousness, and they frequently intermarry with other Americans without regard to national background.

In studies of this kind one often comes away with an impression that the sum of the parts equals far more than the whole. "Contributions" can be exaggerated. What would most Utahns say if asked to name their contribution to the state? It is not really assumed that one should come up with something dramatic to justify his existence. Most work, pay taxes, and vote in elections. Most try to be good citizens. Thus it may be a valuable indication of the degree of assimilation of the western Europeans now residing in the state that in 1974 most of those who filled out a questionnaire sent out by the authors said something like this: "Our people are industrious, good citizens." They take pride in the reputation they have for hard work and frugality. Some mentioned that a relatively small percentage of their national group had been involved in crime. Most of them have indeed become Americans and Utahns in their basic self-identification. If they retain a lingering nostalgia for the old ways, this is not basically different from other Americans who look back with fondness at the simpler life of their childhood.

It would be inaccurate, on the other hand, to overstate the fondness of the immigrants themselves for Utah. From the beginning some became disenchanted with Mormonism or Utah or both. Some of these left, others stayed. One Dutch immigrant said that he would have returned to the Netherlands if he had not been so poor; even now he does not feel welcome except among those of Dutch background. He does not like the crime rate and finds the cold winters hard to tolerate. Yet the same man considers Utah the best of the states he has visited, including California. Others are more enthusiastic about their adopted land, emphasizing the wide open spaces, the opportunities for outdoor recreation, and the relative immunity of the state from the unrest of the large industrial cities. Mormons who stay usually emphasize the LDS church as one of the positive features; the original lure to attract them, it continues to function as a help and support in their lives.

So supermen they are not, these Utahns from continental Europe. Good solid stock ready to work and save and participate they have been. They have exerted themselves to deserve their reputation for hard work and sobriety. They want to be part of the answer, as the saying goes, and not part of the problem facing society. Inevitably, in many small ways, they have added to the richness of the warp and woof that make up the cultural heritage of Utah.

7 THE PIONEER CHINESE OF UTAH

BY DON C. CONLEY

The distance from the subtropical rice paddies of China's southern-most province to the mountainous desert of the Great Basin spans one-third of the earth's circumference. Along this tumultuous course of Pacific Ocean waves and Sierra Nevada mountain peaks came Chinese men to forge an integral but mostly forgotten link in Utah's frontier life.

The majority of the approximately one hundred thousand Chinese arriving at the port of San Francisco between 1860 and 1880 came from Kwangtung Province.[1] In its capital, Kwangchow (Canton), the first trade between China and western nations flourished from 1760 to 1840.[2] This commercial venture brought news of American current events, such as the California gold rush, that stimulated the imaginations of adventuresome Cantonese. The confrontation of two civilizations determined the future of many Chinese who found themselves toiling in factories, mines, chop-houses, laundries, and building the first railroads in North America.

In the nineteenth century floods, typhoons, droughts, and general poverty were the endemic forces on the Pearl River delta of which Kwangchow was the city center. Besides insufficient pro-tection from natural catastrophe, further insecurity stemmed from the loose and faltering central government in Peking, twelve hundred miles north of Kwangtung,[3] an abundance of local bandits roaming the hills, ethnic disputes among the three main districts (Hakka, Punti, and Tanka), local official corruption, heavy taxes which drained a large portion of meager earnings, and unparalleled popula-tion density.

---

[1] Mary Roberts Coolidge, *Chinese Immigration* (New York, 1909), p. 498.

[2] John K. Fairbank, *The United States and China* (Cambridge, Mass., 1948), p. 140.

[3] George Babcock Cressey, *Land of the 500 Million: A Geography of China* (New York, 1955), p. 150.

The family was the single institution providing some stability in that chaotic society.[4] Hardship was reality to the Chinese; and if leaving such circumstances for an opportunity of self and familial improvement for a sometimes lengthy but usually temporary period could by chance alleviate such burdens, why remain in predictable immobility? And so, the opportunity was welcomed by thousands of Chinese who packed a few worldly belongings in straw baskets, balanced on bamboo shoulder poles, and set off for the riches of America.

The discovery of gold in California was initially the chief attraction. Besides the obvious motive of quick wealth, the Chinese idealized the Confucian teaching of an extended family (joint-family).[5] Central to this ideal was financial security that provided Chinese education in the classics for male heirs. This education, in turn, brought land ownership, membership in the scholar-gentry class, and substantial living quarters where many generations could be housed under one roof. The ideal was achieved by an elite minority, mostly those already in the upper social strata.[6] Nevertheless, it permeated all levels of society, existing dreamlike in the minds of the people. Whether philosophical or practical, there was no want of motives for going.

The emigrants made their way to Hong Kong and from there to San Francisco, a journey averaging about two months.[7] The earliest groups were sponsored as indentured servants by one of the Chinese Six Companies, all centered in San Francisco. Because this proved ineffective, it was replaced by the credit-ticket system, wherein a Hong Kong brokerage firm advanced the forty-dollar passage and a connecting firm in the United States found work for the immigrant and collected the voyage debt from his eventual earnings. This credit-ticket system was used by most immigrants unable to pay their own way.[8]

The construction of the Central Pacific from Sacramento to Promontory brought the first Chinese into what is now the state of

[4] Gunther Barth, *Bitter Strength: A History of the Chinese in the United States, 1850–1870* (New York, 1955).

[5] Olga Lang, *Chinese Family and Society* (New Haven, Conn., 1946), p. 16.

[6] John K. Fairbank, ed., *China's Response to the West: A Documentary Survey, 1839–1923* (Cambridge, Mass., 1964), p. 4.

[7] Barth, *Bitter Strength*, p. 69.

[8] Thomas W. Chinn, ed., *A History of the Chinese in California: A Syllabus* (San Francisco, 1969), p. 15.

Utah. At one point there were more than twelve thousand Chinese employed in the building of the Central Pacific.[9] E. B. Crocker, brother of Charles Crocker, Central Pacific general superintendent, was among the first to suggest using Chinese laborers.[10] Charles Crocker tried to persuade his Irish construction superintendent, J.H. Strobridge, to employ Chinese, but he resisted until labor became scarce and then consented to experiment with fifty Chinese. These fifty did so well that no limit was placed on Chinese employment.[11]

Confidence in the Chinese laborer was confirmed by Leland Stanford, the governor of California and one of the "Big Four" railroad bosses, when he wrote Andrew Johnson:

> As a class they are quiet, peaceable, patient, industrious, and economical. Ready and apt to learn all the different kinds of work required in railroad building, they soon become as efficient as white laborers.[12]

They not only laid track with consistent precision but also became legendary in their blasting of tunnels and ridges with nitroglycerin while lowered in baskets over cliffs fourteen hundred feet above the American River Canyon.[13] Their Chinese food was more conducive to good health than the meat and starch diet of American workers and their tea-drinking protected them from diseases transmitted through polluted water.

After moving across Nevada into Utah, the Central Pacific met the Union Pacific at Promontory. Chinese participated at the joining of the rails. In preparation for driving the Golden Spike

> a slicked-up team of the Union Pacific's best Irish track-layers had already swung the west rail across the gap in the track and spiked it down, except on the missing tie. Now a gang of Chinese, in clean blue jackets, moved out to put the final, east rail in place.[14]

In all the talk that took place at Promontory on that occasion, no mention was made of the Chinese contribution; but the Chinese

---

[9] George Kraus, "Chinese Laborers and the Construction of the Central Pacific," *Utah Historical Quarterly* 37 (1969) : 42–44.

[10] Alexander Saxton, "The Army of Canton in the High Sierra," *Pacific Historical Review* 35 (1966) : 141–52.

[11] Wesley S. Griswold, *A Work of Giants: Building the First Transcontinental Railroad* (New York, 1962), p. 111.

[12] Kraus, "Chinese Laborers and the Construction of the Central Pacific," p. 45.

[13] Griswold, *A Work of Giants*, p. 123.

[14] *Ibid.*, p. 326.

were not altogether forgotten. At a Sacramento celebration, Charles Crocker "in his brief, proud speech was the only one of the day that recognized the role of the Chinese." "In the midst of our rejoicing," he said, "I wish to call to mind that the early completion of this railroad we have built has been in great measure due to the poor, destitute class of laborers called the Chinese—to the fidelity and industry they have shown. . . ." [15]

On the centennial of that memorable event at Promontory, May 10, 1969, in a speech given by Secretary of the Treasury John Volpe the gargantuan task, the sweat, lifeblood, and genius of the Chinese railroad man was left unmentioned. [16]

Promontory became the gateway for most Chinese coming into Utah in frontier times. Between 1870 and 1880 the greatest population of Chinese in the state lived within the boundaries of Box Elder County, employed almost entirely as section hands on the railroad. [17]

In the late 1880s and early nineties, when W. A. "Pappy" Clay was just a boy, he was allowed entrance into a world unknown to most, excepting the Chinese who possessed it. Wallace Clay was born March 11, 1884, three hundred feet from that historic spot where "the golden spike" joined the Union Pacific and the Central Pacific. From 1884 to 1893 his father was the telegraph operator and Central Pacific agent at Blue Creek where Wallace Clay's childhood was surrounded by the objects and people of the railroad in its day of glory. The precocious observations of the child were still present in the man of ninety years when he was interviewed:

> After they used them [the Chinese] in the construction of the Central Pacific roadbed, then about every twelve or fourteen miles they had a section house along to keep the track up after it was built, and at each one of these section houses they had a section boss and he was usually a big, burly Irishman, and then he usually had about thirty Chinese coolies working under him as section hands, and that was the set up all the way from Ogden to Roseberg, California. . . . [18]
>
> My name being Wallace Clay, was changed by those Orientals to "Wah Lee, Melicum Boy," and I more or less

[15] Robert West Howard, *The Great Iron Trail: The Story of the First Transcontinental Railroad* (New York, 1962), pp. 336–37.

[16] Francis L. K. Hau, *The Challenge of the American Dream: The Chinese in the United States* (Belmont, Calif., 1971), p. 104.

[17] 1870 Census.

[18] Interview with Wallace E. Clay, Hot Springs, Utah, December 2, 1974.

lived with them from 1889 to 1892, and only slept with my parents and had breakfast at home mostly at Blue Creek Water Tank Station during one-half of each twenty-four hours.[19]

Because he was inquisitive, bright, and just a child, Wallace Clay was allowed to see and experience first hand what was only conjecture and mystery to most Caucasian Americans of that era. He explained in fascinating detail the intricate and well-camouflaged construction of an opium den and of the dream world in which the opium smoker moves—a process Clay observed rather than actually experienced. He spoke of moments of sharing, of an interchange of knowledge and friendship:

> When not "raising taps and tapping ties" those good China-men, among whom were "my very best friends" were many who probably got homesick for their wives and children in China, so they took me as a sort of pet and they gave me much Chinese candy and firecrackers and Chinese money and they asked many questions about American life and I asked them many questions about life in China. . . .

> I will now describe how my "Chinese friends" lived at old Blue Creek Station in 1891. The antiquated box-car they lived in had been remodeled into a "work-car," in one end of which a series of small bunk beds had been built as a vertical column of three bunks one above the other on both sides of the car-end from floor to ceiling so that around eighteen Chinamen could sleep in the bedroom end of the car, while the other end of the car served as a kitchen and dining room wherein there was a cast iron cook stove with its stove pipe going up through the roof of the car and with all kinds of pots and pans and skillets hanging around the walls, plus cubby holes for tea cups and big and little blue china bowls and chop sticks and wooden table and benches—about like we now find in forest service camp grounds—occupying the middle of the car.

After twelve-hour shifts on the railroad roadbed, these men who conquered some of the most rugged terrain in the West let their thoughts turn toward loved ones. Clay often saw them "writing long letters back home to China wherein they used little paint brushes to make their Chinese hieroglyphics or picture writing. . . ." The Chinese also indulged in the age-old remedy for aching muscles, taking "time

[19] Wallace E. Clay, "Personal Life of a Chinese Coolie 1869–1899," Unpublished paper written January 2, 1969.

to prepare a nice hot evening bath" in a big wooden tub of steaming water.

Since even the sound of music in the West was alien to the Chinese, with their own traditions of sacred, dramatic, and popular music—written in an entirely different scale from western music—the men Clay knew played two common instruments, the *lo* (large gong) and, possibly, the *nu k'in* (two-stringed fiddle). The familiar sounds may have eased their loneliness.

The men also took pride in preparing and sharing delicious-sounding meals. As heirs of one of the world's great classic cuisines, these Chinese obtained the necessary ingredients and combined and ate them with gusto. While the meal was a single course and not so elegant as Peking duck, it was surely satisfying to hungry workers.

> The cooks built their own type of outdoor ovens in the dirt banks along side of the sidetrack, and their stake pot spits along side their bunk cars, where they did most of their cooking when the weather permitted. Each cook would have the use of a very big iron kettle hung over an open fire and into it they would dump a couple of measures of Chinese unhulled brown rice, Chinese noodles, bamboo sprouts and dried seaweed, different Chinese seasonings, and American chickens cut up into small pieces. . . . When the cook stirred up the fire and the concoction began to swell until finally the kettle would be nearly full of steaming, nearly dry brown rice with the cut-up chicken all through it.

> Each Chinaman would take his big blue bowl and ladle it full of the mixture and deftly entwine his chopsticks between his fingers and string the mixture into his mouth in one continuous operation, while in the meantime he would be drinking his cup of tea and still more tea. I was the curious, watching kid so the cook would ladle up a little blue bowlful for me (Little Wah Lee) and hand me a pair of chopsticks and with them I would try to eat like the rest of my buddies, but I never could get the "knack" so I would end up eating with my fingers which would make the Chinese laugh and I would get no tea.[20]

Besides Wallace Clay, there were other earlier (but none so excellent) eyewitnesses of Chinese life in Box Elder County. Among the earliest recorded observations were those by a group of excursionists from Cincinnati experimenting with the new-found luxury of railroad travel. Here is their report written September 7, 1869:

[20] *Ibid.*

"EIGHTH LETTER" PROMONTORY

It was there that the excursionists saw the Chinamen. Sam Hing and Ah Lee have little huts adorned with signs, vouching for "good washing and ironing done here." A gang of Chinese laborers, in loose blue muslin garments and peaked parasol hats of straw, were grading a new switch at the station. Their slow, measured way of plying their shovels, explosive cackle of conversation, and frugal midday meal, and manner of eating, amused those who watched them.[21]

Corinne, the once-booming railroad center, had a Chinese community in its heydey. The artifacts of an old Chinese laundry are among the memorabilia housed in the railroad museum there. An editorial from the *Utah Reporter* provides a vivid, although ethnocentric, impression of its international atmosphere:

> Corinne is just now a fine place for the study of ethnology. We have in and around the city some five hundred Indians, *two or three hundred Chinese,* and quite a number of citizens of African descent. Our streets are gay with red blankets, paint and feathers, with Mongolian blue and purple, and with all the varieties of costume affected by hunters, miners, merchants, ranchmen and freighters of the "superior race". . . .[22]

The same newspaper reported the first known Chinese wedding, attesting to the presence of Chinese women in the territory.

> . . . on the evening of Saturday, the twenty-third, by Justice Sewell, Mr. John Tip ["John" was a nickname applied to all Chinese males in frontier times.] to Miss Ma Choy both of the Flowery Kingdom, but now residents of Corinne. The affair took place at the restaurant of Mrs. Clemmens and the happy bridegroom indulged in quite a handsome "set out" of cake, wine and other delicacies. Several ladies and gentlemen of the Anglo-Saxon "Persuasian" were present by invitation and the novel affair was by them pronounced a very pleasant occasion. We understand that the history of the lovers has been a romantic one, and that John secured his fair one by a regular American runaway. The surroundings were well worthy of the first Mongolian wedding in Utah.[23]

---

[21] *Cincinnati Excursion to California,* Indianapolis, Cincinnati and Lafayette Railroad, 1870, pp. 38–39.

[22] *Utah Reporter* (Corinne), April 26, 1870. Emphasis added.

[23] *Ibid.*

Terrace, like Kelton and many other legendary Utah ghost towns, boasted a large Chinese community in frontier days. Terrace was located about one hundred miles west of Promontory; little remains of it since a fire drove out its few remaining inhabitants in 1900. According to the 1880 Census there were fifty-four Chinese in Terrace, only one of whom was a woman. Most of the men were railroad employees, but others were independent small businessmen. One man named Hong Lee "kept a store," another, Wah Hing, ran a laundry. Ching Moon was a grocer, and the only woman, true to frontier expectations, was a twenty-eight-year-old prostitute. One Wong Tz Chong performed the handiwork of a tailor, and another, Ah Lei, raised vegetables in his own garden. Apparently there were two Chinese laundries in Terrace, because Wa Hop was a laundry proprietor also.

How valuable are the census records? Regarding the history of the pioneer Chinese in the West, census records are perhaps more informative than the few other records available. Such simple statistics as names, ages, occupations, and literacy, in the dearth of written history about the Chinese in the state, help clarify certain misconceptions: many of these first Chinese could read and write, which puts to rest the faulty notion that they were all *coolies*. Far from being unskilled, a number of the Chinese took advantage of the economic potential of the new towns to leave the ranks of labor and open their own businesses.

In recent times, Frank Tinker told of souvenir-seekers in Terrace discovering evidence of the lives of those persons listed on the census rolls: Chinese pottery, coins, and assorted artifacts.[24]

Tinker has also recorded the familiar experiences of a few old-timers, George Grose and the Hersheys, who observed the attempts to keep cultural customs alive even while enduring the isolation imposed upon so many Chinese men in mining and railroad towns throughout the old West.

Once a year, on their New Years Day, the Chinese made long strips of white coconut candy which the youngsters of the village came to beg. There were no wives here and no children. When the men died they were taken to a cemetery west of

[24] Frank Tinker, *Salt Lake Tribune*, January 26, 1964.

town which defies location today. Later some of the remains were shipped back to China. . . .[25]

The practice of burying the body for a period of five to ten years, exhuming it, and shipping the bones back to the homeland to be placed in the ancestral tomb may be compared in part to the desire of many people for burial in native soil. Ancestor reverence, a significant aspect of religion in China (Buddhism, Taoism, and Ancestor Reverence), apparently motivated this custom among Chinese.

As the railroad center for Utah, Ogden witnessed the development of a Chinatown with census figures rising from 33 Chinese in 1880 to 106 in 1890.[26] The Chinese section was characterized by "many rows of low wooden structures . . . built along Twenty-fifth Street from the Broom Hotel to the railroad station, four city blocks west of Washington Boulevard, and many of these establishments were operated by the Chinese." [27]

Among laundries operated by Chinese in Ogden were: Ching Wah, 2438 Grant Avenue, Hang Yei, 2222 Grant Avenue, Sam Wah, 271 Twenty-fifth Street, Sue Wah, 123 Twenty-fifth Street, and Wong Lee at 229 Twenty-fifth Street.[28]

Wong Leung Ka was one of the earliest established Chinese merchants in Ogden. He arrived around 1880 but did not come with the influx of railroad workers. However, like many other Chinese of that period, he came to this country without wife or family. Unlike settlers from northern Europe, most Chinese had not left their homeland permanently, and most intended to return. What little is known about Wong Leung Ka was revealed by his son, Wong Siu Pang of Salt Lake City. Wong Siu Pang, who had never known his father, learned of him from family members, mostly from an older brother, the only other child in the family, who lives in Wyoming and has been in the United States for over fifty years. Wong Leung Ka resided in Ogden for forty-six years. During those years, he returned to his family in China twice. Each visit lasted less than a year because he traveled with a business visa that did not allow him to remain away longer.

"Sing Lung Store" was the name of Wong Leung Ka's shop in Ogden. The store carried groceries, canned goods, and Chinese

[25] *Ibid.*

[26] 1880, 1890 Censuses.

[27] Kate B. Carter, comp., "The Early Chinese of Western United States," in *Our Pioneer Heritage,* 17 vols. (Salt Lake City, 1958–), 10:478.

[28] *Ibid.,* 10:475.

imported items. Above the store, in the upper level of the building, were sleeping rooms. Wong Leung Ka was known for his compassion and generosity. When times were hard and men were unemployed, Chinese in the area sought Leung Ka's store as a place of refuge. Sleeping rooms and meals were provided. When, and if, employment was found, the men would pay back what they could.

In 1927, while waiting to embark to China for a third time, he died suddenly at the age of sixty-nine. His dream of returning to see his youngest son and enjoy a reunion with his family was unfulfilled.[29] The basic pattern of the sojourn of Wong Leung Ka was repeated thousands of times by other Chinese.

> . . . Because some Chinese had such difficulties living in America, so he hoped his children would not come here to live. . . .[30]

This was the message of Wong Leung Ka to his sons. But like their father, a spirit of adventure and faith brought them to this country where they have made their homes. Sometime after the youngest son Wong Siu Pang emigrated with his wife, three sons, and daughter in 1964, he and his older brother drove to Ogden and stood on the site of "Sing Lung Store." It was no longer there, and everything all around was changed. The old proprietor's grandchildren were being educated at the University of Utah and other institutions of higher learning. Among them are two promising artists, a scientist, and an inventor, children of Wong Siu Pang.

In the 1870s a controversial theory that Chinese immigration to the United States should be suspended because of high unemployment and job shortage was initiated in California, rapidly filtered into all states and territories of the United States, and was especially defended by those areas with Chinese populations. It was also argued that unemployment was high and jobs were scarce because the Chinese, willing to work for lower wages, were usurping jobs rightfully meant for white Americans. Newspapers in Utah shared the attitude of editors throughout the western region: the Chinese must go. The uproar culminated in the passage of the Chinese exclusion laws beginning in 1882. An editorial in the *Ogden Junction* said:

> . . . But when every argument in favor of the Chinese is exhausted, the case of today is not covered; for times are hard,

[29] Interview with Wong Siu Pang, Salt Lake City, November 27, 1974.
[30] *Ibid.*

work in places is difficult if not impossible to get and the wages of white men, as a consequence, have dwindled to such an extent that there is at least but a trifling difference between the prices paid for work performed by the white man and that done by the copper-colored incubus.

The first care of the nation should be the welfare of its subjects, and when we are brought into competition for day's labor, something must be done. There are unquestionably more workmen than there is work to be performed; and to divide what little there is with the inferior and alien race, is not a good nor a just policy. . . .[31]

The editorial made no note of Chinese-owned businesses that contributed to the economic health of the area by creating jobs and markets for goods and services. Also ignored was the employment of Chinese on the Central Pacific Railroad out of desperation because not enough local citizens were willing to hazard such work.[32]

Since 1900 the largest Chinese population in Utah has been consistently in Salt Lake City. After railroad employment diminished for the Chinese in Box Elder County, the greatest number of Chinese remaining in Utah gravitated to the capital city. The 1890 Census counted 271 Chinese in Salt Lake City, whereas Box Elder County had only 147 for the same period.

Plum Alley ran north and south dividing the city block between Main and State streets, the cross streets being First and Second souths. Within and around Plum Alley the Chinese developed a microcommunity with grocery and merchandise stores, laundries and restaurants. Henry Ju, as a child in the 1930s, recalled accompanying his father Joy to Plum Alley on special occasions:

> They used to have those little shops where you could go and buy Chinese groceries that they sent from Frisco to here . . . then you'd look in the back and see a bunch a guys settin' around tables gambling; and how some of 'em used to sit there and smoke their water pipes.

> On New Year's Day [Chinese Lunar New Year] they had a big New Year's celebration sponsored by the tong in Plum Alley and they'd invite the police chief and mayor and all the dignitaries and they'd set around there and eat all the goodies and some of them old guys [the old Chinese men] would come over and give us the red envelopes with money in them [A Chinese tradition: the older married people give

[31] *Ogden Junction,* January 29, 1879.
[32] Griswold, *A Work of Giants,* p. 11.

money to the young people, mostly children, in red decorated envelopes, the contents known as "lucky money"]; that's all us kids looked forward to. . . . That was quite a haul, when you'd get up there you might get twenty bucks—they used to give silver dollars. . . .[33]

Salt Lake City architect William Louie, grandson of a pioneer Chinese railroad worker, said that according to ancient custom the men probably paid all their debts before the dawning of the Lunar New Year, and in camp the cook would have plenty of hot water ready for the required bath. After a midnight feast of abalone and other special foods not eaten every day, the first day of the new year was a fast from all meat. Coming from a family-oriented culture where children are prized, the men were noted for their generosity toward American youngsters, especially on Lunar New Year. Mr. Louie recalled that they always seemed to put lots of money in the traditional red packets for the children in Ogden.[34]

Holidays provided occasion for greater merging between the Chinese community and the majority populace. A New Year's parade during the 1890s in Salt Lake City is recalled by Ivy C. Towler:

A prominent feature of nearly all New Year parades was a huge Chinese dragon two hundred feet long which progressed along the street like a gigantic centipede. The dragon itself, which swayed from side to side, had a head six feet tall spitting fire from its vicious red mouth. The back of the creature of red, yellow and green painted canvas was suspended on arched staves, supported by poles from within, placed at regular intervals, giving its body a muscular appearance. The curtained sides hung down within two feet of the ground showing the legs and sandled [sic] feet of many Chinese marching in regular rhythm.[35]

Jimmy Wong, a Salt Lake restaurant owner, told of the history of the Bing Kung Tong, the Salt Lake chapter of the Chinese Benevolent Society with headquarters in San Francisco. He said, "There are chapters in Los Angeles, Denver, Sacramento, Oakland, Fresno, Portland, Seattle, and other major cities with large Chinese contingencies throughout the West." The first quarters for the tong were located in Plum Alley before the turn of the century, but Wong

[33] Interview with Henry Ju, December 3, 1974, Magna, Utah.
[34] Salt Lake Tribune, February 15, 1972.
[35] Carter, "The Early Chinese of Western United States," 10:456.

could not pinpoint the exact year it was first organized in Utah.[36] William J. Christiansen's research into the objectives and functioning of the old tong concluded:

> . . . As in other larger western cities, the Salt Lake City Bing Kung Tong's main function was economic. It provided jobs and job counseling, transportation, translating services, lawyers, and letter writing services. Meetings were held often and economic matters were discussed. Another function was the provision of social activities such as gambling.[37]

Another major Utah Chinatown existed in Park City, the once-famous mining town, from its earliest days. According to the 1890 Census, 131 Chinese resided there. The first railroads into Park City were constructed in part by Chinese labor.

> All the men working on the Echo and Park City Railroad have been discharged and Chinese labor substituted in their place. The former class were being paid 1.75 per day; the latter require only 1.10. Some day when we are looking through a very powerful microscope we would like to examine the soul of a corporation like the Echo and Park City Railroad Company.[38]

This project, in addition to mining, which always attracted Chinese to provide community services, was probably what encouraged the development of the Park City Chinatown. Fraser Buck, an old-time Park City resident, had the following to say about the Chinese in the mining settlement:

> The Chinese moved into an area back of Main Street about a block above the post office; they had about fourteen or so houses there. They were very nice, they didn't cause the people in town a lot of trouble. There are still two or three houses standing left from the old Chinatown sector.
> There was a Chinaman came here called, "Old Grover" [nicknamed for Grover Cleveland] and he passed away just a few years back, but he was an old, old-timer. He was quite progressive—he acquired a house or two and rented until he built himself quite a thing. He had a son, "Joe Grover" come from China who lived with him and he inherited the houses

---

[36] Interview with Jimmy Wong, December 3, 1974, Salt Lake City.

[37] William J. Christiansen, "Chinese Ethnicity and Network Relationships in Salt Lake City" (Spring 1972), University of Utah, paper for Dr. Tom Collins, p. 8.

[38] *Silver Reef Miner,* June 10, 1882.

that he had. Sometimes we used to say that he had eighty houses, but I don't think that's possible.

There were a few women—and there was China Mary—she lived down here on Main Street and was well received by the town.

The mines all had Chinese, one or two, and when they got going, they had up to five Chinese, most of them. They took care of the cleaning [in the mines and for the miners] and all that kind of work, and the cooking. . . .[39]

A landmark in old Park City was the "China Bridge" that stretched across Chinatown from Rossie Hill, the residential section of Park City.

They built the "China Bridge"—people in Rossie Hill—they didn't like to come down through Chinatown.

Chinese laundries and restaurants were scattered in different parts of the town. Wash houses were not allowed on Main Street.[40]

An advertisement in the *Park Record* tells of a Chinese restaurant in old Park City:

Charley Ong Lung has lately opened up a first class restaurant, opposite the Marsac Mill, where can be had choice meals at all hours. Oysters in every style. Meal tickets—twenty one meals for $7.[41]

Fraser Buck's impression was that most of the town did not resent the Chinese. However, this was not always true:

Yesterday a smart aleck thought to exhibit his smartness in front of Greenewald's by attacking an inoffensive Chinaman, who was passing along the street molesting no one. He grasped the Celestial and threw him down and pulled his queue rather too severely for John's liking. The Chinaman hastened to his feet and gathered up an armful of rocks and started for the S.A., who threw his hand back to his hip pocket under the pretense of drawing a pistol. This movement had not the effect of checking the Chinaman, who pressed him so closely and hurled stones so rapidly that the S.A. was forced to take to his heels for safety.[42]

[39] Interview with Fraser Buck, November 29, 1974, Park City, Utah.

[40] *Ibid.*

[41] *Park City Mining Record,* June 5, 1880.

[42] *Park City Mining Record,* August 7, 1880.

The Chinese continued to be victims of sporadic, racially inspired difficulties into the first decade of the 1900s. During 1902 and 1903 the miners union campaigned to boycott Chinese restaurants and laundries, to end employment of Chinese, and to prohibit the selling and buying of Chinese goods. The acting consul general in San Francisco sent a petition of redress from See Lee and others in Park City, with a sample of articles published in the *Park Record* and a handbill, to the Chinese chargé d'affairs in Washington, D.C. The articles, entitled "White or Chinese" and signed "Saltair," complained that ninety-eight widows were forced to compete with Chinese restaurants and laundries.

> Shall the widows famish while the heathen Chinese feast? . . . All members of organized labor are in duty bound to patronize only white labor, and such establishments as employ only white labor. . . . The unorganized laborers of the camp who patronize the Oriental competitors of our race . . . are a greater menace . . . than an equal number of "scabs." Either the widows or the Chinese must go.

The handbill was also anonymous:

Patronize Home Industry

> By spending your money with your own race, or braid your hair in a pig tail and move to Hongkong. . . . Benedict Arnold was a traitor to his country but he never stooped so low as to patronize Chinese.[43]

Of the early Chinese in Tooele County, none was more famous than Sam Wing, known as "Doc Chinaman" to his fellow townspeople in Mercur. Besides practicing medicine [Chinese herbal], he was the proprietor of a laundry that employed four Chinese men.

In the early years of her marriage (1904–5), Evalee McBride Fackrell was the next door neighbor of the doctor and his wife Molly, both of whom, she said, spoke English well. Mrs. Fackrell expressed great faith in Sam Wing as a physician:

> When the doctors out there [Mercur] had a case that they didn't know how to cure, and got so bad—they sent for him and that man pulled many a case through that the doctors

[43] Governor's Correspondence, Utah State Archives, State Capitol, Salt Lake City.

From the top: *Signpost commemorating the feat of the Chinese in the race to Promontory. Chinese camp and outfit cars where engineers lived, Nevada, 1868. Twelve thousand Chinese worked on the Central Pacific that met the Union Pacific at Promontory, Utah, May 10, 1869. Chinese railroad maintenance workers filling in the Secrettown trestle, east of Sacramento, 1877.*

Above: *Chinese dragon
float in Pioneer Semi-
Centennial celebration,
1897, Salt Lake City. An
early Chinese resident of
Salt Lake City, Chin Sig,
ca. 1880.* Left: *Chinese
cook standing in doorway
of Buckhorn mine
boardinghouse at Ophir,
Tooele County, 1903.*
Below: *Paving Plum
Alley, Salt Lake City,
where many Chinese lived
and kept shops.
Whitewashed building is
noodle parlor.*

Above: *Seto Shee at age sixteen in Canton, China, before coming
to Ogden as the bride of Wing Louie. Chinese herbalists advertised
widely and served a large clientele. Frank Louie, one of the earliest
pilots of Chinese ancestry, at the Ogden airport, November 1933.*

Below: *The well-known King family: first row: Dr. Ernest King;
father Charles and mother Ruth Y., both Congregationalists from
Canton; and Raymond, commercial photographer; second row: Lily;
Walter, Salt Lake newsman; and Dr. Ruth M., like Ernest a doctor of
medicine. The Kings sold Chinese goods and repaired china dolls in
their King Doll Hospital.*

From the top: *Poolhall in Helper, Carbon County, where WPA workers found residents from thirty-two nations in the early 1930s. Veterans William W. Louie, World War II, and Ogdenite Lee Fook, World War I. Lt. Arthur K. Chinn, of Ogden was the only serviceman of Chinese ancestry from Utah to be killed in World War II. The Bing Kong Tong, a Chinese social organization in Salt Lake City.*

would have lost. Everybody thought if they just had the "Doc" to take care of them, they'd be all right.[44]

On one occasion when Mrs. Fackrell's baby was crying during the early morning hours, the "Doc," recognizing symptoms of colic, came into the Fackrell home and rubbed a "Chinese peppermint oil" around the baby's mouth and navel. The baby ceased crying immediately and his mother thought the "Doc" had drugged him. Sam Wing assured her that the baby would be all right, and his words proved true.

Mrs. Fackrell described Molly's home:

> Just a beautiful little home, just a little home. . . . with two rooms, and the men that run the laundry lived back further— I never went into their apartment at all. They had their laundry in the back part of the home.

Molly often came to visit Mrs. Fackrell, particularly to admire her baby boy. She would hold him on her knee and bounce him saying, "A pretty baby, a nica baby." Mrs. Fackrell said, "She [Molly] had children, and they were in China, and they couldn't bring them over here, and she was lonesome." Molly pined for her children and the "Doc" finally insisted she return to China. In later years Mrs. Fackrell remembered seeing Sam Wing often at the New York Cafe in downtown Salt Lake. After leaving Mercur he ran the Chinese Herbal Medicine Store near the Salt Lake railroad terminal. Whether he ever returned to China is not known.

In Carbon County during the 1880s, the Chinese worked in Pleasant Valley as coal miners. No one seemed to care if they ran laundries, sold vegetables, repaired cane-bottom chairs, or cooked their ancient cuisine. But the free enterprise system could only tolerate so much freedom in the 1880s.

> At the reopening of Utah mine, Chinese were sent in. On their behalf I will say that there is still standing a portion of the mine entry that was driven by them and it is as beautiful a piece of work as one could wish to see in a coal mine. Evidently no powder was used for blasting. Entry was driven exclusively with pick work. The sides are perfectly straight to a certain height and the roof is semi-arched. Due to the method of working this entry will stand indefinitely.

[44] Interview with Evalee McBride Fackrell, December 5, 1974, Holladay, Utah.

A short time after the Chinese were imported into Pleasant Valley, white labor started to come in and naturally resented the presence of the yellow men. When white labor was strong enough they brought the situation to a climax and took the law into their own hands. One day they herded the Chinese into a box car, fastened the doors and started the car down grade. Fortunately, the car kept the track until it reached a place near Hales where there is an adverse grade. It stopped there and evidently the "Chinks" traveled the rest of the way on foot. At least they have not been seen in Pleasant Valley from that day to this.[45]

In the Uinta Basin during the late 1880s and the early part of this century, few personalities stand out with such prominence as Wong Sing. He had a humble beginning as a laundryman at Fort Duchesne in 1889, but during the twenties he owned and operated a merchandise store which boasted an inventory of between sixty and seventy thousand dollars.[46]

Phoebe Litster remembered as a girl in Vernal that:

Wong Sing and two other Chinese set up a washing and cleaning shop. I was about ten or twelve . . . . [1891] and then I got married and we were transferred to Fort Duchesne, he had that store there all the time. . . . Everybody traded with him, and always, before the depression, he put a sack of candy in people's groceries before they went home. When my boy Robert was born, he came to see the baby and put a dollar in the baby's hand. He was thoughtful, he was good; he was good to all the people.[47]

Besides general merchandise, the store handled furniture, ready-to-wear, meat, and groceries and acted as general agent for machinery companies and other firms.[48] Phoebe Litster's son-in-law, Oliver Bradley Cloward, joined Wong Sing as an order boy in 1921. Mr. Cloward was impressed by his benefactor.

He was a stocky built man (about five feet six inches, five feet seven), he wasn't a flashy man, he was just a common, everyday man. He just wore kinda pants, and he usually had a yellow shirt on. . . .

[45] Thursey Jessen Reynolds, et al., eds., *Centennial Echoes from Carbon County*, (Price[?], 1948), p. 37.

[46] Carter, "The Early Chinese of Western United States," 10:464–69.

[47] Interview with Phoebe Litster, December 5, 1974, Salt Lake City.

[48] Carter, "The Early Chinese of Western United States," 10:464–69.

The remarkable thing about him was he had very much patience—that didn't seem to matter to him as long as you was honest. . . . He'd try to train you in his way, and he did. He taught me to figure, and he taught me to write better, and how to treat people and how to meet 'em. . . .

He had an old pair of overshoes sitting around that'd been on the shelves you know, for a long while —and some poor family come in there— they got those overshoes free; or if anybody had a fire in the neighborhood, Wong Sing was there, and usually contributed the most to help those people out. . . .

People respected him; they came from Vernal to trade with him, they came from Lapoint—all over the Basin—I've known cattlemen to come from around Vernal there and spent two hundred dollars at once with him.

I never heard of him being dishonest with any man in all of my life.

I was kinda backward—and he brought that out of me— he really made something out of me. He really taught me. He never taught me anything bad. He'd always say, "Let's do it this way," and if I ever made a mistake—I don't know of him ever bawling me out.

He trusted people so, I guess he lost lots of money by trusting, but he just seemed like he couldn't see a family in need.[49]

Wong Sing spoke the Ute language and displayed a knowledgeable interest and respect for Indian culture. His annual calendars were always designed with an Indian motif.[50]

. . . The Indians would trust him—I never seen anything like it the way they trusted him. He [Wong Sing] could speak it [the Ute language] fluently. He could tell you from memory the different things that'd happened [Uinta Basin Indian history]. When I worked there, there was still some of the old chiefs, that'd come there, and he'd tell me about them. He knew, I believe, every Indian on that reservation, their character, and what they'd do, better than any man (I think) that'd ever lived out there.[51]

[49] Interview with Oliver Bradley Cloward, December 6, 1974, Orem, Utah.
[50] Carter, "The Early Chinese of Western United States," 10:464–69.
[51] Cloward interview.

When Wong Sing died in a 1934 auto accident, sixty Ute men assembled at the office of the Indian agency to mourn his passing.[52]

Other Chinese lived throughout Utah in the nineteenth century. In Washington County, the boom town of Silver Reef had a total Chinese population of fifty-one in 1880. Of these, ten were women.[53] Prominent Utah author Juanita L. Brooks recalled hearing that

> some of the white men knew that the leader of the Chinese had a white mistress—they tried to burn him out, I think they lit the fire—he didn't leave.[54]

During her father-in-law's declining years, Eva L. Miles wrote down his memories of life in Silver Reef:

> When a Chinese man or woman died they were buried in a grave yard east and a little south of Bonanza Flat. . . .
>
> When they would take a person (corpse) to the grave yard, they would carry them on a litter and one or two Chinamen would go ahead of them, carrying a lot of small pieces of paper about two inches square. They would throw these in every direction in front and to the sides.[55]

This paper was "spirit money," used to detract and appease the evil spirits who would otherwise deter the soul's successful journey heavenward.

> They thought that if the man or woman who was buried was going to heaven, they'd need to have time to eat or drink while they went. So they'd have a lot of nice aromatic roast pork and other delicacies to take down for this person to eat and a bottle of liquor.
>
> Well, they'd put it on the grave and go away. When evening came, the Indians would come and eat the pork and drink the liquor. . . .[56]

Juanita L. Brooks also recalled that:

> One of the men [a scholarly Chinese] tried to teach him [George F. Miles] Chinese. . . . He was young, inquisitive,

[52] Carter, "The Early Chinese of Western United States," 10:464–69.

[53] 1880 Census.

[54] Interview with Juanita Brooks, December 5, 1974, Salt Lake City.

[55] A handwritten memoir by Eva L. Miles, sister of Juanita Brooks, sent to the author in a letter dated June 1, 1975, from St. George, Utah.

[56] *Ibid.*

and a brilliant, little chap. So he was friendly enough, that they took time with him, for him to learn to read.[57]

Silver Reef's Chinese community advertised a variety of services in the *Silver Reef Miner:*

Call around to Hop Lee's establishment and be convinced that there is no better repairer of chairs in the Reef.[58]

Other items and advertisements in the *Silver Reef Miner* were:

SAM WING
First Wash-house
Bonanza
(lower Main Street)
Washing, ironing and fluting. Work done
promptly and in best of style.[59]

(It is possible that this Sam Wing is the same Sam Wing [Doc Chinaman] who later had a laundry in Mercur along with his Chinese medical practice.)

Charley Legget, the well-known Oriental caterer, has established a bakery in upper Chinatown, next to Hop Lee's store, where can be found at all times a supply of bread and table pastry. The more poetical name of the dealer in baked dough is Ah Fung.[60]

The Chinese New Year was appropriately celebrated here this week. Firecrackers, Celestial music, lots of fun and forgiving of past grievances were the orders of the day.[61]

During pioneer times, the number of Chinese converted to Christianity in Utah was minimal. But this is not to say that various denominations did not show an interest in the Chinese and a sympathy for their problems. Mormon leader James E. Talmage was one.

Talmage, at Brooklyn tabernacle, last night, denounced the anti-Chinese law, said come the Chinese had, come they would, come they should. God liked the Chinese physiognomy so well that he had made four hundred millions of them, while he had only made one Kearney [the instigator of the anti-

[57] Juanita Brooks interview.
[58] *Silver Reef Miner,* December 2, 1882.
[59] *Ibid.*
[60] *Ibid.*
[61] *Ibid.*, February 10, 1883.

Chinese movement]. Talmage liked the paganism which endured insult uncomplainingly better than the Christianity which mauls and stones them. The Nation that got the inside track with them would be the richest nation of the globe.[62]

Among members of the Congregational church of Salt Lake City were some Chinese. An 1897 newspaper article described "a Chinese Christmas entertainment" that took place at the church "in a hall ornamented with diverse kinds of Oriental creations until it presented a very pretty and picturesque scene. The entire program was carried out by the Chinese (Sunday School scholars) themselves." [63]

The decades between 1900 and 1930 were the years of growing Chinese activity around Plum Alley. In Ogden, Chinese businesses dotted Twenty-fifth Street and spread to Grant and Lincoln avenues north. As in most Chinese communities, there were few families. In Ogden, four or five families provided the rare presence of women and children. However, during the depression years a declining population took its toll of launderies, stores, and restaurants, and by 1940 the number of Chinese in the two principal cities reached a low of fewer than five hundred. It was in this setting that the second-generation Chinese grew up.[64]

During World War II most of the eligible men served with the armed forces. Of the twelve in overseas units, one failed to return. Lt. Arthur Chinn from Salt Lake City was shot down in France while flying a mission in a P-51. Kingsley Wong, a Third Army infantryman, received several Purple Hearts and other medals, including the Silver Star for gallantry in action in Germany. Many returning American-Chinese veterans capitalized on their hard-earned opportunity to attend college under the G. I. Bill, receiving an education that would probably have been an impossibility had this financial aid not been available.[65]

When the Chinese Exclusion Act was repealed in 1952, Chinese immigrants again began to settle in the United States. In Utah, many university students from Hong Kong and Taiwan discovered the beauty and opportunities in the state and remained to become

[62] *Ogden Junction,* February 5, 1879.

[63] *Deseret News,* December 20, 1897.

[64] Typescript by William Wong Louie.

[65] *Ibid.*

citizens. Presently Utah universities, hospitals, and corporate businesses are dotted with names such as Lee, Wong, Chang, and Yee.[66]

The 1960–70 decade has seen a marked increase of 7.5 percent in Chinese population in Utah; 1,281 were listed in the 1970 Census.[67] Almost half are cooks, bus boys, waiters, or owners of Chinese restaurants.[68] Inability to speak English has kept many Chinese immigrants in jobs paying less than four hundred fifty dollars a month. The language barrier is being perpetuated among children from Hong Kong and Taiwan who speak little English.

Chinese immigrants and their children have serious difficulties between them. Communication is limited: ". . . the parents learn only enough English to get by, while the children learn only enough Chinese to converse in household conversations." [69] Parents attempt to impose traditional Chinese values on their children: they expect their children to marry and to have social relations only with Chinese; and they disapprove of American leniency toward young people. Although the children are far more Americanized than their parents, they are not completely assimilated into American life and have conflicts with both cultures.

Little has been known about the Chinese and their problems because they have been a quiet people, helping each other as best they could. Many in need of social services have been unaware that such agencies exist. Until recently the Bing Kung Tong was an important organization for Chinese in Salt Lake City. It provided translating services, letter writing, legal help, found work for new arrivals, and was a meeting place where the immigrants could enjoy speaking their native tongue. However, second-generation Chinese are not interested in joining the tong and today a few more than one hundred members belong to it. The tong no longer offers letter writing, translating, and legal services, but it still tries to help find work for the unemployed and continues to sponsor the Chinese New Year's party for the community. Its recreation hall provides games, television, and magazines for all ages, yet it has become a club for elderly men who are unmarried or who were unable to bring their families to the United States.[70]

[66] Ibid.

[67] Ibid.

[68] See Angela Chan Conley, "The Social Problems of the Chinese in Salt Lake City," (M.S. thesis, University of Utah, 1973).

[69] Ibid., p. 24.

[70] Ibid., 24, 25, 27.

The Utah Chinese are showing a new vitality with an increasing awareness of their own unique background and culture. Plum Alley is no more, a victim of progress; a seven-story concrete parking structure now straddles what was once Chinatown. But the spirit remains, and in the screech of brakes one can almost hear the angry complaint of Hop Sing—late of 9 Plum Alley.[71]

[71] Louie typescript.

8

THE OFT-CROSSED BORDER: CANADIANS IN UTAH

BY MAUREEN URSENBACH AND RICHARD L. JENSEN

Probably the first significant meeting of two Canadians in what is now Utah took place on the banks of the Weber River, east of present Ogden, on May 23, 1825. There, around mid-morning, Peter Skene Ogden, a Quebec-born Anglo-Canadian, leader of a Hudson's Bay Company expedition, greeted a company of competitor trappers, "3 Canadians, a Russian, and an old Spaniard . . . under the Command of one Provost," the French-Canadian Etienne Provost, born in Chambly, not twenty miles from Montreal where Ogden grew up.[1]

There was no love lost between these two men; though the accounts indicate they parted in peace that same morning, there lay buried under their Canadian skins antipathies, the remnants of which burrow still into Canadian sensibilities—one was English-speaking, the other French. Not only that, the two men were competing for the same furs—reports suggest that Ogden's orders were to make a fur desert of the area, so the American companies would lose interest in the region—and they were also jockeying for the loyalty of their men—at least one of Provost's Canadians was a deserter from the Hudson's Bay employ. Following the pattern of the English-French skirmishes in Canada the century before, the French-Canadian's group had suffered an attack by Indians, riled to battle by the horse thievery of the British company's men. That the two

---

[1]David E. Miller, ed., "William Kittson's Journal Covering Peter Skene Ogden's 1824–1825 Snake Country Expedition," *Utah Historical Quarterly* 22 (1954): 137. Cf. David E. Miller, ed., "Peter Skene Ogden's Journal of His Expedition, 1825," *Utah Historical Quarterly* 20 (1952): 181. The basic material on Ogden is from Ted J. Warner, "Peter Skene Ogden," *Mountain Men and the Fur Trade*, ed. LeRoy R. Hafen, 10 vols. (Glendale, Calif., 1965–72), 3:213–38, and that on Provost, from Hafen's own chapter, "Etienne Provost," 6:387–98 of the same work.

Canadians parted amicably is more to be wondered at than expected; the chauvinism of French-speaking and English-speaking Canadians in this century might not have been so easily restrained under such circumstances.

The backgrounds of the two men represent the two major thrusts of the Canadian national character. Provost, the French-Canadian trapper, born 1785 of Albert and Marianne Provost, *Québecois* of the farming community of Chambly, was typical of the *coureurs de bois,* the adventurous trappers who followed the rivers in search of wealth and excitement. Heading south, Provost joined the Chouteau-DeMun, an American fur company; he headed west and had been to New Mexico twice by 1823. An expedition took him over the Wasatch into the Great Basin by 1824, and a skirmish with the Snake Indians, possibly on the Jordan River, may have given him the first white man's view of the Great Salt Lake.[2]

Peter Skene Ogden represents the other major Canadian population stream, the British-linked, English-speaking group. Although there have been in Utah some few immigrants with the French background, certainly the major portion of the Canadian population in Utah comes from a background like Ogden's.

At the time of the Revolutionary War, and for a decade afterwards, there was a flow into Canada of "Loyalists," British sympathizers who, uncomfortable with either the idea of revolution or the estrangement from their mother country, fled to British North America, the Canadas, Upper and Lower. Spreading out along the Saint Lawrence as far east as the Maritime provinces of New Brunswick and Nova Scotia and as far west as the tip of Ontario's Niagara Peninsula, they merged with the British-Canadian life, and found welcome. The United States-Canadian boundary continued to be, as it had been from the earliest colonial times, an oft-crossed border, as descendants of the Loyalists and descendants of their American cousins, antipathies forgotten, met and married and reared their families on either side, in either of two generally friendly countries.[3]

---

[2] Hafen, "Provost," pp. 373–74.

[3] Fred Landon, *Western Ontario and the American Frontier* (Toronto, 1941), p. 61 quotes a droll comment on Canadian-American intermarriage shortly following the war of 1812. One Adam Fergusson, a visitor in Canada, received this reply to his query as to the likelihood of another United States–Canadian war: "Well, sir, I guess if we don't fight for a year or two, we won't fight at all, for we are marrying so fast, sir, that a man won't be sure but he

Ogden's was one of those American-colonial families that found itself split in the 1776 trial of fealty. His Tory father Isaac, after an initial return to Britain, brought his family back to North America, to Quebec, Lower Canada. There, in 1794, his later famous son was born, and christened Peter Skene in honor of a Loyalist uncle. Immediately thereafter, the family moved up the Saint Lawrence to Montreal, a few miles from Chambly where Etienne Provost was a nine-year-old in his father's house. But the two boys might as well have been on opposite sides of the continent, so divergent were their cultures. It was an economic, not a national force that brought them together for that brief meeting on the banks of Utah's Weber River in 1825.

While the fur trade was sending "gentlemen adventurers" and "Nor'westers" into the Mexican territory that would someday be Utah, another force was gathering momentum in the East for a westward push. In upstate New York, the boy prophet Joseph Smith was gathering about him groups of believers who would follow him and his successors in stages to Ohio, Missouri, Illinois, and into the western wilderness, the Great Basin of the Rocky Mountains. That force would draw many Canadians in its magnetic field, pulling them along with its proselytes from New England, Great Britain, and eventually most of the countries of Europe.

Canada's first introduction to Mormonism—the doctrines that shaped the Church of Jesus Christ of Latter-day Saints—came in the summer of 1830, at Kingston, the Upper Canada city at the eastern edge of Lake Ontario. There, where the Saint Lawrence begins, was a stronghold of Loyalist stock, home of first prime minister, Sir John A. Macdonald, and breeding ground for the confederation that would come later. As well as being a politically active city, Kingston was religiously concerned. When Methodist preacher Phineas Young, brother to later prophet-leader Brigham Young, took the newly translated Book of Mormon to the Canadians at Kingston about one hundred fifty miles from his Mendon, New York, home, it was to a Methodist congregation that he preached the new gospel, to people who had already been forced to choose which camp of Methodism they would adhere to, the American or the English. Religious excitement was a part of their lives; it is no wonder the Mormons found a hearing in their midst.

may shoot his father or his brother-in-law." The original source is given as Adam Fergusson, *Practical Notes Made During a Tour in Canada and a Portion of the United States in MDCCCXXXI* [1831], 2d ed. (Edinburgh, 1834), pp. 147–48.

Phineas Young, now a Mormon, returned to Kingston in 1832, and other missionaries followed, to other Canadian communities. Kirtland, Ohio, the second gathering place of the Mormons, was hardly a day's wagon ride from Lake Erie and boat transportation across to Canada, and not much longer by wagon around the lake. From Kirtland traveled Joseph Smith himself into the Niagara Peninsula on the first of his two Canadian missionary journeys in 1833. From his and other missions converts were brought back, singly or in companies, to build the Zions of the new dispensation in Ohio and in the Independence, Missouri, area. Missionaries in Canada traveled chiefly among the English-speaking Canadians, for obvious reasons, proselytizing along the settled shores of the Great Lakes, through the Saint Lawrence Valley, into Quebec's Eastern Townships, and on to Nova Scotia and New Brunswick in the first decade after the church's founding. Among British immigrants— later church president John Taylor was one—they found their greatest successes.

There is as yet no published count of the numbers of converts the Mormons attracted in the two Canadas, but Richard Bennett, preparing a master's thesis on the history of the church in Ontario, suggests that of the approximately fifteen hundred Ontario converts of the first two decades, probably a quarter emigrated, meeting the main body of the Saints at their stopping places along the devious trail to Utah. Add to that number the converts from other parts of Canada, and subtract from it the numbers who straggled along, some arriving in Utah, some never making the final push across the Great Plains. Then realize that of the people converted in Canada, not all were Canada-born; it is entirely reasonable that the 1850 Utah Census shows a total of 368 identified by their birthplace as Canadians.[4] That number increased to 647 in the 1860 count, nearly leveling out to 686 by 1870, these being the years during which nearly all the Canadian immigrants to the Great Basin were Mormon proselytes gathering to their Zion in the West.

The Canada Centennial Project publication *A History of the Mormon Church in Canada*[5] tells of the various Mormon missions

[4] While the official compendium of the census for 1850 lists only 338 born in British America, at least 368 can be counted in the manuscript census.

[5] *A History of the Mormon Church in Canada* (Lethbridge, Alberta, 1968). A pioneer work in the area, the book draws heavily (though deleting some of the most significant material) on the dissertation of Melvin S. Tagg. It is hoped that detailed studies of Mormons in Canada will follow this general overview.

to and emigrations from Canada in more detail than is possible here. Instead of merely making of that feast a hash, let us here have recourse to a few representative individuals, and permit their story to suggest that of so many like them.

David Moore was born, the youngest of ten children, in Eardley, on the Ottawa River in what was then Lower Canada.[6] His parents were American, the father having been born in New York, and the mother in the same county of Vermont that later would be the birthplace of Joseph Smith. Shortly after their marriage, the two moved to Canada, settling first on the Saint Lawrence, and then moving northward to the vicinity of Bytown, the present Ottawa. There the family was born, and there most of the ten children lived, bred prolifically, and died.

Of his family only David and his wife accepted the Mormon message to the point of baptism, along with a neighbor, Barnabas Merrifield, and his wife. In 1842, a year after their conversion, David succumbed to the familiar "spirit of gathering": "Duty and my salvation called me to the headquarters of the Church," he recorded later. The Moores and the Merrifields spent the summer preparing for their journey, and were about ready when David wrote, "I was informed by some of my friends that they heard several state their intentions of upsetting and mashing our wagons when we were passing Aylmer. I . . . concluded that they would have to catch me first." A night was spent in preparations, and then:

> About 3 o'clock in the morning of [August] 16th, I bid my father, mother, and the rest goodbye, and left the house. . . .
> I, having a splendid horse for traveling, soon found myself near Aylmer Village. Barnabas and his wife [were] close behind, he having a wagon and two horses. It was not yet light, and we passed by the place and did not so much as see a person in the street or about any of the houses. We passed on to Bytown [Ottawa] ferry and crossed over the river by the time the sun was an hour high in the morning.

The journey onward was relatively uneventful. Near Kingston the two families picked up a Brother Richard Sheldon, adding an extra load to their wagons. There, too, they were accosted by a

---

[6] David Moore, Autobiography and Journal, in "Compiled Writings of David Moore," typescript, Archives Division, Historical Department, Church of Jesus Christ of Latter-day Saints, Salt Lake City. All the David Moore material in this account is drawn from this source, supplemented with the account in the "Journal History," a daily compendium assembled in the LDS Archives, s.v. "David Moore."

Baptist minister who "readily saw by our mode of traveling that we were Mormons." Moore does not identify what distinctive features marked their party, but the comment suggests that Mormon migrations in the Niagara Peninsula were not uncommon, a conclusion borne out by the naming of Archibald Gardner's road from his settlement in Alvinston to the highway, the "Nauvoo Road."

At Detroit the immigrants had to pass through customs. There was no office of immigration to demand any kind of visa; until 1907 no record was kept even of names, let alone nationality, of immigrants. But their goods were assessed and taxed. David Moore noted the arbitrariness of the assessment with some bitterness when, after he had paid his $12.60, leaving himself only fifty cents to his name, his friend Barnabas was let off with an easier, cheaper assessment of $8.00 because he was unable to pay his full toll. Such leniency towards immigrants bespeaks again the open invitation tendered to Canadians immigrating to the United States.

Once in the United States, the travelers suffered the frequent fate of brothers in the faith newly thrown together. Their falling-out left David and his wagon going on to Nauvoo alone and arriving there, after a six-week journey, with no home and no friend except his passenger Richard Sheldon. Even he would have deserted his benefactor had not Moore pressed his case earnestly. So Sheldon took him to the one-room cabin of his friends, a Canadian family, where the Moores found begrudging hospitality. Their sojourn in Nauvoo followed the inauspicious precedent set by the first week, during which the hay Moore hauled for his host and himself was stolen for a widow next door, he came down with the "chills and fever" which would plague him all that winter, and he heard the Prophet Joseph Smith predict that though the Saints "should never be driven from their habitations in Nauvoo . . . he would not promise that they would not be coaxed to leave."

Moore's account of his Nauvoo experience details the marshaling of opposition to the Mormon presence, the murder of Joseph and Hyrum Smith, the takeover by Brigham Young and the Twelve, the repealing of the Nauvoo Charter, and his own activities as a member of Nauvoo's whittling and whistling militia. (Their arms confiscated, Nauvoo defenders would escort the unwelcome from their city by moving ominously near, whittling away with their large knives as they came.) All in all, Nauvoo was a dark period in the lives of David and Susan Moore.

By May 1846 Moore and his family were on their way west. During a three-year layover in Bentonsport, Iowa, David, obviously considering himself as qualified to vote as his American-born neighbors, involved himself in the local politics. His vote, however, was challenged, not because he was Canadian, but because he was Mormon. Finally, in April 1849, he loaded his wagon once more for the last leg of the hegira, and on October 20, 1849, he entered the valley.

Moore was more happily absorbed into the Deseret society than he had been in Nauvoo. Settling early in Ogden, he became the first recorder there, then county clerk and city and county treasurer. He served on the city council, on the stake high council, and in the Utah militia. As befitting to his ecclesiastical role, he took two more wives shortly after his entrance into the valley and by them raised a posterity long since interwoven into the fabric of Utah's people. It is probable that the Canadian segment of their background is long since forgotten.

David Moore's earliest Mormon antecedents in the Great Basin kingdom were the six (at least) Canadians of Brigham Young's pioneer company who entered the valley in July 1847.[7] Three of them might well have known each other as converts in Canada; Barnabas Adams, William Empey, and Charles David Barnum all lived near Brockville, on the Saint Lawrence River, when they heard and accepted the Mormon doctrine and moved their families to Nauvoo. Two other Canadians in the pioneer company came from remoter regions: John Pack from New Brunswick and Howard Egan from Montreal. Roswell Stevens was fruit of Joseph Smith's 1833 mission into the Niagara Peninsula. It is more the rule than the exception that Canadians do not clan together; except for Barnum, who eventually settled not far from his compatriot Adams, the group seems to have formed no lasting bonds based on shared nationality.

A pioneer of September 1847, Joshua Terry is part of a remarkable family saga that, in its wider implications, suggests the elements of the Canadian experience in pioneer Utah.[8] His grandfather, Pennsylvania-born Parshall Terry II, deserted the Revolu-

---

[7] Andrew Jenson, *LDS Biographical Encyclopedia*, 4 vols. (1901–36; reprint ed., Salt Lake City, 1971), 4:693–725, lists with biographical notes the members of Brigham Young's first company, including the six mentioned here.

[8] Nora Hall Lund, comp., *Parshall Terry Family History* (reprint ed., Salt Lake City, 1963).

tionary Army and fled to Canada. However, Joshua's father, Parshall III, was later born in New York. Parshall III had seven children born in Palmyra and the last six, including Joshua, at Albion, Upper Canada. The parents and most of the children converted to Mormonism in 1838, emigrated to Missouri, and followed the body of the Mormons to Illinois and then to Utah. Joshua became a mountain man and associate of Jim Bridger, and his first two wives were Indians. When most of his family came west in 1849, he and Bridger helped them along their way at Fort Bridger with six fresh oxen to pull the wagons on the last leg of the trek.

Joshua's sister Amy married one of Brigham Young's early Canadian converts, Zemira Draper, who, with his brother William, founded Draper, Utah. Many of the Terry family moved there, some for the rest of their lives. But Zemira and William Draper and James and Jacob Terry were called to the Cotton Mission and settled in faraway Rockville. There Zemira helped build a sawmill, a molasses mill, and a cotton mill, all of which used water power from the Virgin River.

Joshua eventually settled down at Draper and often served as a link between the whites and the Indians of the Great Basin. His half-breed son George, appointed by church leaders to work with the Shoshones, eventually became one of their chiefs. Thus the family blended into the Utah environment and even into the native populace of the area.

A long look through the 1850 United States Census for Utah picks up the names of many Canadians whose stories form a significant part of the Utah picture. Some of them, like Stephen Chipman, had children who later figured prominently, one of them, James, as Utah National Bank president. An indication of mobility and adventuresome spirit, twenty-one year old Washburn Chipman, James's brother, was picked up twice in the census: once at his parents' home in Great Salt Lake County, and later, at age twenty-two, in Iron County. Robert and Neal Gardner, sons of Scottish-born Archibald Gardner who built grist mills first in Ontario and then in Utah, appear as the only members of their family to show Canadian origins, having been born in Alvinston, the Ontario town their father founded. Only one Canadian family is listed in the Manti region; and the extended family of Dudley and Lemuel Leavitt, from Lower Canada, represents the larger part of the

Canadian population of Tooele County.[9] (A third Leavitt, Thomas, became one of the counter-movement, emigrating from Utah to Canada in 1887.) Most of the immigrants shown on this census originated in either Upper or Lower Canada, though some indicate Nova Scotia or New Brunswick origins. Not surprisingy, the only French-sounding name, Lamoreaux, belongs to people with Anglo-sounding Christian names, suggesting that the Mormon message had not yet reached the *Canadiens*.

Most of the Canadian-born converts to Mormonism who moved to Utah arrived before 1860. Few Canadians came during the next decade. Indeed, very little effective Mormon missionary work was done in Canada during the last half of the century, and only a few straggling faithful remained in Canada or the Midwest to make the trip to Utah after the "Utah War" of 1857–58.

Canadians in Utah had slid inconspicuously into the pattern of life and commerce in developing Utah Territory in the 1860s when Halifax-born George B. Ogilvie, lumbering in Bingham Canyon in 1863, made a discovery that reshaped the economic life of Utah, and with it the Canadian population of the territory: there was silver-bearing ore in the rocks of the canyon. Utah's mining boom had begun.[10]

The mines and the arrival of the railroad in 1869 initiated the wave of non-Mormon Canadians that reached Utah in the 1870s. By the 1880 Census, they, along with the earlier Mormon Canadians, had fit into nearly every aspect of life in the territory. Most were listed as being associated with farming and mining, either directly or in supporting enterprises. Besides those there were merchants— dry goods, liquor, tobacco, lumber; doctors; a music teacher; a probate judge; a dressmaker; weavers and spinners; a printer and a saloon keeper. There even was a Canadian prostitute, a Miss Vinnie Snow, as she called herself, doing business on East Temple Street in Salt Lake City. The interesting quirk in the 1880 Census report on Canadians in Utah is the cluster of them in Summit and Beaver counties; a closer look finds them, many of them from mining communities of Canada's Maritimes, working at the Frisco and Park City mines. And of the Canadians in mining, none are more interesting, if atypical, than the bosses of the Silver King mines.

[9] A more complete account of the family is contained in Juanita Brooks, *On the Ragged Edge: The Life and Times of Dudley Leavitt* (Salt Lake City, 1973).

[10] S. George Ellsworth, *Utah's Heritage* (Salt Lake City, 1972), p. 262.

French-Canadian Etienne
Provost, adventurer and
trapper, explored Utah
in the 1820s. The city
of Provo is named for
him.

Peter Skene Ogden, born
in Quebec, Canada, of
English-speaking parents,
led Hudson's Bay
Company trappers into
Utah. Ogden city
memorializes his name.

In 1867 Canadian Ira N. Hinckley was sent to Millard County to
build Cove Fort, a major stopping place on the route south and the
only important Mormon fort of the period still standing. It is a
National Register Place.

er Bingham Canyon was known as Frog Town because of the
ch-Canadians who lived there.

From left: *Canadian Joshua Terry, mountain man and associate of Jim Bridger, furthered Indian-white relations; Canadian-born Howard Egan kept a journal, later published, of the 1847 pioneer company; Phineas Young, a brother of Brigham, took the Book of Mormon to Canadians at Kingston; William Empey, a Canadian, filled several LDS church positions and helped in the settlement of southern Utah.*

Seeking a haven from federal authorities in Utah, Charles Ora Card was sent to Canada where he built this home in 1887 at Cardston, Alberta.

From the top: *Ontario-born William Henry Lawrence was a founder of Kimball and Lawrence, one of the earliest retail stores in Salt Lake City. Thomas Kearns and David Keith purchased the* Salt Lake Tribune *at the turn of the century. The two natives of Canada made their fortunes in the Park City mines. The Ontario mine where both men worked at one time.*

David Keith was a foreman at the Ontario mine when young Thomas Kearns reported to him in the spring of 1883.[11] The stories of their lives to that time are as intriguing as is the history of their mutual accomplishments after their meeting. Keith had come by circuitous route from Mabou on Nova Scotia's Cape Breton, where he was born in May 1847, the youngest of thirteen children of a Scottish immigrant miner who died when David was fourteen. In the gold mines of Nova Scotia the young man won his grubstake, and in 1867 left for California. Within two years he had found a place in Virginia City, Nevada, where he continued until 1883, the year he was summoned to Park City to install at the Ontario mine the great Cornish pumps used to clear the shafts of water during construction. There he met Thomas Kearns, fifteen years his junior, a fellow Canadian. It is doubtful that their being compatriots was much more than an interesting coincidence to the Scotsman's son Keith and Kearns, Canadian-born Irish Catholic whose family had left Woodstock, Ontario, where Thomas was born, for a colony of Irish in Nebraska. Probably more significant than shared national origin is the sharing of an adventuresome spirit which is necessarily part of the mentality of any hardy soul who will try life in the less hospitable regions of North America. Kearns felt the wanderlust even younger than Keith. By the age of twenty-one he was on his way to Butte, Montana, having already worked as a freighter and a miner in the Black Hills, as a cowboy in the Dakotas, and as a miner and a teamster in Tombstone, Arizona. At Pocatello, Idaho, on his way to Butte and "the richest hill on earth," someone told him of Park City. He entered the boom town of three thousand population in June 1883 and there met his future partner, who had arrived just two months earlier.

The story of the Mayflower mine and its subsequent expansion into the Silver King Coalition Mines is a long and exciting one, dealt with in sources readily available.[12] That not only Kearns and Keith but also Windsor V. Rice [13] and James Ivers [14] of the initial

[11] "Thomas Kearns," and "David Keith," *Utah Since Statehood*, Noble Warrum, ed., 4 vols. (Chicago and Salt Lake City, 1919–20), 2:5–9, 26–30; Kent Seldon Larsen, "The Life of Thomas Kearns" (Master's thesis, University of Utah, 1964).

[12] Oscar F. Jesperson, Jr., "An Early History of the Community of Park City, Utah" (Master's thesis, Brigham Young University, 1969); Dean Franklin Wright, "A History of Park City, 1869–1898" (M.S. thesis, University of Utah, 1971).

[13] "Windsor V. Rice," *Sketches of the Inter-Mountain States* (Salt Lake City, 1909), p. 169.

[14] "Hon. James Ivers," Warrum, *Utah Since Statehood*, 2:570–71; "Hon.

group were Canadians is a detail that slips past the researchers. Ivers and Rice both left their Quebec homes, young and alone, just as Keith and Kearns did, and who knows how many other young Canadian adventurers whom fate, or luck, for good or ill, led to Utah. These four left footprints that remain these years later: Keith O'Brien store, the Kearns Building, records in the United States Senate and the Utah state legislature (Kearns and Ivers, respectively), two mansions still standing on Salt Lake City's South Temple Street, the *Salt Lake Tribune,* and independent fortunes now diffused among descendants of the four magnates.

During those beginning days of the mining and railroading booms in Utah, when non-Mormon itinerants were finding their ways into the territory, there finally appeared a *Québecois,* identifiably and distinctly French-Canadian. Amable Alphonse Brossard, "Frenchy" to his Utah comrades, was born the seventh generation in Canada in 1846 at Laprairie, near Montreal.[15] He may have left Laprairie for the same reasons that Etienne Provost left Chambly: for adventure, for fame, for the chance to make his fortune. But the times were different; rather than trap the streams for fur as Provost had done, Brossard worked the hills for gold. He worked in the mines in the Fort Benton, Montana, area, and then ran a dairy there for a time. Finally, a freighting line brought him to Utah, to a rooming house in Richmond, Cache County. There he met and married pretty Mary Hobson, and two deep heredities coalesced: Mary was as many generations American as Alphonse was Canadian. They reared their children in Cache Valley; in 1971 the count of their descendants had reached 168, among them, Edgar B. Brossard, chairman of the United States Tariff Commission for many years and twice president of the French LDS mission. The French culture seems not to have passed in the rest of the family beyond Alphonse, though, and only the purposeful search for family connects the Utah Brossards to their French Canadian past.

Canadians continued their influx into Utah in moderate numbers until about the time of World War I, with a marked increase immediately after the turn of the century. Some of them were apparently associated with the mines in Juab and Tooele counties

James Ivers," *Biographical Record of Salt Lake City and Vicinity* (Chicago, 1902), pp. 132–33.

[15] Edgar Brossard, *Alphonse and Mary Hobson Brossard* (Salt Lake City, 1972).

during periods of high activity there. Increasingly they concentrated in the metropolitan areas, in Salt Lake County, where there were nearly a thousand Canadian-born in 1910, and in Weber County.

Meanwhile, a meeting between Charles O. Card and Mormon church president John Taylor, both in hiding from federal marshals seeking to arrest them on the "unlawful cohabitation" charge under which polygamists were prosecuted, led to the migration which, reversing itself, would in the long run provide Utah with most of its Canadian immigrants.[16] Card, pioneer settler and stake president in Cache County, had concluded to take part of his extended family—he had three wives at the time—and move to Mexico, but the president's approval was necessary. Card family history recounts the response of Taylor, an English immigrant who had lived in Toronto for several years: "No, . . . go to the British Northwest Territories. I have always found justice under the British flag." Whether the quotation is accurate or not, it became a part of the attitude that the settlers who followed Card into Canada built into their children, and the expectation was not without grounds.

The story of Card's 1886 exploration of southern British Columbia and Alberta, and his subsequent choice of the Lee's Creek site (later Cardston, Alberta) is an oft-told tale in the histories of the Mormons in Canada, as is the account of the arrival of the first settlers the following spring. Of the forty-one Utah men who, with their families, had originally agreed to follow Card to refuge in Canada, eleven made the trip, moving in small companies of one or two families each. The journey paralleled in many ways the Winter Quarters-Great Basin trek of forty years earlier, including the poignancy of the arrival reflected in the tearful comment of four-year-old Wilford Woolf on being told this grassy prairie would be home: "Ma," he quivered, "where's all the houses?" [17]

Settlement moved rapidly. Sterling Williams wrote back to his Utah grandmother after a week in Canada that already the settlers had four acres of the dark, rich earth planted in wheat, oats, and potatoes, and that a bed of coal had been found three miles away.[18] The unseasonal snow which had fallen the first night of their arrival

[16] A. James Hudson, "Charles Ora Card, Pioneer and Colonizer" (M.A. thesis, Brigham Young University, 1961).

[17] Ibid., p. 112.

[18] Sterling Williams to Zina D. Young, June 13, 1886, Zina D. Young Collection, in private possession. The letter is mistakenly dated; it should read 1887.

presaged a long cold winter, so houses were speedily erected, and a town sprang up. They named it Cardston.

Whether they actually felt it or not, the Mormons made it apparent to the old settlers that they meant to stay in their new colony, and their immediate neighbors in Lethbridge and Macleod received them warmly. Some Gentile opposition to the Mormon incursion was registered in newspapers as far away as Montreal, but local observers foresaw only good to come of the settlement. The Canadian government, using the recently completed railroad as a drawing card, had been encouraging settlement of the "Palliser triangle," the southern portions of Alberta and Saskatchewan. A Mormon delegation to Ottawa, though they did not return with the concessions they asked—no, Mormons may not practice polygamy in Canada—did obtain the same welcome tendered to all immigrants.

From their arrival in Canada there had been an ambiguity in the Mormons' own attitudes towards their new homeland, an ambiguity still present in the grandchildren of the early settlers. William Woolf, born in Cardston in 1890, remembered that "We never spoke of 'Utah'; it was always 'down home.' " When the July 1 Dominion Day celebration took place that first year in the new colony, it was designed as much to win the approval and confidence of the old settlers as to instill in the new ones a loyalty towards Canada. What happened to that observance in later years, however, suggests the paradox of the community's attitude: from July 1 to July 4 became one long celebration, including a program of speeches praising, on the First, Canada's fair government and good land; on the Third, Cardston's founding; and on the Fourth, the American heritage of freedom and liberty dating back to the Revolution. The interim was filled with baseball, tug-o-war, dances, band concerts, horseshoes, foot races, horse-pulling contests, and horse races in which the Indian contestants from the nearby Blood reserve invariably showed well.[19] And later the same month, on July 24, the entrance of Brigham Young into the Salt Lake Valley would be celebrated with equal enthusiasm. That all these loyalties could be maintained in the consciousness of a single community attests to the basic similarity of the mores and customs of Canadians, Americans, and Mormons. Many Canadian-born Utahns to this day claim they hold "dual citizenship," a legal status now nonexistent. Valid or

[19] Interview with William L. Woolf, July 23, 1974.

not, the claim itself is significant: it represents the wish to hold to both loyalties at once.

Card and his associates probably intended their stay in Canada to be temporary: once federal prosecution for polygamy ceased, they expected to return. The October 1890 LDS conference in Salt Lake City, however, brought with it a series of surprises to Card, and reshaped the lives of Utahns of his generation and at least three to follow.

Expecting to face a trial and fine for his own "illegal cohabitation," Card instead found himself listening in conference to Wilford Woodruff, then president of the church, rescinding the practice of polygamy in his famous Manifesto. A mixture of responses greeted the announcement: "To day the harts of all ware tried, but looked to God and Submitted," wrote Card's mother-in-law Zina Young, widow of Brigham Young.[20] She and Card, most certainly, expected the recall from Canada for him and for her daughter, his wife. But there were other plans, and Card found himself released from his ecclesiastical responsibilities in Cache Valley and assigned indefinitely to Canada. The new colony, already more than mere temporary refuge for beleaguered polygamists, was to become a permanent settlement to support and be supported by the Utah church, a nucleus for an expanded Mormon colonization complex. Card and his brethren in the faith acquiesced, took out Canadian naturalization papers, and encouraged all new settlers to do likewise, and to claim lands under the Canadian homestead act.

Mormon settlements in Alberta radiated out from Cardston. By 1894 some 674 settlers, most of them from Cache, Weber, and Box Elder counties, were expanding the four main settlements. By the turn of the century the church was calling irrigation missionaries, and towns as far away as Taber, east of Lethbridge, were growing. Mormon apostle John W. Taylor, then living in Cardston, persuaded Utah financier Jesse Knight to invest in cattle lands in the area. At Raymond, Knight built a factory for refining beet sugar, and soon the church established a high school there, calling teachers from Utah and Idaho to staff it.[21]

Not all the settlers, of course, were officially sent. Homer M. Brown, for example, was feeling the crunch of land availability for his large family in the Salt Lake Valley and so moved his wife Lydia

---

[20] Zina D. Young, Diary, October 6, 1890, holograph, in private possession.
[21] J. Orvin Hicken, comp. and ed., *Raymond, 1901–1967* (Lethbridge, Alberta, 1967), pp. 19, 30–31.

and their twelve children north to Spring Coulee in 1898, where their last child was born in 1901. They settled finally in Cardston, where their second son, Hugh B., later to become prominent in Utah legal and government affairs, and counselor in the LDS church First Presidency, met Zina Card, daughter of Cardston's founder, whom he later married. They eventually brought their family back to Utah. Brown, reflecting on his mixed Canadian-American background, found it difficult to declare a first loyalty; he had been an officer in the Canadian armed forces, had been a Utah state commissioner and candidate for the United States Senate, and had practiced law in both countries. While he had willingly become a Canadian citizen with his family, he had as willingly become a naturalized, repatriated American.[22]

Not all Canadian-American settlers of the Alberta colonies felt Brown's ambivalence; his mother Lydia, for example, was deeply hurt at leaving Utah, as were many of the women. Mildred Cluff Harvey, for one, moving with her husband Richard C. from Heber Valley, where there was no room, to Mammoth, Alberta, where there was nothing but space, remained, her daughter later recounted, "a Utahn to her death." Richard, on the other hand, was "a Canadian from the time he first set foot on Canadian soil," where, in his own words, "when I saw the abundance of feed and grass everywhere and nothing to feed but my cattle, I thought this was paradise indeed!" Their daughter, Mildred Jennie, aged nearly four at their arrival in Canada, cried to return "home to Utah." And did, years later, to become superintendent of nurses at the Budge Hospital in Logan.[23]

This Mildred Harvey was part of a tide that has swept Canadian descendants of Utahns back to their parental homeland since the first generation of pioneer children matured: the pursuit of higher education. Even if the University of Alberta had been founded earlier than its 1906 beginning, it is likely that the Mormons would have still returned to Utah. Many had relatives in Cache Valley, where Brigham Young College was offering religious as well as practical and academic courses. As early as 1894 John A. Woolf from Cardston was attending there, and by 1900 three others had followed. Enrollment of southern Alberta Mormons rose steadily to

---

[22] Interview with Hugh B. Brown, August 19, 1974.

[23] "A Brief History of Richard Coope Harvey (1865–1950)," *Four Leaves From History,* comp. and ed. Lucile H. Ursenbach, (Calgary, Alberta, 1973), p. 16; interview with Lucile H. Ursenbach, August 20, 1974.

eleven in 1903, dropped, then peaked again with twenty students in various departments in 1907. In the meantime the reputation of Utah State Agricultural College (now Utah State University) was spreading, and in 1902 Seymour Smith registered as the first Canadian student there. The same year, four students from the Alberta colonies enrolled at Brigham Young University in Provo. The stream of Canadian Mormons to that school has continued unabated to the present, most likely because parents see their offspring there as resting safe in the lap of the church. The last available report from that school, recording 1973 attendance, shows 505 Canadian students there.

Strangely, the University of Utah attracted only a dribble of the Canadian student migration; its records show no more than two Canadian students in any term up to 1916, whereas BYU had reached twelve in 1914 and USU fourteen in 1916. The University of Utah showed in 1973 only thirty Canadian students. There were and are other factors than Mormon-linked ones affecting enrollment, of course, but no analysis of foreign student population in Utah is available delineating causative forces.

The student population has been dealt with in this context for one basic reason: a very loose survey of Canadians currently living in Utah, and those of the generation just deceased, shows that a preponderance came south first as students, then stayed to practice their trades and professions here. Until 1968, when immigrating workers were first required to meet stringent labor certification requirements, procuring a visa was almost *pro forma* for Canadians; so all that was required of a graduating student wishing to remain, or any Canadian, for that matter, wishing to take up residence in Utah, was a few forms to fill out and a few months' patience. Prior to 1924 not even a visa was required, and after that the help of a "sponsor," a well-established resident willing to vouch for the candidate, smoothed the way. In 1965, however, Canadians, like all other nationals, were put on a "preference quota system," and the shape of Canadian immigration changed sharply as a result.[24]

From World War I until the 1930s the number of Canadians in Utah decreased almost as rapidly as it had increased before. But in 1940 a resurgence of Canadian immigration began, and the Canadians in Utah more than tripled their numbers between 1930

---

[24] Interview with Gerald O. Fasbender, officer in charge, Salt Lake City office of U.S. Immigration and Naturalization Service, July 25, 1974.

and 1970. Immigration figures for the past two decades reveal that fluctuations in Canadian immigration to Utah have paralleled those to the United States as a whole to a striking degree, indicating that national immigration policies and economic conditions have become more important determinants of this immigration than any particular conditions in Utah. Canadian immigration to Utah rose to a peak of 311 persons during the year 1965, and although it dropped dramatically after the application of the quota system, Canada has supplied more immigrants to Utah than any other country each year since 1962. At last count there were slightly more than four thousand Canadians in the state, including about seven hundred students, and about another seven thousand persons having one or more Canadian-born parents.[25] That relatively few of the immigrating Canadians have become United States citizens in the recent years is perhaps the best indicator of the ambivalent attitudes of the immigrants: they feel themselves strangers in neither location and so sense little pressure to abjure either country's citizenship.

In a recent interview Gerald O. Fasbender of the United States Immigration and Naturalization Service office in Salt Lake City, affirmed that nearly all—he estimated 95 percent—of the recent Canadian immigrants landing in Utah initiated their applications through the United States consulate in Calgary, the nearest office to the Southern Alberta concentration of Mormons. In the absence of complete figures, but on the basis of his experience in the Utah office, Fasbender suggested that the majority of Canadians emigrating to Utah choose this location "because of the [LDS] church."

What of the Canadians in Utah now? In a western setting, the Anglo-Canadians are easily lost in the crowd, unidentified except by a very astute listener who detects a slightly different dialect. "Canajan," as a recent book transliterates it, is recognized by the shortening of the vowels, especially the *ou* diphthong, and a frequent inclusion of the shibboleth "eh?" into the middle or, more frequently, at the end, of sentences.[26] Even this difference all but disappears

[25] 1970 Census, vol. 1, part 46, pp. 113, 134, 279, 282. There is a discrepancy of 1,443 persons between the figures given on p. 282 and all the other totals given for Canadian-born persons. Certainly this cannot be entirely explained by differences in sampling. The authors have assumed that the higher figure given on p. 282 must be more accurate in view of the relatively heavy influx of Canadians during the 1960s. If the lower figure were correct this would indicate that there has been an amazingly high turnover of Canadian immigrants in Utah through death and emigration.

[26] Mark M. Orkin, *Canajan, Eh?* (Don Mills, Ontario, 1973). The book is a clever poke at Canadian speech and Canadian ways. Its description of the use of "eh?," pp. 35–38, is delightful as well as observant.

in the accent of the southern Alberta Mormons whose own "Mormon drawl" distinguishes them in Canada but assimilates them in Utah. French Canadians, of course, are easier to identify. Although a phenomenally large number of present-day *Canadiens* are bilingual, there is nearly always a trace of the mother tongue in their English. The attitudes Canadians express are even more revealing: French Canadians may let slip a trace of the resentment they feel towards the Anglo-Canadian domination of their economy. By the same token, Anglo-Canadians may show resentment of the American big brother, an attitude, says Wallace Stegner, similar to that of the American westerner towards eastern influences on his culture.[27]

No melting-pot, Canada has rather preferred to weave its people, native, British, French, eastern European, and others, into a variegated fabric that encouraged their distinctness. Multi-culturalism is now explicitly the official policy governing social legislation in Canada. The loyalties of Canadians in Utah, then, are more likely directed towards a region than towards the country itself. The Canadian Club in Salt Lake City is an example. At least as early as the 1950s, Canadians would gather in Liberty Park on the First of July, Dominion Day, and make their own national observance. There would be a Canadian flag on the piano, and "O Canada" to begin the ceremonies. A speech, a few musical numbers, and then "God Save the King" (or Queen) to round out the program. There would follow games for the children, a potluck supper, and the inevitable visiting of friends from former years. One year recently, however, the organizers of the picnic advertised the event in local newspapers. The usual crowd of southern Alberta Canadians, most of them Mormon, was augmented by several eastern Canadians who brought the more typically Canadian accoutrements of a celebration: their beer and other bottles. The mixture of religious and regional backgrounds was a stronger divisive force than Canadian nationalism was a unifying one; the celebration the following year returned to the limited observance of the few "old-timers." The celebration in 1974 involved some three families.

Canadians in Utah now, as in the past, have found ingress into the whole commercial and professional life of the state. Some have distinguished themselves in their fields; many have made notable contributions. Any list of such people would be at best spotty, but let there be here a few representative names.

[27] Wallace Stegner, "Letter from Canada," *American West* 11 (January 1974): 28–30.

It is reasonable to expect numbers of Canadians to be involved in education in Utah, since so many of them came here originally for higher training in teaching and school administration. DeVoe Woolf and Marion G. Merkeley came from the Mormon colonies to become, respectively, high school principal and state superintendent of schools in Utah. Stewart Grow, Heber Wolsey, and Curtis Wynder are BYU administrators, and Harold W. Lee and Oliver Smith are faculty members there. Increasingly, however, educational institutions are attracting as faculty other than their own graduates, and Canadians are coming to Utah via institutions elsewhere. Maxwell M. Wintrobe, hematologist of the University of Utah's College of Medicine, came from Manitoba via Tulane University in 1943 to help establish the four-year medical school here. Ukranian Canadian Orest G. Symko finished his student work in physics at Oxford before joining the faculty at Utah. At USU, Canadian William H. Bennett was dean of the College of Agriculture; James Bennett and William Lye are heads of departments; and Bruce Anderson is director of international programs.

In medicine, Morgan Coombs, Harris Walker, Ulrich Bryner, and LeRoy Kimball are representative of Canadians who practice or practiced in Utah. Kimball Fisher and Wallace Johnson represent pharmacists. Canadian lawyers Wilson McCarthy and Emmett L. Brown served here both as attorneys and as judges. McCarthy is more remembered for his contributions in the Reconstruction Finance Corporation and for having taken over receivership of the Denver and Rio Grande Railroad and reviving the company.[28]

In music are Canadian brothers Ralph and Harold Laycock; in sports, Alan R. (Pete) Witbeck; among authors, W. Cleon Skousen. LDS religious leaders N. Eldon Tanner, of the church's First Presidency, the late Hugh B. Brown of its Quorum of the Twelve, William H. Bennett, an assistant to the Twelve, and Presiding Bishop Victor L. Brown are all Canadians, adopted or originally.

It is impossible in practical terms to delineate the impact of Canadians on the social, cultural, political, and economic life of Utah. Canadian stock has long since woven itself into the whole fabric of the state, and newly arrived Canadians blend almost without a trace into the changing pattern. But if the individual fibers can no longer be distinguished, still the fabric itself has been strengthened by the added strands.

[28] Robert A. Athearn, *Rebel of the Rockies* (New Haven and London, 1962), pp. 307–12.

9 ITALIANITA IN UTAH: THE IMMIGRANT EXPERIENCE

BY PHILIP F. NOTARIANNI

> Many years later I was to realize that, to a child of nine years, emigration to America meant a new birth, to which a certain inevitable continuity with the past had given an added significance.
>
> —Angelo M. Pellegrini

The Italian immigrants who settled in Utah faced a strange, nebulous environment. Their numbers were relatively small, yet they settled in four major counties and contributed to the life and labor that characterizes Utah history. These immigrants, almost all of them confined to mining and railroad centers, brought with them language, religion, beliefs, and customs, products of cultural distinctiveness.

The primary forces motivating Italian migration at its height from 1880 to 1920 were overpopulation, agricultural depressions, and discontent among the *contadini,* the "peasants." [1] The United States was in a position to receive the newcomers. Technological advances in the country, railroad expansion, and new demands for coal and ores created a need for unskilled labor. These conditions in Italy and the United States led to the emigration of millions of Italians to America.

The great exodus of emigrants is one of the most striking features of Italy's modern history. The northern Italians had adapted themselves to seasonal migrations but had always returned to Italy.

[1] From 1820 to 1948 Italian immigration into the United States was second only to that of Germany. Exact figures are: Germany—6,064,653 and Italy—4,752,735. However, Great Britain and Ireland accounted for 8,937,879. Figures from U. S., Immigration and Naturalization Service, *Annual Report for Year Ending June 30, 1948* (Washington, D.C., 1948), Table 4.

The early emigrants who left the country permanently were either casual wanderers or political refugees, mainly from the North.[2]

The *Risorgimento,* Italy's national revival, culminated in the unification of the country in 1870. Despite the term "unification," a political and cultural divisiveness continued to exist between the industrial-prosperous North and the agrarian-poor South. The distinction between northerners and southerners found its way to the United States. Until restrictive legislation was passed in the early twenties, the Immigration Bureau issued separate statistics for each group. The mass migration consisted mainly of southern Italians and began in the late 1880s and early 1890s.[3] From the middle of the nineteenth century and extending into the early twentieth century, Italy's population increased markedly. At the same time, an agricultural depression occurred; foreign markets for grapes and citrus fruits were lost to southern Italian farmers. Thousands were left destitute.

The South, *Mezzogiorno,* was the neglected portion of Italy. The lack of industry and the dependence upon agriculture confined the southern *contadini* to a harsh life. Further, an "agricultural backwardness" existed in the South. This backwardness, as defined by Leonard Covello, resulted from "climate, water scarcity, seismic phenomena, floods, deforestation, depleted soil fertility, lack of roads, archaic methods of cultivation, the *latifondi* ("large estates"), taxation, usury, bondage, and corrupt administration of civic affairs." [4] The *contadini,* left poor and desperate, were attracted by emigration posters and agents and looked to new lands. These people, mostly from the Abruzzi, Calabria, and Sicily, in contrast to northerners, had never traveled beyond their village.[5]

Northern Italians wandered to European countries and to South America, mainly Argentina and Brazil, for seasonal work. However, from 1860 to 1870, Argentina was beset with political disturbances, a financial crisis, and war with Paraguay; consequently, southern Italians wanting to emigrate looked away from South America toward the United States.[6] Another decisive factor in turn-

[2] Denis Mack Smith, *Italy: A Modern History* (Ann Arbor, 1959), p. 239.

[3] U. S., Congress, House, *House Reports,* 77th Cong., 2d sess., 1942, VIII, p. 239.

[4] Leonard Covello, *The Social Background of the Italo-American School Child* (Leiden, 1967), p. 34.

[5] Alexander DeConde, *Half Bitter, Half Sweet: An Excursion into Italian-American History* (New York, 1971), p. 79.

[6] *Ibid.,* p. 80.

ing their attention to the United States was the "myth of America." The myth embodied fact, fable, romance, and imagination, and culminated in the Horatio Alger dream of "rags to riches." This myth of America has always been one of the principal incentives for emigration; and the myth, in turn, has been perpetuated and modified by the experiences of the immigrants in their actual contact with the New World.[7]

Once the tide of immigration began, the momentum continued. Additional factors added fuel to the fire. From 1884 to 1887 a cholera epidemic in southern Italy forced many people to evacuate the area. The Italian government had been inconsistent toward the exodus from the country, at times indifferent, at times deploring it.[8] By 1888 it recognized the benefits of relieving the population pressure and passed a law that not only allowed Italians to migrate but actually encouraged it.

The United States became the major magnet to attract the Italians. Ellis Island in New York, the main immigration station, received as many as fifteen thousand Italians a day. Steamships, whose steerage rate from Naples to the United States rose from fifteen dollars in 1880 to twenty-eight dollars in 1900,[9] brought in thousands of individuals, packed in compact areas of the vessels. From 1900 to 1910, during a high point of industrial expansion, 2,104,309 Italians arrived in the country.[10]

The first waves of Italians settled in the industrial centers of the East, but as immigrants continued to arrive, congestion resulted. Opportunities became scarce; consequently, new arrivals often looked to the American West, and many to the state of Utah. One immigrant, asked when his father came to Utah, replied:

> I don't recall the very first, but I believe that it was back in 1894, '95 or something like that. . . . Well, he came to New York and from New York he heard the West was better conditions, it was better, it was new and he came West here.[11]

The West in the late nineteenth and early twentieth centuries was an area of expansion. Railroad and mining industries were grow-

[7] Carlo Levi, "Italy's Myth of America," *Life*, July 7, 1947, pp. 84–85.

[8] DeConde, *Half Bitter, Half Sweet*, p. 80.

[9] Andrew F. Rolle, *The Immigrant Upraised* (Norman, Okla., 1968), p. 31.

[10] Robert F. Foerster, *The Italian Emigration of Our Times* (Cambridge, Mass., 1924), p. 327. Total immigration for the period was 8,795,386.

[11] Interview with Angelo Calfo, Salt Lake City, Utah, July 10, 1971.

ing at such a rate that demand was high for unskilled laborers. Italian immigrants came to fill that demand.

The environment in Utah was also changing at the turn of the century. Population growth, increasing urbanization, the importance of mining and manufacturing, as well as an expansion in trade and transportation, all contributed to change the economic and social life of Utah during the first decade of the twentieth century.[12] Utah did not attract a great number of Italians; yet, they were one of the largest foreign-born groups of southern and eastern European stock in the state. They settled, for the most part, in Carbon, Salt Lake, Weber, and Tooele counties.

The first noticeable number of foreign-born Italians in Utah appeared in 1870 and totaled seventy-four.[13] These early immigrants, Protestant Vaudois of the Waldensian persuasion from northwest Italy, were the result of Mormon missionary activity in Italy from 1849 to 1861. Almost all settled in the fertile areas of Ogden where they began to farm. Joseph Toronto, who had given Brigham Young $2,500 of his savings to help build the Mormon temple in Nauvoo, Illinois, assisted Lorenzo Snow in the founding of the Italian Mission in 1849.[14] A Latter-day Saints publication stated that

> Emigration was a factor keeping the membership of the Italian mission and its successors small. At the time of its amalgamation with the Swiss Mission in 1854 there were three branches, sixty-four members, and records of fifty emigrations to Utah.[15]

However, the majority of Italian immigrants were attracted to Utah for its labor opportunities in mining and railroading.

The first Italian laborers, predominantly from the North, began arriving in Utah in the late 1890s in response to the opening of the Carbon County coal fields. The development and expansion of the Denver & Rio Grande Railroad into Utah in the 1880s was a catalyst to the state's coal mining industry. Four major camps

---

[12] Sheelwant B. Pawar, "An Environmental Study of the Development of the Utah Labor Movement: 1860–1935" (Ph.D. diss., University of Utah, 1967), p. 194.

[13] 1870 Census.

[14] A description of the Italian mission is given in Kate B. Carter, comp., *Heart Throbs of the West,* 12 vols. (Salt Lake City, 1939–51), 4:282–89.

[15] Albert L. Zobell, Jr., "In Italy. . . The Sunny Land," *The Improvement Era* 53 (1950): 733.

emerged: Clear Creek (1882), Winter Quarters (1882), Castle Gate (1888), and Sunnyside (1900).[16] Many of these early laborers were lured to Utah by agents representing coal companies.[17] A newspaper article concerning the camp at Castle Gate reported that Italian miners came in groups—as contract laborers did. It read: "About fifty to twenty Italians have arrived in town, presumably to work in the mines here or at Sunnyside." [18]

Throughout the United States early Italian labor was furnished by a *padrone,* a boss who would exact tribute from an immigrant in return for employment. The system was nationwide.[19] Although Greeks in Utah were subjected to a Greek *padrone,* the Italian experience remains unclear.[20] The possibility that a single Italian *padrone* existed is remote; rather, it is possible that various *padroni* of limited influence might have existed at one time or another. Later arrivals, however, were "called" by friends and relatives to come to Utah where employment was readily available. A paucity of source material may forever preclude a definitive study of the *padrone* system in Utah.

Upon their arrival in Carbon County, the immigrants settled in one of the four main camps, usually Castle Gate or Sunnyside. The coal companies (Pleasant Valley Coal and Utah Fuel) furnished a few of the workers with company-owned houses on company-owned property and compelled the laborer to trade at the company-owned stores.[21] Trading at company stores was inevitable, since miners were issued scrip instead of currency. The company town

[16] Thomas G. Alexander, "From Dearth to Deluge, Utah's Coal Industry," *Utah Historical Quarterly* 31 (1963) : 237. Carbon County was actually organized in 1894.

[17] Interview with Vincent Massari, Pueblo, Colorado, September 14, 1974.

[18] *Eastern Utah Advocate* (Price, Utah), November 30, 1899.

[19] Humbert S. Nelli, "The Italian Padrone System in the United States," *Labor History* 5 (1964) : 157.

[20] For a study of the Greek *padrone,* see Helen Zeese Papanikolas, *Toil and Rage in a New Land: The Greek Immigrants in Utah,* 2d. ed. rev. reprinted from *Utah Historical Quarterly* 38, no. 2(1970): 121–33. Mose Paggi, publisher of *Il Minatore* and Italian consular agent for Utah in 1910, entered into a partnership in 1912 with L.G. Skliris, who was the Greek *padrone* unmasked in the Bingham strike of 1912. This suggests that Paggi could have also been a *padrone.* He was well educated, had consular power, and was an Italian notary public. For details of the partnership see: *Pacific Reporter,* 197 (St. Paul, 1919) : 739–40.

[21] The Pleasant Valley Coal Company operated the Wasatch store. Approximately 225 houses were built on company property by the miners themselves. See Allan Kent Powell, "The 'Foreign Element' and the 1903–4 Carbon County Coal Miners' Strike," *Utah Historical Quarterly* 43 (1975) : 143.

became a prominent feature of western mining life. These towns
have been glorified and condemned, but immigrants who lived in
them were subjected to horrible living conditions. For example, the
rent charged by Utah Fuel Company depended on the number of
rooms in a house. In one boxcar on company property a cloth
curtain was used to divide it into two quarters. When company
inspectors approached, a family member would tear down the
partition in order to be charged for one room instead of two.[22] In
describing the camp at Sunnyside, a writer has stated:

> . . . many put up tents in the southern part of the canyon,
> and this section became known as "Rag Town" by local resi-
> dents. Company-owned houses were hastily erected framed
> structures, not plastered inside, but about 1915 the company
> began a program of building better homes and modernizing
> the town.[23]

The majority of the residents of Rag Town were Italian immigrants.

The mining and railroad opportunities in Salt Lake County
also attracted Italian immigrants at the turn of the century. Italian
laborers funneled into the mining town of Bingham. As early as
1880 there were thirty-five in the camp, mostly Piedmontese, who
were called "Short Towns" because of their stocky builds.[24] Bingham was a bustling community of many diverse nationalities,
described as "a town of 22 saloons and 600 sporting girls." [25] Like
Carbon County, Bingham was susceptible to labor strife. The Utah
Copper Company, incorporated in June 1903, became the foremost
employer of residents of Bingham Canyon.[26]

Towns that were dependent upon mining and smelting companies developed in Magna, Garfield, and Murray. Northwest of
present-day Magna, a Little Italy grew west of Jap Town and
Greek Town. According to long-time residents of the town, in 1914

[22] This incident was reported to the writer by Monsignor Jerome Stoffel,
who is a member of the advisory board of editors for the *Utah Historical
Quarterly* and a former resident of Carbon County.

[23] James B. Allen, *The Company Town in the American West* (Norman,
Okla., 1966), p. 13.

[24] Helen Z. Papanikolas, "Life and Labor among the Immigrants of
Bingham Canyon," *Utah Historical Quarterly* 33 (1965): 290. State of Utah,
*First Report of the State Bureau of Immigration, Labor and Statistics, 1911–
12*, listed the Italians in Bingham as follows: "402 Italians (north), 237 Italians
(south)."

[25] Interview with Joe Tomè, Sandy, Utah, July 31, 1974.

[26] Beatrice Spendlove, "A History of Bingham Canyon" (M.S. thesis,
University of Utah, 1967), p. 60.

there were approximately twenty-five families and a few single men living in the area. Little Italy was:

> . . . just a bunch of shacks that they built themselves. I mean, you built your own shack, and the copper company let you build your shack there. . . . No bathrooms, of course, we had to use the number three tub. . . . It was usually a single-boarded shack, you know. Some of them had sheet iron roof on them, and then covered with tar paper, you know. And single board, that's pretty rough, you know, in those winters.[27]

Garfield, a town of the American Smelting and Refining Company, was remembered by one immigrant as follows:

> He [his brother] was working Garfield. They went over there and never had no houses, they had a boxcar. Him and his brother was to live on a boxcar over there. In the morning they never had no dishes, they had coffee can. And they fill up the coffee can with milk, coffee, and eat some bread, and that is all the breakfast they had.[28]

In Murray, Italians were also employed by the American Smelting and Refining Company.

A later center of Italian settlement was Salt Lake City, with a residential and boardinghouse district on the west side of the city. By 1900, 102 of the 170 Italians who resided in the county lived in Salt Lake.[29] Immigrants were employed by the Union Pacific and the Denver & Rio Grande Western railroads; but Italians also owned saloons, grocery stores, and tailor shops. The lack of a mining town atmosphere with its potentially explosive character differentiated Salt Lake City and Ogden from other Italian localities. In Salt Lake, Italians took part in celebrations and parades that promoted good will between the Italian and non-Italian communities.

In Tooele County, which began as a Mormon farming community but later developed mining and smelting industries, immigrant labor was in demand. The three main mining areas were Stockton, Ophir, and Mercur. The largest settlement of Italians was in Mercur, according to an article in *Il Minatore,* a Salt Lake Italian

---

[27] Interview with Mike and Joe Lewis, Magna, Utah, June 26, 1974.

[28] Interview with Charles Barber, Salt Lake City, Utah, November 28, 1971. However, there were company houses at Garfield.

[29] 1900 Census.

newspaper. In 1904 a Catholic church was erected in the town.[30] At the Tooele smelter later arrivals found employment; and immigrants, mostly southern and eastern Europeans, who eventually settled in Tooele established a section of the town known as New Town.

Italian converts to the Mormon church had arrived in Ogden in the 1850s and 1860s, many of them in handcart companies. The greater number of Italians, however, lived in the Ogden area to work on section gangs for the Union Pacific, Oregon Short Line, and the Lucin to Corinne route of the Southern Pacific. There were also Italian farmers working the fertile lands in north Ogden; several owned dairies.

Italian involvement in labor is significant since immigrants were the core of Utah's labor force. Utah's first important experience with labor strife occurred in the 1903 Carbon County strike that involved, predominantly, Italian miners. The strike was called by the United Mine Workers in connection with the coal mining strike in Colorado. Pleasant Valley Coal Company Vice-President G. W. Kramer, speaking of the Italians, said:

> The Castle Gate mine is what we might call an Italian mine because of the large number of Italians there to the number of other miners. At Castle Gate there are 356 Italians, 108 English speaking, Austrians 10. This is not true, however, at the other mines. At Sunnyside there are 358 English, 246 Italians, 222 Austrians; at Clear Creek, 128 Finns, 172 Italians, 95 English speaking; at Winter Quarters, 181 English speaking, 126 Finns, 74 Italians and a few others.[31]

In addition, Kramer asserted that he wanted to make the Castle Gate mine an English-speaking mine. The Italian miners were the initially dissatisfied group.

The strike received wide press coverage and left readers with a more intensified, stereotyped image of the Italian immigrant as a bloodthirsty, nonwhite, stiletto-in-hand villain. In reference to nonforeign miners who wanted work, an editorial in the *Deseret Evening News* stated:

> And if English speaking men come forward in sufficient numbers, they will not be required to labor in company with

[30] Louis J. Fries, *One Hundred and Fifty Years of Catholicity in Utah* (Salt Lake City, 1926), p. 101.

[31] *Eastern Utah Advocate,* December 3, 1903. See Powell, "The 'Foreign Element' and the 1903-4 Carbon County Coal Miners' Strike," pp. 125-54.

foreigners of the class that has become obnoxious and objectionable.[32]

The *News* revealed the fears of radical influence prevalent in the country:

> The fact is indisputable that among the strikers are many red-handed anarchists who respect no law and feel it a sort of religious duty to exterminate and destroy all opponents. . . . So long as this class has a respected voice in the strikers councils the presence of the militia will be necessary to prevent a reign of terror.[33]

Much of the above editorial was leveled against Charles (Carlo) Demolli, who was sent by the UMW from Colorado to Utah and put in charge of organizing the Italian miners.

Charles Demolli, born in Brussels, Belgium, in 1870 of Italian parents, was educated at the Institute of Milan, served three years in the Italian army, and later worked in the silk mills of Como. While at Como, he was involved in the 1895 strike and revolution there and was exiled from Italy. He then emigrated to the United States, wrote for Italian-language newspapers in the East on Socialist topics, and worked in the coal mines of Pennsylvania. Demolli made his way to Colorado where he founded *Il Lavoratore Italiano* that became the organ of the UMW among the Italians. The *Salt Lake Herald* characterized Demolli as a "silver-tongued" speaker "whose influence with his fellow countrymen is so feared by the Utah Fuel Company officials. . . . with his level head, shrewd judgment, college education, suave manner and great magnetism, he is regarded as one of the strongest men affiliated with the United Mine Workers and he is idolized by his followers".[34]

Demolli indeed proved to be an influential factor in leading the Italian strikers. The following are excerpts from an interview conducted with an old-time resident of Helper, Utah:

[32] *Deseret Evening News,* December 8, 1903. Similar articles mentioned a "fear of Mafia tactics among the Italians."

[33] *Ibid.* The militia was eventually called. For a complete study of the 1903 strike refer to Allan Kent Powell, "Labor at the Beginning of the 20th Century: The Carbon County, Utah, Coal Fields, 1900 to 1905" (M.A. thesis, University of Utah, 1972).

[34] *The Salt Lake Herald,* December 11, 1903. An opposing view was expressed earlier in the *Deseret Evening News,* December 9, 1903, which stated: "The general [Gen. John Q. Cannon of the National Guard] is pleased at the way Governor Wells talked to Demolli, and says that the agitator is no better really than the average Italian fruit pedler [*sic*]; and this newspaper talk about his fine presence, fine speech, and pleasing address and smartness is all rot."

PN   What in your opinion, what was the main grievance between the miners and the company?

JD   The main grievance was the miners wanted a union. That was, they weren't fighting for wages or anything, they wanted the right to organize. And, of course, the companies refused it, see. There was another one by the name of . . . one of the best organizers that the union had.

PN   An Italian organizer?

JD   Yeah.

PN   Charles Demolli?

JD   Demolli. Charles Demolli stayed with my mother and dad.

PN   Really!

JD   Yeah. Charlie Demolli when he was here boarded with mother and dad.

PN   Did your father ever tell you what kind of man Charles Demolli was?

JD   . . . Both mother and dad thought he was a hell of a swell guy. He was more or less a little bit on the radical side. He was kind of an anarchist. Charlie Demolli was a real fine person and . . . everybody, all the old timers, knew him. In fact, my dad said he had more guts than all, anybody he ever saw. When he went to Scofield . . . he was suppose to go up there and talk to the miners up there. And they [company guards] told him when he got up there they were going to throw him in jail. You know how he got into Scofield? He got into Scofield in a bread box.[35]

Demolli, while dodging company guards and becoming involved with much litigation in the courts, was able to articulate his prolabor views most effectively to his *paesani* by addressing them in Italian. The lack of more complete source material dealing with Demolli's activities in Utah is unfortunate, since his leadership among the state's Italians in 1903–4 might very well parallel that of Italian organizers who labored in the East. The placing of Demolli in the state by the UMW is evidence of union efforts to organize the Italian population. Nevertheless, the strike and unionization were lost.

[35] Interview with Dr. Joseph Dalpiaz, Helper, Utah, February 5, 1972. The bread box was reportedly three feet high, three feet deep, and three feet long.

The majority of Italians involved in the Utah labor movement were northern Italians who had an industrial and social base for unionization. However, reports and articles concerning the strikes in Murray (1908), at Doyle and Schwartz Company (1910), Utah Fire Clay Company (1910), and Utah Copper Company in Bingham Canyon (1912), and in Carbon County (1922 and 1933), attest to continued activity in labor by Italians.[36] The leading figure in the long fight for unionization of the Carbon County coal mines was Frank Bonacci, an immigrant from southern Italy.

Strike participation is typical of other southern and eastern European groups because these immigrants were the unskilled labor force necessary for the development of Utah's railroading and mining industries.

Immigrant laborers, then, became susceptible to union organizing and were embroiled in the strife that accompanied demands for workers' rights. Leaders such as Demolli had only to point out coal company abuses, such as the underweighing of coal taken from the mines. In addition, miners were issued tags that they would tie on cars filled with the coal they had mined. When many of these cars were raised to the surface of the mine, "American" miners would remove the immigrants' tags and replace them with their own, thus perplexing the immigrant laborer as to why he was not receiving his full pay. Such abuses, often supported by the companies, added credence to the rhetoric of organizers and strike leaders. Italian women, especially in the 1903 strike, supported their men by marching in parades of protest against the company, an incredible sight to non-Italians.[37]

Labor violence and abuses led many Italians to leave mining and start businesses of their own or turn to farming. After the 1903 strike, Italians left Castle Gate, a number of them settling in farms along the Price River and many more starting anew in the town of Helper. This group of Italians broke from the labor ranks by utilizing business as a means of social mobility. Numerous immigrants had been apprenticed in various trades in the old country, and once an economic base had been achieved, they left the mines

---

[36] See: *Salt Lake Tribune,* May 6, 1908; Karl Alwin Elling, "The History of Organized Labor in Utah (1910–1920)" (M.S. thesis, University of Utah, 1962), pp. 55–56; Papanikolas, *Toil and Rage,* pp. 121–33 and 166–75; and Helen Z. Papanikolas, "Unionism, Communism, and the Great Depression: The Carbon County Coal Strike of 1933," *Utah Historical Quarterly* 41 (1973): 254–300.

[37] *Eastern Utah Advocate,* November 26, 1903.

From the top: *An Italian D&RGW section gang unde foreman Joe Bonacci, foreground, at Helper in the early 1900s. The youngest immigrant worker was often the water boy as on this sect gang in Spanish Fork Canyo in 1914. The Italian camp a Sunnyside, Carbon County, where company houses replaced the tents and shac of Ragtown.*

From the top: *Caterina Pessetto Bottino hid the famed labor leader Mother Jones from Helper authorities in the 1903, coal miners' strike. The Helper Italian band, 1919. The Double Rock Store, Helper, 1912, with owner Mike Bergera, Mr. Rogers, Mrs. Frank R. Slopanskey and her daughters, Mr. Morrow, Anna Bergera, and Lena Lange.*

From the top: *Columbus Day, 1929, celebrated by Federazione Columbiana, Lodge no. 68, Bingham Canyon. The Bonacci rooming house behind the Denver and Rio Grande Western depot, Price. Sam DeAngelas's saloon in Park City.*

From the top: *A funeral procession walking toward the first Catholic church in Helper. Almost every community had an Italian band or orchestra: Tomaso Angotti, Alfonso Cairo, and Filippo Notarianni played for Magna Italians for several decades. An Italian wedding in Helper.*

Above: *Float honoring Columbus in Pioneer Day parade, ca. 1924.*
Below: *Celebration of the naming of A.F. Giovannoni as a monsignor, December 24, 1925, at Price.*

Right: *Italian and Catholic dignitaries at the Salt Lake Airport, October 1936: Fortunato Anselmo, consul; Archbishop (later Cardinal) Francis J. Spellman; Eugenio Cardinal Pacelli (later Pope Pius XII); Bishop Joseph E. Kearney; Count Enrico Gallazzo; Monsignor A.F. Giovannoni.*

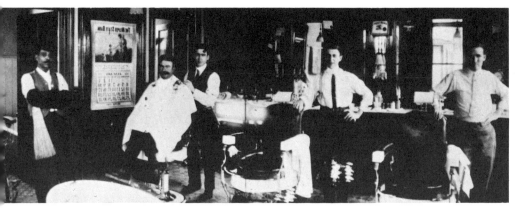

Above: *The Paul Pessetto barbershop in Helper, 1924.* Left: *The Helper Furniture Store, ca. 1925, with Joe Bionde, Floyd C. Bertolina (mayor of Helper in 1923), Riccardo Tensini, Joe and John Quilico.*

e wedding of Bernardina Falvo Bonacci and Thomas Bonacci, 1e 1917 at Helper.

or railroads and embarked upon their craft. This was particularly evident in Salt Lake City and Ogden where shoe shops and tailor shops, as well as grocery stores and taverns, sprang up in Italian residential areas.

A 1913 guide for Italian immigrants mentions Italian farmers in Utah enjoying good success in the fertile valleys near the Great Salt Lake. Farmers in areas of Carbon County,[38] Ogden, and Salt Lake City engaged in growing many varieties of fruits and vegetables. In Salt Lake this produce was often trucked to the Grower's Market on West Temple and Fifth South.

Italian goat ranchers in Carbon, Tooele, and Salt Lake counties found Utah adaptable for herding their animals. As early as 1902, a Utah newspaper reported an Italian starting a goat-raising business in Castle Gate.[39] A rancher in Salt Lake County shipped most of his cheese and meat products outside the state, but also traveled to Bingham with his wagon *affollato* ("crowded"), shouting "ricotta, formaggio, crapa!" [40] This goat milk curd, cheese, and goat meat were eagerly purchased by Italian and Greek miners— foods that were reminders of their southern European cultures.

Life in Utah was indeed a new experience, but Italian immigrants, maintaining continuity with the past yet accommodating to the new environment, discovered, in the words of Alexander De Conde, that it was *mezzo amara, mezzo dolce* ("half bitter, half sweet"). The bitterness commenced from the outset as Italians met antiforeign sentiment—nativism.[41]

Nativism in Utah began with an ignorance of Italian culture and was compounded by Italian participation in the 1903 strike and stereotyped images presented in numerous press reports, both nationally and locally. A typical example was a newspaper article entitled: "Whisky, Knives, and Bad Blood." [42] As early as 1893, the Building Trades Congress reported at their meeting of June 10 that the Culmer Jennings Paving Company of Salt Lake City was em-

[38] *Guida Degli Stati Uniti Per L'Immigrante Italiano* (New York, 1913), p. 32. In the *Eastern Utah Advocate,* April 30, 1908, reference was made to the San Rafael irrigation project indorsed by Dr. A. W. Dowd and Joe Ronzio. Ronzio wished to open land to Italians once it had water.

[39] *Eastern Utah Advocate,* April 3, 1902. The rancher was Frank Cavello; also reported was the starting of a chicken ranch.

[40] Interview with Luigi Nicoletti, Midvale, Utah, July 23, 1971.

[41] The material on nativism is taken primarily from Philip F. Notarianni, "The Italian Immigrant in Utah: Nativism (1900–1925)" (M.A. thesis, University of Utah, 1972).

[42] *Eastern Utah Advocate,* July 24, 1902.

ploying "dagoes" and passed a motion to communicate to the city council, asking them to remedy the "dago" situation by insisting that the company abide by their contract to employ "white men." [43] The above factors were combined with a Mormon genealogical doctrine that classed peoples as either of the House of Israel (Mormons believed they were from the lineage of Ephraim) or Gentiles. England, Germany, Norway, Switzerland, Denmark, Sweden, Holland, and Belgium were said to be the countries containing "a considerable number of the blood of Israel amongst their people which must be gathered." [44] Although some Protestant Italians did convert to Mormonism and emigrate to Utah, southern Europeans were classified as Gentiles.

Newspaper reports and editorials of the early quarter of the century are replete with anti-Italian, antiforeign sentiments. In Lucile Richens's "Social History of Sunnyside," she states:

> I was raised with a whole hearted contempt for Greeks, Italians, and other southern Europeans who lived there. . . . Intermarriage with foreigners was considered almost as bad as death. If they had become Americanized it was not so bad.[45]

Thus, children instilled with hatreds and prejudices for "foreigners" grew to perpetuate further the notion of the inferiority of southern and eastern European immigrants.

A 1914–15 thesis, entitled "On the Housing Problem in Salt Lake City," was submitted and approved by the Sociology Department of the University of Utah. The study began as an investigation of housing on Salt Lake's west side but ended as an undocumented degradation of southern and eastern Europeans, primarily Italians and Greeks:

[43] Minutes Book of The Building Trades Congress, June 10, 1893, Western Americana Division of the Marriott Library, University of Utah.

[44] Nathaniel Baldwin, *Times of the Gentiles. Fulness of the Gentiles. A Discussion with Scriptural References* (Salt Lake City, ca. May 1917), p. 1. Doctrine and Covenants 64:36 states: "For verily I say that the rebellious are not of the blood of Ephraim, wherefore they shall be plucked out." Italian involvement in the strike of 1903 may have made this passage more significant, since Italian miners, as well as most southern and eastern European laborers who participated in labor strife, were considered the foreign element responsible for the situation. In the 1903 strike, Angus Cannon, president of the Salt Lake Stake, announced in the tabernacle that employment was available in Carbon County. Some reports stated that he encouraged Mormons to respond to the call, a move that can be interpreted as "antiunion" and "antiforeign."

[45] Lucile Richens, "Social History of Sunnyside," Manuscript #A 211, WPA Collection, Utah State Historical Society.

> The Greeks and Italians are perhaps the most careless and shiftless people found. . . . Comfort to them is unknown unless it is in the form of a smoke by the fire or a drink. Not only is this true of the hundreds of men who rent a house for themselves. . . . but of the families as well. . . . The standard of living among them [Italians] is lower than of any other nationality.[46]

The author also noted:

> Of all people that do not have sufficient recreation, the Italians are by far the worst off. They seem to have no initiative or resources of their own. . . . They lack a fighting and persevering spirit that might lead them to a better life. Even the children attending school are tortured and left out of the play of other children.[47]

The writer failed to recognize the initiative needed to emigrate from one's mother country. Oral interviews have substantiated her assertion concerning Italian children.

JL   We had to fight in our schools. When we went to school, they just had us in there, because I don't know why, but the kids . . . if you ever wanted to talk to one of the girls why you thought. . . .

ML   Some punk would come along and tell you you couldn't . . . . black men couldn't talk to that girl. . . .

JL   They wouldn't dance with you.

ML   Couldn't even play ring-around-the-rosey . . . the girl would [n't] drop the bean bag. Christ, you never had the bean bag dropped behind you. . . .

JL   Never got a Valentine in my life at school.

ML   Neither did I.

JL   Never one Valentine. Yes, that's right.[48]

Another Italian related that as a child, he was ashamed to admit to his friends that he ate spaghetti.[49]

Parents and children were torn between two cultures. American society demanded the adoption of "American" customs (and

---

[46] Katharine E. Groebli, "On the Housing Problem in Salt Lake City" (M.A. thesis, University of Utah, 1914–1915), p. 40.

[47] *Ibid.,* p. 44.

[48] Lewis interview.

[49] Interview with Sam Siciliano, Salt Lake City, Utah, January 3, 1972.

the English language), but the home was centered about Italian customs, food, language, religion, and the teachings of parents. Compulsory education laws after World War I made Italians feel that their language and backgrounds were viewed as inferior. This proved contradictory because immigrants were told that America was the land of many peoples; therefore, they often wondered, under these pressures to Americanize,[50] just what constituted the ideal prototype of an American? The prejudices and discrimination they experienced provided negative examples.

Antiforeign sentiment reached a peak in the 1920s. In regard to the 1922 strike in Carbon County, one newspaper article asked, "Is Carbon County a Part of the State of Utah or is It a South European Dependency?" It continued: "Hundreds of Red-Blooded American Men with Families want to Know why they Have to Submit to the Blatant Lawlessness Effrontry of South European Domination." [51] These attitudes led to the formation of the Ku Klux Klan in Utah. Klan activity, at a peak in 1924 and 1925, manifested itself in parades, demonstrations, and threats. A fiery cross was burned at Helper in September 1924, with hooded Klansmen seen in the vicinity of the Mormon church.[52] In 1925 articles of incorporation of the Knights of the Ku Klux Klan were filed in Salt Lake City by W. M. Cortner, Harry B. Sawyer, and L. W. Taverner. The doctrines of the Utah Klan were similar to those of other branches, ". . . to uphold Americanism, advance Protestant Christianity, and eternally maintain white supremacy." [53]

Klan activity reached a high point in Salt Lake City in 1925. In retaliation to a municipal antimask law, the Klan instigated a measure that resulted in the banning of false whiskers worn by Santa Clauses during Christmas time. The first state convention in 1925 was held at Ensign Peak, north of the city, with burning crosses illuminating the area.[54] In that same year the Klan was active in Magna, Bingham, and Provo, as well as in areas of Carbon County.

[50] A compulsory Americanization law was passed in Utah in 1919. For details consult Leroy Eugene Cowles, "The Utah Educational Program of 1919 and Factors Conditioning its Operation" (Ph.D. diss., University of California, 1926).

[51] *The News Advocate* (Price, Utah), June 29, 1922.

[52] Papanikolas, *Toil and Rage,* p. 181.

[53] *The Sun* (Price, Utah), November 14, 1925. John Higham, *Strangers in the Land: Patterns of American Nativism 1860–1925,* (New York, 1967), pp. 287–88.

[54] David M. Chalmers, *Hooded Americanism: The First Century of the Ku Klux Klan 1865–1965* (Garden City, N.J., 1965), pp. 223–24.

The Ku Klux Klan of Utah created tension, anger, and fear. Many immigrants lived in a state of uncertainty. They became concerned at the possibility of Klan lynchings and violence, such as existed in the neighboring state of Colorado. In response to these tensions, nationalities banded together for mutual aid. Individuals were unsure of what the Klan was trying to achieve; their impulse was to steer clear. When asked who the Klan members were, one immigrant replied, "Well if he tell you this is a Ku Klan you say goodbye, you never talk to him any more. That is it." [55]

In Magna, children, many of them Greek and Italian, watched a Klan parade down Main Street en route to the Gem theatre for a meeting. As the robed and hooded order passed, the children recognized a local resident who walked with a distinguishable limp. The children shouted "You can't fool us! There goes old Joe Ferris." [56] The tensions created in Utah by the Klan culminated in the lynching of Robert Marshall, a Negro "accused" of murder in Carbon County. [57]

The immigration legislation of the 1920s greatly reduced the number of Italians coming into the United States. [58] With the passage of such laws the intense nativism of earlier years began to ebb. Immigrant life seemed to proceed on a route to accommodation with other residents of the state. Children were learning English and American customs, as well as being educated in American schools.

Yet life for Italian immigrants was not one of total alienation from their traditional life in Italy. Values, customs, beliefs, and practices endemic to Italians were carried from the old country to Utah. The "sweetness" in Italian life was best exemplified in the love of music and musical instruments, a value taught to Italian children in their villages. This affinity for music was carried to Utah. Leonetto Cipriani, an Italian aristocrat journeying through Salt Lake in 1853, befriended a Neapolitan music teacher, Gennaro Capone. Also, Capt. Domenico Ballo directed an instrumental band that came to Salt Lake after traveling across the Plains. [59]

[55] Barber interview.

[56] Incident reported to the writer by Frank Maddy, Mike Lewis, and Joe Lewis, long-time residents of Magna, Utah.

[57] Papanikolas, *Toil and Rage*, p. 180 (includes photograph).

[58] The Immigration Restriction Acts of 1921 and 1924 are discussed in Notarianni, "The Italian Immigrant in Utah," pp. 85–101.

[59] Rolle, *The Immigrant Upraised*, p. 204. Also, Giovanni Schiavo, *Italian-American History*, vol. 1 (New York, 1947), pp. 236–37, 279; and

In the 1903 strike, parades held at Castle Gate and Helper were led by an Italian brass band. Dr. Joseph Dalpiaz of Helper recalled:

> The majority of the band members were Italians . . . . they organized a band years and years ago . . . . Before the strike . . . . Yeah, they had a band in Castle Gate. That is the one that played when they built the bowery up there and had the celebration [July 4]. [60]

Italian strikers, locked in bull pens by company guards, cooked spaghetti in coffee cans, sang songs, and danced the tarantella to relieve tensions.

The Sunnyside Italian band received considerable acclaim for its excellence and repertoire. It was "one of the best anywhere." [61] The band, originally organized in the mid-1910s, was upgraded in the latter portion of 1917 by the talents of Prof. Giovanni D. Colistro from Grimaldi, Italy, as the group's director.[62] The band first performed at a funeral in Sunnyside and thereafter on Sundays during the summer months using the bandstand in front of the amusement hall in Sunnyside. Antonio Guadagnoli, a member, said, "Oh, we played operas and. . . . Oh yes, we played a lot of operas. . . ." [63] Verdi operas, *La Traviata, Il Trovatore,* and *Rigoletto,* were often played by the band in front of the courthouse in Price. The musicians were invited to perform in a parade in Salt Lake City on May 24, 1918, in honor of the third anniversary of the entrance of Italy into World War I and also on October 13, 1919, at the first celebration of Columbus Day as a legal state holiday,[64] occasions with which both Italians and non-Italians could identify.

In the early 1920s an Italian fraternal organization, Societa' Cristoforo Colombo, organized a marching band in Salt Lake City.

Giovanni Schiavo, *Four Centuries of Italian-American History* (New York, 1958), pp. 170–72.

[60] Dalpaiz interview; Powell, "Labor at the Beginning of the 20th Century," p. 119; *Eastern Utah Advocate,* February 18, 1904.

[61] *The Sun,* May 31, 1918. Also called the Sunnyside Community Band.

[62] One member of the band recalled that Professor Colistro was brought from Italy by band members; while other accounts maintain that the Utah Fuel Company possibly sponsored the group and paid Colistro's salary.

[63] Interview with Antonio Guadagnoli, Price, Utah, August 9, 1974.

[64] *Salt Lake Tribune,* May 24, 1918 and May 25, 1918; *Salt Lake Telegram,* October 13, 1919. Fortunato Anselmo, Italian vice-consul in Utah for almost a quarter century, was instrumental in having Columbus Day established as a legal state holiday.

The brass band, in ornate uniforms, played in parades and dances that were held at the Odd Fellows Hall in Salt Lake. The Vito Carone orchestra, a six-man group composed of mandolins, guitars, banjos, and a bass fiddle, also played at lodge functions in the city.

Bingham, Magna, Ogden, and Tooele all had Italian bands or orchestras that entertained at private homes, weddings, and baptisms. In the 1920s Italians of the Magna area would gather at the goat ranch of Luigi Nicoletti, located at Bacchus, for Saturday night festivities. Food, comprised of ricotta and various types of Italian salami (*capocollo* and *soppressata*), wine, and song helped ease some of the strain Italians encountered in daily life. An Italian band comprised of Filippo Notarianni, Tomaso Angotti, and Alfonso Cairo provided music for the group, who danced the tarantella until the late hours of the evening. Even in the remote area of Promontory station, Utah, Italian section hands for the Southern Pacific serenaded the local residents.[65]

In the mid-1940s Italian war prisoners were interned at Ogden, Fort Douglas, Tooele, Deseret, and other Utah and Idaho locations. The Ogden camp was particularly proud of its thirty-piece orchestra, known as the "Camp Ogden Army Service Forces Italian Service Unit Brass Band." [66]

The Catholic church had a varied impact upon Utah's Italian population. In the words of an Italian Catholic priest, born in Utah, ". . . there were those who had the faith that were well versed from the old country. There were those who were ignorant." [67] Among women, both young and old, Mass attendance was imperative; but the men went to the church only for special occasions: holidays, baptisms, weddings, Christmas, and Easter.

A major force in the Italian Catholic community of Utah was Monsignor Alfredo F. Giovannoni, an Italian priest, who brought Catholicism closer to many Italian families. The dominant personality of the priest, who not only represented but also embodied the church, cast a tremendous influence upon the Italian community.[68]

[65] Interview with Bernice Houghton Gerristen, Ogden, Utah, September 3, 1974.

[66] *Intermountain Catholic Register* (Salt Lake City), October 22, 1954; Ralph A. Busco and Douglas D. Alder, "German and Italian Prisoners of War in Utah and Idaho," *Utah Historical Quarterly* 39 (1971): 55–72. The camp near Ogden was reported to have had two thousand Italian war prisoners.

[67] Interview with the Reverend Francis Pellegrino, Salt Lake City, Utah, November 27, 1971.

[68] Covello, *The Social Background,* p. 136.

Numerous oral interviews attest to Monsignor Giovannoni's success in his forty-four years as a prelate in Utah.

In southern Italy there existed a dual-faceted religious system: the official Roman Catholic church and the folk beliefs of the people. These beliefs in the occult and superstition were continually fed by the impotence to control natural forces—earthquakes, volcanic eruptions, and floods.[69] One such belief shared at one time by many southern Italian families in Utah was that of human envy; certain men and women had an inborn power, the *mal' occhio* ("evil eye"). With a mere glance their envy could cause sickness and injury.

An account of the *mal' occhio* was as follows:

> Well they [the women] said whenever you get a severe headache . . . aspirin or anything wouldn't help. They would say that somebody had given you the evil eye. . . . I can't remember just how they did it, but there was oil and water in some way and they would make the sign of the cross on your forehead and let the oil drip into the water. Through some formation that it had they could tell whether it was that or whether it was just a natural headache which you had.[70]

Divinities were viewed as protectors from the evils that might befall one. In southern Italy, the Catholic church gave the peasant support for these beliefs with church cults of the Madonna and the saints, as well as in religious festivals. Such *feste* were sporadically celebrated in Utah Catholic churches. Accounts range from a procession in honor of Santa Lucia in Saint Patrick's Church in Salt Lake City to a feast in honor of La Madonna della Carmine ("Our Lady of Mount Carmel") in Tooele. Statues of the respective saints were carried on top of a platform, much in the style of old-country observances.[71] These feast-day celebrations, as well as others, faded away because their importance was attached to local old-country traditions and had little significance to later generations of Italians in Utah. Also, the relatively small number of Italians in the state

[69] *Ibid.,* p. 104.

[70] Interview with Paul Razzica, Magna, Utah, June 13, 1971.

[71] Interview with Mrs. Catherine Fratto, Hunter, Utah, November 13, 1971; interview with Charles and Rose Leonelli, Tooele, Utah, August 2, 1974. Mrs. Leonelli related to the writer that the Italians of Tooele also celebrated *Carnevale,* "fat Tuesday" (the last day before Lent), at which time they would dress in costumes and visit from home to home.

combined with the multi-ethnic membership of the church—largely Irish who maintained different cultural values—to make their continuance more difficult.

An unusual aspect of immigrant life was the involvement of numerous Italian men in various Masonic lodges throughout the state.[72] The Roman Catholic church refuses its members participation in the Freemasons. Italians of Carbon, Salt Lake, and Weber counties, however, found the Order of Freemasons a means of social mobility and aid, especially during the 1930s. While there is a paucity of manuscript source material concerning this area, various oral narratives help in understanding this development.

> PN Were there any social benefits to be reaped from being a Mason, or economic benefits?
>
> FP Oh, economic, yes, as far as work goes. And money, yes.
>
> PN How was this?
>
> EP Well, they were helped by their fellow Masons. They were certainly given jobs. They had preference over those who did not belong to the Masons. And socially they had their social activities. . . .[73]

Traditional North-South tensions among Italians were continued in Carbon County. Separate Italian lodges were organized at Castle Gate: Stella D'America (1898), whose fifty-seven founding members were from the North, and Principe Di Napoli (1902), whose members came from the South. In 1903, during the wake of the strike, the following account appeared in the *Salt Lake Herald*:

> There is no better citizen than the Italians of the north, nor can there be any more undesirable citizen than the southern Italian of the ignorant class. Unfortunately the men who have created the trouble in the coal camps of Utah are mostly of this latter class. . . .[74]

While the above assertion perpetuated North-South distinctions, the

---

[72] Sources of documentation for this are the *Proceedings Grand Lodge, Free and Accepted Masons of Utah*. These are the yearly reports and date from 1872 to 1972.

[73] Pellegrino interview.

[74] *Salt Lake Herald,* November 25, 1903.

reporter was mistaken in his assumption, since the Italian strikers were predominantly from the North.[75]

Newspaper articles not only mentioned nationality in reporting crimes but also revealed regional distinctions, for example, "Fred Macino, a Southern Italian, wanted for murdering a countryman at Sunnyside." [76] In 1912 the *Eastern Utah Advocate* reported a stabbing incident, maintaining that "The incident seemed to stem from the hatreds of the North and South in the 'old' country." [77]

Old World antagonisms culminated in what Carbon County residents referred to as Black Hand activity. The Black Hand, associated with southern Italians, was characterized by threats and extortion directed against prominent northern Italian bankers, lawyers, and businessmen. The full extent of such activity is difficult to assess because of a lack of source materials. One description maintained that it was highly organized, extracting money from people by force. Threats were often made graphically in the form of a black hand attached to one's door or window. The late Judge Henry Ruggeri of Price stated that he received such threats, especially against his family when he served as Carbon County attorney in the early twenties.[78] Another respondent said:

> I will tell you years ago they had what they call 'Black Hands'. . . . But they no was the Black Hands. They was older single men you know. They know that you had a few dollars so they write you a letter for $1000 or $500 and you had to give it to them. Well, they wait for you some place. Oh, they kill four or five . . . in the 1920s.[79]

Similar Black Hand activity was reported in other areas of the state, but almost all was confined to Carbon County. Time has reconciled the factions; present-day Italian life in Utah, while still marked with some North-South strain, is basically characterized by harmony and understanding between the Italian people, in the first as well as the second and third generations.

[75] Investigation of the lodge rolls for Stella D'America and Fratellanza Minatori, Sunnyside, compared with reports of arrests and other various accounts prove that most of the strikers were from the North. Also, in an interview with Stanley V. Litizzette, of Helper, Utah, Mr. Litizzette stated that from his study of the Castle Gate area, the first wave of Italians were predominantly from the North.

[76] *Eastern Utah Advocate,* July 29, 1910.

[77] *Eastern Utah Advocate,* September 5, 1912.

[78] Interview with Henry Ruggeri, Price, Utah, December 18, 1971.

[79] Barber interview.

Italian fraternal and mutual aid societies were an important development throughout the state.[80] In Carbon County there were: Stella D'America, Castle Gate (1898), Principe Di Napoli, Castle Gate (1902), Fratellanza Minatori, Sunnyside (1902), Societa' Cristoforo Colombo, Castle Gate (ca. early 1910s), and the Italian-Americanization Club (1919); in Salt Lake County: Societa' Cristoforo Colombo, Salt Lake City (1897), Societa' Di Beneficenza, Bingham Canyon and Mercur (ca. 1907), Club Dante Allighieri, Salt Lake City (1908), Figli D'Italia, Salt Lake City (1915), and the Italian-American Civic League, Salt Lake City (1934); and in Weber County: Societa' Cristoforo Colombo, Ogden (date unknown). These early organizations began as a means of mutual aid among single miners and laborers, as well as in response to the nativism that had developed in the state.

Organizational functions eventually helped in bettering relationships both within the Italian community and between the Italian and non-Italian peoples. Mergers took place between societies (bringing northerners and southerners together); parades and celebrations reflected mutual interests between Italians and non-Italians; and Italian participations and contributions in civic affairs, especially through the Italian-American Civic League, provided ways through which Italian group interests were expressed to the rest of the community. These interests were often common aspirations of the public as a whole: providing for orphans at Christmas.

Early Italian life in Utah was able to maintain a distinct continuity with the past. This *Italianita'* ("Italianness") was wedded to the Italian language. A sporadic Italian press existed in Utah. In 1908–9 *Il Minatore,* published by Mose Paggi in Salt Lake City, was a labor-oriented newspaper that reported news of mining camps in Utah and the entire Intermountain region. *La Gazzetta Italiana* was published in Salt Lake City by G. Milano of the Italian Publishing Company, from approximately 1911 to 1917. In 1926 *La Scintilla,* printed by Alfonso Russo and Milano, appeared but by 1929 had merged with *America* to form *Il Corriere D'America.* It was published in Salt Lake City by Frank Niccoli and managed by Alfonso Russo.[81] The paper reported local news within the Italian community in addition to topics of national interest.

[80] A full discussion of Italian mutual aid organizations in Utah by this writer is found in "Italian Fraternal Organizations in Utah, 1897–1934," *Utah Historical Quarterly* 43 (1975): 172–87. A briefer account appears in Notarianni, "The Italian Immigrant in Utah," 54–77.

[81] *Il Minatore* and *Il Corriere D'America* (in part) are available on micro-

Utah's Italian population was not totally isolated from the Italian-language press that existed in other areas of the United States. Newspapers from the West, *L'Italia* (San Francisco), and East, *La Follia di New York* and *Il Progresso Italo-Americano,* were subscribed to by numerous Italian families.[82] However, the Italian press in Utah was ephemeral. This, combined with the multiethnic character of the Catholic church and the lack of Italian language schools (such as the Greek schools) aid in explaining why second, third, and fourth generation Italians have not preserved the language.

The Italian immigrants, upon their arrival, kept aspects of life with which they were most familiar. Language, customs, basic religious beliefs, family life, and food were important. Numerous reports reveal how customs such as *boccie* (played on courts in Helper, Bingham, and Salt Lake); the art of wine-making [83] and sausage-making; and nightly promenades by husband, wife, and family, as well as frequent visits to homes of friends and relatives characterized early Italian life. The Italian community also had midwives and folk cures (a panacea for gastric ailments among infants was chamomile tea).

Much of Italian culture, brought by the early arrivals, has now disappeared. The smallness of the Italian community within Utah is a key factor in its failure to preserve a distinctive ethnic character. Nevertheless, in assessing the history of the Italians in Utah, *Italianita'* has added and given significance to the children and descendants of Italian immigrants in Utah. This is embodied in the immigrant experience itself and becomes germane to our lives with the understanding that the present in which we find ourselves is a product of the past encountered by our immigrant forebears, a past that has produced a future founded on the interaction between the Italian character and a country replete with opportunities.

film at the Marriott Library, University of Utah. Mention of *La Gazzetta Italiana* was made in the *Report of the State Bureau of Immigration, Labor and Statistics,* for the years 1911–1916.

[82] In one case, it was discovered that the Italians of Wattis and Kenilworth, Utah, were very much aware of Riccardo Cordiferro, an outspoken critic of American society and an ardent anticleric. Several published letters, by Achille Monteforte of Utah, were found in the Papers of Alessandro Sisca, pseud. Riccardo Cordiferro, located at the Immigrant Archives, University of Minnesota.

[83] An article appeared in the *Bingham News,* October 31, 1925: "Italians in Bingham have been making wine for their personal use and now residing officers, headed by County sheriff, have arrived in camp with search warrants to clean up the Bingham District of all wine in the possession of these people. The Italians are reported to be the best workers in the mine camp and Bingham is afraid this wine confiscation will drive them on to Calif. . . ."

10 JAPANESE LIFE IN UTAH

BY HELEN Z. PAPANIKOLAS AND ALICE KASAI

The mists rise over
The still pools at Asuka.
Memory does not
Pass away so easily.
—Akahito

For centuries the Japanese were content to live isolated in their wooded land of crags, mists, and ample waters, but the outside world would not allow it. In the early 1600s, fearing the encroaching activities of foreign sea merchants in and about the divine islands, Japan severed commerce with the West and destroyed all seagoing junks to prevent her subjects from traveling abroad. Almost two hundred fifty years later, in 1868, as Japan emerged out of feudalism, Emperor Meiji's government lifted the restriction to allow about fifty contract laborers to take passage for Hawaii.

This shattering of Japan's insularity was the result of Commodore Matthew C. Perry's first incursion, in 1853, into the Bay of Yedo (Tokyo) with four conspicuously armed steamships. In 1859 diplomatic relations began between the United States and Japan; the following year Japanese envoys were sent to Washington.

Source materials used in this essay for the historical and cultural background of *Issei* (first-generation Japanese) and *Nisei* (second-generation Japanese) are: *Orientals and Their Cultural Adjustment,* Social Science Source Documents, no. 4, Fisk University (Nashville, Tenn., 1946); Edwin O. Reischauer and John K. Fairbank, *East Asia: The Great Tradition* (Boston, 1958); Ruth Benedict, *The Chrysanthemum and the Sword: Patterns in Japanese Culture* (Boston, 1946); Bill Hosokawa, *Nisei: The Quiet Americans* (New York, 1969); Hisa Aoki, "Functional Analysis of Mono-Racial In-Groups: Nisei Congeniality Primary Groups on the University of Utah Campus" (M.A. thesis, University of Utah, 1950); Steven Kiyoshi Abe, "Nisei Personality Characteristics as Measured by the Edwards Personal Preference Schedule and Minnesota Multiphasic Personality Inventory" (M.A. thesis, University of Utah, 1958); Isao Horinouchi, "Educational Values and Preadaptation in the Acculturation of Japanese Americans," Sacramento Anthropological Society, paper 7, (Sacramento, Calif., 1967); Alice Kasai, "History of the Japanese in Utah," typescript, Asian Studies Center, University of Utah; Leonard J. Arrington, *The Price of Prejudice* (Logan, Utah, 1962); Elmer R. Smith, "The 'Japanese' in Utah," *Utah Humanities Review* 2(1948).

It was not until the liberalization of Japanese emigration laws in 1885, however, that Japanese were allowed to emigrate to other countries including the United States, where they were explicitly denied any hope for citizenship. A decade earlier the Meiji Restoration had cut off pensions to the disbanded *samurai,* the exalted warrior caste, leaving large numbers of men without livelihood. Soon afterwards the Chinese Exclusion Act of 1882 suddenly curtailed the prime source of labor for road and railroad building in the United States. American industrialists took advantage of unrest and unemployment in Japan to insure "cheap" labor for their expansion plans. This accounts for the drastic change in Chinese and Japanese populations in the United States within a twenty-year period: in 1890 there were 107,488 Chinese in the country and 2,039 Japanese; in 1910, 71,531 Chinese and 72,157 Japanese. Fifty-five thousand of the 1910 immigrants had settled in California where long-standing racial hatred against the Chinese was extended to the Japanese and set the pattern for the whole United States.

Since 1885, when the first heavy flow of Japanese migrated to Hawaii, later immigrants had often stopped there before continuing on to the ports of Seattle and San Francisco. From these cities paths fanned out to other western states. One of these immigrants, Joe Toraji Koseki, left his father's mulberry bushes and silk worms in Fukushima and with an old family spear and *samurai* sword traveled to Yokohama to board ship for Hawaii. In Yokohama he saw for the first time the ocean—and a "blue-eyed Caucasian . . . first time I had ever seen a Caucasian. Isn't that funny? . . . eyes are so big, you know . . . so big that they were way out. . . ." [1]

In Honolulu, Hawaii, he joined his brother who was working on a sugar and pineapple plantation. Many of the plantations were owned by white men from the United States and Koseki became accustomed to big-eyed Caucasians. He saw, also for the first time, electricity, telephones, streetcars, and larger steamships than the one that had brought him from Japan. Other Japanese barely landed in Hawaii before they took one of the big steamships for California, but Joe Koseki was to work in a store, volunteer for the United States Army during World War I, cross the ocean to Los Angeles where he did housework, go to San Francisco and back to Los Angeles fleeing the cold weather (he was used to "straw-hat weather"), travel to Chicago and earn a degree in physical therapy from a college of chiropractry, return to Hawaii and leave during

[1] Tape-recorded interview with Joe Toraji Koseki, American West Center, University of Utah.

the bad times of the Great Depression for Los Angeles where he became a deputy county registrar, be driven to the Turlock, California, assembly center after Pearl Harbor and assigned first to Tule Lake, California, then to the Gila River, Arizona, relocation camps, and find his way to Utah after World War II.

Joe Koseki's travels were more varied than those of most Japanese immigrants; his American education and occupations were also atypical. Yet Japanese did not fit into the mold of the new immigrants who arrived in the country at the turn of the century.

Unlike the Balkan and Mediterranean immigrants who were almost totally from the poorly educated classes, Japanese aliens included artisans, merchants, students, professionals, and bankers. (The first to come were political refugees who arrived in 1869 and formed the Wakamatsu Silk and Tea Farm Colony in El Dorado County, California.) No matter what classes they came from, the *samurai* ideals governed their lives.

Japan's feudal society had been abolished for several decades and *samurai* were no longer allowed to wear their two swords, the reverent symbols of their caste. The code of feudalism, though, continued: courage and loyalty to one's people, esteem for stylized politeness, the courteous treatment of inferiors, and exalted respect for elders. Children were taught through the *bushido* code that they must do nothing that would cause others to laugh at them or bring disgrace upon their families—identical to the principle of *filotimo* that Greek immigrants cherished. The Japanese carried the hiding of feelings even further, bringing Occidentals to call their controlled expressions "inscrutable" and "mysterious."

Like the Balkan and Mediterranean immigrants, the Japanese intended to return to their fatherlands with money enough to buy land and other property that would raise their status and free them from grasping moneylenders. For many years those destined for the railroads of the American West came from the poorest section of Japan, four southwest prefectures around Hiroshima. Japanese who emigrated from Hawaii were even more impecunious and uneducated. Had it not been for Japanese labor agents who sent ships to bring them to America, a great number of Japanese could not have left their country.

Whatever their background, almost all Japanese began their life in America by working in fields or on railroad section gangs. Until they formed Japanese Associations to protect and aid them, they worked as many hours as they were told, for as little as fifty cents a day, slept in crowded bunkhouses with poor sanitation, and asked only that they be given their native food: rice, fish, Japanese vegetables sprinkled with soy sauce, and tea. Before and after the Gentlemen's Agreement of 1907—President Theodore Roosevelt's diplomatic maneuver that restricted Japanese laborers from coming into the country—educated Japanese were employed as migrant workers in Pacific Coast fields and orchards.

In Utah, Japanese had been working on railroad gangs since the turn of the century. The first Japanese seen by Utahns, however, had been in 1872. The *Deseret News* of February 7 of that year described a visit of approximately fifty members of Ambassador Extraordinary Iwakura's party. The visitors were forced to remain a week because of a heavy snowstorm. Territorial Gov. George L. Woods and Mayor Daniel H. Wells headed a public reception for them at City Hall. Members of the state legislature's judiciary as well as Lt. Col. Henry A. Morrow of Camp Douglas arranged a formal welcome for them.

Ten years after these impressive visitors, the first immigrant Japanese came to Utah. Their arrival began a history called *Sanchubu-to Nihonjin* ("Intermountain Japanese People"), published on October 30, 1925, by the Japanese-language newspaper *Rocky Mountain Times*. How these first Japanese left Japan while the emigration prohibition was in force is not known. They were women, brought as prostitutes for Chinese and Caucasian railroad workers. The women had lived respectable lives elsewhere in the United States; but tragedies, often the death of husbands, forced them into prostitution to support themselves and, for some, their children. The newspaper conjectured that the women could also have been shanghied by brothel owners or their agents. They were contemptuously ostracized.

Increasing numbers of Japanese came into the state during the 1880s to fill jobs on railroad gangs that Chinese had abandoned when riots in Rock Springs and Evanston, Wyoming, and in Carbon County, Utah, mines sent them fleeing to California. Yozo Hashimoto was the earliest Japanese labor agent to supply workers for Intermountain West industries. One of his laborers was a nephew, born in Wakayama Prefecture in 1875, the son of a poor fisherman; he would have had little future in his native country where the eldest son inherited whatever property the father had.[2]

---

[2] Tricia Corbett, "The Ambidextrous Irishman," *Utah Medical Bulletin*, January 1973, pp. 3–6; interviews with Dr. Edward I. Hashimoto, April 12 and 16, 1975; and typescript by Dr. Hashimoto were used for biographical details of Edward Daigoro Hashimoto's life.

As soon as he arrived in the United States in 1890 fifteen-year-old Edward Daigoro was sent by his Uncle Yozo to work as a cook on the Great Northern Railroad in Montana. That his nephew knew nothing about cooking had not bothered Yozo. Barely had Daigoro begun learning, however, when vigilantes, riding under the Yellow Peril banner, drove out all Asians and killed many of them. Hiding and running by turns, the men scattered westward.

Edward Daigoro hid in the fields by day and walked by night until he reached Salt Lake City where his uncle had opened a labor agency. In 1902 Daigoro established the E. D. Hashimoto Company at 163 West South Temple in growing Japanese Town. By then he was known as "Daigoro Sama" ("Great Man") to the Japanese and "E. D." to American business associates. The Hashimoto Company furnished section gang workers to the Western Pacific and to the Denver and Rio Grande and supplied them with imported Japanese foods, rice, and clothing. Payrolls were sent out through Daigoro; money orders mailed to the men's families in Japan; credit extended; and numerous legal and governmental forms and applications, difficult for immigrants with limited education to understand, taken care of. Japanese working on labor gangs looked forward to their rare visits to Japanese Town and Hashimoto's store. By 1904 Daigoro was called Salt Lake City's Mikado by Americans.

To facilitate placing laborers on railroad gangs, a second Hashimoto agency was opened in Los Angeles just before the San Francisco earthquake of 1906. There Daigoro became friends with A. P. Giannini who had risen from a push-cart peddler of fish to become founder of the Bank of Italy, later known as the Bank of America. Daigoro Hashimoto's name became well known among American financiers and Japanese immigrants alike. The Japanese were anxious to leave California and Daigoro had no difficulty manning railroad section gangs.

Prejudice against the Japanese increased as more of them arrived in California and worked in fields for Americans until they had saved enough to buy or lease their own land. This thriftiness was called "taking up California's lands" by the Asiatic Exclusion League and other anti-Japanese organizations. Newspapers inflamed Americans with statements later generally refuted by the report of California's Special State Investigation of 1909. Besides being called "unhygienic," "shack dwellers," not "good" (passive) laborers like the Chinese, under the "complete control of the Mikado," "clannish," "unassimilable," lacking in respect for women by keeping brothels (as if prostitution had been unknown in the country until the Japanese entered it), they were described as incapable of becoming good citizens, when citizenship, the right to which all European immigrants had from the beginnings of the nation, was denied them.

Solemn discussions were held on the extent to which Japanese physical characteristics would be transmitted to interracial offspring, with blatant disregard for the obvious Japanese preference for their own people that excluded even Chinese and other Asians. Yellow Peril was the consuming concern of the day.

With impressive statistics as to yield, acreage, and quality and kinds of crops, the Special State Investigation of 1909 proved conclusively that Japanese were exceptional farmers who could have taught Americans better farming methods. Yet in Sidney Gulick's *The American Japanese Problem,* of 1914, a picture has the caption: "This illustrates the stooping work for which Japanese farmers are peculiarly adapted. White men find berry culture exceedingly irksome." [3]

Japanese have traditionally held farming in esteem because "it feeds the nation"; just below the *samurai* class were the farmers. Their special aptitude for farming led to California's Anti-Alien Land Law of 1914 that prohibited their buying land and restricted their leasing it to three years. Many Japanese became discouraged— it took five years, for example, to establish a grape vineyard—and they left looking for other work.

Setsuzo Uchida, a graduate in economics from the University of Todau in Japan, left his wife Take Yamamoto, who was a rarity, a woman college graduate of Aoyamagakuin College, a Methodist mission school, came to California, and found work picking oranges. His wife arrived in 1914 and with the money Uchida had saved, they rented a farm and raised peas and tomatoes. Prevented from buying the farm, the Uchidas tried fishing to supply canneries in San Pedro and gold mining in Mexico after hearing a Japanese general in the Mexican army speak of the opportunities there. Now eighty-six years old, Mrs. Uchida remembers the young farm laborers:

> Yes, some of our workers were Japanese friends, most of
> them students at the time. As students they came, some

[3] See Sidney L. Gulick, *The American Japanese Problem* (New York, 1914) for California's anti-Japanese response.

of them had a curiosity to do that. But 100 percent farming instinct, farming minds.[4]

This "farming instinct" that had immediately become apparent to Californians and had led to many farm owners showing them preference when hiring laborers brought another segment of Japanese to Utah. The 1909 Report of the Bureau of Immigration, Labor, and Statistics counted 1,025 Japanese farm workers. The first had come to Utah in 1898 to work on section gangs and had turned to farming at the earliest opportunity. Besides West Coast Japanese looking for land to farm, there were section workers losing their jobs to a deluge of Balkan and Mediterranean immigrants. To help "his boys," Daigoro Hashimoto established the Clearfield Canning Company and began raising sugar beets for a company later known as the Utah-Idaho Sugar Beet Company. The attraction of farming for the immigrants resulted in Daigoro's opening a branch sugar-beet center in Delta, Utah.

Japanese farmers settled primarily in Box Elder, Weber, and Salt Lake counties. They were to produce the nationally acclaimed Sweetheart and Jumbo celeries and the Twentieth Century strawberries. The patent on these everbearing strawberries was held by Taijiro Kasuga and made him a millionaire.

Yet for the first fifteen years of the 1900s, the section gangs were the main source of employment for the Japanese; their foremen remained far longer with the railroads, some of them until Pearl Harbor. Japanese section workers were less welcome than farmers. Section workers were almost always unmarried, and single immigrants brought implications of wantonness to Americans; farmers were usually married, giving a sense of permanence and solidity to their life. The Railroad Notes column in the Ogden *Standard* of July 26, 1900, quoted Superintendent Young as saying, "A number of Japanese are being employed because contractors can't depend on white men although they prefer to employ white labor."

The dependability of the Japanese to withstand the lonely, desolate railroad maintenance work was soon acknowledged by roadmasters, and Daigoro chose from among them men to become foremen over Japanese and other immigrant crews. One of them, Jinzaburo Matsumiya, worked as a section foreman in Jericho near Tintic where two rails converging in the distance, a section house,

---

[4] Tape-recorded interview with Mrs. Take Uchida, American West Center.

and a water tank set in the sagebrush were all that could be seen. He remained there until 1917 when he returned to Japan, married, and brought his bride to Jericho. The only people the young bride saw were the railroad men who stopped the freights at the water tank, an occasional Indian, and Mexicans who made up the section crew. During shearing time, Mrs. Matsumiya, now in her late seventies, remembers sheep driven near the section house, and tents and a big shed, for shearing, set up. "It was just a little town." She recalls, too, the desert in bloom:

> . . . and cactus blooming so pretty . . . all the little flowers and the cactus are blooming . . . all over blooming . . . I thought I'm going to pick . . . I saw this big dog by the kitchen, a pretty one, too. I said, "Where did that dog came from?" And Granpa said, "That's a coyote." [5]

In the desert she cared for her children, raised three hundred chickens at a time, ripped the seams of her husband's clothes to make patterns for new ones that she sewed on a treadle machine, and was one of the shearers herself when the sheep were driven to the water tank. The Matsumiyas ordered their Japanese food from Los Angeles because the freight was cheaper than that from Salt Lake City.

While Jinzaburo Matsumiya lived his lonely life in the 1900s, a Japanese Town was growing in Salt Lake City. Several stores besides Daigoro Hashimoto's supplied the needs of Utah's 417 Japanese, and boardinghouses were opened as more immigrants came to work on labor gangs. There were already a few graves in the Japanese section of the city cemetery, including two of infants, buried in 1905, Estella and Oroville Arima. A passerby wonders today if they were children of mixed marriages or simply given Anglo names. They could be the first *Nisei* born in Utah.

The growth of Japanese population was small but steady. In 1910, 2,110 were counted in the census; in 1920, 2,936. With the increase came more stores and services. The first Japanese Noodle House opened on West Temple in 1907. In the same year the *Rocky Mountain Times* began a tri-weekly publication and was followed by the *Utah Nippo* seven years later, which is still being published. In 1912 a Buddhist church was established. Oriental goods stores, restaurants, noodle houses, barber shops, hotels, laundries, dry cleaning stores, fish markets, a *tofu* bean-cake factory, and produce stands filled the needs of the industrious community.

[5] Tape-recorded interview with Mrs. Chiyo Matsumiya, American West Center.

The newer arrivals continued to be sent by Daigoro Hashimoto to section gangs and to the Utah Fuel Company mines in Sunnyside and other Carbon County coal camps. As Greeks and Italians came by the thousands in the 1900s, learned section-gang work from the Japanese and replaced many of them, more Japanese began going into the mines. Daigoro had contracted with Daniel C. Jackling in 1910 to supply Japanese and Korean laborers for the Bingham-Garfield Railroad construction. The Japanese remained to work in the Bingham copper mines as "bank men," the most hazardous of all labor. Lowering themselves over the banks of the tiers by ropes tied around their waists, the Japanese swung picks into the ore, hundreds of feet above the open-pit chasm. The Japanese were paid more than the Greeks who lived in Greek Town, next to their Jap Town, and with whom they spent paydays gambling. The higher wages of the Japanese was a grievance of the Greeks in the Bingham strike of 1912—a minor one compared to their frustration in trying to force Utah Copper to discharge their own labor agent, Leonidas Skliris. Yet when the Greeks joined the strike called by the Western Federation of Labor, the Japanese followed.

> The Greeks, it is said, did not consult them before striking but when the walkout occurred the Orientals took it for granted that work was suspended. Among them is Coney Shibota, said to be the champion wrestler of the camp. He is a powerfully constructed man for his race and has downed many stalwart Greeks. The other Japanese have tacitly appointed him leader.[6]

The failure of the Bingham strike led to the blacklisting of many union men, including Greeks, the largest segment of miners. Mexicans were recruited to take their places—many of them had come in as strikebreakers—and Daigoro Hashimoto became their labor agent. President Venustiano Carranza met Daigoro and made him honorary Mexican consul in Utah. He was only one of many noted people of Daigoro's acquaintance that included President William Howard Taft. In 1908 he had married Lois Hide Niiya, a graduate of Kobe College in Japan and the University of California, and built a home for her at 315 South Twelfth East. Many well-known businessmen and politicians of the day were entertained there, and often Gov. William Spry of Utah. Into this center of social life a son, Edward Ichiro ("First Born") was born February

---

[6] Helen Zeese Papanikolas, "Life and Labor among the Immigrants of Bingham Canyon," *Utah Historical Quarterly* 33 (1965): 295.

25, 1911. He remembers as a boy taking apart gold watches brought as gifts by these important visitors and being summarily punished.

Daigoro's labor agency assured Utah industry of Asians and Mexicans to meet every need and emergency. All mill, smelter, and mining towns had Japanese boardinghouses that camp bosses ran themselves and later, when the Picture Bride Provision of 1910 allowed women to emigrate, with their wives. Daishiro and Kyoichi Sako housed their men in Little Tokyos located in Magna and Garfield.

The Latuda, Carbon County, Japanese camp was managed by Eiji Iwamoto and his wife. They were second cousins whose marriage would have been unthinkable in Japan: Suga, the wife, came from a *samurai* family; Eiji from farmers. Their mothers were first cousins and arranged the marriage between Eiji, an only son, and Suga to keep the family closely bound. Knowing the marriage would bring derision on their children if they stayed in Japan, they sent them to America.[7]

In Latuda the *samurai* daughter awoke at four-thirty in the morning to light a coal stove, prepare breakfast for the boarders, and fill their lunch buckets. Between six and seven the boarders dressed, ate breakfast, and left at seven-thirty with carbide lamps on their heads and lunch buckets in their hands. The eight o'clock mine whistle blew to signal the start of the day shift and again at four o'clock when the men came out of the mine and the afternoon shift began. The Japanese miners returned home, bathed in a large wooden tub in the Iwamoto's back yard bathhouse (Caucasian miners used the company showers) and ate dinner between five and six. They went to bed early every night except Saturdays when they gambled until dawn. They were enthusiastic card players, and in their bachelor lives Saturday card games were the main diversion.

Whether the Japanese lived in mining towns under "camp bosses" like Eiji Iwamoto or in mill, smelter, or farming areas, neither they nor their children were subjected to continual harassment as were other new immigrant groups. They were derisively called "Japs," but the explosive antagonisms that the Greeks, Italians, and Slavs experienced were seldom directed toward them. There were many reasons for this: the Japanese did not attempt to enter into American social life; they endured slights without retaliation, because of their cultural training in patient acceptance and

[7] Alice Kasai, "My Family," typescript in authors' possession.

because they most often thought of themselves as temporary workers in America; of all people they were the most law abiding; and their children, trained under the *bushido* code, were well behaved, often exceptional students because their home training insisted on diligent studying.

In comparing the Japanese with Greeks in Utah, the former led hard-working, predictable lives. The Greeks were leaders in the Bingham Strike of 1912 and the Carbon County Strike of 1922; the Japanese were followers. Greeks demanded their rights and flaunted public attitudes (hiring American girls in their restaurants and candy stores and being seen with them at movies or in their new cars). Japanese kept within the family and church circles. The Ku Klux Klan campaign of 1924 hardly touched them in Utah, but a new affront came to them that same year. The Japanese Exclusion Act prohibited any Japanese from entering the country and relegated them to the position of the Chinese forty-two years earlier.[8] California's anti-Japanese lobbying had at last been successful. Deprived of citizenship, they were doubly stigmatized as inferior people.

The Japanese coped with the Act as Balkan and Mediterranean immigrants with low quotas did; many of them swam ashore from boats anchored in harbors or were smuggled across the Canadian and Mexican borders by compatriots. The children of the immigrants, the *Nisei,* were growing older and were becoming aware of this exclusion and restrictions that affected them directly: in larger Utah towns and in Salt Lake City, Asians were barred from the "better white" restaurants and had to sit in the balconies of theatres.

There were stirrings against the Exclusion Act and the earlier Cable Act of 1922 that deprived *Nisei* women who had married *Issei,* first generation Japanese, of their citizenship, but as yet the Japanese did not have effective spokesmen. However, an *Issei,* Henry Y. Kasai, was becoming increasingly active in working with public officials to abolish discrimination in restaurants and in public places, such as swimming pools, but gains were as yet small.

Henry Y. Kasai had come to America with his father and two uncles in 1902 at the age of twelve. His father had been a constable and silkworm farmer; his mother had remained in Japan with the younger children. In Mountain View, California, and in Idaho Falls, Idaho, he boarded with American families and learned their language and ways. He then began a fifty-year career in

[8] See Julia E. Johnsen, *Japanese Exclusion* (New York, 1925).

343

Top: *Edward "Daigoro" Hashimoto,
influential labor agent and merchant
in Salt Lake City in the early 1900s.*
Above left: *Sunnyside coal camp boss
Nakagi and his family.* Above right:
A leading Issei *of Utah, Henry Y. Kasai,
seated center, surrounded by his cousin,
uncle, father, and uncle.*

Left: *Japanese Church of Christ picnic at Lagoon, 1921.* Below: *Composing room of the* Utah Nippo *with publisher U. Terasawa at right, 1917.*

ight: Shiro Iida nded the Rocky untain Times *in alt Lake City in the early 1900s. is photograph is dated 1918.*

From the top: *The Salt Lake Nippon baseball team at Liberty Park in 1919. A funeral in the late twenties with the old Salt Lake Buddhist Church in the background. The first folk dancing yokyo (entertainment) given by the women's organization Fujinkai, 1925; musical instruments are samisens.*

Above: *The first obon dance in Salt Lake City, summer 1936, held on street.*

Left: *A Kabuki play, 1955, by* Sonenkai *members: Taka Kida, Jiuy Sakano, Lessie Yamamoto, Masasuke Tanaka, Yoshiko Hashimoto, Toshimasa Lioasaki, and Jimmy Kido. Procession marking the fiftieth anniversary of the Salt Lake Buddhist Church.*

Below: *Mrs. Izyo Sauki (Madame Ogyoku), well-known teacher of flower arranging.*

Right: *Grocery store owned by the Frank Endos of Oakland, California, was hastily disposed of when Japanese were evacuate from the West Coast after Pearl Harbor.*

Above: *The Topaz relocation camp in central Utah desert wit Marc Goto in foregrou*

Right: *Fred Wada, center, leased thousana of acres at Keetley, Wasatch County, and with other evacuees gr «victory food.»*

Above: *JACL bowling team from Salt Lake City: Pap Miya, Chas Sonoda, Wat Misaka, Dr. Jun Kurumada, and Ken Takeno. Mike Masaoka and his wife at the testimonial in his honor during the national convention of JACL in Washington, D.C., 1972.*

Above: *Dr. Edward I. Hashimoto, professor of anatomy at the University of Utah Medical School for forty years. Members of the Japanese Church of Christ in Salt Lake City in 1924.*

349

Utah with New York Life Insurance and became well known among businessmen.

The communication most *Issei* had with the American community was strictly in business: selling produce to wholesale markets and retailing it—their displays of fruit and vegetables were luxuriously artistic; providing laundry, dry-cleaning, and gardening services. Children translated back and forth between their parents and Caucasians. The perpetuation of the Japanese language to insure continued *Nisei* familiarity in communicating with and for their parents and being proficient in it when *Issei* and their families returned to Japan, as many believed they would, were the reasons for establishing Japanese schools wherever a sizeable community of immigrants lived. The first school had its inception in Salt Lake City in 1919.

The coldness and indifference outside the Japanese Towns were more than compensated by the richness of life within them. Social activities were concentrated around the churches. Although predominately Buddhist, the Japanese communities included a substantial number of immigrants who had been converted to Christianity in Japan. Following an initial period when Christian missionaries met martyrdom there, a variety of religions were accepted without discrimination. It is not unusual to find *Issei* who hold membership in two religions.

In 1918 a Japanese Church of Christ was established in Salt Lake City. A Church of Christ church was next established in Ogden and a Buddhist church in Honeyville. A Salt Lake Nichiren Buddhist church had its inception in 1954. Other religious organizations with a small membership are: Church of World Messianity, and Seicho-No-Ie Salt Lake Shinto Soai Kai ("Home of Infinite Life, Wisdom, and Abundance") with precepts of healing similar to Christian Science. A Mormon Japanese ward is called Dai-Ichi ("Number One") Branch. Besides these churches, every Christian faith counts Japanese as members. The social functions of each church are attended by nonmember Japanese.

The New Year was, and still is, the most celebrated event of the year. Houses were thoroughly cleaned and the last bath of the year was taken to wash off the "old year's dirt." For days in advance festive food was prepared to be eaten during the first week of the year. The golden *Tai* fish (red sea bream, the "King of Fish") or Japanese carp was baked whole with eyes wide open, fins and tail spread in a fan shape and the body arched as if it were alive and flipping over ocean waves (shredded white radishes). *Mochi* (sweet rice pounded into glutinous cakes and topped with tangerines) denoted abundance and was also a symbolic dish. All debts were paid, greeting cards exchanged, and *sake* (rice wine) drunk.

During July, the Obon, comparable to American Memorial Day, was commemorated by Buddhists with prayer services at the church and cemetery. Street dancing was held in the evening. Christmas early began to be celebrated, even by Buddhists, in the traditional American way. Summer picnics gathered Japanese from the entire state in nature's setting, the love of which they had brought from Japan. Children and adults ran races and played games. *Sushis* (rice cakes) and *nigiri* (rice balls) with chicken teriyaki was served, followed by ice cream, soft drinks, and melons. Wrestling contests were the popular attraction, for *sumo* was Japan's national sport. Young *Issei* played baseball and as the *Nisei* grew up it replaced wrestling.

Fund-raising programs for the Japanese-language schools were much anticipated events, with practising of songs, dances, and singing of poetry (*shigin*). Instruments used were the *samisen* (a three-stringed, banjo-like instrument with long neck), the *shakuachi* (bamboo flute), and the *okoto* (horizontal harp that is placed on the floor). In Salt Lake City and in Ogden, *kabuki* dramas were performed with wigs, stylized makeup, and elaborate costumes of the old feudal era. Japanese movies were regularly shown, and occasionally performers from Japan stopped on tour to entertain.

Until the Second World War, the *Issei,* ineligible for citizenship, observed the emperor's birthday and Japan's Foundation Day. On Girls' and Boys' Festival Days, family doll sets were used to teach girls the significance of tea ceremony and flower arrangement—"to promote good breeding"; boys were told to be courageous and to surmount obstacles as signified by a paper carp that was flown over each house that had a son. Reverence for education, obedience and respect for parents and elders, loyalty to one's family, friends, and country were all part of the children's training. "I think," Toraji Koseki said, "it comes from the *samurai* way of life, and children . . . obey . . . just comes natural."

Children's obedience to parents included their submission in marriage arrangements. Neither attraction nor personal feeling was taken into account. Each marriage had a *baishakunin,* a "go-between." The *baishakunin* decided who were the best mates for the children, counseled them, and remained as godparents to the family. This role terminated with the *Sansei* (third generation), but most of the *Nisei* followed the tradition. When the 1924 Exclusion Act prohibited brides coming from Japan, many *Issei* men waited around for the first *Nisei* girls to become of marriageable age, resulting in big age differences between the couples.

Until the depression years of the 1930s, the Japanese Towns expanded with more immigrants and *Nisei* children, but the economic decline cut off jobs first among nonwhites. During the decade, 1,059 Japanese left the state. Many moved to California and sought help from countrymen who had come from the same ken or prefecture in Japan. Others returned with their savings to Japan where the cost of living was lower.

There were two important legislative acts of these years, both passed in 1931, the result of lobbying by a young organization, the Japanese American Citizens League. The 1922 Cable Act was amended, regaining American citizenship for *Nisei* women who had married *Issei* men; and American citizenship was granted to 700 World War I veterans. In Utah, legislation in 1937 reduced license fees for *Issei* from twelve dollars to three, the same as for citizens. The gains had increased. Near the end of the decade, Mike Masaru Masaoka, a brilliant young Salt Lake City *Nisei* Mormon and instructor in the University of Utah speech department, overcame misgivings and involved himself in the JACL. He became the extremely effective spokesman that Japanese needed during and after World War II. He was encouraged and helped by a former teacher at the University of Utah, who had served a Latter-day Saints' mission to Japan in his youth, United States Sen. Elbert D. Thomas.

Japanese in the United States were stunned by the bombing of Pearl Harbor on December 7, 1941. The traumatic mass movement of the Japanese from the West Coast began.[9] Under the infamous Executive Order 9066, the army was empowered to oversee the "enemy alien problem." Houses, shops, and property of the deportees were sold for a fraction of the cost or abandoned. Decades, even generations, of hard work were swept away with the arrival of the United States soldiers.

In Utah, as elsewhere in the United States, reactions to the Japanese varied from threats to bewilderment. Japanese and people who had known and worked with them were uneasy at facing each other. Dr. Edward Ichiro ("First Born") Hashimoto, son of the

[9] See Hosokawa, *Nisei,* for the internment and relocation epoch and Mike Masura Masaoka's work during this period.

Mikado, entered his gross anatomy class at the University of Utah Medical School, where he was to teach for forty years, to a profound silence. "What are you fellows staring at?" he said. "I'm Irish. I was home in Dublin at the time!" With relief and delight, Dr. Hashimoto's students relaxed. Known for being able to draw human figures with both hands simultaneously, the doctor was called, from then on, the "Ambidextrous Irishman."

Dr. Hashimoto's father had died at age sixty-one, five years before Pearl Harbor. He had added significant accomplishments to his name: helped establish Tracy Bank and Trust Company; held a franchise from National Baldwin for the Asian distribution of radio earphones; drilled one of the first oil wells in Casper, Wyoming; organized the Red Feather Stages in 1926 (a subsidiary of the present Greyhound Bus Lines); was involved in gold and silver mines in Guerrero, Mexico; opened a mine near Salmon, Idaho; and was an organizer of the Mountain City Copper Mine in Nevada. Had he lived, his leadership and achievements would have had to be ignored under American policy for interning noted Japanese.

Ten relocation camps were hastily built to house a hundred ten thousand Japanese Americans. Neither German nor Italian nationals were subjected to this kind of treatment. The evacuation was under the direction of Gen. John L. De Witt, commander of the Western Defense Command. His derogatory pronouncement "A Jap's a Jap" and his curfew orders from 8:00 P.M. to 6:00 A.M. still rankle in the memory of Japanese Americans and their sympathizers.

The Japanese were given as little as six days to dispose of their property and be ready for evacuation. There was pandemonium, with certain areas interpreting army orders more strictly than others. Initially the evacuation was to be voluntary; the Japanese were to find inland locations to settle themselves. Men left their families and traveled to the Mountain States hoping for help from relatives and friends. Fearful of what could happen to their families in their absence, of the possibility of mob action as they drove on, of the signs in Idaho, Utah, and Colorado, "No Japs Wanted Here," they slept in their cars and ate cold food at the side of the road. The voluntary program was a failure; the inland Japanese were overwhelmed by public hostility, loss of jobs, and the internment of their leading members.

One "successful" voluntary evacuee, Frank Endo, who owned the Yamato Grocery Store in Oakland, California, came with a

353

brother-in-law to Salt Lake City to solicit help from his friends, the Ikuzo Tsuyukis, owners of the U. S. Cafe. There were many men like him in the city searching and not finding assistance. Frank Endo met Fred Wada, a former Utahn who was negotiating with Sheriff George A. Fisher of Keetley, Wasatch County, to lease 3,909 acres of sagebrush land. Endo asked to bring his family of twelve brothers and sisters, their families, including parents-in-law, to join the colony. Hurrying back to his family, he disposed of as much of his store goods as was possible. Caucasians rushed to buy it at half cost; some of it was taken back by wholesale houses at a loss to the Endos, but Japanese food had no market.

The Endos loaded all staples and nonperishables into a Union Pacific railroad car and sent it on to Keetley to help feed the Endo clan. The families drove their cars from Oakland to Utah. When the Frank Endos reached Sandy, they stopped at a cafe. A sign in the cafe window read "No Dogs, No Japs." Two of Frank Endo's brothers were already in the United States Army; two younger brothers, one of whom would die in the Korean War, sat in the crowded car. "I wonder," one of them said, "when I'm old enough to be drafted, what they would do if I walked in wearing my army uniform." [10]

Under Fred Wada's leadership, the families, part of a ninety-member colony, cleared the land of sagebrush, tilled the valley and mountainsides, cultivated the soil, and raised "victory food." They lived in a motel next to a building used as a meetinghouse and office. One night a bomb was thrown against the building and demolished it, but no one was inside at the time. The *Deseret News* used a half-page to denounce the bombing.

Joe Toraji Koseki, who had seen his first blue-eyed Caucasian in Yokohama, was on National Guard maneuvers in Hawaii when Pearl Harbor was bombed. An American Legionnaire, Commodore Perry Post, he was forced to resign from the National Guard and board an evacuation ship for California. There the evacuees were read the prohibition against their keeping arms, cameras, and radios. Koseki gave his ancient spear and *samurai* sword to a Pasadena high school principal whom he had heard collected Japanese arms. Other Japanese buried their *samurai* swords in their back yards hoping to return to dig them up.

The Matsumiyas were visited by the roadmaster in their Jericho section house and told to leave within three days. Railroads

[10] Interview with Mr. and Mrs. Frank Endo, March 13, 1975.

and mines had been classified war industries and closed to Japanese. After thirty-five years of section work, Matsumiya went from one farm to another in the Payson area looking for work. Years of uprooted life followed with Matsumiya thinning and hoeing beets, his wife sewing for Caucasians for as little as ten cents an hour, then moving to Salt Lake City where Mr. Matsumiya did janitor work for the Mayflower Restaurant, the kitchen of which was completely staffed with Japanese, and Mrs. Matsumiya altered suits for Hibbs Clothing store. Their daughters went to school and did housework for Caucasians; a son was in Alabama learning to "chicksex," a popular vocation for Japanese.

Mrs. Uchida, the Methodist college graduate, and her husband were living in Idaho Falls at the time of Pearl Harbor. Her husband was secretary of the Japanese Association there and she taught Japanese school. (Until World War II, many Japanese still expected to return to Japan and often took the ashes of their dead to be buried there.) On December 8 the Federal Bureau of Investigation sent the local sheriff to take them into custody. Orders were given to remove all important *Issei* to internment camps "to leave the Japanese leaderless." Uchida was sent to camps in North Dakota and Louisiana and his wife to Missoula, Montana, Seattle, Washington, and then to Seagoville, Texas, where she was placed in charge of Japanese women and children from California, Peru, and the Panama Canal Zone.

Another leader interned was Henry Kasai, the insurance agent who had begun the fight against discrimination in the twenties. He had married a *Nisei*, many years his junior, Alice Iwamoto, daughter of the Latuda mine camp boss. Kasai was in Teton, Idaho, the day of Pearl Harbor at a wedding celebration. He had effected a conciliation between the parents of the bride and groom who had objected to the marriage because it would unite farmers with *etas*, the lowest in the Confucian hierarchy. The *etas* were animal slaughterers and hide tanners; they were from northern Japan, often blue-eyed, from a Caucasian strain, believed to be Russian.

During the wedding feast, the sheriff of Rexburg, on orders from the FBI, came to the house and took Henry Kasai to jail. He was sent to Missoula and Livingston, Montana, and then to Albuquerque, New Mexico. His wife and children remained in Salt Lake City and lived by taking in boarders and withdrawing $150 a month from their savings account, the maximum allowed families of internees. His mother-in-law, daughter of the *samurai*, was shocked into illness and asked that her ashes be buried in Japan with her family's. Two months later she died.

Tomoko Watanuki Yano, daughter of a community leader, said:

> My father not only lost his job and seniority rights but the dignity and honor of a proud man. He was employed by the Tooele smelter as a camp boss. As a bilinguist, he also taught Japanese language classes. Since father was taken away so abruptly, mother was left without any means of support. She was ordered to leave her home . . . with no place to go. Within a week, my mother was destitute, homeless, scorned and shunned by her community friends—after living there for twenty years. No one would rent them a house, so they accepted the offer of another Japanese family to use their upstairs storage space. There, my mother, sister, brother and his family, and three elderly *Issei* men from camp lived from day to day in very confined quarters under most inconvenient conditions.
>
> When my younger brother was inducted into the service, my father was abruptly released after two years confinement. He came back a thoroughly dispirited and beaten person. . . . He had never been sick a day in his life, but in camp he contracted a lung disease and died in 1948 of cancer. Over the years, this injustice has rankled and festered my conscience every time I see my eighty-three-year-old mother and realize more fully what she had to endure.

The stories of the Endos, Kosekis, Matsumiyas, Uchidas, Watanukis, and Kasais can be echoed a hundred thousand times. Stranded, desolate, in panic, they needed the conscience of the nation to arise in their defense. Sporadic, weak defenses did come from a few individuals, but it was left to Mike Masaoka and the Japanese American Citizens League to fight a tidal wave of irrational, anti-Japanese hysteria. Feverishly working to help the Japanese evacuees, Masaoka was jailed in North Platte, Nebraska, and held incommunicado for two days. He was then allowed to make a telephone call but warned not to say he was in jail. "I'm stuck here in North Platte, Nebraska," he told a colleague. "I'm at the, ah, the Palace Hotel." A return call to the Palace Hotel revealed where Masaoka really was and a telephone appeal to Sen. Elbert D. Thomas effected his release. Masaoka boarded a train west only to be taken off at Cheyenne, Wyoming, when local police officers walked through and arrested him because he was an Asian. Again

Senator Thomas intervened and Masaoka continued west to the Japanese in their great crisis.[11]

Eight thousand evacuees were sent to the Central Utah War Relocation Center that came to be called Topaz after the nearby mountains. The cold, drafty barracks were built on nearly twenty thousand acres of arid land at a cost of five million dollars. Another five milion was spent yearly for upkeep. A young evacuee said of Topaz: "Topaz looked so big, so enormous to us. It made me feel like an ant. Every place we go we can not escape the dust . . . dust and more dust, dust everywhere. . . . I wonder who found this desert and why they put us in a place like this. . . ." [12]

The fine silt dust demoralized them all. Mine Okubo said on glimpsing Topaz, "the Jewel of the Desert" as it was sardonically called:

> . . . suddenly, the Central Utah Relocation Project was stretched out before us in a cloud of dust. It was a desolate scene. Hundreds of low black barracks covered with tarred paper were lined up row after row. A few telephone poles stood like sentinels and soldiers could be seen patrolling the grounds. The bus struggled through the soft alkaline dirt . . . when we finally battled our way into the safety of the building we looked as if we had fallen into a flour barrel.[13]

In nominating Topaz for the State Register of Historic Sites over thirty years later, LaVell Johnson, long-time resident and historian of Millard County, said, "We were afraid of the Japanese in the camp. I don't know why. It seems strange now that we were."

In the three years of its existence, only one incident of violence occurred at Topaz. An elderly man wandered toward the off-limits, outer barbed-wire fence in search of rocks and was shot by the sentry. The entire camp attended his funeral and a delegation angrily protested to camp officials. Several young men became enraged and were sent to the camp at Tule Lake, California, where security was tighter.

Three thousand students were enrolled in the Topaz school system and taught by both Japanese and American teachers. They were taken on field trips to hunt fossils, arrowheads, and topaz crystals. The *Topaz Times* was published by the evacuees; art classes

[11] Hosokawa, *Nisei*, p. 227.
[12] Maisie Conrat and Richard Conrat, *Executive Order 9066: The Internment of 110,000 Japanese Americans* (Los Angeles, 1972), p. 73.
[13] Hosokawa, *Nisei*, p. 344.

were held, using sagebrush and other desert materials to create art forms for their barren quarters. The people behind barbed wire made valiant efforts to make adjustment easier for their children, but it was a time of bitterness and loss. The following haiku was composed by Miyuki Aoyama while in the Heart Mountain, Wyoming, camp:

> Snow upon the rooftop,
> Snow upon the coal;
> Winter in Wyoming—
> Winter in my soul.[14]

Until 1946 the evacuees endured Topaz while Japanese elsewhere in the state had comparative freedom but suffered continued oppression. After the FBI unsuccessfully searched "enemy aliens" for everything from dynamite to invisible ink, they kept the Japanese under close watch. Veterans groups were vociferous in condemning *Issei* and *Nisei* alike. President Elmer G. Peterson of Utah State University refused admittance of *Nisei* students. The Utah Fish and Game Commission denied fishing licenses to the Japanese. State Sen. Ira A. Huggins sponsored a bill that became law allowing aliens to lease land only on a renewable, yearly contract. Union miners effectively stopped the hiring of evacuees at Bingham. Business licenses were denied throughout the state. In Orem a large group of white youths attacked five young *Nisei*, part of the labor force of Japanese brought in to harvest the fruit crop.[15]

Japanese rallied to help each other, and influential Utahns aided them in many ways. When the national headquarters of the Japanese American Citizens League and the Buddhist church were temporarily moved to Salt Lake City, Mayor Ab Jenkins waited at the state border to welcome caravans from San Francisco and escort them into the capital. Former Gov. Henry Blood, Gov. Herbert B. Maw, Sen. Elbert D. Thomas, and Claude T. Barnes, prominent attorney, gave assistance and quelled irrational demands, such as outcries to cut down the Japanese cherry trees on the State Capitol grounds.

The Japanese-American Relocation Aid Committee collected contributions and raised several thousand dollars for books and recreational equipment for the school children in Topaz. A *Nisei* Victory Committee was organized for the USO (United Services

[14] *Ibid.*, p. 337.

[15] Michael Ross Strode, "The *Salt Lake Tribune* Account of Utah's Discrimination Against the Japanese Americans, 1942–1944," typescript, Asian Studies Center, University of Utah.

Organization). The *Nisei* army volunteers from the ten relocation centers were all trained and processed at Fort Douglas, in Salt Lake City. With headquarters at the YWCA, one of the few places still open to Japanese, the Victory Committee sponsored socials, sent packages to soldiers, and made visits to Bushnell Hospital in Brigham City where *Nisei* solders were recuperating from injuries suffered in Italy and France. (The *Nisei* 442d Regimental Combat Team was the most highly decorated regiment during the war.) Eighteen names of war dead from Utah are engraved on the *Nisei* War Monument in the Salt Lake City Cemetery.

At war's end the Japanese dispersed throughout the United States. Little Tokyos and Japanese Towns were not rebuilt, and assimilation became swift. Many evacuees remained in Utah; the 1950 Census reported an increase of 1,183 Japanese in the state. Fred Wada, head of the Keetley farm colony, returned to Los Angeles and became a member of the Harbor Commission. The Frank Endos, also with the colony, remained in Salt Lake City and opened a dry-cleaning establishment. The Uchidas settled in Ogden; Joe Toraji Koseki made Salt Lake City his permanent residence and did not again see his *samurai* sword; and the Matsumiyas never returned to their section house in Jericho. Twelve years afterwards, Eiji Iwamoto, who had become blind in 1935 while working as camp boss, returned to Japan with his wife's ashes and stayed there to die.

After the war the JACL held its first convention since 1941 in Denver. At this 1946 meeting the members resolved to gain citizenship for the *Issei* and to ask indemnity for evacuation losses. Mike Masaoka was sent to lobby for these causes and, according to the *Readers' Digest,* became "Washington's Most Successful Lobbyist." The Evacuation Indemnity Claims Act passed in 1948 provided payment of one-tenth of the evacuees' property losses. The total loss was estimated at $400 million; $38 million was paid to 26,560 claimants.

A year earlier in Utah the alien land law was repealed; two years later, in 1949, *Issei* were granted hunting licenses. In 1951 the armed forces recognized Buddhism as a major religion and the following year the Walter-McCarran Immigration and Naturalization Act granted *Issei* citizenship. In 1963 Utah repealed its antimiscegenation law that had caused tragic problems with racially mixed marriages unrecognized in the state, the number greatly increased by soldiers returning with Asian brides. Two years later

Utah passed fair employment and public accommodation measures that included validation retroactively of racially mixed marriages. In 1968 new quotas for immigrants were fixed: 170,000 for the Eastern Hemisphere and 120,000 for the Western Hemisphere. In 1970 Title II of the Internal Security Act of 1950 was repealed, withdrawing federal authority for arbitrary prevention, detention, and concentration camp internment.

Two events of the forties presaged these changes in attitude toward the Japanese in Utah. Wat Misaka of Ogden became the first *Nisei* member of a University of Utah varsity basketball team. He was one of the "Cinderella Kids" from Utah who won the National Invitational Tournament in 1944—now a mechanical engineer and active civic worker. In 1947 George Shibata of Garland became the first *Nisei* appointed to West Point through the sponsorship of Sen. Elbert D. Thomas. He received his commission in the Air Force in 1951.

Utah *Nisei* are among the leaders in Japanese-American affairs. Mike Masaoka won the 1950 *Nisei* of the Biennium, JACL Award for distinguished leadership. Henry Y. Kasai was the JACL recipient in 1964, and ten years later Raymond S. Uno, Salt Lake City attorney, was similarly honored.

Although the population of Utahns with Japanese ancestry was estimated at only forty-seven hundred in 1970, a high percentage have advanced college degrees: doctors, dentists, lawyers, architects, educators, engineers, and social workers. When feudalism was abolished in Japan, not family status but personal ability and achievement judged a person. Education became a goal of first magnitude and parents and children led hard-working, Spartan lives to accomplish this aim. "I will be glad to eat only one meal a day to support you through medical school," an *Issei* told his son.[16]

A considerable number of Utah *Nisei* with graduate school degrees work for the disadvantaged. Architect Carl Inoway is director of Assist (non-profit community planning organization); Jimi Mitsunaga is founder and chairman of Legal Defenders; many others work in mental health and social work programs.

Nisei are also entering politics. Yukus Inouye of American Fork serves as Utah County commissioner, and other contestants have shown strength at the polls. The third generation *Sansei* with

[16] Horinouchi, "Educational Values and Preadaptation in the Acculturation of Japanese Americans," p. 41.

greater verbal skills and less passivity are expected to become increasingly active in politics.

Another outstanding contribution of the Japanese is in cultural and aesthetic values. Mrs. Izyo Kiyoshi Sauki, whose professional title is Madame Ogyoku, has given many years' dedication to the annual *Salt Lake Tribune* Flower Show. Her students participate in larger numbers each year with unusual exhibits that show through the art of flower arrangement the balanced relationship of man, earth, and heaven.

The Japanese community worked with Mrs. Otto Weisley of the Salt Lake Council of Women to fulfill her life's goal of an International Peace Garden in Jordan Park. The Japanese section was the first completed, at the farthest end of the garden. Not only the Japanese in Utah but those of the Intermountain area contributed to the project. Friends in Japan sent stone lanterns, a bronze statue of the Goddess of Peace, a tea house, and a gateway. Annually the Japanese-American gardeners, always in demand for their special talent, aid the city parks' employees by pruning, shaping, and weeding the Peace Garden.

Each year the public anticipates the Obon and Asian Festivals. The Buddhist church still observes its Memorial Day with a street celebration: music, lanterns, and Obon dancing with participants dressed in bright kimonos. The Japanese Church of Christ presents a program that includes exhibits, dancing, singing, food, and games.

The Judo Clubs in Salt Lake City and Ogden have trained many boys and girls in self defense and each November are hosts for the Intermountain Tournament.

Honors to the Japanese of Utah have also come from Japan whose people had once looked down on immigrants to this country. Through the office of the prime minister, recognitions have been bestowed on septuagenarian *Issei* for their contributions in improving relations between their mother mountry and their adopted land.

In 1965 Henry Y. Kasai was decorated with the Order of the Sacred Treasure Fifth Class for his work in cultivating understanding between Caucasians and Japanese-Americans in Utah. He also received, posthumously, the American Phi Delta Kappa "Man of the Year" award for distinguished work in international education.

In 1968 Mrs. Kuniko Terasawa, publisher of the *Utah Nippo*, also received the Order of the Sacred Treasure Fifth Class for her efforts through the press to help the Japanese people of Utah in many ways, including counseling in domestic problems.

In 1969 Mrs. Take Uchida was given the Order of the Sacred Treasure Sixth Class for her work in teaching English to *Issei* and Japanese to *Nisei* and for community leadership.

In 1968 Mike M. Masaoka received the highest honor that Japan bestows on a foreigner in a special ceremony held in Tokyo. Premier Eisaku Sato presented him with the Order of the Rising Sun Third Class.

In 1960 Japan and the United States celebrated the centennial year of the treaty that opened diplomatic relations between the two countries. Further significance was given the event in Utah by the silver anniversary of the Salt Lake Chapter of the Japanese American Citizens League with their only *Issei* president, Henry Y. Kasai, in attendance.

Today increasing intermarriage and assimilation are rapidly changing Japanese-American communities. The *Sansei* have freed themselves from many restrictions of the *samurai* code, particularly submissiveness to elders and full and rigid responsibility for their standing in life—sources of conflict for their *Nisei* parents. Their assimilation has been easier than that of their parents: they were not bound to truck farming and to stoop labor as their parents and grandparents were, and their parents had achieved middle-class status during the *Sansei's* growing years. Not many knew the debasement and bitterness of internment and other extreme forms of discrimination. Few attend Japanese schools and most do not speak the language of their grandparents. When marriages take place among *Sansei*, there is no thought given to classes: *samurai*, farming, merchant, or *eta*.

In 1966 Japanese Town was demolished and the Salt Palace convention center built in its place. The Buddhist and Japanese Christian churches on the block west of it are all that exist of the old Japanese area. They stand as proud reminders of a Japanese immigrant life that laid the foundation for the economic and cultural enrichment of succeeding generations and added a unique quality to Utah's history.

11

FALCONS IN FLIGHT: THE YUGOSLAVS

BY JOSEPH STIPANOVICH

Oh, rocky Lika,[2] your soil is poor and barren, but for every one of your stones you have a gray falcon.[3]

—Traditional

Serbs, Croats, and Slovenes began arriving in Utah in the last decade of the nineteenth century. The majority of them came to seek employment in the mines, smelters, and railroads of the state. They settled primarily in Bingham Canyon, in the Midvale-Murray area, and in the coal camps and towns of Carbon County. They were more often called Austrians than Slavs and lived in neighborhoods called Bohunk Towns. The exact number of Yugoslavs who came to Utah will probably never be determined, but various indicators point to the presence of at least four thousand of them, including all generations, at the time of the enactment of the restrictive immigration legislation of 1924. They were a small group in comparison with others, such as the Scandinavians who preceded them, but because of their concentration in laboring occupations in the smelting and mining industries, they formed a significant portion of the industrial working class in the state of Utah.[4]

The South Slavs came from Austria-Hungary, from the provinces of Croatia-Slavonia, Carniola, Dalmatia, Bosnia, and Herzegovina. They came for the most part from farming villages that were homogeneous units in culture, language, and religion. The

[1] The Yugoslavs, or South Slavs, are those ethnic, linguistic, and cultural groups known as the Slovenes, Croats, Serbs, Macedonians, and Bulgarians. Only the Slovenes, Croats, and Serbs from Croatia, however, are treated in this paper. The terms "Yugoslav" and "South Slav" refer only to these three groups, unless otherwise indicated.

[2] Lika is a region of Croatia, on the Adriatic Sea. Approximately 50 percent of the Yugoslav immigrants in Utah came from this region.

[3] "Gray falcon" is a poetic image connoting "hero."

[4] A detailed description of the causes and the techniques of immigration from South Slav lands to Utah is contained in Joseph Stipanovich, *The South Slavs in Utah: A Social History* (San Francisco, 1975), p. 119.

Slovenes and Croats were Roman Catholics; the Serbs were Serbian Orthodox, an autocephalous national church in Christian Orthodoxy. The Slovenes spoke a distinct language and used a Latin alphabet for writing with modifications for Slavic sounds; the Serbs and Croats spoke several major dialects. There is controversy as to whether the Serbs and Croats spoke separate languages, but despite the differences they were mutually intelligible. The Serbs, however, used the Cyrillic alphabet while the Croats used the same modified Latin alphabet as the Slovenes, with only a minor deviation.[5]

The South Slav villages were composed of single nationalities. Serb villages may have been located in proximity to Croat villages and vice versa, but it was extremely rare for them to be mixed. Contacts with outside areas were few and subsistence farming and cottage industry occupied most of the time of the villagers. Compulsory legislation for the education of children was enacted toward the end of the nineteenth century by the imperial government, but it was enforced unevenly. The work in the household and in the fields required the assistance of the children in the poorer areas, especially during planting and harvesting of crops.[6] As one Croatian woman explained:

> Yes, yes . . . we go to school maybe a couple of years. That's all we go. Maybe a couple of years. You see, my mother and nobody be home but me, I oldest one there. And then I didn't go to school. Have to work home, you see.[7]

Because of the day-to-day grind for survival, the sons and daughters of the poor farmers were required to sacrifice the long-term benefits of education in order to ease the economic burdens that laid heavily upon all of them. The frustration resulting from the cycle of poverty was the strong element in the decision to emigrate. The wealth of *Amerika* had become common knowledge and the

[5] The early development of the Slavonic languages is treated in Dmitri Obolensky, *The Byzantine Commonwealth: Eastern Europe, 500–1453* (New York, 1971), p. 445.

[6] For descriptions of life among the South Slav peasants in Austria-Hungary prior to World War I see Emily Greene Balch, *Our Slavic Fellow Citizens* (New York, 1910), p. 536; R.J. Kerner, ed., *Yugoslavia* (Berkeley, 1949), p. 558; C.A. Macartney, *The Habsburg Empire, 1790–1918* (New York, 1969), p. 886; and R.W. Seton-Watson, *The Southern Slav Question and the Hapsburg Monarchy* (1911; reprint ed., New York, 1969), p. 463.

[7] Interview with Tonka Bolic, August 14, 1972, Salt Lake City, Utah; American West Center Minorities Collection No. C-2, University of Utah, Salt Lake City.

subject of a thousand rumors in the inns and coffeehouses of the villages.[8]

The grim nature of South Slav peasant existence in the pre-emigration period is difficult to exaggerate or ignore; its impact can lead one to forget that very real as well as symbolic forces were at work in the emigration-immigration processes.

In the regions where Yugoslavs emigrated, agriculture was unable to provide adequate food, fodder, and fibers for the indigenous populations without periodic interruptions. When crops failed or were below average in yields, famines occurred or conditions were created that insured famine would come the following year. The problem was compounded by the continual rise in population, particularly in the nineteenth century. The people lacked the means of acquiring money that would have enabled them to buy the food they failed to produce. When opportunities for emigration to industrial areas appeared, they seemed a solution to the Malthusian dilemma that was shared by the majority of South Slav peasants in Austria-Hungary. With the memory of famine and its concomitant ills fresh in their minds, the original immigrants found the industrial environment much less forbidding than it appears in retrospect.

Once the Yugoslav immigrant committed himself to his existence as an industrial worker in America, a profound change took place in his attitude. The dangers of industrial work were much more swift in their realization than had been true of the dangers of subsistence agriculture. In the coal mines, the metal mines, and the smelters, death and disabling injury were frequent. The daily struggle for bread became a struggle to survive: *borba za opstanak*. The commitment to unionization can only be understood in this context, for this commitment became a continuation of the Yugoslavs' earlier struggles against the Turks and the German-Austrians. Industrial managers and corporations controlled their environment; the Yugoslavs felt that if they could not modify the conditions, they would be destroyed.[9]

Many of the South Slav villagers had always sought seasonal employment in the industrial areas of Austria and Germany. At first

[8] Jozo Tomasevich, *Peasants, Politics, and Economic Change in Yugoslavia* (Stanford, 1955), p. 80–131.

[9] For an individual statement of this position see interview with Mile Dragosavac, June 22, 1972, American West Center Minorities Collection No. C-12.

they went at the instigation of labor agents and, later, on their own initiative. They traveled north to work for several months, to save as much of their wages as they could, and then to return home in early spring. The Slovenes were among the first to go. The fabled wealth of America, however, soon overshadowed the harsh German industrial environment, despite the latter's nearness to the South Slav lands. One Serb reflected the change when he told of his experience:

> I work in Germany eight months. I made money in Germany and I saved. And I don't think it cost me more than sixty dollars . . . to buy ticket for America.[10]

The labor gangways and factories of Germany and Austria thus began to serve as the training area for many future Utah workers and to provide a means of accumulating the fare to America without going into debt. This was an important consideration for those who were primarily concerned with saving their wages and returning to their villages, rather than going to a distant land to work out their lives as industrial laborers.

The movement to America was at first similar to the seasonal migrations to Central Europe. The greatest difference lay in the scale of the trans-Atlantic movements: the distances traveled and the time spent working in the new lands were both much greater. Most of the workers in this period returned to their villages if they survived the dangers of industrial work, and a great many of them made the journey several times. One Serb explained how his family was affected by this process and how he interpreted the significance of the process:

> Well, just like the rest of the immigrants, you know, my father didn't figure to stay. He earned a little bit of money and then go back home. That's where he made a great mistake, you know. In those days people think a lot about home. . . . They didn't care much, they didn't know the language, the English, and that was why they got lost. All they could speak was, those days, the German language (besides their native tongues). That's why those days you could get pretty good jobs if you spoke German language.[11]

[10] *Ibid.*

[11] Interview with Joseph Church, October 28, 1972, Leadmine, Utah, American West Center Minorities Collection No. C-18.

As sons began to follow fathers, subtle changes took place in attitudes toward immigration. The idea of getting one's daily bread by working for cash wages for a lifetime slowly took hold. One Serb, who arrived before his sixteenth birthday, recalled the mood of the people:

> At that time people just started to come over to this country and everybody said that there was wealth here and you make fast money and all that. My father was already here and come back. He was working down here in Midvale smelter and he come back to the old country . . . But that was hard life when I come here and start working and wasn't easy like now. . . .[12]

And so the gradual transition from short-term migrants to long-term immigrants began. The transition was never complete, for aged immigrants still returned to the old country, or *stari kraj*, for prolonged stays or even in old age to retire there on their Social Security payments.

Many of the short-term migrants did not survive the illnesses and accidents resulting from industrial work. The death of the head of household placed greater strains upon other male members of the family to emigrate and to replace the relative who had been sending cash to help support the family. The small farms could afford the absence of several males because of the general rural overpopulation that existed in the South Slav lands in Austria-Hungary throughout the nineteenth century. As one woman pointed out:

> They didn't need every man. Just woman work. Woman work. Woman work harder than a man in the village.[13]

And in the decade between 1904 and 1914 a great number of males, between the ages of fourteen and thirty years, went to America and some to Utah.

The period of migration to America tended to be longer than the period of migration to Austria and Germany had been. One result of this was the emigration of women to Utah, and to other places in America, to join husbands already there or to marry. The arrival of the first woman in each South Slav community was

[12] Mile Dragosavac interview.
[13] Bolic interview.

a memorable event for the men and for the arriving women. One of the original Serbs in Midvale recalled what occurred there:

> They had saloon there in Midvale and some Serb used to run saloon there. First woman come there. His wife come there. . . . God, well, you know, we crazy. See her, first woman from, come from Yugoslavia. We give her $800 that night. Wedding present . . . you know how people use to marry. They never give anything but money.[14]

The raising of a family on American soil proved to be an important element in the decision of many Yugoslavs to remain. As children were born, it became almost impossible for the workers to save the money that would make their return to the village economically feasible. Recessions, depressions, and panics consumed precious savings. When this happened, some people with money went home, while those who had none went into debt. One man recalled the effect of the Panic of 1907:

> [My father] came right here in Midvale and worked in the smelter until 1907. There was a panic in here for about seven months and they had no money and most of them that had money went back home.[15]

The dangers of industrial work and the cyclical fluctuations of the American economy required the South Slavs to develop additional means of acquiring and maintaining stable economic positions. These dangers also required them to depend upon many of their traditions that assumed added significance in their new industrial environment.

Godfatherhood, the extended family, fraternal organizations, and boardinghouse life gave the Slav immigrants solidarity in an unwelcome environment. *Kumstvo,* or godfatherhood, among the Serbs and Croats, insured the immigrants that their children would be protected if they died. The roles of the male *kum* and the female *kuma* (*boter* and *botra* among the Slovenes) antedate Christianity among the South Slavs. One Croat told of the meaning of the godfather to the Slavic immigrants:

> *Kum,* yeah, that means "godfather." I'm godfather to several. . . . I'm godfather both in the Roman Catholic church

[14] Interview with Joseph Mikić, January 27, 1973, Midvale, Utah, American West Center Minorities Collection No. C-23.

[15] Interview with Joseph Hinich, June 27, 1972, Salt Lake City, Utah, American West Center Minorities Collection No. C-23.

and the Orthodox church. . . . You see, a *kum* is a very important part of the Slav people's background. What I mean, if you're a *kum* or godfather, if anything happened to you, to your mother or father, it is my responsibility to see that you have a proper bringing up both in education and healthwise and physical wise. . . . they stress that quite a bit . . . it was a sacred thing in the Slav people's language. They make fun of, the American people make fun of it by this *Godfather* deal. . . . actually a godfather, in the Slav, among the Slav people is a fellow that is looked up to and is very well thought of. . . .[16]

In the mines and smelters of Utah many Yugoslav workers lost their lives, and the godfather and godmother often fulfilled their maximum duties.[17]

The tradition of the extended family gave security in alien surroundings and tempered longings for home. Called *zadruga,* the extended family, like the *kumstvo,* traces back to pre-Christian times.[18] In America the extended family appeared as more and more male members of one patronymic group clustered together in one geographical space. In Utah this happened frequently among the Serbs and Croats in Bingham Canyon and in Midvale, and among the Slovenes in Carbon County. For example, one man came to Highland Boy in 1907 from a Serbian village in Croatia. By 1910 three brothers with their wives and children had joined the man as had their father. The three-generation *zadruga* that was formed continued to function for approximately ten years.[19] Such familial groupings were common among the Yugoslav people in Utah; it

[16] Interview with George Pezell, July 17, 1972, Salt Lake City, Utah, American West Center Minorities Collection No. C-1.

[17] For frequency of industrial accidents see, for example, *Utah, Facts and Figures Pertaining to Utah (Second Report of the State Bureau of Immigration, Labor, and Statistics)* (Salt Lake City, 1913); Death Benefit Payment 1904–1924, by lodge, SNPJ Collection, Immigrant Archives, University of Minnesota; and Isaac F. Marcosson, *Metal Magic, The Story of the American Smelting and Refining Company* (New York, 1949), p. 313.

[18] Literature on the *zadruga* and kinship ties among the South Slavs is extensive. Some helpful works include Philip E. Mosely, "The Peasant Family: The Zadruga or Communal Joint Family in the Balkans and its Recent Evolution," C.F. Ware, ed., *The Cultural Approach to History* (New York, 1940), pp. 95–108; Eugene A. Hammel, *Alternative Social Structures and Ritual Relations in the Balkans* (Englewood Cliffs, N.J., 1968), p. 110; Joel M. Halpern, *The Serbian Village* (New York, 1958), p. 325; and Vera St. Erlich, *Family in Transition: A Study of 300 Yugoslav Villages* (Princeton, N.J., 1966), p. 469.

[19] Interview with Gray Melich, January 24, 1973, Murray, Utah, American West Center Minorities Collection No. C-22.

was a subtle blending of elements of their own cultural past with the realities of industrial employment and immigration.

Fraternal organizations, too, helped mitigate the ill effects of industrial employment in a strange environment. These were different types: some were politically oriented like the Jugoslav Socialist Federation; others were oriented to the basic economic and artistic needs of the people. Insurance for deaths, disabling accidents, and unemployment arising from sickness or economic slowdowns was provided by several national and regional organizations. *Slovenska Narodna Podporna Jednota* ("Slovene National Benefit Society"), or "Snappy J" as it is referred to affectionately, was created in 1904 in Cleveland, Ohio, to serve Slovenian workers in America. SNPJ lodges were created simultaneously in Bingham Canyon, Murray, and Carbon County, Utah, that same year. Most of these lodges continue to function.[20]

Hrvatska Bratska Zajednica ("Croatian Fraternal Union") dates back to 1894.[21] The first Croatian lodge in Utah was founded in Bingham Canyon in 1908. It served the Croatian communities in Midvale and in Bingham Canyon. There are two Croatian lodges functioning in Midvale at the present time, and there are others in Murray and Carbon County. The *Srpski Narodni Savez* ("Serb National Federation") organized a lodge in Bingham in 1928 on the framework of a lodge that was originally established in the canyon in 1908. A remnant of this lodge continues to function, but the majority of the Serbs now belong to the Slovenian or Croatian lodges or to the *Zapadni Slavenski Savez* ("Western Slavonic Association"), an insurance organization in Denver, Colorado, that serves all Slavs in the western United States.[22]

Although the South Slav insurance organizations paid out thousands of dollars in benefits to their members in Utah, they provided other functions that were of equal if not greater importance. Each organization printed newspapers in the Slovenian or Serbo-Croatian languages, and later in English, that gave news and views of America, the old country, and the world to their readers. The SNPJ printed *Prosveta* ("Enlightenment"); the Serb Na-

[20] *Slovenska Narodna Podporna Jednota,* Manuscript Collection, Immigrant Archives, University of Minnesota.

[21] George J. Prpic, *The Croatian Immigrants in America* (New York, 1971), pp. 125, 264.

[22] Interview with Milka Smilanich, December 1972, Leadmine, Utah, American West Center Minorities Collection No. C-21.

tional Federation printed *Amerikanski Srbobran* (American edition of "Serbian Defense"); the Croatian Fraternal Union published *Zajedničar* ("The Unionist"); and the Jugoslav Socialist Federation printed the *Proletarec* ("Proletarian"). Also, these organizations provided literary works, dramatic and musical entertainment group tours, and books and pamphlets to the Slav communities in Utah and across the nation through the *matica* ("cultural society"). Each South Slav organization maintained a *matica,* and it was through these organizations that the national literature, the national romantic history, and the then current cultural activities of the Yugoslavs in America and in the old country were transmitted to the Yugoslav communities scattered throughout the United States.[23]

The work of these formal institutions tended to be secondary, however, to the oral traditions maintained in many South Slav families. For centuries the Slovenes, the Croats, and the Serbs in Croatia had maintained their culture and historical consciousness primarily through their separate oral traditions.[24] This occurred because the majority of the people were unable to read or write and because it was not until the nineteenth century that the Slovenes, Croats, and Serbs developed their modern grammatical styles. The oral tradition was carried over to the Yugoslav communities in Utah. The following passage from a much longer discourse on the origin of Žumberčani, a subgroup of the Croatian people, made by a man who had emigrated from Žumberak to America, reflects this:

> See, this Croatian come. Greek Catholic came away from Serbia when the Turks and Serbia had war. Maria Theresa, queen of Austria, she declare war on the Turk and take Serbia away. And Maria Theresa she wanted everybody to join Catholic Church to Rome. And a lot of people says, "Well, I be good honest soldier to you, but don't take my cross." See, the Greek cross with three fingers and Catholic with one hand. So she divided the part of Croatia I come from, from Serbia, away from the Turks. And [the people] said, "We'll be honest to you as soldiers, fight for you, die for you, but let [us] believe [our] religion." So we used to hold the Christmas on January 7, like old ordered us to do, of

[23] *Prosvetna Matica, JSZ,* Manuscript Collection, Immigrant Archives, University of Minnesota.

[24] For a critique and theory of South Slav epic poetry see Albert Bates Lord, *The Singer of Tales* (Cambridge, Mass., 1960), p. 309.

From the top: *The wedding of Mr. and Mrs. Joe Melich in Pueblo, Colorado, 1907. The man at left is wearing the bandolier of the Serb National Federation. Immigrants from the Balkans and the Mediterranean displayed their national flags on all social occasions. The Forbes and Melich saloon in Bingham Canyon. Joe Melich, center, was a prominent businessman and president of the Serb National Federation. Helper in the early 1900s was a focal point for South Slavs from the surrounding coal camps.*

Left: *Playing cards at Highland Boy.*
Below: *Baptismal dinner at
Highland Boy in the early 1900s
when only a few women were among
the Balkan immigrants in Bingham
Canyon.*

bian lodge gathering at Highland Boy, Bingham Canyon, 1907.

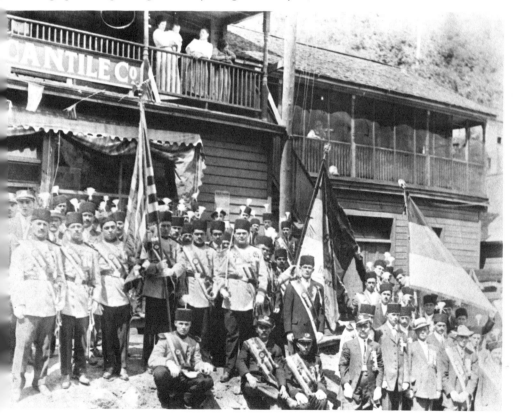

South Slavs in Midvale, 1922, bury one of their own. Men have turned the badges of the Serbian Benevolent Society to reveal the black satin covering with white crosses of mourning. First man on right of grave is Mike Dragos, a leader in the Carbon County strike of 1933. To the left of the grave is Nick Bogdanovich wearing the bandolier of the lodge.

Right: *Miners at Castle Gate shortly before the explosion of March 8, 1924, that took 172 lives.*

Below: *Sunnyside lodge was chartered in 1906. Fraternal organizations helped Yugoslavs adjust to American life.*

From the top: *Slovenian Catholics followed ancient custom of having members of the same sex as principals at funerals. Older girls would carry coffin of infant Olga Plute who died in 1916 at Sunnyside. Smaller girls would carry flowers. South Slav coal miners at the end of the shift in Carbon County in the early thirties. Croatians, Slovenes, and Serbs are shown with other railroad workers on the D&RGW at Helper.*

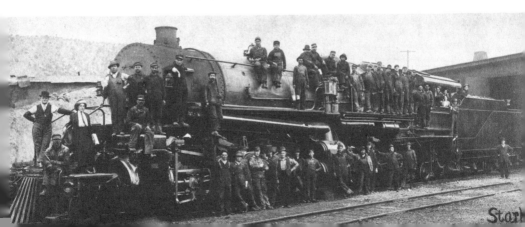

Serbia. But [they] says, "We'll believe in the Rome." So they start believing in the Rome, but they still had Christmas on different than Catholic day. Austria think better to split up three brothers [Serb, Croat, Slovene] like this so they can't get together and be afraid, maybe, that they work against the government of Austria. . . .[25]

The oral tradition was continued in the lodges of the national and regional fraternal-insurance organizations. The local of the Serbian national organization in Bingham Canyon and in Midvale was named *Milosh Obilich i Tsar Dushan*.[26] In Serbian legend and the *narodni epi* ("national epics"), Milosh Obilich was the Serbian knight who rode into the Turkish camp after the Serbian defeat at Kosovo Polje (June 28, 1389) and slew the Turkish sultan, Murad II. Tsar Stephen Dushan, the greatest of the Nemanjid emperors of Serbia, in his last years, challenged the Turks and the Byzantines for political and spiritual control of the Balkan peninsula. The Croats and the Slovenes named their lodges in a similar fashion, drawing upon the imagery and symbolism of their history to reinforce their identity in the new environment.

Added to godfatherhood, the extended family, and fraternal organizations, the boardinghouse completed a circle of protection and support around the South Slavs. Boardinghouses were developed by workers, industrial management, and entrepreneurs wherever housing was in short supply. In a variety of ways they were utilized by workers of many different nationalities and races, and, except for the huge company-managed boardinghouses, they tended to be segregated according to the race or nationality of the occupants. Boardinghouses varied in size from the small, usually private home that boarded two or three countrymen, to the large, often company-owned structure that could house more than a hundred workers. For the average Yugoslav family taking in boarders meant a little extra income and a lot of extra work for the woman or women of the household. Laundry, cleaning, and cooking chores were increased for those already burdened with children, communal plumbing, and primitive cooking and laundering facilities. The Yugo-

---

[25] Interview with John Dunosković, September 20, 1972, Midvale, Utah, American West Center Minorities Collection No. C-3.

[26] Dunosković Manuscript Collection, South Slav Archives, Western Americana, Marriott Library, University of Utah.

slav women strove to end the boarding system in their homes and were relieved when the practice died out after 1924.[27]

The *kumstvo,* the extended family, the national and regional fraternal-insurance societies, and the taking-in of boarders were just a few devices that the Serb, Croat, and Slovene immigrants used in their efforts to improve and maintain their economic status in the industrial environment in Utah and in other industrial areas of the United States. All stressed the ethnic bonds which united the Yugoslav people even before their arrival in the United States. The South Slavs, however, were also participants in organizations that were not based on ethnic exclusiveness but reflected interests common to other people as well as themselves. The most prominent of these organizations were the labor union and the church.

Labor unions attracted the interest of the most transitory of Yugoslav workers in Utah, perhaps as a result of their exposure to the German and Austrian trade union movement. In 1903 South Slav coal miners in Utah supported Italian coal miners in a strike in Carbon County.[28] Many of the Slavic coal miners, who did not first emigrate to Germany or Austria, were also exposed to trade unions and their beneficial effects prior to their arrival in Utah. One Slovene recounted his exposure to unionism:

> Well, I go from Colorado then I went to Red Lodge, Montana. . . . This was coal mine, Butte was metal mine. And they was paying dues, they had union up there. And so that's where I went and they were paying better wages up there than they were here so that's where I went. I stayed there for two years.[29]

A large number of other Yugoslav miners passed through the coal mines of the Red Lodge area and came to the coal mines of Carbon County, already in possession of their membership cards in the United Mine Workers of America (UMWA). As a result of this early exposure to unions and belief in their efficacy, the Yugoslav miners supported other coal industry strikes in 1922 and 1933. In 1933 the South Slav miners were the main supporters of the National Miners Union strike that led directly to recognition of

[27] Interview with Milja Dragosavac, June 22, 1972, Salt Lake City, Utah, American West Center Minorities Collection No. C-12.

[28] State of Utah, *Coal Inspector's Report* (Salt Lake City, 1904), p. 66.

[29] Interview with John Skerl, January 12, 1973, Helper, Utah, American West Center Minorities Collection No. C-7.

the UMWA by the companies. Prior to 1933 and for several years after, the newly recognized union succeeded in achieving little for its membership. The labor union's main function, in effect, was to serve as a social organization that bridged, but did not destroy, the ethnic and cultural differences between Utah workers.

In the Catholic churches in Utah, Slovenes and Croats shared pews with Italians and other nationalities. These churches did not, however, function as "melting pots" where ethnic differences were dissipated, as has been postulated by some scholars.[30] Except for the Mass, the people used the church in ethnic groups, not as a congregational whole. For example, the christening of a Croatian child would be attended by Croats and an Italian wedding by Italians. In addition, many men from all nationalities did not attend even the Mass because of the demands of their work and disinclination. A similar relationship developed between the Orthodox Serbs and Greeks in the Greek Orthodox churches in Utah. The first marriage to be solemnized in the newly built Holy Trinity Greek Orthodox Church in Salt Lake City in 1905 was Serbian.[31] The Serbs continued to use the "old" calendar and to celebrate Christmas on January 7, even though the Greek Orthodox adopted the "new" date of December 25.

In part a carry-over from pre-Christian attitudes and in part because of a mistrust in conspicuous displays of piety by lay church members since conversion to Christianity, the South Slavs displayed ambivalence toward the formal manifestations of their religions. The acceptance of the basic religious values, as evidenced through customary behavior and by social interchange with one's neighbors, was the true worth of religion to many Yugoslavs. As one man put it:

> Churches all the same, just different religion. But if people
> believe any church . . . you won't be bad fellow.[32]

Because of the opposition of the Catholic church to labor unions, many conflicts arose between Catholic workers and the local clergy. This tended to reinforce the ambivalent attitudes of the South Slavs toward formal religion and its role in their lives. A

---

[30] For a view of the ethnic community church functioning as a "melting pot" see Timothy L. Smith, "New Approaches to the History of Immigration in the Twentieth Century," *American Historical Review* 71 (1966): 1265–79.

[31] Stefanos Lazarovitch and Anna Bonasovitch were married by Father Parthenios Lymberopoulos on November 9, 1905.

[32] Dunosković interview.

crisis between Catholic Yugoslav workers and the clergy developed in 1933 when, out of desperation, the former supported the Communist National Miners Union (NMU) in a strike. Although the NMU was broken, the strike led directly to recognition of the UMWA and to deep antagonisms between the Yugoslav workers and their priests. The wounds of this period did not heal for a decade.

The central theme of Yugoslav immigration to Utah is that of struggle for existence. The South Slavs called the struggle *borba za nasušni hleb,* or "the fight for daily bread." It involved all members of the family, and it required a great deal of their energies. Such struggle did not originate in America. Most of the immigrants' attitudes toward the conflict were partially formed through the prism of their previous collective and individual history. These attitudes received their final shape in the crucible of industrial conflict in America.

A sense of isolation and defensiveness had developed between the Yugoslavs and their work environment. Occasionally, this sense of hostility developed between Serbs, Croats, and Slovenes, and between the Slavs and their Mormon neighbors. Because religion was central to their concept of nationality and culture (i.e., adherence to Roman Catholicism for Slovenes and Croats, and Orthodoxy for Serbs), there developed fertile ground for internecine conflict primarily between Serbs and Croats, and, secondarily, between the Yugoslavs and the Mormons.

Feuding continued between Serbs and Croats in Bingham Canyon from 1908 to 1918. It was based on several disparate factors, most of which were rooted in the experience of the old country. In some areas of Croatia, for example, there had existed a tradition of hostility, or at best, friendly competition, between Serbs and Croats. As one immigrant remembered:

> Well, of course, I didn't have no problem, but in my village there wasn't any mixed religion at all. They was all Serbian people. But, generally, between those peoples, Serbs and Croats, there was an unfriendly feeling between them. . . . Never was too friendly, anyhow.[33]

The vague hostility was fed by political events in the Balkans in 1908 when Austria-Hungary annexed Bosnia-Herzegovina lands

---

[33] Interview with Joseph Hinich, June 19, 1972, Salt Lake City, Utah, American West Center Minorities Collection No. C-22.

that were desired by the kingdom of Serbia and whose people would probably have preferred union with Serbia rather than with Austria. Ultranationalist Serbs in Bingham Canyon used such events to provoke arguments with the Croats who were already displeased with Serbian labor contractors who hired Croatian workers for Utah Copper Company.[34] A Serb who was residing in Midvale at the time recalled his fears of going to Bingham, especially Highland Boy, and his feelings about the general situation:

> In *stari kraj* we use to celebrate Christmas and have a good time [together]. And up the son of a gun Bingham Canyon there was murder. Born in same country, talk same language, and everything else and just because of church. Well, that's that damn couple of guys up there making the trouble between the people.[35]

The conflict reached ominous proportions when World War I began and the United States entered the war against the Central Powers.

The Croats and Slovenes in Utah were not anxious to serve in the United States Army in World War I because they dreaded the possibility of fighting their relatives, many of whom were serving in the Austrian and even the German armies.[36] The Serbs in Utah, on the other hand, looked upon the war as a veritable crusade and as the concluding episode in the five-hundred-year struggle for national liberation. More than two hundred young Serbian men from Bingham Canyon volunteered and served in the Serbian and French armies during 1917 and 1918.[37] As the Serbs watched their sons and brothers marching off to war while the Croats and Slovenes did not, hostilities began. The absence of young male Serbs proved a blessing for community relations in Bingham Canyon; it removed a vociferous and energetic element that had kept the feuds alive. With the cessation of hostilities and the creation of the kingdom of Serbs, Croats, and Slovenes (renamed Yugoslavia, Land of the South Slavs, in 1929) the tensions between the Serbs and Croats were lessened.

---

[34] For information concerning Serbian labor contractors see the copies of Utah Copper Company Employment Records (1908–1918) presently housed in the American West Center, University of Utah.

[35] Mikić interview.

[36] Dunosković interview.

[37] *Bingham Press Bulletin*, March 22, 1918, and Church interview.

World War I had an interesting side effect on the Yugoslav community in Utah. Many Slovenes and Croats who had served in the Austrian army emigrated to Utah between 1919 and 1924. A large number of these men had served on the Russian front and had been captured. As prisoners of war they witnessed the Russian Revolution of 1917 and the Bolshevik coup d'etat of the same year. Many of the South Slavs joined the Bolsheviks in the course of the Russian Civil War, including one Joseph Broz who was to become President Tito of Yugoslavia in 1945. One Serb immigrant recounted what happened to his brother:

> That's my brother, yes. He is in Russia since the First World War. And he's got three doctors in his family. One son and two daughters is doctor. . . . First World War we was under Austrians. He don't like Austria and he went over to Russia. To fight against the Austrians. He stayed there, yes, he did and he married there twice.[38]

A Slovene who fought in Russia for the Austrians told of his experience:

> They sent my company to Russia, you know, to fight Bolshevik. We fight those communists there in Russia and I stay in Russia one year. . . . I don't care what kind of soldier come into your country, you're not going to like it. I don't care what it is. Now American is in Germany, you know German hate American. . . . When I been in Russia they like me personally, but they don't like us being there. They tell me, "You go to your territory. That's mine. You got nothing here. That's nothing but right, isn't it? That's the way its supposed to be." [39]

These later immigrants brought not only a cosmopolitan element to the South Slav communities in Utah but also firsthand information of momentous events in Europe, including the Russian situation, the Italian occupation of parts of Slovenia and Croatia, and the formation of the new South Slav kingdom.

The secondary area of interethnic friction for the Yugoslavs lay in their relations with the Mormons. Much of this friction was generated by socio-economic factors, especially the competition between Yugoslav and Mormon workers and between Yugoslav and Mormon businessmen. (Other nationalities from southern and east-

---

[38] Mile Dragosavac interview.

[39] Interview with Anton Klarich, January 13, 1973, Price, Utah, American West Center Minorities Collection No. C-9.

ern Europe, primarily the Greeks and Italians, were also competitors.) The ideological background to the conflict was based in the separateness that the Yugoslavs maintained in language, culture, and community and in the primacy that the Mormons felt was their birthright in the land that their ancestors had settled and subdued.

Labor disputes brought mutual antipathies into public view and deepened antagonisms that developed over several decades. Mormon businessmen and political leaders took advantage of labor strife to stress the "un-American" and "Bolshevik" proclivities of the Yugoslavs and other ethnic workers. Epithets such as "No-name-ovich" and "Bohunk" were used in identifying the Yugoslavs. They were held up to ridicule for their accents and their "obscure" origins by the progeny of the "blood of Israel." The result of these social encounters, particularly those that occurred during the twenties and thirties, was to strengthen the internal bonds of each group and to perpetuate, albeit to a lesser degree, the suspicions and fears that each group held for the other.[40]

The overall impact of the immigration experience in Utah upon the Yugoslavs and their descendants is almost impossible to determine with the data that is presently available. Vital information, for example, remains restricted from historians in the manuscript census collections that have been taken by the United States government since 1910. Various local sources of information, including newspapers that were printed by the South Slavs in Utah and personal records, are still being sought for collection, deposit in library or museum, and for analysis. It will take more time and effort, however, to amass and sift the materials for comprehensive analysis. Three general observations about the Yugoslavs in Utah and their history can nevertheless be made.

First, the South Slavs in Utah are still in the immigration and accommodation process. The decisions made by each succeeding generation determine the overall meaning of the experience of the original immigrants. Continually, behavior, values, and organizations are changed, discarded, or developed anew; and it is extremely hard to make observations beyond the superficial and the

[40] For detailed accounts of one conflict between Mormons and the ethnic workers, see Rolla West Manuscript, American West Center, University of Utah, and Helen Z. Papanikolas, "Unionism, Communism, and the Great Depression: The Carbon County Coal Strike of 1933," *Utah Historical Quarterly* 41 (1973): 254–300.

truistic. The lodges are still flourishing, for example, but they have lost many of their cultural and social functions. The *kumstvo* is still in use as are various forms of the extended family. Slovenian and Serbo-Croatian are still used as linguistic mediums in the press and in everyday communication. Recently a *Slovenski Dom* ("Slovenian Home") was established in Helper to serve the cultural and social needs of the South Slavs in Carbon County.[41] The continuity between past and present is strong and causes the observer to look for the end to the migration cycle.

Second, the Yugoslav communities in Utah form only a part of an extensive network of Yugoslav settlements that still exist in the western United States. The coal mines of southeastern Colorado and Washington, southwestern Wyoming, and northern New Mexico attracted the South Slavs as did the copper mines of Nevada and Montana. The communities in Utah are the geographical and historical center of these Yugoslav settlements in the Intermountain West. Better undersanding of these other settlements will result in a better understanding of the settlements in Utah. Comprehensive programs of oral history and documentation should be undertaken for all of them.

Third, and in conclusion, a word should be said about the role of ethnic history. A noted historian of American immigration has written that:

> The histories of single ethnic groups . . . are open to the criticism that they neglect the common aspects of that experience which transcend ethnic differences.[42]

It can be contended, however, that the most common aspect of the transcendental in American history is that we are all ethnics. The acceptance of this hypothesis does not require the filiopietal worship of our ancestors, but it frees us from the rigidity of the concept of the new American man; and it forces us to explore the ethnic dimensions of our social, economic, and cultural history with a critical eye, grace, and compassion. Such an injection into the realm of American history could bring more quality to our scholarship and, perhaps, to our lives.

[41] Interview with Joseph Chesnik, January 12, 1973, Helper, Utah, American West Center Minorities Collection No. C-8.

[42] Rudolph J. Vecoli, "European Americans: From Immigrants to Ethnics," *The Reinterpretation of American History and Culture,* eds. William H. Cartwright and Richard L. Watson, Jr. (Washington, D.C., 1973), p. 93.

12 FROM BABYLON TO BABYLON: IMMIGRATION FROM THE MIDDLE EAST

BY ROBERT F. ZEIDNER

Syria has always been an inhospitable place to live in and a splendid place to leave.

— Philip K. Hitti

INTRODUCTION

The Middle Eastern peoples who settled in Utah—and in the entire nation—represent a congeries of the state's smallest immigrant elements in terms of absolute numbers.[1] Although the Syro-Lebanese and Armenians, who began to land on American shores during the late 1880s, comprise the great bulk of Utah's Middle Eastern ethnic mixture, recent years have seen the arrivals of modest numbers of Egyptians, Iranians, Palestinian Arabs, Iraqis, Jordanians, and even a few Turks and Libyans. The early immigrants were almost all adherents of various Christian denominations, but Moslems have as-

© 1975 Robert F. Zeidner

---

[1] The 1910 Census reflects the entire Middle Eastern population of Utah as merely "Turkey in Asia" or "Turkey in Europe" with a net strength of only 361 foreign-born (215 from Asia), comprising a mere 0.5 percent of the total foreign-born element of Utah. When combined with their 36 offspring as the Middle Eastern "foreign white stock" of Utah, however, they encompassed only 0.2 percent of that same total. These percentages closely match nationwide trends for the same census. The above source sets the foreign-born from all of Turkey in Utah for the previous census (1900) at a mere 18 persons. The 1910 Census reveals the following county distribution of the Middle Eastern-born of Utah: Salt Lake 229, Carbon 31, Weber 30, Utah 30, Summit 15, Sevier 8, Uintah 7, Juab 6, Morgan 2, and 1 each for Grand, Wasatch, and Washington.
    Although failing to record any speakers of Armenian or Turkish, the 1960 Census does set Utah speakers of Arabic at—1960: 94(all urban), 1940: 100, 1930: 144, 1920: 162, 1910: 118. Thus, if all the above statistics are accurate, it seems reasonable to assume that the bulk of the state's Syro-Lebanese immigrants arrived in Utah between 1900 and 1920. The 1920 Census confirms the presence of eighty foreign-born Armenians in Utah.

sumed an increasing proportion among recent additions to our Middle Eastern population. Nevertheless, the Christian element remains by far the dominant group of the two.

Throughout the period of maximum emigration from the Middle East (1890–1918), two Islamic states encompassed the entire area: Iran (Persia) and the Ottoman Empire. Hence, immigrants from the region frequently found themselves identified here, in terms of national origin, as "Persians" and "Ottomans" (or "Turks") respectively. However, aside from nation of residence, the issue of ethnic identification, and of group loyalties, throughout the Middle East has long revolved about the twin axes of religion and mother tongue. Thus, several "Persian" immigrants of the early 1920s might more properly be identified as "Assyrians"— Syriac-speaking members of the long-oppressed Nestorian communities of northwest Iran and northern Iraq. In view of the harsh treatment they often experienced at the hands of their nomadic Moslem neighbors during the late nineteenth century, these people cling tenaciously to their Assyrian identity; and they continue to emigrate to this date. Similar cycles of oppression and emigration launched the exodus of masses of Armenians and Christian "Syrians" during the same period. Whereas the United States has admitted over a quarter million of these two peoples, even larger numbers emigrated to Latin America, especially to Brazil and Argentina.

Despite popular American notions ascribing a general "sameness" to all Middle Eastern peoples, the various cultural units of that region are very much aware of their respective differences. (The *Millet* system, wherein each faith maintained its own laws, courts, schools, welfare agencies, and systems of taxation contributed to this awareness.)[2] This is especially true of those elements that began to migrate to the New World during the late nineteenth century: the Christian Lebanese and the Armenians, who are still arriving in United States ports in modest numbers. All of the peoples native to the Middle East have long displayed a fierce attachment to faith, family, cultural tradition, and their home soil. Therefore, despite the great upheavals suffered by many peoples, particularly the Christian minorities, of the area during the nineteenth century, emigration remained relatively subdued in terms of absolute numbers. Moreover,

---

[2] For further details on the *Millet* System, plus identification, population, distribution, and doctrinal differences of the various sects contained within it, see: Sir Harry Luke, *The New Turkey and the Old* (London, 1955), pp. 66–

restrictive policies on emigration among the states of the region and limited immigration quotas set for their nationals by the United States combined to discourage migrations of the scale witnessed in Europe throughout the latter half of the nineteenth century. Further, the Middle East as a whole has not suffered the strains of overpopulation and consequent pressures on the available arable land, with the obvious exceptions of Egypt and Lebanon, until recent times.

On the other hand, two relatively small but distinctive ethnic units of Middle Eastern society, the Armenians and the Christian Lebanese, have demonstrated over a period of centuries a readiness to emigrate in the face of adverse living conditions at home, or of opportunities for self-improvement abroad. A diaspora of both peoples had already commenced well before the launching of the great European exodus to the Western Hemisphere. Armenian merchants and tradesmen had founded colonies from London to Bombay by the turn of the seventeenth century; and Muhammad Ali Pasha, in the course of his founding of the modern Egyptian state, imported thousands of Christian Lebanese and Armenian clerks and petty officials during the early decades of the nineteenth century.[3]

An early attachment to western educational traditions among the urban elements of both peoples, reinforced throughout the nineteenth century by continuous infusions of western Christian missionaries among their urban and rural segments, plus high rates of literacy and a flair for learning western languages, especially French and English, facilitated the mobility of both the Lebanese and the Armenians. Significant numbers of both groups, by virtue of education and linguistic versatility, found employment and even dual citizenship among the western commercial firms that burgeoned throughout the Middle East during the nineteenth century.[4] Thus,

101; A.H. Hourani, *Syria and Lebanon* (London and New York, 1954), pp. 121–45, 386; George Haddad, *Fifty Years of Modern Lebanon* (Beirut, 1950), pp. 10–19; Harvey H. Smith *et al.*, *Area Handbook for Lebanon* (Washington, D.C., 1969), pp. 45–57, 59–65, 123–33, 159–79; Richard F. Nyrop *et al.*, *Area Handbook for Syria* (Washington, D.C., 1971), pp. 55–100; Philip K. Hitti, *The Syrians in America* (New York, 1924), pp. 35–43. The author is particularly indebted to Professor Hitti and the last cited work for much of the content of the Syro-Lebanese portion of this chapter.

[3] Abstracts of the Egyptian census, contained in: Edward Lane, *The Manners and Customs of the Modern Egyptians* (New York, 1963), p. 23; and J.C. McCoan, *Egypt* (New York, 1900), p. 23, estimate 5,000 "Syrians" and 2,000 Armenians for the census of 1847–48 and 7,000 "Syrians" and 10,000 Armenians for the census of 1859, respectively. Also see: Philip K. Hitti, *Lebanon in History* (New York, 1967), pp. 473–74.

[4] This is not to claim that the Syro-Lebanese who came to America were an educated group. On the contrary, they were more often illiterate than not, because most of them were from the peasant class.

the stage was set for large overseas migrations among the Armenians and Lebanese when strife broke out between them and their neighbors in the latter half of the nineteenth century.

THE SYRO-LEBANESE

Although the Christians of Lebanon comprise one of the major ethnic groups of the Middle East to emigrate to this country and elsewhere commencing in the late 1880s, a great deal of confusion regarding national origins persists among such immigrants, and among United States immigration and census officials as well. Much of this confusion stems from the late arrival of Lebanon within the society of independent nations (1943). More specifically, many of the Lebanese settled in the United States and elsewhere were identified upon arrival in their new homelands as "Syrians." Many such immigrants continue to this day to think of themselves as such— whereas their native land was, in fact, Lebanon. United States immigration and census statistics persist in reflecting a far larger "foreign stock" of Syrian origin than justified by current realities.

The full "Syrian" immigration statistics will never be known, because many Syro-Lebanese entered this country *sub rosa,* via Vera Cruz and a surreptitious northward crossing of the Rio Grande River. These were principally diseased persons and victims of horror tales of Ellis Island, told by steamship agents in Beirut, Naples, and Marseilles, plus a substantial number of people already refused entry for a variety of reasons at eastern port cities.[5]

An eminent Syro-Lebanese scholar, himself an immigrant to this nation, records a loss of one-quarter (one hundred thousand) of the entire population of autonomous Lebanon through emigration

[5] U.S., Commissioner-General of Immigration, *Annual Report for 1903,* pp. 86, 88–89; and Lawrence Guy Brown, *Immigration: Cultural Conflicts and Social Adjustments* (New York and London, 1933), pp. 194–95. The former source alleges that a constant stream of 500 "Syrians" per month sailed to Mexico for ultimate destinations in the United States.

Ottoman Nationals Admitted to the United States, 1881–96.

Year	Turkey in Asia (total/males)	Turkey in Europe (total/males)
1881	5/5	72/54
1886	15/14	176/132
1891	2488/1774	265/224
1896	4139/2915	169/118

Compiled from Imre Ferenczi, ed., *International Migrations* (New York, 1969), vol. 1, *Statistics,* pp. 418–31.

between the years 1900 and 1914;[6] the Christians of the coast, the south, and the Beqaa must have departed in even greater numbers. Almost all of the many Lebanese families in Utah interviewed by the writer hail from the latter regions, more specifically from the vicinities of Zahle in the Beqaa and of Saida and Sur on the southern coast. However, a few did emigrate from the slopes above Beirut and from modern Syria proper.

Peasants and, to a lesser degree, petty artisans and clerks, formed the great bulk of Syro-Lebanese emigrants in terms of numbers. Young males held a heavy majority among those bound for the New World, and many of them harbored initial intentions of returning to the Levant with their savings. Thus, many—if not most—left wives and children behind in the care of the extended family. On the other hand, a few years of the "good life" on these shores, plus the general devastation of the Levant by the Young Turks during the First World War,[7] sufficed to make permanent Americans of most of the "Syrian" immigrants. An extraordinary talent for adaptation among the Syro-Lebanese, born of centuries of politico-economic vicissitude and constant association with diverse peoples in

"Syrians" Admitted to and Departed from the United States, 1899–1924

Year	"Syrians" Admitted (total/males)	"Syrians" Departed
1899	3708/2446	Unknown
1904	3653/2480	"
1909	3668/2382	464
1914	9023/6391	949
1919	231/157	53
1924	1595/801	8

Compiled from Ferenczi, *International Migrations,* pp. 432–43, 498.

[6] Hitti, *Lebanon in History,* p. 474.

[7] For accounts of the devastation suffered by the "Syrians" during the war, see: Hitti, *Lebanon in History,* pp. 483–86; Zeine N. Zeine, *The Emergence of Arab Nationalism* (Beirut, 1966), pp. 23–40; George Haddad, *Fifty Years of Modern Lebanon* (Beirut, 1950), pp. 46–50; Salom Rizk, *Syrian Yankee* (Garden City, N.Y., 1943), pp. 1–47; and George Antonius, *The Arab Awakening* (Beirut, 1955), pp. 185–91, 202–42. Additional data on "Syrian" emigration from the Levant are available in: Hitti, *Lebanon in History,* pp. 473–77; Haddad, *Fifty Years,* pp. 10, 18–19, 134–36, 163; Smith, *Area Handbook,* pp. 47–48; Elie Adib Salem, *Modernization without Revolution: Lebanon's Experience* (Bloomington, Ind., 1973), pp. 27–29, 44–45, 139; and Hitti, *Syrians in America,* pp. 47–61. Subsequent to the completion of this chapter, an entire issue of *ARAMCO World Magazine* 26 (March–April 1975), was devoted to Arab immigrants in America.

their native land, greatly facilitated their cultural absorption in the United States and elsewhere. This trend was especially true of those who, like their brothers in Utah, did not congregate in the large "Syrian" ghettos of New York, Boston, Patterson, Detroit, Philadelphia, Cleveland, and Chicago. The ghetto-dwellers usually managed to import their respective churches —and even their Arabic presses—and thus maintained a modicum of their former culture on this continent, so much so that New York, in 1905, saw a brief outbreak of "Syrian" intracommunal violence of the sort long since deemed endemic among the varied ethnic elements of the Levant.[8]

As suggested above, the vast majority of Syro-Lebanese immigrants settled in areas east of the Mississippi River and north of the Ohio River.[9] Nonetheless, the modern Levantines remain the cultural heirs of their Phoenician forebears insofar as commerce is concerned, and business or employment opportunities have impelled them to migrate widely throughout this continent. One can find a "Syrian" colony, however small, in every American city boasting a population of 500,000 or more. Although most of the Levantines who settled in New England and the Atlantic Seaboard found work in the textile mills of those regions, many, if not most, of those who migrated south and west started their new lives as peddlers of "notions"—souvenirs of the Holy Lands, laces, embroidered linens, and silk goods (especially lingerie and kimonos).

Many of the native housewives of rural America first learned of the existence of these luxuries through the door-to-door visits of wandering "Syrian" merchants. Blessed with world-famous business acumen, these peddlers soon discovered that access to American housewives in the sale of "personal" goods was generally more open to women than to men and they began to employ their own womenfolk in this role. Moreover, many a male peddler, who had hoped to return to the Levant eventually, sent for or acquired a mate in the homeland. Hence, the web of migrant "Syrian" involvement in America slowly grew taut, and dreams of seeing the motherland again gradually receded with the establishment of families here. In the meantime, Syro-Lebanese frugality generated capital among the peddlers, and many of them opened dry-goods and grocery stores,

---

[8] Hitti, *Syrians in America,* pp. 84–85.

[9] *Ibid.,* p. 64, presents a valuable map depicting the distribution of "Syrian" immigrants throughout the United States in the year 1919. However, this map reflects no such immigrants in Utah, nor in any of the Intermountain states.

particularly in the Midwest and the West. Probably the most successful of such ventures was that of the Farah family of El Paso, Texas.

Even a decision to settle permanently in New York, Texas, or
Utah, however, did not signal a clean break with the Levant. The
ties of kith and kin remain strong among Syro-Lebanese immigrants,
even into the second generation of the native-born. Hence, the initial
waves of "Syrians" to surge upon American shores, having decided
to remain here rather than to return, began to import relatives of
both sexes. The modest resources of immigrant families imposed
severe limits to the numbers of persons they could sponsor for emigration, and many family members preferred to remain in the home
country. As a result many Levantine-Americans retain a strong attachment to their native towns and villages to this day. Philip K.
Hitti has portrayed this attachment in simple but vivid terms in citing
the many Lebanese villages renovated or expanded, especially after
the depredations of the First World War, through the massive cash
remissions of concerned expatriates.[10] Moreover, like their Greek
counterparts, many Levantine immigrants have visited their former
homes and taken their American-born children to meet "Syrian"
cousins and grandparents. Some naturalized Syro-Lebanese here
even retain dual citizenship, a status actively encouraged by the
government of Lebanon.[11]

Like most immigrants from Eastern Europe and the Mediterranean basin, the Middle Easterners in this hemisphere have tended
to flock to and remain in the large cities of their new homelands. On
the other hand, relatively few of the latter group have undertaken
heavy labor as a means of family support. As already suggested,
most Levantine stock sought employment in the manufacture or
sale of textiles. This is hardly surprising in view of the extent to
which spinning and weaving are still known and practiced in rural
Middle Eastern households. Textile work, or sales, appealed to many
unskilled and frequently illiterate immigrants who might otherwise
have found only the most menial positions in heavy industry.[12]

[10] Hitti, *Lebanon in History,* pp. 474–76. Haddad, *Fifty Years,* p. 136,
states that the expatriate remissions of 1924 exceeded the value of all Lebanese
exports for that year.

[11] George Grassmuck and Kamal Salibi, *Reformed Administration in
Lebanon* (Beirut, 1964), pp. 43–44. According to this source, the Lebanese
Ministry of Foreign Affairs maintains a benevolent surveillance over expatriates
and assists them in protecting their interests (e.g., real property) in the homeland. However, under U.S. law dual citizenships are not recognized.

[12] Hitti, *Syrians in America,* pp. 69–73; on p. 67 of his work, he has compiled a list of the nation's fourteen largest "Syrian" urban colonies with estimated
populations.

A marked departure from this trend, however, was blazed by the earliest Syro-Lebanese to settle in Utah. The very first of these identified by the author, 'Brahim (Abraham) Howa, having arrived in Carbon County as a peddler of carpets and jewelry about 1896, tried his hand at both mining and farming. He conformed with other immigrant Levantine patterns in sponsoring the immigration to Utah of three brothers and a sister. Their descendants here have adhered to the general urbanizing trend and gradually migrated to Price, Provo, and Salt Lake City.[13]

'Brahim Howa's niece, Sarah George, came from Dibbel, Lebanon, in 1907 with her uncle John Howa and his wife, landing in Mexico and traveling from Texas to Utah. Sarah was thirteen years old and had been betrothed in Lebanon to sixteen-year-old John Attey, already in Utah. John and his father painted boxcars in the railyards, later managed an ice cream shop, and worked at the Garfield smelter and in a brickyard. Sixty-eight years later Sarah Attey said:

> Yes, I wanted to come to America. Streets paved with gold, everyone said. I was so homesick when I come. I cried all the time for my parents and home. My father had a farm. He raised melons, grapes, silkworms. Two years after, I married my husband in the Salt Lake Catholic Cathedral. We had big dinner at my aunt and uncle's house. Roast lamb, *pilaf, dolmas* [meat and rice wrapped in grape leaves], chicken, honey pastries. Dancing, music.
>
> We lived on the west side, by Greek Town, with Lebanese neighbors. You know, when you are far from home, you want to be with your people. Lebanese Town it was called. Three Lebanese were very successful. Bonos Shool had a grocery store in Greek Town, on Second South. George Katter and Kalil Fadel also, dry goods, stores. George Katter got men jobs at Bingham copper mine.
>
> Lebanese men peddled, sold lot of jewelry to Greeks. They peddled lace, linens, cloth, bedspreads all over Utah. They bought from New York stores. Lebanese men in some labor jobs made ten cents an hour for ten hours a day. That's why some Lebanese women took in boarders. They had to.
>
> When the Greeks had weddings and baptisms in their first church on Fourth South, we used to go there to watch them dance in the churchyard. Namedays [saints' feast days] were

[13] Interview with Joseph P. Howa, June 25, 1974, Salt Lake City.

big holidays for us, but Easter was the great holiday of the year.[14]

Other early arrivals among the Levantine settlers in Utah, the Malouf family of Salt Lake City and Logan, first entered a variety of mercantile ventures in and around Richfield before gravitating to Provo, Salt Lake City, Ogden, and Logan. The Maloufs constitute a classic example of the products of Syro-Lebanese frugality, commercial shrewdness, and passion for education in a milieu of opportunity. Although their earliest arrivals were virtually illiterate, in a single generation they established several flourishing businesses in Richfield, before moving to Salt Lake City to found the Western Garment Manufacturing Company, subsequently developed by Anees B. Malouf and his kin as the nationally known Mode O'Day, a women's garment manufacturing and sales firm. Meanwhile, both physicians and university professors of note, not to mention the current leadership of Mode O'Day, have emerged from the ranks of the first and second generations of the native-born Maloufs of Utah.[15] Similarly, both the Howa and Sheya families of Carbon County have produced conspicuously successful members among the professions—again reflecting the trend toward urban migration among the Syro-Lebanese of Utah's central counties.[16]

Later arrivals, those who came to Utah after 1905, seem to have concentrated in Salt Lake and Weber counties and comprise the bulk of the state's current "Syrian" element. Although a substantial number among them started life here as peddlers of clothing and notions in the mining and farming communities of northern Utah, perhaps even more males eventually took up labor at the Utah Fire Clay Company, formerly located at 1078 South First West in Salt Lake City. And, in consequence, a miniscule Little Syria blossomed during the 1920s and 1930s in the vicinity of the residences and stores centered on Third South and Fifth West. Among the most prominent members of this colony the late Gibran (George) Katter, who arrived as a peddler in 1901, founded the Salt Lake Grocery

---

[14] Interview with Sarah Attey, April 29, 1975, Salt Lake City.

[15] Interview with Dr. Phelon J. Malouf, December 3, 1974, Salt Lake City.

[16] Most of what follows is a synthesis of many interviews with Utahns of Lebanese extraction. To cite all of them would prove tedious to both reader and writer. Nonetheless, the author wishes to acknowledge the valuable assistance and keen perception of the following persons who were interviewed at length: Interview with George Haddad, August 2, 1974; interview with John L. and Helen S. Anton, September 16, 1974; and interview with Michael S. Allam, September 23, 1974.

and Dry Goods Company (now defunct) and opened a boarding-house for miners in Bingham Canyon. His involvement with labor recruitment for the Utah Copper Company continued until his death in late 1937. His marriage to the former Mary Elizabeth Hussoun Boyer in 1915 marked one of the major social events among the entire foreign-born community of Salt Lake City for that year. Extensive news coverage of this occasion presents a vivid description of all-night Lebanese dancing, music, and food. The entire neigh-borhood was invited as were all of the local police.[17]

Although both Syro-Lebanese immigrants and their United States-born children have demonstrated a strong preference for marrying among their own kind, to include religion, in all districts of Utah, the degree to which the traditions of the homeland have been preserved in home life varies sharply between the relatively large colonies of Salt Lake City and Ogden on one hand, and the dis-persed elements of the rest of Utah on the other. As one might ex-pect, "Syrian" lifestyles prevail far more among the former group than among the latter. Were it not for their surnames, one would scarcely recognize the children of the latter group as first-generation native-born. Most of them profess to know little Arabic, and, in consequence, they speak flawless Utah folk-English. Many of the first generation native-born among the former group still reveal traces of a "Syrian" accent when speaking English, and, perhaps more significant, they cling tenaciously to the values and customs peculiar to their forebears. The author has encountered here a sprinkling of such individuals who appear to have strayed less from the lifestyle of late nineteenth-century "Syria" than relatively recent arrivals from that area or the current inhabitants of the region. One finds among the children of the Salt Lake City enclave of Levantine immigrants many who continue to serve "Syrian" dishes at home and who can play the *oud*, the *def*, or the *tabla*—or dance the *dabke* to the strains of these ancient musical instruments.[18]

Whereas Hitti has anguished at considerable length over the clannishness and individualism of his countrymen and the consequent

---

[17] Interview with Helen F. Jones (nee Katter) and Frieda Katter, August 10, 1974, Salt Lake City. *Salt Lake Tribune,* December 20, 1915, and December 4, 1937.

[18] Respectively, the forerunner of the lute, the tambourine, and the bongo-drum. The *dabke,* national folk dance of Lebanon, is a communal activity wherein the performers form a line, side-by-side, hold hands, and follow the movements of a leader.

lack of cohesion among them,[19] Levantine fraternal associations, newspapers, and churches founded in America have served to enhance and preserve the memory of native customs and traditions among United States–born offspring. Since the Syro-Lebanese immigrants found themselves engulfed everywhere amidst other, larger ethnic elements, they derived much comfort and a sense of solidarity from their own organizations. The sole entity of this sort formed in Utah to date is the Phoenician Lodge of Salt Lake City, originally chartered in 1936 as The United Syrian-American Society. Membership, since the inception of the club, has varied between thirty and forty persons and includes several residing in Ogden and Provo. The major social events of the association, however, frequently command attendance by as many as ninety from the Levantine community.[20]

Despite their small numbers and their reputation for adaptability, the Levantine settlers of Utah have endured the full range of nativistic hostility and bigotry shared by immigrant Italians, Greeks, Blacks, and other "swarthy" peoples at the hands of the culturally dominant Anglo-Saxon majority of the population. Thus, bitter memories of cries of "dago" and "greaser" and "nigger" still linger among the Middle Eastern residents of Salt Lake City and Ogden; and, under the pressures of such treatment, much of the mutual distrust and suspicion that divided the various religious sects in the motherland has gradually vanished, and sectarian mobility and intermarriage has ensued among Christians. A few Levantines have even entered the Church of Jesus Christ of Latter-day Saints.

Although the Maronites (who use the Syriac liturgy, are governed by the patriarch of Antioch, and acknowledge the Roman pope as supreme) boast the largest sectarian membership of the "Syrian" Christian groups, the entire Maronite population of Utah is not sufficient to warrant the importation of a priest of that denomination; and the Utah Maronites have merged with the local Roman Catholic diocese. Nor have the Greek Orthodox or the Protestant Levantines banded together to form their own ecclesiastical communities. Like the Maronites, they too have joined local churches of their respective faiths.[21] Again, due to the modest size of

---

[19] Hitti, *Lebanon in History,* pp. 476–80; Hitti, *Syrians in America,* pp. 23–24, 94–97.

[20] Hitti, *Syrians in America,* appendices A–F, pp. 125–35, lists "Syrian" churches of all denominations and publications extant in the United States as of 1924. He discusses fraternal organizations on p. 90, citing a few in Boston and New York.

[21] The author's estimate of the present sectarian composition of the Levantine community of Utah is 70 percent Maronite, 10 percent Greek Orthodox, 10 percent Protestant, 5 percent Mormon, and 5 percent Moslem.

Nafy Sawaya and
Sabeh A. Sawaya,
in Lebanese
costume.

From the top: *Lebanese immigrants in Salt
Lake's Greek Town in the early 1900s. John M.
Howa, at left mixing cement, was a partner in
Hiawatha poolhall, 1920. Lebanese patriarchs
in Carbon County, 1921: Abe ('Brahim) Howa
Mose Howa, Sam Sheya, John M. Howa, and
Amen Sheya.*

Right: *Eighteen-year-old John Attey and his bride, fifteen-year-old Sarah George, Salt Lake City, 1909.* Below: *Sabeh A. Sawaya in his Kemmerer, Wyoming, store, 1918. John Attey, son of John and Sarah Attey, wearing his godmother's dowry necklace. Salt Lake Lebanese attending a picnic in Logan in the late 1920s.*

397

*Right: Armenian
converts to the
Mormon church:
Sheranians, Kezerians,
Gagosians, and
Tavoians in Zara,
Sivas province,
Armenia, 1901.*

*Below: Armenian
Latter-day Saints in
Aintab, Armenia, 1905,
among whom are:
Aposhians, Ouzounians,
Plowgians, Gengosians,
Hindoians, Polosagians,
Nolbontians, Golishians,
and Vezerians.*

Above: *Herond Nishan Sheranian, seated in foreground, with others in his University of Utah anatomy class, 1917. Dr. Sheranian was a general practitioner in Murray for many years before specializing in ophthalmology. Hagop Gagosian kept a diary of his experiences as an LDS convert.* Left: *Rebecca Sheranian as a child in Zara.* Below: *Zara, Sivas province, Armenia.*

the "Syrian" element in Utah, no Arabic publications have emerged here nor any media of any sort or language directed at Middle Eastern peoples. The only attempt to perpetuate local knowledge of the Arabic language uncovered by the writer, other than informal instruction in the home, was undertaken six years ago by Michael S. Allam, formerly a young schoolteacher in southern Lebanon, when he voluntarily conducted classes in Salt Lake City. This instruction lasted for only a few months. Allam remains the chief link in correspondence between many Levantine residents of Utah and their relatives in the motherland. He is frequently asked by the former to translate their messages into the Arabic language and script and to read and translate letters from the latter.

Other than their remarkable achievements here in the spheres of business and the professions, Levantine immigrants and their children have accrued a most enviable reputation for respect for law and order. Even during the violent strike at the Utah Fire Clay Company in 1910, the "Syrian" laborers there emerged without mention in either the newspapers or the police "blotters" of the time.[22] Further, as a dramatic indication of the continuing strength of family ties, one finds that divorce among Utah Levantines is extremely rare. Their traditional respect for their women and their elders, moreover, seems undiminished by their long residence in Utah. However, a steady trend toward migration to the Pacific Coast and elsewhere, increasing intermarriage, and other inevitable forces of cultural absorption even now foretell the eventual extinction of the Syro-Lebanese Utahns as a communal entity. In the meantime, the impact of their coming here upon the lives of many outside their own ranks stands out far more significantly than mere demographic data would suggest.

THE ARMENIANS

Unlike the "Syrians," the Armenians of the Middle East, and particularly those subject to the Ottoman throne, were impelled to emigrate in large numbers to Egypt, Western Europe, Russia, the Balkans, and the Western Hemisphere during the late nineteenth century as an urgent matter of immediate survival. A long series of bloody Armenian massacres, widely believed to have been instigated by Sultan Abdul Hamid II, commenced throughout the Ottoman

[22] Hitti, *Syrians in America,* pp. 82–87, displays obvious pride in this aspect of the "Syrian" experience in America.

Empire in 1894. The causes of these assaults, initially launched only against the defenseless Gregorian, or Apostolic, sect are far too complex to merit analysis here.[23]

The chief incentive behind the initial waves of Armenian immigrants of all faiths to America in the 1890s centered on personal safety and survival. Although the massacres of 1894–96 did not recur at a significant level until 1909, a haunting fear of recurrence among all Armenians of the Middle East sustained a steady flow of departures from that region until the outbreak of the First World War. However, the final agony of the "Armenian Question" did not commence until the year 1915, when the Young Turk regime, fearful of Armenian collaboration with invading Russian armies in eastern Asia Minor, decided upon a massive evacuation of all Armenians from that area to the vicinity of Deir ez-Zor in eastern Syria, on the surface, a reasonable and relatively harmless measure for any state in time of war. The implementation of this scheme proved cynical and inhumane beyond description. At least one Armenian immigrant of Salt Lake City, Mary B. Ouzounian, survived this bloody ordeal; and, although she was a child at the time of the march, the many atrocities she witnessed, including the loss of her parents, remain boldly etched in her memory.[24]

The slaughter of 1915 marked the high tide of Armenian suffering, but the termination of the war did not bring security to those who resided in Turkish Cilicia and the trans-Caucasian provinces of Russia. The population of Turkey today exceeds thirty-six million people; the Armenians of all sects remaining there total less than one hundred thousand, most of whom now live in Istanbul, Izmir, and Ankara. In short, World War I and subsequent, ancillary struggles totally uprooted the entire Armenian population of the Ottoman Empire.[25]

The majority of the Ottoman Armenians who survived these events settled in Syria, Lebanon, and Egypt where significant numbers of their compatriots had long before established thriving com-

---

[23] For a detailed exposition of this issue, with extensive bibliographic notes, see the author's forthcoming article, "Britain and the Launching of the Armenian Question," in *The International Journal of Middle East Studies* 7 (April 1976).

[24] Interview with Mary B. Ouzounian, July 3, 29, 31, 1974, Salt Lake City.

[25] For a moderate Turkish view of the Armenian problem, see: Ahmet Emin (Yalman), *Turkey in the World War* (New Haven, 1930), pp. 212–23. The views of an Ottoman apologist, who played a major role in the Armenian evacuation, are offered in: Djemal Pasha, *Memories of a Turkish Statesman: 1913–1919* (New York, 1922), pp. 241–302. The western liberal view of the issue, to include many alleged eyewitness accounts of the atrocities of 1915, is

mercial colonies. In 1945 Albert H. Hourani, a noted authority on Middle Eastern minority peoples, estimated the Armenians of the Levant at almost one hundred twenty thousand in Syria and nearly sixty-nine thousand in Lebanon, almost 5 percent of the total population in each case. The greatest concentrations of them are still found in Aleppo and Beirut. However, a paroxysm of anti-Christian sentiment throughout Syria in the wake of the founding of Israel and the first Arab-Israeli war heralded the start of a constant flow of Armenians from the former city to the latter. This migration continues to this day and lies at the source of most Armenian movement to the United States in recent decades.[26]

Like the "Syrians," most of the Armenians admitted to this country have settled east of the Mississippi River and north of the Ohio River, and in California, particularly in the farming community around Fresno. And again, similar to trends set by the Levantines, Armenian immigrants have concentrated in the greatest numbers in the cities of New England and the Atlantic Seaboard, where most found work in the manufacture of leather goods (especially shoes) and textiles.[27] Also, Armenian merchants, like their Levantine contemporaries, engaged in the importation and sale of carpets and other costly fabrics. Yet again like the "Syrians," some Armenians have entered this land by way of Mexico—having been refused admittance to eastern ports due to diseases (usually trachoma) or a lack of proof of means of financial support.

probably best presented by Arnold J. Toynbee, *The Armenian Atrocities: The Murder of a Nation* (London, 1915). The *Armenian Review* of Boston, produced by the large Armenian colony there, although often lacking in objectivity, has printed many articles on the issue as seen from the Armenian point of view.

Armenians Admitted to and Departed from the United States, 1899–1924

Year	Armenians Admitted (total/males)	Armenians Departed
1899	674/471	Unknown
1904	1745/1315	"
1909	3108/2601	464
1914	7785/6533	1117
1919	285/196	1
1924	2940/1226	16

Compiled from Ferenczi, *International Migrations*, pp. 432–43, 498.

[26] For an exhaustive study of the Armenian community in the Levant, consult: Avedis K. Sanjian, *The Armenian Communities in Syria under Ottoman Domination* (Cambridge, Mass., 1965). Richard G. Hovannisian, "The Ebb and Flow of the Armenian Minority in the Arab Middle East," *Middle East Journal* 28 (Winter 1974): 19–32, examines post-Ottoman developments.

[27] The Fresno area comprises the sole significant Armenian farming community in the United States. Niles Carpenter, *Immigrants and their Children: 1920* (Washington, D.C., 1927), pp. 364–84, presents tables to reflect the national distribution of our Armenian colonies per the census of 1920.

Thanks to the development of a relatively superior system of education within the Gregorian communities of Turkey and Russia during the latter half of the nineteenth century, plus the general concentration of efforts among western missionaries on the rural Armenians of the Middle East, the literacy rate among Armenian immigrants compared favorably to American standards; and newly arrived Armenians enjoyed relatively rapid and painless advancement here in employment. A national reputation for industriousness enhanced this process considerably.

Nevertheless, an enduring propensity for clannishness and haggling for prices in the marketplace, also peculiar to the Levantine immigrants, exposed the Armenians to the usual nativistic patterns of suspicion and hostility.[28] Armenian clannishness, stemming as in the case of the Syro-Lebanese from the restrictions of sectarian communal life in the Middle East, remains strong among the Gregorian and Catholic ghettos of New York, Boston, Detroit, Philadelphia, Jersey City, and San Francisco. True again to the fashions set by Levantine settlers, the larger Armenian colonies have reinforced their old lifestyle in importing both their presses and their native churches; and they have formed many fraternal, philanthropic, and scholastic associations, some on an international scale.

However, an apparent passion for business, the professions (especially medicine), and the arts among the more affluent ranks of Armenians is steadily breaking down old barriers; and the relentless forces of cultural assimilation, including migration from the ghetto and intermarriage, have spawned at least two generations of utterly acculturated Armeno-Americans.[29] This marks the extent of similarities in trends set to date by America's major groups of immigrants from the Middle East, particularly so in the case of those in Utah.

A recent ethno-historical survey of the employment records of the Utah Copper Company for the period 1910–20 revealed almost one hundred fifty Armenian laborers' names and terms of service. Few of these surnames can be found today in the telephone directories of the major communities of this state. One is thus forced to

[28] Emory S. Bogardus, *Immigration and Race Attitudes* (New York, 1928), pp. 14, 25, 53–54, 196.

[29] Jeremiah W. Jenks and W. Jett Lauck, *The Immigration Problem: A Study of American Immigration Conditions and Needs* (New York and London, 1917), in Table 5 (Occupations abroad), pp. 493–501, presents data concerning the former vocations of Armenian (and "Syrian") immigrants. In Table 9 (Industrial distribution of immigrant wage earners), pp. 516–19, they offer similar data after immigration.

conclude that these Armenians, most of them railroaders by trade, migrated from Utah toward the close of the First World War, barring, of course, the distinct possibility that some died here without male offspring or had anglicized their surnames, such as: Krikorian to Gregory, Hagopian to Jacobson.[30] Current Utah telephone directories did yield slightly over one hundred Armenian surnames, over one-half of which fall in Salt Lake and Weber counties. Interviews among the forty-four families of Armenian extraction located by the author in Salt Lake County have produced few trends in arrival dates and employment preferences. In keeping with national patterns, however, Utah Armenians are well represented in education and medicine, far out of proportion to their modest numbers in this state. Contrary to the general trend set among the Syro-Lebanese population, the Armenian immigrants of Utah, like those of the entire nation, hail from all walks of life in the old country: urban and rural, rich and poor, highly educated and scarcely literate.

Without access to the worksheets and individual questionnaires compiled during the 1960 census of population, it is impossible even to estimate the current Armenian "foreign stock" of this state.[31] Although native speakers of Arabic (and their children) became a matter of record in that census, no other Middle Eastern language warranted mention. The omission of Armenian-speakers from the inventory of "foreign stock" in 1960 obviously suggests that the number of such persons discovered fell considerably below the ninety-four Arabic-speakers recorded. That a substantial segment of Armenian immigrants claim Turkish, rather than Armenian, as their native tongue may help to explain this void. The sole hint available regarding the size of the Armenian community of Utah comes from the census of 1920, which records the Armenian foreign-born element of this state at eighty persons. The Armenian colony is too small and available data on dates of arrival here, trends in employment, and places of residence too disparate to permit generalization by the

[30] It is equally possible that native male Utahns, returning from military service in World War I, claimed the jobs formerly held by these transient Armenians, or that the latter departed this country for the newly established Armenian republic in trans-Caucasia. After World War II Armenians emigrated from all over the world to the Armenian SSR in response to Soviet blandishments.

[31] The 1960 Census is more useful, for purposes of comparison, than that of 1970, because the Arabic-speaking, foreign-born element of Utah dropped sharply from 94 to 50 persons during this interval. Also the 1960 Census offers similar data from past censuses (1910–40), and the 1970 Census does not.

writer. One must therefore conclude tentatively that most of the non-Mormon Armenians came here from the northeastern states and California in response to unique opportunities for self-improvement or to join relatives.

On the positive side of the ledger, however, a great deal of information is available through church records and personal journals on local Armenians of the Mormon faith.[32] Slightly over one-half of all the Armenians identified in Utah by the author are Latter-day Saints, and their ancestors started to arrive here from the vicinity of Sivas in central Anatolia about 1897. Other Mormon families began the long trek to Utah from Aintab (the Gazi Antep of modern Turkey) in southern Asia Minor about the same time. About twenty such families had arrived here by the outbreak of the First World War. The war not only put a stop to Mormon missionary work in Anatolia but drove the Mormons out of both Sivas and Aintab into the Levant, whence they have been emigrating in a slow but steady rivulet since the war. Some who arrived in recent years had awaited an immigration quota in Aleppo or Beirut for over twenty years.

One of the earliest arrivals from the Sivas area, Hagop Thomas Gagosian, has left a brief, fascinating journal of his odyssey that begins:

> I Hagop Thomas (Tumas) Gagosian, son of Tumas and Marrow Sherinian Gagosian, was born an Armenian in the town of Zara, State of Sivas, Country of Turkey, . . . on January 25, 1868. I lived in Zara until I was 45 years old, then emmigrated [sic] to the United States of America. . . . We had joined the Church of Jesus Christ of Latter-Day-Saints so were anxious to come to America, the land of our dreams.

Years of penury and thwarted planning preceded the arrival of Hagop Gagosian to Utah. As a boy he was hired out to a farmer to get stacks of wheat ready for threshing. "This plank was too heavy for a fourteen-year-old boy to handle alone. I hurt my back and have

---

[32] See: Viola Woodbury Kelsey, "Diary of Hagop Thomas (Tumas) Gagosian," trans. F.H. Gagosian (Price, Utah, 1961); Reuben Ouzounian, untitled autobiography (Salt Lake City, n.d.); and Herond Nishan Sheranian, *Odyssey of an Armenian Doctor* (Los Angeles, 1970). Historical sketches of Mormon missionary efforts in the Middle East are available in: Kate B. Carter, ed., *Heart Throbs of the West,* 12 vols. (Salt Lake City, 1939–51), 4: 295–300; and Abraham Hindoian, "A short history of the Church of Jesus Christ of Latter-day Saints in the Middle East," trans. Joseph Jacobs (Salt Lake City: n.d.).

been bothered with it all my life." He was later apprenticed to a barber, a distant relative of his mother.

> So, I started on my career of learning how to cut hair, to pull teeth, as well as how to prepare and serve Turkish coffee, all for one Krush a day (4¢ in American money) and my board and room. It was also my job to sleep at the barber shop, clean it up after hours and serve as a watchman. . . .

While working as a plasterer several years later, Gagosian heard of F.F. Hintze of Holladay, Utah, who chose "to go to Constantinople as a Mormon missionary to do good instead of staying home to face punishment as a polygamist because he felt he could not desert any of his [three] wives." From Constantinople, Hintze came to Zara. "The Mormon church started in Zara 6 of October, in 1888." Gagosian was baptized against his wife's wishes by Nisham K. Sherinian, May 27, 1894, in the river Zara.

It took Gagosian three years to reach Utah to see if "there really was a prophet at the head of the church with two Councilors and twelve Apostles like in Christ's Church of olden days." Armenians had extreme problems with obtaining passports and Gagosian's membership in an anti-Turkish party added danger to his efforts. Leaving his wife with three children, and a bakery to run, Gagosian "started walking like an American hobo," with a borrowed lira [the equivalent of five American dollars] and a rug on which to sleep. While he worked his way to the sea for a few cents a day, sleeping in stables, and sailing on to Cyprus, the first wave of Armenian massacres swept through Anatolia.

After incredible misery in Egypt, France, and London, Gagosian arrived in Salt Lake City on July 10, 1897, in time for the fiftieth anniversary celebration of the arrival of the Mormon pioneers in Utah. Six months later he was told that he must accompany F.F. Hintze and Anthon Lund "to the Old country to buy land in Jerusalem on which to colonize the Armenian Mormons." Gagosian had destroyed his passport to keep from ever returning. "Oh, my! How I did resist. I had just reached the Holy Land, now they wanted me to go back."

It was twelve years before he returned to America, "a free country, away from Turkish bondage." From Salt Lake City he and his family traveled to Saint George where their eldest daughter, Nimzar, lived. She had married John T. Woodbury, a Mormon missionary to Turkey, a year earlier.

In Saint George, Gagosian worked as a laborer on the construction of Dixie College. From there he moved to Nevada to farm, then to Nephi and to Price, with hard work and many setbacks in each place. His faith in his American religion never altered, although,

> I am sorry to say that all of us that emegrated [sic] to Utah started changing. We began getting weaker in our beliefs. . . . We, that loved each other so much, now started to be like the people around us. Even though we were poor before we came to America, we were rich in our faith and we were contented with each others love. What happened to us? What changed us? I cannot truly explain but I pray that the Lord be with us and help us to live to the end in faith.

Hagop Gagosian died five years after his son Ferdinand took him to Salt Lake City in 1947 for the one hundredth anniversary celebration of the Mormon pioneers. "It was a rare priviledge [sic] and a great celebration," he said.

Another early arrival from the Sivas area, Herond Nishan Sheranian, became a prominent ophthalmologist in Salt Lake City where he founded both a hospital and a clinic before moving to Los Angeles in 1933. And Col. Kerrigan M. Manookin, a Utah immigrant from Adana in Turkish Cilicia, commanded the U.S. Army Proving Ground at Dugway during the Second World War.

Dr. Sheranian said, in *Odyssey of an Armenian Doctor:*

> Mother was considered to be the most expert of all rug weavers in all of Sivas County in Turkish Armenia which was then the center of the rug weaving industry. . . . she sheared her own wool, made her own yarn, chose her own patterns, made her own colors. . . . Apostle Lorenzo Snow of the [Latter-day Saints] Church wrote her a letter of gratitude for a large rug she wove and presented as a gift to the Temple in Salt Lake City, December 13, 1899.[33]

Despite the leveling influence of the church, Mormon Armenian immigrants have married among themselves to an intense degree— especially so among the children and grandchildren of the first settlers. Among the more recent arrivals and the third generation of the earlier settlers, marriage outside the Armenian community has become commonplace. The sacrifices endured by all in the course of coming to Utah are most impressive; many have exchanged lucrative businesses in the old country for the most menial sort

[13] P. 487.

of work in Salt Lake City. The devotion of this small community is a great credit to their church.

MISCELLANEA

In the past twenty-five years, small colonies of Iranians, Egyptians, and Palestinian Arabs, many of them Moslems, have bloomed in the larger urban communities of this state. However, in all cases the numbers of immigrants involved remains too modest to merit mention in the census of 1960 or 1970. Iran has enjoyed the consultative services of agronomists at Utah State University since 1939. This relationship has generated a burgeoning stream of Iranian students to all of the institutions of higher education in northern Utah, and an increasing number of graduates foresake their former homeland each year.[34] In Egypt, on the other hand, the strains of overpopulation finally moved the government to encourage emigration in the mid-1960s. Thus, many professional people and administrators who had seen higher education in Europe and America began to respond to employment opportunities here. The United States government, since the creation of Israel, has allowed special immigration quotas to displaced Palestinian Arabs, and a modest number of them have settled in Utah, most of them in Salt Lake County.[35]

The staff and faculty of the University of Utah probably boast the largest Middle Eastern work force in the state. A survey of the staff and faculty portion of the campus directory reveals many Middle Eastern names, spread throughout every college and major staff agency. Finally, the university claims one of the few Middle East centers founded in recent years among American institutions of higher learning.[36] Although the Middle Eastern ethnic faculty of the center is quite small, they spark some of the major social events today among the entire Middle Eastern community of Utah and, through courses, publications, and public appearances, contribute to American understanding of the Middle Eastern peoples.

[34] For a history of this relationship, see: Gwen H. Haws, ed., *Iran and Utah State University: Half a Century of Friendship and a Decade of Contacts* (Logan, Utah, 1963). The Melcomian and Simonian families of Salt Lake City emigrated from Iran which continues to host large Armenian colonies in Isfahan and Tehran. Ardeshir Zahedi, Iranian ambassador to the United States and himself a graduate of Utah State University, during an address before celebrants of the Iranian New Year in Salt Lake City, on March 22, 1974, estimated the Iranian student population of Utah then at over five hundred men and women.

[35] Interview with Dr. Fikri Gahin, October 7, 1974, Salt Lake City.

[36] The center is directed by Professor Khosrow Mostofi, an Iranian immigrant holding a doctoral degree from the University of Utah. The previous director, Distinguished Professor of History Aziz S. Atiya, emigrated from the Coptic Christian community of Egypt.

13

THE EXILED GREEKS

BY HELEN Z. PAPANIKOLAS

Small bird, there where you fly to *Ameriki,*
Tell me, where does my son sleep?
When he is sick, who tends him?
　　　　　　　　　　—Folk song of immigration

At the beginning of the century, thousands of young Greeks began coming to Utah to live their first years of exile in a new land. Like myriad Greeks since ancient times, forced to leave their rocky land that could not sustain them, they vowed to return within a few years. Any life outside *patridha,* "the fatherland," was exile. Not knowing what the three *Moiroi,* "the Fates," had decided for them during their first three days of life, many brought a bit of earth in an amulet or small bottle. If their destiny was death in American exile, a priest would have a pinch of Greek earth to sprinkle over them as they lay in their caskets.

The boys and young men had grown up in one of the most devastating periods of Greece's turbulent history. Struggling in the decay left by 400 years of Ottoman rule, their northern provinces still under Turkish control, many of their islands governed by the English and Italians, Greece became bankrupt in 1893. In 1897 the Greeks were defeated by the Turks and further humiliated by the Great Powers' imposing financial control over them.[1] The education of this generation, then, was poor, often completely lacking, their opportunities stultified.

When the main industry of Greece, the currant crop, failed in 1907, families mortgaged their land at usurious rates to send sons to America. It was their only hope to survive penury and to provide daughters with necessary dowries. The few yearly emigrants standing on wharves with their scant belongings multiplied into thou-

This essay is based mainly on the author's *Toil and Rage in a New Land: The Greek Immigrants in Utah,* 2d ed. rev., reprinted from *Utah Historical Quarterly* 38, no. 2 (1970).

[1] L.S. Stavrianos, *The Balkans Since 1453* (New York, 1966), p. 467.

sands, among them men wearing white kilts or Cretan breeches. Villages were left with only women, children, and old men to harvest crops and to tend goats.[2] Previous generations had gone to Rumania, Russia, and Egypt. Sailors were wont to jump ship in outposts throughout the world. The young at the turn of the century sat in village squares and in coffeehouses listening to priests reading letters from *Ameriki* and gazing at photographs of former villagers dressed in American finery. Work was everywhere, the letters said, especially on the *sidheró dhramés* ("rail lines").

Often the well-dressed emigrants themselves returned as labor agents for American industrialists. Although contract labor had been made illegal after the inundation of Irish immigrants a half century earlier, it had continued covertly. Into remote mountain villages of Greece, labor and steamship agents climbed to entice the destitute who were eager to indenture themselves to reach *Ameriki*. With their families' pool of silver sewed inside the lining of their jackets or pinned to their homespun underwear, some with clarinets and stringed instruments under their arms, they boarded crowded ships at Piraeus, Patras, and Heraklion. Many of them were forced to wait a week or more in Naples and other European ports for space on ships crossing back and forth to the United States. They stood on the crowded lower decks with hope and anxiety, hope for a new life, anxiety that they would be turned back by officials at Ellis Island who every day rejected thousands of immigrants. Gheorghios Zisimopoulos, who would change his name to George Zeese and become the owner of a grocery chain in Utah, feared that he would be sent back because of a missing index finger. George Cayias, who became a leading Utah insurance man, was nine years old when he reached Ellis Island. Through a misunderstanding his older brother was not there to meet him. He was put back on board ship, got off in Spain by mistake, and after many harrowing adventures, again sailed for Ellis Island. The island was a symbol of what awaited them in America.

The Greeks came later to America and to Utah than the Italians with whom they are often compared. Italians had been in Carbon County mines since the late 1890s and were followed by relatives and countrymen. Yet a greater number of Greeks came to Utah.[3]

[2] *Ibid.*, p. 481. The 1910 Census lists immigrants from Greece as follows: 1850–86; 1860–328; 1870–390; 1880–776; 1890–1,887; 1900–8,515; 1910–101,282.

[3] *Ibid.* In 1910 Utah's population was 373,351. Greeks numbered 4,039 or 6.4 percent of the foreign-born population; Italians 3,117 or 4.9 percent.

It was the intense activity of Greek labor agents that brought thousands of their *patrioti* to that section near the Salt Lake City railyards called Greek Town. Of these, Leonidas G. Skliris, became a *padrone* of immense power. All Greek labor agents in the West either worked directly for him or had a reciprocal relationship with him. Americans called him the "Czar of the Greeks." Pictures of Skliris and other leading Greek immigrants appear in a 1908 issue of *O Ergatis* ("The Worker"), a Greek-English newspaper printed in Salt Lake City. Skliris is correctly described as a native of Sparta and incorrectly as the first Greek in Utah. (Nicholas Kastro was the first, coming to Utah in the 1870s; he was a friend of Brigham Young, an Indian fighter, and pioneer Bingham Canyon mining man.)[4] The back page of the newspaper advertises Greek steamship lines with branch offices in Greek Town.

Commissions from steamship companies for fares and from immigrants for finding them work were lucrative for the *padrones* during America's burst of industrialization. The Czar advertised in Greek newspapers in America, Greece, and Crete. His advertisements in the journal of the Denver and Rio Grande and Western Pacific reads:

L. G. Skliris

The Reliable Labor Contractor

Headquarters: 507 W 2d So., Salt Lake City.

Branch offices: New York, St. Paul, Chicago,

Kansas City, Denver, San Francisco and Sacramento.[5]

Skliris was the authorized labor agent for both the Denver and Rio Grande and Western Pacific railroads, the Utah Copper Company (now Kennecott Copper Corporation), and coal mines in Carbon County, Utah. Through arrangements with other Greek labor agents, he sent laborers to the Union Pacific and Oregon Short Line railroads, Wyoming and Colorado mines, Pueblo steel mills, and Nevada metal mines. Skliris's czardom accounts for the 1910 Census recording the largest concentration of Greeks in America as living in the Mountain States.[6] Between the 1910 and

---

[4] Greek Archives, Western Americana Division, Marriott Library, University of Utah. Nicholas Kastro, according to the *Holy Trinity Greek Orthodox Church of Salt Lake City Fiftieth Anniversary Book* (Salt Lake City, 1955), pp. 38–39, returned to Greece at the age of 80. His descendants altered their name to Casto.

[5] *The Scenic Lines Employees' Magazine, Official Railroad Journal of Denver and Rio Grande-Western Pacific,* September 1917, p. 38.

[6] Greeks in Utah numbered 4,039.

1920 Censuses, the Garfield smelter was opened (1914), and eleven more coal mines began producing, bringing more Greeks into Utah.

Padrones in the West supplied strikebreakers as well as workers. With a telephone call or telegram to western coffeehouses, Skliris could have hundreds of newly arrived, unemployed Greeks traveling to distant mines and railyards. When reaching their destination, the perplexed immigrants found they had to run through picket lines. Although the workers did not win their demands, the Greeks were impressed that lowly laborers had the effrontery to complain about employers. Unlike northern Italians and South Slavs, Greeks did not leave their country for seasonal employment in northern countries where radicalism was prevalent among workers. For supplying strikebreakers alone, mine and railroad management found Skliris invaluable.

In the first years of the century, Skliris sent lieutenants to Greece for his labor gangs. Among them was a contingent brought over to break the Carbon County strike of 1903.[7] Skliris's advertisements made the journeys unnecessary. Greeks were coming into the country in such numbers that the Czar sent recruiters to coffeehouses in the Greek section of Chicago's Halstead Street and to those in Denver and Pueblo, Colorado. These dispatches also became superfluous, except during strikes; Serbians, Albanians, and Lebanese, as well as Greeks, came to Skliris.

Greeks without countrymen already employed in Utah worked their way across the country laying rails over the prairies, building roads, digging sewers, disposing of offal in slaughterhouses, and clearing land of sagebrush. They rode freights, munching bread and dried beans, trying to learn a few words of the new language from small, gilt-edged, Greek-English dictionaries bought in New York and Chicago. They climbed onto wrong freight cars, their food giving out, always alert for railroad detectives their countrymen had warned them against. They hid from town officials who would charge them a three-dollar head tax and jail them if they could not pay it. They were stunned by the hate of Americans. "The scum of Europe," "depraved, brutal foreigners" they were called in print, taunted and jeered when they asked for work. In coffeehouses along the way, they heard of attacks on Greeks: the burning of Omaha's Greek Town and the routing of a gang of Greeks clear-

[7] *Wyoming Labor Journal* (Cheyenne), June 16, 1922.

ing sagebrush south of Boise, Idaho, by masked men on horses, whips and guns in their hands.[8]

They arrived at last at the Salt Lake City railyards, the life-blood of immigrants in the state. Greek Town encircled the yards and in the Parthenon, Open Heart, and Hellenic coffeehouses were Skliris's men waiting to sign on the new arrivals. Each Greek agreed to pay an initial fee averaging twenty dollars—out of his wages if he did not have the money—and was given a document to sign. It was printed in English that the men could not read.

> . . . I ——————— for myself, my heirs, executors adminis-trators, and assigns, do hereby irrevocably assign and set over to L. G. Skliris, of the City and County of Salt Lake and State of Utah, the sum of One Dollar ($1,00) [sic] per month out of any wages earned or which may hereafter be earned by me in the employment of ——————— and I do hereby irrevocadly [sic] authorize, empower and direct said Railroad Company to deduct said amount . . . and to pay same to L. G. Skliris. . . .[9]

The laborers were told to trade at certain Greek businesses or they would lose their jobs. The owners of these meat, grocery, and clothing stores were all agents of Skliris. Although the workers fumed at Skliris's living off their labor, at his diamonds, and at his luxurious suite in the recently constructed Hotel Utah, they considered themselves fortunate to have work. It enabled them to send money orders to Greece, a practice that was used in all propaganda attacks against them. Because Skliris had the *messa* ("means") of patronage that the poor did not have, the men accepted his extortion in America as they would have in Greece.

Labor men throughout the country complained that the immigrants were taking jobs from "bona-fide" Americans by working for less pay. Newspapers printed scornful descriptions of their crowded, unhealthy living conditions. No one, except the American Federation of Labor, blamed industrialists who hired this "cheap labor" and provided insufficient housing or none at all. A Greek woman journalist berated R. C. Gemmel, general manager of Utah Copper Company, for the tents and shacks in which Greek workers

[8] Thomas Burgess, *Greeks in America* (Boston, 1913), pp. 165–67; Theodore Saloutos, *The Greeks in the United States* (Cambridge, Mass., 1964), pp. 62, 66–69; John G. Bitzes, "The Anti Greek Riot of 1909—South Omaha," *Nebraska History* 51, no. 2 (1970): 199–224; Papanikolas, *Toil and Rage,* p. 112.

[9] American West Center, University of Utah.

413

lived, and where water for drinking and sewage streams trickled nearby. "They choose their own habitations," Gemmel said, "and if we built them new quarters, they would prefer to stay where they are." [10]

Greeks steadily arrived, found temporary sanctuary in Greek Town, and were sent to the Carbon County mines, Murray-Midvale smelters, Bingham Canyon mines, Magna mill, Garfield smelter, north of Ogden for railroad-gang work on the Oregon Short Line (later Union Pacific), and the Denver and Rio Grande in Utah and Colorado. Those from nine to fourteen years of age became water boys.

The greatest number of men were sent to railroad section and steel gangs where pay was as low as twenty dollars a month and where they were isolated for months until winter when they were laid off. Besides extensive branch-line building, narrow-guage tracks were being replaced by wider, standard track that would allow freight to proceed from one line to another without having to be unloaded and reloaded. Laying track and keeping it in repair was a major industry and a wholly immigrant occupation. Census-taking was haphazard and Greeks known to have been in Utah working on railroad gangs are not found in Polk's city directory.

The men lived in tents and in railroad cars and worked under Japanese foremen, later replacing many of them. Although the Greeks were reviled as "undesirable aliens" and not "white," the more distinctive appearance of the Japanese caused their ruthless displacement. The early association of Greeks and Japanese lasted during their prolonged bachelorhoods. They wrestled, vied with each other in feats of strength, and were favorite card-playing companions.

Between jobs on section gangs the men returned to Greek Town. Although they were fulfilling family obligations decreed by Greek tradition, for the first time in their lives they had steady work and could spend a portion of their savings in coffeehouses, restaurants, saloons, candy stores, and bakeries. In crowded, pungent-smelling importing stores, they bought octopi, Turkish tobacco, olive oil, goat cheese, liqueurs, figs, and dates. They gathered in coffeehouses for their most satisfying recreation, discussions based on the stands taken by Greek-language newspapers. These invariably turned into brawls over Greek politics: the men were either royal-

[10] Maria S. Ekonomidou, *E Ellines Tis Amerikis Opos Tous Eda* ("The Greeks of America as I Saw Them") (New York, 1916), p. 85.

ists upholding King Constantine or partisans of Premier Eleftherios Venizelos.

Peripatetic showmen from Greece regularly brought puppet shows, the *Karaghiozi*, to the coffeehouses. *Karaghiozis* was a sly, hunchbacked, illiterate Greek peasant who successfully cheated wily Turks and pompous Greek officials. Night and day, coffeehouse phonographs rasped out old guerrilla songs from the centuries of struggle against the Turks. For the Cretans the days of liberation were but a few years past, in 1897. Many of them had been guerrillas, singing then as they sang in Utah coffeehouses, songs of necessary cruelty:

> When will the sky clear, when will it be February
> to take my rifle, my lovely mistress,
> To come down to Amalo, on the road to Mousoure,
> to make mothers sonless, and wives widows.

The young men—few older men and no women came in the first onrush—clasped hands and danced in circles, waiting their turn to lead, to show their manliness, their *leventia*. With leaps and twirls, they bent backwards and lifted chairs with their teeth or balanced a glass of *ouzo* or *mastiha* on their foreheads. In their songs and dances, nostalgia for *patridha* lay heavy in rooms, blue-layered with tobacco smoke.

The men brought with them an ambivalence toward priests, but not to their religion. They built a small, one-domed brick church on Fourth South between Third and Fourth West. It was dedicated on October 29, 1905, and served the Greek, Serbian, Christian Albanians, and Russian people.[11] The immigrants were now assured of the Eastern Orthodox ceremonial rites of life and death. Bearded, long-haired priests, wearing black robes, glinting pectoral crosses, and tall black cylindrical hats (*kalimafkions*), walked the streets of their Greek Town domain, performed the mysteries (sacraments), arbitrated disputes, and helped in matchmaking by writing letters to Greece for illiterate immigrants—although they were often barely literate themselves.

The Holy Trinity Church was the mother church for Greek immigrants in the Intermountain West. Until Greek churches were built in McGill and Ely, Nevada; Denver and Pueblo, Colorado; Rock Springs, Wyoming; Pocatello, Idaho; Great Falls, Montana;

---

[11] *Holy Trinity 50th Anniversary Book*, pp. 41–44.

and Price, Utah, the Salt Lake Greek church was the center of Greek life in these states. Archbishops and bishops, in robes and *kalimafkions,* with black veils falling backwards, elaborately carved staffs of office in their hands, came to Salt Lake City as to a far-off outpost. From there they were escorted to Greek "colonies" hundreds of miles away.

If immigrants could not come to the church, priests went to them. They rode trains and stages to marry men to picture brides, to baptize a prolific number of children, and to bury the many young men killed in industrial accidents. These burials, called Death Weddings in Greek folklife, required the unmarried dead to be dressed as for marriage, the most important event in a person's life, one of the seven mysteries. With white-blossomed wedding crowns on their heads and gold wedding rings on their right hands—the hands that make the sign of the cross—the dead were buried with a sprinkle of Greek earth.[12]

If the Greeks could have chosen their jobs, they would have stayed in Salt Lake's Greek Town near their church. Their main objective, though, was to find work in the mines where wages were twice as high as on the railroads and where the camps were filled with *patrioti.* Utah Copper employment records, Utah immigration reports, and Carbon County newspaper accounts attest to Greeks being by far the largest group of immigrants in mining towns.[13]

In mining camps the men lived in crowded boardinghouses, in tents, and in shacks they built themselves out of explosives boxes on company land. Sanitation was deplorable. Yet the men would live under any conditions in return for steady wages. It was the company doctors they feared, who, they said, carelessly cut off arms and legs. Injured men were hidden at times and spirited away to boardinghouses where a Greek folkhealer was brought to administer cures before "the butchers got them." The loss of a leg or an arm or blindness from mine blasting meant return to Greece and destitution, help to parents and dowries for sisters a lost fantasy.

American life was jarring for the Greeks. Their 23 percent illiteracy rate left many of them at the mercy of their compatriots as

---

[12] This custom is traced to antiquity. See John Cuthbert Lawson, *Modern Greek Folklore and Ancient Greek Religion* (New Hyde Park, N.Y., 1964), pp. 545–62.

[13] Employment records of Utah Copper Company 1880–1920, in R. C. Gemmel Hall, Bingham Canyon; yearly Coal Mine Inspector's Reports in State of Utah documents.

well as of Americans.[14] They had come from societies accustomed to paying Turkish and Greek authorities bribes for every small service and found the practice continued in America by Greek "interpreters" who knew a few more words of English than they. In contrast there was also in each coffeehouse an older man "with reason" who admonished the young men against card players and "bad" women and who extricated them from disturbance-of-peace charges, so common as to be routine—the Greeks would take no slight to their nationality. Vice-Consul Stylian Staes (Stylianos Stagopoulos) of Salt Lake City and Price was foremost among these "men with reason."

The coffeehouse was the men's true home. In its gregariousness, they found security against nativist hostility. Mormons looked at them as strange beings; the Greeks, in turn, derided the "White Heads" whose polygamy in the recent past was, to them, another version of Turkish harems.

Cut loose from the authoritarian rule of parents, the men discovered freedom; it also brought them "that homesickness that has no cure." The patriarchal structure of their society gave women a lowly role. Men were waited on from birth to death with slavish subservience. In the male society of labor gangs and mining camps, the men were vulnerable and longed for return to *patridha*.

There were fewer than ten Greek women in Utah by 1910. The men's namedays passed with makeshift celebrations of roast lamb and a drink of liqueur at best; the days of feasts and religious services to honor them were memories. The Greeks had no women to prepare the fast foods before the great church events, Christmas, Easter, and the Dormition of the Virgin on August 15. When one of them died, women did not sit by the casket to keen the *mirologhia,* the "Words of Fate," nor forty days later to prepare the memorial wheat, boiled, sweetened, sprinkled with nuts, raisins, and pomegranate seeds, wheat and seeds, symbols of immortality.[15]

To help each other and to keep their ethnic identity, the men joined Pan Hellenic Unions. These organizations were fostered by Greece itself to keep alive the idea of return. With the Pan Hellenics, their immigrant church, and their customs, the men led a Greek-

[14] *Annual Report of the Commissioner General of Immigration to the Secretary of Commerce and Labor for the Fiscal Year Ended June 30, 1905,* chart II following text.

[15] Memorial feasts have their roots in ancient Greek life. See Lawson, *Modern Greek Folklore,* pp. 486, 532–41.

centered life. Only men isolated in areas far from Greek Towns were without roots. They married Mormon women and although only two of them converted to the Latter-day Saints church, they were lost to their culture.[16]

The Greeks continued coming to Utah, continued paying extortion to the Czar. In 1912 the Western Federation of Labor called a strike in the Bingham copper mines.[17] The federation had tried to interest the Greeks in unionization for several years but had not been successful. The Greeks still expected to return to the fatherland. Their only interest in labor was to get enough money to get out of it, each to become his "own boss." It was important to the Western Federation to have the support of the Greeks, the largest group of workers. In saloons and boardinghouses, the labor organizers, called Bolsheviks, Wobblies, and agitators, made a pact with the Greeks: if the Greeks became members of the federation, a condition of the strike would be the firing of Skliris as their labor agent. The Greeks joined in a body and jubilantly ran up and down the streets of Bingham shooting off guns.

Fifty National Guard sharpshooters on order of Gov. William Spry and twenty-five deputy sheriffs from Salt Lake City were sent into the town. Gambling halls were closed and mines and railroad crossings were floodlighted. The strikers took blankets and guns and barricaded themselves on the mountainside.

The union spoke of wages, but the Greeks, almost all Cretans, "famed as men who, when the spirit moves them to fight, are difficult to control," made the firing of Skliris their first goal. The Cretans were supported by the second Greek-language newspaper to be published in Salt Lake City, *O Evzone,* named for the white-kilted Greek palace guard. (The editor was a champion of laborers. He exposed a self-proclaimed banker who ostensibly represented the National Bank of Greece, but instead deposited the workers' money each night in a Salt Lake City bank and collected the interest for himself.)[18]

The Greek priest, Father Vasilios Lambrides, wearing his black robes and *kalimafkion,* climbed the mountain to exhort the men to

---

[16] Harry George Greaves and Sarah Smith Greaves, "Hellenic Latter-day Saints," vol. 1, Greek Archives, University of Utah.

[17] Helen Zeese Papanikolas, "Life and Labor Among the Immigrants of Bingham Canyon," *Utah Historical Quarterly* 33 (1965): 289–315.

[18] Tape-recorded interviews with Paul G. Borovilos, Louis Lingos, John Demeris and Theodore Marganis, and John Kotsovos, in American West Center, University of Utah; and reminiscences of author's parents.

refrain from violence. The Greeks took off their caps to him in respect but became enraged when Utah Copper manager Gemmel steadfastly upheld Skliris. Strikebreakers were brought in, the greater number of them unemployed Greeks sent on Skliris's orders through his connections with Greek labor agents in Pocatello, Idaho, and Denver, Colorado. The strikebreakers were from the Greek mainland; enmity between them and the Cretan strikers never healed.

Gunfights among strikers, deputies, and strikebreakers erupted, killing two Greeks and wounding many men on both sides. The strike caused intense suffering among the union members and their families; business and transportation were seriously affected throughout the county; and ore production fell drastically through the inefficiency of the strikebreakers. The strike gradually ended with the Western Federation unrecognized. However, it broke the power of Leonidas Skliris and forced him out of Utah.

The Greek strikers began leaving Bingham. Church services were held for those who joined approximately two hundred Utah Greeks who went back to fight for Greece in the Balkan Wars of 1912–13. Greece recognized no other citizenship for anyone born on its soil, and men, who had served in the Greek army and others who had not, returned in high spirits to fight for the Great Idea, the redeeming of Greek lands taken by the Turks centuries before. Others knowing they were blacklisted for their participation in the strike left the state to search for work.

Greeks who could have returned to Greece at this time wanted to defer their repatriation until they had increased their savings. It was unrealistic to postpone marriage, and picture brides began to arrive on every train. In the Carbon County coal camps, Italian bands met them, their operatic melodies mingling with the shrill of mine and train whistles. Other Greeks journeyed to Greece to return with brides for themselves and several women for their friends. Immigration authorities suspected white slavery and sent women detectives to follow the travelers.[19]

The week-long wedding festivities in Greece, which began after the haggling over the dowry was completed, had to be done away with in America. There was not time in the industrial, shift-work days; Americans looked down on immigrant customs; and parents did not come with the young to insist on all of the old customs. Weddings were solemnized on Sundays, the holy day for weddings,

---

[19] Interview with George Zoumadakis, April 21, 1966.

Above: *Leading* padrone *of the West, Leonidas G. Skliris, "Czar of the Greeks," was forced out as labor agent during the 1912 Bingham strike. The traditional final picture taken outside the first Holy Trinity Greek Orthodox Church, dedicated in 1905.* Below: *The first Politz Candy Store, corner of State and Third South streets, 1921. From the left: Ernest G. Mantes, state senator from Tooele and Juab counties for six terms; George Karas, confectioner; Mrs. Andrew Politz; Mrs. Tom Politz; Tom Politz, owner. Second and third from right: Louis Limberis and Con Chlepas.*

From the top: *Greeks from Crete had their picture taken for old-country relatives with bottles and guns as signs of affluence; sprigs of basil are a symbol of friendship. A gathering of brides and young Greeks in 1912 with the Garfield smelter in the background. Greeks outside the first Orthodox church on Palm Sunday before returning to fight for Greece in the Balkan Wars of 1912 and 1913. Jim Gavrilis wearing the* foustanella *of mainland Greeks and Steve Grillos in Cretan* vrákes.

Above: *The Open Heart coffeehouse in Greek Town, Salt Lake City in the twenties. Owner Emmanuel Katsanevas is standing.* Below: *The Americanization of immigrants: the decorated Christmas tree was unknown in Greece. Mr. and Mrs. Gregory Halles and friends at the baptismal dinner for Georgia Markakis, left, in her mother's arms, whose father was killed in the Castle Gate explosion, 1924.*

Left: *Greek Town, adjacent to Jap Town, where Bingham miners lived.*

Below: *Mrs. Nick Mageras ("Magerou"), midwife to two generations of Greek, Italian, and Slav women in the Magna-Midvale-Tooele area. She was renowned for her folk cures.*

ɔove: *The three main Greek musical instruments ought to America: the Cretan* lýra *played by ellios Mavrakis, the* claríno *played by Louis osta, and the* laoúto *played by Andrew Bathemess, ding Greek musician. Letters edged in black re received regularly by immigrants; this one ls George Karas that his mother "died without ving had her fill of him."*

423

Right: The flowered tomb of Christ is carried around Holy Trinity Church on Good Friday while dirges are sung. The two tombs represent separate liturgies; until Prophet Elias Church was built in Holladay, the great number of parishioners required a second service in the Memorial Hall.

Below: Sam Sampino with hat upside down and tablecloth on shoulders mimics a priest at a Scofield picnic, 1929. Marriage license issued at Canea, Crete. To circumvent the immigration laws of 1921 and 1924, Greek women sometimes married strangers in mock ceremonies that enabled them to enter the U.S.

Above left: *The wedding of Mr. and Mrs. James Latsis in Layton, 1923.* Above right: *Plays on the theme of revolt against the Turks were important social events. Harry Kambouris, standing left, wrote many plays for the Star theatrical company. Isadore Nackos, seated left, played the part of a woman as Greek propriety frowned on married women participating without their husbands.* Left center: *picnics with lambs roasting and folk dancing were favorite recreation of summer.* Below left: *The Greek school at Bingham with teacher Andonios Voyagis, left, and the priest, Father Stephanos Angelopoulos.*

Ἑλληνόπαιδες
τοῦ Ἑλλην. Σχολείου Bingham, utah
May 29-1929· Φωτ. Ι.Δ. Σαγρῆς

baptisms, and funerals, and were followed by feasts in backyards of mine company houses, boardinghouses, and in the church basement. The Cretans kept their customs longer. For three days after a wedding, they ate, sang, danced, and stayed away from work.

By 1915 thousands of Greeks were working in the Carbon County mines and on railroad gangs in eastern Utah and western Colorado. A second Greek church, the Assumption, was dedicated in Price, the county seat, on August 15, 1916.[20] Special trains ran from all the coal camps and brought Greek miners shooting off guns in celebration.

Around every mine, mill, and smelter town in Utah, there was now a cluster of Greek families. (Real-estate clauses in many instances barred their living in the "good" sections.) The houses in these Greek Towns were three- and four-room frame ones, often painted a sky blue, the color of the Greek flag. Peddlers called out their wagon loads of butchered lamb, kid, and barrels of goat cheese. Luxuriant gardens were watered by irrigation streams, a joy to the women; in the old country they had had to walk miles over rocky goat paths to fill jugs with water. Next to the gardens were chicken coops, rabbit hutches, coal and wood sheds, and wash houses where bachelor Greeks slept on cots. In domed mud ovens bread baked and sheep pelts hung on wire fences to dry. As more children were born, lean-tos were added to the houses.

For the young mothers, life was continual childbearing and unending work. There was the added burden of boarding the young Greeks for village women. "City" women were exempt.

> We boarded forty men. They came in the morning for breakfast and we filled their lunch buckets. In the evening they came for the big meal. We washed their clothes, going to the river far from the house to get water. I had only four children, but most of the women had eight or more. Four men relatives lived with us.[21]

In retrospect the mothers remember the fatigue but also the relief that their children would never be hungry. They had left behind the immemorial fear felt by village Greeks: whether there would be enough corn for bread to get them through winter. In Utah's springtime, they went off, talking and laughing to the outskirts of towns, dishtowels tied about their heads, children hanging

---

[20] *Fiftieth Anniversary Book of the "Assumption" Greek Orthodox Church of Price* (Price, 1966), Greek Archives, University of Utah.

[21] Interview with Mrs. James Koulouris, June 16, 1971.

on their skirts, to pick the first dandelion greens of the season. They would eat them for their tart flavor, not to supplement the winter diet of corn and beans they knew in *patridha*.

Except for constant apprehension of industrial accidents that would make them widows with orphan children in exile, the mothers were secure in their Greek Towns. Their customs and religious rites were transplanted almost intact to their neighborhoods. This isolated them from American life and eased their exile. Beyond their borders they knew were the *Amerikani* and the *Mormoni* who did not want them in their country, but not until World War I did they experience new anxieties. With the United States' entrance into the war, the chronic fear of the native-born that the burgeoning numbers of immigrants "would take over" burst into an irrational campaign against Germans and all aliens.

In Utah the Greeks were castigated in newspapers for refusing to enlist immediately. Still expecting to return to their country, they were wary that the war would again give powerful nations the opportunity to further cut up portions of Greece under the guise of being her protectors. This Greek nationalism was a puzzle to Americans: why this concern for the land they had left? Not only were the Greeks "unassimilable," but they were

> whelps who think nothing of getting American dollars under the American flag but who would not turn a hand over to save that flag from being dragged in the dirt by the Kaiser's dirty cutthroats.[22]

As hysteria against Germany mounted, Greeks began enlisting, but animosity swelled. Two lynchings of Greeks were thwarted at this time, one of a Greek who had killed the brother of fighter Jack Dempsey, the other of a Helper Greek who had allegedly contributed to the delinquency of a minor—a ride in his new car had precipitated the mob action.[23] In both incidents, Greeks armed themselves and arrived in time to prevent the lynchings.

After the war, the American Legion led a virulent campaign against all aliens, especially the Greeks. The Legion resented Greeks' establishing schools for their children, speaking their native language on the streets, reading Greek newspapers in coffeehouses, and leaving the mines, mills, and section gangs to enter business.

---

[22] *News Advocate* (Price), January 3, 1918.

[23] Papanikolas, *Toil and Rage*, p. 155; Helen Zeese Papanikolas, "The Greeks of Carbon County," *Utah Historical Quarterly* 22 (1954): 153–54.

By the early twenties, Greeks had become proprietors of stores, bought real estate, and entered the sheep business. Sheepmen had ironically returned to the very occupation they had left Greece to avoid. Supplying Greek boardinghouses with meat had given them a foothold in a thriving business. Sheepmen and owners of successful "Greek stores," many of them World War I veterans, were condemned for "not knowing their place," and were indiscriminately classed with Greek cardplayers and idlers whom they themselves denounced.

The third Greek-language newspaper weekly, *To Fos* ("The Light"), printed exhortations to their readers to become American citizens that "they could travel freely in America." *To Fos* praised Greek immigrants for their successes on leaving labor for business ventures and condemned those who "sullied the Greek name by involvement in bad businesses." (Throughout the text were American words transliterated into Greek: *stool pigeon, frame-up, bootlegger*.)[24]

American Legion attacks increased. When the Greek miners of Carbon County joined the unsuccessful national coal strike of 1922, the Legion had its most potent propaganda weapon: striking was the epitome of un-Americanism. The *Wyoming Labor Journal* accused coal operators of inciting prejudice against Greek businessmen to gain support of Americans who had become alarmed at this new competition.[25]

Near Scofield, guards and strikers fired on each other wounding a guard and two Greeks. Gov. Charles R. Mabey came to the mining camps and promised armed aid to the coal operators. Two weeks later a Greek striker, John Tenas, was killed in a Helper orchard by Deputy Sheriff R. T. Young. The Greeks of the county rose up at the killing. Several hundred of them followed the casket to the church and graveyard carrying small blue and white Greek flags. Newspapers spoke of Tenas's having "attempted to murder R. T. Young," whose family were "oldtimers of Price."

On June 14 the governor announced that the National Guard was being sent to Carbon County; machine guns and equipment had already arrived there. The day the troops went in to occupy the coal fields, strikers tried to stop a train reportedly carrying strikebreakers to Spring Canyon. Deputy Sheriff Arthur P. Webb was

[24] *To Fos,* Greek Archives, University of Utah.
[25] Papanikolas, *Toil and Rage,* pp. 167–75.

killed and H. E. Lewis, general manager of the Standard Coal Company, was wounded. A seriously injured Greek was arrested and, later, helped by his countrymen to escape. The militia rampaged through Helper and the strikers' tent colony south of the town searching for him. Greeks were driven out of Spring Canyon by sixty men wearing masks or with blackened faces. Searching for guns, the guard raided coffeehouses and poolhalls in Helper. They forced strikers out of the tent colony into the Helper school yard and ordered them to form lines. Lewis then walked down each line and chose men whom he said had fired on the train. Fourteen men and one Italian were arrested. "Men were chosen who weren't there [Spring Canyon train incident] and men who were there were not." [26]

The trials were long and resulted in twelve of the men receiving sentences from ten to thirty years. "A vicious element," the *Sun* called the Greeks, "unfit for citizenship . . . must America be a haven for foreign born, criminally inclined persons?" The same issue reported the arrest of Greek Vice-Consul Stylian Staes as he tried to enter Kenilworth to talk with Greek strikers. His diplomatic immunity was ignored.

An editorial in the July 13, 1922, *News Advocate* blamed the nation's citizens for not demanding forceful immigration laws to keep out "undesirables" and Americanization schools where the aliens would be forced to learn the English language:

> The local Greek priest has been in America twelve years and can not speak or understand a word of English. . . . If he doesn't want to learn the American language so that he can converse with local people, he should go back to where Greek is the national language.

During the court trials, the Castle Gate Mine Number 2 exploded on March 8, 1924, killing 172 men who left 417 dependents. Fifty Greeks were killed. A few of the nineteen Greek widows returned to Crete. The rest of them and their children remained in the state, their black clothing a constant reminder of the tragedy.[27]

Simultaneously, a revived Ku Klux Klan appeared, purporting, among other principles, to protect American womanhood and

[26] See Sam A. King, *Utah Statement and Brief Concerning the Coal Operation of Utah Against Organized Labor and the Unionizing of the Utah Coal Fields,* June 25, 1923, which was sent to the U. S. Coal Commission, in the Greek Archives, University of Utah; Zoumadakis interview.

[27] Papanikolas, *Toil and Rage,* p. 177.

429

to prevent fire.[28] The Klan paraded down Salt Lake City's Main Street and burned crosses on Ensign Peak. They marched in Magna, burned crosses on the Oquirrh foothills, and at night drove through Greek Town at high speeds with clattering wash tubs tied to cars. A Magna Greek who had eloped with an American girl found a cross on fire in front of his store and another in the yard of his wife's family home. During a Klan march down Magna Main Street, the Stamoulis brothers, who owned the Ford agency, noticed the distinctive, highly polished tan and beige colored shoes of their bookkeeper under his flapping white robes. Young Greeks followed the Klan to the park, pulled off their robes, and exposed several prominent citizens.[29] It was not a social stigma to belong to the Klan.

In Helper the Klan burned crosses at the railyards and on a mountain slope. Catholics answered the Klan with a circle of fire on the opposite mountain. Greeks, Italians, South Slavs, and Irish-Catholic railroad men formed an elaborate spy system that revealed who the Klansmen were. Wary, then fearful, the Klan disbanded. There was one fatality, an Italian who surprised Klansmen painting KKK signs on his barn chased them with a hoe and fell dead from a heart attack.

For all this turbulence from without their enclaves and dissensions within over political crises in the fatherland and the establishment of the Greek Archdiocese in America, the twenties were still the prime of Greek life in Utah. Greek schools multiplied. Greek Towns teemed with births; illnesses; one of America's many wonders, the canning of fruits and vegetables; and soap, bread, and noodle making. Children went from house to house on New Year's Day, sang *Kalenda* to welcome the coming year, and were repaid with sweets and coins. Children and adults dressed in costumes to sing and to revel before the forty days of austere Lent when neither meat nor meat products were eaten.

Each Greek Town had a matriarch or patriarch who was looked to for advice. In Magna, a renowned midwife, Mrs. Nick Mageras (Magerou), not only delivered babies to Greek, Italian, and South Slav women, but arranged marriages and used folk cures for a variety of illnesses: a wandering spleen, burns, fevers, and infections. She also dispelled the evil eye and set bones.[30]

[28] *Ibid.,* pp. 177–81.
[29] Interview with Mr. and Mrs. Andrew Dallas, June 26, 1972.
[30] Papanikolas, "Magerou: The Greek Midwife," *Utah Historical Quarterly* 38 (1970) : 50–60.

In Helper, John Diamanti was sought out to interpret dreams, using a dream book ordered from New York. In addition, *Barba Yiannis* ("Uncle John") was a *praktikos*, a folk healer. As a patriarch, he read the shoulder blade of the paschal lamb every Easter and predicted from the demarcations what the year would bring. Pregnant women asked him to foretell the sex of their babies. Looking away from embarrassment, he gave his predictions. Legend says he never made a mistake.[31]

Another *praktikos*, *Barba Andreas* ("Uncle Andrew"), was noted for setting bones. In response to urgent telephone calls, he would board the Bingham stage for the Salt Lake area to use the Greek folk method for broken bones: egg whites mixed with clean sheep's wool packed around the reset bones then firmly bandaged with white cloth. Like *Barba Yiannis,* he would not accept pay.

In the twenties, the Pan Hellenic Unions of earlier days were disbanded in favor of organizations representing different provinces in Greece; the names of the local chapters were those of legendary heroes and leaders in the 1821 Revolution against the Turks. Burial expenses were among the benefits provided. The larger lodges formed women's auxiliaries and youth groups. Whatever their origin in Greece, almost all men belonged to the national lodges, either AHEPA (American Hellenic Educational Progress Association) or GAPA (Greek American Progressive Association).[32] The AHEPA was founded in 1922 to counteract hostility toward Greeks. It espoused assimilation and used the English language in meetings. "Ahepans" emulated American lodges with conventions in leading hotels, balls, and queens. Under this veneer, however, the Ahepans remained Greek-oriented. The GAPA was established in 1923 as a reaction to the AHEPA in fear that Greek heritage in America was threatened. "Gapans" were conservative. Their favorite gathering was the mountain picnic with lambs roasting on spits.

In the twenties, almost all Greeks became American citizens. Their children dutifully attended the Greek schools where proverbs and axioms were taught in the stilted, purist *katharevousa*. (Rebellion came later, in the thirties.) In Greek Towns a few sheepmen's wives were still carding wool, not through necessity but through habit. In mud ovens bread still baked. Boys, heads shaved to make

---

[31] Helen Zeese Papanikolas, "Greek Folklore of Carbon County," in *Lore of Faith and Folly,* ed. Thomas E. Cheney (Salt Lake City, 1971), pp. 61–77.

[32] Saloutos, *Greeks in the United States,* pp. 246–57.

their hair strong, wore knee-length rubber boots and trampled on grapes in galvanized tubs. Girls sat on front porches and embroidered pillowcases and dishcloths for trousseaus, the American dowries.

Picnics were held regularly on Sundays in nearby canyons. Often Greeks from the Salt Lake area and those from Carbon County met halfway to share the day. Men went to the picnic sites before daybreak to roast lambs. Mothers made cheese pastries and honey and nut delicacies with an extra supply for bachelors to take to their hotel rooms and boardinghouses. For hours men played *lyras, laoutos,* and *clarinos* while young parents and their children sang centuries-old songs and danced.

Plays were produced on the topic of the Greek-Turkish war and given on March 25, the anniversary of the Greek revolt. In Salt Lake City, a small group of literate immigrants formed a coterie that met often. Several of them wrote stories and poems, published in *To Fos,* that spoke of longing for *patridha* and alienation in American exile. A leading member, James Skedros, wrote poems and stories on themes of Greek life that were as vivid to the immigrants as if they had never left *patridha.* In "Heroes Who Are Watchful," written after the disastrous 1922 Greek rout by the Turks in Asia Minor, he says,

> Is that roar, do you think, the fluttering souls
> Of heroes who watch with secret pain
> The Fatherland whose honor there they guard
> Against a dishonorable, murderous foe?
> There in the earth, newly dug.[33]

Women whose families had been forced out of Asia Minor came as picture brides and enlivened this circle of poetry writers and readers. Having lived among many peoples, the women spoke several languages and were cosmopolitan compared with the villagers of the mainland.

Prosperity continued for all Greeks during the 1920s—except for labor agents. The immigration laws of 1921 limited the number of incoming Greeks to 100; in 1924 this was raised to 384. The heretofore inexhaustible supply of Greeks needing jobs was cut off, and older workers who had been in the country for a time had freed themselves from the extortion of labor agents. Now the *padrones* who had lived solely, and well, on the labor of workers were forced

---

[33] *To Fos,* August 2, 1923.

to make a living. Many became destitute. Men who had combined a business with supplying labor for Skliris as a sideline were the earliest of Utah's successful Greeks. Their days as labor agents dimmed and the origin of the money that bought their businesses and property was almost forgotten.

With mines, mills, and smelters working at full capacity, an exodus began from Greek Towns to middle and, for a few, to upper-middle-class neighborhoods. Not only were mud ovens, wash houses, and gardens left behind, but the dispersal brought an end to singing the New Year's *kalenda* and masquerading before Lent. Children of the immigrants found themselves in schools where they were among a small number of "foreigners," stripped of the psychological haven of their old neighborhoods, even more exposed to derision because of their strange names and their Greek-school attendance. Yet at this time a penchant and aptitude for business that the Greeks evinced had made many of them prosperous newspaper advertisers. The businessmen began to demand an end to newspaper accounts that described Greeks in pejorative terms and after several years the practice stopped.

The exodus continued until the stock market crash of 1929. In Carbon County, where mines closed or worked half shift, families moved to California hoping to find work with countrymen in grape fields and canneries. Sheepmen neared bankruptcy as the price of sheep fell from eighteen dollars to three dollars a head. There were not enough buyers at three dollars and sheep were abandoned in the Chicago stockyards.

Communal activities, picnics, and plays went on despite the bleak years. The two churches provided the Easter feast of Agape (Christian Love) because many could not afford the traditional paschal lamb. The Greek Revolution plays filled the church basements and rented halls. In Carbon County, the schoolgirl members of the Athena Club played all parts, male and female. Many of the Salt Lake City plays were written by Harry K. Kambouris, and all were presented by the Hellenic Theatrical Club "Star." Only when husbands had parts in the plays did married women also participate; otherwise the rigid Greek custom of separation of the sexes would have initiated gossip about the women. When wives and daughters were not available to play female roles, men took the parts. Strange-looking "women" with heavy makeup and odd voices minced or stamped about the stage boards.

Following the Second World War in which 565 sons of Utah Greeks served, 20 of whom died,[34] Greek immigrant life ceased. The first American-born generation had reached maturity, and some children of immigrants were marrying into other cultures. Many of the immigrant generation returned to visit *patridha* and supplied dowries, installed water lines to their villages, repaired churches, and brought relatives to the United States, but they were eager to come back to America—no longer their exile—and to their lifetime of tangible and emotional ties.

Thousands of the first Greeks, who, with immigrants of other cultures, did the industrial work that changed Utah from a rural state, did not remain in its mining and smelter towns. They "passed through" Utah and with their savings settled elsewhere, a considerable number of them becoming prosperous. A Greek who sold shoelaces and pencils on Salt Lake streets in 1910, established a chain of laundries in California. Others used their money to educate themselves in the professions.

After the Second World War, the lifting of quotas enabled a new influx of Greeks to come to Utah; 749 were counted in the 1950 Census. Unlike the first immigrants who came to America without skills, these later ones included "many skilled laborers, intellectuals and entrepreneurial talent," depleting Greece of their greatly needed services.[35] All have shown the same ambition as the early immigrants, but their accommodation has been easier and faster. (They did not bring amulets of Greek earth with them.) Even the village-born are less provincial: education had been made compulsory in Greece, and roads connect villages to towns and cities. Utah, and all America, no longer holds the intense, anti-alien feelings of the past. These later immigrants have given a new vitality to Greek life in the state.

Children of these newer immigrants and grandchildren and great-grandchildren of the first immigrants continue to attend Greek schools, but there are far fewer students in comparison with the large numbers enrolled in Sunday schools. Increasingly, the Sunday schools are composed of the offspring of two cultures, mainly Greek and Mormon. The four Greek churches in the state, two in Salt Lake City, one in Price, and one in Ogden, are the centers of Greek ethnic life.

[34] Greek church records of Salt Lake City and Price.

[35] George Christos Papadatos, "Greek Labor Migration and Its Dimensions in the Greek Economy" (M.A. thesis, University of Utah, 1971), p. 6.

Greek immigrant life in Utah, begun in the oppression of hostility and ostracism, nevertheless brought economic independence to the first generation and exceptional success to the second generation through education in the professions and in business. A survey conducted after World War II showed over ninety Greek-owned businesses in Salt Lake City's downtown area.[36] It is a paradox, uniquely American because of the great opportunities industrialization of the country presented, that this Greek immigrant life may have been negligible, or altered, had it not been for the notorious *padrone*, Leonidas Skliris, the Czar of the Greeks.

The Greek Towns have long been gone. Coffeehouses have closed; there are not enough old men to support them. Old-country customs of mourning have fallen away; *mirologhia*, the keening for the dead, have not been sung since before the Second World War; memorial wheat is no longer elaborately decorated but enclosed in small, stapled plastic bags. Ikons and vigil lights remain.

---

[36] Made by Constantine J. Skedros, in Greek Archives, University of Utah.

14

AFTER ESCALANTE: THE SPANISH-SPEAKING PEOPLE OF UTAH

BY VICENTE V. MAYER

> Poor Mexico! So far from God and so near to the United
> States.   —Attributed to Porfirio Diaz

To the Spanish is owed the distinction of being the first Europeans
to explore, map, and describe the area of present-day Utah. However, not until the twentieth century, and almost one hundred fifty
years after the 1776 Dominguez-Escalante expedition, were their
Hispanic descendants to become a numerically significant community
in Utah. Chronologically, they were the last major immigrant group
to establish residence in the state, parts of which together with all
of California, Arizona, New Mexico, Texas, Colorado, and Nevada
had been the northern half of Mexico before the Mexican-American
War of 1846–48.

Prior to the twentieth century, the number of Spanish-speaking
inhabitants in Utah was probably small, although it is difficult to
arrive at a figure. The residual trade connections between the Utah
Territory and New Mexico that persisted after the Mexican-
American War revolved around a traffic in Indian slaves. These
were finally dissolved by the Walker War of 1853 and by Mormon
opposition to the role of New Mexico traders in this enterprise.[1]

After 1850 it appears that only a small number of Spanish-
surnamed individuals made Utah Territory their permanent home.[2]
There was little to attract others to Utah during this period. A

---

[1] Leland Hargrave Creer, *The Founding of an Empire: The Exploration
and Colonization of Utah, 1776–1856* (Salt Lake City, 1947), pp. 28–39; also
Joseph J. Hill, "Spanish and Mexican Exploration and Trade Northwest from
New Mexico into the Great Basin 1765–1853," *Utah Historical Quarterly* 3
(1930): 3–23 (hereafter referred to as *UHQ*).

[2] One available, if not totally reliable, source that contributes to this conclusion are the censuses of 1850, 1860, 1880, and 1890. Early references to
Mexicans in Utah usually referred to the small numbers found with the army
working as herders or laborers. See J. H. Simpson, *Report of Explorations of
the Territory of Utah for a Direct Wagon-route from Camp Floyd to Genoa,
in Carson Valley in 1859* (Washington, D.C., 1876), p. 5.

Spanish-speaking community, in terms of numbers, was nonexistent, and sizeable communities were necessary to give support to Mexican Americans, who had lived in the new United States Southwest since Spanish colonial days, and to Mexican immigrants from below the revised boundaries of Mexico—an insubstantial support at best. The Treaty of Guadalupe-Hidalgo (1848) that was to insure the Mexicans equal treatment and protection under the law, recognition of their land titles and religious rites, and the preservation of their culture, including language, was flagrantly violated. Wholesale stealing of their lands, vigilante lynchings, peonage, and most tragically, complete disregard for the education of their children made the Spanish speaking "strangers in our own land." [3] In Utah the religious and social exclusiveness of Mormon society discouraged any significant influx of Spanish-speaking settlers, or any non-Mormon settler.

Throughout much of the West in the late nineteenth century, railroads, and especially the mining industry, acted as occupational lures to large numbers of Spanish-surnamed laborers. Mining, an important industry in Utah, early became the province of other immigrant laborers. As the Bingham Canyon mines developed in the 1880s, they began to employ Irish laborers. The Irish gave way to other immigrants from the British Isles, mainly Cornish miners. By 1890 Finns, Swedes, and Italians in turn were replacing these immigrants. After 1900 Italians, together with eastern Mediterranean and Balkan peoples (Greeks, Slavs, Croatians, and Serbs), dominated the labor ranks of the mines. A similar process was repeated in the coal mines of Carbon County during this period.[4] In contrast, census records for the period 1850–1900, Catholic baptismal registers, labor rolls of the major mining areas, and newspapers of the period all confirm the dearth of any significant Spanish-speaking population in Utah.

In 1900 the United States Census listed only forty individuals of Mexican nativity living in Utah. In addition, Catholic baptismal records for the Utah diocese revealed only eleven Catholic baptisms of Spanish-surnamed children (both Mexican and Mexican Ameri-

[3] David F. Gomez, *Somos Chicanos: Strangers in Our Own Land* (Boston, 1973).

[4] Helen Zeese Papanikolas, "Life and Labor among the Immigrants of Bingham Canyon," *UHQ* 33 (1965): 289–315; "The Greeks of Carbon County," *UHQ* 22 (1954): 143–64; and *Toil and Rage in a New Land: The Greek Immigrants in Utah*, 2d ed. rev. (Salt Lake City, 1974), reprinted from *UHQ* 38, no. 2 (1970). Elroy Nelson, "The Mineral Industry: A Foundation of Utah's Economy," *UHQ* 31 (1963): 179–91. 1910 Census.

can) for the decade 1900–1910.[5] By 1910 the number of inhabitants of Mexican nativity had increased slightly to 166, a number undoubtedly augmented by Mexican Americans who had moved to Utah from surrounding states, particularly Colorado and New Mexico. Population estimates for this period (1900–1910) are tenuous at best. Although only a fledgling Spanish-speaking population emerges for this first decade, several small *colonias* appeared along the Wasatch Front in northern Utah and in southeastern Utah.

Culturally, the Spanish-speaking population of southeastern Utah, principally San Juan County, has been linked to the *Hispano* population of southern Colorado and northern New Mexico. At the turn of the century, a number of families had settled in and around the southern Utah town of Monticello. Almost all had come from northern New Mexico—from Tierra Amarilla, Coyote, Gallina, and Abiquiu. Moving to southern Utah, they found work as sheepherders and ranch hands with a small number homesteading ranches and farms of their own in the area.[6] Having come from New Mexico and Colorado, they were American citizens. Their *colonia* contrasted with those in Ogden and Salt Lake City whose Mexican immigrant population was much larger if not predominant.

Mexican Americans and Mexican immigrants have been the two major groups making up the Spanish-speaking population of Utah, although the immigration patterns of each group have been distinct in terms of time and numbers after 1910, the beginning of the ten-year-long Mexican Revolution. During the initial years of Mexican immigration into Utah, the immigrant was often a single male, or a man who had left his wife and family behind in Mexico in order to search for work in the United States. One early member of the nascent Mexican community of Salt Lake City, Señor Santos Cabrera recalled:

> Yes, I came up from Texas in 1918, while the war was still on in Mexico, and there were very few families in Salt Lake City. A few from Old Mexico, and a few from Colorado and New Mexico, but very, very few families . . . here

[5] Cathedral of the Madeleine, Baptismal Records, holograph, individual entries from January 1900 to January 1910, Salt Lake City.

[6] 1910 Census. Also interview with Cosme Chacon, July 15, 1973, Monticello, Utah, Chicano Oral History Project No. 3–109, S–110, and S–111; Bill and Cleofes Manzanares, Project No. S–123. Tapes and transcripts currently located at the American West Center, University of Utah, Salt Lake City. These will soon be transferred to the Marriott Library, University of Utah.

in this area when you saw a Mexican woman, it was like
seeing your mother.[7]

The subsequent growth of the Spanish-speaking population in
Utah between 1910 and 1930 was distinguished by an increase in
Mexican immigration over that from the Southwest. The immigration was stimulated by the start of World War I that reduced the
numbers of European and Asiatic immigrant laborers. Mexican
dictator Porfirio Diaz, using foreign capital, had built railroads into
Mexico's interior, and for the first time mass transportation to the
American Southwest was available for millions of peons freed from
rich *haciendas* by the revolution.

After 1910 a classic push-pull relationship developed between
North American capital and Mexican labor. While the havoc of the
Mexican Revolution stimulated the flight (push) of an estimated
one million Mexicans northward, expanding economic conditions
in North American agriculture and industry provided a great
economic incentive (pull) for at least semi-permanent residence
there.[8] The vast numbers of Mexicans displaced by the Mexican
Revolution quickly filled this labor vacuum. However, like their
Asian and European immigrant predecessors, the Mexican introduction to life in the United States was often dreary and exhausting
at best, and at its worst, exploitative and violent. Mexicans, though,
met far deeper-rooted prejudice than European immigrants—instilled in Americans from the days of the Alamo and the annexation
of Texas. To justify thievery of land that required the dispensing
of justice, a stereotype of Mexicans as devoid of moral and intellectual
worth, indolent, and of inferior culture was conjured by government
officials and kept alive by fanatically prejudiced journalism. As
late as the 1930s John Steinbeck would write of the Mexicans as
a people inclined to sleep a great deal and to put off for tomorrow
(mañana) what should have been done that day.

Although prompted by economic motives, many like Señor
Isidro Marrufo had come with views of America as a land of promise
as well as fascination:

I [wanted] to know the United States. . . . They used to
say whoever knows Los Angeles [knows] the glory and the

---

[7] Interview with Santos Cabrera, January 4, 1971, Salt Lake City, Chicano
Oral History Project No. S–6.

[8] Manuel Gamio, *Mexican Immigration to the United States* (New York
1971), pp. 23–30. See also Leo Grebler, ed., *The Mexican American People:
The Nation's Second Largest Minority* (New York, 1970), pp. 63–64.

heaven. I didn't want to die before I saw the glory and the heaven in person; I had that on my mind. That's why I came to the United States. . . .[9]

The increase in the size of Utah's Spanish-speaking population did not really appear until after 1915. By 1920 inhabitants of Mexican nativity numbered 1,666, an incomplete figure representing only part of the Spanish-surnamed population.[10] There are, of course, no figures for clandestine immigration that far exceeded legal admissions.

Mexican immigration into Utah between 1910 and 1920 was apparently of a secondary nature. Utah was not the primary settlement area for Mexicans who eventually entered the state. The major reason was tied to the circumstances of labor demand. Only slowly did Mexican and Mexican-American workers begin to appear in Utah's labor force. Until 1915 mines, smelters, and railroads were still the domain of southern European immigrant labor—especially the Italians and the Greeks. This late arrival into Utah's labor market together with the wide acceptance of the Mexican stereotype added further difficulties for the immigrants. Even though Balkan, Mediterranean, and Japanese immigrants had had to pay tribute for their jobs, they were represented by labor agents who had become influential with industrialists by providing the cheap labor they wanted. The Spanish surnamed had no agents to speak for them. Their illiteracy (35.6 percent for rural inhabitants, according to the 1930 Census) was also far greater than that of earlier immigrants and would continue to reinforce their poverty role.

A survey of the employment records of the Utah Copper Company (now Kennecott Copper Corporation) between 1908 and 1920 makes the employment pattern clear, at least for the Bingham copper mines.[11] Not until 1918 and 1919 did large numbers of Mexican, Mexican-American, and Spanish miners begin to appear on Utah Copper Company's labor rolls. One exception was the year

[9] Interview with Isidro Marrufo, March 13, 1973, Salt Lake City, Chicano Oral History Project No. 82.

[10] 1920 Census.

[11] Employment records of Utah Copper Company 1880–1920, R. C. Gemmel Hall, Bingham Canyon. Access to these records is possible only with permission of Kennecott Copper Corporation.

For a description of Italian and South Slav labor in Bingham see Philip Frank Notarianni, "The Italian Immigrant in Utah: Nativism (1900–1925)" (M.A. thesis, University of Utah, 1972) and Joseph Stipanovich, *The South Slavs in Utah: A Social History* (San Francisco, 1975).

1912 when Utah Copper brought in hundreds of "Mexicans" (both Mexicans and Mexican Americans) as strikebreakers in the 1912 strike. However, relatively few remained, at least in the mines, upon settlement of the strike.[12]

In the same year the first appointment of a Mexican consul for Utah was made in Salt Lake City. Although a possible reflection of the growing presence of Mexican immigrant labor, it is more probable that it was established in response to, or in preparation for, the sudden influx of large numbers of Mexican strikebreakers. The role and activities of the various Mexican consuls during the periods 1912 and 1920 lend further evidence to this.

For example, in 1916 the duties of the Mexican consul in Salt Lake City fell to a gentleman with the improbable name (for a Mexican consul) of E.D. Hashimoto. The appointment bruised the pride of the local Mexican community; however, that he was of Japanese extraction and in no way a Mexican national apparently bothered neither the president of Mexico nor the Utah officials.[13]

Hashimoto's duties as Mexican consul were for the purpose of bringing laborers into the mines, mills, smelters, and railroads. He placed most Mexicans on railroad section gangs under Japanese foremen. During this period of immigration, Mexicans worked under other immigrant foremen, never under their own countrymen. Their entrance into Carbon County, for instance, was on a large labor gang under a Greek contractor bringing a water line through the mountains of Price Canyon into the county. The ditches were dug by hand, but because of postwar shortages, the pipe was not delivered in time and snows caved-in the ditches, necessitating their being dug again in the spring. Many of the Mexicans found work in the Carbon County mines after the water line was completed.[14]

The payroll records of the Union Pacific Railroad clearly illustrate the growing significance of Mexicans and Mexican Americans

[12] *Deseret Evening News,* November 3, 1912; *Deseret Evening News,* November 14, 1912; Papanikolas, "Life and Labor among the Immigrants of Bingham Canyon," pp. 294–307.

[13] William Spry to Mexican government, 1912, President Carranza to Spry, 1916, Hashimoto to Spry, 1916, in Governor's Correspondence, Box M and SE-1, 18.4, Boxes 43 and 45, Utah State Archives, State Capitol, Salt Lake City.

[14] Interview with George Zeese, contractor for the water line, May 21, 1975.

as track laborers during the 1920s.[15] As early as 1923 the payroll records of the Los Angeles and Salt Lake Railroad, a subsidiary of the Union Pacific, show that Spanish-surnamed labor made up nearly 20 percent of the permanent track labor on the sections between Salt Lake City and Milford. As the decade progressed, their numbers increased until Spanish-surnamed individuals made up over 30 percent of the permanent track labor forces on the Utah portion of the Los Angeles and Salt Lake Railroad. The temporary labor utilized on extra gangs during the busy summer months pushed the numbers of Spanish-surnamed track laborers as high as 70 percent.[16] Those who were fortunate enough to work on a railroad section often shared quarters with other single men in a company bunkhouse, while those working on large extra gangs on remote stretches of the railroad lived in the cramped quarters of railroad cars.

In the northeastern part of the state, payroll records for the Union Pacific's Wyoming Division, specifically those sections between Evanston, Wyoming, and Devil's Slide in Morgan County, Utah, also show that many Spanish-surnamed workers were employed early in this decade. As on other Union Pacific lines in Utah, the temporary summer labor on extra gangs was composed primarily of Spanish-surnamed workers.[17]

The activities of later consuls, after 1920, changed considerably from that of facilitating worker importation to giving increasing attention to the needs of the Mexican community. Part of this was no doubt because of the rapid growth of the Mexican community. Between 1920 and 1930 the Mexican population grew to over four thousand inhabitants. Although the total Spanish-speaking popula-

---

[15] The Union Pacific Payroll Records are presently located in the annex of the general offices of the Union Pacific Railroad in Omaha, Nebraska. The records date only from 1923 for all UPRR divisions, including the Los Angeles and Salt Lake Railroad. These records are accessible only at the convenience of the UPRR. However, statistical summaries of representative years between 1923 and 1945 are available at the American West Center, and very shortly at the Marriott Library.

[16] For example, in June of 1927, of 889 men employed as section hands between Salt Lake and Milford, 596 were Spanish surnamed. The number of permanent laborers on this section of the Los Angeles and Salt Lake Railroad throughout this decade averaged about two hundred fifty men, of whom between 35 and 45 percent were Spanish surnamed. Union Pacific Payroll Records, Fifth, Sixth, and Provo districts, January 1923 to June 1931.

[17] The earliest available payroll records show that in 1925, 69 of the 187 permanent track laborers were Spanish surnamed. In June of 1926, the number of workers on the Wyoming Division rose as high as 556 out of a total 797. Until the early years of the depression, Spanish-surnamed labor represented between 25 and 30 percent of the permanent track force and close to 35 percent of the summer labor force.

tion of Utah included a significant number of Mexican Americans, the distinguishing characteristic in this period was that it was still predominantly made up of Mexican immigrants.[18]

The rapid growth of the Spanish-speaking population in that decade was influenced by national events. Utah industry and agriculture, like that in other parts of the country, was faced with a steadily diminishing labor supply. World War I had temporarily shut off the traditional southern European sources that had provided cheap immigrant labor. After the war, the resurgence of nativism and the subsequent restrictive immigration legislation in 1921 and 1924 effectively cut off this source of immigrant labor.[19] Following a pattern established earlier throughout the Southwest, Spanish-surnamed labor in Utah, especially immigrant labor, began appearing in increasing numbers in those areas traditionally open to them: agriculture, railroads, and mining.

This labor became important to an expanding sugar beet industry. In the small northern Utah farming community of Garland, an agricultural *colonia* appeared in response to the demand for sugar beet labor. Sixty Spanish-speaking families composed the nucleus of this *colonia,* which had been established in Garland in 1918. Their number was augmented in the harvest season by some one hundred fifty Mexican laborers. In the absence of such focal points of unity as the Catholic church or the Mexican consul, the Mexican residents of Garland went ahead with their own Independence Day celebrations and projects, including the building of a schoolhouse.[20] There were also small *colonias* in other sugar beet areas of Utah, such as Delta and Spanish Fork.

Life in these *colonias* and in city neighborhoods was little different from life in Mexico. The nearness of their native country to the Southwest and hence to Utah made the extension of the immigrants' language and culture into their new life a natural continuation. Japanese, Greeks, Italians, and Slavs, nationalistic though they remained in America, were cut off from their countries by thousands of miles and the Americanization of their children proceeded rapidly. Also, their stay in immigrant neighborhoods seldom exceeded two decades. Whether they left labor for business or stayed in laboring jobs, their ethnic towns dispersed and were taken over

[18] 1930 Census.

[19] John Higham, *Strangers in the Land: Patterns of American Nativism 1860–1925* (New Brunswick, N.J., 1955), pp. 202–4, 300–330.

[20] *Salt Lake Tribune,* June 13, 1920.

by later immigrants, mainly the Spanish speaking. The static role of the Spanish speaking in the lowest paying work kept them bound to their original neighborhoods from which few have ventured outward.

In their neighborhoods and *colonias,* the patriarchal society of Mexico continued. Mothers were the mainstay of the family, but fathers were the authority. Children showed deep respect for their parents. Families were close-knit with a high sense of loyalty to one another and included not only parents and children but also grandparents, aunts, uncles, cousins, godparents, and in-laws. One of the main responsibilities of the family was the chaperoning of unmarried daughters. Any hint of improper behavior on the part of girls reflected disgrace on their families and compromised their hope for good marriages. Señora Luz Solorio and Señora Bertha Mayer, early Salt Lake residents, recalled:

> Mayer: Well, I was always with my brother. He always went along with us. If we went to the park, they were around there, Luis, or one of my brothers.
>
> Solario: . . . sometimes he [my father] let me go to the show or something with my friends, and after I was a block or two away from home I thought, "Oh, I'm going by myself," and I would start dancing because I was so glad that no one was watching me. Then I would look across the street, and my dad would be watching me. They really didn't let you go alone or with somebody, your friends, or with anybody unless somebody was looking after you. . . . We understood that this was the custom and that's why we put up with it.[21]

Young men and women hardly had the opportunity to know each other under this kind of tradition and were often nearly strangers when they married. A marriage proposal was a solemn and formal occasion. The groom, accompanied by his parents, a priest, or a nun, made a visit to the bride's house and asked for her hand. The answer was never given immediately and the groom had to wait an indefinite time for it. Marriages and baptisms were celebrated with an abundance of food, drink, music, and dancing. The "poet" of the *colonia* would sing or recite appropriate verses in honor of the occasion.

The need to come together, to be secure in the company of relatives and friends and temporarily forget the unfriendly world

[21] Interview with Bertha Mayer and Luz Solorio, July 13, 1972, Bountiful, Utah, Chicano Oral History Project No. 5–42 and S–43.

that surrounded them, made for a humble but active social life. Parties began spontaneously in the back of Mexican shops or in houses. Sunday was spent in visiting; there were hours of talk on summer days under the shade of trees with lemonade to drink, or, for the men, homemade wine or beer if they had the money to buy it. The oral tradition was strong among the Spanish speaking, and familiar stories were told whenever people gathered. The story of Rafael Lopez has been retold so often, he has become a folk hero.

Lopez was one of the strikebreakers brought in during the Bingham copper strike of 1912. He had been unjustly arrested, pistol whipped, and further harrassed by law officers for several weeks. Months later Lopez killed another Mexican, Juan Valdez, in a fight. Some Mexicans said that Valdez had sometime earlier killed Lopez's brother, others that the men had quarreled over Mexican politics. Taking clothes, gun, and ammunition, Lopez walked into the snow-covered hills around Utah Lake. Four posse members followed and searched in the underbrush for him. Three shots rang out leaving three of the men dead. The fourth deputy returned to Bingham where several hundred men were organized for the search. For several days Lopez eluded them and then hid in the tunnels of the Apex mine. Guards were placed at all exits and a bale of hay was lighted at the entrance of the mine to smoke him out. Lopez fired killing one deputy and injuring another. Lump sulphur, damp gunpowder, and cayenne were then lighted at the mine entrance, and the fires kept going for five days. Ten days later deputies entered the mine, but Lopez had disappeared. How he had escaped is not known, but a myth persists among the Mexicans that he found his way to Mexico and joined the revolutionist Pancho Villa.[22]

Another important cultural feature the Spanish speaking brought with them was the belief in *curanderismo* ("folk healing") that continues for lower income people to the present day.[23] Although technically illegal and not approved by the Catholic church, *curanderismo,* in variant forms that have evolved from five centuries of Indian-Spanish culture, has until recently been more important in curing than the medical profession. The expense of professional medical care, language barriers, condescending attitudes of doctors

[22] See Thomas Arthur Rickard, *The Utah Copper Enterprise* (San Francisco, 1919), pp. 42–43 and Vicente V. Mayer, Jr., *Utah: A Hispanic History* (Salt Lake City, 1974), pp. 50–51.

[23] See E. Ferol Benavides, "The Saints Among the Saints: A Study of Curanderismo in Utah," *UHQ* 41 (1973): 373–92.

and nurses, the strange environment of hospitals and clinics keep many of the Spanish speaking loyal to their folk healers. *Curanderismo,* also, "rarely instills the patient with hopelessness. Statements to the effect that the patient must learn to live with his pain or that medical science hasn't conquered this disease are not made by folkhealers." [24] Therefore, for many diseases from apparent physical ones to psychological ones that Anglo physicians would ridicule, such as, *mal ojo* ("evil eye"), *empacho* ("surfeit"), and *susto* ("fright"), the poor turn to folkhealers.

Curanderas in Utah have included a Mrs. Blanco whose cures were dependent on prayers; Incarnacion Florez, well known in Utah and surrounding states, who used prayers, ritual, and medicine until her death in 1968; and Te Valdez of Ogden who cured mainly with herbs. None of the *curanderas* has accepted money or advertised their services. To the poorest of the Spanish speaking, the migrants, *curanderismo* is especially necessary.

After 1930 migrants increasingly came to fill the demand for agricultural labor and the earlier agricultural *colonias* disbanded. Part of this migrant labor was made up of Spanish-speaking farm workers who lived in towns along the Wasatch Front during the winter and followed the planting and harvesting of crops through northern Utah, Idaho, and Oregon during the remainder of the year. For those migrants whose subsistence was almost solely dependent on this source of employment during the depression, life was reduced to a grim proposition. For Señora Francis Yanez, it was an early introduction to the harsh realities of migrant life:

> We started working on the farm, from the time I was about seven years old. . . . We started topping beets in the early season. You were down on your knees, like when you go to church and pray, but this was hour after hour . . . and the sun would be beating on you, and it would rain on you, and this is the kind of work we did. Of course, lots of times I'd cry, you know . . . I couldn't understand why I had to be out there. But we were hungry, that's the only thing our parents would tell us. "We have to do it — to feed the younger ones." [25]

With the depression both permanent and temporary Spanish-surnamed track labor was rapidly eliminated. By 1932 they had

[24] *Ibid.,* p. 392.

[25] Interview with Francis Yanez, May 21, 1971, Salt Lake City, Chicano Oral History Project No. S–5.

447

Above: *Carlos M. Gaxiola, Mexican consul, 1926–31, was active in the Chamber of Commerce.*

Left: *First page of the journal kept by Fathers Domínguez and Vélez de Escalante of their 1776–77 expedition through Utah.*

When Mexican girls turned fifteen they often were given a special party with fifteen girl guests and a special birthday mass as in this photograph taken outside a church in Guadalajara. The custom was observed in Utah, too.

Above: *Advertisement for an early Spanish-speaking establishment in Salt Lake City.* Right: *A Mexican extra gang. Mexicans replaced Japanese, Greeks, and Italians on railroad crews.* Below: *The Sisters of the Perpetual Adoration came from Mexico to serve at the Mission of Our Lady of Guadalupe, 1927–39.*

Lucero Ward members at a Mexican celebration in the Salt Lake Tabernacle, ca. 1925.

Lucero Ward Relief Society members, ca. 1938.

Members of the LDS Mexican Branch when it was located at 448 South Third West in Salt Lake City, ca. 1929.

Left: *A large influx of
Spanish-speaking
workers came to the
Bingham Canyon mines
during World War II.*

Below: *Father Collins (priest on left), some of his "kids," Sisters of
the Perpetual Adoration, and parish workers outside the mission,
ca. 1935.*

Above left: *Fourth of July parade float, 1951, of the Sociedad Mutualista Mexicana in Bingham Canyon.* Above right: *Incarnacion Florez, a Salt Lake City curandera who was known throughout the Intermountain Area for her cures.* Below: *Lucero Ward at its present location, 232 West Eighth South, Salt Lake City.*

Above: *Posters advertising two important Mexican celebrations in Bingham Canyon, the Sixteenth of September and the Fifth of May.* Below: *Many Spanish-speaking service men during World War II were brothers—one such family from Ogden: Ross Salazar, Nick Salazar, Tom Medina, Jim Salazar, and Tony Salazar.*

453

Our Lady of Guadalupe Church at its present location on Salt Lake City's westwide, 740 West 300 North, serves a large congregation of Spanish-speaking members. The church's Hacienda provides many community services.

La Morena Cafe provides jobs, a source of income for community projects, and a gathering place for the Spanish speaking.

Above: *Dancers of Utah's Ballet Folklorico preserve the Spanish-speaking cultural heritage and serve as good-will ambassadors for the state. Migrant workers perform arduous labor harvesting various crops in Utah. Right: Mrs. Gonzales, seated center, was a volunteer English teacher to the Spanish speaking, and also to Greeks, in Bingham.*

been reduced to a mere 14 out of 264 names that made up the permanent track force working on the sections between Salt Lake and Milford, a reduction undoubtedly representative of the situation on other railroad lines. To the northeast, all Spanish-surnamed labor had also been eliminated by 1932 on the sections between Evanston and Devil's Slide.[26] José Medel, who had begun working on Utah's railroads in 1927, recalled this period when competition for jobs became intense:

> He [the foreman] was one guy who wanted eight hours work, pulling ties . . . He don't want you drinking too much water or talking, just keep working. He [would] fire men every day or every week and kept bringing new ones because we don't have no unions.[27]

Despite the hardships, José Medel counted himself as one of the lucky ones who was able to find work during this period. Not until the beginning of World War II and the resulting manpower requirements did Spanish-surnamed track labor again become significant on Utah's railroads.

At the beginning of the depression, the more than four thousand Mexican residents were numerically superior to any other non-European ethnic minority. Family units had begun to be even more important in the sociological makeup of the community. Nearly a quarter of the Mexican population of four thousand in 1939 was under ten years of age.[28]

The growth and character (its immigrant characteristic) of the Spanish-speaking population in Utah expressed itself in the first real efforts at social mobilization and organization in the 1920–30 decade. In the early twenties, a number of temporary organizations, mainly in Salt Lake City and Ogden, had appeared and disappeared with rapidity. The majority were formed for the specific purpose of working with the Mexican consul to prepare the Mexican Independence Day celebrations of the Fifth of May and the Six-

[26] Union Pacific Railroad Payroll Records, Fifth, Sixth, and Provo districts, January 1923 to 1931; also Wyoming Division, January 1925 to June 1945.

[27] Interview with José Medel, October 9, 1970, Salt Lake City, Utah Chicano Oral History Project No. S–1.

[28] Cathedral of the Madeleine, Baptismal Records, January 1921 to December 1927; 1930 Census.

teenth of September.[29] Homage was paid to the village priest Father Hidalgo who on September 16, 1810, rang the church bell to proclaim an end to Spanish rule and called his people to fight with courage and patriotism. These programs invariably included several patriotic speechs followed by a number of traditional songs and dances with participants wearing native dress. For the Mexican community, these Independence Day celebrations were important social occasions in which both children and adults actively participated. They gave opportunities to visit with old friends from other parts of the state and, more importantly, to recreate and immerse themselves in the culture of a society they had left behind.

The needs of a growing Mexican community also gave rise to other more permanent organizations. For example, a formal organization, *La Cruz Azul,* the Mexican Blue Cross, was also established in Salt Lake City during this period. The impetus for the organization came from the Mexican community with support from the Mexican consul. Operating as a mutual aid organization, its expressed purpose was to help the needy and indigent within the Mexican community by using initiative and resources.

With a growing contingent of Spanish-speaking mine workers and their families, the Bingham Canyon area also responded with similar organizational efforts. The most prominent organization was a mutual aid society known as the *Union y Patria.* Within several years the name and concept of the Bingham organization was changed to conform as a chapter of the *Comisión Honorífica Mexicana,* a larger, more nationally oriented organization. In Utah, as in other states, these chapters which were closely associated with the Mexican consul often came to serve as the community spokesman.[30] As a mutual aid organization, the Bingham (and later Salt Lake and

[29] *Salt Lake Tribune,* September 17, 1920. Interview with Louis Amador, Salt Lake City, December 8, 1970, Utah Minorities No. S–4; Interview with Maria Luz Solorio and Bertha Mayer, Salt Lake City, July 13, 1972, Utah Minorities No. S–42; Interview with Ellen Cordova, Salt Lake City, June 15, 1973, Utah Minorities No. S–7; Interview with Jesus Avila, Lark, Utah, May 6, 1973, Utah Minorities No. S–99.

[30] The *Comisión* was originally established in Los Angeles in 1921 by the Mexican consul there, Eduardo Ruiz. Its original purpose was to assist Mexican nationals until consular aid could be obtained. Matt S. Mier and Feliciano Rivera, *The Chicanos* (New York, 1972), p. 239. See also Avila interview and interview with Filomena Ochoa, Midvale, Utah, July 1972, Utah Minorities No. S–34 and No. S–35, pp. 22–23.

Further information on both Bingham organizations, the *Union y Patria* and the *Comisión Honorífica Mexicana,* can be found in a collection of organizational consular documents (correspondence, meeting minutes, budgets, and organization rosters, etc.) now kept at the American West Center.

Ogden) chapters of the *Comisión* assisted the entire Spanish-speaking population. However, its close relationship with the Mexican consul channeled its orientation to the interests and needs of the Mexican immigrants.

Concern for the spiritual welfare of the growing Spanish-speaking population was also noticeable in this period. In 1920 the Mormon church responded by establishing the Provisional Lamanite Branch, a fledgling missionary effort. The idea for the formation of a Spanish-speaking congregation of Mormons originated not with church officials but with three laymen, two Mexicans and a Spaniard, whose insight and efforts initiated and sustained the small branch.

The Provisional Lamanite Branch was the first organized in Salt Lake, with Margarito Bautista as its president. Later it was reorganized into the local Mexican Mission under the direct jurisdiction of the Mexican Mission of the Latter-day Saints church. Initially, the restaurant of Juan Martinez was used for the meetings of this small group. In an effort to enlarge membership, meetings were also held in Pioneer Park, a favorite point of congregation for many of the Spanish-speaking residents of Salt Lake City. Convinced of the viability of the organization, Mormon authorities finally organized it officially as the *Rama Mexicana,* or Mexican Branch, in 1923. Under Spanish-surnamed leadership, the initial organization of the branch included auxiliary groups such as the women's Relief Society. Efforts were made by members of this group to begin missionary efforts among the Spanish-speaking population in the Salt Lake Valley and in northern Utah farm communities.[31]

By 1927 the Catholic church had also established a mission for the benefit of the Mexican community in Salt Lake City. It had evolved from an earlier mission effort among the Italian population of Salt Lake. As the neighborhood around the Italian Mission, the west side of Salt Lake City, came to be increasingly dominated by

---

[31] Betty Ventura, "La Historia de la Rama Lucero" ("The History of the Lucero Wards"), manuscript, Lucero Ward, Salt Lake City; also, Mexican Branch; Priesthood Minute Book, 1922. See also manuscript, "Brief History of the Mexican Branch of the Mormon Church in the Salt Lake Valley," and Paul Morgan and Vicente Mayer, "The Spanish Speaking Population of Utah: From 1900–1935," *Toward a History of the Spanish Speaking People of Utah,* Mexican American Documentation Project, American West Center, 1973, Western Americana, Marriott Library.

Spanish-speaking residents, the focus of the mission shifted toward that group.[32]

The Mexican Mission was administered for a short time in 1927 by Padre Perfecto Arellano, a Mexican priest. He was followed by two brothers, Padres Antonio and Turibio Galaviz, both singers and guitarists. Padre Turibio was also an accomplished pianist and organist. Another "Padre Mexicano" followed. In 1930 the mission was given a separate status from Saint Patrick's Parish, from which it was administered. Officially, and appropriately, it was designated as the Mission of Nuestra Senora de Guadalupe, or Our Lady of Guadalupe, with Father James Earl Collins as administrator.

Under Mexican direction from 1927 to 1930, the Catholic Mission initiated various programs that included music and summer school classes for the children. Assisting these Mexican priests were Mexican nuns of the Order of Perpetual Adoration. Arriving in 1927, they began to help in the mission's programs, three of the sisters serving for twelve years.[33] While the activities of the Guadalupe Mission constituted a cultural oasis for Spanish-speaking residents of Salt Lake City, to many others the mission represented the joy of once again hearing sermons in Spanish.

The dedication of Father Collins for the mission's people, particularly his "kids," gave a strong identity to the mission. Father Collins was thirty-one years old when he arrived in Salt Lake City. Another later priest of the Guadalupe Parish, Father Jerald H. Merrill, as energetic and resourceful as Father Collins, wrote in "Fifty Years with a Future: Salt Lake's Guadalupe Mission and Parish":

> For twenty-seven years the people of the mission and later the parish, saw in the figure of Father Collins their church in action and their "Lord among them." Living in poverty—his only extravagance was the mission—Father Collins patched his suits and glued composition soles to his shoes. His salary was shared with his people.
>
> Each year in order to visit his mother in Albany, New York, he borrowed on his insurance and repaid the loan month-by-month in the following year. He bore in silence much infuriation with the "good Catholic ladies" who tried to help but who betrayed snobbish and condescending

---

[32] Jerald H. Merrill, "Fifty Years with a Future: Salt Lake's Guadalupe Mission and Parish," *UHQ* 40 (1972): 246.

[33] *Ibid.*, pp. 249–50. Also Solario and Mayer interview.

attitudes toward the poor Spanish-speaking women with their ever-present babies and small children.[34]

Father Collins's summer schools were attended by as many as two hundred fifty Mexican, Greek, Italian, Syrian, Armenian, English, Scandinavian, Irish, and "American" children a day. Religious instruction, softball and volleyball, and handicraft classes ended with cookies or other treats and a two-reeler Charlie Chaplin, Keystone Cops, or William S. Hart movie. The mission had a parish song that was sung to the music of a Mexican Marian hymn:

> We're down on Fourth South, far from luxury,
> Down where the viaduct spans the D&RG
> Most unpretentious, but somewhat quaint
> With Guadalupe as our patron Saint.[35]

The years 1920 to 1930 stand out as particularly important in the history of the Spanish-speaking population in Utah. Not only was it a period of heavy Mexican and Mexican-American movement into the state but also the initial period of organization and activity on the part of this group. A sense of community cohesiveness began to appear with the Spanish-speaking community and, with activities and organizations centering around the Mexican consul, the immigrant characteristic of the population was clearly reflected.

The size of the Spanish-speaking community, the number of organizations, and their varied activities reflected a growing importance in Utah's population in the first three decades of the twentieth century. However, this growth which had occurred primarily in the 1920s was reversed after 1930. A sharp decrease in the size of the Spanish-speaking community in Utah took place during the years of economic depression that gripped the United States in the 1930s.

Although the depression was a period of hardship for all workers in the United States, its effect was especially harsh on Mexican labor immigrants, the Mexican American, and indeed all those people who were relegated to the lowest positions on the social and economic ladder in American society. As economic conditions became worse in the United States, Mexicans and Mexican Americans found themselves competing with Anglo workers for the dwindling number of jobs available.

---

[34] *Ibid.*, p. 251.
[35] *Ibid.*, p. 254.

One solution to this growing unemployment problem was to deport large numbers of Mexican immigrants who had come to the United States between 1910 and 1930 to fill the labor needs of the booming economy. Between 1930 to 1940 from two hundred fifty thousand to five hundred thousand Mexican immigrants returned to Mexico either voluntarily or through forced deportation. A number who were deported involuntarily were United States citizens.[36]

In Utah the depression also affected the Mexican immigrants who had settled here. The 1930 Census showed that 4,012 persons of Mexican origin were living in the state. Of this number more than twenty-three hundred were born in Mexico, but by 1940 the number of Mexican-born immigrants living in Utah dropped to 1,069, reducing the Mexican immigrant population of Utah by one-half. After this marked reduction in the Mexican population in Utah, a second and larger wave of Spanish-speaking people arrived during and after the years of World War II.

The advent of World War II pulled the country out of the Great Depression, but the ensuing four years of war had particularly significant effects on the population and economy of the West. The sudden need for labor in the many war-related industries and in agriculture created a large labor shortage almost overnight. People looking for work moved quickly to those areas in the West where labor shortages existed. In Utah, for example, the rapid establishment and growth of government facilities and the need for workers was probably the single most important factor that attracted Mexican Americans from surrounding states.

The new federal supply depots in Utah, the Ogden Arsenal, the Tooele Army Depot, and the United States Naval Supply Depot in Clearfield, created a demand for labor that the Utah population could not supply. In the Ogden area alone nearly fifty-two thousand jobs were created by these government facilities during the war. This number equaled the jobs available in Utah's agricultural industry.[37]

The war also brought a labor shortage to the copper mines in Bingham Canyon, coal mines in Carbon County, agriculture, and railroad companies. The plentiful employment opportunities in

[36] Meir and Rivera, *The Chicanos*, pp. 161–62. See also, Leo Grebler, ed., *The Mexican American People* (New York, 1970), p. 526.

[37] Leonard J. Arrington and Thomas G. Alexander, "They Kept 'Em Rolling: The Tooele Army Depot, 1942–1962," *UHQ* 31 (1963): 11–12, and "Supply Hub of the West: Defense Depot Ogden, 1941–1964," *UHQ* 32 (1964): 99.

the region produced a rapid increase in the size of the Spanish-speaking population in Utah. Unlike the immigration of the preceding three decades, this increase was principally made up of Spanish-surnamed individuals who had moved to Utah from other states, expecially from Colorado and New Mexico. This interstate migration was increased by the active recruitment programs conducted by private industry and the federal government to fill the wartime labor needs of Utah.[38]

In contrast, the number of immigrants from Mexico who arrived and remained in Utah during this period was small. Census figures show that only 327 new immigrants from Mexico settled in the state between 1940 and 1950, although the census failed to record Mexicans who came to Utah to stay for limited periods as migrant labor.

During the Second World War, the labor needs were so great that the United States turned once again to Mexico for labor. Under a series of government-supervised programs, which grew out of treaties with the Mexican government, large numbers of workers were brought from Mexico to work in the United States. These Mexicans worked mainly in agriculture and on railroads in the West.[39] In comparison to states such as Texas and California, Utah employed relatively few workers from Mexico. At the peak of the war in 1944, Utah agriculture employed between six hundred and seven hundred Mexicans, while a smaller number were employed by the railroads.

In addition to labor from Mexico, Utah also imported workers from Puerto Rico and Jamaica. Indeed, the establishment of a Puerto Rican community in Utah was a direct result of Utah's wartime labor shortages. A number of Puerto Ricans, recruited to work in the copper mine at Bingham Canyon, stayed and established their homes, thus adding to the growth and variety of the Spanish-speaking community in Utah.[40]

[38] National Archives, Records of the War Manpower Commission, Record Group 211, Utah Es. 533.15, Box 3, 1943, (memos, telegrams, etc.), Washington, D.C.

[39] National Archives, Records of the War Manpower Commission, Record Group 228, Box 409, Division of Review and Analysis. (Mexican laborers folder).

[40] National Archives, Records of the War Manpower Commission, Record Group 211, Box 1, War Food Administration, Office of Labor. Also, Record Group 228, Box 409, Mexican laborers folder. Also, Record Group 211, Box 3–1533, Memorandum from John E. Gross, "Utah Stabilization."

In the postwar period, the distinctive characteristic in the growth of the Spanish-speaking population in Utah was its varied demographic origins. Mexican immigrant, Mexican American, Puerto Rican, South and Central American—each of these areas contributed to the growth and diversity of this population in Utah. Although bound by a common Hispanic tradition, especially in the form of language, the various national groups retained their distinctive cultural traditions. For example, the differences in the national music, dance, or food of a Mexican and a Peruvian in many cases may prove as dissimilar as those between a North American and a Mexican.

Despite the growth of the Spanish-speaking population in Utah, organizations such as the *Comisión Honorífica* tended to decline during the war years of 1942 to 1945. This was similar to the experiences of other organizations of Spanish-speaking communities throughout the West during this period.[41]

However, after World War II the number of organizations of the Spanish-speaking community in Utah showed a resurgence. The *Centro Civico Mexicano* was organized in Salt Lake City in 1944; the *Sociedad Mexicana Cuahotemoc* (Mexican Lodge) in Helper in 1949, and the *Sociedad Fraternal Benito Juarez* in Ogden in 1952. Together with the older *Comisión Honorífica Mexicana* and its three chapters, all remained associated with the Mexican consul in Salt Lake City and were oriented toward social and cultural activities primarily for the Mexican immigrant. In addition to the celebration of Mexican Independence days and upholding cultural traditions, these organizations continued to serve as a means by which the Mexican consul remained close to the Mexican immigrant community in Utah.

The contrast between the Spanish-speaking community before and after World War II in Utah was reflected not only in demographic origins of this population but also in the activities and goals of their organizations. The earlier organizations, such as the *Comisión Honorífica,* the *Union y Patria,* and later the *Centro Civico Mexicano,* were strikingly similar to those of other immigrant groups, and indeed, illustrate the immigrant experience in America.

Like other immigrant groups coming to Utah, the Spanish-speaking population had to deal with prejudice and discrimination in schools, housing, and employment. Mutual aid and fraternal

---

[41] Mier and Rivera, *The Chicanos,* p. 244.

organizations such as the *Cruz Azul* and the *Comisión Honorífica* aided the immigrant in adjusting and coping with a new, and at times hostile, social environment. As immigrants they reconciled themselves to such social realities, although they still found such prejudicial treatment galling. This was especially true of that part of the Spanish-speaking population in Utah who were American citizens by birth and whose families had lived in the Southwest long before annexation of the area by the United States.

School experiences were bitter for Mexican and Mexican-American children. They began their school days knowing little English and were immediately ostracized by other students and tolerated, ignored, and even abused by many teachers in whom the stereotype of the Mexican as inferior and unteachable was ingrained. The superiority of Anglo culture was stressed and Mexican culture was blatantly denigrated. For the sake of their children many parents identified themselves as Spanish. In the polyglot area around Helper, Utah, a common expression of those years was: "You won't find a single Mexican in the county. They're all Spanish."

Children stayed in school for a few years and dropped out, with poor reading and writing skills. The negative school experiences gave rise to an anger and frustration that manifested itself in distrust of American institutions. Law enforcement officials added to the damage done to the psyche of Mexican and Mexican-American children. Any deviation from what they considered proper Anglo standards gave them license to hound and harrass. In the early 1940s the Spanish-speaking adolescent's "ducktail" hair style and "zoot suits" (wide-shouldered suitcoats, festooned with watch chains, and full, pleated trousers, tapered at the ankles) brought quick, repressive action from officers.

Because of their American citizenship, the Mexican Americans had a somewhat different perspective of Anglo-American society and their place in it. Such a viewpoint was expressed in the postwar organizations that attracted Mexican Americans in Utah.

During the 1940s and 1950s organizations were formed that reflected the presence and needs of the large number of Mexican Americans who had moved to Utah from surrounding states and who constituted a majority of the Spanish-speaking population of Utah. One of these, the *Sociedad Proteccion Mutua de Trabajadores Unidos* (the "Mutual Protection Society of United Workers"), was organized in Ogden in 1946 by Demetrio Trujillo. The Ogden group was a chapter of a large fraternal society that had been established in Colorado in 1900. It was one of a number of similar societies throughout the Southwest that helped meet the needs of Mexican-American citizens for some form of financial security. A number of these organizations provided sickness and death benefits and in some cases life insurance.[42]

Another postwar organization established in Utah was the American G.I. Forum. The Forum, begun in Texas in 1947, was initially formed to help needy and disabled Spanish-speaking veterans. Quickly spreading throughout the West, the Forum oriented its activities increasingly toward civic and political action. Mrs. Molly Galvan, who was an active member of the G.I. Forum in Colorado, was instrumental in the initial organizing efforts of the G.I. Forum in Utah.

Transplanted to Utah in the period following World War II, the Utah chapters of the American G.I. Forum mirrored the changing orientation of the Spanish-speaking community in Utah. Rather than stressing Mexican nationalism, this more than any other organization up to that time aimed at dealing with the problems of the Mexican Americans in an Anglo-American society.

Abel Medina served as the first chairman of the G.I. Forum's Ogden chapter which was established in 1954; Larry Jaramillo headed the Salt Lake chapter, organized in 1955. The G.I. Forum immediately began to seek civic involvement. This ranged from challenging hiring practices at Hill Air Force Base to sponsoring back-to-school drives and providing scholarships in an effort to combat the high dropout rate among children of the Spanish-speaking people.[43]

Throughout the 1950s the activities of the G.I. Forum, the Mexican Civic Center, the *Comisión Honorífica,* and church-related activities such as those sponsored by the Catholic and LDS churches dominated the lives of the Spanish-speaking people in the state. Although several of these groups became increasingly concerned with community affairs, the focus of these activities remained local.

[42] For example, *La Sociedad Proteccion Mutua de Trabajadores Unidos* served not only as a fraternal organization, but offered life insurance to its members.
José Timoteo López, *La Historia de la Sociedad Protecció de Trabajadores Unidos* (New York, 1958). See also, interview with Cirino Chavez, July 27, 1974, Utah Minorities No. S–166.

[43] In Utah, the G.I. Forum did not establish a chapter until 1954 when one was begun in Ogden under the organizing leadership of Molly Galvan. *G.I. Forum News Bulletin,* October 1954; also the issues of January 1955 and August 1955.

The Spanish-speaking people remained in their neighborhoods, attended their churches, worked in low-paying jobs, and watched their children drop out of school with frustration but acceptance of the social order in which they found themselves. Newspapers duly noted the yearly celebrations of Mexican independence from Spain. Children, dressed in national costumes, still danced, sang, and put on plays. Patriotic speeches were given, and, as all immigrant groups did, the Spanish speaking invited public officials to address them.

But in the 1960s newspapers began giving coverage to new, aggressive activities among the Mexican and Mexican-American population. Reflecting the new activism brought on by liberal opposition to the Viet Nam War and the thrust for Black power, peaceful marches were held to present petitions asking for investigations in housing, neglect and abuse of Chicano students, lack of employment opportunities, and prejudice of law enforcement officials against youthful Chicanos. The young activists, following the Black experience, rejected the Anglo notion that their Mexican culture was inferior and began discovering and learning of their heritage: the advanced Aztec civilization, the heroic Aztec warriors led by Cuahtemoc who defended that civilization, fiercely but tragically; the Indians who never surrendered to the Spaniards; the repulsion of forces of Napoleon III in 1862; the young cadets in 1847 who held the Castle of Chapultepec against Gen. Winfield Scott's invading American army and when overpowered draped themselves in Mexican flags and jumped to their death. It was a time of "being more Chicano than thou." [44]

In Utah, activism of the Spanish-speaking community was also affected by national events. The American G.I. Forum showed a resurgence in activities and membership after a decline in the late 1950s. Other organizations appeared, but not until 1968 and the formation of SOCIO (Spanish Speaking Organization for Community, Integrity, and Opportunity) was there a broadly based statewide organization to represent the largest ethnic minority in the region.

In December 1967 a meeting was held in Salt Lake City to establish a permanent organization that could help in dealing with the economic and social problems of the Spanish-speaking community in Utah. Under the leadership of Jorge Arce-Laretta, Father Jerald Merrill, and Ricardo Barbero, SOCIO gained between

[44] *Salt Lake Tribune,* November 30, 1971.

four hundred and five hundred members in its first year. By 1974 membership had grown to nearly twenty-seven thousand persons with nine chapters in counties throughout Utah.[45] Through activities such as these, SOCIO has come to serve as the largest, although not the only spokesman, for the interests of the Spanish-speaking population in Utah. SOCIO has also proven to be the most successful effort in organizing Utah's largest ethnic minority and in giving voice to the more than forty-three thousand Spanish-speaking people who live in Utah today.

Commitment to the welfare of migrants is one of the priorities of SOCIO, the Migrant Council, and other related organizations. In the book *Somos Chicanos: Strangers in Our Own Land,* the author, a young Catholic priest who had turned away from his heritage, says:

> I don't know when I stopped thinking like a Catholic priest and became a Chicano. It was a long and complicated process, but maybe it began in Utah where I was first assigned to work. . . . Many of the families had no choice but to settle in the dilapidated shacks and huts located in the ruins of an abandoned sugar refinery. Inside the shacks there was no running water and outside there was only a single shower unit for 200 people. The toilet facilities were crumbling wooden outhouses which most of the people were afraid to use. . . . A few months after their return, Manuela [an intelligent, overworked girl] died from an acute and fatal form of anemia.
>
> When the news eventually reached me, I felt like burning down the migrant camp and getting a gun to go after everyone responsible for the conditions there: The Utah and Idaho Sugar Company who owned the land the camp was on. The Mormon farmers who leased the land and allowed their hired workers to live in filth and squalor. The county health and welfare officials who did absolutely nothing to help my people.[46]

The history of the Spanish-speaking people in Utah is a long one that stretches back to Escalante and to the Spanish and Mexican traders who followed in the last half of the eighteenth century. Yet, at the same time it is relatively recent history—indeed, in terms of a Spanish-speaking community it is a twentieth-century experience.

[45] Interview with Father Jerald H. Merrill, Salt Lake City, November 27, 1971, Utah Minorities No. 12–A, 12–B, and 12–C.

[46] Gomez, *Somos Chicanos,* pp. 20–22.

This experience follows that of all immigrants, but the stigma of prejudice continues and has a longer history for the Spanish speaking whose setting out from the *barrios* and into Anglo life has not yet begun. It will happen, and just as the Spanish speaking followed the new immigrants from the Balkans and the Mediterranean who in turn followed the old immigrants from the British Isles, Scandinavia, and northern Europe, other immigrants will follow the Mexicans and Mexican Americans and bring their distinctive cultures to face similar and yet peculiarly unique attitudes and circumstances, but in the end they will call themselves Americans.

THE AUTHORS

THE EDITOR

Helen Z. Papanikolas was born in the little town of Cameron, Carbon County, of Greek immigrant parents. Later, her family moved to Salt Lake City where she completed her education, receiving a bachelor's degree from the University of Utah. She has written and lectured extensively on Utah history and folklore. Her publications include the well-known *Toil and Rage in a New Land: The Greek Immigrants in Utah* and a variety of articles on Utah's immigrant and mining communities. She is a member of the Board of State History, a Fellow of the Utah State Historical Society, and coordinator of the Greek Archives, Western Americana, Marriott Library, University of Utah. With her pioneering research, writing, and collecting of materials on immigrant culture, Mrs. Papanikolas has encouraged many young scholars to explore this important aspect of social history.

THE CONTRIBUTORS

Fred Conetah Born at Fort Duchesne, Utah, Mr. Conetah has worked for the American West Center, University of Utah, under a grant from the National Endowment for the Humanities and as Ute tribal historian. He is presently serving as director of the Ute Indian Tribal Museum at Bottle Hollow near Fort Duchesne.

Clyde J. Benally Mr. Benally was born at Montezuma Creek, Utah, and is presently working to further Navajo participation in local education in San Juan County. A graduate of Fort Lewis College, Durango, Colorado, he was engaged as an oral history translator at the American West Center, University of Utah.

Floyd A. O'Neil Born in Roosevelt, Utah, Dr. O'Neil received his doctoral degree in history from the University of Utah and is associate director for documentation and oral history programs at the American West Center. His publications include *Ute People: An Historical Study* and *The Southern Utes: A Tribal History.*

Frederick S. Buchanan An immigrant from Scotland, Dr. Buchanan is an associate professor of cultural foundations of education at the University of Utah. He received his doctoral degree from Ohio State University. Professor Buchanan has written and lectured publicly on a variety of educational topics and on Scots in Utah.

Ronald G. Coleman Mr. Coleman, a doctoral candidate and an instructor in history at the University of Utah, is a native Californian. A member of the executive committee, Institute for the Study of Black Life and Culture at the university, he has been active in promoting Black history and has been a frequent guest lecturer on the subject.

William Mulder A professor of English at the University of Utah, Dr. Mulder was born in the Netherlands. His doctoral dissertation at Harvard University was published in 1957 as *Homeward to Zion: The Mormon Migration from Scandinavia.* He is a founding director of the Institute of American Studies and the Center for Intercultural Studies at the University of Utah.

Jack Goodman A native of New York, Mr. Goodman was educated at New York University and came to Utah in 1945. During his career as a journalist, he has worked for the *Salt Lake Tribune,* local radio and television stations, and as area correspondent for the *New York Times* and *Newsweek.* He is an Honorary Life Member of the Utah State Historical Society.

Davis Bitton Dr. Bitton, a professor of history at the University of Utah, received his graduate degrees from Princeton University. He is the author of books and articles on Mormon history and European intellectual history. A native of Idaho Dr. Bitton is an assistant church historian for the Church of Jesus Christ of Latter-day Saints.

Gordon Irving A native of Salt Lake City, Mr. Irving is a history graduate of the University of Utah and is presently a historical associate with the Historical Department of the Church of Jesus Christ of Latter-day Saints. In 1974 he received the Mormon History Association award for the best article on Mormon history by a young scholar.

Don C. Conley Mr. Conley, a native of Idaho, received his master's degree in Asian studies from Brigham Young University where he wrote his thesis on "The Pioneer Chinese of Utah." A missionary for the Church of Jesus Christ of Latter-day Saints in Hong Kong, he first became aware of the Chinese contribution to Utah through his wife, Angela Chan.

Maureen Ursenbach Dr. Ursenbach was born in Canada of parents who as children were uprooted from Utah and transplanted to Mormon colonies in Southern Alberta. She received her doctoral degree from the University of Utah and is currently editor and senior historical associate in the Historical Department, Church of Jesus Christ of Latter-day Saints.

Richard L. Jensen Mr. Jensen, a native of Provo, Utah, is a graduate of Utah State University and received his master's degree in history from Ohio State University. He is currently engaged in historical research and writing for the Historical Department, Church of Jesus Christ of Latter-day Saints, on subjects such as the Canadians in Utah.

Philip F. Notarianni A son of immigrant Italian parents who settled in Utah, Mr. Notarianni received his bachelor's and master's degrees in history from the University of Utah and a master's degree in history from the University of Minnesota where he was a research assistant at the Immigration History Research Center.

Alice F. Kasai Mrs. Kasai was born in Seattle, Washington, and, later, her family moved to Carbon County, Utah, where she was educated. She is presently volunteer coordinator for the Salt Lake Board of Education. Mrs. Kasai has been active in the Japanese-American Citizens League since 1939 and served as the local chapter's only woman president to date in 1946.

Joseph Stipanovich Born in Kansas City, Kansas, the grandson of Serbian immigrants, Mr. Stipanovich is presently a doctoral candidate in United States social history at the University of Minnesota and a research assistant at the Immigration History Research Center. He is the author of *The South Slavs in Utah: A Social History.*

Robert F. Zeidner Born in Seattle, Washington, of British and Central European stock, Colonel Zeidner was graduated from the United States Military Academy at West Point and served in various governmental positions in the Middle East for twenty-five years. He is presently a teaching fellow and a doctoral candidate at the Middle East Center, University of Utah.

Vicente V. Mayer Dr. Mayer, a native of Salt Lake City, received his doctoral degree in history from the University of Utah where he was involved in the American West Center's minorities oral history and documentation project and edited *Utah: A Hispanic History*. He is presently attached to the United States embassy in Panama.

INDEX

Abbeglen, ———, Swiss immigrant, 243

Abel, Elijah, Black Mormon priesthood member, 119–20

Abel, Mary Ann, wife of Elijah, 119

Abplanalp, ———, Swiss immigrant, 243

Abraham Lincoln Club, Black Republican organization, 134–35

Abrahams, Levi, Jewish immigrant, 193

Abravanel, Maurice, Utah Symphony conductor, 215, 247

Adams, Barnabas, Canadian immigrant, 285

Ah Fung, Chinese baker, 274

Ah Lee, Chinese laundryman, 257

Ah Lei, Chinese farmer, 258

Alemania Club, soccer organization, 247

Alexander, Daniel, backer of Clarion colony, 210

Alhandra, Ute leader, 40

Allam, Michael S., Syro-Lebanese teacher and translator, 400

Allensworth, Allan, Black army chaplain, *127*, 132

Alle Vermark Is Ous (AVIO), Dutch organization, 230, 240

Allied Metals, 213

America, Italian newspaper, 330

American G. I. Forum, Spanish-speaking veterans organization, 465, 466

American Hellenic Educational Progress Association, Greek lodge, 431

American Legion, activities of, against immigrants, 427, 428

American Smelting and Refining Co., Italians worked for, 309

Amerikanski Srbobran, Serbian newspaper, 371

Andersen, Jens, Danish immigrant, 157

Anderson, Bruce, Canadian educator, 301

Anderson, Emma, Scandinavian immigrant, 182

Anderson, Marian, Black concert singer, 136

Anderson, Nephi, Norwegian novelist, 184

Anderson, Niels, Scandinavian sheepherder, 171

Anderson, Peter, Scandinavian immigrant, 170

Angelopoulos, Stephanos, Greek priest, *425*

Angotti, Tomaso, Italian musician, *317, 326*

Ankatosh, Ute leader, *32*

Anselmo, Fortunato, Italian consul, *318*

Antelope Jake, Gosiute Indian, 57

Anti-Defamation League of B'nai Brith, 218

Aoyama, Miyuki, Japanese internee, 358

Appah, Ute leader, 42

Arce-Laretta, Jorge, SOCIO organizer, 466

Arellano, Perfecto, Catholic priest, 459

Arima, Estella, Japanese infant, 340

Arima, Oroville, Japanese infant, 340

Armenians: Americanization of, 403, 404; culture and customs of, 403; immigration of, 385–88, 400–402; in manufacturing and merchandising, 402, 403; massacres of, 400–401, 406; in mining, 403

Arnowitz, Irving, Jewish lawyer, 214

Arny, Willy, trader, 22

Ar-reep, Ute leader, 40

Arthur, Christopher, Welsh immigrant, 74, 109

Arze-Garcia expedition, 31

Ashley, William Henry, trapper, 31

Assist, community planning organization, 360

Associated Newspapers, LDS foreign-language press, 183

The Assumption Greek Orthodox Church, 426

Atchee, Ute leader, 40

Athena Club, Greek organization, 433

Atkin, William, English immigrant, 108

Attey, John, Lebanese immigrant, 392, *397*

Auerbach, Frederick, Jewish merchant and community leader, 194, 198, 200

Auerbach, George, backer of Clarion colony, 210

Auerbach, Mrs. Samuel H., daughter of J. G. Brooks, 191

Auerbach, Samuel H., Jewish merchant and community leader, 194, 199

Auerbach's department store, 194, 196, *203,* 208

Auerbach, Theodore, Jewish merchant, 194

Axelrad Furniture, 213

Baer, Adolf, backer of Clarion colony, 210

Baird, James, and music, 77

Ballantyne, Richard, Scottish civic and church leader, *86*

Ballet Folklorico, *455*

Ballo, Domenico, Italian band leader, 324

Bamberger, Herman, Jewish merchant, 208, 209

Bamberger, Jacob, Jewish businessman, 209

Bamberger, Louis, Jewish businessman, 209

Bamberger Railroad, *205,* 209

Bamberger, Simon, Jewish businessman and governor, 197, *205,* 208–10, 215, 219

Bankhead, Alexander, Black slave, 121, 122

Bankhead, Don Freeman, first freeborn Black in Utah, *126*

Bankhead, George, slave owner, 121

Bankhead, John, slave owner, 121

Bankhead, Mary Lucille Perkins, descendant of Black pioneers, 115, *125*

Banks, John, Morrisite leader, 90, 92

Baptist church, 176

Barber, George, English immigrant, 109

Barbero, Ricardo, SOCIO organizer, 466

Barnett, Andrée, French educator, 245

Barnum, Charles David, Canadian immigrant, 285

Barton, ———, LDS bishop, 151

Bathemess, Andrew, Greek musician, *423*

Bautista, Margarito, Spanish-speaking LDS leader, 458

Beanland, ———, railroad agent, 133

Beckwourth, James P., Black trapper, 115–16, *124*

Beeley, Arthur L., social worker, 112

Beesley, Ebenezer, English musician, 77, *80*

Begay, Hilda, Navajo weaver, 23

Belafonte, Harry, Black entertainer, 136

Belgians: immigration of, 224; prejudice against, 229–30

Bennett, James, Canadian educator, 301

Bennett, William H., Canadian educator, 301

Bennion, Samuel, English immigrant, 109

Benson, Ezra T., LDS leader, 144

Bergera, Anna, *315*

Bergera, Mike, Italian retailer, *315*

Bergman, Abner, rabbi, *204,* 217

Berman, Daniel L., Jewish attorney, 214

Berstrup, Soren Larsen, Danish farmer, 156

Bertolina, Floyd C., Helper mayor, *319*

Bertrand, Louis, French sericulturist, 243

Bikuben, Danish newspaper, 158, 173, 183

Billy, Ute leader, 40

Bingham Canyon, Canadian camp in, *289*

Bingham-Garfield Railroad, 341

Bing Kung Tong, Chinese Benevolent Society, 262–63, *269,* 276

Bionde, Joe, Italian, *319*

Black Hand, 329

Black Hawk, Ute leader, 38

Black Hawk War, 38

Blacks: in military, *127, 128,* 130–32, 133; prejudice against, 136–40; as railroad workers, 132–33; as slaves in Utah, 116–18, 120–23; social life of, 133–35; as trappers and explorers, 115–16

Blake, F. W., apostasy of, 91–92

Blanco, Mrs., Spanish-speaking *curandera*, 447

Blood, Henry H., governor, 358

Blood, William, English immigrant, 109

B'nai Brith, Jewish organization, 139, 201, 216

B'nai Israel, Jewish Reform congregation, 199, *206*

Bodenheimer, Mr. and Mrs. Edgar, Jewish law professors, 216

Bogdanovich, Nick, Serbian lodge member, *374*

Bonacci, Bernardina Falvo, wedding of, *319*

Bonacci, Frank, Italian union leader, 313

Bonacci, Joe, Italian railroad foreman, *314*

Bonacci rooming house, *316*

Bonacci, Thomas, wedding of, *319*

Bonelli, Daniel, Swiss LDS winemaker, 242

Bonnemort, Elizabeth, Scottish sheep rancher, *86*

Borgeson, Anders, Scandinavian immigrant, 171

Borglum, Gutzon, Danish sculptor, 141

Borglum, James, Danish woodcarver, 141

Borglum, Solon Hannibal, Danish sculptor, 141

Bottino, Caterina Pessetto, Italian who hid Mother Jones, *315*

Bottle Hollow resort, 44

Boyer, Mary Elizabeth Hussoun, wife of G. Katter, 394

Brewster, Sheldon, realtor, 137

Bridger, Jim, trapper, 31, 115, 286

Brigham Young University, 245, 298, 301

British immigrants: culture and customs of, 75–79, 88–89; and native pride, 98–111; number of, 64–65; and religion, 89–98; settlements of, 66–68; trades and skills of, 68–75

Broad Ax, Black newspaper, 122, 134

Brooks Arcade, business building, 191

Brooks, Juanita L., and Chinese, 273

Brooks, Julius Gerson, Jewish businessman, 190–91, 193

Brooks, Isabell (Fanny), Jewish milliner, 190, 191, 193

Brossard, Amable Alphonse, Canadian immigrant, 293

Brossard, Edgar B., U.S. Tariff Commission chairman, 293

Brown, Benjamin, Jewish businessman, 211

Brown, Emmett L., Canadian attorney, 301

Brown, Homer M., immigrant to Canada, 296–97

Brown, Hugh B., LDS leader, 297, 301

Brown, James, and Scandinavian LDS converts, 155

Brown, Lydia, wife of Homer M., 296–97

Brown, Victor L., LDS leader, 301

Bruno Cession, took Ute lands in Colorado, 39

Bryner, Ulrich, Canadian physician, 301

Buchman, Louis, Jewish businessman, 219

Buck, Fraser, and Chinese, 263–64

Buckhorn mine boardinghouse, *267*

Buddhist church, 340, *346*, *347*, 350, 351, 358, 361

Buehner, Carl W., German immigrant, 240

Buher, Fred, Swiss cheesemaker, 243

Building Trades Congress, 320–21

Bureau of Indian Affairs, 25–26

Burgess, John, British immigrant, 101

Burton, Robert T., and Morrisites, 90

Cable Act, 343, 352

Cabrera, Santos, Spanish-speaking immigrant, 239–40

Caine, John T., British immigrant and delegate to Congress, 75, 95

Cairo, Alfonso, Italian band member, *317*, 326

Calder, David O., British immigrant, 75

Calderwood, Alexander, Scottish immigrant, 110

Caledonia Club, Scottish social organization, 103

Caledonia Football Club, Scottish organization, 103

Caledonia Pipe Band, Scottish organization, 103

Caledonia Society, Scottish Mormon organization, 103

Callis, Helmut, German educator, 245

Calvary Baptist Church, 134

Cambrian Association, Welsh organization, 111

Cambrian Society, Welsh organization, 104–5

Camelia Arts and Crafts Club, Black organization, 135

Campbell, James S., Scottish immigrant, 112

Campbell, Lottie, Black pioneer, *126*

Campbell, Robert, British actor, 76

Campbell, Robert L., British educator, 112

Camp, Williams Washington, slave owner, 122

Canadian Club, 300

Canadians: in education and medicine, 301; French and English backgrounds of, 279–81, 299–300; as immigrants, 283–87, 293–94, 298–99; as Loyalists, 280–81; in mining, 287, 292–93

Cannon, Angus M., Manx immigrant, 73

Cannon, Frank J., U.S. senator, 131

Cannon, George Q., LDS leader, 92, 93, 94–95

Cannon, Martha Hughes, Welsh physician and politician, 73, 82

Capone, Gennaro, Italian music teacher, 324

Captain Jack, Ute leader, 40

Card, Charles O.: founder of Canadian LDS settlement, 294–96; home of, *290*

Card, Zina, wife of H. B. Brown, 297

Cardon, Alfred, and LDS church, 92

Cardon, Paul, French-Italian sericulturist, 243

Cardon, Susanna, French-Italian sericulturist, 243

Cardon, Alfred, British immigrant, 108

Careless, George, and music, 77

Carone, Vito, Italian orchestra leader, 326

Carranza, Venustiano, Mexican president, 341

Carson, Christopher (Kit), frontiersman, 23, 115

Carter, Kate B., Daughters of Utah Pioneers president, 145 n. 4, *163*

Carvalho, Solomon Nunes, Jewish artist-photographer with J. C. Fremont, 191–93

Casement, John S., railroad foreman, *84*

Cathedral of the Madeleine, *236*

Catholic church: and Italians, 326–28, 331; and Spanish-speaking, 438, 458–60, 465

Cayias, George, Greek insurance agent, 410

Centennial Eureka mine, 209

Central Pacific Railroad, construction of, by Chinese, 252–54, 261

Central Utah War Relocation Center (Topaz), Japanese interned at, 357–58

Centro Civico Mexicano, fraternal organization, 463, 465

Chambers, Amanda Leggroan, Black pioneer, *125*

Chambers, Samuel D., Black pioneer, *125*

Chapoose, Connor, Ute leader, *27*

Chappuis, Flore G., French immigrant, 231

Chappuis, Gaston, Swiss handball and chess champion, 248

Chavanaux, Ute leader, 40

Chemnitzer Vereinigung, German organization, 231

Cherenik, Edward, World War II casualty, 216

China Mary, Park City resident, 264

Chinese: and Christianity, 274–75; culture and customs of, 252, 256, 258–59, 261–62, *267, 268,* 273, 276; immigration of, 251–52, 260–61, 275–76; as miners, 270–71; prejudice against, 253, 260–61, 264–65, 271, 274–75; as railroad workers, 252–56, 261, 263, *266*

Chinese Benevolent Society, 262

Chinese Exclusion Act, 275, 334

Chinese Herbal Medicine Store, 270

Chinese Six Compånies, 252

Ching Moon, Chinese grocer, 258

Ching Wah, Chinese laundryman, 259

Chinn, Arthur K., World War II casualty, *269, 275*

Chin Sig, Chinese immigrant, *267*

Chipeta, Ute leader, 30

Chipman, James, banker, 286

Chipman, Stephen, Canadian immigrant, 286

Chipman, Washburn, Canadian immigrant, 286

Chisholm, W. W., mine owner, 209

Chlepas, Con, Utah Greek, *420*

Chorus Harmonie, German choir, 246

Christensen, Carl Christian Anton, Danish artist, 153, 154, *165*

Christensen, Christian, handcart pioneer, 155

Christensen, Hans, Scandinavian immigrant, 152

Christensen, Willam F., Ballet West director, 185

Christian Reformed Church of America, 241–42

Christophersen, Martin, Norwegian gardener, 184

Church of Jesus Christ of Latter-day Saints: in Canada, 282–83, 287, 294–98; and Jews, 195, 200–201, 210, 217, 218; missionary activity of, 1–2, *50*, 62, 68–69, 141, 143, 144–46, 150, 151–52, 222, 224–25, 226, 227, 240, 306; and non-English-speaking members, 9, 179–81, 231, 238–39, 350, 395, *398*, 405, 406, 407–8, *450, 452*, 458, 465; racial and ethnic dogmas of, 5, 139, 321

Church of World Messianity, Japanese organization, 350

Church of Zion, Godbeite organization, 90

Civil War, effects of, in Utah, 37, 38, 123, 194, 197

Clarion, Sanpete County, Jewish agricultural colony in, *203,* 210–11

Clawson, Hiram B., and culture in pioneer Utah, 75

Clayton, William, British immigrant, 76, 77

Clay, Wallace A., "Pappy," and Chinese, 254–56

Clearfield Canning Co., establishment of, by E. D. Hashimoto, 339

Clearfield Naval Supply Depot, 461

Clemmens, Mrs. ———, Corinne restaurant owner, 257

Cline, A. B., Jewish merchant, 201

Cloward, Oliver Bradley, and Chinese, 271–72

Club Dante Allighieri, Italian fraternal organization, 330

Clyman, James, trapper, 115

Cohen, Henry, backer of Clarion colony, 210

Cohen, H. M., pioneer Jew, 197

Cohen, Max, Jewish merchant, 201

Cohen, Mr. and Mrs. Briner, Jewish hotel owners, 209

Cohen, Sid, Jewish film exhibitor, 213

Cohoe, Ute leader, 40

Colistro, Giovanni D., Italian band leader, 325

Collins, James Earl, Catholic priest, *451, 459*–60

Columbus Day, *316, 318,* 325

Comisión Honorífica Mexicana, mutual aid organization, 457–58, 463, 464, 465

Congregational church, 175, 275

Connor, Patrick Edward, commanding officer at Camp Douglas, 72, *84,* 88, 102

Contributor, Utah periodical, 106

Coombs, Morgan, Canadian physician, 301

Cooper, Joseph, British immigrant, 107

Corinne, Box Elder County, 196–97, 257

Il Corriere D'America, Italian newspaper, 330

Cortner, W. M., Ku Klux Klan organizer, 323

Cove Fort, Millard County, *288*

Creedon, Mrs. ———, Bingham landlady, 102

Critchlow, John J., Indian agent, 39

Croatian Fraternal Union, 370, 371

Croats. *See* Yugoslavs

Crocker, Charles, and Central Pacific Railroad, 253, 254

Crocker, E. B., and Central Pacific Railroad, 253

Crosby, Martha, wife of Green Flake, 118

Crosby, Oscar, Black pioneer of 1847, 116, 118

La Cruz Azul, Mexican mutual aid organization, 457, 464

Cullen, Matthew, and mining, 72

Culmer Jennings Paving Co., 320–21

Curecante, Ute leader, 40

Cutler, John, governor, 112

Daily Union Vedette, Camp Douglas newspaper, 88, 110

Dalpiaz, Joseph, Italian dentist, 312, 325

Dalsgaard, Christen, Scandinavian artist, 146

Dan, Black slave, 122

Danes. *See* Scandinavians

Danske Broderskap, Danish lodge, 182

Danske Klub, amateur theatrical group, 182

Danish Evangelical Lutheran Church, 177

Danish Publishing Co., 184

Dart, Isom, Black cowboy, 123, *125,* 130

Davies, Benjamin, Indian agent, 37

Davies, John Jones, Welsh immigrant, 109

Davis, Benjamin, Welsh immigrant, 66

Davis, D. D., Welshman, 105

Davis, Lonnie, Black hotel owner, 133

Davis, Richard, Welsh immigrant, 66

Davis, Thomas, Welsh immigrant, 66

Davis, William, LDS bishop, 169

Dawes Act, 42

Daynes, Joseph, and music, 77

Deadwood Dick (Nat Love), Black cowboy, 130

DeAngelas, Sam, Park City saloon of, *316*

DeBouzek, Jean A., engraving company of, *235*

DeBry, William, Dutch publisher, 231, 238

Deep Creek Reservation, 58, 59

deJong, Geritt, Jr., Dutch educator, *234,* 245, 246

Delmonico Hotel (White House), 209

Democratic Headlight, Black newspaper, 134

Demolli, Charles, Italian labor organizer, 311–12, 313

Dempsey, Jack, boxer, 427

Denver & Rio Grande Western Railroad: baseball team sponsored by, 134; and immigrant workers, 309, 337, 411, 414; in receivership, 301

Desaules, Henri Edouard, Swiss carpenter, 228

Deseret Dramatic Association, 77

Deseret Musical Association, 75–76

Deseret News: and coal miners' strike, 310, 311; and immigrant groups, 99, 103, 105, 147, 179–80, 217, 228, 336, 354; and Indians, 36–37; and sericulture, 243

Deseret Pottery, 69

Deseret Typographical Association, 70

Deus, Manfred R., LDS leader, 240

Deutsches Theater, German drama group, 247

DeVoto, Bernard A., historian, 95

DeWitt, John L., general, 353

Diamanti, John, Greek dream interpreter, 431

Diaz, Porfirio, Mexican president, 437, 440

Dietrich, Joseph Walter, German publisher, 231

Dinwoodey, Henry, British furniture maker, 73

Dixie Land, Black nightclub, 135

Dodson, Jacob, Black explorer, 116

Dolowitz, David, Jewish physician, 214

Dominion Day, celebration of, by Canadian Mormons, 295, 300

Domínguez-Vélez de Escalante expedition, 31, 46, 437, *448*

Donnellan, John W., and mining, 72

Dooley, James, NAACP leader, *129*

Dorcheus, John T., Danish immigrant, 172

Dorius, Augusta, Scandinavian midwife, 168

Dornbush, Lu, Jewish delicatessen owner, 216

Double Rock Store, Helper business, *315*

Douglas, Camp (now Fort), 102, 106, 131–32, 326

Dow, Alexander, and Morrisites, 90

Doyle and Schwartz Co., strike against, 313

Dragos, Mike, 1933 coal miners' strike leader, *374*

Draper, William, Salt Lake County settler, 286

Draper, Zemira, Salt Lake County settler, 286

Droubay, Paul, Tooele County commissioner, 246

Duchaine, trapper, 31

Duchesne, Fort, 42, 130

Dugway Proving Grounds, 133
Dunbar, David, and music, 77
Dunbar, W. C., Scottish immigrant, 103
Dunford, George, English immigrant, 109
Dupler, Joe, Jewish furrier and mink rancher, 213
Dusserre, Henry, French sheepman, *235*
Dutch: immigration of, 224, 225; periodicals for, 231, 238; and religion, 222, 238, 239, 241; and soccer, 247–48; social organizations of, 230
Dwyer, James, bookstore of, 78, *85*
Dwyer, Robert J., Catholic historian and archbishop, 67, 102

Eastern Orthodox church, 378, 395, 415–16, 417, 430
Eastern Utah Advocate, Carbon County newspaper, 328
Eccles, David, British financier, 73, 95
Echo and Park City Railroad, construction of, by Chinese, 263
Ecker's Hill ski jump, *165,* 185
E. D. Hashimoto Co., Japanese employment and services center, 337
Edmunds, Nathaniel, Welsh immigrant, 66
Egan, Howard, Canadian immigrant and missionary, 47, 285, *290*
Egloffstien, ———, topographer with J. C. Fremont, 192
Eimco, industrial equipment firm, 208, 213
Einersen, Axel, Scandinavian settler, 170
Einstein, Albert, *207*
Eliason, Anders, Swedish immigrant, 151
Elkin, Heiman J., rabbi, 199
Ellis, James, Jewish merchant, 195
Ellis, Nathan, Jewish merchant, 195, 198
Elocution Society, 88, 89
Elsinore Hotel, Sanpete County, *162*
Emancipation Day, celebration of, by Blacks, 134
Empey, William, Canadian immigrant, 285, *290*

Endo, Frank, Japanese grocer, farmer, and businessman, *348,* 353–54, *359*
Engh Floral, 185
Ephraim LDS chapel, *160*
Episcopal church, *21,* 26
O Ergatis, Greek-English newspaper, 411
Ericksen, Carl C., Danish editor, 184
Erickson, Hilda Anderson, Swedish midwife, *167*
Erickson Pharmacy, 185
Eriksen, H. T. W., educator, 149
Ernest, Thomas A., Black soldier, 131
Ershler, Irving, Jewish physician, 214
Esquire Club, Black social organization, *129*
Evacuation Indemnity Claims Act, 359
Evans, Jennett, mother of David O. McKay, 97
O Evzone, Greek newspaper, 418
Executive Order 9066, 352

Fackrell, Evalee McBride, and Chinese, 265, 270
Fadel, Kalil, Syro-Lebanese merchant, 392
Farnham Hotel, 119
Fasbender, Gerald O., immigration official, 299
Federal Bureau of Investigation, 355, 358
Federazione Columbiana, Italian lodge, *316*
Fenian Brotherhood, Irish organization, 102
Ferguson, James, Scottish actor, 76
Ferris, Joe, Ku Klux Klan member, 324
Figlia D'Italia, fraternal organization, 330
Finns, as coal miners, *163*
Finn's, restaurant, 185
First Baptist Church, 176
First Christian Reformed Church, 241
First Church of Jesus Christ Congregation, 198
Fisher, George A., sheriff, 354
Fisher, Kimball, Canadian pharmacist, 301
Fitzgerald, Ella, Black entertainer, 136
Fitzpatrick, Thomas, trapper, 31

Flake, Abraham, son of Green Flake, 118

Flake, Agnes, slave owner, 118

Flake, Green, Black pioneer of 1847, 116, 118, *124*

Flake, James M., slave owner, 118

Flake, Liz, Black servant, 118

Flake, Lucinda, daughter of Green Flake, 118

Florez, Incarnacion, Spanish-speaking *curandera*, 447, *452*

Floyd, Camp, 193–94

Flygare, Niels C., Scandinavian immigrant, 158

La Follia di New York, Italian newspaper, 330

Fook, Lee, Chinese World War I veteran, *269*

Forbes, and Melich saloon, *372*

Forsgren, Erika, wife of William Davis, 169

Forsgren, John Erik, Swedish immigrant and missionary, 144, 145, *166*, 168–70, 175

Forsgren, Peter, Danish weaver, 169

To Fos, Greek newspaper, 428, 432

Foundation Day, celebration of, by Japanese, 351

442d Regimental Combat Team, highly decorated *Nisei* unit, 359

Fox, Sid, Jewish television and radio pioneer, 213

Francis, Samuel, English immigrant, 74

Frank, Arthur, Jewish merchant, 201

Frankel, Lionel, Jewish lawyer and educator, 214

Frank, Louis, Jewish merchant, 201

Fratellanza Minatori, Italian lodge, 330

Free Christian Church, 175

Freed, Robert E., civil rights worker, *129*, 136–37

Fremont, John C., explorer, 116, 191–93

French: immigration of, 224, 225–26, 231; and LDS church, 222; prejudice against, 229–30; and sericulture, 243

Freund, Charles, rabbi, 210

Fritz, Albert, Black civil rights advocate, *129*

Gagosian, Ferdinand, son of Hagop T., 407

Gagosian, Hagop Thomas, Armenian immigrant, *399*, 405–7

Gagosian, Marrow Sherinian, mother of Hagop T., 405

Gagosian, Nimzar, daughter of Hagop T., 406

Gagosian, Tumas, father of Hagop T., 405

Gallazzo, Enrico, Italian count, *318*

Galligan, Thomas, Catholic priest, 96

Galaviz, Antonio, Catholic priest, 459

Galaviz, Turibio, Catholic priest, 459

Galvan, Molly, veterans organizer, 465

Gardner, Archibald, Canadian immigrant, 284, 286

Gardner, Neal, Canadian immigrant, 286

Gardner, Robert, Canadian immigrant, 286

Gavrilis, Jim, Greek immigrant, *421*

Gaxiola, Carlos M., Mexican consul, *448*

La Gazzetta Italiana, Italian newspaper, 330

Geldzahler, David, Jewish lawyer, 214

Gemmel, R. C., Utah Copper Co. general manager, 413–14, 419

George, Sarah, Lebanese immigrant, 392, *397*

German-American Federal Credit Union, 231

Germania Club, soccer organization, 247, 248

Germans: immigration of, 223–24, 225, 227; and LDS church, 222, 238, 239, 246; and Lutheran church, 241; prejudice against, 228–29; and soccer, 247–48; social organizations of, 230, 231; as war prisoners, *237*

Giles, Thomas Davis, Welsh harpist, *83*

Giovannoni, Alfredo F., Catholic priest, *318*, 326–27

Gittins, Alvin, British artist, 112

Gladstone, Gladys, Jewish concert pianist, 215

Glazier, Harold, World War II casualty, 216

Godbe, William S., English businessman and Godbeite leader, 71–72, 79, 89, 90

Golden Rule Store, Beaver business, 201

Goldberg, Gumpert, and Liberal party, 197

Gonzales, Mrs. ———, volunteer English teacher in Bingham, *455*

Goodman, Louis, Jewish physician, 214

Goodyear, Miles, and Fort Buenaventura, 63

Gordon, Samuel, rabbi, *204,* 216, 218

Gosiute Indians: contact of, with early travelers, 54–55; culture and customs of, *52, 53,* 55–56, 58–59; legends of, 56

Goto, Marc, Topaz internee, *348*

Goulding's trading post, *18*

Grand Central, chain store, 211

Grant, Jedediah M., LDS leader, 100

Grant, William, British immigrant, 106

Greek American Progressive Association, fraternal lodge, 431

Greek Orthodox church. *See* Eastern Orthodox church

Greeks: Americanization of, *422;* and Balkan Wars, 419, *421;* in Bingham and Carbon County strikes, 418–19, 428–29; culture and customs of, 409, 414–15, 416, 417, 419, *421, 422, 423, 424, 425,* 426, 427, 430–32, 433, 435; immigration of, 409–10, 412, 432, 434; and labor agents, 410, 411–12, 413, 418, 432; in mining and railroading, 411–14, 418–19, 426; prejudice against, 412–13, 414, 426, 427, 428, 429–30, 433; and religion, 415–16, 417, 419, 426, 430, 434; schools of, *425,* 430, 431, 433; in sheep and other businesses, 428, 433

Greek Town, *423*

Green, Jake, Black policeman, 135

Greenwood, William, British immigrant, 107

Gregory, Nettie, Black civic leader, 135

Grillos, Steve, Greek immigrant, *421*

Grose, George, and Chinese, 258

Grover, Joe, Park City Chinese, 263–64

Grow, Stewart, Canadian educator, 301

Guadagnoli, Antonio, Italian band member, 325

Guero, Ute leader, *32,* 40

Guertler, Siegfried, German theatre director, 247

Hafen, John, Swiss artist, *232, 247*

Hagg, Herman H., artist, 247

Halles, Gregory, Greek immigrant, *422*

Halles, Mrs. Gregory, Greek immigrant, *422*

Hals, Hans Jensens, Scandinavian immigrant, 168

Hamblin, Jacob, LDS missionary to Indians, 47, 48

Hamilton, Henry, British immigrant, 73

Hampton, Lionel, Black musician, 136

Hang Yei, Chinese laundryman, 259

Hansen, Hans Christian, Danish immigrant, 145

Hansen, Peter Ole, Danish missionary, 144, 145

Hansen, Ramm, Norwegian architect, 184

Hardie, James, British actor, 76

Hardie, Janet, British midwife, 73

Harker, Joseph, English immigrant, 107, 109

Harmonien, Swedish musican group, 182

Harmony, Fort, 47

Harrison, E. L. T., English immigrant and Godbeite, 76, 79, 89, 90

Harvey, Mildred Cluff, immigrant to Canada, 297

Harvey, Mildred Jennie, nurse, 297

Harvey, Richard C., immigrant to Canada, 297

Hashimoto, Edward Daigoro: escape of, from vigilantes, 337; business interests of 337, 339, 340, 341, 342, *344,* 353; death of, 353; as Mexican consul, 442

Hashimoto, Edward Ichiro: birth of, 341–42; as professor of anatomy, *349,* 352–53

Hashimoto, Yoshiko, in Kabuki play, *347*

Hashimoto, Yozo, Japanese labor agent, 336–37

Hasoppe, Joseph, Belgian contractor, 243

Heap, ———, Parowan resident, 192

Helbling, Robert E., Swiss educator, 245

Held, John, Swiss band leader, *232*

Hellenic, Greek coffeehouse, 413

Hellenic Theatrical Club "Star," 433

Helper, Carbon County, *269, 315, 319, 372*

Henderson, Fletcher, bandleader, 135

Henderson, Horace, nightclub owner, 135

Henderson, James, Scottish immigrant, 110

Henry, Alberta, Black civic leader, *129*

Heywood, Martha Spence, Irish immigrant, *84, 89*

Hibbs Clothing, retail store, 355

Hidalgo, Father, Mexican hero, 457

Hill Air Force Base, 133, 465

Hi Marine, Black social organization, 135

Hintze, F. F., LDS missionary, 406

Hirschman, Herbert, Jewish insurance agent, 213

Hitler, Adolph, 200, 206, 218, 229

Hobson, Mary, wife of A. A. Brossard, 293

Hogar Hotel, Basque headquarters, *235*

Hoier, Christian, Norwegian forty-niner, 144

Holladay, John, farmer, 2

De Hollander, Dutch periodical, 238

Hollandia Club, soccer organization, 248

Holy Trinity Greek Orthodox Church, 378, 415, *420, 421, 424*

Hong Lee, Chinese store owner, 258

Hooper, William H., slave owner, 122

Hop Lee, Chinese craftsman, 274

Horne, Nate, Jewish merchant, 201

Hotel Newhouse, 136

Hotel Utah, 136

Howa, 'Brahim (Abraham), Lebanese immigrant, 392, *396*

Howa, John M., Hiawatha poolhall owner 392, *396*

Howa, Mose, Lebanese immigrant, *396*

Howard, William, distiller, 74

Howell, Martha J. Perkins, granddaughter of Green Flake, *124, 125*

Howell, Paul Cephas, Black policeman, *127, 135*

Hrvatska Bratska Zajednica, Croatian lodge, 370

Hubbell, Don Lorenzo, trader, 22

Huber, ———, Swiss immigrant, 243

Hudson's Bay Co., 63–64, 279

Huggins, Ira A., state senator, 358

De Huisvriend, Dutch periodical, 231

Hyrum Dairy, *166*

Iida, Shiro, Japanese publisher, *345*

Immanuel Christian Reformed Church, 241

Independence Hall, 198

Indian Peaks Reservation, 49

Indian Reorganization Act, 44

Ingalls, George W., and Indians, 48, 58

Inouye, Yukus, *Nisei* politician, 360

Inoway, Carl, *Nisei* architect, 360

Intelligenz-Blatt, German newspaper, 231

Internal Security Act of 1950, 360

International Peace Gardens, 361

Irish, O. H., Indian agent, 38

Israelsen, Andrew M., Norwegian immigrant, 156

Italian-American Civic League, 330

Italian-Americanization Club, 330

Italian Publishing Co., 330

Italians: Americanization of, 323, 324, 330; culture and customs of, *317,* 324–26, 327, 330, 331; as farmers and ranchers, 320; immigration of, 303–8; and labor movement, 310–13; in mining, smelting, and railroading, 306–13, *314;* and North-South factions, 304, 328–29, 330; prejudice against, 320–24, 328–29; publications of, 330–31; social organizations of, 330

Ivers, James, Canadian mine owner, 292–93

Iwamoto, Alice, wife of H. Y. Kasai, 355

Iwamoto, Eiji, Japanese camp boss, 342, 359

Iwamoto, Suga, wife of Eiji, 342

Jackling, Daniel C., mining magnate, 341

Jackson, Ruth, descendant of Green Flake, *125*

James, Isaac, Black pioneer, 118–19

James, Jane Manning, Black pioneer, 118–19

James, Mary Ann Perkins, Black pioneer, *126*

James, Silas, Black pioneer, 118

James, Sylvester, Black pioneer, 118–19

James, William, Black pioneer, *126*

Japanese: in agriculture, 335, 336, 338–39, 354, 358; assimilation of, 360–62; culture and customs of, 335, 336, 342–43, *346, 347,* 350–52, 361; immigration of, 334–36, 339, 343, 352; in mining and railroading, 335, 336, 337, 339–41, 342, 354–55; organizations of, 335, 351, 352, 356; prejudice against, 334, 337, 342–43, 352–59; publications of, 336, 340; and religion, 340, 350; relocation and internment of, 335, 352, 353–59; schools for, 350, 351; in U. S. armed services, 334, 352, 354, 358–59

Japanese American Citizens League (JACL), 139, 352, 356, 358, 359, 360, 362

Japanese-American Relocation Aid Committee, 358

Japanese Church of Christ, *345, 349,* 350, 361

Japanese Exclusion Act, 343

Jaques, John, and music 77

Jaramillo, Larry, veterans group chairman, 465

Jarvis, Robert, Indian agent, 57

Jazz Bo, Black nightclub, 135

Jensen, Anders, Scandinavian immigrant, 155

Jensen, Christiansen and Co., Richfield store, *161*

Jensen Creamery, *162*

Jensen, Hans, Danish blacksmith, 152

Jensen, Hans Peter, Danish iron founder, 172

Jensen, Harald, pastor of Danish Evangelical Lutheran Church, *161*

Jensen, James, Scandinavian farmer, 152

Jensen, Lars, Green River ferryman, 170

Jensen, Minnie, wife of Lorenzo Snow, 172

Jensen, Niels, Scandinavian potter, 168

Jensen, Sarah Josephine, wife of Hans Peter Jensen, 172

Jenson, Andrew, LDS historian, 92, 183

Jenkins, Ab, Salt Lake City mayor, 358

Jennings, William, British entrepreneur, 72

Jewish Community Center, 213, 220

Jews: and anti-Semitism, 217–18; definition of, 188–89; immigration of, 188–93, 194, 195, 200, 210, 211–12; Main Street businesses of, *202,* in the U.S. armed services, 214, 216; and religion, 189–90, 197–201, 212–13, 216, 219

Jewish Welfare Fund, 216

Johannessen, Christian, Norwegian editor, 184

Johannessen, Grant, concert pianist, 184, 185

Johnson, Chief, Ute leader, 40

Johnson, Frank, 136

Johnson, LaVell, historian, 357

Johnson, Wallace, Canadian pharmacist, 301

Johnston, Albert Sidney, and Camp Floyd, 102, 193–94

Jonas, Abraham, Jewish Masonic leader, 195

Jones, Dan, Welsh immigrant, 62, 66, 144

Jones, Fantley, Black railroad worker, 133

Jones, John, Welsh immigrant, 66

Jones, Shadrach, home of, *83*

Jorgensen, Cecelia, Scandinavian immigrant, 168

Jugoslav Socialist Federation, 370, 371

Ju, Henry, and Plum Alley, 261–62

Ju, Joy, and Plum Alley, 261–62

Julien, Denis, trapper, 31

Junior Soccer Association, 248

Kahn, Benjamin, pioneer Jew, 200

Kahn, Samuel, Jewish merchant, 196, 197, 198

Kahn, Sarah Cohen, Jewish society matron, 202

Kaibab Reservation, 49

Kambouris, Harry K., Greek playwright, 425, 433

Kanosh, Indian leader, 1

Kapteyn, Cornelius, Dutch contractor, 243

Karas, George, Greek confectioner, 420

Kasai, Henry Y.: as businessman, 343, 350; as civic leader, 343, 360, 361, 362, internment of, 355; photograph of, 344

Kastro, Nicholas, early Greek immigrant, 411

Kasuga, Taijiro, Japanese horticulturist, 339

Katsanevas, Emmanuel, Greek coffeehouse owner, 422

Katter, George, Lebanese merchant and labor agent, 392, 393–94

Kearney, Joseph E., Catholic bishop, 318

Kearns, Thomas, Canadian mining magnate and U.S. senator, 292–93

Keith, David, Canadian mining magnate, 292–93

Kelly, Edward, Catholic priest, 96

Kelsey, Eli B., British immigrant, 90, 159, 168

Kempe, Jens Christopher, Scandinavian carriagemaker, 152

Kida, Taka, in Kabuki play, 347

Kido, Jimmy, in Kabuki play, 347

Kiesel, Frederick J., mayor of Ogden, 246

Kimball and Lawrence, retail store, 291

Kimball, Ellen Sanders, Norwegian pioneer, 143, 163

Kimball, Heber C., LDS leader, 143

Kimball, LeRoy, Canadian physician, 301

Kimball, Ranch, resort lessee, 136

King, Charles, Chinese businessman, 268

King, Ernest, Chinese physician, 268

King, Hannah Tapfield, English immigrant, 81, 88, 89

King, Lily, daughter of Charles and Ruth Y., 268

King, Raymond, Chinese photographer, 268

King, Ruth M., Chinese physician, 268

King, Ruth Y., wife of Charles, 268

King, Walter, Chinese journalist, 268

Kletting, Richard K. A., German architect, 236

Knaphus, Torlief, Norwegian sculptor, 164, 185

Knight, Jesse, financier, 296

Knowles, Eliza, English immigrant, 108

Knudsen, Wilhelm, Scandinavian immigrant, 168

Kol Ami, Salt Lake City Jewish congregation, 189, 199, 217

Kolff, Willem, medical researcher, 245

Koosharem Reservation, 49

Kooyman, Frank I., Dutch editor and bookkeeper, 238

Korean War, 9

Koseki, Joe Toraji, Japanese immigrant, 334–35, 351, 354, 359

Kosta, Louis, Greek immigrant, 423

Kramer, G. W., mine official, 310

Krikstein, Joseph, rabbi, 216

Krotki, Max, Jewish merchant, 201

Krotki, Sol, Jewish merchant, 201

Kuhr, Otto, Lutheran minister, 241

Ku Klux Klan, 7, 218, 323–24, 343, 429–30

Kurumada, Jun, and JACL, 349

Ladies Civic and Study Club, Black organization, 135

Lagoon resort, 136, 137, 205, 209

Lamar, L. Q. C., secretary of war, 42

Lambert, Charles, English stonecutter, 70

Lamb, M. T., Baptist pastor, 173

Lambrides, Vasilios, Greek Orthodox priest, 418–19

Lammers, Johanna Carolina, Dutch immigrant, 240

Lammers, P. J., Dutch LDS missionary, 238

Lamoreaux, ———, Canadian immigrant, 287

Landa, Esther, Jewish community leader, 215
Lange, Lena, *315*
Larkin, Elijah, English immigrant, 106, 109–10
Larsen, Hans "Pram Stikker," Scandinavian builder, 153
Latsis, Mr. and Mrs. James, wedding of, *425*
Il Lavoratore Italiano, United Mine Workers newspaper, 311
Lawrence, Henry, and Godbeites, 90
Laycock, Harold, Canadian musician, 301
Laycock, Ralph, Canadian musician, 301
Lay, Hark, Black pioneer of 1847, 116, 118
Leavitt, Dudley, Canadian immigrant, 286
Leavitt, Lemuel, Canadian immigrant, 286
Leavitt, Thomas, Canadian immigrant, 286
Lebanese. *See* Syro-Lebanese
Lee, Harold W., Canadian educator, 301
Lee, Joe, trader, 25
Lee, John D., 25
Legal Defenders, 360
Legget, Charley, Chinese baker, 274
Leggroan brothers, Black baseball players, 134
Lessing Hotel, 201
Lester House Hotel, 209
Levy, Morris, and Jewish religious activities, 200
Lewis, H. E., Standard Coal Co., general manager, 429
Liberal Hall, 174
Liberal party, 90, 197
Liebler, H. Baxter, Episcopal priest, 26
Liljenquist, Ola Nilsson, Swedish tailor and LDS bishop, 152, *166*
Limberis, Louis, Salt Lake City Greek, *420*
Lindquist Mortuary, 185
Lindsay, James, Scottish immigrant, 110
Lindsay, John, actor, 76
Lioasakim, Toshimasa, in Kabuki play, *347*
Lister, Phoebe, and Chinese, 271

Liverpool, England, docks at, *80*
Llewellyn, John, Welsh immigrant, 66
Lochrie, Peter, county attorney, 112
Lockerby, ———, town named for, ·171
Lohner, Margrit Feh, Swiss choral director, 246
Longstrath, Stephen, British immigrant, 108
Lopez, Rafael, Spanish-speaking folk hero, 446
Los Angeles and Salt Lake Railroad, 443
Loscher, J. Peter, LDS mission president, 240
Louie, Frank, Chinese pilot, *268*
Louie, William W., Chinese architect and World War II veteran, 262, *269*
Love, Nat, Black cowboy, 130
Lovenberg, H., Nevada rabbi, 198
Lowenstein, Harry, Jewish merchant, 201
Lucerne Land and Water Co., 147
Lund, Anthon H., Danish LDS leader, 142, 406
Lund, Christian, Scandinavian immigrant, 151–52
Lund, Augusta, Danish immigrant, *162*
Lund, Joseph L., son of Danish immigrants, *162*
Lutheran church, 147, 149, 176–77, 241
Lye, William, educator, 301
Lyon, John, poet, 78

Mabey, Charles R., governor, 428
McCarthy, Wilson, Canadian attorney, 301
McCook, Ute leader, 40
McCornick, W. S., mine owner, 209
McCullough, John, drama critic, 77
Macdonald, John A., Canadian prime minister, 281
McDonald, John Taffe, Scottish candymaker, *86*
McEwan, Henry, Scottish printer, 70

MacFarlane, John M., and music, 77, 97

McGillis, Charlie, Jewish newspaper distributor, 213

Ma Choy, Chinese bride, 257

MacIntosh, Daniel, Scottish immigrant, 110

McKay, Charles, trapper, 64

McKay, David, father of David O., 97

McKay, David O., LDS president, 87, 97–98, 110

McKenzie, David, Scottish actor, 76, 77, 110

McLeod, Norman, Protestant minister, 96

McMillan, Duncan J., Presbyterian minister, 96, 174, 175

McMillan, J. S., Presbyterian missionary, 174

McNiece, Robert G., Presbyterian minister, 96, 174–75

McPherson, J. Gordon, Black publisher, 134

McPhie, Joseph H., Scottish immigrant, 110

Madsen, Carl, Scandinavian carriagemaker, 151

Maeser, Karl Gottfried, German educator, 237, 244

Maestas, Spanish officer and interpreter, 31

Mageras, Mrs. Nick (Magerou), Greek midwife, 423, 430

Mahleras, Harry, Greek sheepman, 235

Maiben, Henry, English immigrant, 61, 68

Malmstedt, Frank, Swedish vice-consul and editor, 184

Malouf, Anees B., Lebanese clothing manufacturer and retailer, 393

Malsh, Julius, and Liberal party, 197

Makoff's, clothing store, 213

Manifesto, 95, 296

Manning, Isaac, brother of Jane Manning James, 119

Manookin, Kerrigan, M., commanding officer at Dugway Proving Ground, 407

Mantes, Ernest G., state senator, 420

Manuelito, Navajo leader, 23

Marcus, Louis, Salt Lake City mayor and motion picture pioneer, 213, 215

Margetts, Phil, British actor, 76

Markakis, Georgia, baptismal dinner for, 422

Marrufo, Isidro, Spanish-speaking immigrant, 440–41

Marshall, Robert, lynching of, 137, 324

Martin, Edward, English artisan, 70

Martinez, Juan, restaurant owner, 458

Martin, Rev. and Mrs. G. W., in Mount Pleasant, 181

Masaoka, Mike Masaru, Japanese community leader, 349, 352, 356–57, 359, 360, 362

Masaoka, Mrs. Mike, 349

Massachusetts, Fort, 36

Matsumiya, Chiyo, wife of Jinzaburo, 340, 354–55, 359

Matsumiya, Jinzaburo, Japanese railroad foreman, 339–40, 354–55, 359

Mauritzen, Anna, Norwegian settler, 172

Mavrakis, Stellios, Greek immigrant, 423

Maw, Herbert B., governor, 358

Mayer, Bertha, Spanish-speaking resident, 445

Mayflower mine, 292

Mayflower Restaurant, 355

Medel, José, Spanish-speaking railroad worker, 456

Medina, Abel, veterans group chairman, 465

Medina, Tom, serviceman, 453

Meeker, Nathan C., Indian agent, 39–40

Meinig, D. W., geographer, 100

Mejia, Abraham, Spanish-speaking restaurant owner, 449

Melich, Joe, wedding of, 372

Melich, Mrs. Joe, wedding of, 372

Melling, Ellen Knowles, and music, 77

Merkeley, Marion G., Canadian educator, 301

Merrifield, Barnabas, Canadian immigrant, 283–84

Merrill, Jerald H., Catholic priest, 459, 466

Messenger, Manti newspaper, 181

Methodist church, 175–76, 281, 338

Mexican Americans. See Spanish-speaking people

Mexican-American War, 31, 32, 437

Mexican Blue Cross, mutual aid organization, 457
Mexican Revolution, 7, 439–40
Mexicans. *See* Spanish-speaking people
Meyer, Philip, Jewish architect, 200
Michelsen, Christian, Scandinavian immigrant, 155
Middle Easterners. *See* Armenians, Syro-Lebanese
Midsommarfest, Swedish celebration, 185
Migrant Council, 467
Milano, G., Italian publisher, 330
Miles, Eva L., and Chinese, 273
Miles, George F., and Chinese, 273
Millennial Star, LDS mission periodical, 79, 147, 191
Milosh Obilich i Tsar Dushan, Serbian lodge, 376
Il Minatore, Italian newspaper, 330
Misaka, Wat, *Nisei* athlete and mechanical engineer, *349, 360*
Mitsunaga, Jimi, founder of Legal Defenders, 360
Miya, Pap, and JACL, *349*
Moapa Indian Reservation, 48, 49
Mode O'Day, clothing store, 393
Moench, Louis F., German educator, 244
Montefiore, Conservative Jewish congregation, 199, 200–201, 216
Moore, David, Canadian immigrant, 283–85
Moore, Susan, wife of David, 284
Moran, Patrick J., Irish contractor, *85*
La Morena Cafe, *454*
Morgensternen, Danish periodical, 157, 170, 183
Morley, Isaac, Manti colonizer, 169
Mormons: exclusiveness of, 438; and Indians, 36, 46–49, 437; relations of, with immigrants, 379, 381–82; 416, 418, 434; as slave owners, 117–18, 121–22
Morris, Elias, Welsh immigrant, 104
Morris, Isadore, Jewish religious activities of, 199, 200, 201
Morris, Joseph, and Morrisite schism, 90–91
Morrison, William, Scottish immigrant, 67, 98
Morrow, Henry A., Camp Douglas officer, 336
Morrow, Mr. ———, *315*

Mortensen, Andreas, and Lutheran missionaries, 174
Moser, ———, Swiss immigrant, 243
Moses, Nathan, and Jewish religious activities, 200
Mosisco, Ute leader, 42
Mount Nebo Literary Association, 89
Mount Tabor Lutheran Church, 185
Mulder, William, Dutch educator, 238, 245
Murdoch, John, Scottish sheepherder, 69–70
Musical and Dramatic Co., 77
Musser, Elise Furer, Swiss politician and civic leader, *233,* 246
Muster, Oscar, cantor, *204*
Mutual Protection Society of United Workers, Spanish-speaking organization, 464–65

Nackos, Isadore, in Greek play, *425*
Naegle, John C., Swiss winemaker, 242
Naisbitt, Henry, and music, 77
Nakagi, ———, Japanese coal camp boss, *344*
Narbona, Navajo leader, 23
National Association for the Advancement of Colored People (NAACP), 137, 139
National Miners Union, in 1933 coal miners strike, 377–78, 379
National Store, 213
Native American church, 43–44
Nauvoo Brass Band, 75
Nauvoo Legion, 38, 90
Navajo Indians: effect of Spanish on, 17, 22, 23; culture and customs of, 14, 15, *18, 19, 20, 21,* 22; family and social organization of, 17, 23, 25; land of, 13–14; religion of, 14, 15–17; removal of, to Bosque Redondo, 23; traders among, 23–25
Navajo Reservation, 23, 26
Nazism, 200, 216, 218, 229
Neibaur, Alexander, Jewish immigrant, 193
Nelson, Andrew (Anders Nielsen), Presbyterian convert, 175
Nelson, Alice, Navajo weaver, 23

Nelson, Lowry, sociologist, 175

Nettie Gregory Community Center, 135

Neuhausen, Carl M., German architect, *236*

Neumann, Hermann, German soccer player and organizer, 248

Newhouse, Samuel, Jewish businessman, *203*, 210, 219

News Advocate, and 1922 Carbon County coal strike, 429

New York Cafe, Chinese restaurant, 270

Nibley, Charles W., Scottish immigrant and LDS leader, 73, 95, 96, 110

Niccoli, Frank, Italian publisher, 330

Nicoletti, Luigi, Italian goat rancher, 326

Nicholas, David, Welsh immigrant, 66

Nielsen, Christian, Scandinavian immigrant, 169, 170

Nielsen, C. M., Norwegian judge, 184

Nielsen, Jens, handcart pioneer, 148, 152

Nielsen, Peter, 149

Niiya, Lois Hide, wife of E. D. Hashimoto, 341

Nilsson, Anna B., Baptist missionary, 176

Nimble Thimble Club, Black social organization, 139

Ninth Cavalry, Black troops stationed in Utah, 130–31

Norden Society, 182

Norske Literaire Forening, Norwegian literary magazine, 184

Det Norske Sangkor, Norwegian glee club, *167*

The Northern Light, Danish-English periodical, 184

Notarianni, Filippo, Italian band member, *319,* 326

Norwegian Constitution Day, 185

Norwegians, Fox River, Illinois, colony of, 143–44. *See also* Scandinavians

Obon, Japanese festival, *347,* 351, 361

Ogden Arsenal, 461

Ogden, Chinese community in, 259–61

Ogden, Camp, 326

Ogden, Isaac, father of Peter Skene, 281

Ogden Junction, and Chinese, 260–61

Ogden, Peter Skene, Canadian leader of Hudson's Bay Co., 279–81, *288*

Ogden Standard, and Japanese, 339

Ogilvie, George B., Canadian immigrant, 287

Oglesby, Belle, descendant of Green Flake, *124*

Ogyoku, Madame, Japanese flower arranger and teacher, *347,* 361

Okubo, Mine, Japanese interned at Topaz, 357

Oliver, D. H., Black attorney, 135

Olsen, A. P. Kjersgaard, Scandinavian farmer, 156–57

Olsen, Hans Peter, home of, *161*

Ontario mine, *291*

Open Heart, Greek coffeehouse, 413, *422*

Oregon Short Line Railroad, 310, 411, 414

Ottinger and Weggeland, art studio, 247

Ottinger, George M., artist, *81*

Ouray, Ute leader, 30, *32,* 40

Our Lady of Guadalupe Church, *454,* 459–60

Ouzounian, Mary B., Armenian immigrant, 401

Pacelli, Cardinal Eugenio, *318*

Pack, John, Canadian immigrant, 285

Paggi, Mose, Italian publisher, 330

Pahvant Indians, 43

Palmer, James, English immigrant, *80*

Palmer, Mary Jane Ewer, English immigrant, *80*

Pan Hellenic Union, Greek fraternal organization, 417, 431

Park, Boyd, British jeweler, 73

Park City, Chinese in, 263–65

Park City Mining Record, and Chinese, 264, 265

Parker, James, cavalry captain, 41

Parkinson, Charles, British immigrant, 74

Park, William, Scottish immigrant, 106

Parthenon, Greek coffeehouse, 413

Paul, Priscilla, Cornish businesswoman, 72

Peak, Ute leader, 40

Peart, Jacob, British immigrant, 113

Peck, Joseph H., physician, 58–59

Pedersen, Hans A., Norwegian businessman, 184

Peep O'Day, published by E. W. Tullidge and E. L. T. Harrison, 79

Perkins, Mary, wife of Sylvester James, 119

Perkins, Sylvester, Black pioneer, *126*

Pellegrini, Angelo M., Italian immigrant, 303

Penrose, Charles W., LDS leader, 78, 93, 95, 101

People's party, 95

The People's Store, 194

Pepper, Milton, Jewish physician, 214

Perpetual Emigrating Fund, 78, 94, 154–58

Pessetto, Paul, barbershop of, *319*

Petersen, Frederik, Scandinavian potter, 168

Petersen, Rasmus, Danish immigrant, 168

Peterson, Canute (Knud), Norwegian immigrant, 143, 144

Peterson, Charles Shreeve, Scandinavian immigrant and LDS bishop, 170

Peterson, Elmer G., educator, 358

Peterson, J. A., steamship agent, 158

Peterson, Sarah Ann, 158

Philbrick, Joe, Wyoming deputy sheriff, 130

Phillips, Moses Caspar, and Jewish religious activities, 198, 199

Phoenician Lodge, Syro-Lebanese organization, 395

Pinney, Dr. ———, slave owner, 121–22

Pitt, William, English bandleader, 75

Pleasant Valley Coal Co., 307, 310

Plum Alley, Chinese area of Salt Lake City, 261, 262, *267*

Plute, Olga, funeral of, *375*

Podet, Mordecai, rabbi, *206*

Poke, and Posey War, *34*

Politz Candy Store, *420*

Politz, Mrs. Andrew, *420*

Politz, Mrs. Tom, *420*

Politz, Tom, Greek candy store owner, *420*

Polysophical Society, 88, 89

Pomerance, Sherman, World War II casualty, 216

Popper, Charles, Jewish merchant, 195

Porters and Waiters Club, Black social organization, 133, 135

Posey, Chief, and Posey War, *34*

Posey, Jess, and Posey War, *34*

Powell, John Wesley, 3, 30, 47, 54, 58

Pratt, Parley P., in Las Vegas and San Bernardino, 192

Presbyterian church, 174–75

Price, John, Welsh miner, 66, 111

Prier, Peter Paul, German violin maker, 244

Principe De Napoli, Italian lodge, 328, 330

Il Progresso Italo-Americano, Italian newspaper, 330

Proletarec, Yugoslav newspaper, 371

Prosveta, Slovenian newspaper, 370

Provost, Albert, father of Etienne, 280

Provost, Etienne, Canadian trapper and explorer, 31, 279–80, 281, *288,* 293

Provost, Marianne, mother of Etienne, 280

Puerto Ricans. *See* Spanish-speaking people

Pugmire, Jonathan, English blacksmith, 70

Quilico, Joe, Helper Italian, *319*

Quilico, John, Helper Italian, *319*

Rainbow Gardens, and Blacks, 136, 137

Ransohoff, Nicholas Siegfried, Jewish merchant, 194, 195, 196

Rasmussen, Hans, Scandinavian immigrant, 157

Rasmussen, Elsie, handcart pioneer, 148

Red Cap, Ute leader, *35*, 42

Redd, John Hardison, slave owner, 121

Redd, Martha, Black slave, 121–22

Red Feather Stages, 353

Red Moon, Ute leader, 40

Reed, Chambeau, Ute Indian, 31

Reenders, Martin M., Dutch businessman, *234*

Rees, Henry, Welsh immigrant, 66

Rees, John, Welsh miner, 66, 111

Rees, Thomas, Welsh immigrant, 66

Reynolds, George, LDS leader, 93

Rice, Windsor V., Canadian mine owner, 292–93

Richards, Franklin D., LDS leader, 64

Richards, William, Welsh immigrant, 66

Richmond, Mignon, Black civic leader, 139

Rider, John, Irish immigrant, 74

Roberts, Brigham H., LDS leader, 93

Robidoux, Antoine, trapper, 31

Rocky Mountain Times, Japanese newspaper, 336, 340

Roe, Ben M., Jewish community leader, 201, *207,* 217

Rogers, Mr. ——, *315*

Romick, Morris, World War II casualty, 216

Romney, Miles, English architect, 63, 70

Roosevelt, Franklin D., *233*

Roos, Louis, LDS leader, 240

Rosenblatt, Joseph, Jewish businessman, 208, 219

Rosenblatt, Morris, Jewish businessman, 208

Rosenblatt, Nathan, Jewish businessman, 200, 208

Rosenblatt, Simon, Jewish businessman, 208, 217

Rosenwald, Julius, backer of Clarion colony, 210

Ross, Alexander, trapper, 64

Royal Hotel, 133

Ruggeri, Henry, Price judge, 329

Russo, Alfonso, Italian publisher, 330

Rydman, Otto, Swedish editor, 179

Sailor Jack mine, 209

Saint Christopher's Episcopal Mission, *21*

Saint David's Day, Welsh celebration, 104, 105

Saint John's Lutheran Church, 185, 241

Saint Patrick's Church, 327, 459

Saint Vincent's School, 112

Sakano, Jiuy, in Kabuki play, *347*

Sako, Daishiro, Japanese camp boss, 342

Sako, Kyoichi, Japanese camp boss, 342

Salazar, Jim, serviceman, *453*

Salazar, Nick, serviceman, *453*

Salazar, Ross, serviceman, *453*

Salazar, Tony, serviceman, *453*

Saltair, 130, *236*

Salt Lake Athletic Club, soccer organization, 247

Salt Lake City Cemetery, 359

Salt Lake Chamber of Commerce, 201

Der Salt Lake City Beobachter, German newspaper, 183, 231

Salt Lake City Police Department, 135

Salt Lake Colored Political Club, 135

Salt Lake Council of Women, 361

Salt Lake Grocery and Dry Goods Co., 393–94

Salt Lake Herald, 311, 328

Salt Lake Nichiren Buddhist Church, 350

Salt Lake Nippon baseball team, *346*

Salt Lake Scots Pipe Band, 103

Salt Lake Telegram, 198

Salt Lake Telegraph, 88, 197

Salt Lake Theatre, 76, 153, 169

Salt Lake Tribune, 79, 131, 198, *291,* 293

Saltwater, Mrs., Navajo weaver, 23

Sam Hing, Chinese laundryman, 257

Sampino, Sam, Greek immigrant, *424*

Samuels, Leo, Jewish physician, 214

Sam Wah, Chinese laundryman, 259

Sam Wing, Chinese laundryman, 274

Sandack, A. Wally, Jewish lawyer, 214

Sandack, Helen, Jewish women's leader, 215

Santschi, Eugene, Swiss mayor of Hiawatha, 246

Sapavanaro, Ute leader, 40

Sauki, Mrs. Izyo Kiyoshi (Madame Ogyoku), Japanese flower arranger and teacher *347*, 361

Savage, Charles R., British photographer, *81*

Sawaya, Nafy, Lebanese immigrant, *396*

Sawaya, Sabeh A., Lebanese immigrant, *396, 397*

Sawyer, Harry B., Ku Klux Klan organizer, 323

Scandia Kaffe House, 185

Scandinavian Choir of Salt Lake City, 157–58

Scandia Male Chorus, 185

Scandinavian Democratic Club, 182

Scandinavian Dramatic Club, 182

Scandinavian Mercantile Association, 182

Scandinavian Publishing Co., 183

Scandinavians: acculturation of, 149, 150, 178–83; celebration of, *164;* immigration of, 158–59, 168–70; as settlers, 168, 170–72; numbers of, in Utah, 141–42; trades and skills of, 151–54

Scandinavian Shop, 185

Scanlan, Lawrence, Catholic bishop, *85,* 96–97

Schiff, Jacob, backer of Clarion colony, 210

Schindler, Emil, LDS leader, 240

Schmalz, Charles, German contractor, 243

Schreiner, Alexander, Tabernacle organist, 246

Schubach brothers, optical business of, 213

La Scintilla, Italian newspaper, 330

Scottish Club, 103

Scottish Missionary Reunion, 103

Scots, culture and customs of, *87.* *See also* British immigrants

Seicho-No-Ie Salt Lake Shinto Soai Kai, Japanese church, 350

Seixas, Joshua, taught Hebrew to Mormons, 195

Selvin, Sol, Jewish state senator, 215

Serb National Federation, 370–71

Serbs. *See* Yugoslavs

Seto Shee, wife of Wing Louie, *268*

Seventh Day Adventist Hospital, 26

Sewell, ———, Corinne justice, 257

Shaarey Tzadek, Orthodox Jewish congregation, 212

Shapiro, Alex David, Bar Mitzvah of, *204*

Shapiro, Eric Simon, Bar Mitzvah of, *204*

Shapiro, Joel, and Zionism, 217

Shapiro, Joshua, and Jewish religious activities, 200

Shapiro's Luggage, 213

Shapiro, Simon, and Zionism, 217

Sharp, John, British entrepreneur, 72

Shavano, Ute leader, *32*

Shearman, William, and Godbeites, 90

Sheldon, Richard, Canadian immigrant, 283–84

Sheranian, Herond Nishan, Armenian ophthalmologist, *399*, 407

Sherinian, Nisham K., LDS missionary, 406

Sheranian, Rebecca, Armenian immigrant, *399*

Sheya, Amen, Lebanese immigrant, *396*

Sheya, Sam, Lebanese immigrant, *396*

Shibata, George, *Nisei* West Point graduate, 360

Shibota, Coney, Japanese miner, 341

Shool, Bonos, Lebanese grocer, 392

Siegel brothers, Jewish merchants, 195, 196

Siegel, Solomon, Jewish merchant, 196, 198

Silver King Coalition Mines, 287, 292

Silver Reef Miner, and Chinese, 274

Silver, William, British engineer, 73

Simon, Adolph, backer of Clarion colony, 210

Simon, Fred, Chamber of Commerce president, 201

Simpson, J. H., and Gosiutes, 54–55

Simpson, Sir James, Edinburgh physician, 73

Sing Lung Store, Ogden grocery, 259–60

Sion, Eliza, daughter of Fredrick, 120

Sion, Ellen, wife of Fredrick, 120

Sion, Fredrick, Black Mormon convert from England, 120

Sisters of Perpetual Adoration, *449, 451*

Sisters of the Holy Cross, 97

Sjodahl, J. M., Swedish publisher, 229

Skandinaviens Stjerne, LDS mission periodical, 147, 168, 183

Skedros, James, Greek author, 432

Skliris, Leonidas G.: Greek labor agent, 341, 411–12, 413, *420,* 433, 435; firing of, demanded by 1912 Bingham strikers, 418–19

Skousen, W. Cleon, Canadian author, 301

Sloan, James, Nauvoo city recorder, 62

Slopanskey, Mrs. Frank R., *315*

Slovene National Benefit Society, 370

Slovenes. *See* Yugoslavs

Slovenska Narodna Podporna Jednota, Slovenian fraternal organization, 370

Smith, Alvin, Jewish lawyer, 214

Smith, George Albert, and Jews, 217

Smith, Hyrum, 284

Smith, Joseph F., LDS leader, 93

Smith, Joseph Fielding, LDS leader, 119

Smith, Joseph, Jr., LDS prophet, 62, 68, 79, 143, 144, 195, 281, 282, 283, 284, 285

Smith, Joseph III, Reorganized LDS leader, 144

Smith, Oliver, Canadian educator, 301

Smith, Seymour, student, 298

Smith, Thomas L. (Pegleg), trapper, 31

Smith, William R., LDS bishop, 201

Smoot, Abraham O., slave owner and LDS leader, 121, 172

Smoot, Reed, U.S. senator, 172

Snelgrove, Edward, English shoemaker, 70

Snow, Erastus, LDS leader, 99–100, 144, 159, 168

Snow, Lorenzo, LDS leader, 172, 306, 407

Snow, Vinnie, Canadian prostitute, 287

Sociedad Fraternal Benito Juarez, Spanish-speaking fraternal organization, 463

Sociedad Mexicana Cuahotemoc, Spanish-speaking fraternal organigation, 463

Sociedad Mutualista Mexicana, Fourth of July float of, *452*

Sociedad Proteccion Mutua de Trabajadores Unidos, Spanish-speaking fraternal organization, 464–65

Societa' Cristoforo Colombo, Italian fraternal organization, 325, 330

Societa' Di Beneficenza, Italian fraternal organization, 330

Solorio, Luz, Spanish-speaking resident, 445

Sonoda, Chas, and JACL, *349*

Sorensen, Virginia Eggertsen, novelist, 185

South Americans. *See* Spanish-speaking people

Southern Pacific Railroad, 132, 310

Southern Paiute Agency, 48

Southern Paiute Indians: culture and customs of, 45–46, *50, 51;* economic status of, 49; gatherings of, *51, 52;* and Mormons, 46–49, *50;* religion of, 45, 54; reservations for, 48–49

South Slavs. *See* Yugoslavs

Sow-a-wick, Ute leader, 40

Spanish-American War, 132

Spanish Speaking Organization for Community, Integrity, and Opportunity (SOCIO), 466–67

Spanish-speaking people: in agriculture, 444, 447, *455,* 461, 462, 467; culture and customs of, 439, 444–47, 456, 463, 464, 466; deportation of, 461; immigration and migration of, 437, 438–44, 460–63; in mining and railroading, 441–43, 447, *449, 451,* 456, 461–63; organizations of, 457, 463–67; prejudice against, 438, 440, 464, 468; and religion, *448, 452,* 458–60, 465; during World War II, *453,* 461–62

Spellman, Francis J., Catholic archbishop, *318*

Spillman, Juanita, descendant of Green Flake, *125*

Spitz, David, backer of Clarion colony, 210

Sport Abzeichen, German physical fitness program, 248

Sports Club Berlin, soccer organization, 247

Sports Club Rapids, soccer organization, 247

Spring City LDS chapel, *160*

Spry, William, English immigrant and governor, *81,* 112, *203,* 210, 341, 418

Srpski Narodni Savez, Serbian lodge, 370

Staes, Stylian (Stylianos Stagopoulos), Greek vice-consul, 417, 429

Staines, William C., English immigrant, 78, 107

Stamoulis brothers, Greek automobile dealers, 430

Stanford, Leland, California governor, 253

Standard Coal Co., and 1922 Carbon County strike, 429

Standard Optical, 213

Stansbury, Howard, and Gosiutes, 56

Steele, Catherine, Irish immigrant, 102

Steele, James, Scottish immigrant, 106

Steele, John, Irish immigrant, 102

Stein, Sam, Jewish merchant, 201

Stella D'America, Italian lodge, 328, 330

Stenhouse, Fanny, British immigrant, 79, 88

Stenhouse, T. B. H., British immigrant, 79, 88, 89

Stephens, Evan, British composer, 77

Sterling, Harry, cantor, 206

Stevens, Henry, Sanpete County settler, 168

Stevens, Lucinda Flake, descendant of Green Flake, *124*

Stevens, Roswell, Canadian immigrant, 285

Stewart, Justin C., lawyer, 218

Stoffel, Charles M., pharmacist, *237*

Stoof, K. B. Reinhold, LDS mission president, 240

Storstrom, Johan, handcart pioneer, 155

Straaberg, Josef, Norwegian author, 184

Strang, James J., schismatic leader, 144

Strauss, Leon, rabbi, 199

Strauss, Levi, Jewish merchant, 195

Strobridge, J. H., railroad superintendent, 253

Sue Wah, Chinese laundryman, 259

Sutherland, John, British immigrant, 74

Svanevelt, Conrad, Scandinavian immigrant, 168

Svanevelt, Josephine Brighamine, daughter of Conrad, 168

Svea, Swedish organization, 182

Svenska Gleeklubben, Swedish musical organization, 182

Svenska Härolden, Swedish periodical, 183

Swedes. *See* Scandinavians

Swedish Baptist Church, 176

Swedish Evangelical Lutheran Church, 166

Sweet, Corrinne, Jewish community leader, 215

Sweet, Leon, Jewish businessman, 213

Swiss: immigration of, 223, 225; and LDS church, 222; prejudice against, 229–30; social organizations of, 230–31; and wine and cheese production, 242, 243

Swiss Chorus Edelweiss, 246

Symko, Orest G., physicist, 301

Symphony Singers, 246

Syro-Lebanese: culture and customs of, 392–93, 394; fraternal organizations of, 395; immigration of, 385–94; as merchants and businessmen, 390–91, 392, 393; prejudice against, 395; and religion, 395, in Salt Lake City's Greek Town, *396;* as textile workers, 391

Teasdale, George, LDS leader, 93

Tabby-to-Kwana, Ute leader, 38

Tabernacle Choir, 77, 246

Tadje, Frederick, LDS mission president, 240

Takeno, Ken, and JACL, *349*

Talmage, James E., LDS leader, 93, 274–75

Tanaka, Masasuke, in Kabuki play, *347*

Tanner, N. Eldon, LDS leader, 301

Taverner, L. W., Ku Klux Klan organizer, 323

Taylor, John, LDS leader, 69, 93, 94, 99, 282

Taylor, John W., and LDS in Canada, 296

Taylor, Julius, Black publisher, 234

Taylor, William W., Black publisher, 134

Teec Nos Pos, Navajo weaving district, 22

Teerlink, Nicholas J., Dutch LDS leader, 240, 246

Temple B'nai Israel, *206*

Tenas, John, death of, Greek striker, 428

Tensini, Riccardo, Italian, *319*

Terasawa, Mrs. Kuniko, Japanese publisher, 361

Terasawa, U., Japanese publisher, *345*

Terry, Amy, wife of Z. Draper, 286

Terry, Jacob, Dixie settler, 286

Terry, James, Dixie settler, 286

Terry, Joshua, Canadian immigrant, 285–86, *290*

Terry, Parshall II, and Revolutionary War, 285–86

Terry, Parshall III, Canadian immigrant, 286

Thalia, Swedish dramatic society, '179, 182

Thistle Social Club, Scottish organization, 103

Thomas, A. L., territorial governor, 104–5

Thomas, Charles J., British musician, 76

Thomas, Elbert D., U. S. senator, 352, 356–57, 358, 360

Thomas, Evan, Welsh immigrant, 66

Thomsen, Anders, Scandinavian immigrant, 169

Thomsen, Peter, Scandinavian immigrant, 151

Thornburg, Fort, 41

Thornburg, Thomas, army officer, 40

Thurman, Wallace, Black author, 135

Tinker, Frank, and Chinese, 258

Tip, John, Chinese bridegroom, 257

Tooele Army Depot, 461

Topaz, Japanese relocation camp at, 8, *348*, 357–58

Topaz Times, Japanese newspaper, 357

Toponce, Alex, French mayor of Corinne, 246

Toronto, Joseph, Italian immigrant, 306

Towler, Ivy C., and Chinese, 262

Townsend, Thomas J., pastor of Trinity African Methodist Episcopal Church, *128*

Tracy Bank and Trust Co., 353

Treaty of 1868, and Navajos, 23, 26

Treaty of Guadalupe Hidalgo, 23, 438

Tri City Oracle, Black newspaper, 134,

Trinity African Methodist Episcopal Church, *128,* 134

Trujillo, Demetrio, fraternal society organizer, 464

Tsau'-wi-at, Ute leader, 30

Tse-ne-gat, and Posey War, *34*

Tsuyuki, Izuko, Japanese restaurant owner, 354

Tullidge, Edward W.: as author and publisher, 74, 75, 76, 79; and Godbeites, 89, 90

Tullidge, John E., English musician, 76, 79

Tullidge, John, Jr., English artist, 76, *82*

Twenty-fifth Infantry, Black troops stationed in Utah, 130

Twenty-fourth Infantry, Black troops stationed in Utah, 130–32

Uchida, Setsuzo, Japanese immigrant, 338, 355

Uchida, Take, Japanese immigrant, 355, 362

Uintah and Ouray Reservation, 34, 37–42

Unca Sam, Ute leader, 40

Uncompahgre Indians, *35*

Union Pacific Railroad: completion of, 254; labor agents for, 411; workers for, 132–33, 309, 310, 414, 442–43

Union y Patria, Spanish-speaking organization, 457, 463

United Jewish Council, 216

United Mine Workers Union, 310, 311–12, 377–78, 379

United Services Organization (USO), 358–59

United Syrian-American Society, 395

University of Utah, 245, 297, 301, 353, 360, 408

Uno, Raymond S., Japanese lawyer, 360

Urban League, 139

Ursenbach, Octave, Swiss sericulturist and watchmaker, 243, 244

U.S. Cafe, Japanese restaurant, 354

Utah Bladet, Swedish periodical, 184

Utah Colonization Fund, for Jewish colony at Clarion, 210

Utah Copper Co.: and immigrant workers, 394, 413–14, 416, 441–42; L. G. Skliris labor agent for, 411; and 1912 Bingham miners strike, 313, 418–19, 442, 446

Utah C. V. Federal Credit Union, German organization, 231

Utah Danske Amerikaner, Danish magazine, 184

Utah Fire Clay Co., 313, 393, 400

Utah Fuel Co., 307, 308, 311–12, 341

Utah High School Activities Association, 248

Utah High School Soccer Association, 248

Utah-Idaho Sugar Co., 339, 467

Utah Korrespondenten, Swedish newspaper, 179, 183

Utah Magazine, 79, 89

Utah National Bank, 286

Utah National Guard, and 1912 and 1922 miners strikes, 418, 428

De Utah Nederlander, Dutch periodical, 238

Utah Nippo, Japanese newspaper, 340, 361

Utah Pipe Band, 103

Utah Plain Dealer, Black newspaper, 134

Utah Posten, Danish newspaper, 179, 183

Utah Poultry Cooperative Association, 211

Utah Reporter, and Chinese, 257

Utah Skandinav, Scandinavian periodical, 183

Utah Soccer Association, 247

Utah State Fish and Game Commission, 358

Utah State Register of Historic Sites, 357

Utah State University, 298, 358, 408

Utah Symphony, 215, 247

Utah Territory, legal status of Blacks in, 120–22

Utah Territorial Penitentiary, 95

Utah War, 193–94, 195, 197

Ute Indians: ancestral lands of, 27–28; culture and customs of, 29–30, *32, 33, 34,* 36, 38, 44, 45; effect of Spanish on, 30–31; and Mormons, 36–38; religion of, 28–29, 43–44; and Sioux, 42–43

Valdez, Juan, death of, 446

Valdez, Te, Spanish-speaking *curandera,* 447

van Dyke, R., Dutch LDS missionary, 238

Varden, Norwegian periodical, 184

Vasa Orden, Swedish organization, 182

Venizelos, Eleftherios, Greek premier, 415

Vidnesbyrdet, Norwegian and Danish Methodist newspaper, 176

Vikings, soccer club, 185

Villa, Pancho, Mexican revolutionist, 446

Volpe, John, secretary of the treasury, 254

Voyagis, Andonios, Greek teacher, *425*

Wada, Fred, Japanese leader, 348, 354, 359

Wagener, Henry, brewery of, *237*

Wah Hing, Chinese laundryman, 258

Wa Hop, Chinese laundryman, 258

Wakamatsu Silk and Tea Farm Colony, founding of, by Japanese in California, 335

Wakara (Walker), Indian leader, 1, 192

Walker Bank, 72

Walker brothers, pioneer merchants, 194, 195, 196

Walker, Charles L., southern Utah settler, 172

Walker, David, English merchant, 72
Walker, Harris, Canadian physician, 301
Walker, Joseph, English merchant, 72
Walker, Matthew, English merchant, 72
Walker, Samuel, English merchant, 72
Walker War, 36, 437
Wall Street Baptist Church, 134
Walsh, Patrick, Catholic priest, 96
Walter-McCarran Immigration and Naturalization Act, 359
Warets, Ute leader, 32
Warshaw, Maurice, Jewish merchant, 211
Wasatch Academy, 174
Washakie, Indian leader, 1
Washington, James W., Black pastor and publisher, 134
Wass, Ute leader, 40
Watters, Abraham, Jewish merchant, 195
Watters, Ichel, Jewish merchant, 195, 198
Watters, Leon L., Jewish historian, 190, 193, 207, 209
Watt, George P., 91
Weber Stake Academy, 244
Webb, Arthur P., deputy sheriff, 428–29
Weekly, Billy, club manager, 133
Weggeland, Danquart A., Norwegian painter, 153, 165
Weibye, Jens, Scandinavian tailor, 152
Weihe, Willard, Norwegian violinist, 184
Weinstock, Jack, Jewish insurance agent, 213
Weisley, Mrs. Otto, and International Peace Gardens, 361
Welles, Capt. ———, and Fort Buenaventura, 63
Wells, Daniel H., Salt Lake City mayor, 192, 336
Wells, Heber M., and Scandinavians, 182
Wells, John, LDS leader, 95
Welsh, and music, 82, 83. See also British
West, Caleb, territorial governor, 201
Western Federation of Labor, and 1912 Bingham strike, 418–19
Western Garment Manufacturing Co., 393

Western Pacific Railroad, 377, 411
Western Slavonic Association, insurance organization, 370
White House, Salt Lake City hotel, 209
White, James A., Jewish businessman, 213
White River Agency, and Meeker Massacre, 40
Widtsoe, Anna, Norwegian immigrant, 156
Widtsoe, John A., Norwegian scientist and educator, 1, 156, 164, 171, 184
Wilbeck, Alan R. ("Pete") Canadian sportsman, 301
Wilkins, Roy, NAACP leader, 129
Williams, Albert "Speck," Black ferry operator, 123
Williams, Esther, Navajo weaver, 23
Williams, Price, Welsh immigrant, 66
Williams, Sterling, and Canadian Mormon settlement, 294
Williams, Thomas S., slave owner, 122
Wilson, David D., pastor of Trinity AME Church, 128
Wilson, Mary, named Ben Lomond, 67
Winder, John R., LDS leader, 93, 95
Wing, Molly, wife of Sam, 265, 270
Wing, Sam, Chinese herbal doctor, 265, 270
Wintrobe, Maxwell M., Jewish Canadian hematologist, 214, 301
Wolfe's, sporting goods store, 213
Wolsey, Heber, Canadian educator, 301
Wolthuis, Bart, Dutch mayor of Ogden, 240, 246
Wong, Jimmy, Chinese restaurant owner, 262
Wong, Kingsley, World War II veteran, 275
Wong Lee, Chinese laundryman, 259
Wong Leung Ka, Chinese merchant, 259–60
Wong Sing, Chinese merchant, 271–73
Wong Siu Pang, son of Wong Leung Ka, 259, 260
Wong Tz Chong, Chinese tailor, 258
Woodbury, John T., LDS missionary, 406

Woodruff, Wilford, LDS leader, 132, 192, 296

Woods, George L., territorial governor, 336

Woodward, Absolom, and Gosiutes, 57

Woolf, DeVoe, Canadian educator, 301

Woolf, John A., student, 297

Woolf, Wallace, Jewish businessman, 219

Woolf, Wilford, and Mormon settlement in Canada, 294

Woolf, William L., and Mormon settlement in Canada, 295

World War I, effect of, on immigration and immigrants, 7, 223–24, 226, 228, 380–81, 389, 401, 405, 427, 440, 444

World War II, effect of, on immigration and immigrants, 8, 9, 224, 352–59, 461

Wyasket, Ute leader, 40

Wynder, Curtis, Canadian educator, 301

Yabeney, Emma, Navajo weaver, 23

Yamamoto, Lessie, in Kabuki play, 347

Yamamoto, Take, wife of Setsuzo Uchida, 338

Yamato Grocery Store, Oakland, Calif., business of F. Endo, 348, 353

Yano, Tomoko Watanuki, and Japanese internment, 356

Yanez, Francis, Spanish-speaking agricultural worker, 447

Yost, Charles, Scandinavian immigrant, 171

Young ———, railroad superintendent, 339

Young, Brigham, 71–72, 75, 77, 94, 109, 118, 170, 174, 192, 306; and immigration and immigrants, 68–69, 144, 154, 156, 159, 169, 194, 196, 197; pioneer company of, 118, 285, 295; and schismatics, 89, 90, 91, 92; leadership and policies of, 2, 36, 38, 106, 107, 178, 193, 284

Young, Phineas, took Book of Mormon to Canadians, 281–82, 290

Young, R. T., deputy sheriff, 428

Young Women's Christian Association, and Japanese, 359

Young, Zina D., wife of Brigham, 296

Ystendatter, Aagaata Sondra (Ellen Sanders Kimball), Norwegian pioneer, 143

Yvanti, Lillian, Black singer, 136

Yugoslavs: boardinghouses of 376–77; and Catholic church, 364, 368, 371, 378, 379; culture and customs of, 368–70, 371, 373, 374, 375, 376, 378, 383; fraternal organizations of, 370–71, 373, 374, 376, 377; immigration of, 363, 364–68; in mining, smelting, and railroading, 363, 365, 369, 374, 375, 383; and old-country politics, 379–80; prejudice against, 382; publications of, 370–71; relations of, with Mormons, 381–82; and Serbian Orthodox church, 364, 369, 371, 379; and unions, 365, 377, 379, 382

Zander, Arthur, soccer player and organizer, 248

Zajedničar, Croatian newspaper, 371

Zapadni Slavenski Savez, Slavic insurance group, 370

Zara, Sivas province, Armenia, 398, 399

Zion's Cooperative Mercantile Institution, 195, 196, 197

Zeese, George (Gheorghios Zisimopoulos), Greek merchant, 410

Zionism, 216–17

Zion Lutheran Church, 185

Zobell, Hans, Danish weaver, 152, 156

Zucker, Ethel, and Zionism, 217

Zucker, Louis C., Jewish scholar, 204, 207, 212, 214, 216, 217

Acme, 233; Rebecca Alvera, 452; Helen Shool Anton, 396; Archivo
General de la Mexico, 448; Adele Attey, 397; Sarah George Attey,
397; Ballet Folklorico, 455; Mary Lucille Perkins Bankhead, 124, 125,
126; Mrs. Tony Barrutia, 316; Mrs. Andrew Bathemas, 423;
Mrs. M. B. Bertolina, 315, 319; Zorka Bogden, 373, 374; Mrs. Joe
Bonacci, 314, 316; Sophie Melich Borich, 372, 373; Frederick S.
Buchanan, 87; Lucy Bonacci Capalbo, 319; Dr. Ruth King Chang,
268; John Chipian, 424; Church of Jesus Christ of Latter-day Saints,
127, 267, 290; Jenalyn G. Cline, 83; Helen L. Crane, 162; Gerrit de
Jong, Jr., 234; Denver Public Library, 125; *Deseret News,* 87, 127,
160; Dea Diamanti, 235; Peter C. Dimas, 425; Fred Endo, 348;
O Ergatis, 420; Marie Floor, 421; Mrs. Robert Freed, 129; James
Galanis, 424; Glenbow-Alberta Institute, Calgary, Alberta, Canada,
290; Dr. Edward I. Hashimoto, 344, 345; John Howa, 396; Japanese
American Citizens League, 349; Mrs. Dee Johanson, 423;
Konstandinos Kambouris, 425; George Karas, 420, 423; Alice Kasai,
344, 347; Mrs. Emmanuel Katsanevas, 422; Rose Tavoian Kezerian,
398, 399; Mrs. John Klekas, 423; Steve Knaras, 420; Dr. Jun
Kurumada, 349; Stanley Litizzette, 315; William Wing Louie, 268,
269; Mrs. L. O. McMichael, 423; L. V. McNeeley, 269, 450, 452,
454; Esther Aposhian Magdiel, 398; Bernadette Marshall, 129;
Vicente V. Mayer, 451, 453; Joe Merabelle, 318; Maria Muñoz, 448,
452, 455; Ted Nagata, 235; National Archives, 33; National
Migrant Information Clearinghouse, 455; *The New Era,* 125; Frank
Norton, 314; Filippo Notarianni, 317; Our Lady of Guadalupe
Church, 449, 451; Lillie Gagosian Pecorelli, 399; Guido Rachiele,
317; Rudolph Rebol, 317; Mrs. M.M. Reenders, 234; Mrs. Henry
Ruggeri, 318; Salt Lake Buddhist Church, 346, 347; Salt Lake City
Public Library, 291; *Salt Lake Tribune,* 53, 318; Steve Sargetakis
collection, 421, 422; Judge James S. Sawaya, 396, 397; Joel B.
Shapiro, 204; Dr. Herond Nishan Sheranian, 399; Andrew Siouris,
421; Smithsonian Institution, 18, 32, 33, 35, 50, 51; *Survey Graphic,*
348; Mrs. Miwame Tatai, 345, 346, 349; Jackson Thode collection,
314; David T. Thomas, 163; Gary Tomsic, 315, 374, 375; Tony
Torres, 450; Trinity African Methodist Episcopal Church, 127, 128;
Union Pacific Railroad, 449; Utah Heritage Foundation, 288; *Utah
Medical Bulletin,* 349; *Utah Nippo,* 345; Utah State Historical
Society collections, 18, 19, 20, 21, 32, 33, 34 (courtesy Hayden C.
Clark), 35 (courtesy Floyd A. O'Neil), 50, 52, 80 (courtesy John
Palmer), 81, 82 (courtesy Sam Weller), 83, 84, 85, 86 (courtesy
Mrs. Robert Thomas), 124, 160, 161, 162, 163, 164, 165, 166, 167,
202, 203, 205 (courtesy *Salt Lake Tribune*), 206, 207, 232, 233, 235,
236, 237 (courtesy John A. Widtsoe family), 237 (courtesy Msgr.
Jerome Stoffel), 266 (courtesy Bernice Gibbs Anderson), 267

(courtesy *Salt Lake Tribune*), 268, 288, 289 (courtesy Russell G. Frazier), 290 (courtesy John A. Widtsoe family), 291, 316, 348, 448, 449; Fred Voll, 269, 319, 372; Louis L. Vuksinick, 374; Zelpha Skriner Vuksinick, 375; Western Americana, Marriott Library, University of Utah, 204, 206, 207, 314; *Wordpower*, 129; Virginia Latsis Zamboukas, 425.

The Peoples of Utah / edited by Helen Z. Papanikolas. — 1st ed.
— Salt Lake City : Utah State Historical Society, c1976.

499 p. : ill. ; 24 cm.

Includes bibliographical references and index.
ISBN 0-913738-26-3 : $7.50

1. Minorities—Utah—History.   2. Frontier and pioneer life—Utah.   3. Utah
—Emigration and immigration.   4. Utah—History.   I. Papanikolas, Helen
Zeese.   II. Utah State Historical Society.

F835.A1P46   301.29'792   76-12311
                                                       MARC

Library of Congress   76